# The Idea of Historical Recurrence in Western Thought

G. W. TROMPF

# The Idea of Historical Recurrence in Western Thought

## FROM ANTIQUITY TO THE REFORMATION

UNIVERSITY OF CALIFORNIA PRESS
Berkeley • Los Angeles • London

*À ma chère Fortune*
*qui vient de me revenir*

University of California Press
Berkeley and Los Angeles, California

University of California Press, Ltd.
London, England



ISBN 0-520-03479-1
Library of Congress Catalog Card Number: 77-76188
Printed in the United States of America

1 2 3 4 5 6 7 8 9

# Contents


ABBREVIATIONS vii

PREFACE ix

INTRODUCTION 1

1 THE POLYBIAN *ANACYCLŌSIS* OR CYCLE OF GOVERNMENTS 4

A. Polybius as a theorist of historical rather than cosmological recurrence, *6* B. The Polybian "anthropology," *15* The two-staged "anthropology" and its background, *16* The "anthropology" and the three-stationed biological principle, *22* C. The anacyclic zigzag, *25* D. The *Anacyclōsis* viewed synoptically and the importance of Plato, *37* E. The application of the *Anacyclōsis*, *45* The problem of mixed constitutions, *45* The constitutional development of Rome, *49*

2 POLYBIUS AND THE ELEMENTARY MODELS OF HISTORICAL RECURRENCE IN THE CLASSICAL TRADITION 60

A. Cycles and alternation as paradigms of recurrence, *61* Fortune's wheel, *62* i. General, *62* ii. Polybius, *63* The biological principle, 66 i. General, 66 ii. Polybius, *69* Age theory and the rise and fall of empires, *75* i. General, *75* ii. Polybius, *78* B. Reciprocal paradigms of recurrence, *84* The rectified mean, *85* i. General, *85* ii. Polybius, *88* Principles of retribution, *93* i. General, *93* ii. Polybius: key lines of approach, *97* iii. Polybius on the special case of Rome, *101* C. Other models of historical recurrence, *106* Conventional *metabolē* theory, *106* i. General, *106* ii. Polybius, *107* The appeal to the permanent traits of human nature, *110* *Addendum:* Special cases of recurrence, *112*

3 NOTIONS OF HISTORICAL RECURRENCE IN LUKE AND THE BIBLICAL TRADITION 116

A. Luke-Acts and the reenactment of significant events, *121* Central cases of reenactment, *122* The question of typology, *128* Lukan geography, *130* Old Testament background, *134* The reenactment of Old Testament events in Luke-Acts, *139* Luke-Acts and the reenactment of significant events in Gentile history, *147* B. The recurrent actualization of retributive principles in Luke-Acts and the biblical tradition, *155* The Deuteronomic historian, *156* The Chronicler, *160* Later Jewish writing, *164* Luke, *170* C. Notions of rise and fall and of successive Ages, especially in Luke, *174*

4 FROM LATER ANTIQUITY TO EARLY RENAISSANCE 179

A. Beliefs about the decay of Rome, *185* B. The body-state analogy applied to Rome, *188* C. The Roman Principate and fortune's wheel, *192* D. Age theory from later antiquity to the early Renaissance, *200* Later pagan views, *200* Patristic writers, *204* Medieval writers, *212* Early humanism, *220* E. The rise, fall and succession of empires: Patristic and medieval themes, *222* F. Special cases of cyclical thinking: Origen, Gemisthius Plethon, Nicephorus Gregoras, *229* G. Principles of retribution from later antiquity to the early Renaissance, *231* H. History's lessons for future behavior, *241* I. Notions of cultural rebirth or renaissance, *243*

5 MACHIAVELLI, THE RENAISSANCE, AND THE REFORMATION 250

A. Machiavelli and the cycle of governments, *251* Models in the *Discorsi* I,2 and the *Istorie* V,1, *252* Machiavelli on *Corpi Misti* and the constitutional history of Rome, *259* The recurrent lapse of republics into tyranny: Rome, *265* Reciprocal change within unstable republics: Florence, *268* *The Prince* and constitutional history, *269* Theories of constitutional change before and after Machiavelli, *274* B. Sixteenth-century themes, *278* Natural processes, rise and fall, *278* Feints of fortune and rules of reciprocity, *283* Other Renaissance themes, especially concerning human nature and the utility of history, *291* New Age theory for a new world, *295* The reenactment of significant events and other Reformation themes, *303*

Reflections 313

Excursus 1. Polybius on the Constitution of Sparta and Its Decline 317

Excursus 2. Luke as Hellenistic Historian: Background Comments 321

Excursus 3. Exegetical Notes on Luke 325

Excursus 4. Age Theory and Periodization from Joachim to the Early Humanists 335

Excursus 5. Notes on Machiavelli's *Il Principe* 338

Excursus 6. Notes on Sixteenth-Century *Metabolē* Theory and Age Theory 343

Select Bibliography 347

Index 355

# Abbreviations

| | |
|---|---|
| CSHB | *Corpus scriptorum historiae Byzantinae* |
| ERE | *Encyclopaedia of Religion and Ethics* |
| MGH | *Monumenta Germaniae historica* |
| OCD | *Oxford Classical Dictionary* |
| PG | Migne's *Patrologiae cursus completus: Series Graeca* |
| PL | Migne's *Patrologiae cursus completus: Series Latina* |
| RECA | Paulys' *Realencyclopädie der classischen Altertumswissenschaft* |

*ET*, *FT*, *GT* refer to English, French, and German translations.

# Preface

Even today it is commonly held that history repeats itself. The idea of historical recurrence has a long and intriguing history, and this volume concerns the period of time in the Western tradition when its expressions were most numerous and fervent. As we shall show, this idea is not to be confined to its cyclical variety, for it also entails such notions as reenactment, retribution, renaissance, and such like, which belong under the wider umbrella of "recurrence." Moreover, it will be argued that not only the Greco-Roman but also the biblical tradition contributed to the history of this idea. The old contrast between Judeo-Christian linear views of history and Greco-Roman cyclical views will be seriously questioned.

Beginning from Polybius, historian of the Roman empire, we examine the manifold forms of recurrence thinking in Greek and Roman historiography, but then turn our attention to biblical pictures of historical change, arguing that in the work of Luke-Acts and in early Jewish writings there was clearly an interest in the idea of history repeating itself. Jewish and early Christian writers initiated and foreshadowed an extensive synthesizing of recurrence notions and models from both traditions, although the synthesis could vary with different contexts and dogmatic considerations. In the Renaissance and Reformation the interrelationship between classical and biblical notions of recurrence reached a point of consummation, yet even in the sixteenth century some ideas distinctive to both traditions, such as the Polybian conception of a "cycle of governments" and the biblical notion of the "reenactment of significant events," were revived in stark separation from each other. We find ourselves dealing with a continuing but not always fruitful dialogue between the two great traditions of Western thought, a dialogue which has been carried on to the present day. The present volume represents the first half of a long story to be continued with a study running from Giambattista Vico to Arnold Toynbee.

Some will question whether what follows is the history of separate ideas rather than the history of one idea. Taking my cue from J. B. Bury's *The Idea of Progress*, I should reply that it is both. Thus, as the idea of progress is in fact a number of related ideas which may be gathered into one, so we shall discover in analyzing the great exponents of historical recurrence that these thinkers made use of a variety of paradigms to affirm the same truth or illuminate the same basic conception. The idea of historical recurrence, we may hasten to add, is likely to gain in popularity and credibility at the expense of the idea of progress. The belief in human progress may have outlived two World Wars and been strengthened in recent years by both the remarkable achievements of Chinese society and hopes for steadier development in the Third World. Yet although I have prepared this work at a time when our globe was not suffering from any overwhelming crisis, many of my contemporaries have come to recognize around them the symptoms of major ecological and political disasters in the years to come. I have written this book because it is relevant to mankind's present situation, because I believe the ideas contained in it, though many were not fully articulated or developed by their spokesmen, will provide the basis for new visions of history and change in the future. It is an unruly opinion of mine that the ideas and manifestations of recurrence will overtake our ideologies and impel them to change face.

This work is a revision of my doctoral thesis, which I began as a Research Scholar in the History of Ideas Unit at the Australian National University, and completed while teaching at the University of Papua New Guinea. A year's comparative respite at the University of California at Santa Cruz, which came with the generosity and stimulus afforded by the Fellows of Merrill College, has enabled me to prepare the thesis for publication. Unfortunately, I am unable to name all who have assisted me, but I am especially indebted to Professors Eugene Kamenka, John Pocock, Peter Munz, Christopher Evans, and Drs. Robert Banks and Evan Burge, for their constructive criticism of the work as a whole. For help on specific points I am grateful to Sir Steven Runciman, Professors Peter Ackroyd and Noel King, Cn. Laury Murchison, Princ. Mervyn Hindbury, Drs. Carl Loeliger, Ken Mackay, Robert Maddox, and Garth Thomas, and Messrs. Robert Barnes and Quentin Skinner. Alain Hénon of the University of California Press was understanding and supportive; and Ms. Jane-Ellen Long did a wonderful job as copy editor. In giving thanks which cannot repay their love, I mention Robin and Bronwyn Pryor, my two sets of parents, Annie Udy, and especially dear Bobbie, my wife and assiduous student of medicine, to whom this book is dedicated.

GWT

Sassafras,
Victoria, Australia
20 December 1977

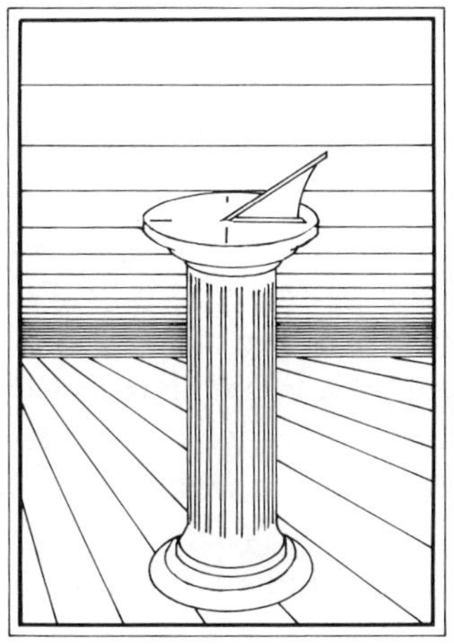

# Introduction

The idea of historical recurrence has played an important rôle in the development of Western historiography, especially from antiquity to the Reformation. The view that "history repeats itself" is commonly seen as characteristically Greek, and is principally associated with a general belief in cosmic and social cycles. It is natural, therefore, to begin our investigations with the Greek *cyclos*. The idea that history repeats itself, however, is wider than its cyclical formulation. It includes such notions as retribution, rebirth, reenactment, and even imitation. The present volume is an attempt to trace the progress of the idea of historical recurrence, from antiquity to the sixteenth century, in its richness and variety, and to draw out the various, often competing, models and paradigms used by those who speak of historical recurrence. In considering non-cyclical as well as cyclical ideas of recurrence we need to look beyond classical or Greco-Roman writers to Hebrew and early Christian literature. We will also see that some of the relevant paradigms are present in both great traditions of Western thought.

Recognizing these complexities enables us to make a more realistic comparison of Greek and Judeo-Christian views of history. A number of scholars have been inclined to draw too sharp a contrast between these two views. This contrast has been interesting and fruitful, emphasizing as it does the difference between Greek philosophical doctrines of eternal recurrence and biblical beliefs about history from creation to the eschaton. Yet it has tended to assimilate Greek views of historical repetition into cyclical views, and to limit almost all Judeo-Christian writers to a strict linear-eschatological outlook on history. This thesis attempts to correct that approach. Contributions to a reassessment, of course, have already been made: by Ludwig Edelstein, for example, in a recent book on ideas of progress in classical antiquity; by Arnaldo Momigliano in his denial that any extant classical historian had a cyclical understanding of time; and by a few scholars who wish to elicit cyclical notions from the Bible.

This is not an essay in the philosophy of history, however. I have only intended to write an historical account of how historians have used recurrence models to make sense of the past. I have therefore often dealt with the material exegetically rather than philosophically, and special attention has been paid to the historical writings of Polybius, Luke, and Machiavelli. Polybius has usually been regarded as a theorist of cyclical recurrence, but in fact he made use of a variety of recurrence paradigms. Luke has been taken to hold a linear view of history, but a number of recurrence notions, if not directly cyclical ones, are also present in his work. Luke's narrative reflects the impact of Hellenization on Judeo-Christian thought and sets the stage for the subsequent interlacing of recurrence ideas from two major traditions. The history of these ideas from later antiquity to the early Renaissance is interesting in its own right, and it also helps us to understand the sixteenth century, when ancient and medieval ideas of recurrence were either transmuted or revitalized, most remarkably in the writings of Niccolò Machiavelli and of the radical Reformation.

In emphasizing the number and variety of paradigms which enter into the notion of historical recurrence, we are not saying that they can always be sharply distinguished or logically opposed. Some views of recurrence prove more difficult to disentangle than we might assume; some are not easy to relate because the languages used in expressing them arise from different areas of discourse. Before proceeding, it would be helpful to set out in a preliminary way the major views and paradigms which form the subject matter of this volume.

*The cyclical view*: the belief that history or sets of historical phenomena pass through a fixed sequence of at least three stages, returning to what is understood to be an original point of departure, and beginning the cycle again.

*The alternation (or fluctuation) view*: the view that there is a movement in history wherein one set of general conditions is regularly succeeded by another, which then in turn gives way to the first.

*The reciprocal view*: the view that common types of events are followed by consequences in such a way as to exemplify a general pattern in history. The doctrines that departures from a mean are continually rectified, and that good and bad actions recurrently evoke their appropriate desert, are two particular and important varieties of this view.

*The reenactment view*: the view that a given action (usually taken to be of great significance) has been repeated later in the actions of others. The imitation view, which acknowledges recurrence because a person has consciously copied the actions or habits of another, is a variety of this.

*Conceptions of restoration, renovation, and renaissance*: these entail the belief that a given set of (approved) general conditions constitutes the revival of a former set which had been considered defunct or dying.

The view that certain kinds of social change are typical and are to be described by a recognized terminology. The recurrences of these changes do not necessarily belong within a cyclical, alternating, or reciprocal process. An example of this would be *conventional* metabolē *theory* (see Chapter 2, section C).

The view proceeding from a belief in *the uniformity of human nature*. It holds that because human nature does not change, the same sort of events can recur at any time.

Other minor cases of recurrence thinking include the isolation of any two specific events which bear a very *striking similarity*, and the preoccupation with *parallelism*, that is, with resemblances, both general and precise, between separate sets of historical phenomena.

Connected with almost all the above is the view that *the past teaches lessons for present and future action*. When this view is espoused, it is commonly (though not automatically) presupposed that the same events or sorts of events which have happened before are recurring and will recur again.

The idea of exact recurrence, we may note, was rarely incorporated into any of these views, for in the main they simply presume the recurrence of *sorts* of events, or what I have termed event-types, -complexes, and -patterns.

This volume begins with a case study, that is, with an analysis of a crucial and intricate model of recurrence in the ancient history written by Polybius. This model will initiate us into many of the major preconceptions, paradigms, and views occupying our attention through the whole work, and will serve as an excellent introduction to the methods and sensibilities of those who interpret the past in recurrence terms.

# Chapter I

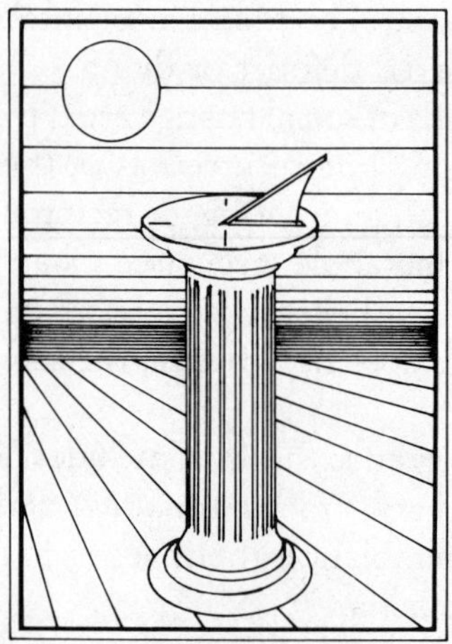

# The Polybian *Anacyclōsis* or Cycle of Governments

By the middle of the second century BC Rome had subjugated almost all of the then known world, including such formidable powers as Macedon and Carthage. Polybius of Megalopolis wrote his *Historiae* to explain how this had happened. The thirty-nine books received their final form after 146 BC, although he probably began writing before he was exiled from Achaia to Rome in 170. At first interested in Greek affairs, his experience of Rome and her rapidly expanding empire dramatically altered his perspective. He attempted what he called universal (rather than ethnic, "national," or local) history, the kind of history which Rome's new world dominion had made possible. At one time an official of the Achaian League, a celebrity in the circle of brilliant Romans surrounding Scipio Aemilianus, and an intrepid traveler, Polybius was better equipped to write of Rome's rise to power than most of his contemporaries. He wrote with confidence, believing his work to be of immense practical value for the politician and the student of history.[1] He is best known for the sixth book of this history, the book in which he considered the merits of Rome's constitution and argued that a crucial factor in her success was the stability of her political institutions. The opening sections of that book will occupy most of our attention in this chapter, for there he sketched a model of historical change which he termed ἀνακύκλωσις πολιτειῶν (the cycle of governments).[2] The *Anacyclōsis* forms an excellent beginning point for our investigations into the idea of historical recurrence. It is a key example of that cyclical thinking about history so commonly associated with the Greek view of life. What is more, it reflects the attempt to bring into a systematic relationship several ideas of recurrence so as to form a coherent theory.

According to Polybius, the *Anacyclōsis* was the natural course or order in which constitutions change, are transformed, and return again to their original stage (*Hist.* VI,ix,10). Identifying six types of constitutions, he tried to show how they followed one another in a fixed sequence.[3] The first type, kingship (*basileia*), was the just reign of one man by hereditary succession. This constitution degenerated into tyranny, an unjust hereditary rule which is the vicious form allied to kingship (and sometimes called monarchy).[4] Tyranny was replaced in turn by aristocracy, the worthy rule of a few influential citizens, but this also lapsed into its degenerate counterpart, oligarchy—the régime of the irresponsible and greedy few. Democracy, an orderly rule by the whole people, arose on the destruction of oligarchy, but it, too, changed into its vicious complement, mob rule (*ochlocratia*), thus completing the series.[5] Polybius presented two accounts of this process in summary form (VI,iv,7–10, v,4–ix,9) and in the

1. For Polybius' career and its background, see esp. E. Täubler, *Tyche: historische Studien*, Leipzig, 1926, pp. 76–84; M. Gelzer, "Die Archaica im Geschichtswerk des Polybios" in *Abhandlungen der preussischen Akademie der Wissenschaften: philosophische-historische Klasse* no. 2, 1940, esp. pp. 8–31; K. Ziegler in *RECA*, vol. 21, pt. 2, cols. 1444ff.; K. von Fritz, *The Theory of the Mixed Constitution in Antiquity: A Critical Analysis of Polybius' Political Ideas*, New York, 1954, ch. 1; F. W. Walbank, *A Historical Commentary on Polybius*, Oxford, 1957, vol. 1, pp. 1–3; cf. A. E. Astin, *Scipio Aemilianus*, Oxford, 1967, esp. pp. 294ff. For Polybius on universal and pragmatic history, see esp. *Historiae* I,iv,6, xxxv,9; cf. P. Pédech, *La Méthode historique de Polybe*, Paris, 1966, pp. 26ff.

2. Or "the process whereby constitutions move in recurring cycles." See *Historiae* VI,ix,10; cf. iv,6–ix,9. The texts used include those of J. Schweighaeuser, *Polybii megalopolitani historiarum*, Leipzig, 1795, 8 vols.; J. L. Strachan-Davidson, *Selections from Polybius*, Oxford, 1888; W. R. Paton, *Polybius: The Histories* (Loeb Classical Library), London, 1922–7, 6 vols., and T. Buettner-Wobst, *Polybius: Historiae* (Bibliotheca Scriptorum Graecorum et Romanorum Teubneriana), Stuttgart, 1962–7, 5 vols. For lexical aids, see Schweighaeuser, op. cit., vol. 8; A. Mauersberger, *Polybios Lexikon* (im Auftrage der Wissenschaften zu Berlin), Berlin, 1961–8, three parts (unfinished).

3. In VI,iv,6 Polybius refers to six *genē politeiōn*, yet in 6–10 appears to consider seven: for the explanation see below, sect. B, pt. 2.

4. Polybius can use *tyrannis* and *monarchia* interchangeably: VI,iv,6, and cf. esp. iii,9; VIII,viii, 4–7. See also F. W. Walbank's discussions in "Polybius on the Roman Constitution" in *Classical Quarterly* XXXVII, 1943, p. 76 and ff., and in *Polybius* (*Sather Classical Lectures XLII*), Berkeley and Los Angeles, 1972, pp. 140–1. *Monarchia* can be used of the primitive rule preceding the establishment of *basileia* (cf. VI,v,9), or of one-man rule in general (iii,10, iv,1–2). Paton erroneously takes *monarchia* rather than *basileia* to be the subject of iv,8.

5. VI,iv,7–10. *Ochlocratia* is interchangeable with *cheirocratia*: cf. ix,8–9, lvii,9.

second he attempted to isolate the causes of the transformations from one type of government to another. He also made it clear that the series began and ended with the same socio-political order—an elementary form of monarchy. This monarchy preceded kingship in the first instance and followed mob rule in the last, and it was understood to be the natural rule over men when their behavior and conditions of existence are the most animal-like.[6] With this at the beginning and end of the sequence, the whole natural process appears capable of continuous repetition, even if Polybius bequeathed us no historical example of such a recurrence in the life of a given political entity, and even though he spent remarkably little time on the theoretical idea of an orderly cyclical process continuing ad infinitum.[7]

Thus the *Anacyclōsis* covers a series of stages, including a zigzag line of change (*metabolē*) between worthy and unworthy constitutions, as well as a return to an original point of departure where the fixed sequence of stages begins again. According to Polybius, one could therefore prognosticate not only the most likely immediate destiny of a given constitution but also the eventual reversion of all political societies to a primitive state, a state which he associated with bestiality or the vulgar herd, and with the emergence of a strong monarchical master.[8]

Such a comprehensive picture of recurring political processes is unique in classical literature. Among Greek and Roman writers whose works have survived, Polybius is the most advanced theoretical exponent of historical recurrence. He had imbibed enough of the specialist's world of Academicians, Peripatetics, and Stoics to formulate abstract philosophical principles of his own, shown nowhere more ostentatiously than in the *Historiae* Bk. VI. Whether he created or reproduced the theoretical model of *Anacyclōsis*,[9] that model enabled him succinctly to combine numerous traditional lines of Greek thinking about ordered change, growth and decay, the nature and fate of all things, into one systematic overview. We must emphasize, however, that Polybius was primarily interested in human affairs rather than in the general laws of nature or in metaphysical questions about changing phenomena. In consequence, there seems no apter way to begin investigating his important anacyclic model than by discussing his decidedly historical interests.

## A. Polybius as a theorist of historical rather than cosmological recurrence

Book VI of the *Historiae* is largely devoted to Rome and her mixed constitution, and it is important to recognize that Polybius delineated his cycle of govern-

6. VI,v,9, ix,9; cf. iv,2, 7.

7. VI,ix,9–10 is the key passage, but cf. also v,4–6 and discussion below, sect. A.

8. See esp. VI,iv,11–12, ix,10–11. On bestiality, see ix,9, and on herds, v,7–9.

9. VI,iv,7–10 could have been based on a source: cf. H. Ryffel, ΜΕΤΑΒΟΛΗ ΠΟΛΙΤΕΙΩΝ; *Der Wandel der Staatsverfassungen* (*Noctes Romanae II*), Bern, 1949, p. 202, and cf. pp. 185, 195, but as

ments as a preface to a much longer discussion. His model was intended to serve this subsequent exposition, and Rome's special achievements, including her constitutional soundness, were to be assessed in the light of the anacyclic process. That certainly establishes the paramountcy of his socio-political concerns. On the other hand, the *Anacyclōsis* itself contains a sufficient number of features which also invite us to reflect upon the differences between Polybius' approach to recurrence and the approaches of those before him.

In the second, more complex, delineation of his model, Polybius attempts to relate the *Anacyclōsis* to actual facts, and begins by a rather guarded appeal to the traditional idea of societies originating from among the remnants of a long-past disaster. At this point (and it is the only point in his whole work where he does so) Polybius shows himself aware of what may be termed Greek "catastrophe theory," that is, those theories which postulate great periodic upheavals interrupting the life of the whole cosmos, including one of its most significant components, the human race. But he is careful to avoid philosophical contention in this connection. He begins his treatment by asking, "What are the beginnings of political societies and where do they first emerge?" and answers that they spring from those who survive a great destruction of the human species such as has been and will "many times again" be caused by "flood, famine, crop failure, or similar cause" (v,4–5). Significantly, Polybius' position on the beginning of human life is ambiguous; he cautiously skirted the vexing debate between those who upheld the eternity of the cosmos and those who believed that the existing universe had a fixed starting point and end. There is in fact no evidence that he ever committed himself to anything like the Peripatetic view that the cosmic order was ageless or to the traditional Stoic doctrine which saw the whole universe, with all its inhabitants, as undergoing periodic dissolution and reconstitution (*ecpyrōsis* and *palingenesia*). Not that he was ignorant of the relevant debates, for the leading Roman Stoic, Panaetius of Rhodes, a philosopher who has claims to being Polybius' closest colleague, was famous for rejecting the notion of cosmic dissolution.[10] Yet Polybius was no cosmologist. It is important that he considers catastrophe theory only from an historical point of view; he was a theorist of historical rather than of cosmological recurrence.

This last distinction may be elucidated by placing the *Anacyclōsis*, especially Polybius' approach to catastrophe theory, against the background of Greek

---

we have no comparable theoretical statement of *anacyclōsis* before Polybius, we must regard this view as an unhelpful *argumentum ex silentio*. Idiosyncratic usages of *monarchia* and *monarchos* probably arose from the needs of theoretical reflection on one-man rule (against Walbank, *Polybius*, who posits a special source).

10. On this rejection, see *Panaetii Rhodii fragmenta* (ed. M. van Straaten), (*Philosophia Antiqua V*), Leiden, 1952, Frgs. 64–9. On Panaetius' connections with Polybius, Frgs. 2, 15–6, 21, and Cicero *De re publica* I,xxi,34 (although the evidence that the two actually met and taught together is slender: cf. C. O. Brink and F. W. Walbank, "The Construction of the Sixth Book of Polybius" in *Classical Quarterly* N.S. IV, 1954, p. 103 n. 3). On Stoics who had previously questioned the doctrine of conflagration see F. H. Sandbach, *The Stoics* (Ancient Thought and Culture), London, 1975, p. 79.

cosmological thinking. Since Thales, Greek philosophy had never ceased to reflect an interest in questions concerning generation, change, and decay. When Polybius commented briefly (toward the end of Bk. VI) that "all existing things are subject to decay and change" and that this was "a truth scarcely needing proof" (lvii,1), he put himself in line with the mainstream of Greek philosophical speculation on these matters. But when Greek philosophers speculated about change and decay in terms of recurrence or periodicity or cycles, they were almost invariably concerned with the material universe, its constituents or components, and its overall destiny. The early Eleatic Xenophanes (sixth century BC), for example, purportedly contended that the earth is being continually mixed with the sea, that in time it would be dissolved into moisture, becoming a mud in which all mankind would be destroyed, and that "then there is another beginning of coming-to-be (or generation), this foundation applying to all worlds."[11] In this he may have drawn much from his Ionian predecessor Anaximander, who probably held a similar view,[12] and certainly his speculations set the stage for the more elaborate Empedoclean cosmic cycle.

According to Empedocles, the world underwent a continual but very slow alternation between tendencies which integrated and tendencies which separated the four elements, between the formation of "whole-natured creatures" and the appearance of bodily aberrations (monsters, separated limbs), between the forces of harmony and the principle of evil, or, in the most all-embracing terms, between the powers of Love and Strife.[13] Basically, those who saw cosmic processes in this way assumed that the primary substances of the All were indestructible, so that the world was only temporarily transformed through great elemental processes or the agency of Strife. Beneath persistent change lay an awesome agelessness (the Greek philosophers were no less fascinated by duration than by change),[14] and this quality of the everlasting was reflected in the recurring succession of states through which the cosmos/world came to be and passed away.

By Polybius' time the chief proponents of this type of approach were the Stoics, yet they adopted this way of viewing the universe only with interesting modifications, because on the surface their doctrine of dissolution prescribed a much more definite end of the existing world than seems to have been envisaged by Xenophanes or Empedocles. However, although this doctrine must have

11. *Die Fragmente der Vorsokratiker* (ed. H. Diels and W. Kranz), Berlin, 1952 edn. (henceforth Diels-Kranz), vol. 1, Frg. B33.

12. See esp. G. S. Kirk and J. E. Raven, *The Presocratic Philosophers: A Critical History with a Selection of Texts*, Cambridge, 1969, p. 140 (henceforth Kirk-Raven); cf. Diogenes Laertius *Vitae philosophorum* ix,21. On further background in Hesiod's teaching about chaos, see K. Reidemeister, *Das exacte Denken der Griechen*, Darmstadt, 1972, p. 96.

13. D. O'Brien, "Empedocles' Cosmic Cycle" in *Classical Quarterly* N.S. XVII, 1967, pp. 29ff.; idem, *Empedocles' Cosmic Cycle: A Reconstruction* (Cambridge Classical Studies), Cambridge, 1969, pp. 1–3 and passim; cf. C. H. Kahn, "Religion and Natural Philosophy in Empedocles' Doctrine of the Soul" in *Archiv für Geschichte der Philosophie* XLII, 1960, esp. pp. 15–24.

14. J. Burnet's insistence on this point hardly needs reinforcing: cf. his *Early Greek Philosophy*, London, 1930 edn., p. 9.

been used as a weapon to contradict Platonists and Peripatetics who were teaching the eternity of the world,[15] the Stoics who propounded the idea of world conflagration did not understand it as a total destruction—certainly not as a destruction of "pure matter" and "acting force." That would have meant defecting to another position equally if not more disturbing, the view upheld by the atomistic-Epicurean tradition that there was not one world, but an infinity of them, each single world living out its separate and relatively short existence, then lost forever in an endless, meaningless void. For the Stoics conflagration and restoration were, rather, *mundi aeternae vices*,[16] and Chrysippus (third century BC) with his followers put much emphasis on the cyclical or periodic return of the same world and the same people,[17] so that in fact they had much in common with those pre-Socratics who had talked about an alternating succession of cosmic states. Even what was peculiarly their own was claimed by them to have pre-Socratic antecedents, for concerning the world's reversion to elemental fire they appealed to the early Ionian Heraclitus,[18] and their notion of an exact (or, as it was called, "numerical") repetition of all things may well have been derived from the Pythagorean stock of ideas.[19]

For the Stoics and those who foreshadowed them, regular cosmic periods were described in terms of *archē* (beginning) and *telos* (end), and of momentous events which radically altered the condition of the universe. For the Platonists and Peripatetics, however, it was the ever-moving circular courses of the planetary bodies which formed the basic image of periodicity. The world was eternal; that was a fundamental Aristotelian doctrine opposed to any belief in total transformation and re-creation.[20] In his so-called *Politicus* myth Plato implicitly satirized the Empedoclean cycle by depicting a cosmos which, once it had passed through a three-staged process (a process Plato significantly calls *anacyclēsis*), was established by its divine Maker as "immortal and free from decay."[21]

15. Polybius *Hist.* XXXIII,ii,8–10 = Aulius Gellius *Noctes Atticae*, VI,xiv,8–10 is important among the skimpy pieces of evidence on the polemical use of this doctrine.

16. I.e., "changes of the eternal world," to follow J. von Arnim (ed.), *Stoicorum veterum fragmenta*, Stuttgart, 1902–4, vol. 2, p. 183; cf. esp. Philo Judaeus *De aeternitate mundi* viii.

17. Chrysippus (and others), Frgs. 623, 625–8, etc. (von Arnim, vol. 2, pp. 189–91); cf. Zeno, Frgs. 98, 109 (vol. 1, pp. 27, 109) and Panaetius, Frgs. 65–9 (van Straaten, p. 19).

18. On the apparently erroneous interpretation of Heraclitus: Chrysippus, Frg. 430 (von Arnim, vol. 2, pp. 141–2); Diogenes Laertius *Vit. philos.* ix,8; Clement of Alexandria *Stromateis* V,civ,1 (from a Stoic source); cf. Plutarch *Consolatio ad Apollonium* 106E–F; Marcus Aurelius *Meditationes* III,iii; etc.

19. Chrysippus, Frgs. 624, 627 (von Arnim), and on numerical repetition among the Pythagoreans, Eudemus of Rhodes (in *Die Schule des Aristoteles: Texte und Kommentar*, ed. F. Wehrli, Basel, 1967–9, vol. 8), Frg. 88 (p. 41); cf. Porphyry *Vita Pythagorae* xix. See also E. Zeller, *The Stoics, Epicureans and Skeptics* (ET), New York, 1897 edn., p. 166 n. 2.

20. Esp. Aristotle *De caelo* I,280a–284b; Eudemus, Frgs. 38–40 (Wehrli, pp. 27–8); Theophrastus in Philo Judaeus *De aeternitate mundi* xxiii,117; Simplicius *In Aristotelis physicorum commentaria*, e.g., on 227b21ff. (ed. H. Diels in *Commentaria in Aristotelem Graeca*, Berlin, 1895, vol. 10, pp. 884ff.). Cf. Dicaearchus, Frg. 47 (Wehrli, 1967, vol. 1, p. 22); Diodorus Siculus *Bibliotheke* I,iv,3.

21. Plato *Politicus* 273E for the phrase; cf. *Timaeus* 29A. On Plato's use but ultimate rejection of the Empedoclean system, see esp. J. B. Skemp, *The Theory of Motion in Plato's Later Dialogues*, Cambridge, 1942, pp. 21–7 and ch. 4. On the term *anacyclēsis* in Plato see *Politicus* 269E. Despite

In a cosmos without real genesis (Plato wrote of creation only concessively and mythologically),[22] and in which degeneration never attained to the extremity of a total conflagration, large-scale changes affecting man became a matter of outside astral influences which caused more confined, yet nevertheless catastrophic, events on an indestructible earth. Transformations at the cosmic level were replaced in Platonic and Aristotelian writings by limited cataclysms and regional disasters by fire.[23] Cyclical thinking about cosmology was thus in a special sense transferred to the realm of "history" or of the human species. One should be careful here, of course. After all, it was Plato who glorified the circular revolutions of the seven heavenly bodies, who conceived time in cyclical terms as the "moving image of eternity," and who also accepted the great truth that all things grow and die.[24] The altered stress, however, had to do with those great time lapses which certain pre-Socratic cosmologists had understood to be cycles, those periods which they divided into stages and took to end and begin again with the same or similar conditions. In Plato's view the incontrovertibly eternal universe did not succumb to any general mutation; great cyclical processes were only experienced by parts of the cosmos, not by the All. Concerning man, he wrote of many great eons of time which were separated from one another by the fact that, in each, human existence was bounded by cataclysm and extensive destruction (cf. *Leg.* III,677A). It was in fact Plato who first popularized the idea, later to appear in Polybius, that political societies emerged from the remnants of such disasters.

Significantly enough, however, Plato did not insist that the process governing the development and destruction of human groups and civilizations reproduced the kind of formal patterning, regularity, and alternation found in the normal movements of the heavens or in such a system as Empedocles'. Admittedly, he stressed the virtual innumerability of the cataclysms,[25] and in reading the third book of his *Laws* one is left with the impression that in *every* immediately post-cataclysmic situation men must start on the same slow journey, from the simple-mindedness of the mountaineering herdsmen who survive a deluge to the establishment of the city-state (677B–680E). In contrast to the slow reversion to mud, though, or the steadily increasing influence of Strife, Plato's cataclysms come

---

his apparent satire, it does not follow that he excluded the idea of the cosmos turning in opposite directions over great periods of time (*Politicus* 270B). In the *anacyclēsis* of the *Politicus*, however, there are only three identifiable stages. The first has the cosmos rotating normally before the Great Reversal (269C, 270A, 272E); the second is the Age of Kronos and the Earthborn (the Age of the Great Reversal) (269D–E, 270D ff., 273Aa); the third Age being the present one, the continuing degeneration of which God managed to forestall (273Ab–E).

22. P. Friedländer, *Plato (III: The Dialogues, Second and Third Periods)* (ET), London, 1969, vol. 1, pp. 198ff. Aristotle took the *Politicus* myth too literally in *Physica* VIII,251b and *De caelo* 280a.

23. Plato *Leges* III,677A, *Timaeus* 22D, 23A, *Critias* 111A, 112A; Aristotle, esp. *Meteorologica* I,351b, *Politica* 1269a4ff., Fragments [*Aristotelis fragmenta selecta*, W. D. Ross (ed.), Oxford, 1955, Frg. 8 = R²2, R³13, W8]. Note also *Protrepticus*, Frg. 53 in Iamblichus *De communi mathematica scientia* III,26; cf. W. Jaeger, *Aristotle: Fundamentals of the History of His Development* (ET), Oxford, 1948, pp. 71–2.

24. *Timaeus* 37C–39E, 80D–81E, *Respublica* VIII,546A.

25. *Leg.* III,676B–C, 677A, *Timaeus* 23B.

unexpectedly; they are effected through planetary deviation rather than representing the completion of an even, uniform movement in the heavens (*Tim.* 220E). And Plato consciously created room for variation. Although the idea of continual recurrence is suggested when he asks:

Have not thousands upon thousands of city-states come into existence, and on a similar computation, have not just as many perished? And have they not in each case exhibited all kinds of constitutions many times everywhere? (*Leg.* III,676B–C),

his sense of multiformity and of the differing possibilities of change (*metabolē*) in human affairs was remarkably strong.[26] He did not advance the teaching that each inter-cataclysmic period was a simple repetition of the preceding. By implication, perhaps, the same sorts of political societies were understood to arise during each grand time lapse, as were parallel historical situations, but if we can take his description of antediluvian Athens and Atlantis seriously (and Plato seems to wish us to do so),[27] then we realize that he has drawn out the essential differences between one period of civilization and another.[28] If anything, Plato advanced the view that the earliest was best; whether one considers the blissful Age of Kronos, or the time when the gods invented the arts and divided the lands, or even the period when ancient Athenian heroes thrust back Atlantid aggrandizement, those ages prior to the present one were closer to a state of perfection.[29] This view complemented Plato's picture of the material universe as a "creation" lacking the perfection of the divine One lying behind all reality, and of the ideal polity (the "Republic") which eventually comes to slide into the mire of self-interest, false freedoms, and tyranny.[30]

Aristotle in turn evidently took the essentials of Plato's catastrophe theory for granted, occasionally alluding to cataclysms when he discussed very early societies.[31] For Aristotle, these great eruptions formed part of the world's fixed and natural operations; they were not the result of heavenly deviation. Although he wrote of a Great Winter or inundation, for example, as if it coincided with the special positioning of the heavens (at the end of the Great Year),[32] he still took

26. C. Mugler, *Deux thèmes de la cosmologie grecque: devenir cyclique et pluralité des mondes* (*Études et Commentaires XVII*), Paris, 1953, esp. pp. 93–7.

27. Cf. *Critias* 110A–B, *Tim.* 22E–23C, 25E, where Plato places a peculiarly historical stress on the fact that Egypt, which escaped the regional deluge last affecting Hellas, held documents relating to the ancient era of the Atlantids which the Athenian Solon had been able to examine. R. Weil, *L' "Archaeologie" de Platon* (*Études et Commentaires XXXII*), Paris, 1959, pp. 14ff.

28. On Plato's idealization of the antediluvian Athenians, see B. Knauss, *Staat und Mensch in Hellas*, Darmstadt, 1940 edn., pp. 39ff.; Friedländer, op. cit., vol. 3, pp. 385ff.

29. *Politicus* 269Cff., and cf. *Leg.* IV,713C–D (Kronos, the Earthborn creatures); *Polit.* 274B–D, and cf. *Philebus* 16C (gods and arts) (cf. *Polit.* 273B, *Gorgias* 523B on the Age of Zeus); *Critias* 110C–E; *Tim.* 23C–25C (period of heroes).

30. *Tim.* 27Cff. (on Creation and the Demiurge, cf. *Politicus* 273C–D); *Resp.* VIII–IX (543–92) (on the decline of the ideal political society).

31. *Meteorol.* I,351b24–8, and cf. 7–14; *Politica* 1268b-1269a; *Fragm.* (Ross), No. 8 ($R^2$2, $R^3$13, W8).

32. The Great Year was the period required for the heavenly bodies to return to their original (and aligned) positions: cf. Aristotle *Protrepticus* in Frg. 19 ($R^3$, 2S, W19). I. Dühring, in *Aristotle's Protrepticus: An Attempt at Reconstruction* (*Studia Graeca et Latina Gothoburgensia*), Gothenburg,

its incidence to be unexpected because one could not be sure which region it would affect.[33] The important point remains, however. For Plato and Aristotle great upheavals were not cosmic; they became regionalized or confined geographically, or (as in the case of the Great Winter) were treated as specifically meteorological rather than as general cosmological events.[34] Although the evidence is scattered, Aristotle apparently concurred with Plato in assuming that various periods of civilization saw repetition only in a very general sense, the earliest men in each post-cataclysmic situation having to form the groups and rediscover the skills on which future political societies were to be based.[35]

Basically, then, Polybius inherited two traditions of speculation concerning violent disruptions to human life. One, the Platonic-Aristotelian tradition, was more historically oriented than the other. For Plato and Aristotle there was really only one "history," stretching back into time immemorial even if cut off from human knowledge by the destructions of flood and fire,[36] and catastrophes were primarily important for their effect on mankind. The Stoics and some of their pre-Socratic predecessors, by contrast, placed far greater stress on the cyclical processes undergone by the whole cosmos. For the Stoics, further, there was more than one "history," or better still, there was one "history" which was repeated an infinite number of times.[37] The cyclical element is not absent from the Platonic-Aristotelian position, however, since it was possible for them to speak of cataclysms occurring "periodically," and since for them such regional disasters demarcated cycles of civilization. Nevertheless, the Stoics' vision is much more impressively circular. Their grand cycle included every single event in world history, so once the cosmos returned to its original point of departure, all previous events and conditions would be repeated down to the finest detail.

The *Anacyclōsis* bears the marks of both these lines of approach. The apparent carefulness of its description, in fact, persuades one both that it has been framed in deference to competing philosophical positions and that it has been endowed

---

1961, excludes this fragment from his reconstruction. For discussion of the crucial passage from Censorinus see F. Solmsen, *Aristotle's System of the Physical World: A Comparison with his Predecessors*, Ithaca, 1960, p. 426 and n. 136. *Meteorol.* I,352a31–4 does not constitute sufficient proof that Aristotle propounded the idea of a Great Year. On this idea in Pythagoras, see esp. J. A. Philip, *Pythagoras and Early Pythagoreanism* (*Phoenix: Journal of the Classical Association of Canada, Supp. Vol. 7*), Toronto, 1966, p. 74; in Heraclitus, see esp. Mugler, op. cit., pp. 28–9; in Aristarchus and others, T. Heath, *Aristarchus of Samos: The Ancient Copernicus*, Oxford, 1913, pp. 314ff.; cf. pp. 132ff., 286ff. Cf. also Plato *Tim.* 39D, and see below, Chapter 2, sect. A; Chapter 4, sect. D, pt. 1.

33. *Meteorol.* I,352a30–2 (within the context of 352a17–353a31) on slow changes.

34. *Meteorol.*, esp. I,352a33–5, 352b16–21, 25ff.; Plato, esp. *Critias* 111B. See also R. McKeon, "Plato and Aristotle as Historians: A Study of Method in the History of Ideas" in *Ethics* LI, 1940, p. 92.

35. Aristotle's notion of mankind learning skills over and again (*Metaphysica* 993b, 1074a38–b14, *Politica* 1329b; cf. Plato *Leg.* III,677D, and below, Chapter 4, sect. I) is probably linked with catastrophe theory. Cf. Plato *Leg.* III,677C, 678D, 679D on the reacquisition of skills after a Deluge.

36. For Plato's heightened perception of immense past time, see esp. *Leg.* III,678B; cf. 676A–C and A. E. Taylor's significant comments about its originality in *Plato: The Man and His Work*, London, 1948 edn., p. 472. For Aristotle on infinite time, see esp. *Physica* 217b ff.

37. I am thinking of the older Stoics; on later modifications of the Stoic theory of conflagration, see Zeller, op. cit., p. 169 and below, Chapter 4, sect. D, pt. 1.

with a special, if not original, thrust of its own. Polybius' respect for alternative cosmologies is certainly exemplified from the start, by his vagueness about ultimate beginnings. Even if he may have recognized the recurrence of catastrophes, thus recalling before all else Plato's *Laws*, it was not Plato's sense of a virtually immeasurable past that he stressed (and so by implication the eternity of man), but the *future* likelihood of the destruction of men many times again.[38] Perhaps it is typical of Polybius to be concerned about foreseeing the future (for he believed that the study of the past better enabled one to prognosticate; see Chapter 2, esp. sect. C), but since he was at this point talking less about political realities than about theoretical possibilities, it may be inferred that he chose words both to acknowledge the Platonic view and to safeguard the position of the Stoics and others who taught that history had restricted boundaries.[39] Consciously avoiding philosophical subtleties, Polybius constructed his model to suit the "common intelligence" (*Hist.* VI,v,2), and thus the suspicion that he was attempting to combine differing outlooks, and to pay respect to the major traditions of Greek thought as generally conceived, is not ill-founded.

Along with concessions to well-established views, however, even those brief comments on catastrophes which begin the detailed description of the *Anacyclōsis* carry a quite distinctive impulse. From the start Polybius makes it plain that his cycle operates strictly within historical bounds. Certainly this historicization is more in agreement with Plato and Aristotle than with the Stoics.[40] It is curious, though, how the unexpected cataclysm is no longer the key focal point from which cyclical movement in history is defined. In Polybius, catastrophes and the bare facts of survival become no more than a stage setting; once men start along the road toward civilization, it is, according to the *Anacyclōsis*, their own collective career and what happens to their socio-political creations which inscribe the circle. If, after alternating between good and bad constitutions, a society returns to its first state, that is not the omen of an imminent downpour or a physical catastrophe, it is just the signal for a political, social, human, and therefore essentially historical, process to begin again. Polybius certainly began by conceiving the general state of early human life (in *Hist.* VI,v,4–vi,12), yet on referring to the beginning of a new cycle (in ix,9), he seems to have assumed that recommencement only applies to particular societies. Neither Plato nor Aristotle touched on the return to social primitivism in exclusively political terms, although they had only regional cataclysms in view. What is more, the *Anacyclōsis* is more heavily cyclical in the sense that its stages and its renewal point are much more historically definite than is the case with Plato's intercataclysmic periods. Polybius' position is unusual, for he seems to have carried some of the theory of cosmic cycles and alternating processes into the domain of

38. *Hist.* VI,v,5: πάλιν πολλάκις ἔσεσθ' ὁ λόγος αἱρεῖ.

39. With a view to morality, Stoics emphasized future repetitions rather than the innumerable recurrences of the past. Chrysippus, Frg. 596 (von Arnim, vol. 2, pp. 183–4); Cicero *Somnium Scipionis* vii,23, *De natura Deorum* ii,118; Seneca *Naturales quaestiones* iii,30; etc.

40. See also Polybius' Peripatetic-looking comments in *Hist.* IV,xl,4–10, xlii,1–5 on the infinity of time in connection with the silting up of the Pontus. Cf. Aristotle *Meteorol.* I,351a19ff., 352a on land-sea transformations (being related to the infinity of time in 353a15–24; cf. 351b8–13).

history. As the *Anacyclōsis* is not closed off by a catastrophe, it conveys the impression of an alternation between the "primitive" and the "civilized" (as well as between good and bad constitutions), rather than a model grounded in catastrophe theory. Yet despite these shades of pre-Socratic theory, Polybius emancipated himself even more convincingly from cosmology than either Plato or Aristotle, since those two philosophers' ideas of recurring civilizations continued to have some real ties with quasi-cosmological beliefs, with the notion that extraterrestrial movements have great consequences for the destiny of mankind.

The *Anacyclōsis*, then, represents a rather special adaptation of classical cosmologies. However, we cannot appreciate it fully without also recognizing that other thinkers had been pondering the relationship between cosmology and "history" right up to the second century BC. Efforts to amalgamate some of the older pre-Socratic cosmological systems with Platonic and Aristotelian structures form part of the more immediate theoretical background to Polybius. Stoic thought was not without syncretistic elements, of course, but most relevant to Polybius' case is a piece of popularist Hellenistic philosophy on the nature of the Universe by "Ocellus Lucanus" (second century BC). This writer upheld the eternity of the world like any good Peripatetic, yet he inclined to the view that there were alternating processes in the life of elements and plants,[41] and in writing about man, Pythagorean and some Stoic tendencies clearly got the better of him. He taught catastrophe theory rather than cosmic dissolution, yet his cataclysms were major ones marking a clear line of demarcation between the separate great periods of humanity.[42] Significantly enough, however, each great period was understood to see the recurrence of exactly the same events. Thus, in Athenian history there were reappearances of the ancient Inachos, and with successive cycles came repetitions of the same barbarian invasion of Greece.[43]

Without requiring the conclusion that Ocellus directly influenced Polybius, we may note how similar tendencies of thought were important for the formulation of the *Anacyclōsis*. Plato had hinted at historical regression, at an increasing isolation of man from his earliest, most perfect condition. A teleological aspect was revealed in his thinking: history had overall direction. But both Ocellus and Polybius made the cycle of civilization decisively non-teleological; taken as a whole their models have been axiologically objectified, rather like the universe of the Stoics in which every phase of the great cycle was natural, necessary, and a mark of eternal cosmic stability. Both Plato and Aristotle had written of catastrophes as regional, and although Ocellus and Polybius did not take issue with this they rather stressed the effect of these upheavals on the human race as a whole. Thus certain features of the *Anacyclōsis* seem related to more recent reflection on cosmic cycles and the overall patterns of human existence.

41. For his terms, see *De universi natura* I,xiv,20–1 (ed. R. Harder, *Neue philologischen Untersuchungen I*, Berlin, 1925, p. 14, sect. 16); cf. xii,6–xiii,19 (p. 14, sects. 14–6). For further discussion of them, see Ryffel, op. cit., pp. 204–7.

42. III,iv,4–7 (Harder, p. 21, sect. 41); cf. Harder's notes, pp. 115–9.

43. III,iv,4–v,14 (Harder, p. 21, sects. 41–2), with v,9–12 on Inachos and the barbarian invasion. (Inachos the Argive, sometimes represented as a river god, yet often also as a mortal ancestor of the Argive kings, may be taken as the earliest human figure in Greek legend.)

There are differences, however. Polybius made his cycle so essentially historical that it ceased to be a mini-cosmology, as it had been in Ocellus. And although the anacyclic process was taken to recur, Polybius nowhere propounded a doctrine of exact recurrence. Only the general configurations, the shifts from one form of constitution to another (as well as the causal factors operating these changes) undergo repetition, even if his acceptance of a fixed historical pattern is in part a concession to Pythagorean and Stoic lines of thought. Furthermore, Polybius went beyond Ocellus in treating catastrophe theory as a secondary issue for historical study. That stance accords well with other known tendencies to historicize and demythologize traditional deluges by ranging them, as did Dicaearchus in the early third century, alongside all those other forces which brought about the destruction of men.[44] When Polybius briefly mentioned catastrophes, he wrote of "floods, pestilences, crop devastations, and other such causes" destroying the human race. Whether or not he was quoting here some of Dicaearchus' very words,[45] his intention was to affirm quite simply that catastrophes were common among mankind, that they were hardly to be limited to deluges or conflagrations, and that they were in no special sense removed from, but on the contrary were very much a part of, the province of "pragmatic history." The weight of recurrence was consistently thrown upon political rather than upon more naturo-historical events. Polybius, the first historian known to have formed a coherent theory of cyclical recurrence, used all his powers of synthesis to demonstrate how mankind's institutions, not just the sweeping changes of nature, conformed to a circling path.

## B. The Polybian "anthropology"

We are now in a more strategic position for analyzing the cycle of governments in greater depth. According to Polybius, those who survived a cataclysm were naturally weakened and clung together for protection. Like animals, they placed their trust in the strongest and bravest of their number, and so there arose a rule best called *monarchia*, the physical prowess of the ruler being the sole rationale behind this most "primitive" of social arrangements (v,9). Men had children, however, and taught their young ones a sense of duty (vi,7; cf. v,10–vi,9). Soon they obeyed their overlord no longer "through fear of his force, but rather their judgment approved him" (vi,11). They now chose and rallied around rulers not on account of their "brute courage" but of "their intellectual and reasoning capacities" (vii,3). Hence kingship replaced primitive monarchy (vi,12–vii,1, 6) because men had naturally acquired feelings of sociability and learned notions of "goodness, justice, and their opposites" (v,10), and because rationality, a

44. Dicaearchus, Frg. 24 (Wehrli, op. cit., vol. 1); pseudo-Hippodamus in Stobaeus *Anthologium* IV,xxxi,71; cf. Ovid *Metamorphoses* XV,240ff. In Plato and Aristotle, however, great flood and fire are not the only natural causes of human destruction: cf. Plato *Leg.* III,677A, V,740E–741A; Aristotle *Meteorol.* I,351b14–6; Frg. 8 ($R^2$2, $R^3$13, W8).

45. Polybius VI,v,5: ὅταν ἢ διὰ κατακλυσμοὺς ἢ διὰ λοιμικὰς περιστάσεις ἢ δι'ἀφορίας καρπῶν ἢ δι'ἄλλας τοιαύτας αἰτίας. . . . Dicaearchus, Frg. 24 (in Cicero): *qui collectis ceteris causis eluvionis, pestilentiae, vastitatis, beluarum etiam repentinae multitudines,* . . . .

faculty peculiar to humans (vi,4), had instructed men's offspring to preserve rather than to reject these first principles of noble conduct (vi,2–9).

How these adjustments also relate to the destined *return* of a political society to its primal condition is not explicitly shown here; yet, looking at the whole model, we are clearly expected to believe that the beginning and the end of the *Anacyclōsis* have something in common. This issue was an awkward one for Polybius, since in carefully describing a situation immediately following a catastrophe he was dealing with social beginnings far more fundamental than any recommencement of the anacyclic process. Had Polybius delineated in more detail the savage elementary state of affairs *between* two separate anacyclic moments, the one concluding with mob rule and the other beginning once more with a primitive monarchy, he probably would not have emphasized all those features which applied to a post-diluvian crisis. There would be no question of a few survivors, for example, and arts and crafts would not necessarily have perished amid socio-political chaos as they did in the vast disruption of a cataclysm.[46] This tension between two different kinds of beginnings remains unresolved, and yet Polybius' lack of tightness and consistency had largely arisen out of his eclectic, accommodating attitude toward well-established yet often competing opinions about man's origins and destiny.

## *The two-staged "anthropology" and its background*

The idea of mankind progressing from a state of primitive helplessness to the civilized condition of flourishing city-states and sophisticated technics was not foreign to Greek thought.[47] Before Polybius it had been advanced in a variety of different ways and by thinkers as dissimilar in their interests as the atomist Democritus and the rhetorician Isocrates. Some had stressed man's productive use of gifts, such as fire, which the gods had originally bestowed on him;[48] others preferred to think of his progressive emancipation from superstition and his arrival at true knowledge concerning the order of things.[49] Some had highlighted humanity's painfully slow upward path toward political organization and civilization,[50] while others concentrated their attention more on the general

46. See v,6. In his description of the barbaric tribes in northern Italy, however, we may have a hint that the two situations were comparable: cf. II,xvii,10–2, IV,v,7–8.

47. L. Edelstein, *The Idea of Progress in Classical Antiquity*, Baltimore, 1967, passim; cf. A. O. Lovejoy and G. Boas, *Primitivism and Related Ideas in Antiquity* (*A Documentary History of Primitivism and Related Ideas, Vol. 1*), Baltimore, 1935, esp. pp. 192ff.; E. A. Havelock, *The Liberal Temper in Greek Politics*, London, 1957, esp. pp. 52ff.

48. Protagoras in Plato *Protagoras* 320D ff.; Aeschylus *Prometheus vinctus* 101ff.

49. Xenophanes, Frg. B18 (Diels-Kranz) = Frg. 191 (Kirk-Raven); Prodicus, Frgs. B2–4 (Diels-Kranz); Critias, Sisyphus Frg. B25 (Diels-Kranz); cf. M. Untersteiner, *The Sophists* (ET), Oxford, 1954, pp. 209–11, 333–5. On Democritus and Hecataeus (after Diodorus Siculus *Bibliotheke* I,vii,8ff.), see K. Reinhardt, "Hekataios von Abdera und Demokrit" in *Vermächtnis der Antike: gesammelte Essays zur Philosophie und Geschichtsschreibung* (ed. C. Becker), Göttingen, 1960, pp. 114–7; cf. A. T. Cole, *Democritus and the Sources of Greek Anthropology* (*American Philological Association, Philological Monographs XXV*), Chapel Hill, N.C., 1967. See also Theophrastus *Peri Eusebias*, Frgs. 2ff. (W. Pötscher).

50. Anaxagoras, esp. Frgs. B21b, A102 (Diels-Kranz); Democritus, Frgs. B144, 154 (Diels-Kranz);

circumstances or on the psychological and educational factors which made the life of the city-state possible.[51] On the other hand, there is a more pessimistic outlook to be reckoned with. Perhaps surprisingly few Greeks painted a picture as indelible as Hesiod's description of the five Ages of mankind, with its gloomy view of the contemporary condition and its idealization of both the heroic Age and the primeval reign of the god-king Kronos.[52] Yet there was a widespread sense of decay overtaking all things. With permanency impossible, then, every human organism and structure had to suffer an end—even if a relative end—to its life.

These different threads of Greek anthropological thought show up in the *Anacyclōsis*, stuffed as they are into Polybius' creation to be a reflection of the "common intelligence." Since Polybius concentrated on socio-political rather than on general cultural developments, moreover, he managed to retrieve some of the traditional theories of progress while at the same time recognizing the inexorability of transience. To begin with, his apparent dissociation of the history of science from the history of constitutions removed the necessity of discussing arts and crafts as if they were subject to periodic cessation and return (as per Aristotle),[53] and of setting too much store by technical improvement as a prerequisite for the social life (a tendency of some Sophists).[54] The important idea of continuing technological progress was thus allowed to retain a right to independent credibility.[55] In handling the formation and fate of polities Polybius fastened primarily onto the moral condition of man, so that questions of progress and regress or of growth and decay became questions of whether mankind was enlightened by rationality or overcome by bestiality, not whether it had acquired skills in the general sense.

Even concerning this moral issue, however, Polybius seems consciously ambivalent so as to do justice to divergent standpoints of anthropological thought. On the one hand, neither the journey to rationality, when man discovered "goodness, justice, and their opposites," nor the establishment of a "true kingship" was accomplished without a struggle.[56] Not only was the primitive monarchy contrasted with this kingship as a rule of ferocity which yielded to the supremacy of reason (VI,vi,12), but the forces of violence lurk in the background

---

Hecataeus (?) in Diodorus Sicul. I,viii,7; Plato *Leg.* III,676Aff.; Isocrates *Panegyricus* xxxii; *Evagoras* vii; Dicaearchus, Frg. 49 (Wehrli, p. 24); etc.

51. Protagoras in Plato *Protagoras* 322 on the early learning of virtue; Polos in Plato *Gorgias* 448C on learning techniques by experience; cf. Hecataeus(?) in Diodorus Sicul. I,viii,7–9. Hecataeus (9) has necessity as the teacher of early men: cf. Aristotle *Politica* 1329b on necessity as the mother of invention. Also, Protagoras (322), Hecataeus (5), Plato (*Leg.* 678C), on the importance of self-protection.

52. Hesiod *Erga* 110ff.

53. Who probably linked such cessation and return with catastrophe theory: see below, Chapter 4, sect. 1; cf. A. Stigen, *The Structure of Aristotle's Thought: An Introduction to the Study of Aristotle's Writings* (*Universitetsforlagets Trykningssentral*), Oslo, 1966, pp. 64ff.

54. Protagoras (esp. 322A–B) and Prodicus; cf. Untersteiner, op. cit., 61, 210. In using the word "Sophist" I am at the mercy of convention: cf. Philostratus *De Sophistis* proem. 479, I,480–1.

55. Note also *Hist.* IX,ii,5, X,xlvii,12; cf. II,xvii,10, III,lviii,5–lix,8, VIII,vi–vii.

56. *Hist.* VI,vii,1; cf. vi,6a, 11b, 26.

behind the whole *Anacyclōsis*, and though temporarily restrained, they reemerge in their fullness at the end of the cycle, when men's renewed search for a *despotēs* or *monarchos* coincides with their degeneration back into bestiality (ix,7b, 9). Looked at from this viewpoint, man's early animal-like condition was not the subject of idealization. Men had to progress out of it to acquire reason and morality. On the other hand, Polybius made concessions to the more primitivistic vein in Greek thought, for it was in this early situation that a sense of duty took root, and in fact he suggested that the very same ruler who was a *monarchos* became by degrees a king (*basileus*) (vi,10–12, vii,1).

What becomes apparent, then, is that for Polybius there were two stages of the elementary, preconstitutional life of mankind, the earliest and first being marked by man's fragility and animal-like instinct for self-preservation (cf. v,8), and the second being the stage when moral awareness was strong enough to establish a polity which, through the excellency of the ruler's judgments, provided security and abundance for the people (vii,3–4). It is this second phase which reflects those more primitivistic features in Greek thought. Both stages taken together suggest the idea of progress toward the social life, but with the second, traditional notions of early man's pure virtues and of an ideal primeval king show beneath the surface. Thus Polybius' anthropology, in the cunning of its construction, neither completely excludes human progress nor openly disallows the view that in the earliest we may discover the best. We are somehow persuaded that both notions can be accommodated even if neither is openly espoused.

Polybius' "anthropology" may be appreciated more fully if one explores his possible use of sources. It is both natural and profitable to begin with Plato. Plato was the one philosopher Polybius actually named in connection with the *Anacyclōsis*, and if anything came first to the reader's mind in pondering his treatment of catastrophe theory, it would certainly be the seminal dialogue in Plato's *Laws* Bk. III. Polybius significantly admitted that the subject of the natural changes of societies into their different forms had been treated with more precision and subtlety by Plato and certain other unnamed philosophers (v,1). One naturally asks, then, whether Polybius understood Plato to have taught a form of the doctrine of *Anacyclōsis*. Aristotle had concluded that in the *Republic* Bk. VIII Plato conceived a cycle running from his ideal polity through different constitutional forms to tyranny and back to the ideal again. Was Polybius familiar with this interpretation? Probably not. He does not seem to have read Aristotle's *Politica*,[57] and Plato's *Republic* itself contains no reference to such a cycle, nor to the sort of early and elementary human conditions found in the Polybian *Anacyclōsis*.[58] What is most likely is that Polybius conceived two quite separate items of Plato's social and political theory, namely the account of societal growth (*epidosis*) in the *Laws* Bk. III, and the analysis of degeneration

57. Polybius probably read Aristotle's lost *Constitutions* (cf. *Hist.* XII,v–xvi), but the influence of the *Politics* and *Nicomachean Ethics* seems indirect (cf. Walbank, *Commentary*, vol. 1, p. 643).

58. *Resp.* II,369B–374E may be noted but is unrelated to Polybius' concerns.

(*phthora*) in the *Republic* Bk. VIII, as two parts of the same nexus of ideas. It is not hard to imagine a mind as unphilosophical and historically-oriented as Polybius' assimilating the "progressive" and "regressive" elements of Plato's work into one consistent system. Indeed, it is necessary to reckon with this probability if one is going to make any sense of Polybius' association of the *Anacyclōsis* with Plato's name, for in the *Laws* Plato had narrated how the various yet familiar constitutions of the Hellenic world had emerged from a primitive stage, with no more than a few, albeit suggestive, hints concerning their eventual decay as a whole set of phenomena,[59] while in the *Republic* one finds no relevant, historical-looking treatment of conditions preceding the ideal polity and no catastrophe theory, but only a stage-by-stage account of socio-political decay.[60]

We shall see later that, granted Polybius did effect this conjunction between the *Laws* Bk. III and the *Republic* Bk. VIII, it was easy for him to derive from Plato the order of constitutional types which one finds in his anacyclic model. At this stage, however, it suffices to note two crucial facts. First, in the *Laws* Plato explained how groups of mountaineering herdsmen who had survived the last cataclysm slowly gained enough courage to establish relationships with one another, to form clans and migrate to lower terrain where, on the analogy of the family, each clan accepted a one-man rule of power (*dynasteia*), or "a kingship which of all kingships was the most just."[61] And second, the line of degeneration described in the *Republic* stops short of the worst kind of government, tyranny, a despotism which is the result of the mob clamoring for a champion.[62] Now, unlike Aristotle, Polybius did not reckon with any subsequent reemergence of the ideal republic in the Platonic series. For Polybius that ideal was irrelevant to the facts of history (cf. VI,xlvii,7–10), so that in taking Plato to be teaching some more complicated version of *anacyclōsis* he apparently took the Platonic picture of degeneration into tyranny to mean a reversion to an elementary human condition, one partly analogous to a post-cataclysmic situation and one in which people had to learn all over again the ethical foundations of political life. By this reading, Plato's tyrant, set up by the furious mob, can be equated with the *monarchos* at the beginning and end of the Polybian cycle, and Plato's "just king" in the *Laws* can be identified with Polybius' "true king" who replaces the rule of brute force by the power of reason. Thus at the beginning and end of Polybius' cyclical process lay the same situation in which no polity, in any conventional sense, existed, and if Polybius owed to anyone the double truth that mankind both climbed out of *and* degenerated into these circumstances, it was to Plato.

59. *Leg.* III,701B–C; cf. VIII,832B, and below, sect. D.

60. *Resp.* VIII,548Eff., 553Aff., 558Dff., 571Aff. (cf. *Epistulae* VII,326D); J. Gould, *The Development of Plato's Ethics*, Cambridge, 1955, pp. 183ff.; cf. R. G. Bury, "Plato and Progress" in *Philosophical Review* LV, 1946, pp. 651ff.; J. Luccioni, *La Pensée politique de Platon* (*Publications de la Faculté des Lettres d'Alger* XXX), Paris, 1958, ch. 1.

61. *Leg.* III,677B, 678C–D, 680B, D, E, 682B–C.

62. *Resp.* VIII,562A ff., 565C–566C, 569C, 575C, 576D; cf. *Politicus* 302E.

Polybius, of course, distorted Plato. He made him more of a cyclical theorist of history than he actually was. Furthermore, not all the details of Plato's "anthropology" suited Polybius. The philosopher's herdsmen were more virtuous than Polybius' early men. They were not brutish or violent so much as "more simple, brave, temperate, and in every way more righteous" than succeeding generations, and hence established the most just of kingships.[63] Besides, Plato made no explicit reference to their submission to any *monarchos*, that is, to one who either preceded or changed into the "just king," while their establishment of the first constitution had more to do with the results of familial and group organization than with the growth of a sense of duty.[64] On the other hand, Plato gave an account of the Cyclops, and if taken seriously, one could easily read into his rather abstruse phrases the idea of a savage one-man rule existing prior to the emergence of a patriarchal kingship (*Leg.* III,680B, D). Moreover, Plato's discussion of herdlike behavior, early virtues, parental training, and the bravery of the younger generation are hardly unimportant clues; they confirm the *Laws* as a major source. But it is not likely that Polybius had a Platonic text in front of him—he was probably relying on his good memory—and one should also remember his readiness to accommodate conflicting traditions.

Polybius' eclectic tendencies suggest that he was not likely to reproduce Plato, and certainly not those aspects of Platonic thought which conflicted with other well-settled anthropologies. Plato had placed emphasis on the painful slowness of growth toward organized political life, and had forged a close connection between the progress of skills and the growth of political consciousness (cf. *Leg.* III,677C–D, 678D, 679D, etc.). Polybius could retain neither component because both vitiated his concept of a continuing cycle. Along with others, Plato emphasized such slowness to verify the eternity of the world,[65] yet we already know how on such disputable cosmological matters Polybius effected a compromise among a diversity of views. Despite the apparently impressive influence of Plato, in fact, compromises still remain present in his "anthropology." We might say that to treat Plato as so decidedly cyclical a thinker was, if anything, Aristotelian; certainly the idea of mankind's upward path from natural weakness to political (and more highly-developed technological) life was a well-known Sophistic teaching, linked with the Sophists' doctrines about man's capacity to learn by experience.[66] The idea that early man had started his career in a fragile condition could also be said to be Sophistic, and it is not, strictly speaking, present in Plato. Polybius, we must note, spoke very generally of this weakness, allowing for the idea of war or of danger from wild animals (or, in other words, different lines of interpretation) to be covered.[67] Again, the notion

63. *Leg.* III,678E, 679D, 679E (for the quotation), 680E.

64. *Leg.* III,680D–E; cf. Aristotle *Politica* 1257a19ff.

65. *Leg.* III,680A; cf. Isocrates *Paneg.* xxxii; Dicaearchus, Frg. 47 (Wehrli, p. 22).

66. Above; cf. also Isocrates *Evagoras* vii.

67. *Hist.* VI,v,7; cf. Protagoras (322B, C); Hecataeus(?) in Diodorus Sicul. I,viii,5–7; Lucretius *De rerum natura* V,1419ff. (Atomist source?); Prodicus (Untersteiner, 210). Also Panaetius, Frg. 118 (van Straaten), yet cf. Plato *Leg.* III,678E–680E.

of one-man rule as the first kind of social control was neither peculiarly Sophistic nor Platonic; its roots went back to earlier teachers of wisdom and it had enjoyed wide currency since. The divine ruler Kronos continued to lurk in the background of speculation about the first men,[68] and there was a frequent tendency to idealize the ancient kings.[69]

Polybius' image of the first rule was stark by comparison, and a clever semantic and institutional distinction between monarchy and kingship entered into his discussion. Hints of this distinction may be found in Alcmaeon, Critias, and the "anonymous" Iamblichus among the pre-Socratics,[70] but it was the architect of the *Anacyclōsis* himself (in my view Polybius) who was the innovator at this point, and this was largely because he sought to render his theory both acceptable and convincing.[71] His colleague Panaetius may have depicted the ancestral king as an honest man able to protect the weak from the violent and the poor from the rich; but for Polybius the ruler was brave first and morally excellent afterward. Polybius had the cycle of governments to contend with. In his view, a social condition with no real polity, with absence of custom, and with a susceptibility to lawlessness and animalization was the key concept which linked the two ends of his cyclical process and confirmed its continuity. Once that link was made, Polybius found it easy to be concessive about others' idyllic images, although it is nevertheless true that the second stage of his "anthropology" was not meant simply to reflect traditional views about the reign of a "just king." Moral training also occupied Polybius' attention. He evidently argued (with the Sophists?) that civic virtue could be taught.[72] In a special sense he also held that man was by nature a political animal;[73] man in his elementary state was a creature inclined to self-propagation like other animals, yet he possessed the power of reason to guide the conduct of his progeny for his own future well-being and the welfare of the group. On that point Polybius was significantly close to the Stoic Panaetius.[74] Training for duty and training to destroy brutishness were important ideas for Polybius, and his interest in the way the forces of

68. Hesiod *Erga* 110ff.; Pindar *Pythian Odes* III,4, and cf. Xenophanes, Frg. B12 (Diels-Kranz); Plato *Politicus* 271C ff.; *Leg.* IV,713C–D, on Zeus as king and father.

69. Plato *Leg.* III,680E; Aristotle *Politica* 1285b4ff.; Isocrates *Panathenaicus* cxxi ff.; Panaetius in Cicero *De officiis* II,xii (van Straaten, Frg. 120); Cicero *De re publica* I,xxxv,54 (Stoic source?); *De legibus* II,ii; Sallust *Catiline* I,2; Lucretius *Rer. nat.* V,1105ff.; Tacitus *Annales* I,2; Poseidonius in Seneca *Epistulae* XV; Dionysius of Halicarnassus *Archaeologiae* I,lxxv ff.; Trogus in Justin *Epitome* I,1. Cf. also Gorgias, Frg. B11a (Diels-Kranz, vol. 2, p. 297, *ll.*19–26); Diodorus Sicul. I,ix,2ff. (= Hecataeus?); etc.

70. Alcmaeon, Frg. B4; Critias, Frg. B25; Anon. Iamblichus, Frg. 7 (all Diels-Kranz, the last reference in vol. 2, p. 404).

71. Plato (in *Politicus* 291E) and Aristotle (*Ethica Nicomachea* VIII,x,3) consider *monarchia* as one-man rule with kingship and tyranny as its two aspects (cf. Polybius *Hist.* VI,iii,9). Isocrates, in *Panathenaicus* cxxi comes closer to Polybius.

72. Cf. A. W. H. Adkins, *Moral Values and Political Behaviour in Ancient Greece: From Homer to the End of the Fifth Century*, London, 1972, pp. 99ff.

73. So Aristotle *Politica* 1253a3.

74. *Hist.* VI,vi,1–3; Panaetius, Frgs. 79–81 (van Straaten); cf. Aristotle *Polit.* 1253a10ff. Also see E. Graeber, *Die Lehre von der Mischverfassung bei Polybios* (*Schriften zur Rechtslehre und Politik LII*), Bonn, 1968, p. 55, on the Stoic understanding of man as a political animal.

bestiality were restrained by education, and in the growth of morality (as distinct from skills, beliefs, even purely civic virtue) in its primitive setting, probably have their closest connections with certain Stoic preoccupations.[75]

It is apparent, then, that more than one traditional anthropology lies behind Polybius' description of how man attained to a polity. The shadow of Plato is the most definite, but Polybius wished his general truths to be based on a range of existing, even if divergent, theories. His readjustments to others' thoughts were not merely for syncretism's sake, moreover, but were governed above all by his aim of producing a coherent, convincing rule of thumb concerning historical recurrence. Not a few thinkers interested in anthropology remained unconcerned with cyclical or recurrence ideas, speaking as they did of either progress or regress; yet Polybius still used their varying opinions to fulfill his aim.

### *The "anthropology" and the three-stationed biological principle*

The special nuances of Polybian "anthropology" aside, we now need to reflect on its implications for the general shape of the *Anacyclōsis*. In his first brief account of the sequence of constitutions Polybius made a significant distinction between the coming-to-be of primitive monarchy and that of the kingship which followed. The former's emergence came "unaided and naturally," while the latter's was "with [artificial] preparation and the rectification of defects" (VI,iv,7). From his more elaborate outline, too, we can distinguish the first stage of his "anthropology," which was natural (*physikōs*), from the second, which was one of moral preparation (v,4–9, and cf. v,9–vii, 1). One may detect the implication, then, that Polybius' *Urmonarchie* belongs to a special category, distinct from the six constitutional forms following it. Although he wrote of the whole *Anacyclōsis* as a natural order of events, he clearly wished to assert that the changes between the six major constitutions were effected by human will, aim, preparation, political self-interest, and so on, but that the grounds upon which the primitive monarch arose were those of unreasoning instinct, necessity, brute force, and the elementary laws of nature (v,7, 8, vi,2, 7, 12). We will soon be discussing Polybius' suggested reasons for political change along the zigzag line from kingship to mob rule, but here it suffices to note his efforts to expose the emphatically *natural* basis of the primitive monarchy and its emergence. Moreover, although this monarchy provided the historical basis for the kingly and tyrannical *politeiai* (VI,iv,6–7), he nevertheless associated it with a situation in which the ordinary conditions for civic life did not exist. It will be appreciated that the word *politeia* carries a certain ambiguity, since it can mean a specific constitution as well as "polity" or "the state," that is to say, the

75. With *Hist.* VI,v,10, vi,2, 4, 8, and see IV,xx,1–xxi,6 (on the reasons for bestiality in Arcadia); cf. Panaetius, Frgs. 79–81, 120; Seneca *Epistulae* VII; Graeber, op. cit., p. 62. However, related ideas pervade Greek (and some earlier Roman) educational thought in one form or another: W. Jaeger, *Paideia: The Ideals of Greek Culture* (ET), Oxford, 1946–7, esp. vol. 2, pp. 224ff.; M. Taylor, "Progress and Primitivism in Lucretius" in *American Journal of Philology* LXVIII, 1947, pp. 187f.; etc.

conditions under which civic life, as against non-civic life, is maintained. Polybius implied that conditions of polity did not really come into being until men attained the necessary degree of ethical awareness. Thus his "anthropology" and his treatment of the early monarch hang very closely together, and both have been appended to the constitutional zigzag, telling us still more about the composite character of the *Anacyclōsis*.[76]

Quite clearly, the monarchy of force does not relate readily to the major sequence of constitutional change in the *Anacyclōsis*; it tends to modify the zigzag line from kingship to mob rule. It is too simple, for instance, to speak of the passage from monarchy to kingship as a transference from a bad to a good constitution, and it is difficult to see the zigzag applying in the case of mob rule degenerating into a state of bestiality. What is equally important, however, is that there are other analyses of constitutional change still extant, and these conform to a six-part rather than a seven-part series. In Bk. VIII of the *Nicomachean Ethics*, for example, Aristotle introduced three forms of *politeiai*: kingship, aristocracy, and timocracy (a "constitutional form of government"), with their corresponding perversions and corruptions, tyranny, oligarchy, and democracy (VIII,x,1–3). Although these constitutions were not linked in a developing chain, Aristotle nevertheless listed them in an order similar to Polybius'. He at least noted how kingship degenerated into tyranny, aristocracy to oligarchy, timocracy to democracy (the last nomenclatures being altered in the *Anacyclōsis*), even if he made no mention of any passage from tyranny to aristocracy or from oligarchy to timocracy (let alone from democracy to a returning kingship).[77] Furthermore, Plato had discussed three lawful constitutions and their three lawless deviants in the *Politicus* (although he could find no appropriate political terms to distinguish good from bad democracy), and again the material follows the order: one man rules/minority rules/majority rules.[78] After Polybius, one finds Arius Didymus, Emperor Augustus' teacher, with a six-part framework that recalls the *Anacyclōsis*.[79] In none of these presentations, however, does a primitive monarchy make an appearance. Thus our suspicions are confirmed that Polybius combined two sets of material derived from separate areas of theoretical speculation: he wedded an "anthropology" to an hexadic framework of constitutional change, and his "anthropology," with its *monarchos*-figure, was intended as the basis for understanding conditions at either end of the major constitutional sequence. These conditions became the *termini ad quem et a quo* of the cycle, and it is justifiable to write of them as conditions of non-polity because with them the normative life of the city-state has either been dissolved or has not yet come into being.

76. Cf. T. H. Cole, "The Sources and Composition of Polybius VI" in *Historia* XIII, 1964, p. 455. On the ambiguity of *politeia*, see Schweighaeuser, op. cit., vol. 8, p. 486.

77. Aristotle's aim was to draw analogies between political forms and the structures of family life: see *Eth. Nic.* VIII,x,1–6; cf. *Ethica Eudemia* 1241b25–33, *Politica* 1279a17–b10.

78. *Politicus* 291C–292A, 300E–303C (and on terminology, 291E–292A).

79. See Chapter 4, introd.

We may now begin to see that the anacyclic model contains a far more significant synthesis of ideas than we have brought out so far. Since the work of Heinrich Ryffel, scholars have come to acknowledge that Polybius actually appealed to two "laws" of constitutional change which clearly excluded each other.[80] The first was the law of a fixed sequence and course, involving the path from one-man rule to mob rule; while the second was more simply and conventionally structured:

Every body or state or action has its natural stage of growth (*auxēsis*), then of prime (*acmē*), and finally of decay (*phthisis*), and . . . everything in them is at its best at the zenith. (VI,li,4)

Ryffel termed the first the law of *Anacyclōsis*—it comes so very near to the heart of Polybius' model as it is best remembered—and the second he termed the "biological" or "three-station" principle, taking the three stations to be growth, acme, and decline.[81] The apparent contradiction between these two theoretical formulae resides in the fact that the *Anacyclōsis* has no identifiable acme, but rather the three high points of kingship, aristocracy, and democracy. One might be tempted to conclude that it is not necessary to resolve the tension here, that for Polybius the three-station theory applied to the general development of states like Rome and Carthage whereas the *Anacyclōsis* was concerned strictly with changes in the forms (*eidē*) of constitutions. Yet such an interpretation blurs the extent to which Polybius integrated different ideas. Granted that the *Anacyclōsis* has no clear zenith, we have already discovered at least one way in which the biological principle may nevertheless be reflected in the anacyclic process as a whole. The rise from primitiveness to kingship and the decline from mob rule into bestiality are so much more decisive than the other types of change within the model that the largest of his cycles in the *Anacyclōsis* emerges as the passage from conditions that are *urpolitisch* to the state of polity, and then back to the elementary situation once more. As we shall see, there are other, smaller cases of growth and decay within the *Anacyclōsis*, and when discussing the place of the mixed constitution in Polybian thought we will find another crucial way in which the "zigzag" and the biological principle may be integrated. But this very general curve also demands the recognition it has not yet received: not only does the space devoted to anthropological issues confirm its importance, but it is also true that it invokes traditional themes from Greek social theory. Although Polybius wrote too much under the shadow of the great fourth-century critics of democracy to accept this tradition on its own, I think especially of the democratic-Athenian tradition in which a polity became a reality only after the people removed a violent and arbitrary tyranny.[82]

80. Ryffel, op. cit., pp. 186–221; cf. Walbank, *Commentary*, vol. 1, pp. 645–7; Pédech, op. cit., pp. 308–9.

81. Op. cit., pp. 209ff.

82. Attic Scolion (*Scolia Anonyma* 10, 13); Alcmaeon, Frg. 24B4, and Democritus, Frg. 68B251 (both Diels-Kranz); Demosthenes *Philippics* II,21; Isocrates *Paneg.* xxxix; and on the monarchy-polity dichotomy underlying Aristotle's *Polit.* V, see W. L. Newman, *The Politics of Aristotle*,

In review, then, the *Anacyclōsis* appears to be reducible to a single cycle, one with similar conditions at both the beginning and the renewal point, and one characterizable in terms of organic growth and decay.[83] Let us be cautious, however. It is not unfair to represent the cycle in the three (biological) stations: growth (toward a polity), acme (a polity), and decay (away from a polity). Yet there are other ways of expressing the more general changes of the anacyclic process. One could speak, for instance, of an alternation between the general conditions of non-polity and those of political societies. Having finished his account of the *Anacyclōsis*, moreover, Polybius significantly wrote of the reversion to an original state of affairs as a return to "opposite" conditions (*palin eis hauta katantā ta kata tas politeias*) (VI,ix,10), alluding to the antithesis between civic life and its absence in such a way as to reinforce the impression of an alternating process. Cyclical movement and alternation were not hard to bring together—that had certainly been done before, perhaps most remarkably by Empedocles—but the combination adds yet another aspect to Polybius' eclectic tendencies. The interconnection between cyclical and alternating motion becomes still more important when we examine the most memorable and prominent feature of the *Anacyclōsis*, the zigzag line between worthy and unworthy constitutions.

## C. The anacyclic zigzag

The zigzag may be considered either as one block of material or as three separate units: it will be more rewarding to be analytic first and synoptic afterward. Although Polybius first introduced his six types of constitution as two triads, the three constitutions "on everybody's lips" and their three "vicious counterparts" (VI,iv,6, 8; cf. x,7), he in effect treated them as three pairs strung together. One is thus reminded of Aristotle's dyads in the *Nicomachean Ethics* (and elsewhere),[84] even though the philosopher did not place them in one extended sequence. With this consideration of kingship and tyranny, aristocracy and oligarchy, democracy and mob rule as twins, one enters that amorphous field of Greek political speculation best described (again in Ryffel's useful term) as *metabolē* theory, or theory of change.[85] This encompasses, perhaps a little too

Oxford, 1887–1902, vol. 1, p. 521. For the paradigm case of the Cleisthenic settlement following the Peisistratid tyranny in Athens, see Aristotle *Athenaiōn Politeia* xx–xxiii; cf. Herodotus *Historiae* V,61ff.; Aeschylus *Suppliants ll.*694ff.; and see V. Ehrenberg, "Origins of Democracy" in *Historia* I, 1950, pp. 517–24. On the same theme much later, see Lucretius *Rer. nat.* V,1120–47; and on Polybius' treatment of Achaia's early history, see *Hist.* II,xli,1–5, IV,i,5; cf. T. H. Cole, loc. cit., p. 454.

83. Explaining the apparent disparity between the anacyclic zigzag and the biological principle in terms of a source behind VI,iii–ix, or of Polybius' intellectual development, only tends to multiply hypotheses. Against Ryffel, op. cit., pp. 185, 195, 202; O. Cuntz, *Polybios und sein Werk*, Leipzig, 1902, pp. 40ff.; G. De Sanctis, *Storia dei Romani*, Florence, 1907–23, vol. 3, pt. 1, pp. 206ff.; cf. Walbank, *Commentary*, vol. 1, p. 646; Pédech, op. cit., pp. 310–1.

84. *Eth. Eud.* 1241b27–32; *Polit.* 1279a28–66. Cf. Arius Didymus, below, Chapter 4, introd.

85. Ryffel, op. cit., pp. 23–79.

unconditionally, a great variety of reflections which go back at least to the sixth century, on the causes and major types of political change, especially degeneration from "good" into "bad" government. With the *Anacyclōsis*, however, one has to reckon with other features not fully developed in early *metabolē* theory. There is the rather Peripatetic preoccupation with classifying constitutions into different types (although Aristotle would have wished for a more exhaustive inquiry and a greater awareness of historical variety than Polybius allowed for), and there remains that concern to trace a long, even if not factually defensible, line of constitutional development which hails, above all, from Plato. It will be profitable to proceed through the constitutional sequence stage by stage in order to isolate the peculiarities of Polybius' position and gauge the influence of background ideas.

One naturally begins with Polybius' treatment of kingship and its breakdown into tyranny. He contended that true kingship was based on goodness and justice, and that its power was really maintained by the people, who chose their kings for life and harbored no ill will toward them because of the security and provisions they bestowed. But once kings received their office by hereditary right and gained a certain inviolability, their living habits became far less frugal and more licentious.

> Those habits having given rise in the first place to envy and injury, and in the second to an outburst of hate and hostile resentment, the kingship became a tyranny. (VI,vii,8; cf. vii,1–7)

Now, much thinking within the compass of *metabolē* theory was concerned with tyranny. The traditional and most widely-supported approach ascribed the causes of despotical régimes to the shift in the attitude of kings toward their offices, their refusal to care for the subjects of the state, and their efforts to establish the lawless, self-seeking rule of absolute power.[86] The emphasis on the misuse of authority was present in alternative approaches, but with these the element of degeneration from kingship was excluded. A predominantly Athe-

86. K. F. Stroheker, "Zu den Anfängen der monarchischen Theorie in der Sophistik" in *Historia* II, 1953–4, pp. 387ff. Cf. also Herodotus *Hist.* III,16ff., 80, V,61ff., VII; Plato *Leg.* 694A–696B; *Gorgias* 483D–E, 525C ff.; *Menexenus* 293D ff. Using Dorian traditions, Plato emphasized the weaknesses of the first Heraclidae kings: *Leg.* III, 685C–686C. 691A–D, 692B; others blamed their downfall on the recalcitrant populace: Isocrates *Archidamus* xxii, Ephorus, after Pausanias *Descriptio* II,xix,2 and in Frgs. 116–7 (F. Jacoby, ed., *Die Fragmente der griechischen Historiker*, Berlin, 1926–58, pt. 1, vol. 2a, pp. 72–3) (Jacoby hereafter *FGH*); cf. A. Andrewes, "Ephorus Book 1 and the Kings of Argos" in *Classical Quarterly* N.S. I, 1951, pp. 39ff. Further on tyranny: Aristotle *Eth. Nic.* VIII,x,2–3, *Polit.* 1310b18–20; Thucydides *Hist.* I,xiii,1; pseudo-Hippodamus in Stobaeus Anthol. IV,v,95 (ed. O. Hense, vol. 4, p. 36, *ll.*2–4); Euripides, Frg. 282; Isocrates *De pacis* cxi ff., *Helen* xxxii; Theophrastus in Dionysius of Halicarnassus *Archaeol.* V,lxxiv,1–2; Tacitus *Annales* III,26; Lucretius *Rer. nat.* V,1144, and cf. also below, Chapter 4, introd., on Roman interpretations of their early kings. For the special case of Timaeus, who probably conceived a sequence of governments for early Syracusan history down to the reign of Theron (488–72 BC), and whose reputation was significantly resented by Polybius, see T. S. Brown, *Timaeus of Tauromenium* (*University of California Publications in History LV*), Berkeley and Los Angeles, 1958, p. 58; cf. F. W. Walbank, "Polemic in Polybius" in *Journal of Roman Studies* LII, 1962, esp. p. 10.

nian line of explanation, for example, took tyranny to arise because the masses backed a champion to redress wrongs inflicted by oppressive oligarchs, while others wrote of tyranny as rule before the establishment of any genuine polity.[87] Polybius adopted the first approach (the last had already been established in the ambiguity surrounding the *monarchos*), yet he evidently intended to account for a range of one-man rules and to recognize different bases of monarchical power (force, reason, benefaction, popular consent, courtly splendor, personal aggrandizement).

This concern is comparable with an attempt by Aristotle to classify kingships into five types. Although Polybius mapped out the types and stages of monarchical rule a little differently,[88] he was hardly uninterested in and certainly not ignorant of the variety of possible political forms. However, if we take only his anacyclic model, he was quite unlike Aristotle (and the Peripatetics) in neglecting the variety of *contexts* in which different kinds of governments and constitutional change could manifest themselves. The facts of history taught Aristotle that various forms of kingship could exist in quite separate contexts, that kingship was capable of changing into aristocracy, and that both democracy and oligarchy might be removed by a popular tyrant,[89] but the *Anacyclōsis* had no provision for such changes, narrowed as it was by its fixed sequence and cyclicism. On the other hand, by limiting history's possibilities Polybius was able to capitalize on other approaches and traditions: chief among these were the ideas of Plato, who significantly took over much conventional *metabolē* theory. Obviously, Plato does not look so useful for Polybius on kingship and tyranny, for although in the *Laws* Bk. III he referred to the lapse of the former into the latter, he also placed a tyrant at the end of his series in the *Republic* Bk. VIII. But assuming that Polybius equated the tyrant of the *Republic* with his *monarchos*-figure, it is the *Laws* which becomes important at this point. And in effect the only really impressive statement Plato ever made about the *recurrence* of constitutional change has to do with kings degenerating into tyrants. Commenting on two sons of Heracles, early Laconian kings who failed to live up to expectation and became tyrants because of their depravity and not their want of skill,[90] he averred:

> This was the course of events then, and is so still; and whenever such events occur, will be so in the future. (*Leg.*, III,688D; cf. 683Dff.)

87. The former approach: Herodotus *Hist.* I,58ff.; Aristotle *Ath. pol.* xiii f.; *Polit.* 1286b16–7, and cf. 1305a7ff., 1310b15–6; pseudo-Hippodamus (Hense, p. 35, *ll.*17–8). The latter: see esp. T. H. Cole, loc. cit., p. 456; cf. above, sect. B. Against both approaches, see Xenophon *Hiero* i,1ff.

88. Aristotle's types in the *Politica* run: hereditary kingship with limited functions exercised through popular consent during the heroic Age; the barbarian type, hereditary and despotic but constitutional; an elective tyranny or dictatorship; Spartan hereditary generalship; and the absolute sovereignty of one enjoying authority over the state as a father does over his household (1285a–1286b).

89. *Polit.* 1286b10–14 (kingship to aristocracy), 1305a7ff. (democracy to tyranny), 1286b14–17 (oligarchy to tyranny).

90. On depravity (*kakia*) as an ethico-political term (in Sophistic writing), cf. Ryffel, op. cit., pp. 52, 82.

Aristotle, too, recognized this as a basic model of *metabolē* theory (cf. *Eth. Nic.* VIII,x,3), so that Polybius' concern for the decay of kingship into tyranny largely tends to the mainstream line of thought about regular change and one-man rules.

In connection with one-man rules, however, there are some special syncretisms which still have to be reckoned with. These have to do with the relationship between Polybius' monarchy and his tyranny. On the one hand, he wished his *monarchos*-figure to symbolize the condition of non-polity, even if, on the other, there was a point at which the primitive monarchy marked a necessary stage in the growth out of utter bestiality. Now this meant that the tyrant he depicted as the depraved type of king had to be someone less brutal and more innocuous than the *monarchos*, and that is precisely what he was. Within the zigzag, the real sting has been taken out of the most unpleasant of all governmental forms. Apart from the traditional labeling of tyrants as men of *hybris* (political insolence) (VI,vii,9),[91] Polybius tells us little more than that they were overindulgent and sexually licentious, and that they provoked resentment and conspiracy. General political lawlessness (*anomia*), or any stress on the unwelcome rule of force, or, above all, enslavement (*douleia*), is absent.[92] It would be too facile, though, to construe Polybius' treatment as a whitewash. After all, his treatment of kingship and tyranny relied on age-long categories of thought about luxury as the cause of a régime's dissipation. "First there comes to the state dainty effeminacy," runs an old saying ascribed to Pythagoras, "and thereupon petulance, insolence, and after that, destruction," and Polybius was telling essentially the same story about kings and tyrants.[93] It remains true, however, that he ranked tyranny as a form of government. Perhaps that was in accord with more favorable or lenient attitudes toward tyranny,[94] but it simply suited Polybius here to consider it as the bad side to kingship and not as the utter ruin of political life. And his point about tyranny as a specific constitution was clinched by his next telling point—that aristocracy originated at the very onset of tyrannical power.

The passage from tyranny to aristocracy was effected by nobleminded, brave men of the city-state who could not tolerate the insolence of the tyrant (VI,vii,9). These men acted in the interests of the populace (who continued to be a determining background factor), and as "nobles" they became the new leaders

91. On *hybris*, esp. in Herodotus, see below, Chapter 2, sect. B, pt. 2(i). Cf. Ryffel, op. cit., pp. 17f.

92. On these terms in classical *metabolē* theory see Ryffel, op. cit., pp. 17ff., 50ff. Also see Herodotus *Hist.* VII,102, IX,90; Plato *Menexenus* 239E–240E; Isocrates *Paneg.* xcvi; cf. Polybius *Hist.* XXVIII,ii,1–4, on the Great King as the bearer of enslavement for Greece; and Plato *Leg.* III,695D–E; Aristotle *Eth. Nic.* VIII,x,4; Isocrates *Paneg.* lxxxviii–xc, on the Great King symbolizing arch-tyranny.

93. Cf. Stobaeus *Anthol.* IV,i,80.

94. Tyranny could be viewed phenomenologically rather than condemned ethically: e.g., Thucydides *Hist.* I,17; Plato *Leg.* IV,712D and *Epis.* VII,326D; Aristotle *Polit.* 1314a15–1315b39; Isocrates *Evagoras* xlvi, *Nicocles* xxi, *Archidamus* xliv–xlvi; cf. Archytas of Tarentum in Stobaeus *Anthol.* IV,i,137.

of the people. Monarchy in the sense of one-man rule was abolished, and aristocracy took its place (viii,1–2). The descendants of the aristocrats, however, were unable to keep up a paternal concern for the common interest, and gave themselves over to grasping selfishness, avarice, convivial excess, and licentiousness, thus producing oligarchy (4–5).

Concerning minority rule Polybius was rather sketchy: one might be tempted to characterize his account as a mere adaptation of the analysis on one-man rule. Nevertheless, considering that he had less traditional material to play with, he remained concerned about reflecting established lines of interpretation and adjusting them for his own purposes. A passage from Aristotle is most pertinent here. In the *Politica* Bk. III it is contended that kings ruled in early times because "it was rare to find men who greatly excelled in virtue." When men with comparable virtues appeared in great numbers, however,

> they would no longer submit [to one-man rule], but sought to set up a community in the form of a political society. When men became worse, however, and began to make money out of the community, wealth became the road to honor, and so, we may reasonably say, oligarchies sprang up. (1286b9–16)

Here we see a three-part frame: virtuous men not submitting to one-man rule (*basileia*); virtuous men establishing a community (*koinon*) and a political society (*politeia*) (*aristocratia* not named); then oligarchy. The Polybian structure is quite close: noble men intolerant of tyranny; their establishment of an aristocracy; oligarchy. We must also take into account how democratically-inclined writers had distinguished a genuine polity from pre-political one-man rule by pointing to its magistracies, and aristocracy presupposed magistrates just as readily as any democracy.[95] Plato reflected this line of approach when he referred to aristocracy after the "just king" (*Leg.* III,681D).[96] Plato's shadow falls on the scene darker yet, since the Polybian picture of oligarchic avarice had an important precedent in the philosopher's analysis of oligarchy in the *Republic* Bk. VIII (550C–555A), and it is also interesting that both Plato and Polybius, unlike Aristotle, do not appear to associate oligarchy with a decrease in the number of those ruling.[97] Thus once more the historian wrestled with notions of regular *metabolē* and synthesized different lines of approach.

What of the next segment of the *Anacyclōsis*? The oligarchs meet the very same disastrous end as the tyrant. At first supporting anybody brave enough to oppose the greed and lechery of the oligarchs, the people finally succeed in overthrowing them. Through fear of tyranny, however, the people do not revert to one-man rule, but create a democracy, "taking public affairs to be a matter of their own responsibility and conduct" (VI,ix,3; cf. 1–2). This new constitution lasts only so long as its many participants place a high value on equality and

95. For background see A. Fuks, *The Ancestral Constitution*, London, 1953, esp. pp. 107–11.

96. For complications, however, see below, sect. D.

97. Polybius *Hist.* VI,viii,4–6, ix,2; Plato *Resp.* VIII,550D ff. and *Politicus* 291E, 292C, 301A; yet cf. Aristotle *Politica* 1293a11ff.

freedom of speech, but once later generations fail in this, then bad men of means "tempt and corrupt the people" in "their senseless mania for reputation" (ix,5–7). Democracy then turns into its bad counterpart which in Polybius' first, briefer account of the *Anacyclōsis* was called mob rule but in his second a rule of "force and the strong hand" (*bia kai cheirocratia*) (iv,10, ix,7; cf. 8b). In isolating the faults of both oligarchy and mob rule Polybius appealed to traditional language about the qualities of degenerate states (injustice, insolence, lawlessness, greed), and about a weakening of the polity through loss of civil equality and free speech;[98] and in writing about transition from aristocracy to oligarchy and from oligarchy to democracy, he invoked notions of political change well-known from major texts of Greek political theory.[99] Nevertheless, his discussion of the downfall of democracy was rather special. Earlier writers had approached democracy, as they had approached monarchies, from differing viewpoints, and Polybius was here forced to do justice to a greater variety of theories. In addition, he was confronted with the fact that the cycle of governments, in his rendering of it, was about to arrive at its *terminus ad quem*.

It is well-known that the two great fourth-century philosophers, Plato and Aristotle, had been democracy's critics, not its supporters.[100] On the other hand, Polybius was not unfavorably disposed toward effective democracy, and those virtues he ascribed to it in his *Anacyclōsis*, namely equality and free speech, were the principles for which he praised the Achaian constitution he lived under and knew so well (cf. II,xxxviii,6). As an Achaian, he naturally prized liberty and associated the security conferred by liberty with democracy.[101] Yet it is not necessary to conclude that democracy represented the acme of the *Ancyclōsis* any more than did kingship or aristocracy. Although a zenith in terms of the people's involvement, democracy preceded the complete degeneration of political society.[102] In highlighting liberty on the one hand, then, and the great dangers of corrupt democracy on the other, Polybius paid his deference to the pro- and anti-democratic positions in Greek political theory.

According to Polybius, there were three stages in the decay of the democratic constitution: first, the rise to influence of men of means who in their lust for reputation and power entice and lead the common people astray through bribery (VI,ix,6–7); second, the rise of a party leader (*prostatēs*) who is without means, and whom the masses themselves push to the fore—having become over-dependent on the gifts of the opulent, the masses bring about "a rule of the

98. Iv,9; viii,5 (*adikia*); iv,10, viii,5 (*hybris*); iv,10 (*paranomia*); viii,5 (*pleonexia*). Cf. Ryffel, op. cit., pp. 13–82 on these terms in Sophistic *metabolē* theory. Note viii,4, ix,4–5 on equality, etc.

99. Aristocracy to oligarchy: Aristotle *Eth. Nic.* VIII,x,3, *Politica* 1307a22–3, 34–5; Plato *Politicus* 301A; cf. Herodotus *Hist.* III,82. Oligarchy to democracy: Plato *Resp.* VIII,555B ff.; Aristotle *Polit.* 1301b55ff.; cf. *Ath. pol.* v–xiii.

100. Plato *Polit.* 303A–B, *Resp.* VIII,555A ff.; Aristotle *Eth. Nic.* VIII,x,1, 3; cf. A. H. M. Jones, *Athenian Democracy*, Oxford, 1957, ch. 3. For other critics: Solon in Aristotle *Ath. pol.* xii(3); Thucydides *Hist.* III,62; Isocrates *Areopagiticus* lxix–lxx; etc.

101. Esp. II,xxxvii,6–xxxix,5, esp. xxxviii,6; cf. M. Gelzer, loc. cit., pp. 5f.

102. T. H. Cole, loc. cit., p. 464, takes democracy as the anacyclic zenith; yet cf. Walbank, *Commentary*, vol. 1, p. 646.

strong arm," and assemble en masse "executing, banishing, and redistributing land" to their own gain (ix,8–9a); finally, there is the degeneration of all these violent men into a state of bestiality "until they once more search for a master and a monarch" (ix,9b).

Various accounts of the failure of democracy seem to be absorbed into this picture. One recalls, for example, the famous debate in Herodotus about the best constitution. Darius argued that democracy does not last because corrupt men mutually support one another to the detriment of the state. The disorder they produce persists until there arises a champion of the people (*prostas tis tou dēmou*), and he puts an end to the troubles, soon being instated as monarch (III,82). These statements are admittedly polemical and in defence of monarchy,[103] but it remains true that Darius' words were not far away from the assessed facts of the past. Peisistratus had been understood to be in the first place an extreme democrat (to take widely-known Athenian history), the people voting him a bodyguard during the turmoil which followed Solonic "democracy."[104] Although Aristotle recognized more than one means by which democratic constitutions might change, he fastened on demagogy as the chief factor, and at least generalized (with Peisistratus partly in mind) that "in ancient times, when a single man was both demagogue and general, democracy tended to change into tyranny" (*Polit.* 1305a7ff., 23ff.). These lines of thought seem to lurk behind Polybius' analysis, even if he did not explicitly identify the leader as a demagogue, nor claim that either kind of figure became the monarch at the end of his cycle.

The phases in the Polybian treatment, however, have their most obvious connections with Plato's *Republic*, where Socrates isolated three groups important for democracy's downfall—energetic politicians already engaged in public business, a small group who have arisen out of the masses and become rich, and the masses themselves, who become active once they realize they can acquire "a share of honey" from the second group (*Resp.* 564D, E, 565A). The leaders of the third group rob the rich, keep most of the proceeds, and distribute the rest to the people (565A). Once this has been done the roots of tyranny have been laid, for the populace eventually places its hope in one particular leader (*prostatēs*). This leader obtains

> control of an utterly beguiled mob and does not withhold his hand from shedding blood. . . . Exiles, murders, hints of debt cancellation and land division follow, until the man who instigated them is necessarily destroyed by his enemies or else changes from man to wolf and becomes a tyrant. (565E–566A)

The Polybian and Platonic accounts admittedly differ. Polybius made more of demagogues, some rich, one other poor.[105] That emphasis was natural enough. In a post-Thucydidean world it was almost universally held by Greek theorists that

103. Cf. also Isocrates *Nicocles* xviii.
104. Aristotle *Ath. pol.* xvii–xx; cf. A. Andrewes, *The Greek Tyrants, London*, 1956, pp. 106f.
105. In Plato demagogy emerges from his third group only: *Resp.* VIII,565A, B.

demagogues destroyed the foundations of democracy.[106] Again, the causal chain between demagogy and tyranny is less direct in Polybius than in Plato. If Plato found it easy to see how one of his popular leaders could become a tyrant, Polybius found that conception awkward. The *Anacyclōsis* was certainly moving toward a return to one-man rule, but only by way of the degenerate form of democracy—mob rule. Thus, in Polybius' picture, although the demagogue figures seem to dwindle in number the masses increase in power at the same time. It is they who effect the new rule, the evil counterpart of democracy, the "constitution" of mob rule. It is the people as a mass who succumb to bestiality, and then once more find a master and a monarch.[107]

Despite these differences, however, Plato's general approach is akin to the historian's. In his own way Plato would have agreed that demagogy was just one aspect of a more general process of socio-political decline. For both Plato and Polybius "exiles," "murders," and hints of "land division" were a prelude to one-man rule,[108] a rule associated with bestiality and the veritable collapse of civic life. We should remember that Polybius evidently took the Platonic tyrant to be the *monarchos*-figure standing at the renewal point of the anacyclic course. It is of crucial importance that at one point in the *Historiae* he went out of his way to insist that the Platonic "bestial" ruler was not to be confused with the conventional tyrant or the *constitutional* form which followed kingship (VII,xiii,7).[109] Thus Polybius clearly made use of the picture in the *Republic*, but in a modified form. Above all, he was bent on making a statement of recurrence at this stage, and on explaining how human affairs returned to an original point of departure.

The zigzag line from kingship to mob rule only serves to underline the complexities of recurrence thinking in Polybius. As we have seen, many of the special changes within the *Anacyclōsis* fall within the rubric of *metabolē* theory. They involve the idea of historical recurrence in the sense that they are *typical* changes (kingships, for instance, often become transformed into tyranny), and are described by a recognized terminology (for example, words exposing the moral inadequacy of a régime). By comparison, these very changes also suggest a fluctuating process. It is true that no two of the constitutions in the zigzag are the same, yet Polybius still meant to convey the impression of alternation; there

106. Thucydides *Hist.* II,65f.; Theopompus in *FGH*, pt. 1, vol. 2B, Frgs. 90–6 (cf. W. R. Connor, *Theopompus and Fifth Century Athens*, Washington, 1968, pp. 36f.); Aristotle *Ath. pol.* xxviii, *Polit.* 1304b19–1305a10; Isocrates *De pacis* cxxvi–xi; etc. For Polybius himself see *Hist.* XX,vi,3, XXIV,vii,2–3; cf. IV,lxxxi,13, VI,xliv,9, XIII,vi,3.

107. If Polybius at one point confused mob rule or *cheirocratia* with bestiality (VI,x,5; cf. x,2–6), it was because he wished to make a double point. Mob rule was a constitution, the bad brother of democracy and the station of decay in the life cycle of majority rules (VI,iv,6, 10, x,5, 7; cf. ix,7, 8b, lvii,9), yet it could aptly be called "the worst condition of all human (political) affairs" (lvii,9b), because political societies slid through it into a state of non-polity.

108. Plato *Resp.* VIII,566A (apparently the work of the tyrant); Polybius *Hist.* VI,ix,9 (of the masses). Cf. also Thucydides *Hist.* VI,60.

109. Commenting on Philip V of Macedon and his changing character, Polybius contended that "it was not a change from man to wolf, as in the Arcadian myth mentioned by Plato, but from a king into a pernicious tyrant."

is a shift, by turns, from a worthy to an unworthy constitution. Furthermore, he endeavored to integrate this alternative element with the three-stationed biological principle as applied to particular constitutions. He sought to apply the stations of growth, acme, and decay to each individual (*hekastos*) major constitution,[110] and how he then interrelated the biological paradigm with the whole zigzag becomes an interesting question.[111] His integration is not easy to represent accurately. We must avoid concluding, for instance, that primitive monarchy marked the growing stage of one-man rule *qua* constitution, with kingship its acme and tyranny its decay.

Concerning one-man rules, Polybius' most important appeal to biological notions was in connection with true kingship. Once the people have acquired a moral sense, kingship then has its "beginning and generation" (vii,1). As a form of government it grows to its maturity from this point, not from an earlier stage, and its decay and dissolution come with tyranny. A similar pattern arises with the rules of the few and the many. Perhaps one might anticipate aristocracy being born in the conspiracies of the nobleminded against the tyrant, yet only after one-man rule is abolished does aristocracy have its "beginning and generation" (viii,1b). And it is only when oligarchy, the decayed form of aristocracy, has been eliminated that democracy emerges (ix,1–3). On this reading, then, two kinds of symmetry lie behind the "backbone" of the *Anacyclōsis* (see Diagrams I and II), even if they cannot be put together so readily in plastic terms (see Diagram III).

There is still more to be said, however. It follows from the above interpretation that there are three separate movements of alternation in the *Anacyclōsis*, and three biological cycles each having its beginning at the end point of another. While it appears true that these two paradigms remain slightly disengaged, Polybius brought them closer together by characterizing the historical preparations for the three major constitutions of kingship, aristocracy, and democracy. These three constitutions result from reactions against defective governments, or, in the case of kingship, arise after socio-political dissolution. As a Marxist might put it, one major form of constitution was conceived in the womb of another, although this extension of the biological analogy is not worked out in Polybius.[112] Again, one should not overlook Polybius' interest in human generations. His position is not clearcut, but the tendency toward decay in the careers of the three major constitutions within the *Anacyclōsis* seems to come always with second-generation politicians, that is to say, with those who inherit rather than create the constitutions of kingship, aristocracy, and democracy. Generations, just as organic development from birth to death, had often

110. For Polybius' interest in the life cycle of each single (major) constitution see VI,iv,11, 12; cf. K. F. Eisen, *Polybiosinterpretationen: Beobachtungen zu Prinzipien griechischer und römischer Historiographie bei Polybios*, Heidelberg, 1966, pp. 42f. Notice how Aristotle does not apply the biological principle to types of rules in *Eth. Nic.* VIII,x.

111. Not the *whole* anacyclic model: cf. above, sect. B, pt. 2.

112. For a variation on this theme see Chapter 4, sect. D, pt. 3 (on Joachino di Fiore).

Diagram I The Anacyclic Zigzag

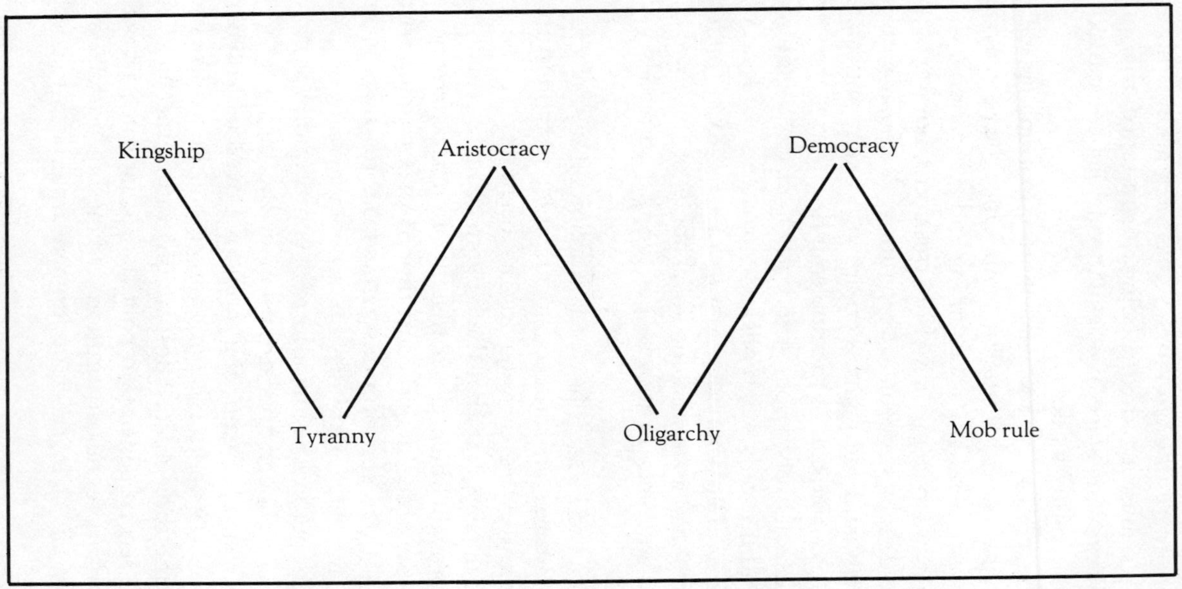

Kingship

Tyranny

Aristocracy

Oligarchy

Democracy

Mob rule

Diagram II The Polybian *Anacyclōsis*: Alternating and Biological Change

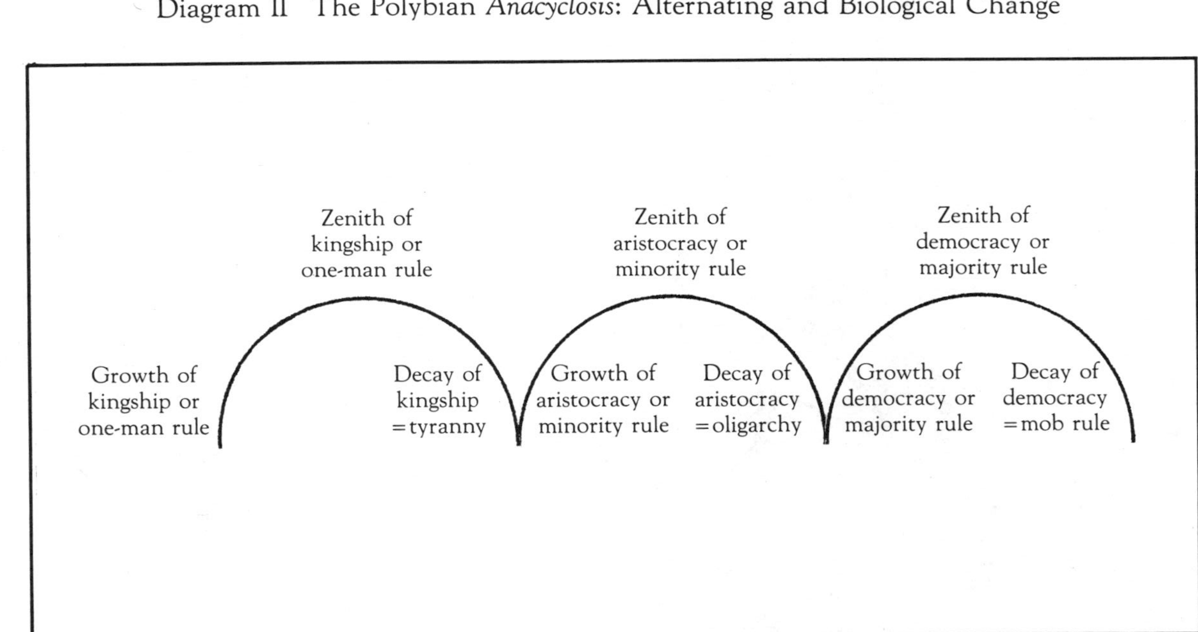

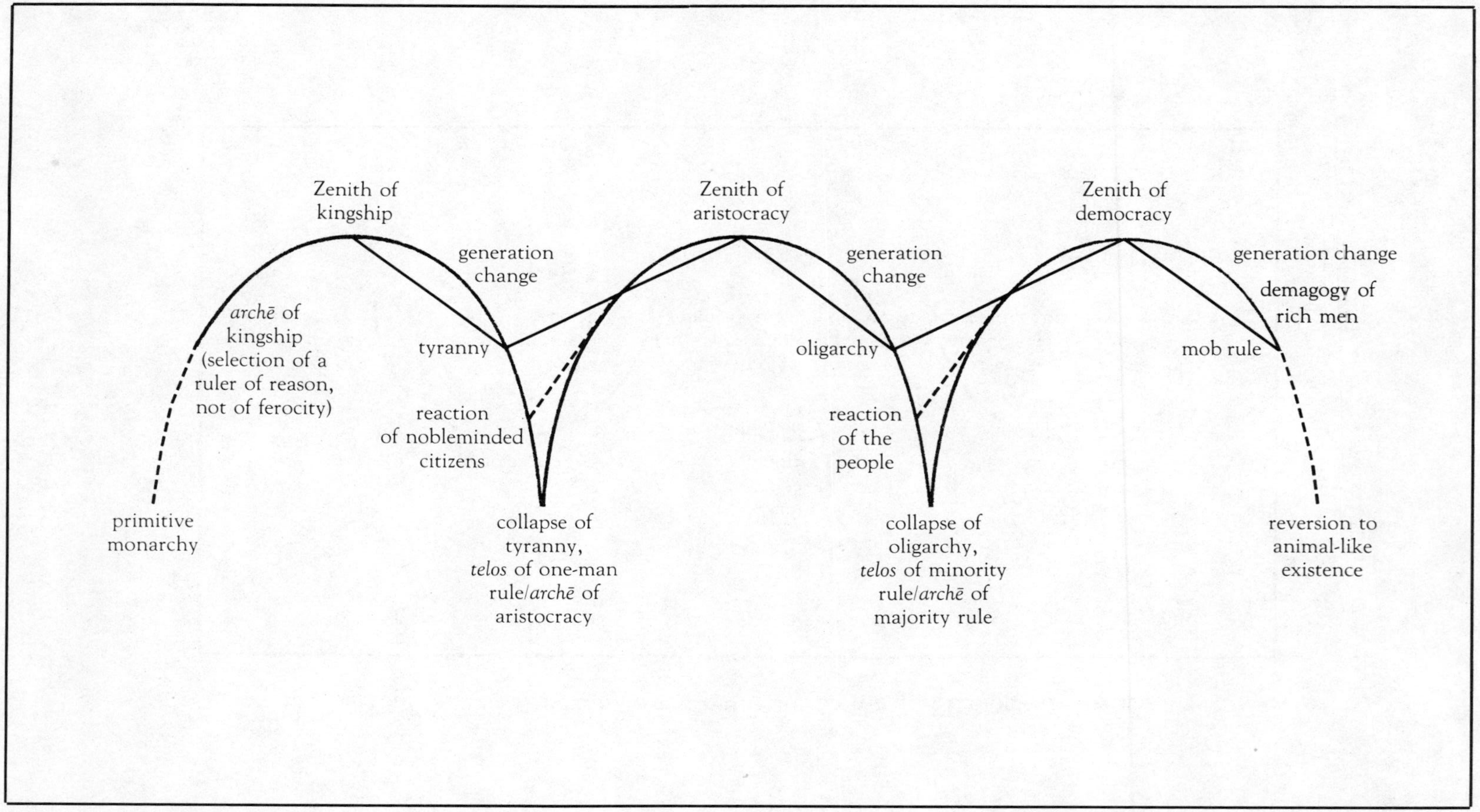

Diagram III The Polybian *Anacyclōsis*: Combining Patterns of Alternating and Biological Change

been conceived of as cycles,[113] so that yet another notion of cyclical recurrence was covered by his framework.[114]

The anacyclic zigzag, therefore, is a complex interweaving of both cyclical and non-cyclical models of recurrence. Polybius' ingenuity lies as much in his combination of conceptual structures as in his accommodation of various opinions. Although the complex passage from kingship or mob rule certainly has an interest and importance of its own, one hardly needs reminding that it is wedded to an "anthropology," and it is now time to gather up the numerous threads we have followed and to discuss the grand framework as a whole.

## D. The *Anacyclōsis* viewed synoptically and the importance of Plato

Apart from the *Anacyclōsis*, were there other self-contained and summary manuals on the changes and cycles of government? The debate in Herodotus' *Historiae* Bk. III (80–82) is the earliest one extant. Its peculiar unity lies in the reasonably balanced recognition of the strengths and weaknesses of the three major constitutional types, as well as in the accumulative effect which comes into play when Darius defends monarchy against oligarchy and democracy and against his two opponents, who argue for the abolition of one-man rule. This treatment of the good and bad sides of governments, as well as Darius' argument that either oligarchy or democracy eventually leads to a "champion" and a monarch, has significant affinities with the zigzag and the final stages of the *Anacyclōsis* (although whether or not Polybius had read Herodotus remains an unresolved question). Again, the classification of constitutions in Aristotle's *Nicomachean Ethics* may be called to mind. Although it contains no governmental form akin to primitive monarchy, and although the terms describing popular rules are different, Aristotle's three pairs of "right" and "deviant" constitutions generally match the zigzag, and Polybius could have inherited his hexadic classification from an interim Aristotelian writer (Dicaearchus?), who altered his master's nomenclatures.[115] A parallel ordering of material, however, was not enough to form the basis of the *Anacyclōsis*. There had to be some understanding of a dynamic, historical relationship among all the forms before the Polybian model became possible. Despite at least one false claim that Aristotle did once develop such a relationship and depict a cycle of governments,[116] it is undeniable that no long-term historical thrust appears in the relevant portion of his *Ethics*. In the *Politics*, moreover, where he did actually

113. See Chapter 2, sect. A, pt. 2(i).

114. Esp. VI,vii,6, viii,4, ix,5. In being imprecise as to the length of a generation, Polybius may have given deference to Hesiod and his influence. See Hesiod *Erga* 106ff. (on *geneai*); Plato *Leg.* VII,798C–D, *Meno* 93E ff.; yet cf. Aristotle *Rhetorica* 1367b29ff.

115. Cf. Dicaearchus, Frgs. 70a–72 (from the *Tripoliticus*) (Wehrli, pp. 28f.). For Polybius' knowledge of Dicaearchus see above, sect. 4; cf. *Hist.* XXXV,v,11.

116. Appealing to *Polit* 1285b38–1286a2, R. Nisbet (in *History and Social Change: Aspects of the Western Theory of Development*, New York, 1969, p. 40) argues that Aristotle analyzed a sequence of constitutions from kingship to aristocracy to democracy and back to kingship again. Nisbet, however (p. 306 n. 25), was following B. Jowett's misleading translation (cf. *The Works of Aristotle Translated into English*, ed. W. D. Ross, Oxford, 1910–52, vol. 10, *Polit.* III,xv,10–40).

consider chains of development, the parallel with the whole sequence of the anacyclic "backbone" falls down. As for the Herodotean debate, if it contains more of that overall thrust we are seeking, it was nevertheless concerned with a quite limited number of constitutions, as were other arguments about the eventual emergence of democracy after certain unpopular governments.[117] In any case, if that element of directionalism was an essential prerequisite for the *Anacyclōsis*, so was the idea of a fixed sequence of constitutional change, which hardly comes out in any of these authors. In fact, because Aristotle envisaged such a great variety of possible changes he really excluded it (*Polit.* V). Insofar as Polybius allowed for divergences in the expected course of events when writing narrative, and insofar as he nowhere reckoned the anacyclic sequence to be inexorable (rather than "natural"; see *Hist.* VI,iv,11, v,1, ix,10; cf. li,4), he may not have been so far away from Aristotle's position. Yet the *Anacyclōsis* involved only six or seven forms of constitution (Aristotle's *Politics* included various others), and it was still presented as a continuing line of political development with a given order of events. What is more, it was conceived as a cyclical process.

We have to take stock, and we are drawn back to the tentative suggestions offered earlier. Was the cycle of governments constructed primarily (though not exclusively) from two dialogues of Plato, that is, from those important historical analyses of political change found in the *Laws* Bk. III and the *Republic* Bk. VIII? If Plato was the one explicitly-acknowledged author connected with the cycle, if Polybius had certainly read the *Republic*,[118] and if it is quite clear that Plato analyzed constitutional change in terms of relatively fixed sequences,[119] one cannot avoid reckoning seriously, if cautiously, with this hypothesis.

In the *Laws* Bk. III, we may recall, Plato began his account of socio-political development with catastrophe theory: he touched on questions of early morality, he hinted at a savage social order in the time of the Cyclops, and he wrote of the first government as "the most righteous of kingships." All this, in general structure, runs nearly parallel to the Polybian "anthropology." Yet what of Plato's treatment of transformations from one constitution into another? In the *Laws* he "discerned a first, a second, and a third community" (III,683A). The first was the patriarchal kingship, the second was a rule founded on magistrates and legislation and called aristocracy (though Plato conceded that kingship could be another name given to it: 681C–D), while the third was a polity "blending all varieties and forms of constitutions," and founded not in the highlands but on the plain (681D–682D). These succeeding one another, there then appeared a "fourth city, or, if you wish, a nation" (683A). Treating the early Dorian community as such a nation, Plato then showed that of the three related Dorian city-states, Argos, Messene, and Lacedaemon, only the last managed to

117. Esp. pseudo-Hippodamus in Stobaeus *Anthol.* IV,i,95 (probably based on Aristotle *Polit.* 1267b23ff.); Polybius *Hist.* IV,xli, 5–6 (based on an Achaian tradition?).

118. Cf. *Hist.* VI,xlv,1, xlvii,7–10, VII,xiii,7, XII,xxviii,2–3 (and VI,v,4ff., xlviii,2 on the *Laws*).

119. The apparent rigidity of which significantly drew the fire of Aristotle in *Polit.* 1316a20–25.

survive. Evil, insolence, and tyranny manifested themselves in the rulers of the other two societies,[120] but they were avoided in Sparta by a blending of political forms in the right measure (692A).

Following all this, Plato turned his attention to what he termed the "two mother forms of constitutions," one "properly called monarchy and the other democracy" (693D). He made it plain how the former, as in the case of Persia, was liable to bring despotism and political deterioration in succeeding generations (694A–696B). The latter, by contrast, as in the instance of Athens, began with a workable, venerable, and magisterial aristocracy, with the people as willing slaves to the law, but it eventually ended in license or disorder, or with theatrocracy, as he ironically called it.[121] After this last analysis, interestingly, Plato made further comments, and these in a strangely neglected passage:

> Next, after such freedom, comes the condition in which there is a refusal to be subject to rulers, and then a shirking of submission to one's parents and elders, and their pronouncements, and near the final stage comes the effort to disregard laws, the last point being marked by an absolute loss of respect for oaths, pledges, and gods, whereby men display and reproduce the nature of the ancient Titans of tradition, returning to their original state once more, and bearing a hard existence with never a rest from evil. (701B–C)

Curiously enough, Plato then put a "bridle upon his discourse" (701C) and resorted to another theme, but in this short passage he had offered a subtle, perhaps prophetic, utterance about the decline and collapse of the community.

In the *Laws* Bk. III, then, lies a great deal of material relevant to the political changes of the *Anacyclōsis*. This material could easily be linked, moreover, with Plato's discussion in the *Republic* about imperfect societies degenerating in a series, that is, from the ideal state through timocracy, oligarchy, democracy, on to the "champion" of the masses who becomes a tyrant.[122]

Polybius himself noted that Plato's analysis was most "intricate," stated at great length, and by implication, more precise or accurate than his own (*Hist.* VI,v,1). The historian, less in keeping with his profession than we might expect, sought a greater coherency and symmetry than the philosopher, and encapsulated Plato's less interconnected musings in a tightly-compacted model of his own. The unmistakable correspondences clinch this line of argument. In the *Laws* Plato's treatment began and ended with what Polybius could readily understand as savage, primitive rule (Cyclops, Titans), and in the *Laws* and the *Republic* the end points of the historical analyses were marked by the breakdown of ordinary political life, by complete social deterioration. Plato's and Polybius' first constitutions are one-man rules; both accept as normative the breakdown of kingship into tyranny, and democracy into a rule of license and excess of liberty. In the *Republic* Plato discussed the transition from oligarchy to

120. *Leg.* III,684A–692C, esp. 688C, 691C, 692B.
121. *Leg.* III,698D, 699C, 700A, 701A.
122. *Resp.* 544E, 545D, 547C (on *aristocratia* or the "rule of the best" in an ideal sense).

democracy, as well as the factors weakening democracy and laying the foundations of the worst of all régimes. Thus in preliminary outline we may sketch the elicited correspondences as follows:

| *Plato* | *Polybius* |
|---|---|
| catastrophes (*Leg.*) | catastrophes |
| early moral notions and the growth of skills (*L*) | growth of moral notions (and implicitly of skills) |
| Cyclops (*L*) | primitive monarchy |
| just kingship (*L*) | kingship founded on reason |
| monarchs/kings degenerate into tyrants (*L*)[123] | tyranny |
| oligarchy (*Resp.*) | oligarchy |
| democracy (*L* and *R*) | democracy |
| breakdown of democracy to rule of license (*R*) to theatrocracy (*L*), leading to champions of the people (*R*) | mob rule/cheirocracy leading to champions of the people |
| degeneration of the society (*L*)[124] | degeneration of political society |
| tyranny (*R*); cf. the rule of Titans, with the notion of a reversion to an original condition (*L*) | monarch and despot, with the notion of a reversion to an original condition |

The run of parallels is not so neat at one point, of course, since Plato was vague about his second society, about the precise constitutional form which followed upon the true kingship. He simply emphasized that this society was magisterially based and it could be either aristocratic or kingly. Polybius could take this looseness as he pleased. He did not follow the philosopher's analyses for every single special point he desired to make. Thus in forging a link between "just kingship" and oligarchy, Polybius simply had to be freer than usual with his chief mentor. Committed to the idea of a fixed sequence, he assumed that kingship had to degenerate before the establishment of aristocracy, and consequently transposed some of Plato's more readily acceptable material about the transformation of kings into tyrants.

It should be recalled, however, that Plato considered a third and fourth form of society and not just a second. Following magisterial government, he isolated the "mixed polity of the plain," and then the nation, which, because of the weaknesses in Dorian kingship, resulted in the mixed constitution of Lycurgus, which Plato claimed enthusiastically to have been divinely inspired (*Leg.* III,691D–E). Leaving aside the problem of Plato's ideal republic (for Polybius

123. In *Leg.* III,693D–696B (on Persian rule), Plato does not distinguish clearly between monarchy and kingship; yet cf. 685C.

124. Also *Resp.* VIII,560D–562E. Plato on the disintegration of values, esp. in *Leg.* III,701B–C, parallels Polybius VI,vi.

himself disregarded it as historically irrelevant), it was this Spartan constitution, this "half-way house between aristocracy and oligarchy," this Platonic "timocracy," which begins the series in the *Republic* (cf. 554C, 545B–500C), suggesting the link between the analyses of the two Platonic dialogues. The complete sequence extracted from these dialogues may thus be represented as follows:

primitive monarchy
kingship
tyranny
aristocracy

---

mixed polity (*L*)
nation with mixed constitution (Sparta) (*L* and *R*)

---

oligarchy
democracy
mob rule
breakdown of political society
reversion to primitive monarchy

Here, with the mixed polity and the nation, we have isolated an aspect of Platonic thought which does not seem to fit into the *Anacyclōsis*. This special feature is of great interest, however, since immediately after outlining the anacyclic framework Polybius proceeded to deal with the question of a mixed constitution, the formation of which was not taken to invalidate his model, but rather as a means of forestalling the natural processes of political change.[125] Polybius discussed not only the Spartan but also the Roman *politeia* as a mixed constitution, and one of his most central points in the *Historiae* Bk. VI is that Rome, although it came to possess such a mixed constitution, still developed constitutionally "according to nature." It was this state, in fact, to which the anacyclic model best applied. But this is another side to the story which will be considered later.

We may claim, then, that it was Plato's historical and "archeological" discourses which provided the general superstructure for the *Anacyclōsis*. Polybius discovered how, to his own mind (yet despite the philosopher's original intentions), Plato had actually succeeded in picturing a cycle of governments. In other details as well, Plato's influence shines through. In describing the transformations of the three well-known constitutions into their "vicious counterparts" rather than into (Aristotelian) "deviations," and in showing that certain important political changes were due to the supplanting of an older generation by a younger, Polybius seems closer to Plato than to any other known predecessor.[126] Those who consider the cycle of governments to be mainly derivative

125. See esp. Walbank, *Commentary*, vol. 1, p. 648.

126. On "vicious counterparts" see Plato, esp. *Resp.* X,608E–609A; cf. Empedocles, Frgs. 31B26, B81 (Diels-Kranz); Antiphon, Frg. 87B15 (Diels-Kranz); also A. Roveri, *Studi su Polibio* (*Studi Pubblicati dall'Istituto di Filologia Classica XVII*), Bologna, 1964, p. 181. On generations see Plato,

from Plato are thus very much on the right track, although to ascribe it to an intermediary Platonizing source is to hypothesize unnecessarily.[127]

We must remember, however, that Plato's dialogues were not his exclusive source; they provided the catalyst for his own more accommodating and popular vision of history and political change. Polybius had his own purposes to fulfill—to satisfy as wide an audience as possible, and that included Romans as well as Greeks (cf. esp. I,iii,7, VI,xi,5), and to distill the essential truths of Greek "anthropological" and historico-political speculation into one systematic statement. This meant for him the enunciation of a doctrine of historical recurrence, and such a teaching did not come easily from Plato, for one; even though the material was there it had to be forced out. Polybius was only partly controlled by Plato, and his relative freedom is evident from his very first statements about catastrophe theory. If one reflects upon the views of Dicaearchus in the *Life of Greece*, moreover, it will be perceived how much more Platonizing even a Peripatetic could become than Polybius. Dicaearchus not only stressed the painful slowness of man's progress,[128] but resurrected the Hesiodic myth of early bliss, and the age of Kronos so idyllically portrayed in Plato's *Politicus*. Besides that, he conformed closely to a decidedly Platonic picture of early communal life, describing a nomadic, pastoral existence without war or *stasis*, lived out by men with simple virtues, before moral decay brought the need for strongholds, and the development of skills brought the art of agriculture.[129] Polybius did not go this far; he was an Eclectic before he was a Platonist.

A brief reflection on all the traditions of thought lying behind the *Anacyclōsis* elicits a conception of Polybius as a popularizer.[130] Surveying his model as a whole (see the schematic outline of Diagram IV), we may grasp not only his remarkable accommodation of several often conflicting lines of thought, but also the way he packed different models of recurrence into one framework. The large cycle, which can also be described as an alternation between polity and non-polity, included within it three smaller biological cycles and the process of fluctuation between good and bad constitutions. If the paradigm of alternation is virtually lost within the wider cycle, it certainly retains its identity in the case of the zigzag. It does not stand alone, moreover, as a non-cyclical paradigm. Also present in the *Anacyclōsis* are the "typical changes" of *metabolē* theory and the idea of transformations into opposites (cf. VI,ix,10). Polybius even utilized the principle of change from less to more and from more to less. Constitutional

esp. *Resp.* VIII,549C–550B, 553Ab–554C, 558Cb–561Aa, 572Bb–537A, *Meno* 93E ff.; cf. *Protagoras* 326D; "Ocellus Lucanus" IV,4 (Harder, p. 22, sect. 45). So see Polybius VI,viii,4, ix,5; cf. vi,2–3.

127. See esp. E. Mioni, *Polibio (Problemi d'Oggi III)*, Padua, 1949, pp. 66ff.; cf. Ryffel, op. cit., pp. 201, 360; U. von Wilamowitz-Moellendorf, *Griechisches Lesebuch*, Berlin, 1906–13, vol. 2, sect. 1, p. 119. On the supposed close dependence of Polybius on the *Republic* see esp. R. von Scala, *Die Studien des Polybios*, Stuttgart, 1890, pp. 97ff.; von Fritz, op. cit., p. 68 and p. 412, n. 32.

128. Frg. 49 (Wehrli, p. 24, *l.*34).

129. Frg. 49, *ll.*3–14, 20–30, 34ff.; cf. Frg. 48, *ll.*29–31 (p. 22).

130. One might justifiably rank Polybius as a forerunner of the better known Eclectics, i.e., of such men as Antiochus of Ascalon and (two important men he influenced) both Cicero and Arius Didymus. Of relevance here is Polybius' comment on Carneades in *Hist.* XXXIII,ii,8–10.

Diagram IV The Polybian *Anacyclōsis* as a Whole

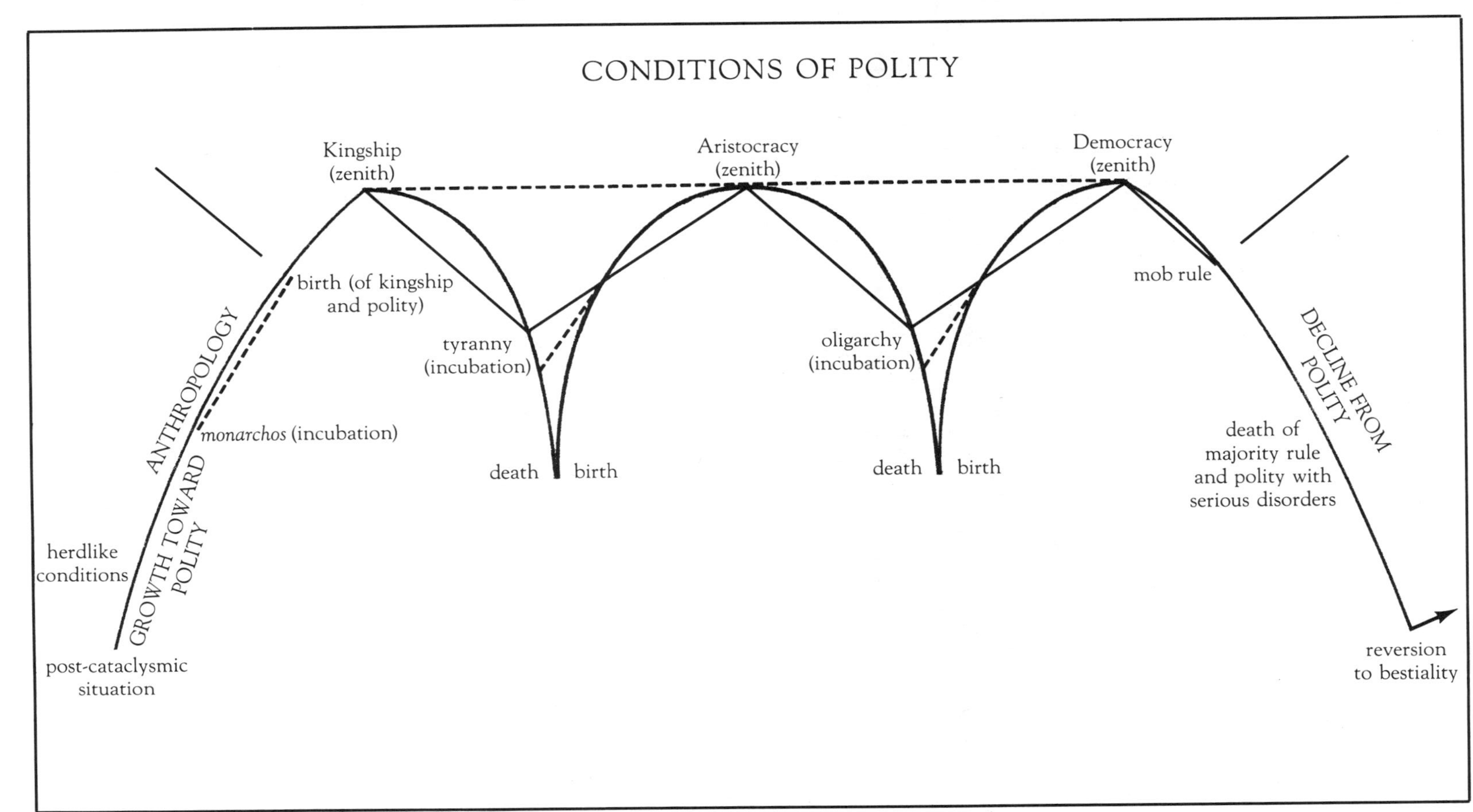

development within the *Anacyclōsis* proceeds from the rule of the one to the rule of the many,[131] and then, with political dissolution, back to the one again. As his model was partly framed by catastrophe theory, there is also the implicit sense in which the human species alternates between virtual (though regional) elimination and multiplicity. It is not too much to claim that this particular motif was drawn from a Stoic background. If the Stoics pictured cosmic history as bounded by dissolution into elemental fire, yet recurrently reconstituted in all its diversity, Polybius consciously historicized this vision, conceiving human affairs to reflect not only large-scale oscillation between few and many in both political leadership and population, but between societal definition and lack of structure as well.[132]

The *Anacyclōsis* was held together not just by a fusion of competing anthropologies or of recurrence paradigms, however, and we cannot conclude this part of our discussion without acknowledging Polybius' important stress on the naturalness of the anacyclic course. We have already noticed how one set of developments in the cycle, namely the stage of elementary, animal-like existence, the rule of brute force and the early growth of morality, seems to be more "natural" than developments in the course of the zigzag. This contrast between pre-political and political conditions remains valid, yet it is also true that Polybius wrote about the whole cycle as both necessary and natural (VI,x,2). Concerning the causal principles lying behind the cyclical process there is a certain ambivalence. On the one hand, the transitions from kingship to mob rule result from the passions and reactions generally characteristic of civic life, and they all imply a series of efficient causes. On the other hand, by presenting a fixed sequence of transitions, by emphasizing the changing attitudes of new generations toward their predecessors, and also by suggesting that the lives of political societies were recurrently in danger of lapsing into bestiality and oblivion, Polybius reveals himself to be necessitarian. This broad vision of a necessary dispensation smacks of Stoicism,[133] yet, as we shall see, Polybius admitted that the anacyclic path could be forestalled or even severed. Paradoxically enough, therefore, its progress was inevitable only if it was not pre-

131. Polybius did not claim the oligarchs to be fewer in number than the aristocrats: see above, sect. C. On the other hand, the three major constitutions emerge and settle with the people; the people are operating politically even under disliked régimes. Overall, though, the people's sphere of influence widens in the course of the transitions from monarchy to mob rule.

132. The notion of change from less to more and vice versa seems inextricably bound up with the cyclo-alternating processes of the *Anacyclōsis*, yet there is room for looking at it in its own right. It is named together with qualitative and organic change by "Ocellus Lucanus": cf. *De univ. nat.* I,iv (p. 11).

133. The Stoics attempted to hold the doctrine of inevitability (or necessity) concurrently with belief in the freedom of the ethical will to conform with the "laws of nature": cf. Diogenes Laertius *Vit. philos.* vii,85ff.; Graeber, op. cit., pp. 75f. Aristotle considered teleological causation in a different light, his final cause being that which brings anything, inert or living, to its proper fulfillment: cf. esp. *Eth. Nic.* I,i. On the Peripatetic background to Polybius' use of the biological principle, however, see Dicaearchus, Frg. 24 (Wehrli, pp. 17f.); cf. Aristotle, e.g., *De gen. et corrupt.* 336b11, *De generatione animalium* 777b17ff. on the phrase "according to nature" (though Aristotle did not apply the biological principle to political analysis in the *Politica* or *Eth. Nic.* VIII,x).

vented from running its natural course. This leads us to the next stage of our analysis, and also looks forward to a wide investigation into Polybius' etiology and to the way he related different causal explanations.

## E. The application of the *Anacyclōsis*

### *The problem of mixed constitutions*

It is on Polybius as a theorist of historical recurrence that our attention has and will continue to be focused, yet it is not possible to shelve another central and problematic issue of Polybian studies which is really worth exhaustive study for its own sake. I refer to his notion of the mixed constitution, of a polity with three evenly-balanced power elements. These elements, it was said, corresponded to the three most basic constitutional forms, kingship (or monarchy in its most widely used, least technical sense), aristocracy, and democracy. Now if Polybius faced some patent difficulties in attempting to interweave different paradigms into one far-reaching anacyclic schema, and in formulating a statement with the widest possible appeal, the greatest difficulty of all arose when he endeavored to forge a connection between the *Anacyclōsis* and a special type of government combining three of the very constitutions which belonged to his set sequence. In neither of his two outlines of the *Anacyclōsis* does there appear to be any provision made for the natural emergence of a mixed constitution (*mixis*), and despite Fritz Taeger's rather ingenious efforts to argue that the anacyclic model contained a "mixed" kingship and a "mixed" aristocracy (because Polybius' "true kingship" and "high-minded aristocracy" were based on popular support), this truth still has to be firmly emphasized.[134] Yet Polybius went out of his way to make some bold yet problem-raising statements about the relationship between the anacyclic path and that one constitution he was most concerned to examine in his sixth book, the mixed constitution of Rome. Book VI of the *Historiae* begins with the expressed intention of examining the Roman constitution (or state) (cf. esp. ii.3, 9, iii,4), and the outline of the anacyclic process only formed its introductory parts. It may be inferred from its extant remains that this book was concerned not only with the peculiar genius and intricacies of Rome's polity (xi,3–xviii,8), but also with her military system (xix,1–xlii,6), her constitution's background history (cf. xi,1–2), and her internal strengths compared to other constitutions such as those of Athens, Thebes, Crete, Sparta, and Carthage (xliii,1–lviii,13; cf. x,1–14). Perhaps one could argue that the *Anacyclōsis* merely forms a conceptual prelude to these subjects, yet it remains true that Polybius considered the application of the cycle of governments in his subsequent discussion.

Immediately after he presented the cycle, Polybius made three very significant affirmations with Rome in view. He first contended that the method which the

134. Cf. F. Taeger, *Die Archäeologie des Polybius*, Stuttgart, 1922, esp. pp. 43–5. Polybius' explicit references to kingship and aristocracy, however, cannot be read as implicit references to mixed constitutions.

*Anacyclōsis* provided for assessing the constitutional situation of any given state was most of all suitable for the study of the Roman constitution (*politeia*) (iv,13a; cf. ix,11–12); second, that this was the case because, more than any other, the Roman constitution developed naturally (iv,13b, ix,13; cf. x,13–14); and third, that the Roman constitution at the time of the Hannibalic War—at its prime—preserved within itself an equilibrium among monarchical, aristocratic, and democratic elements of power (xi,1–2, 12, etc.). Impressive points. Yet how, in Polybian terms, could a state experience both the anacyclic process and a mixed constitution? That is a problem which has frustrated numerous classicists, and it is hard not to believe it was a problem for Polybius also. Let us be careful, though, not to identify his difficulties with those of modern scholarship. We are frequently prone to ask whether Polybius' assertions were logically consistent, because a sufficient degree of inner contradiction might persuade us that the writer changed his mind or that his work lost consistency through his own attempts at redaction.[135] Yet this tends to make the last resort of interpretation what with Polybius of all people should have presented itself as the first likelihood, that the writer was struggling to marry two sets of ideas which were not the happiest of bedfellows, and that he saw the necessity to do this because he wished to pay deference to, and to interrelate, the traditionally stated, most widely-accepted truths of Greek political theory. It is reasonable to assume that the ideas of a political cycle and of a mixed constitution represented for Polybius two key principles of Greek social theory, both of which he took to be essential for understanding Rome's constitution and her unparalleled success.[136] Concerning the second basic *Formprinzip* it may fairly be claimed that Polybius looked at Rome with Greek presuppositions, that he foisted an Hellenic face upon her government, describing it in terms of the tripolitical structure so commonly appealed to by his fellow countrymen.[137] The question naturally arises: Did Polybius understand this special combination of constitutions to arise within the anacyclic process? And (as we are not considering the idea of a mixed constitution for its own sake), what was the significance of the mixed constitution for his views of historical recurrence?

According to a passage primarily centered on Sparta (VI,x), the triadic mixed

135. See R. von Scala, op. cit., pp. 248ff.; E. K. Kornemann, "Zum Staatsrecht des Polybios" in *Philologus* LXXXVI, 1932, pp. 183f.; Walbank, "Polybius on the Roman Constitution," pp. 79ff.; Pédech, op. cit., pp. 333–5 for the most important discussions.

136. Esp. Graeber, op. cit., p. 85.

137. For background see Ion of Chios in Isocrates *Antidosis* cclxviii; pseudo-Hippodamus, Frg. 95 (Hense, vol. 4, pp. 35f.); Plato *Menex.* 238D; Aeschines *Contra Timarchum* iv, *Contra Ctesiphon* vi; Archytas of Tarentum in Stobaeus (Hense, vol. 4, pp. 82–5, Frgs. 135–8); Dicaearchus, Frgs. 70–2 (*Tripolitikos*) (Wehrli, pp. 28f.); Theophrastus in Diogenes Laertius *Vit. philos.* v,45; Panaetius in Diogenes vii,131; Diogenes himself, vii,66, 131; cf. Chrysippus, Frg. 700 (von Arnim, vol. 3, p. 175). Also see Herodotus *Hist.* III,80–3; Xenophon *Cyropaedeia* I,1, *Agesilaus* I,4, *Memorabilia*, IV,iv,12; (pseudo-)Plato *Epistulae* V,321D; Isocrates *Panath.* cxix, cxxxii; cf. J. de Romilly, "Le Classement des constitutions d'Hérodote à Aristote" in *Révue des Études Grecques* LXXII, 1959, pp. 81ff.; G. J. D. Aalders, *Die Theorie der gemischten Verfassung im Altertum*, Amsterdam, 1968, pp. 25–69.

constitution forestalled the natural cycle of governments. Lycurgus, Polybius contended,

> well understood that each of the above changes [in the anacyclic sequence] takes place necessarily and naturally, and realized that every constitutional form which was simple and based on one principle was unsound . . . and foreseeing this, he did not make the *polity* simple and uniform, but united in it all the best and distinctive features of the worthy constitutions so that they would not grow unduly, falling into their perverted counterparts, but that each power, being checked by the other, might neither outbalance nor be subject to one another. (x,2, 6–7)

Thus a condition of equilibrium was preserved in the state, Polybius noting how Spartan kingship was prevented from arrogance through fear of the people, how the common people feared the elders too much to be contemptuous of the (two) kings, and how the elders were always on the side of justice because they were elected from the best citizens (x,7–9).[138] The mixed constitution, then, brought the anacyclic course to a standstill.[139] Like Sparta, Rome also possessed such a constitution to check the process of transition, balancing the monarchical-consular, the aristocratic-senatorial, and the democratic powers within itself, so that only after the government (*politeia*) *qua* state or mixed constitution "has attained to an uncontested sovereignty" does it begin to show the weaknesses brought on by too much prosperity (xi,11–xviii,8, lvii,5). For Polybius the Roman constitution was nearest to perfection during the second Punic War (221–202 BC) (xi,1). A status quo prevailed and a relative immortality was secured; all power sources zealously acted in concord during times of external danger, and none became corrupted in periods of good fortune and prosperity (cf. xviii,1–8).

If the mixed constitution held up the cycle of governments, how could it properly be considered as part of the latter's natural economy? It seems more a new growth grafted upon the normative line of development. If Lycurgus was able to create such a mixed constitution by virtue of his foresight and rationality,[140] however, thus legislating at one special point in Spartan history, Rome, by contrast, arrived at the same result not through reason but "through many trials and troubles," always choosing the best in the light of changing circumstances (x,13–4). In the cases of both states, Polybius refers to special qualities required to effect the extraordinary, but, concerning Rome, he placed a special insistence on the slower, natural growth of a mixed polity. We have already admitted that the natural economy of his cycle did not exclude the exercise of the human will in effecting political change. It should not puzzle us, then, that for Polybius both the cycle of governments and Rome's mixed constitution took shape *kata physin* ("according to nature"; or at least "not interfered with by any

138. Cf. also Plato *Leg.* III,691D ff.; K. M. T. Chrimes, *Ancient Sparta: A Re-Examination of the Evidence*, Manchester, 1949, pp. 397ff.
139. Graeber, op. cit., ch. 3, sect. B.
140. Cf. x,2, 6, 12, xlviii,2, etc.

outside or artificially imposed influence").[141] Not that Polybius claimed Rome to be undergoing the anacyclic process in its pure form, that is, in accordance with the way the process was outlined in *Hist.* VI,iv–ix. His meaning was much more complex than this, and his expression of the relationship between the natural cycle of governments and the natural Roman constitution was especially subtle.

One may recall that after his first description of the zigzag from monarchy to mob rule he commented on the need to attend to the stages undergone by each individual constitution, for each had a "beginning and generation," and each experienced growth, acme, change, and an end (iv,12). He was there thinking of the three basic forms of constitution, but then he proceeded further by asserting that:

> It is above all to the Roman polity that this type of exegesis may successfully be applied, because from its beginning, its formation and growth have been natural. (iv,13)

Again, after setting out the second, more elaborate statement of constitutional change, he reflected on the usefulness of the anacyclic model for assessing the stage of growth or decay any polity had reached (cf. ix,11), and added:

> Especially concerning the Roman *politeia* will this model be of use, providing us with the knowledge of its formation, growth, and acme, and likewise its change toward the reverse of these in the future. For, as I said, this polity, more than any other, has undergone natural formation and growth, and will undergo a natural change to opposite conditions in the future. (ix,12–13)

One cannot but be struck by the fact that in order to discuss the Roman polity in relation to the cycle of governments Polybius had been forced to talk far less about his grand model in general and much more about the biological principle in particular. That was an important shift, yet the reasons for it, upon close examination, become fairly obvious.

For Polybius the Roman constitution attained a zenith, but as already observed, the *Anacyclōsis* reflected no clearly-defined point of acme, even though he appears to have reckoned the general condition of polity as a high point in the large-scale cycle of his model. Moreover, whereas three specific constitutional forms had their life cycles and zeniths within the cycle of governments, he wrote of the Roman mixed constitution as if it had several constitutional developments both in preparation for it and in decline from it. As an individual polity, of course, with a limited span of life, the mixed constitution had a biological cycle of its own. But Polybius wished to say more than just that. The beginning and formation of Rome's mixed type of government and its future decay were bound up with the careers of the separable constitutional forms which preceded and succeeded it. Viewed in this broader light, it is easier to grasp why, according to Polybius, Rome had the most natural of polities. At the inception of its constitutional history there was no *mixis* in sight. That had to be

141. On the distinction between the inner development of a constitution as the realm of nature and the outer more variable relations between states as the realm of chance, see below, Chapter 2, sect. A, pt. 2(ii).

developed by the Romans in response to numerous difficulties, and it arose not through one piece of legislation nor by any artificial means, but by what was claimed to be the natural even if willful responses to circumstances. At Rome's constitutional end point, it follows, the mixed constitution would have long passed.

So what are we to make of Polybius' approach here? Was his strong appeal to the biological principle in relation to Rome simply a way of linking his two great "basic frameworks," enabling him to affirm that both the anacyclic process and Rome's constitutional course were natural, even if they could never be truly integrated? It may seem realistic to answer in the affirmative, but the available evidence compels us to proceed further, showing how Polybius did actually hold that Rome in some sense experienced both the cycle of governments and a mixed constitution. Closely interrelated with this area of inquiry, however, is an even more problematic question: whether or not it is possible to reconstruct what he wrote about the early history of Rome.

### *The constitutional development of Rome*

Polybius stated explicitly in one place and implied in another that he had described the formation of the Roman polity (in Bk. VI),[142] but almost all the relevant material has been lost. The methods used in the Roman "archeology" may be reflected in his short historical accounts of Sparta after the establishment of the Lycurgan constitution, and of the Achaian state before and after it adopted democracy,[143] but probably only in a very pale way, since these were states with constitutional forms settled in the relatively distant past. With Rome it was apparently a matter of explaining (at what length one cannot tell) how the Roman *politeia* reached a state of perfection during the relatively recent second Punic War. Polybius evidently began his background presentation with the early Roman kings;[144] that naturally enough leads one to ask whether he also treated the reign of Tarquinius Superbus, the tyrant who succeeded the sixth king and brought on the downfall of Roman one-man rule,[145] and whether he considered Romulus as the primitive monarch of Rome's political society, since the career of her founder was so strongly associated with animal-like existence and with physical strength. This is not unlikely (Taeger was justified in arguing that it was more than a possibility),[146] so that the search for an historical interrelationship between the Roman mixed constitution and the cycle of governments may not be in vain. One should tread warily, however, for many pitfalls await those attempting to reconstruct the non-extant parts of any ancient text.

We may recollect at this point how Polybius apparently combined Plato's

142. See VI,xi,1–2, ix,12, 14.

143. VI,xlviii–xlix (Sparta), II,xl,5–xliii,6, IV,i,4–6 (Achaia). Eisen (op. cit., p. 38) argues that further materials on the Greek constitutions have been lost.

144. Cicero *De re pub.* II,xiv,27; Polybius, Frg. VI (6,2) (a & b) (following E. Hultsch's order); cf. Taeger, op. cit., pp. 55ff.

145. Cicero *De re pub.* II,xxiii,43–xxix,51; Livy *Ab urbe condita* I,49ff.; Tacitus *Annales* III,26; etc.

146. Taeger, op. cit., pp. 38ff.

*Laws* Bk. III and the *Republic* Bk. VIII. Plato's account of socio-political development included a reference to the formation of the "third community" of the "plain" which blended all forms and conditions of constitutions, and which followed the appearance of an aristocracy.[147] In the *Laws* Plato had gone on to describe the establishment of the Spartan mixed constitution as one manifestation of his fourth society (683A–693C); in the *Republic* he diagnosed the weaknesses of Sparta's form of government (547B–550B). Polybius' cycle of governments, on the other hand, bypassed such developments, assuming a direct passage from aristocracy to oligarchy. Given that the general course of the Polybian cycle of governments was based on Plato's dialogues, and presupposing that Polybius allowed for the appearance of a mixed constitution within the grand cycle, at least in Rome's case, the most likely place for such an appearance was after aristocracy and before oligarchy.

A crucial passage toward the end of Bk. VI bears on this line of thought. In Chapter lvii Polybius spent time describing how a polity fell into decay. Clearly he had Rome in mind, and although *politeia* was used as both "state" and "constitution" in this context, the passage is more easily understood if one takes it to mean mixed constitution (*mixis*). When such a constitution overcomes many perils and eventually achieves an uncontested sovereignty (presumably in both external and internal affairs), then long-established prosperity engenders extravagance among the citizens, and excessive rivalry for office among those most ambitious or most afraid of falling into obscurity. There follows the rise of the populace, motivated both by its grievances against the obvious greed of certain people, and through its pride built up by flatterers (lvii,5–7). The common people, no longer wishing to obey their old leaders, demand "the lion's share for themselves" (8b),[148] and set up a constitution with the finest-sounding of all names, "freedom and democracy," which changes for the worse into mob rule (9). This analysis, one may contend, largely parallels the second half of the anacyclic zigzag, though it is a special version of it. In this case Polybius gave more details about the rise of the people to complete supremacy than in ix,1–3,[149] yet the

147. *Leg.* III,681D. The mixed constitution was not perfect and it was without the divine inspiration of the Spartan polity. Plato admits that it could "possibly have followed a kingship" instead of an aristocracy, but we are arguing that Polybius deliberately avoided discussing this complication.

148. Is this an allusion to Plato's phrase in *Resp.* VIII,565A? The terms and contexts are not dissimilar.

149. W. R. Paton's translation (vol. 3, p. 399) of lvii,6–7 takes the *people* to be responsible for the general "change for the worse" in the state, but one must be careful about subtleties here and about the meaning of the crucial phrase λήψεται δὲ τὴν ἐπιγραφὴν τῆς μεταβολῆς ὁ δῆμος (7a). *Epigraphē* appears to be deliberately ambiguous, probably because two lines of analysis were being brought together in the passage 5–9. Adopting one course in interpretation, we may take the people to "bear the stamp" of this change in the sense that they were involved in the two stages which brought about democracy; they felt unjustly dealt with, on the one hand, and they were flattered, on the other. Taking another course, which presupposes a discussion soon to come, it is probable that if in 5–9 Polybius was describing the line of decay from a mixed constitution to mob rule, he was thinking of the relevant sequence of forms as: mixed constitution with a heavy popular bias (cf. li,6)/oligarchy/democracy/mob rule. Thus with the emergence of oligarchy in this process of decline, the populace "bear the mark" of a change to oligarchy because it was due to

grasping of the (oligarchic) leaders,[150] the resulting grievances among the populace, the people's support for anyone backing their cause, as well as the sequence of democracy and mob rule, are all central features shared by both accounts.[151]

There are, it is true, noticeable differences. His attitude toward democracy in lvii,8–9 (cf. viii,3–4) was quite derogatory; the comparative objectivity of the cycle of governments has been swept away for talk about a people "puffed up" by flattery, filled with "fury" and "passion," and instituting what is ironically called "liberty."[152] Oligarchy, democracy, and mob rule thus appear to form a chain of decay, the anacyclic zigzag being apparently (though not indisputably) forgotten. This shift in axis is evidently due to the fact that in lvii Polybius was considering decline from a mixed constitution, and therefore from an acme that overshadows the three zeniths of the normative zigzag. The pattern emerging, then, has the mixed constitution at the very center of the *Anacyclōsis*, Polybius evidently holding that the first stage of the anacyclic process from monarchy to aristocracy saw the formation and growth of Rome's mixed constitution, while the stages from oligarchy to mob rule (at least) represented its decay. On this reading, Roman constitutional development followed both the anacyclic line (from primitive monarchy to mob rule) and a drawn-out biological path (to and from an acme point). On this reading there is no reason to wonder why Polybius claimed that of all constitutions the Roman developed most naturally.

In deciding whether the above explanation is satisfactory, a brief glance at possible alternatives would be helpful. It has been argued by Fritz Taeger that Polybius' "Roman archeology" can be recovered from the pages of a later document which bears the signs of his influence, namely Cicero's *De re publica* (mid-first century BC).[153] In Bk. II of this work Cicero sketched the history of the Roman constitution from the time of Romulus at least as far as the dictatorship of Lucius Quinctius (458 BC) (II,ii,4–xxxvii,63b). Scipio Aemilianus, chief narrator in the second book, dealt in turn with Romulus (his origins, his founding of Rome, and his creation of both the auspices and the senate), with the period of the kings which ended with the tyranny of Tarquinius Superbus, and then with the constitutional developments that followed—senatorial, aristocratic-seeming government (yet with the consulates and dictatorship as crucial offices), the creation of the plebeian tribunes, and the unfortunate rule of the Decemvirs.[154] The rest of Scipio's narrative only survives in fragmentary form, but

their increased influence in the mixed constitution that oligarchic policies became possible, and because, since oligarchy in this case emerged *between* two popular rules, the common people played a fundamental rôle in the developments covered in 5–7 (and 8–9).

150. That oligarchy is meant (though not mentioned by name) in lvii,5–7, see V. Pöschl, *Römischer Staat und griechisches Staatsdenken bei Cicero: Untersuchungen zu Ciceros Schrift De Re Publica* (*Neue Deutsche Forschungen Abt.Klassische Philologie V*), Berlin, 1936 edn., pp. 62–4.

151. Cf. viii,5, lvii,7b (on *pleonexia* or greed), viii,6, ix,1b, lvii,7–8 (grievances), ix,1, lvii,7.

152. lvii,7, 8, 9; cf. Plato *Resp.* VIII,557C; Herodotus *Hist.* III,80.

153. Op. cit., pp. 16ff.

154. *De re pub.*, esp. II,ii,4, iii,5–6, iv,7ff., ix,5, x,17f., xii,23–xiii,25, xvii,31, xviii,33, xx,35, xxi,37f., xxiii,43, xxvii,49, xxix,51, xxxi,55, xxxiii,58–xxxiv,61, xxxvi,61–xxxvii,63, for the important constitutional details.

Taeger detected a sequence which parallels the *Anacyclōsis*, namely: *Urmonarchie*/kingship (but mixed)/tyranny/aristocracy (but mixed)/oligarchy. Although recognizing more than one tradition behind *De re publica*, he endeavored to reconstruct the Polybian archeology on the supposition that Cicero employed Polybius as his key source.

Taeger's thesis is provocative but tenuous. Admittedly, a mention of Polybius in the dialogue establishes him as one of Cicero's sources (cf. II,xiv,27b), but if there is a seminal work behind *De re publica* Bk. II, it was not Polybius' history but rather, according to Cicero's own admission, the *Origines* of Cato the Elder (i,1–3). In matters of fine detail, moreover, disparities between Polybius and Cicero are sufficiently stark and numerous. For one of Taeger's more important critics, Viktor Pöschl, they actually preclude both the likelihood of decisive Polybian influence on Cicero and the possibility of reconstructing Polybius' early history along Taeger's lines of approach.[155] It should be noted that Taeger took Polybius to be expounding an "accumulative" view of Rome's constitutional development. Cicero claimed Romulus to have founded the senate, and the post-monarchical senate to have created the consuls and tribunes. He was thus describing a process whereby Rome, despite temporary setbacks, gradually accumulated the components of its mixed constitution. Mixed kingship (that is, kingship with the counsels of the senate, and based on popular assent) and mixed aristocracy (senatorial government with checks imposed by consuls and tribunes) replace what have been simply referred to as kingship and aristocracy in the *Anacyclōsis*, and after experiencing decemvirate oligarchy the mixed constitution achieves its peak.[156] According to Taeger, this account derives from Polybius. Despite a certain persuasive symmetry, however, Taeger's argument has obvious weaknesses. He has tended to read into the normative *Anacyclōsis* "mixed" phenomena that are not really present. Not only is there no evidence to show that Polybius wrote of mixed kingship, aristocracy, or even democracy in connection with Rome, but it is also most likely that he placed the Roman mixed constitution within the normative anacyclic zigzag between aristocracy and oligarchy, and not between oligarchy and mixed democracy, as in the "accumulative" schema.[157] We have already given reasons for this conclusion, and we may add how improbable it is that Polybius considered oligarchy as part of the formation and growth of the complex Roman system of government. On top of this, Taeger takes Polybius to have too much knowledge of Roman constitutional history: Cicero, who was eclectic in tendency, followed more than one line of Roman tradition. Besides, Cato's *Origines*, his chief source and a crucial work on the subject of Rome's constitutional history, probably saw daylight only after Polybius had written his sixth book.[158] Coupled with the fact that the

155. Op. cit., ch. 2, esp. pp. 47ff.

156. Ibid., pp. 26ff.; cf. von Fritz, op. cit., p. 419.

157. See Pöschl, op. cit., pp. 63–5; Eisen, op. cit., pp. 84f.

158. The *Origines* are usually dated to between ca. 168 and 149 BC, and the first six books of Polybius' *Historiae* to ca. 150 BC (although these could have been revised in Greece after 146 BC). Cato's *Origines* included an account of the Punic Wars to Cannae (Bk. IV), yet Polybius does not seem to have made use of this work as a source (he consistently mentions and criticizes his key

Achaian's facility with Latin is suspect, this should make one wary of ascribing to him anything more than a general, certainly non-technical, acquaintance with the Roman past. Fabius Pictor, whose history of Rome in Greek was used in Polybius' account of the second Punic War (cf. *Hist.* I,xiv,1, xv,12, lviii,5, III,viii,1, ix,1–3), was in all likelihood the main source for the archeology. There is evidence that Fabius considered Roman history from Aeneas to the Gallic Wars very discursively, and it is by his more annalistic, less legalistic approach that one can best given some definition to the limits of the Achaian's knowledge.[159]

The surviving material from the sixth book of the *Historiae* suggests that Polybius' account of the growth of the Roman polity was in narrative rather than analytic form.[160] In prefacing his description of Rome's polity at its height, moreover, he admitted that Roman readers might well find his approach far too selective, insisting rather defensively that his omissions, which included omissions about the origin of certain matters his readers might have thought crucial, were deliberate and not due to ignorance (VI,ix,3–9; cf. iii,3). In addition, he was not interested in pinpointing any basic constitutional change in Rome after the time of Xerxes' invasion of Greece near the beginning of the fifth century, because by that time Rome already had a constitution meriting special study by the Greeks, and he therefore went straight on to describe its structure during the second Punic War, at the time of its zenith (xi,1).[161] All this points to conclusions radically different from those of Taeger and the "accumulative" view.

Our limited knowledge of Polybian archeology confirms the pattern for which we have argued. We know that Polybius dated the origins of Rome [Frg. 2 (6,2)]; we know that he betrayed a keen interest in the ethical basis of Roman life (probably in an "archeological" context,[162] and his reproduction of the story about Horatius Cocles upon the bridge, even if not in such a context, is relevant here);[163] we know that he presented a narrative of Rome's early kings and taught

sources). It is thus fair to assume that although he knew something of Cato's life and attitudes (cf. *Hist.* XXXI,xxv,4ff.) Polybius had not read his work.

159. *FGH*, Frgs. 1ff. (vol. 2, pt. 3C, pp. 848ff.); cf. Cicero *De Legibus* I,ii,6. Also J. P. V. D. Balsdon, "Some Questions about Historical Writing in the Second Century BC" in *Classical Quarterly* XLVII, 1953, p. 161, on the likelihood that Polybius' predecessors knew little about Roman history between the monarchy and the Punic Wars.

160. So Frgs. V(6,2), VI(6,2); *Hist.* VI,liv,6–lv,4. The moralisms in Frgs. VI(6,1,a & b), VII(6,2) can be explained as pithy statements included at the end of narrative pieces: cf. Frg. VI(6,2) *finis*; *Hist.* VI,lv,4.

161. Thus Polybius evidently believed Rome to have possessed a mixed constitution from ca. 480 BC until his own day, an extremely long period of time. It is unlikely, though, that he knew the constitutional history of Rome over those centuries in any detail. Even his treatment of Roman history from ca. 390 to 216 in Books I–V reflects some vagueness as to the actual workings of the constitution.

162. Frg. IV(6,2). I take the only authentic Polybian section of this fragment to be: παρὰ Ῥωμαίοις δὲ . . . ἀπείρηται γυναιξὶ πίνειν οἶνον. τὸ δὲ καλούμενον πάσσον πίνουσιν; the rest to be ascribed to Athenaeus *Deipnosophistae* X,440E–F. In an archeological context Polybius' observation probably concerned the growth of Roman discipline and sense of duty: cf. VI,iii,3, xlvii,1.

163. *Hist.* VI,liv,6–lv,4; cf. lii,7–11, etc.

that close to the beginning of the fifth century Rome possessed a mixed constitution. It is difficult to imagine that the lost parts of his work did not fill in the gaps, that he said nothing about Romulus (even as a *monarchos*-figure! though the proof is lacking), and that he said nothing about the renowned tyranny of Tarquinius Superbus. And Tarquinius was banished toward the end of the sixth century (conventionally 510 BC), while Rome acquired its mixed constitution, according to Polybius, around the time of Xerxes' invasion (480 BC). Can we not suppose, even if very tentatively, that the time in between was occupied by a senatorial-aristocratic order, out of which the mixed form of government emerged?[164] That would certainly be a convenient means of piecing the jigsaw puzzle together, and both the way in which Polybius apparently interpreted the Platonic sequence of constitutions and the evidence requiring the mixed constitution to be inserted between an aristocracy and an oligarchy make this conclusion very attractive. To take this view, of course, means to say that Polybius did not treat the Decemvirs (451 BC on) as oligarchs; their rule merely formed part of the "many trials and troubles" which were undergone by the constitution itself in the attainment of its highest perfection.[165]

This raises crucial questions, of course, concerning the career and life cycle of the mixed constitution in particular. Once it was established, it apparently was understood to undergo a three-staged process of change. When Polybius compared the constitutions of Rome and Carthage at the time of their contest during the Hannibalic War, he took both to be structurally triadic, combining the regal, aristocratic, and popular powers (li,1–2). Declaring that every body, state, or action must experience growth, acme, and decay (li,4a), he went on to make some of the most interesting observations of the *Historiae*:

It was for this reason that the difference between the two states [*politeumata*] then showed itself.[166] For by as much as both the power and prosperity of Carthage had been earlier than that of Rome, by so much had Carthage already begun to decline. Rome was at its zenith by this time, at least so far as the settled system [*systasis*] of its polity was concerned.[167] Consequently the populace had already acquired the most power in deliberating among the Carthaginians, while at Rome the Senate was on top.[168] Hence in

164. The text is uncertain, but VI,xi,1 may well place the beginning of the mixed constitution at 449 BC, after the Decemvirs (Buettner-Wobst edn., vol. 2, p. 255; cf. Walbank, *Polybius*, p. 148). According to Polybius, twenty-eight years elapsed between the removal of Rome's tyranny and the invasion of Greece by Xerxes (cf. III,xxii,1–2). Dionysius (*Archaeol.* V,i,1) and Appian (*Historia Romanorum*, *proem*.6) may well have been following Polybius in placing an aristocratic rule after Tarquinius Superbus, although we lack evidence that Polybius recognized an oligarchy (in the form of the Decemvirs) between this rule and the mixed constitution.

165. VI,x,14. These troubles were not exclusively, nor even primarily, institutional or internal crises, but we can infer that he sketched the history of the mixed constitution, however complex the subject matter was (iii,3), and despite necessary omission (xi,3ff.), "up to the time of the second Punic War"; cf. F. W. Walbank, "Polybius and the Roman State" in *Greek, Roman and Byzantine Studies* V, 1964, p. 248.

166. = *politeiai*: cf. F. W. Walbank, "The Spartan Ancestral Constitution in Polybius" in *Ancient Society and Institutions* (V. Ehrenberg Festschrift) (ed. E.B.), Oxford, 1966, pp. 305f.

167. For *systasis* cf. Plato *Resp.* VIII,546A, *Leg.* VI,782A; yet note Polybius *Hist.* VI,iv,13.

168. The phrase *akmēn echein* here is probably meant to denote both the acme of senatorial power within the mixed constitution *and* the acme of the life cycle of the mixed constitution.

one case the many were the advisers and in the other the most eminent men. The Roman decisions on public affairs were thus superior, and although they met with disaster, they were eventually able to overpower the Carthaginians in war by the wisdom of all their deliberations. (li,4b–8)

In this passage Polybius simultaneously identified the final zenith of Rome's constitutional development as a whole and the acme of Rome's mixed constitution in particular (when taken as a separate constitution with its own life cycle). From either perspective the zenith lay with a *mixis* in which the senatorial-aristocratic power was preeminent. According to the passage, moreover, a mixed constitution in which the popular power was most decisive was a decline away from this apex, while by implication one dominated by monarchical elements represented a growth toward it.

This interpretation accords well with the different emphases reflected in Polybius' treatment of Roman politics before and after the battle of Cannae, that great military defeat suffered by Rome in the very middle of the second Punic War (216 BC). For Polybius, the factor in Rome's politics which enabled her to avoid defeat and become master of the world was the senate. The senate gave "wise counsels" to save Rome from disaster.[169] It was the senate which more and more came to sanction key negotiations and the submission of conquered territories, consuls and other military appointees awaiting senatorial decisions on the most vital matters.[170] Although great power was wielded by such eminent individuals as Scipio Africanus and Scipio Aemilianus, these men were understood to have lived under a mixed constitution, the chief voice of which was aristocratic.[171] On the other hand, Polybius portrayed pre-Cannaean politics as though the consuls were more important in the conduct of both military and foreign affairs than the senate.[172] Significantly enough, he was only too willing to highlight the deficiencies of Roman politics operating under these earlier conditions. In general, the Romans were unable to defeat the Carthaginians;[173] in particular, to take central examples, Consul Regulus' attempt to undermine the constitution by prolonging his appointment in North Africa brought disaster upon his fellow countrymen (I,xxxi,4–xxxiv,9), and Consul Gaius Flaminius' betrayal of demagogic policies was the first step "in the demoralization of the populace" (II,xxi,8).[174] Unhealthy rivalry among the consuls during Hannibal's invasion of Italy (cf. III,lxxx,1ff.), and the curious appointment of two dictators, with such widesweeping powers that they merely competed with each other (III,clii,4–8 and ff.), added to the Carthaginians' advantages.

169. Esp. III,lxxxv,10, cxviii,9, VIII,ii(iv),7–9; yet cf. IX,vi,5–8, XVIII,xxxv,2.

170. Esp. XVIII,x,1–2, xi,1ff., xlii, xlvii,9, XXI,ii–iii, xviii,1ff., xxxi,1f., xliii,2, XXII,vi, XXIII,i, etc.

171. XXIII,xiv,1 in Suidas *Lexicon* (ed. A. Adler, Stuttgart, 1928, vol. 4, p. 173), S.V. Πόπλιος. *Hoti Poplios philodoxēsas en aristokratikō politeumati* . . . ; cf. VIII,i(iii),3–ii(iv),11, esp. ii(iv),7–10.

172. I,xvii,6–7, xxvi,4–9, xxxi,6–8, xxxviii,5–7, xxxix,1–2, xlix,3–4, lv,2, lxxxviii,8, III,lxxxvi, 6–7, IX,vi,5–8; yet cf. I,xx,1–11, lii,5, lix,8.

173. See below, Chapter 2, sect. B, pt. 1(ii), especially for Polybius' stress on the balance between these two powers in Bk. I.

174. Cf. III,lxxx,3; Roveri, op. cit., p. 186. Significantly, Polybius did not place Flaminius' popular reforms before his consulship, the historically accurate thing to have done.

Thus it appears to have been Polybius' intention to contrast the inadequacy of a mixed constitution biased toward consular authority before Cannae (the mixed constitution in a stage of growth), with the emergence of greater senatorial influence from about the time of that disaster onward (the mixed constitution at its acme).[175] Yet if this senatorial influence marked Rome's highest constitutional zenith, Polybius noted that within his own lifetime the best stage had passed, and problems of luxury, pomp, and moral breakdown had revealed themselves (cf. Chapter 2). It is not necessary to suppose that Polybius thereby isolated the symptoms of a decline into oligarchy. In Bk. VI,lvii he placed such a breakdown in the rather distant future (5; cf. iii,3). Thus it is more likely that when he noted these contemporary tendencies he was referring to the danger of popular power usurping the authority of the senate, that is, to the kind of "democratization" within the mixed constitution which marked a decline from the highest point of Rome's constitutional life. When this third and last stage in the life cycle of the mixed constitution was passed, then its death as a particular constitutional form would be decided, and Rome's return to the normative anacyclic path, to oligarchy and the transformations following it, would be the natural consequence. This reversion is precisely what is covered in VI,lvii, with its downhill movement from a "democratized" mixed constitution to mob rule.

Thus the Polybian archeology or Polybius' comprehension of Rome's whole constitutional career may be set out briefly as follows (the bracketed sections indicating reconstructions by inference):

Growth {
origin of Rome
[Romulus, along with material about the growth of moral values]
early Roman kings
[tyranny]
[senatorial-aristocratic government] } "trials

Zenith {
the mixed constitution[176] } and
[consular role more decisive] : growth } troubles"
senatorial role more decisive : zenith
popular role more decisive : decay

Decay {
oligarchy
democracy
mob rule
[return to *monarchos*-figure]

As the line parallels that which Polybius extracted from Plato's *Laws* and the *Republic*, and as the natural biological and natural anacyclic paths of development are both accounted for, we may fairly take this interpretation to satisfy all the available evidence, to complement our analysis of the anacyclic model and

175. In ibid., p. 187, Roveri comes close to this interpretation.

176. Principles of transition between the three stages in the life cycle of the mixed constitution are not analyzed anywhere in the extant text, but note VI,lvii,5–7 on the passage from this mixed constitution (with the popular voice preeminent) to oligarchy.

its theoretical background, and to give intelligibility to Polybius' claims about the Roman polity.

Not that this interpretation is without its problems. Quite apart from our reliance on inferences and the overshadowing doubt that one might have read too much into Polybius, there are other, even if minor, complications. We may single out at least three of them. First, if Polybius derived his general pattern of constitutional development from Plato, then we must admit that he applied to the career of one particular state what Plato applied to a whole cultural area, and not to any specific community such as Sparta or Athens. Why he chose to use Plato in this way is not easy to answer; that he did so best makes sense of his analyses. Second, there is an apparent contradiction between his statement that Rome's mixed constitution was moving through the three stations of a life cycle, and his exposition of it in static terms as a constitution of checks and balances (cf. VI,xi,11–xviii,8). He nowhere used the language of absolute balance in connection with mixed constitutions, however,[177] and he even wrote of the monarchical, aristocratic, and democratic elements in the Roman *mixis* as if they were separate constitutions themselves, separate though capable of working in unison.[178] Thus the contradiction is not a real one; a constitution was mixed as long as the three elements neutralized each other's powers to a sufficient (yet unspecified) degree, and it did not cease to be such when one or another of the elements played a dominant rôle. We may add a third problem—the difficulty of not being able to possess anything more than a very general Polybian explanation for the emergence of Rome's mixed constitution. The Romans learned from awkward circumstances to choose "the best"—but from which particular circumstances? Perhaps Polybius' assertion that the Lycurgan constitution was set up without the experience of any adversity (x,12) provides a hint. According to Plato, the Lycurgan polity staved off the kind of tyranny which had emerged in Lacedaemonia's sister cities of Argos and Messene (*Leg.* III,683C–688D), whereas according to the reconstructed Polybian archeology Rome actually experienced a tyranny, that of Tarquinius Superbus.[179] But there were many "trials and troubles" faced by the Romans, and this one instance of crisis hardly makes up for the information we lack, including details as to the precise manner in which the Roman polity departed from the anacyclic course and experienced a quite new kind of growth. The least one may say is that Polybius took Rome's mixed constitution to be very complex and that he bypassed many intricate changes and trials appertaining to the formation of the Roman constitution itself, and to the "natural" processes by which the normative *Anacyclōsis* was forestalled as a result. Complexity made it difficult to explain Rome's present character and to prognosticate its future (VI,iii,3), yet Polybius was still able to relate its growth, pinpoint its zenith, suggest the manner of its decline, and declare it the most natural of all polities.

177. Esp. VI,ix,11, xviii,2.

178. VI,xi,12, xii,9, xiii,8, xiv,11, xviii,1; cf. Graeber, op. cit., pp. 33ff., 78–80.

179. According to Aristotle, Carthage had never been subject to a tyranny: *Polit.* 1272b32–3.

These problems, whatever their solution, do not prevent us from drawing conclusions about the application of the cycle of governments to the recognizable facts of history. With characteristic eclecticism, Polybius combined two great theories. Roman history illustrated, first, his cycle of governments, and second, the stability of a mixed constitution. Concerning the cycle's applicability to Rome, he simplified her pre-Cannaean constitutional development to suit his model, and he could do little else than theorize about her future. As for the mixed constitution, he oversimplified the facts when considering not only Rome but also Sparta and Carthage as mixed constitutions with tripolitical frameworks.[180] But for his own purposes he believed he had grasped the truth about Rome. He felt able to explain how and by what form of government Rome managed to conquer the world (VI,ii,1–10; cf. I,i,5), and to show why the Roman polity was superior to others (VI,xliii,1–lvi,15; cf. III,cxviii,11–2).[181]

What can we say, in review, about the general relationship between his analysis of the Roman polity in Bk. VI and his grand statement of anacyclic recurrence? The first thing to be said is that, according to Polybius, Rome by the latter half of the second century BC had only partly illustrated the *Anacyclōsis*. Polybius had certainly not documented a full recurrence of the anacyclic path, even if it is possible that he took the Platonic representation of Greek history in general to be a precedent for Rome's constitutional development.[182] The limited degree of application is very disappointing. But then we are here requiring a "vertical" confirmation of his recurrence model, one taken from events in the same region over a long lapse of time, when in fact Polybius was primarily interested in recent affairs. One needs to be aware of the "horizontal" dimensions of Polybius' recurrence thinking, that is, his concern for illustrating his models from happenings in different regions within a modern, relatively limited period. For this concern, one should look beyond his sixth book to the *Historiae* as a whole.

180. See Excursus 1.

181. On important points of contrast among Athens, Sparta, Carthage, and Rome see VI,x,14b,1ff., xviii,5–6, xliv,2, 8, xlviii,1–xlix,10, l,4–6, lii,1–11.

182. Polybius began writing history as a strong Achaian nationalist: cf. M. Gelzer, "Die hellenische ΠΡΟΚΑΤΑΣΚΕΥΗ im zweiten Buch des Polybios" in *Hermes* LXXV, 1940, pp. 27–37; Täubler, op. cit., pp. 78ff.; Graeber, op. cit., pp. 15–21; M. Treu, "Biographie und Historie bei Polybios" in *Historia* III, 1954, pp. 219ff.; K. E. Petzold, *Studien zur Methode des Polybios und zu ihrer historischen Auswertung* (*Vestigia IX*), Munich, 1969, pt. 2. He wrote then about the unexpected rise of Achaian power not dissimilarly to the way he later wrote of Rome's rise to greatness (II,xxxvii, 6b–11, xliv,2, IV,i,4), offering a discursive "archeological" account of Achaia's constitutional development. Some political transitions were referred to (kingship to tyranny, tyranny to democracy), yet although the notion of an ongoing thrust was present (as it was later in his treatment of Rome), the complicated sequence of the cycle of governments was as yet unformulated, and the element of recurrence, whether in terms of the biological principle or the reversion to original conditions, not added. Although Polybius considered the Achaian League's constitution to be mixed, moreover, there is no indication that he put it forward as a model for the Romans to follow (against M. Grant, *The Ancient Historians*, London, 1970, p. 151, and to a lesser extent against H. Labuske, "Zur geschichtsphilosophischen Konzeption des Polybios" in *Klio* LIX, 1977, esp. pp. 404f., 411).

The *Anacyclōsis*, though, remains immensely important as a special, self-contained statement of historical repetition. Key paradigms, some hailing from the discourse of cosmic recurrence, are intertwined in a complex theory of political change. Not only do we encounter these paradigms and some of their applications, but we discover how one seminal writer sought to interrelate them, the difficulties he found in doing so, and how his preconceptions affected both his reading and his written interpretation of the past. The *Anacyclōsis*, moreover, introduces us to a rich and complex strain of Western intellectual history, a strain which begins before Polybius and persists to our own day.

# Chapter 2

# Polybius and the Elementary Models of Historical Recurrence in the Classical Tradition

The Polybian *Anacyclōsis* is like a figure in papier-mâché: simpler, more basic paradigms of historical recurrence lie beneath its complex exterior. Less sophisticated, more fundamental notions of recurrence, moreover, are scattered throughout the *Historiae* as a whole. That should not surprise us: when Polybius affirmed that the study of history provided a sound training for politics (cf. *Hist.* I,i,2) he presupposed that past events reflected various paradigmatic movements and patterns which would reemerge in current and future affairs. It is the more elementary paradigms and their interrelationships which interest us in this chapter, but we will delve into the classical (especially the Greek) heritage and not attend to Polybius' work alone. What will become apparent is the dominant concern in classical historical thought with "processes of change." Deeds and events lose their singularity and fall into recognizable configurations which appear again and again; thus past circumstances provide the clue not only to future occurrences but to future action as well. This is the binding factor behind the rich variety of recurrence paradigms which lie before us, and which we seek to present in a logical order.[1]

## A. Cycles and alternation as paradigms of recurrence

When the paradigm of a cycle or of circularity was first applied to human affairs is a matter of sheer speculation. The early Greeks met the ordinary circle as part of their everyday concrete experience; it could be found in the human eye, in pots, carts, dances, shields, and eventually in skillfully executed pillars, military formations, and the like. There was magic and wonder in its perfect symmetry, its endless perimeter. It was pregnant with figurative value as an image of both revolving movement and stability, of both alternation and continuousness. Besides, day and night were facts simple and usual enough to associate with circularity: the shapes and paths of the sun and moon, the incessant alternation of light and darkness, waking and sleeping, working and resting, were no less rhythmic than a cart wheel nor less everlasting than a circumference. These facts provided the conceptual basis for *periodoi* (literally, "ways around"), for thinking in periodic terms about the seasons, years, festivals, and even more abstractly about the generations of men or the psychic destinies of individuals.

Early Greek reflection on the seasonal cycle and human generations (which goes as far back as Homer),[2] and speculation about the career of the soul as a continuing procession through different, including animal, existences (which reaches back to so-called Orpheus),[3] were both built upon and enriched by cosmologists.[4] Eastern astronomers taught the Greeks to observe the heavens, and

1. For related comments, but from a broader perspective, see A. Momigliano, "Tradition and the Classical Historian" in *History and Theory* XI, 1972, pp. 284, 286, 291. In concentrating on Greek models of recurrence in this chapter I must make it clear how unwilling I am to make pretentious claims about the common assumptions of large groups. Certainly the *cyclos* and notions of eternal return have been taken to be near the heart of Hellenic consciousness: e.g., O. Spengler, *Der Untergang des Abendlandes*, Munich, 1923, vol. 1, p. 11, and cf. pp. 173ff.; M. Eliade, *Cosmos and History: The Myth of the Eternal Return* (ET), New York, 1959, esp. pp. 87ff.; S. G. F. Brandon, *History, Time and Deity*, Manchester, 1965, pp. 66ff.; J. Needham, "Time and Knowledge in China and the West" in *The Voices of Time* (ed. J. T. Fraser), London, 1968, pp. 129, 622; but I am well aware that there are other, non-recurrence strands of Greek thought. On views of progress, for example, see esp. Havelock, *Liberal Temper*, pp. 52ff.; Edelstein, *Idea of Progress*, passim; on pessimism, see esp. F. Nietzsche in *Gesammelte Werke*, Schlechta edn., Munich, 1966, vol. 2, pp. 245f., 1102f., vol. 3, pp. 353ff.; J. B. Bury, *The Idea of Progress: An Inquiry into its Origin and Growth*, London, 1924, pp. 10ff.; cf. E. Rohde, *Der griechische Roman und seine Vorläufer*, Leipzig, 1876 edn., p. 201 n. 2; on different views of time among the Greeks, see J. Callahan, *Four Views of Time in Ancient Philosophy*, Cambridge, Mass., 1948; and on less theoretical notions of time and history, see, e.g., Z. Barbu, *Problems of Historical Psychology*, London, 1960, pp. 70ff.; C. G. Starr, *The Awakening of the Greek Historical Spirit*, New York, 1968, pp. 57ff.

2. *Iliad* VI, 146ff., cf. Hesiod, *Erga* 107–184, 383–821.

3. W. K. C. Guthrie, *Orpheus and Greek Religion: A Study of the Orphic Movement*, London, 1952 edn., pp. 156ff.; cf. Herodotus *Hist.* II,123.

4. P. Duhem, *Le Système du monde: histoire des doctrines cosmologiques de Platon à Copernic*, Paris, 1954–9, vol. 1, pp. 65ff.; M. L. West, *Early Greek Philosophy and the Orient*, Oxford, 1971, pp. 34ff. and passim; cf. Eliade, op. cit., pp. 87ff.; B. Sticker, "Weltzeitalter und astronomische Perioden" in *Saeculum* IV, 1953, pp. 241ff.

they also broadcast the doctrine of a Great Year, the immense period of time taken for all the known planets to return to their original positions.[5] With general cosmology came not only visions about the shape and structure of the cosmos, but also a fascination with the processes of composition and decomposition and the stages of birth, growth, and decay in plant and animal life.[6] What of cyclical thinking about history? The language of the cosmologists certainly informed it, yet, as with the cyclical strain in early philosophy itself, this kind of thinking goes back still further. It evidently derives from ancient intuitions about the human round, about the way men's lives were regulated by season and custom, and the manner in which generations came and passed away. The gnomic saying κύκλος τὰ ἀνθρώπινα (human things are a circle)[7] probably had its roots in the early agricultural communities of Hellas, and yet it was the sort of profound truth which could be filled out by those who contemplated the fate of souls, or who were struck by complex regularities in urban life or fascinated by dramatic changes in the careers of notable individuals or city-states. It was this last interest, in the remarkable alteration of circumstances, which saw the development of what was in all likelihood the earliest conception of specifically historical recurrence in the West—the cyclical idea of fortune's wheel.

## *Fortune's wheel*

### I. GENERAL

Applied to human affairs, fortune's wheel was a revolving *cyclos* of human life in which "the same man was never allowed to continue in prosperity" (or to experience an uninterrupted measure of happiness).[8] The notion was most usually applied to the fortunate—the sad fate of the astoundingly lucky king Polycrates of Samos is a famous example[9]—but the transience of ill luck was sometimes implied as well, and there arose a popular fancy of a rotation between the two opposite conditions.[10] The wheel was alluded to by moralists and men of religious sensibility when they warned their fellows not to overtest good fortune, or reminded them that the gods were jealous of success.[11] More signifi-

5. Hesiod *Theogonia* 793ff.; Heraclitus, Frg. 22 (Diels-Kranz) (cf. West, op. cit., pp. 155ff.); Empedocles, Frgs. 115, 118, 121 (Diels-Kranz) (cf. Kirk-Raven, p. 352); Plato *Tim.* 39D; Censorinus *De die natali* XXI,3 (Jahn edn., p. 63).

6. Kirk-Raven, pp. 87ff., 139ff., 176ff., 385ff.

7. *Corpus Paroemiographorum Graecorum* (ed. E. L. Leutsch), Göttingen, 1851, vol. 2, p. 492; cf. the Erechtheum Inscription, which spells out "human *pragmata*": *Epigrammata Graeca* (ed. G. Kaibel), Berlin, 1878, no. 1092.

8. Herodotus *Hist.* I,207: "Human affairs are on a wheel (*cyclos*) which in its turning does not suffer the same man to have good fortune forever"; cf. Aristotle *Eth. Nic.* I,x,7 (on men liable to the changes of fortune many times: *pollakis anacycleisthai*); and for a variant see the Chian epigram (*Epigr. Graec.*, no. 233, *l.*7) on the recurrence (*palindromos*) of sorrow. In Latin authors, see esp. Tibullus *Corpus Tibull.* i,5, 70; Ovid *Epistulae ex Ponto* II,iii,56; Cicero *De finibus* V,viii,23; pseudo-Seneca *Octavia* 388–91; the term *orbis* generally being used.

9. Herodotus *Hist.* III,39–45, 120–6.

10. E.g., Anonymous poet in Plutarch *Consol. ad Apoll.* 103F (= W. T. Bergk (ed.) *Poetae lyrici Graeci*, Leipzig, 1843, vol. 3, p. 740): "The wheel (*trochos*) goes round, and of the rim now one/And now another part is at the top." Cf. Theognis 157; Pindar *Olympian Odes* II,9–23, 35–40, etc.

11. E.g., Homer *Iliad* V,436ff.; Theognis 129f.; Herodotus *Hist.* III,40; Aristotle *Eth. Nic.* I,x,6f.

cantly, however, it gained currency among those who wished to understand the passage of momentous historical events. It was employed to endow events with shape and coherence. Perhaps fortune's operations in these events were conceived quite variously, especially in the extent to which they were theologized or integrated with religious ideas about inevitable destiny;[12] yet there remains the one basic theme of reversal, and because of its suddenness or unexpectedness such reversal appeared to be the product of the incalculable. For some, it is true (and these people tended to personify and deify *tychē*), fortune's mysterious ways had ethical meaning, since the proud could be deservedly brought low, and the deprived but worthy man suddenly find riches. At this stage, however, we may concentrate on the more simple idea of a twist or revolution from one state of affairs to another and then back again. Fortune, whether hypostatized or left impersonal, was mutable. There was a tendency toward resignation and far less theodicy when fortune was looked at this way: if impersonal, it could be no more than blind chance; if personified, she could be accused of capriciousness and cruelty.[13] Death and setbacks could fall upon the apparently blessed, war and social distress upon the flourishing state, and riches and happiness upon the distressed or backward.

The Greeks imagined that these shifts for either good or ill formed two sides of one circular movement. Such an intuition was not only based on the observation of remarkable change, but also on the truism that favorable and adverse conditions must succeed each other by turns. We discover here, once again, the difficulty of disentangling the cyclical from the alternating; the idea of changing fortune is hardly far removed from notions of a shifting balance in human affairs or of "change into opposites." But the cyclical image predominated in connection with fortune, and there was a pervasive assumption that men must learn how fortune's wheel inscribes its path and must be prepared for unexpected (though not unrecognizable) change.

## II. POLYBIUS

One does not have to look far to locate the basic notion of fortune's mutability in Polybius. Surprisingly, perhaps, he made no reference to a *cyclos* of historical events, and the term *Anacyclōsis* he used in Bk. VI is the only relevant

12. For critical discussion see esp. G. Herzog-Hauser in *RECA*, vol. VIIA, cols. 1643ff. On *Tychē* (Fortune) as an early deity see, e.g., Hesiod *Theog.* 360, Theognis 1188; cf. F. M. Cornford, *From Religion to Philosophy: A Study in the Origins of Western Speculation*, London, 1912, p. 98. On fusing *tychē* with destiny, see, e.g., Euripides *Alcestis* 780, Menander in Plutarch *Consol. ad Apoll.* 103C–E, Plutarch *Vita Caii Marii* xxiii,1; and on Aristotle's more objective (though still theological) approach, *Physica* II,195b30–198a13. On *tychē* in Greek historiography, see esp. Herzog-Hauser, loc. cit., cols. 1662–5; and on *Fortuna* in Roman thought as background to Latin historiography, I. Kajanto, *God and Fate in Livy* (*Annales Universitatis Turkensis LXIV*), Turku, 1957, pp. 66ff.; cf. W. Jaeger, "Horaz C. I.34" in *Hermes* XLVIII, 1913, pp. 443ff.

13. E.g., Theognis 129–30; Philemon in *Fragmenta comicorum Graecorum* (ed. A. Meineke), Berlin, 1839–57, vol. 4, p. 31; Diphilus in ibid., vol. 4, p. 424; Menander, Frgs. 417, 630 (A. Koerte); cf. Anonymous (proverb) in Diodorus Siculus *Bib.* IX,x,3. On accusing *tychē* see Polybius *Hist.* XVI,xxxii,5; Dio Chrysostom *Orationes* lxiv; and on fortune's cruelty see Demetrius of Phalerum, Frg. 81 (in *Schul. Arist.*, ed. Wehrli, op. cit., pp. 22f.).

instance of cognate terminology.[14] However, simple cyclical models were frequently presupposed in his interpretations; he did not stop to theorize about their intrinsic qualities, but, rather, utilized them as the means of extracting significance from given events. It is evident that he was interested in types of events or event-complexes, and in the characteristic forms with which they were endowed. While any specific reference to a *cyclos* of human affairs is absent, the idea that events can fall within the ambit of fortune's circling wheel, or belief in a process in which prosperity succeeds adversity by turns, was still of great thematic importance for his "history of the world" from ca. 220 to 145 BC.

There are, admittedly, certain difficulties surrounding Polybius' approach to the concept of chance. His most common tendency was to deify fortune, treating it not as a mere impersonal contingency, not as the accidental or the haphazard, but as a quasi-personalized force which moderated and even took direct control of human affairs. On occasions, however, personification is absent, and there were other times when he insisted that certain events did not occur, as some had pretended, through the agency of fortune, but rather in accordance with human will and judgment.[15] Moreover, even if Polybius acknowledged Fortune as director of human affairs (as a crucial factor responsible for the success of Rome, for example),[16] this tendency jars somewhat with a number of his assertions that she was capricious.[17] Yet despite these by no means insoluble problems (cf. sect. B), Polybius' understanding of fortune was still largely dominated by the primary model of finite prosperity and adversity. Moralizing about the career of Philopoemen, his Achaian hero, he quoted "the popular aphorism" that "it is possible for a human being to be fortunate, but impossible for him to be constantly so" (*Hist.* XXIII,xii,3–4) and then went on to contend that the happiest men were those to whom Fortune was kind for most of their lives and who finally met with only moderate mishaps (5–7). At the end of his own labors, Polybius prayed to avoid Fortune's typical envy against all those who seem to have had too happy and too successful a career (XXXIX,vii,2). Thus, seeing good fortune (*eutychia*) predominate in the private lives of certain men, seeing such a skillful general as Hannibal reach the point of almost conquering the whole of Italy, or such a virtuous soldier-statesman as Epameinondas virtually unite the Peloponnesus under Achaia, it was appropriate for him to remind his readers that these men suffered under Fortune's blows (IX,viii, 13–ix,1; cf. XV,vi,6, XXIII,xii,3). But fortune was not always adverse: individuals suffering under misfortune (*atychia*) could meet with the opposite extreme (cf. XII,via,2–3, XV,ii,13–15), and Polybius noted that the world was

14. For other usages see A. Mauersberger, *Polybios-Lexikon*, vol. 1, pt. 3, col. 1443.

15. For the distinctions see Mioni, *Polibio*, pp. 140–7. Cf. *Hist.* IX,xii,3,6–10, xvi,3, X,xxxii,3, xxxiii,7, on the accidental in Polybius; I,lxiii,9, III,cxviii,6–9, VII,viii,1, X,v,8, XI,xiv,2, xvi,4–5, XVIII,xii,2, etc., on skill and purpose instead of fortune; and I,xxxvii,3–6, II,vii,2–3, X,xxxii,7–12, XV,xxi,3, etc., on error and lack of skill instead of fortune.

16. Esp. I,iv,1, 4–5 (cf. III,xxxii,7, IV,ii,4), VIII,ii,3–4, XXXIX, xxvii,11–13, on Rome, and see below, sect. B, pt. 2(i) on fortune as preserver of the moral order.

17. Esp. XI,xix,5–6, XV,vi,8, vii,3f., xv,5, XXV,iii,9b, XXIX,xxi,5f. xxii,2, XXX,x,1, XXXV,ii,14.

replete with instances of both exaltations and abasements of men involved in public affairs (V,xxvi,12; cf. VIII,xxi(ii),11).

As with private careers, so it was with groups and nations. He cited the predictions of the Peripatetic Demetrius of Phalerum that as cruel Fortune had once destroyed Persia, so she would eventually bring the downfall of Macedon (XXIX,xxi,1–6).[18] Fortune, the philosopher had said, was lending good things to Macedonia until she wished otherwise; Polybius concurred with such judgments as though they were divine utterances. The Roman victory over Perseus (167 BC) was a substantiation of them,[19] and Polybius brought a similar principle of interpretation to the fate of other nations he examined: Fortune willed to work either for decline or prosperity. He remarked concerning the Boeotian cities that, although they had enough good fortune to scrape through the critical times created by Macedon's Philip V and the Seleucid Antiochus the Great, they eventually found fortune to be against them (XX,vii,1–2). On another occasion, however, he asserted that because Thebes had suffered so severely at the hands of Alexander the Great fortune changed in her favor and made reconstruction possible (XXXVIII,ii,3–iii,2). Of more significance is his treatment of the Roman-Carthaginian conflict in these terms. He stressed Hannibal's victory at the battle of Cannae as a high point in Carthaginian affairs, yet as the worst of disasters for Rome; it was after treating events up to the date of Cannae that he paused to consider the Roman constitution and its institutions, because it was of some wonder that a virtually conquered state had become a world power.[20] With this emphasis we may perceive how he integrated the image of fortune's wheel with a central purpose of his history—to explain Rome's amazing success.[21] Hannibal's remarkable achievements brought the eventual reversal of fortune's favor, while Rome, since she had faced near-destruction, suddenly found the wheel running in the opposite direction.[22] This could not alone account for the rapid rise of Rome to world dominion, but these principles nevertheless have a place in his understanding of world events and in his philosophy.

Such evidence demonstrates Polybius' willingness to share common Greek, and by that time Roman, assumptions about the vicissitudes of private and public fortunes. His approach presupposes no special source: popular notions about "turns" or "ups and downs" in human affairs are sufficient to account for it.[23] He simply utilized the stock notion of a common transference from prosperity to adversity or vice versa. What was taken to recur were *types* of events which

18. = Demetrius of Phalerum, Frg. 81 (Wehrli, pp. 22f.) = Diodorus XXXI,x,1–2.

19. 7–9; cf. xxii,2, and esp. XXIII,iii,5, x,1–5 on the foreshadowing of Macedonia's fall.

20. III,cxviii,1f., V,cv,10, cx,10, cxi,8, VI,xi,2; cf. I,xii,7, VI,ii,6f. Eisen (*Polybiosinterpretationen*, p. 36) suggests that Polybius wrote much more about the significance of Cannae.

21. I,i,1–6; cf. xii,7, III,i,4–iv,12, and below, sect. B, pt. 2(ii–iii).

22. IX,xxi; cf. vi,5, viii,13–ix,1, etc., on the turn of Carthage's fortunes, in contrast to Rome's new "good fortune" (VI,li,7f.). Polybius may well have omitted certain defeats suffered by Hannibal before Scipio's emergence to accentuate this picture of changing fortune: cf. Plutarch *Vitae* (*Pelopidas and Marcellus Compared*) i,4f.

23. For background see Epicurus, Frgs. 76–7 (Bailey, pp. 136–9) (3rd century BC); Epictetus

reflected the wheel-like movement from one set of conditions to another. Outside of an interesting piece of parallelism drawn between the careers of Hannibal and Philopoemen, who experienced fortune's recalcitrance in "the very same way," nothing approaches the repetition of particulars. Furthermore, Polybius considered the relevant phenomena "horizontally" rather than "vertically," so that he gave no instance of the wheel's complete circuit in the case of any one individual or group. His way of narrating events in recent world history tended to preclude this, and found him passing rapidly from one region or subject to another. Yet he still succeeded in conveying general guidelines for the student of politicians who wished to learn how historical events should be interpreted. One could assess through others' experience, moreover, how far Fortune could be trusted and how her reversals could be borne.

This notion of history's usefulness raises important questions about Polybius' special treatment of Rome, whose ways and achievements merited emulation. Did Polybius take Fortune to be singularly less fickle and far more favorably disposed toward the Roman empire than other nations? At one significant point he praised the judgment of Scipio Aemilianus who, when watching flames engulf Carthage, admitted his personal forebodings about a similar doom for his own country. However, although this suggests that the wheel would eventually turn against Rome as against others, Polybius emphasized the wisdom of this Roman general in reflecting on Fortune's mutability at the very height of success.[24] He attempted to expose certain qualities in Roman actions, policies, and institutions which dissuaded or forestalled Fortune in her normal operations, but these qualities were primarily moral, and we must await an analysis of his understanding of history's moral order before clarifying this matter.

## *The biological principle*

### I. GENERAL

The adage "human things are a circle" must have been pregnant with meaning for Pythagoreans and others who philosophized upon the mystical significance of numbers or shapes, and upon metempsychosis. Although it is difficult to reconstruct their early beliefs, the Pythagoreans probably enunciated a doctrine of exact recurrence. Objecting to their teaching, Eudemus the Peripatetic disputed the possibility that one could find oneself in exactly the same situation, as a teacher with the very same pupils and with rod in hand, for example, at some long-distant future date.[25] Unlike Stoics, Pythagoreans evidently refrained

*Dissertationes* I,ix,1–8, III,xxvi,1–36; Dio Chrysostom *Orat.* XXIV,19–24, XXV (both 1st century AD), on the way moralists encouraged personal resilience when fortunes altered; and Demetrius, Frgs. 79, 81, 121 (Wehrli, pp. 22f., 27) for a writer who philosophized on the inconstancy of human affairs. Cf. Polybius *Hist.*, esp. XV,vi,8, viii,3, xv,5, XXIX,xxi,5, xxii,2, XXX,x,1, etc., on fortune's unexpectedness, and XII,xiia,1, XXXI,xiii,12–4, XXXIII,iv,3, XXXIV,ii,2, etc., on his common use of proverbs.

24. *Hist.* XXXVIII,xxi,1–3 (from Plutarch's *Apophthegmata*).

25. Cf. Pythagoras, Frg. 58 (Diels-Kranz) = 272 (Kirk-Raven) in Eudemus of Rhodes, Frg. 88 (Wehrli, p. 41). Also Porphyry *Vita Pythagorae* xix.

from talk of any cosmic conflagration: one may therefore assume that they took such recurrence to occur within one continuing historical order, and that this repetition was made possible by the eventual return of souls to the same bodies and circumstances.[26] There are in fact two distinct cyclical models entwined in this teaching: recurrence is on the one hand tied in with the processes of birth, death, and rebirth of life forms, and on the other with the passing of huge lapses of time such as a Great Year or an Age (*aiōn*).[27]

Greco-Roman speculations about psychic transmigration are peripheral to our concerns, there being no extant attempt to show how the reembodiment of souls affected historical events.[28] The ideas of recurring life cycles, however, and of the application of the three-stationed biological principle to human affairs are clearly of great relevance. That all bodies come into being and pass away, or are born, grow, and die, was a truism frequently reflected upon.[29] Aristotle exploited this thought consistently in his studies of sublunary change, and he successfully fused the life cycle principle with the more widely applicable idea of periodicity. His fellow-countrymen, he once claimed, habitually conceived of human affairs in terms of circular motion. Concurring, he asserted that such affairs proceeded "periodically,"[30] though he pictured these "natural" movements as undulatory or cycloidal, quite distinct from the heavenly courses.[31] Because earthly motions were rectilinear they did not see any return to exactly the same point; human events were not repeated "numerically," then, but they recurrently took on the same forms (*eidē*), or fell into the same genus (so that certain types of constitutional change, certain types of temperament, and so forth, became evident).[32] Whether he also understood human events to recur on a regular periodic basis is not clear. He admittedly taught that

> the time periods or the lives of each kind of living thing have a number and are thus distinguished, for there is an order for everything, and every life and span is measured by a period (*De gen. et corr.* 336b11–14),

but only in the *Problemata*, in a section which was probably not executed by Aristotle himself, does one find a general statement suggesting a periodic, indeed eternal, return.

26. Esp. Frgs. 268–70 (Kirk-Raven).

27. On whether Pythagoras did actually speak of a Great Year, though, see J. A. Philip, *Pythagoras and Early Pythagoreanism*, p. 74; cf. B. L. van der Waerden, "Das Grosse Jahr und die ewige Wiederkehr" in *Hermes* LXXX, 1952, pp. 129ff.

28. Excluding the odd asseveration, such as Alexander the Great's claim to be Achilles (Quintus Curtius *Historiarum Alexandri Magni Macedonis* IV,vi,29; cf. Arrian *Anabasis* VII,xiv,4), and see below, Chapter 4, sect. F.

29. E.g., Diogenes Laertius *Vit. philos.* I,*proem.* iii; Plato *Resp.* VIII,546A; Polybius *Hist.* VI,lvii,1; Strato in Cicero *De natura deorum* I,xiii,35; Seneca *Epist.* LXXI,15; Epictetus *Dissert.* III,xxiv,9ff.

30. *Physica* 223b24–31, esp. 25: probably an allusion to the proverb discussed above.

31. *Phys.* 223b26–9; on undulations in Aristotle see Lovejoy and Boas, *Primitivism and Related Ideas in Antiquity*, p. 173.

32. *De gen. et corrupt.* 338b11–4; cf. pseudo-Aristotle *Problemata* 916a18–38; Eudemus, Frg. 88 (Wehrli, p. 41).

Just as the turning of the firmament and each of the stars is circular, why should not also the coming-to-be and decay of perishable things be the kind of process in which the same things come into being and pass away? This agrees with the saying that "human things are a circle." Yet to demand that those things [recurrently] coming into being should be numerically identical is foolish; on the other hand, one could more readily accept the theory of the identity of species (*eidos*). . . . If human life is a circle, moreover, and a circle has neither beginning nor end, we should not be prior to those who live in the time of Troy, nor they prior to us, by being nearer the beginning. (916a24–38)

Quite apart from the true authorship of this passage, the West owes that distinctive understanding of the cycle of growth, zenith, and decay in human affairs to the Aristotelian school before all others. Perhaps Aristotle and his followers were reiterating something already commonly held, yet their simple equation of three-staged cycles with periods (or with time lapses covering the existence of recognizable phenomena) provided a workable frame rich in possibilities for historians.[33] This was done, we must insist, at the expense of slightly modifying the seminal image of a circle, since organismic change, with its starting point in birth and its end in death, registers more as a cycloid with three basic stages than a movement which sees the return to an original point of departure. To be old and dying was a long way from being a child, while to have been once poor, then rich, and then unexpectedly poor again was more obviously a process which saw a return to the same circumstances, an important difference between the biological cycle and (in this instance) the wheel of fortune. Even if turns of fortune appear as a fluctuation between two states, the impact of a reversion is more decisive. Either conception, however, was reckoned to be cyclical, and it was even assumed that they involved alternation between the same kinds of dualities—between good and evil, the desirable and undesirable, the favorable and unfavorable.

But we have only been pursuing one avenue of thought, and there is another to consider. The extent to which the biological paradigm conveyed a strong cyclical impression depended on the sphere to which it was applied. With the vegetation cycle the sense of continuity was easily strengthened, because growth and death were tied to the ever-recurring seasons, and because the death of seeds and old vegetation often foreshadowed, on the very same ground, new life. Animal and human death, however, was more irregular and disparate, and it was not the norm that the death of one bespoke the birth of another. In a longer view matters looked different, and one can understand how natural it was for Plutarch (in the late first century AD), for instance, to write of the seemingly

33. Cf. Ryffel, ΜΕΤΑΒΟΛΗ, pp. 209–15 on the "three-stationed principle" or the biological model, growth/acme/decay. The wheel of fortune could also be said to have three segments (e.g., prosperity/adversity/prosperity); thus it is not surprising that changes of fortune were sometimes identified with "natural change," e.g., Thucydides *Hist.* II,64(3) ("It is the nature of all things to dwindle"). Incidentally, we should note that from the viewpoint of conceiving events in plastic terms, the half-circle or arch was as much rooted in common experience as the circle: cf. Seneca *Epistulae morales* XC,32–3.

endless passing of human generations as a cyclical process (*anacyclēsis*).[34] Of even more interest is the fact that, in comparison to the coming-to-be and passing away of living organisms, changes in human affairs (*pragmata*) could be more easily represented as inscribing a circling course along one *un*broken continuum. The individual human being at the end of a cycle died, and the cyclical processes were usually carried on by reproduction (the creation of a "new branch," as it were) long before death. On the other hand, death was relative in human affairs, and because deeds could be reenacted, ideas and schemes revived or continually renewed, and nations and the human species only partially destroyed, one is justified in contending that in a special logical sense the life cycle was more usable and appropriate in the historian's hands than in those of the "biologist."

## II. POLYBIUS

As with fortune's wheel, the biological principle was an important tool of interpretation for Polybius. It has already been observed how the doctrine that all existing things are subject to decay and change, and that every body, institution, and action has its natural stages of growth, prime, and decay, affected his formulation of the *Anacyclōsis* (cf. Diagram IV). Polybius apparently assumed most of the major states he considered to have undergone growth (*auxēsis*) and to have attained an acme of prosperity or success. Perhaps this language seemed inappropriate for some states—for permanently disrupted Crete, let us say, and for governments stunted early on by destruction or foreign occupation.[35] Yet he was committed to it as a means of describing relatively unimpeded, natural developments in the lives of political societies. States such as Macedonia and Rhodes experienced growth just as Rome did, even though he took the development of the Roman state with its mixed constitution to be most "natural."[36] In considering the non-Roman scene, moreover, he could expose some of the variations attending the operation of the biological principle. In Achaia's case, for example, whatever small growth had accompanied the earliest appearance of the League,[37] Macedon's temporary dissolution of the confederation ended it until the cities "effected a beginning once more," and until new

34. *Consol. ad Apoll.* 106F; cf. 106E–107A. See also Plato *Politicus* 269E for another use of the term *anacyclēsis*; and for variations on the idea of successive generations see Hesiod *Erga* 110, 127, 140, 157, 180; Plato *Leg.* III,679D; Isocrates *Antidosis* clxxiv–v. On the "acme method" of the second-century chronographer Apollodorus see F. H. Jacoby, *Apollodors Chronik* (*Philologische Untersuchungen XVI*), Berlin, 1902, pp. 39–59. Taking the age of forty to mark the time of bloom in a person's life, Apollodorus elicited certain patterns of recurrence; he noted, for example, that there was a forty-year interval between the acmes of successive sets of practitioners in the same field (e.g., between teachers and pupils), a view reproduced in a lost work on the successions of philosophers by Sosicrates of Rhodes.

35. See below, pt. 3(ii) on Crete; *Hist.* VIII,xiv,8–10 on Illyria.

36. *Hist.* V,x,1 (Macedonia as a state), III,iii (Rhodian government). On Rome see VI,ix,3; cf. above, Chapter 1, sect. E, pt. 2.

37. II,xxxviii,10–xxxix,12; cf. xli,6, IV,i,5b.

and surprising growth brought it to maturity just before his own day.[38] Again, Athens and Thebes underwent such growth and reached points of prime, but in both instances the development was not *kata logon* ("according to reason"; not following the most rational course open?)[39] and the acme was short-lived (VI,xliii,2ff.).

The *Historiae* affords some key insights into the pragmatic aspect of the biological principle. For Polybius the study of the past taught one how to assess the condition of any political society, whether it was a process of growth or in decline. We may well ask if Polybius held general political growth to be dependent on a measure of soundness in a given state's constitution and on the persistent existence of such soundness. He certainly argued that the secret of Rome's success lay in her "natural" mixed constitution, a phenomenon which represented Rome's constitutional acme after a long time of "growth and formation." It was because Rome eventually achieved a special internal balance that she was able to "grow" into a world power. By contrast, however, the splendor of Athens and Thebes was due not to their constitutions but to their great men (VI,xliii,5–xliv,2), and with Macedonia Polybius emphasized the energy of her royal leaders rather than constitutional stability as the growth factor.[40] Despite Rome's case, then, general political growth and constitutional stability were not rigorously interdependent.[41]

In an important theoretical passage (VI,lvii,1–2), Polybius identified two agencies by which every polity was susceptible to *decay*, the first being an external factor, the second something naturally developing within the polities,[42] the first being an uncertain thing with which science could do little, the second being orderly.[43] If Polybius seemed to begin in this passage by discussing *politeiai* as constitutions (as types: VI,iv,6), it was the eventual collapse of political societies in general which soon became uppermost in his mind (lvii,5a). Although one must keep in mind the possible interrelation between these two senses, it is fair to conclude that Polybius ascribed the fall of states to either outside forces (war, aggrandizement, etc.) or to internal dissipation (extravagance, discord, etc.).[44] The regular biological curve is the appropriate model for inner changes,

38. II,xl,5b; cf. xxxvii,8, xli,9, xlv,1, IV,i,6–7, XVIII,xiii,9, XXIV,x,10a.

39. Nature and reason were never opposed to one another in his history, though here, unusually, they are implicitly identified, and in a way which betokens Stoicism.

40. V,x,1–8 (Philip II and Alexander), XXV,iii,9 (Philip V).

41. In VI,ii,9 Polybius may have contended that the chief requirement of success or its opposite in all public affairs is a settled system of government, but there he was stating for students what *should* happen because it did happen with the *best* state, namely Rome. If Athens and Thebes are the best Polybian examples of growth without sound constitutions, pre-fourth-century Sparta and pre-Philippian Achaia are the best examples of sound constitutions with a minimum of political growth (VI,xlviii,1–5, II,xxxix,5, 9f.). Rome, by comparison, experienced a sound constitution and general political growth (though not simultaneously), and this growth, unlike that undergone by Athens or Thebes, was far more permanent, because of the constitutional factor.

42. Lvii,2; cf. also x,3.

43. 2b. The meaning is "uncertain" and "orderly" *methodologically*.

44. On the Peripatetic background to the distinction between internal changes within bodies and external changes upon them, see esp. Aristotle *Polit.* 1312a39ff.; Critolaus in Philo *De aetern.*

but not for those between conflicting nations. Thus in Bk. VI,lvii, where he was still engaged in his examination of constitutions, he concentrated only on the inward changes which cause a state's downfall—extravagance and rivalry for office among the powerful, resulting grievances among the common people, the emergence of democracy, and, eventually, mob rule (5b–9). Even if he were here primarily concerned with the Roman future (which he believed would ultimately undergo a natural decline; cf. ix,12–13), the passage may still be said to stand as a blanket statement about political degeneration.

Polybius gave numerous hints that the first stages of decay—extravagance and rivalry among the nobles—were underway in Rome. She passed the highest point of her constitutional (which is not to be confused with her imperial) line of development.[45] He quoted the elder Cato's speech against the vices of Roman youths and against the current tendency to price pretty boys and caviar above fields and ploughmen. Agreeing with Cato, he claimed that deterioration had begun to manifest itself with the display of public and private wealth in Rome after the fall of Macedon.[46] The appropriation and misuse of objets d'art from conquered territories troubled him,[47] as did the dissonance and chaos of a very peculiar triumphal march in the capital following Lucius Anicius' capture of Genthius, King of Illyria.[48]

Other states—Achaia, for example—were even closer to collapse than was Rome. Admittedly, difficulties surround Polybius' contentions that Achaia's democracy was a stage in the process of decline. When he originally set out to write his history, his as yet unsurpassed ideal was the democratic polity of the Achaian League with its basis in equality and freedom of speech (cf. II,xxxviii,6, xlii,3), and its constitutional safeguards.[49] But Polybius was eventually forced to reckon with Achaia's weaknesses. He criticized the excessive love of liberty among Achaians in his own day (V,cvi,5; cf. IV,xxxi,4; XXXVIII,ix,8) and in referring to the influence of the pro-Roman Callicrates on the League in 181 BC he insisted that Achaia's acme had passed and the turn for the worse begun XXIV,x,10; cf. 8–9). Equality and free speech were socio-political goals Polybius never shelved (cf. XXVII,iv,7), yet it remains true that he frequently associated the enfeeblement of certain states with the irresponsibility of popular government. Carthage was at a disadvantage against the Romans because the common people had acquired a greater voice; not only constitutionally but in power and prosperity she passed her prime earlier than Rome (VI,li,4–6). Both Athens and

*mundi* 20f., 74; Ocellus *Univ. nat.* I,xi,13 (Harder, p. 14); cf. W. Theiler, "Schichten im 6.Buch des Polybios" in *Hermes* LXXXI, 1953, p. 296.

45. Lvii,10 and li,5 both suggest that the acme of Rome is already a matter of historical reflection (against Paton). Also the Codex Urbinas heading to xi may derive from a non-extant part of the text: cf. (on the state of F), J. M. Moore, *The Manuscript Tradition of Polybius* (Cambridge Classical Studies), Cambridge, 1965, pp. 56–8.

46. XXXI,xxv,4, 7; cf. XVIII,xxxiv,7–xxxv,4.

47. XXXIX,ii,1–3; cf. IX,x,1–13, XXI,xxx,9, XXXIX,iii,3–11.

48. XXX,xxii,1–12; cf. T. R. Glover, "Polybius at Rome" in his *The Springs of Hellas and Other Essays*, Cambridge, 1945, p. 118.

49. II,xxxix,12, XXIII,xii,8; cf. E. Graeber, *Die Lehre von der Mischverfassung*, pp. 13ff.

Thebes lost supremacy in Greece because good leadership was succeeded by headstrong mobs (xliv,3–9), and numerous other Greek democracies were treated as though they had degenerated with the increasing factions of the populace.[50]

Should we draw the conclusion, then, that Polybius understood the decay of a state to be coterminous with excessive growth in the power of the people? That is not an unfair judgment. When he described the effect of popular government on such Greek centers as Cynaetha, second-century Thebes, and the Boeotian cities, on Aetolia, Tarentum in Sicily, Cius in Bithynia, and the like, he was analyzing their decline as states, not just the decay of their democratic constitutions.[51] This interpretation is justifiable, moreover, even while recognizing the distinction between states with mixed constitutions, which begin their decline with an excess of the popular element (so VI,li,6, lvii,5–7), and states tending to follow the normative anacyclic path, which decay toward dissolution after the "third acme" of democracy (ix,1–9). In either case, popularism was a special symptom of general political decay.

Popular influences tended to bring decay only to the state looked at from the viewpoint of its internal history, however. External factors were quite another issue, even though Polybius would have admitted that internal strengths and weaknesses affected any state's ability to withstand outside pressure or to consolidate possessions. The question now arises as to the difference between the two interpretative models Polybius employed in analyzing internal history and external relations. Methodologically, he argued, one could be scientific about inner transformations; they were predictable, regular, and cyclical.[52] But by what method could one put order into external relations, which largely consisted in conflict *between* states? The fact that "the external" (*exōthen*) involved separate entities, rather than one continuous life, was a problem sizable enough even without the hopeless prospect of reducing diplomatic and military interchanges to lawlike generalizations. Yet although Polybius theorized more about internal than external politics, it cannot be said that he turned his back on these difficulties. Significantly enough, external conflicts were worked out largely under the aegis of fortune. To win victories or to be worsted was to experience either good or bad fortune,[53] and although skill, opportunism, discipline, courage, excellence, and their opposites could never be neglected by

50. See below, sect. C, pt. 1(ii) on transitions within democracy.

51. IV,xvii,4 (Cynaetha); XX,iv,1ff., vi,1–3, vii,3–4, XXII,iv,1ff., XXVII,i,9 (Thebes and Boeotia); XXVIII,iv,13b, XXX,xi,1–6 (cf. Livy *Ab urbe cond.* XLI,xxv) (Aetolia); VIII,xxiv,1–3 (Tarentum); XV,xxi,3ff. (Cius); XXX,xii,1–3 (Epirus); XI,xxix,8–10 (general).

52. Interestingly, two of Polybius' important philosophical sources drew the analogy between biological cycles and social developments: Plato *Resp.* VIII,546A, and Demetrius in Plutarch *Consol. ad Apoll.* 104B (Plutarch treated Demetrius as quoting Euripides' *Ino* in both cases—104A and B—and as interposing his own comments between two parts of the quotation, so that Wehrli, on his p. 22, unjustifiably excludes κύκλος γὰρ αὐτὸς καρπίμοις τε γῆς φυτοῖς/γένει βροτῶν τε, . . . etc. from Frg. 79 of Demetrius' work).

53. Esp. II,lxx,2, III,cxviii,6, IX,viii,13, xii,10, xxi, XI,xix,5f., XII,xxve,5f., XV,vi–vii.

the historian, external conflict was the realm in which human illusions, the unexpected, and the incalculable played a very crucial part.[54] With Rome, to take a central example, the strong interdependence between the acquisition of empire and the stability of her internal politics had to be admitted (cf. III,cxviii,5–9, VI,ii,6–7, lii,8ff.). Nevertheless, Rome suffered obvious misfortune despite her splendid institutions, so that it was still justifiable to claim that when matters improved after Cannae it was fortune who gave Rome world dominion.[55] In general, therefore, Polybius' approach reflects a reasonably clear working distinction between inner constitutional developments proceeding "naturally" and the uncertainties of fortune-dominated external relations. The three-stationed biological principle and the model of changing fortune operated in different spheres; even if they were capable of close complementarity, the distinctiveness of their respective applications should be recognized.[56]

Polybius did endeavor to draw these two explanatory devices closer together, however, and the extent to which he did so bears assessment. His idea of growth (used indiscriminately for constitutions and states alike) was practical in describing both the inner and outer relations of politics. Assertions that such states as Athens, Achaia or Rome "grew" complemented, even reinforced, statements that their emergence to power was the work of Fortune.[57] On the other hand, at no point does Polybius write of Fortune governing their inner constitutional development. Concerning decay, moreover, the important passage VI,lvii indicates that, while natural processes govern inward corruption, decay could also involve external affairs (2). Since the language of adverse fortune was appropriate to outside pressures impinging upon a state, it could to that extent be harmonized with the model of a downward biological curve. Polybius' concern with associating decay with misfortune becomes increasingly accentuated in the later books of the *Historiae*. Before every state succumbed to Rome it underwent some kind of inner degeneration: Macedon's kingdom became the tyranny of Perseus,[58] the city-states of once democratic Greece were harassed by the passion of the masses,[59] and on the eve of the submission of all Greece, Polybius observed a prevalent disintegration of moral and mental health among her inhabitants.[60] With other areas one detects similar patterns. Carthage, having conceded excessive power to the populace, eventually ended her career in

54. See above, sect. A, pt. 1(ii).

55. For references see below, sect. B, pt. 2(ii). Against von Scala, *Studien*, pp. 159, 183, and O. Cuntz, *Polybios*, pp. 43ff., I dispute that Polybius downgraded fortune's rôle halfway through his history, to place increasing stress on Roman virtue.

56. Against W. Rehm, *Der Untergang Roms im abendländischen Denken* (*Das Erbe der Alten XVIII*), Darmstadt, 1930, p. 10.

57. VI,xliii,2f. (Athens); II,xxxvii,6b–8 (Achaia); I,i,5, iv,1, 4f. (Rome).

58. XXXVI,xvii,13, XXVIII,x, XXIX,v,1ff., yet cf. XXV,iii,3–8, XXVII,ix,1–x,5.

59. Cf. above, n. 51 (excepting Cynaetha, though she decayed before both Achaia and Aetolia took her).

60. XXXVI,xvii,6ff. (break-up of family life), XXXVIII,i,5, iii,5–iv,2, xii,5, xvi,7f., xvii,7–12.

horrific distress under a brutal tyrant,[61] and in the Middle East there was a regional conflict along with shifts to mob rule and tyranny.[62]

From the viewpoint of external relations, however, Polybius went out of his way to invoke Fortune and her participation in military conflicts. It was Fortune who turned against Macedon and who favored Scipio Aemilianus in the Third Carthaginian War (XXIX,xxi, XXXVIII,xxi,3), it was misfortune which befell all the cities of Hellas (XXXVIII,iii,5–10; cf. xviii,8, III,v,6). Thus two kinds of decline could operate in conjunction, and two of the most basic cyclical models were brought into unison. The old doctrine of fortune's unstable, wheel-like movements, a doctrine applied to historical events by Herodotus and developed in Hellenistic historiography, was brought into partnership with the biological principle. With this cunning harmonization (another of Polybius' eclectic achievements), he felt permitted to proffer his rather awesome generalization about the whole line of development in world history from 220 BC onward: that Fortune (clearly conceived as a providential overlord) guided all the events of the world toward one end—the dominion of Rome.[63] He also felt able to formulate an explanation for the success of Rome in both her inner and outer relations, and in this he treated Rome as what one may term "the great exception." Neither the wheel of fortune nor the biological principle, according to Polybius, had its most typical consequences for the Romans. Fortune had been more liberal than usual with her permissions, but above all the secret of Rome lay in her mixed constitution. When any external threat or misfortune was imminent, her remarkable institutions united the people in defence, and when good fortune and outward peace prevailed, they forestalled the natural decay brought on by idleness and corruption (VI,xviii,1–6).

All this implies a special didacticism. To disclose the correct application of cyclical paradigms, to estimate the point of growth or decay reached by any state, or to gauge the tendencies of fortune: all this was to teach men how to choose the best courses of action in future situations (see VI,ii,8, ix,11–12; cf. III,cxviii,12). That kind of preconception, too, could affect the relating of events. Admittedly, Polybius insisted that the historian's duty was to recount the "true facts" and he criticized others for over dramatizing events and for showing a patriotic partiality.[64] But to grant him relatively modern ideas about "real facts" or about *wie es eigentlich gewesen ist*, would be false.[65] He was bound to subvert the actual and the true he so dearly wished to see preserved, for to tell what happened was at the same time to tender a preferred understanding of the

61. XXXVIII,viii,11–4; cf. XXXVI,vii,3–5, XXXVIII,vii,1ff., xx,1ff.

62. References are too numerous to cite fully: X,xxvii–xxxi, xlix, XI,xxxiv, XIV,xi–xii, XV, xxi,3ff., XXI,vi, x,1–xxi,17, etc.

63. I,iv,1, 3–5; cf. IV,xxviii,3, VIII,ii(iv),4, XXI,xvi,8.

64. II,lvi,11f., XII,v, xii,2–7, x,4ff., XXV,i,1, XXXVIII,iii,5, etc.

65. "The claim to write honestly is more or less standard in ancient historians (for example Thucydides, Polybius, Sallust, Josephus), indeed a cliché, as Seneca's parody of it indicates": F. R. D. Goodyear, *Tacitus* (*Greece and Rome: New Surveys in the Classics IV*), Oxford, 1970, p. 29 (with Seneca *Apocolocyntosis* i,1). Cf. Cicero *De oratione* ii,62, *Leg.* i,4f.

events, which above all meant to grasp their paradigmatic and utilitarian qualities.[66]

## *Age theory and the rise and fall of empires*

### I. GENERAL

In the Pythagorean teaching of exact repetition we detected another vision of cyclical recurrence, the idea of the successive macro-Ages of human existence, according to which the "generations of men" assume far wider proportions. The division of world history into vast segments was a very ancient procedure, probably motivated by the need to put present events or circumstances into context, not so much in their purely historical as in their theologico-historical or mythological context. In the mythologies of the Middle East and the Mediterranean basin, at least to the sixth century BC, man's present relationship with the divine was often held to have been foreshadowed (or even determined) by primeval events of great moment. The time or setting in which these awesome happenings took place was usually radically distinguished from the contemporary Age, yet they were understood to have a crucial bearing on man's current situation.[67]

What relevance does this approach to the past have for recurrence? A superficial glance at two seminal Greek descriptions of great time lapses, the one in Hesiod's *Works and Days*, when he considered the five races of mankind, and the later enunciation of catastrophe theory in Plato's *Timaeus* and *Laws*, could easily lead one to say that it has none. The Hesiodic generations are all different and, with the exception of the fourth or heroic one, represent a steady worsening of the human condition, while Plato, in considering numberless inter-cataclysmic periods and the political societies formed within them, placed great stress on the enormous variety of human phenomena.[68] On the other hand, the relatively biological terms *genea* and *genos* were used to characterize Hesiod's stages, and for both him and Plato each grand stage concluded with the general removal of all or, in the case of Plato, all but very few, protagonists from the historical scene.[69] Thus the barest structures of these eons—their coming-to-be, life career, and death—recurred as great "cycles of human existence,"[70] and both Hesiod and Plato took their mode of initiation, and, with some exceptions,

66. It is not within the scope of this study to detail probable inaccuracies in the *Historiae* which derive from Polybius' methodological preconceptions, but for background see esp. G. A. Lehmann, *Untersuchungen zur historischen Glaubwürdigkeit des Polybios* (*Fontes et Commentationes* V), Münster, 1967, passim; Walbank, *Polybios*, ch. 2; cf. M. Feyel, *Polybe et l'histoire de Béote au III siècle avant notre ère*, (*Bibliothèque des Écoles Françaises d'Athènes et de Rome CLII*), Paris, 1942, pp. 302–5.

67. G. von Rad, *Genesis: A Commentary* (ET), London, 1963 edn., pp. 112ff.; J. Pritchard (ed.), *Ancient Near Eastern Texts Relating to the Old Testament*, Princeton, 1955 (hereafter *ANET*), pt. 1. On Zoroastrian texts see below, Chapter 3, introd.

68. Hesiod *Erga* 109–84 (cf. 156–76 on the heroic Age); on Plato see above, Chapter 1, sect. A.

69. Hesiod *Erga* 138–9, 153–5, 180; yet cf. 140–2, 167–76; Plato *Leg.* III,677A–B.

70. For this phrase see W. K. C. Guthrie, *In the Beginning: Some Greek Views on the Origins of Life and the Early State of Man*, London, 1957, p. 63.

their end, to be virtually the same.[71] We have here, after all, notions of periodicity, and whether these Ages were imagined to be curved, rectilinear, or simply lapses of time, they form the kind of periods Aristotle would have been happy to call "cycles."

One should admit that both Hesiod and Plato leaned toward pejorism, assuming that the glorious epochs of old were irretrievable. This tendency had no lack of support among later poets and moralists,[72] yet there were also writers who turned the stories they told into something of even greater interest from the viewpoint of historical recurrence. I mean those who spoke of the Golden Age rather than of the golden race,[73] and who anticipated the return of the Ages. Among the Stoics, for instance, theories of three or more intermediate Ages of the world gained currency.[74] Outside their barest lineaments, admittedly, these Ages were only envisaged as recurring on "the other side" of a cosmic conflagration, and so this recurrence was cosmological rather than historical. However, the Stoics' special cyclical emphasis acquired a new significance when popularists and syncretists combined the beliefs of different philosophies, and when ancient Pythagorean conceptions were revived. As such a popularist, pseudo-Ocellus Lucanus (third century BC) adopted a thoroughgoing cyclical view of cosmic and human events, yet declined to believe in such an extremity as *ecpyrōsis*. He suggested that past Ages would return within the same historical order.[75] Over one hundred years later Cicero, in his *Somnium Scipionis*, recalled Platonic catastrophe theory with its stress on vast stretches of time and set this in the context of the recurring Great Year, when—after "many Ages (*saecula*) of man" had elapsed—the planets eventually returned to their original positions.[76]

In Roman poetry in the early days of the Empire, moreover, can be found at least three passages concerning the imminent reemergence of the Saturnian Age, the Latin equivalent to Hesiod's golden reign of Kronos.[77] Whether such notions were derived from the Sibylline Books, Etruscan lore concerning the

71. Hesiod *Erga* 109f., 127, 143, 156f., 176f., and see above; Plato *Leg.* III,677B–679C, *Tim.* 22D, 23A; cf. *Leg.* III,677A. Plato may well have been consciously demythologizing and historicizing Hesiod's tale.

72. E.g., Aratus *Phaenomena* 96–136, Ovid *Amores* III,viii,29–44, *Metamorphoses* I,76–215; cf. Seneca *Epistulae morales* XC,36ff., Juvenal *Satires* xiii,26ff., and in general Lovejoy and Boas, op. cit., pp. 41ff.

73. On the Golden Age as a creation of Latin poets see H. C. Baldry, "Who Invented the Golden Age?" in *Classical Quarterly* N.S. II, 1952, pp. 83ff.

74. Four Ages: Chrysippus, Frg. 413 (von Arnim, vol. 2, p. 136); cf. Zeno, Frg. 98 (von Arnim, vol. 1, p. 27); Seneca *Epist. mor.* XC,36ff.; five Ages: pseudo-Seneca *Octavia ll.*402–7; and for three Ages see below, Chapter 4, sect. A on Seneca and Poseidonius. Cf. K. J. Reckford, "Some Appearances of the Golden Age" in *Classical Journal* LIV, 1958–9, pp. 80f.

75. *Univ. nat.* III,i,42 (Harder, p. 21).

76. *Somn. Scip.* vii,23–5 (A. Ronconi edn. pp. 53f.). The reference to *eluviones exustionesque* cannot be taken to mean *ecpyrōsis*; along with mention of the many Ages of man, they recall Plato *Leg.* III,676B–678B.

77. Virgil *Eclogue* IV,5; Calpurnius Siculus *Eclogue* I,42–5; Anonymous (mid-first-century AD) in *Anthologia Latina* (ed. F. Buecheler and A. Rise), no. 726, 22–4. See Ablabius (fourth century AD) in Sidonius *Epistulae* V,viii,2; cf. Horace *Odes* II,xii,1–9 for satirical comments against those as optimistic as Virgil.

Ages, or other literature now lost,[78] they gained a reasonably wide currency among Romans, and the idea of a macrocosmic recurrence of the Ages within the history of mankind probably received its fullest articulation in the work of the Sicilian astrologer Firmicus Maternus (fourth century AD). Firmicus maintained (while still a pagan) that each of five Ages he isolated operated in accordance with the influence of the five planets, apparently recurring in sequence forever.[79] As with most extant writings anticipating the return of a former Age, it seems that Firmicus expected exact recurrence, not merely reappearance of the general qualities or the central features of former Ages. Stoic (or more correctly neo-Pythagorean) ideas thus had their impact, although one can never be sure how literally such poetic effusion as one finds in Virgil's fourth *Eclogue* should be taken, with its vision of a second Argo, "and the great Achilles sent to Troy once more."[80] Be that as it may, it remains important that the earlier conceptions of successive Ages were often cast into directly cyclical molds. The newer approach is even partly reflected in the Polybian *Anacyclōsis*, where the idea of a large cycle containing within itself a procession of separate significant stages also manifested itself.

What mattered for philosophers and poets, however, did not always concern conventional historians. Historiography did not go uninfluenced by cosmology, yet the contours and periods elicited by Greek historians and their Roman successors were decisively grounded in the political. They usually prescribed boundaries for history, going back to the Trojan era or to ancient Egypt or the Middle East, but only rarely back to the Ages of the gods or antediluvian times.[81] Interestingly enough, their researches into the distant past forced them to consider the relative antiquity of foreign cultures, and this factor was crucial for the emergence of ideas about the rise and fall of empires. These ideas, which blossomed under Rome and which advanced by comparisons of Greek and Roman achievements, had their proper seedbed in Age theory rather than in scientific efforts to apply the biological principle to history. Earlier Age theory had involved mythological cultures and empires, but in the more recent, especially in the Hellenistic, inquiry, historians only wrote of past glories for which there seemed real evidence, or else tried to place renowned mythological figures (such as Saturnus) into an acceptable historical context.[82] Born of Age theory, the vision of imperial rise and fall was still further evidence that history was the mirror of recurring configurations. Rise and fall, moreover, whether

78. See below, Chapter 4, sect. D, pt. 1.

79. Firmicus *Mathesis* III,i,11–5 (there being progress through the first four Ages until the last Age of degeneration). Cf. Lovejoy and Boas, op. cit., p. 77; G. E. Cairns, *Philosophies of History: Meeting of East and West in Cycle-Pattern Theories of History*, New York, 1962, pp. 225f.

80. *Eclogues* IV,34–6; cf. 46f.

81. On the heroic Age as background: Hecataeus, Frgs. 300ff. (*FGH*, pt. 1A, pp. 38ff.); Herodotus *Hist.* I,1–6; Thucydides *Hist.* I,i,3; Aristotle *Polit.* 1285a11–4. On Egypt's importance cf. T. S. Brown, "The Greek Sense of Time in History as Suggested by Their Accounts of Egypt" in *Historia* II, 1962, pp. 257ff. On the ancient Near East in Hellenistic historiography see below, Chapter 4, sect. A.

82. On Saturnus, Belus, and Ninus, see also below, Chapter 4, sect. A; sect. D, pt. 2.

conceived as alternation between high point and low point or as a three-staged process of emergence, flourishing, and dissipation, could be tied in with a cluster of cyclical notions—of growth and decay, mutable fortune, or regular heavenly influences upon human affairs (see Chapter 4, sect. D, pt. 1). Together with the idea of successive Ages, however, the theory of rise and fall could throw men's history into very broad relief, so that current affairs tended to lose some of their immediacy within the vast convolutions of time.

## II. POLYBIUS

What bearing do the schematization of world history into Ages and incipient doctrines of rise and fall have on Polybius and his *Historiae*? One should begin by stating that Polybius was very much a functionalist in matters of religion.[83] Without committing himself to any belief in deities, prodigies, or even in an afterlife,[84] he attacked historians who appealed to traditional theological explanations.[85] Homer's mythopoeic world was foreign to his rationalistic outlook, and the time of the Trojan War was a mere preface to history, not a transition period between the Ages dominated by gods and the more mundane events of the present (cf. XXXIV,ii, XXXVIII,xxii,2Bb). Although Polybius apparently appropriated Plato's references to the Cyclops and the Titans for his own purposes (see Chapter 1, sect. D), he did so without a mention of names and with an even greater degree of demythologization than Plato had managed. On the other hand, that special Polybian curiosity-piece, the *Anacyclōsis*, covered a whole range of phenomena which together constituted something like an Age of mankind, or a "civilization." Even if the Homeric period only formed an early segment of this great cycle (with Agamemnon and Priam as early kings, perhaps), its beginning was not so closed nor its end so open that agreement with both Plato and Hesiod about periodic destruction, or about history's tendency toward the worse was precluded. The difficulty remains, of course, that although Polybius began describing the cycle of governments in terms of general human development toward political life, he ended by considering the career and eventual dissolution of one given political entity. We can only infer, therefore, that through his clever eclecticism, and with his concern to accommodate a variety of traditional viewpoints, Polybius was concessive toward Age theory.

Turning to the issue of rise and fall, however, one finds Polybius' position rather different. He lived at a time when Hellas was in a state of conflict and there were severe pressures from the north caused by Macedonian expansionism. It was also a time when much depended on the outcome of the struggle between Rome and Carthage, and Polybius, more than any of his predecessors

83. *Hist.* IV,xxi,1, 3f. (cf. F. W. Walbank, "The Geography of Polybius" in *Classica et Mediaevalia* (*Revue Danoise de Philologie et d'Histoire*) IX, 1947, p. 181), VI,lvi,6–15, IX,xix,1–4, X,xi,7f., xiv,11, XXIX,xvi,1–3.

84. XXXIX,viii,2 is a literary formality; cf. III,v,7, VII,vii,1, VIII,xii,8.

85. III,xviii,8, XVI,xii,7; cf. VIII,ix,13, XII,iv$^{c}$,1, xxvi,1ff.

in interpreting Western affairs to the Greeks, was able to grasp the unprecedented nature of Rome's imperialist enterprise and its significance for the future of Greece.[86] His context is important. If Herodotus, a man of comparable interests writing some three centuries earlier, could analyze the emergence and weakening of various kingdoms, it was only with limited chronological perspective. Possessing little adequate documentation before the middle of the sixth century BC, Herodotus knew next to nothing about Assyria and Media, and made little conceptual distinction between the emergence and fall of small realms like Samos and Lydia and the rise and weakening of Persia, as though one were an analogue of the other.[87]

Herodotus was not able to envisage the long sequence of great imperialisms which Polybius, with the rise of this new and awesome threat to Greece,[88] found himself able to consider. How long Polybius conceived this sequence to be remains a problem. We have it on Appian's authority that upon beholding the destruction of Carthage Scipio Aemilianus shed tears and wept for the enemy.

> After being wrapped in thought for long, and realizing that all cities, nations, and empires, just like men, must meet their doom, that this was what the once fortunate city of Troy suffered, as did the mighty of the Assyrians, the Medes, the Persians, and the very recent and brilliant empire of Macedonia, he uttered, whether voluntarily or otherwise, the words of the poet: "The day shall come when sacred Troy shall perish; as also Priam, with the people over whom spear-bearing Priam rules."[89]

Appian went on to report a conversation between Scipio and Polybius soon after. Scipio revealed that he feared the downfall of his own patrimony after a similar fashion to the collapse of these great empires, and Appian noted that Polybius had recalled these words in his history.[90] It would be interesting to know whether Polybius mentioned such a long string of fallen empires in the closing stages of his work: the list is probably Appian's rather than his, since Appian prefaced his *Roman History* by contrasting the enduring Roman dominion with the short-lived empires of the Assyrians, Medes, Persians, and Macedonians—those very régimes Scipio was taken to reflect upon in the passage above.[91] On the other hand, Polybius did present a similar, though more limited, overview in his introduction when he compared the extent of the Roman empire to the earlier powers of Persia, Lacedaemon, and Macedon (I,ii,1–5). Moreover, it is even possible to extract from his work a very relevant skeletal plan of

86. See Eisen, op. cit., pp. 9–11; cf. *Hist.* XXXIX,vi,3, viii,1.

87. H. R. Immerwahr, *Form and Thought in Herodotus* (*Philological Monographs XXIII*), Ohio, 1966, pp. 153ff.; cf. Herodotus *Hist.* I,96ff., 130.

88. Polybius *Hist.* XXXVIII,i,1f.; cf. III,v,6, XXIV,x,8.

89. Appian *Punica* XIX,132 = Polybius *Hist.* XXXVIII,xxii,1f.

90. *Punica* XIX,132 = *Hist.* XXXVIII,xxii,3. Cf. also xxi,1 (from Plutarch, and closer to the lost Polybian text?).

91. *Hist. Roman.*, *proem.* (I,8–10). Elsewhere Polybius makes no reference to Assyria, and identifies Media with Persia: *Hist.* XVI,xxii,4. My conclusions here are against those of F. Taeger, *Archäeologie*, pp. 114ff.; W. Siegfried, *Studien zur geschichtlichen Anschauung des Polybios*, Leipzig, 1928, pp. 100f.; Rehm, op. cit., pp. 12f.

what he understood to be the key world events between the sixth century and his own day.

The earliest empire which mattered was the Persian, yet Persia's attempted invasion of Greece under Xerxes had failed (XXXVIII,ii,1ff.),[92] and her downfall was sealed by Alexander (XXII,xviii,10a, XXIX,xxi,4). Athens dominated Hellenic affairs after the Persian Wars, but her effort to conquer Sicily ended in disaster,[93] allowing Sparta to succeed to hegemony. Sparta, however, though stable at home, proved incapable and overbearing as an imperial power (VI,xlviii,1–xlix,10, XXXVIII,ii,6–7), and was replaced by a new military factor, Thebes (XXXVIII,ii,8; cf. VI,xliii,2–6). But Philip destroyed Theban power (XXXVIII,ii,13–14) as well as overpowering Athens and the Peloponnesus (V,x,1; cf. II,xli,9), and built up the Macedonian kingdom which was eventually to remove the Middle Eastern sway of the Great King himself.[94] This same Macedon, in fulfillment of Demetrius' almost divine prophecy, was overcome by Rome (cf. XXIX,xxi,4–9). Unlike Athens, Rome was successful in her conquest of Sicily,[95] and before taking all Hellas and extending her control to the Middle East (cf. XXI,xvi,8, XXIX,xxvii,12) she was victorious over a still more ferocious contender for world domination, Carthage. All this reveals the peculiar advantages of a second- (and post-second-) century perspective: Polybius could view over three hundred years in terms of empires, and see a certain "lawlike rhythm of their rise and fall."[96] Whether or not he knew of Assyria and Media, his grasp of a longish succession of empires reveals him as an important watershed figure. Herodotus and Demetrius had dwelt upon the waxing and waning of great kingdoms, Thucydides had analyzed the growth and defeat of the Athenian régime, and Dicaearchus had formulated generalizations concerning "war, sedition, and other misfortunes" which befell all powers.[97] Polybius drew these older threads together and provided at least one sound basis for future, better-known Greco-Roman theories of rise and fall.[98]

For Polybius, we can see, "rise and fall" meant the "biological" growth and decay of the greater powers. Natural processes were chiefly operative within internal politics, but they could also be manifested on a broader scale. Thus a fall, a process of corruption, and a severe turn of adverse fortune could be alternative expressions for the same phenomenon. That raises the interesting question, of course, as to whether degeneration in accordance with closing stages of

92. Cf. II,xxv,7, VI,xi,1a, XVI,xxiia,4; note also IV,xxxi,5.

93. VI,xliii,2f., xliv,1–9, XXXVIII,ii,4f., IX,xix,1–4; cf. XII,xxvk,5–xxvi,9.

94. V,x,1–8; cf. III,vi,9–13, XVI,xxiia,5, XXII,xviii,10a, XXIX,xxi,4.

95. Eisen, op. cit., pp. 156–65 on defensive Rome contrasted with aggressive Athens in Sicily; cf. below, sect. B, pt. 2(iii).

96. Rehm, op. cit., p. 13.

97. Herodotus and Demetrius: see above, sect. A, pt. 1(ii); Thucydides *Hist.* I,97ff., VII; Dicaearchus, Frg. 24 (Wehrli, pp. 17f.).

98. His imperial succession is not likely to have derived from Sura (or Ctesias): cf. F. W. Walbank, "Polybius and Rome's Eastern Policy" in *Journal of Roman Studies* LIII, 1963, p. 8 (and see also below, Chapter 4, sect. A), though where Ephorus fits in remains unclear; cf. G. L. Barber, *The Historian Ephorus*, Cambridge, 1935, pp. 17ff.

the *Anacyclōsis* could amount to the fall of a great and long-enduring power. Was Rome to fall victim to a superior and exterior force like previous empires, or was she destined for a natural decline? Polybius was in no position to be definite, but it is unlikely that, as some argue, he approached this issue as a vehement Achaian "nationalist," either yearning for Rome to be weakened by democratization or anticipating that the Roman conquest of Greece would redeem his beloved Achaia from constitutional and political decline.[99] It is perhaps less unlikely for him to have believed that because Rome controlled the whole world the decline of Rome would mean the destruction of the world. Fascinatingly enough, not only did he suggest that the Roman polity would experience the whole cycle of governments (VI,xi,12–13, lvii,5–10), but he also emphasized that Rome had virtually taken control of the world (even before the Middle East and Egypt had been taken!). As he endowed Rome's path to sovereignty with a structurally distinct "beginning and duration," and with an end marked by supreme power,[100] it is not inconceivable that he took Rome to be the copestone for a whole macrocosmic era, for something like an Age or inter-cataclysmic period. Certainly his almost Stoic stress on the universal proportions of the new empire could carry the implication that the destiny of Rome was the destiny of the human species.[101] But Polybius simply opened up possibilities for the more speculative; nearer to his heart was a simple truth and practical lesson to be learned—that, whether by nature or force, empires recurrently come into being and pass away.

These, then, are the basic cyclical models of recurrence in Greco-Roman historical thought. There are, of course, some interesting minor variations. When Tacitus rendered a Latin version of the saying "human things are a circle," for example, he sought to apply the image of a circle to the altering social attitudes and habits of Roman families, affected as they were by changes in the temper of Rome's rulers.[102] For Tacitus the cycle of fashion and attitude could be paralleled by the movement of seasons, and this idea seems to be a curious and weak variation on the model of growth and decay. It comes nearest to the Aristotelian doctrine that techniques of cultural importance could recurrently disappear and then experience revival,[103] but it concerns fashions and habits rather than skills. Another cyclical notion hard to place emerges from Polybius' analysis of Cretan society, a society he consistently despised.[104] Of events in 181 BC he wrote:

At this time there arose in Crete the beginning of troubles, if it befits to talk about a beginning of troubles in Crete, for owing to the constancy of civil wars and their

99. E. Täubler, *Tyche*, pp. 92–4; Gelzer, "Archaica," p. 31; Walbank, *Commentary*, vol. 1, p. 302; cf. also N. G. L. Hammond, "The Arrangement of the Thought in the Proem and in Other Parts of Thucydides I" in *Classical Quarterly* N.S. II, 1952, p. 132.

100. Esp. III,i,4f., 9.

101. Graeber, op. cit., pp. 54f.; cf. Täubler, op. cit., p. 92.

102. *Annales* III,55.

103. See above, Chapter 1, sect. A, and below, Chapter 4, sect. I.

104. IV,viii,11, liii,5, VI,xlvi,1–6 (cf. xlvi,1–5, 9–11, xlvii,1–5), VII,xi,9, VIII,xix,5, etc.

excessive savageness toward each other, beginning and end are the same in Crete, and what seems a paradoxical way of speaking to some, can there be seen to be continually a matter of fact. [XXIV,iii(iv)]

This is a picture of brutish turmoil, and by alluding to the truth that beginning and end are the same on a circle,[105] Polybius was suggesting that the Cretans experienced a constant round of instability, so that their politics never inclined in any recognizable direction.[106]

There are two other conceptions—more suggestive of alternation than cycles, however—which deserve noting here: the idea of an interchange between the One and the Many, and the notion of change into opposites. The former has great relevance for cosmology, of course, but is of only marginal importance for historiography. Certainly the Stoic picture of a great World Age ending in the reduction of all things to elemental fire is related to this idea, and we have already observed how Polybius seemed to describe a path between the rule of one and the rule of the many (Chapter 1, sect. D); he also made something of the idea of one world, almost under one government, sharing many cultural, political, and geographical aspects. His successor, "Stoic" Poseidonius (ca. 135–ca. 50 BC), apparently went on to draw an analogy between the diversity and unity of human affairs in his own time and the One and the Many of the universe in general (Chapter 4, sect. A). For Poseidonius, then, and for Polybius to a more limited extent, Roman world dominion appears as a fulfillment of human unity: the forces of the universe leaned toward political integration. One might be tempted to conclude that in Polybius' mind the breaking down of this unity would mean an eventual return to multiplicity. These comments, however, must remain tentative.

The idea of change into opposites (*metabolē eis enantion*) has a greater relevance for historical interpretation. Though its real home was within natural philosophy, this principle of change was often applied to human affairs. Aristotle, for example, contended that constitutional types were likely to be transformed into their opposites because human reactions tended to produce the converse to a disliked state of affairs.[107] One popularist position associated such change with the reversal of fortune or with the emergence of what was contrary to expectation.[108] Still another was nicely expressed by Cicero:

105. In writing *tauton archē kai telos*, Polybius probably thought of philosophers who said the same: Alcmaeon, Frg. 2 (Diels-Kranz) = 288 (Kirk-Raven) = pseudo-Aristotle *Prob.* 916a33; cf. Heraclitus, Frg. 126 (Diels-Kranz) = 39 (Bywater) = 232 (Kirk-Raven).

106. Was Crete caught at the beginning or the end of the anacyclic process? Cf. VI,xlvi,3f., 9, xlvii,1, lvii,7–9. On Polybius' interest in *stasis* and the recurring alternation between ethico-political "health and disease," see IV,viii,11, liii,5, VI,x,2–4, XXXIII,xvi,5 (on Crete); cf. I,lxv,8, lxxxi,7, 10, II,xxx,4, etc. (on other societies).

107. E.g. *Polit.* 1316a18ff.; cf. 1307a6ff., 1310b27ff., 1304a34ff., 1307b26ff. As philosophical background, see *De gen. et corrupt.* 319–38; Melissus of Samos, Frg. 8 (Diels-Kranz) = 392 (Kirk-Raven).

108. Herodotus *Hist.* VII,52 (quoting the maxim, "The end is not always to be seen in the beginning"); Philo, see below, Chapter 3, sect. B, pt. 3; pseudo-Heraclitus (first century AD), *Allegories from Homer* liv,1 (Buffière edn., p. 62); Alexander (third century AD), *In librum de sensu*

Everything which is in excess—when, for instance, either in the weather, or in the fields, or in men's bodies, conditions have been too favorable—is usually changed into the opposite; and this is especially true with states, where such excess of liberty either in nations or in individuals turns into an excess of servitude.[109]

Polybius, too, revealed this kind of change in natural, internal politics—in the zigzag between constitutions of opposing value and in the alternation between polity and non-polity.[110] He also saw it at work in external relations, where it stood as an equivalent to reversed fortune and thus as a supplement to a cyclical frame (IV,lxxxi,12, IX,xxi, VI,ii,6, xliii,3, xliv,2).

Considering the major cyclical or cyclo-alternating models, however, together with these variants, we may now reflect on the common preconceptions which lie behind them. In appealing to a cycle or to movements either rotating or fluctuating, men were decoding the complexities of human life. It was not just that elicited rhythms or patterns made history more intelligible as a spectacle, but more significantly that the understanding of change added much to man's measure of self-determination. It bears recalling that the aphorism "human things are a circle" stood before the Athenian public on the walls of the Erechtheum. Men, it implied, ought to anticipate the most likely changes, and either bear with their consequences or turn them to advantage.[111]

This ancient "pragmatism," however, raises some difficult conceptual problems, especially in relation to causation. It presupposed that historical agents need not be subjected to fortune's wheel, growth and decay, changes of fashion, and the like, but that they were actually capable not only of modifying or forestalling recurrences but of adopting effective courses which turned necessitarian-looking processes to their favor. Now of the types of cycles we have disclosed, none was an intrinsically causal factor itself, but all implied causal agencies behind them. These agencies, whether personified (as fortune often was), or left as principles of change ("into opposites," for instance), were most often reckoned as extra- or supra-human. They created an environment in which man had to struggle, to which he had to adapt, and which he could occasionally control. It was only within the limits of a predetermined stage that man could act out his "free" or "purposeful" rôle. His possibilities for self-determination, then, could only be increased by coming to terms with preexisting influences, unless he was understood to be inexorably bound by fate. Thus history imparted wisdom because it showed men in varying relationships both with each other and with extra-human causes.

Because he used such a variety of causal explanations, Polybius and his history have a real interest for us in this connection. Unfortunately, however, even if

---

*commentarium* clxxxi (ed. P. Wendland, in *Comm. Arist. Graec.*, vol. 3, pt. 1, p. 86, *l.*19) (Alexander explicitly denying change between opposites as cyclical).

109. *De re pub.* I,xliv,68; cf. also below, Chapter 4, introd. on excess.

110. VI,ix,10, 14 (see above, Chapter 1, sect. C); cf. VII,xi,10, XX,iv,1–3.

111. Hesiod *Erga* 218 (for distant background); Thucydides *Hist.* I,22; Lucian *Pōs dei historian syngraphein* 42; cf. Tacitus *Annales* III,55. For Polybius on learning from history: *Hist.* III,cxviii,12, VI,ii,8, iii,2–4, ix,1–11, x,2, XV,vi,8, XVIII,xxiii,4f., XXV,iii,9, etc.

Polybius offered sophisticated distinctions between the cause (*aitia*), the pretext (*prophasis*), and the beginning (*archē*) of a given event-complex, especially a given war (cf. III,vi,1–vii,3, XXII,xviii,6),[112] he nowhere adequately defined the relationship among such agencies as fortune, nature, and men. They were treated as separate causes, and it is left to us to suggest their probable interrelationship or to identify the distinct spheres to which they applied. By and large, to distinguish supra-human, natural, and human (or purposive)[113] causes adequately accounts for his levels of explanation. Fortune, sometimes impersonal and capricious yet often personal and providential, was almost always conceived as an outside factor breaking across the "normal," expected course of events, by producing surprise situations (*paradoxon*; sect. B, pt. 1,ii). *Physis*, by contrast, implied a set path along which all things would pass unless interrupted by some external factor; in the *Anacyclōsis* Polybius also envisaged natural processes working themselves out in accordance with a tight-knit causal chain, each state being dependent on what had gone before.[114] We have seen, moreover, that fortune and nature generally operated in separate spheres of human affairs, and as causal agencies they were not meant to exclude one another logically (cf. above, sect. A, pt. 2,ii). As for rational human beings, they had their wills to exercise and they were quite capable of being the causes of their own actions. Men execute their decisions

> from what propels their judgments and opinions most in a given situation, that is to say, from our notions of things, our state of mind, our reasoning about matters, and everything through which we make decisions and effect projects. (III,vi,7)

In this last causal sphere, then, come the positive reactions of men to the circumstances created by fortune, nature, or other governing principles. Thus, on the level of human volition, men may hinder nature or let it be; they may seduce Fortune or succumb to her recalcitrance. Such purposive behavior or decision-making was obviously of central importance to an historian who for the most part had to recount agents' actions and to give reasons why they behaved as they did. Yet it was insufficient for Polybius to confine historical explanation to the study of motives and rationality, and despite the fact that his characteristically eclectic combination of explanatory devices was not clearly thought out, there is a certain brilliance in his view that history is often beyond human control.

## B. Reciprocal paradigms of recurrence

It should be clear by now that belief in cyclical recurrence is not equivalent to belief in exact or even near-exact repetition. Certain Stoic and Neo-Pythagorean views aside, cyclical recurrence only required that configurations or types of

112. A relatively late formulation? Cf. II,xxxviii,5ff., IV,xiii,6.
113. Cf. R. G. Collingwood, *An Essay on Metaphysics*, Oxford, 1939, pp. 285ff.
114. On polity as *Ursache* in Polybius contrasted with it as *Symptom* in Plato (*Resp*. VIII) see Rehm, op. cit., p. 11.

events be repeated, the degree of particularity varying. It was not Polycrates and his career which recurred, for example, but turns of fortune similar to those experienced by Polycrates; nor was it the same Roman families whose tendencies Tacitus so perceptively described, but the same sort of behavior. Early observers of human things learned to recognize or elicit the shape of a given event-complex and to demonstrate that similar shapes manifested themselves at other points in time, even at fairly regular intervals. Cyclical structures were not the only ones to be exhibited, however, and we may now profitably turn to those relevant notions and models I call "reciprocal." With these, common types of events are simply followed by consequences in such a way as to exemplify patterns in history. To examine these reciprocal ideas will help to confirm our early claim that talk about historical cycles does not exhaust talk about historical recurrence (p. 1).

## *The rectified mean*

### I. GENERAL

"Reciprocity" is a handy term for covering a multitude of sins, though its very convenience should make one cautious.[115] Two important varieties of the reciprocal view of recurrence—the doctrines that departures from a mean are continually rectified, and that good and bad actions evoke their appropriate desert—demand most of our attention in this context.

Concerning the idea of a rectified mean, it is useful to reflect once more on pre-Socratic cosmologies. In these cosmologies alternation between two (usually opposing) states, whether between order and chaos, between unity and multiplicity, or between cosmic degeneracy and cosmic purification, was a common theme. The basic components of the universe, moreover, were often said to be in continual flux: the four elements might become slowly mixed (into Xenophanic mud, for instance) and then separated; or "contrary" conditions (hot and cold, wet and dry) might replace one another unceasingly.

Such oscillating processes could be taken to function cyclically, as with the Empedoclean cosmic cycle, but the cycle was not always the paramount image of change. Consider, for example, the fragments from the late sixth-century philosopher Heraclitus. According to his most renowned dictum, "all things flow" and "come into being and pass away," and yet they do this through what Heraclitus does not hesitate to call "strife" (*eris*), that is, by a process of continual warfare between opposing states and variant tendencies in the universe.[116] Without strife the cosmos was unable to perpetuate itself. This strife was paradoxically identified with harmony, since "all things," including opposites, were ultimately "one" (being reducible to one attunement),[117] and because strife and

115. H. J. Rose ("World Ages and the Body Politic" in *Harvard Theological Review* LIV, 1961, pp. 132f.) inspired my usage.

116. Frgs. 218–9 (Kirk-Raven) and Frg. 80 (Diels-Kranz) = 62 (Bywater). For background, see Hesiod *Erga* 804.

117. Frg. 50 (Diels-Kranz) = 199 (Kirk-Raven) = 1 (Bywater); cf. Frgs. 51 (Diels-Kranz), 43, 45–6 (Bywater).

the changes it effected never produced an imbalance. Fire was apparently to Heraclitus the very well-spring and physical paradigm of cosmic energy, yet although the world was "always an ever-living fire" it was something moderated, "kindling in measures and going out in measures."[118] In the last analysis, no one factor had final dominance over the universe. This was not because there was an endless process of cycles, but because the principle governing the cosmic flux—God, reason, nature, fire, psyche, call it what you will—consistently rectified imbalance. Whether Heraclitus wrote of the restrained heat of the sun, of one element living upon the death of another, of warm things becoming cold, of alternating seasons, of the ocean as the purest and impurest water, of the way up and the way down being identical, or of the same point as beginning and end of a circle, he was reaffirming his central teaching that all movement was controlled by a principle which regulated and balanced the strife between opposites, not allowing one force to gain control over another.[119] Yet the processes of rectification were complex and apparently not understood to occur or recur in a fixed sequence; an imbalance could emerge at any point in time, thus inducing the appropriate consequences.

What bearing does this kind of thinking have on the interpretation of human affairs? What Heraclitus said about moderation, we may note, nicely complements much Greek ethical theory, in which balance and restraint were extolled. The Delphic Oracle, for instance, enjoined against excess; metaphorically the Pythagoreans made the same point in the precept: "Do not step across the beam of a balance"; Aristotle taught a middle way between excess and defect.[120] Man was often advised against aspiring to what he could not be—e.g., a god, or the possessor of excessive power over others—because that meant violating the boundaries of one's allotted position in life (or *moira*) and could only bring disastrous consequences.[121] Significantly, Heraclitus joined others in warning against arrogance and excessive desire,[122] and so his other assertions suggesting that no one factor could dominate the cosmos were supplemented by ideas about proportionateness of law in the specifically moral and human spheres.[123]

118. Frg. 30; cf. 31, 90 (Diels-Kranz) = 200; cf. 221–2 (Kirk-Raven) = 20; cf. 21–2 (Bywater).

119. Frgs. 60, 61, 67, 76, 94, 126 (Diels-Kranz) = 69, 52, 36, 25, 29, 39 (Bywater) and (omitting the third) 202–3, 207, 229, 232 (Kirk-Raven); cf. W. Veazie, "The Meaning of Φύσις in Early Greek Philosophy" in *Studies in the History of Ideas* (Dept. of Philosophy, Columbia University), New York, 1918, pp. 27–42.

120. Diodorus Sicul. *Bib.* IX,x,3, on the Delphic maxim "Nothing in excess" (cf. Theognis, 335; Pindar, Frg. 235, etc.); Anonymous Pythagorean in Anaximander *Akousmata kai symbola*, Frg. 6 (Diels-Kranz, vol. 1, 465, *l.*23); cf. Aristotle *Eth. Nic.* II,ix,1ff.

121. E.g., Homer *Iliad* V,4–44; Pindar *Olymp. odes* II,35–42; Theognis 605ff., 653ff.; Herodotus *Hist.* I,206f., VIII,99ff.; Thucydides *Hist.* III, 82(8); Timaeus, Frg. 155 (*FGH*, pt. IIIB, p. 644); etc.

122. Frgs. 43, 110–1, 112, 116; cf. 118 (Diels-Kranz) = 103; 104–7, cf. 73–6 (Bywater).

123. Frg. 44; cf. 33 (Diels-Kranz) = 100, 110 (Bywater). On intertwining the new cosmological terminology with the earlier language of religion and morals before Heraclitus, note Anaximander, Frg. 1 (Diels-Kranz) = 112 (Kirk-Raven). On this important fragment, see Simplicius *In Aristotelis physica commentaria* I,2 (ed. H. Diels, in *Comm. Arist. Graec.*, vol. 9, p. 24); P. Seligman, *The Apeiron of Anaximander: A Study in the Origin and Function of Metaphysical Ideas*, London, 1962, pp. 24ff., 111ff. Also cf. G. Vlastos, "Equality and Justice in Early Greek Cosmologies" in *Classical Philology* XLII, 1947, pp. 156ff.

Comparable admonitions against excess had their place in Greek historiography, although historians were generally not interested in the total cosmic order and, unlike the moralists, they were more concerned to describe actions and consequences than to formulate abstract truths. Ancient historians, moreover, were in the best position to document how the principles of reciprocity were *recurrently* actualized in human affairs. At this point we are especially interested in the idea that when an imbalance is created in human affairs there is a kind of "gravitational pull" in history which tends toward the reclamation of ordered, balanced, and morally better conditions. The recurrences of unevenness and correction were taken to be diversified in space and time, occurring at irregular intervals, with interim events being irrelevant.

Why men succeeded or failed in their enterprises, or why certain societies triumphed or faltered, were problems fascinating for ancient historians. Herodotus and Thucydides, to take important examples, were both seeking to answer the same sort of question: Why did the more powerful of two opposing states fail to gain victory in the contest? Why was the Persian giant sent home in shame, and why was Athens, the school of Hellas, eventually overcome by Sparta, the most isolationist of all the major Greek city-states? A good part of each man's explanation was in terms of requited excess and checked imbalance. An immoderate degree of power, political insolence, or tyranny ultimately brought downfall;[124] to the cyclical side of this way of thinking, they flew in the face of Fortune's changeableness, or provoked the envy of the divine.[125] In Herodotus' history in particular, one finds the strong (almost Heraclitean) implication that transgression of geographical boundaries was a violation not only of human law but of the divinely ordained order of things, and that such violation demanded requital.[126]

The basic image common to these lines of explanation is that of a shifting beam-balance (*rhopē*); there were movements in history on either side of a mean. Admittedly, such tendencies could be considered in terms of cycles and alternation, as a "hybristic cycle," for instance, or as fluctuation between balance and imbalance. One might even take the reclamation of an equipoise to be a return to original conditions. Nevertheless, descriptions in these terms do not account for certain subtleties and complications. To recount past events was rarely a matter of describing easily-conceived imbalances followed by simple rectifications; more than often one deviant tendency was joined with others to form a "colligation" of imbalance; a given imbalance or instance of immoderateness on one side might be followed by immoderateness on the other; there might never be attained a perfect balance, but only occasional approximations of it, in the

124. Herodotus *Hist.* VII,16, VIII,17; cf. VII,49f., 57; Thucydides *Hist.* V,85ff.

125. Esp. Herodotus VII,10; Thucydides V,102–5.

126. I,51–6, 73, 89 (Croesus and the Halys); I,202–214, and cf. I,86f.; 189f. (Cyrus and the Araxes); III,1–3; 13–68 (Cambyses and Egypt); IV,89ff. (Darius and the Danube); and esp. VIII,8 (Xerxes and Europe): cf. K. Reinhardt, "Herodots Persegeschichten" in *Von Werken und Formen*, Godesberg, 1948, pp. 222f. Also C. N. Cochrane, *Christianity and Classical Culture*, New York, 1944, pp. 456ff. (with caution).

endless flux of events and the constant action and reaction of opposing forces. Thus, insofar as the model of a recurrently corrected mean defies representation as a series of cycloids or as a simple process of alternation between two sets of general conditions, it is most satisfactorily characterized by the word "reciprocal." Its basis lies more in a recognition of typical actions followed by typical consequences than in the intuition of a cyclical or alternating process, even if a relative interlacing of different conceptions is possible.

## II. POLYBIUS

The notion of balance or "beam-balance" in human affairs was part of the stock of useful ideas which Polybius inherited.[127] In his context the Achaian was primarily interested in the fact that the balance of history had been tipped in favor of Rome. He evidently understood the normative historical processes to contain "shifts and turns of circumstances" (cf. XVI,xxviii,6), which included alternations between success and failure, and wheel-like turns between favorable and unfavorable conditions. These processes, however, had been upset by the remarkable achievement of Rome. Before her expansion, the Mediterranean scene was not far removed from the traditional Greek world of fairly well-defined boundaries and equal political chances. While still part of that kind of world, Carthage and Rome were poised for combat at the beginning of the First Punic War. They were both "still uncorrupted in morals, receiving moderate help from fortune, and equal in strength" (I,xiii,12), and when the war was in progress its outcome was continually in doubt. Using both pro-Roman and pro-Carthaginian sources,[128] Polybius traced a constant shifting of advantages from one side to the other (cf. esp. I,xx,7). Elsewhere he could evoke the concept of a balance whenever two military forces faced each other for battle; he commonly remarked upon the even matching of arms or men and presented counterposing speeches, heightening the reader's sense of expectation as to how the issue would be decided.[129] In Bk. I on the First Punic War, however, he gave the idea of balance special attention. If we reflect on the general trends in the *Historiae*, we see that the events immediately preceding and including Cannae weighed heavily in favor of a Carthaginian success (esp. III, IX), and those afterward on the side of an expanding Roman empire; yet the First Punic War ended only very slightly in Rome's favor (Ixxxviii,5–12) and was marked throughout by fluctuating fortunes. The initial stages of the war over Sicily saw matters hanging in the balance (xx,5), but by contesting the Carthaginian command of the sea (xix,9–11) the Romans upset the equipoise and set in motion a struggle which at times appeared to proceed in seesaw-like fashion, and at other moments witnessed the reclamation of stability (see Diagram V). In this battle between "game cocks" (cf. lviii,7), new advantages and victories were ascribed to skill,

127. E.g., Alcaeus, Frg. 31 (Lobel and Page edn.); Thucydides *Hist.* V,103, and cf. VII,71; Plato *Resp.* VIII,556E; Aristotle *Polit.* 1295a36–9, cf. Homer, *Iliad*, VIII,72.

128. I,xiv,1ff.; cf. lviii,5f.

129. E.g., XI,xiii,1f., XV,iii–xiii; cf. XI,xxviii–xxix.

## Diagram V The Pattern of Recurrence in Polybius I

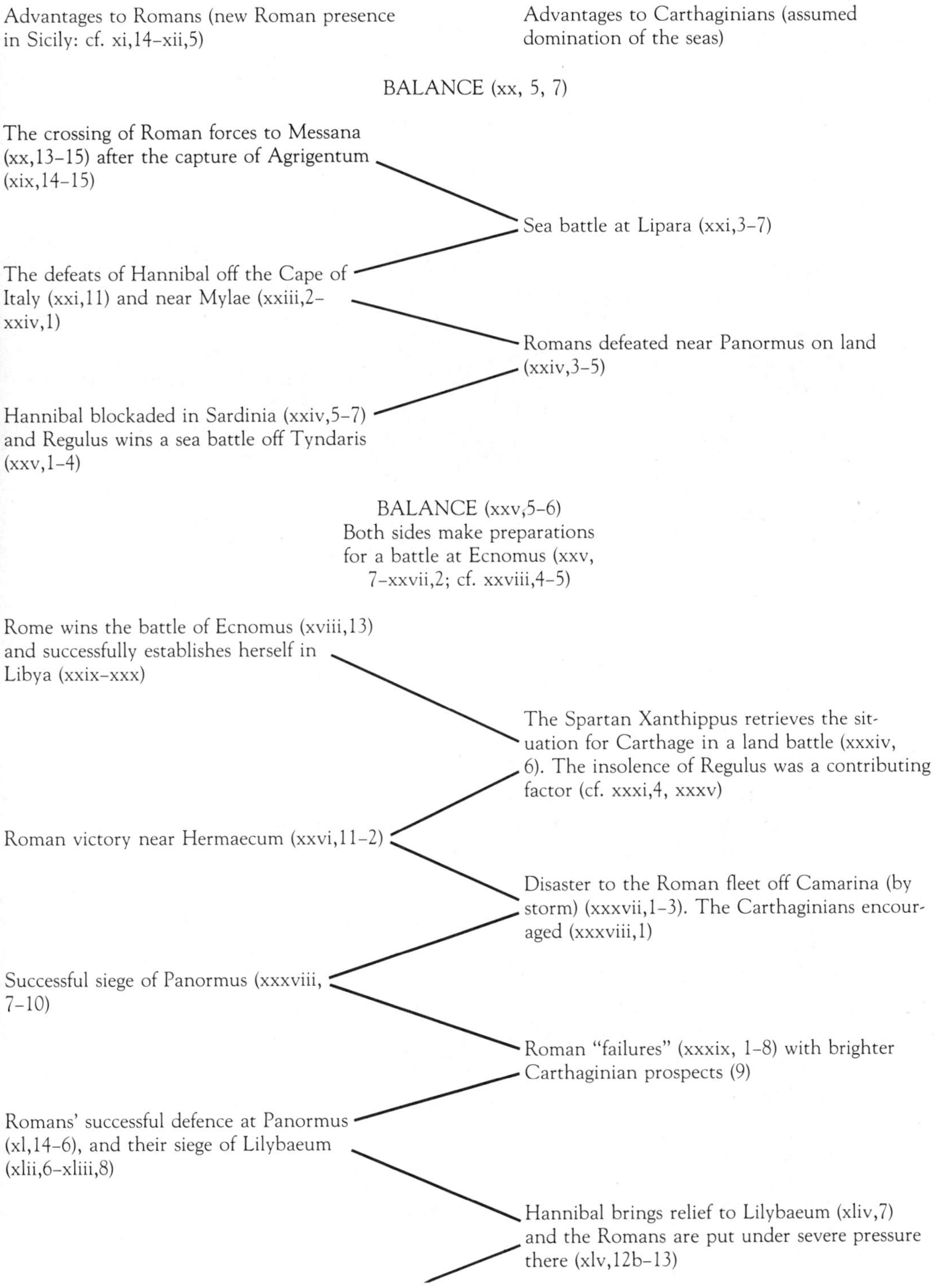

Advantages to Romans (new Roman presence in Sicily: cf. xi,14–xii,5)

Advantages to Carthaginians (assumed domination of the seas)

BALANCE (xx, 5, 7)

The crossing of Roman forces to Messana (xx,13–15) after the capture of Agrigentum (xix,14–15)

Sea battle at Lipara (xxi,3–7)

The defeats of Hannibal off the Cape of Italy (xxi,11) and near Mylae (xxiii,2–xxiv,1)

Romans defeated near Panormus on land (xxiv,3–5)

Hannibal blockaded in Sardinia (xxiv,5–7) and Regulus wins a sea battle off Tyndaris (xxv,1–4)

BALANCE (xxv,5–6)
Both sides make preparations for a battle at Ecnomus (xxv, 7–xxvii,2; cf. xxviii,4–5)

Rome wins the battle of Ecnomus (xviii,13) and successfully establishes herself in Libya (xxix–xxx)

The Spartan Xanthippus retrieves the situation for Carthage in a land battle (xxxiv, 6). The insolence of Regulus was a contributing factor (cf. xxxi,4, xxxv)

Roman victory near Hermaecum (xxvi,11–2)

Disaster to the Roman fleet off Camarina (by storm) (xxxvii,1–3). The Carthaginians encouraged (xxxviii,1)

Successful siege of Panormus (xxxviii, 7–10)

Roman "failures" (xxxix, 1–8) with brighter Carthaginian prospects (9)

Romans' successful defence at Panormus (xl,14–6), and their siege of Lilybaeum (xlii,6–xliii,8)

Hannibal brings relief to Lilybaeum (xliv,7) and the Romans are put under severe pressure there (xlv,12b–13)

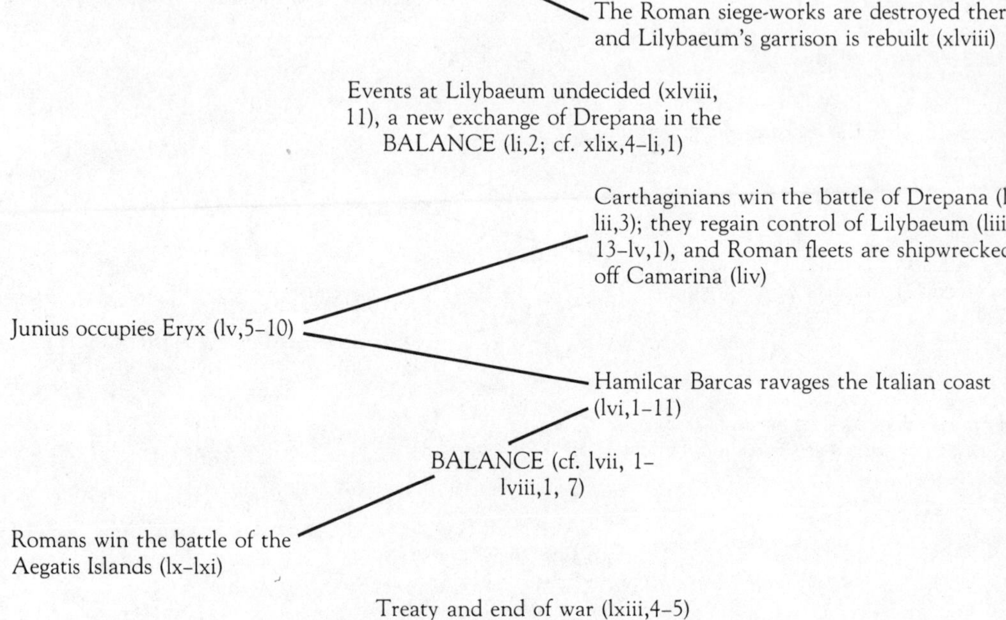


courage, and spirit,[130] and reverses either to lack of preparation and foresight[131] or to an inability to adjust to the unexpected (*paradoxon*) in events.[132] Fortune played a crucial role: she lay behind the contest "like a good umpire" (cf. lviii,1), and she also participated in it by contributing to the outcome of battles, by determining their location, and by generally preserving a balance between the forces.

Thus a recognizable pattern of recurrence underlies most of the *Historiae* Bk. I. Easily recognizable conditions or event-types recur (victories, defeats, accidents, etc.), as do those important tendencies toward either balance or imbalance. Polybius' pattern was to a large extent imposed, of course, and in extracting it he was not strictly fair to the facts.[133] His line of interpretation probably had much to do with the opposing claims of his sources, and these also

130. E.g., I,ix,6ff., xi,15–xvi,3, xvii,11f., xviii,9ff., xx,11ff., xxiii,6, xxvi–xxvii, xxxvi,2f.

131. E.g., I,xxi,5–9, xxiv,3f., xxxv,1f., xxxvii,3f.

132. Esp. xxiv,1 (cf. xxiii,5ff.), xxviii,9, xliv,5; lxxi,2, lxxv,10, lxxvi,7, lxxii,3ff.; yet note xxv,3f.

133. For various examples see Walbank *Commentary*, vol. 1, p. 73 (on I,xix,15–xx,12), 100 (on I,xxxix,6), 121 (on lvii,1f.).

appear responsible for a certain confusion in Bk. I over differing levels of causation. His etiology there is perhaps best looked at in terms of a simple spectrum. On the one hand, the First Punic War was a battle of wits and on the other it was supervised by fortune, yet between these two levels of causation seems to lie the area of the unexpected, which could either be created by human cunning[134] or else be a product of a force beyond human control.[135] The categories were not effectively interrelated, however, and it is not unlikely that they were in large measure derived. Philinus, a key source for Polybius on the First Carthaginian War, evidently appealed to similar causal principles (if it is safe to assume that he lies behind Diodorus Siculus' treatment of the Syracusan-Mamertine War).[136] On the other hand, the accentuated seesaw effect in Polybius I and some of the book's more theoretical statements about balance are probably to be credited to the Achaian's originality,[137] and have much to do with his efforts to characterize the normative processes of history, especially military history, before Rome's emergence as the greatest of all world powers.

This understanding of shifting and rectified balance is well worth disentangling from other related notions of historical recurrence (such as the idea of fortune's wheel), and particularly from an important Polybian preconception evident in the *Historiae.* Polybius held that, as a general rule, external threat to a state or region produced internal, defensive consolidation, while the absence of such a threat engendered internal disorders. Peoples such as the fifth-century Athenians and the Carthaginians in Spain (ca. 230–210 BC) could gain respite from war (after success against competitors), and yet experience the same internal instabilities known in far weaker political entities.[138] Those states well enough constituted to control the worst domestic disorders, moreover, could still be enervated by a long peace (XXXI,xxi,3–4; cf. VI,lvii,5), thus becoming susceptible to defeat from without. By contrast, the disadvantages of war and grave peril often consolidated the resources of a state so that it was able to achieve far more than mere recovery. This happened in Rome's case in consequence of the Gallic and Hannibalic invasions and the Mercenary War.[139] Thus Polybius

134. Esp. I,xx,13, xxiv,1, xxv,3, xxviii,9, xxxiv,11, xxxv, xxxvi,3, xliv,5, xlix,7, lix,9, lxxv,3, lxxxiv,8, etc. Cf. I,i, liii,12, lviii,3, lxxi,2.

135. Esp. I,xxi,11, lxi,7; cf. xxxix,4, liv,8, lxii,1, etc.

136. Polybius gave far less detail on this war than Diodorus (cf. *Hist.* I,ix,1–x,1, Diodorus XXII,xiii,1–9) and does not refer to his causal apparatus in connection with it. Diodorus' report on a battle at Messana in this war is significant: it began with an "even balance," contained unexpected (*paradoxos*) eventualities, and saw the intervention of *tychē* to avert the utter collapse of Mamertine affairs (XXII,xiii,4b, 6, 7). The interpretative manner is probably both pre-Polybian and pre-Diodoran, and it is not unlikely that Polybius' acceptance of fortune as "stage manager" and "stage producer" derives from Philinus; cf. F. W. Walbank, "Polybius, Philinus and the First Punic War" in *Classical Quarterly* XXXIX, 1945, pp. 5, 8f. (though note Diodorus XVIII,liii,1ff.).

137. His use of Philinus as a foil against Fabius' history is important here: see esp. xxx,1–xxxv,10 (cf. Walbank, *Commentary*, vol. 1, pp. 89–93), xlviii,3–11.

138. VI,xviii,6b, xliv,6f., IX,xi,1f., X,vi,5; cf. II,xix,2–4, IV,xxxi,1–xxxii,3, XV,xxi,3–5, and below, pt. 2(ii), sect. C, pt. 1(ii).

139. I,vi,13f., lxxxvii ff., II,xxxiii,1ff., xxi,8b, III,lxxv,8, VI,li,7f.

identified the "forces of compensation" in play during either conflict or peace. Broken down, his interpretation reflects two alternations, one between war and peace, the other between unity and discord (and this is with the life of one particular state in view). The combination of factors made for greater complexity, however, and more than one state could be under consideration. In that case the word "reciprocal" fits better. Furthermore, that term covers the exceptional—the remarkable development of Roman supremacy. According to Polybius, the Romans possessed a government of such excellence and coordination that those working within it acted in zealous concord before an outside foe, and were saved from the corruptions of idleness, insolence, and selfish competition in prosperity (VI,xviii,1–8). Rome's political resilience was unique, then, yet the same reciprocal principles still applied.

In so analyzing recurring political interactions, Polybius created a methodological tool for interpreting internal and external relations at the same time. This tool was probably intended to complement his line of thinking on altering fortune in external affairs and on natural inner changes, but despite the apparent originality Polybius failed to make all the relationships clear. We may presume that if states could stem imminent disaster, this was parallel to a turn from bad to good fortune, though the levels of causation were different. He seemed to treat the tendency toward disunity in prosperity as natural and belonging to the inner life of the state. It was thus akin to constitutional decay "according to nature," though it had more to do with the notion of general moral degeneration, a notion not convincingly integrated with his anacyclic theory.[140]

Whatever the difficulties, Polybius did not encapsulate the above understanding of internal-external relations in a cyclical model. Whereas basic cycloalternating processes (such as growth and decay or rise and fall) were unilinear, Polybius took his special reciprocal principles to operate between states and not just within the separate courses of given political societies. Moreover, the idea of deviations from a mean is absent from simple cyclical frames. That difference continues to apply even when one compares the most elementary wheel of fortune model (sec. A, pt. 1) with the idea of a requited immoderateness (the "hybristic cycle") in Greco-Roman historiography. Although these two conceptions can to some extent be blended, the latter can still be distinguished from the former in respect of a mean. In the "hybristic cycle," one does not simply talk about the impermanence of fortune or the alternation between good and ill fortune, but about the consequences of excess, usually moral excess, committed against moderation. Reference to arrogance (*hybris*) introduces us to those ideas of interaction and compensation which have to do with history's moral order. It was held by certain ancient historians, and Polybius was not least among them, that immoderateness brought adverse retribution, and that historical events

140. Except perhaps in Rome's case, with its most natural of constitutions (VI,lvii,5). The distinction between the constitutional and the moral history of a people was to be drawn and treated ably much later by Machiavelli: see below, Chapter 5, sect. A, pt. 2.

confirmed the inexpediency of servility on the one hand and of arrogance on the other. Such opinions may be included in a wider view of reciprocal principles—the view that good and bad actions consistently evoke their appropriate desert—principles which could be recurrently actualized in history without the regularity and fixed stages associated with cycles and alternation.

## *Principles of retribution*

### I. GENERAL

For those upholding it, the moral order of affairs was maintained by principles of retributive justice. To commend the ways of justice was typical among the Greeks, and they were comforted when it was satisfied, whether by men, by the gods, or by the natural order of things.[141] Thus certain interpreters of history were bent on demonstrating how the good were rewarded and the evil punished in the events of the past. Variables in the enunciation and defence of this crucial idea, however, ought to be acknowledged. Four problem areas come to mind. First, although these retributive principles were usually considered divine, the degrees to which justice (*dikē*) was associated with traditional deities or naturalized into an inviolable law of the universe differed from historian to historian.[142] In much Hellenistic and Roman historiography, of course, the agent of justice was a heavily "hypostatized" fortune, though God or fate, or even just men, could also suit the case. Second, judgments as to good and evil could well vary, and often depended on the measure of a given historian's patriotism. Greeks might rail against the imperialism of Xerxes, for instance, yet countenance the glorious achievements of Alexander. Much depended, moreover, upon what incidents a writer chose to be sensitive or to make moral observations about. Take the case of reporting on deaths, for example. It was a common presupposition that on the battlefield good men died as heroes and bad men obtained their just deserts, that the murder of a good man was a perfidy requiring repayment but that the murder of an evil man was an outcome befitting his crimes. Some

141. On various commendations of justice see Hesiod *Erga* 213–8, 256–70; Theognis 202ff.; Anaximander, Frg. 1 (Diels-Kranz) = 112 (Kirk-Raven); Heraclitus, Frgs. 80, 94, and cf. 23 (Diels-Kranz) = 214; 229 (Kirk-Raven) = 62, 29, and cf. 60 (Bywater); Aeschylus *Agamemnon* 754ff.; Herodotus *Hist.* VIII,77, 106; Aristotle *Eth. Nic.* V,i–ix; Isocrates *Archidamus* xxxv–vi; Demosthenes *Orationes* XXV,xi, xxxv; etc. Traditionalists could insist that the rewards and punishments of the gods were well apportioned (Hesiod *Erga* 213–341; Xenophon *Cyropaideia* I,vi,1–7; Marcus Aurelius *Meditationes* II,iii, IX,i–XII,x, xii; cf. Epictetus *Dissert.* III,xxiv,48; etc.), others could envisage types of post-mortem existence appropriate to one's moral condition on earth: Pythagorean Frgs. 263 *finis*; 268 (Kirk-Raven); Empedocles, Frgs. 468–71, 476–86 (Kirk-Raven) (cf. W. K. C. Guthrie, *A History of Greek Philosophy*, Cambridge, 1965, vol. 2, pp. 244–65); Plato *Phaedrus* 248f., *Resp.* 608C–620; yet cf. Herodotus *Hist.* I,29–33; Aristotle *Eth. Nic.* I,v–xiii, *De anima* 430a10–25. Others paralleled the consequences of human actions to the "impersonal" yet ultimately moderating effects of physical and biological interactions: Anon. Pythag., Frg. 5 (Diels-Kranz, vol. 1, p. 452, *ll.*30ff.); Heraclitus, Frgs. 57, 67, 80, 102, 119 (Diels-Kranz) = 57, 36, 61–2, 121 (Bywater); Epicurus, Frgs. 69, 72, 74–7; 82 (Bailey edn., pp. 136–9); cf. Aristotle *Eth. Nic.* VIII,viii,7; and on the Stoics, see Zeller, *Stoics*, pp. 173–93.

142. In Herodotus VIII,106, and cf. 77 ("God"); in Thucydides III,67, IV,118, VI,61 (requital in human hands); in Polybius III,x,1, XXXI,xvi,2, and cf. XXIII,x,3 (an aspect of the moral order); etc.

authors went to excessive lengths to confirm the evidence for appropriate retribution by presenting a list of the ultimate fates of the impious in given incidents, and others theologized about the brave end of good men.[143] Yet the deaths overlooked were numerous, and they were generally omitted because they were not morally "pointed," or because they did not fit the conventional view, or simply because they had been forgotten.[144]

Turning to a third problem area, we find seemingly vulgar expectations of quick rewards and punishments in sharp contrast to the minimizing of popular supernaturalism and removal of any emphasis on immediacy. Historians were quite capable of flirting with both approaches. They were bound to inherit accounts of hastened divine visitations upon the presumptuous—of the thunderbolt falling on King Scylas, for instance, who dared as a Scythian to become an initiate into the Dionysian mysteries[145]—yet in the main they would demonstrate, from a complex disarray of less spectacular events, how in the end, irregularly or slowly, justice won. Finally, the difference between a moral order dependent upon will—on the will of the gods, Fortune, or men—and one operating according to inexorable destiny or to a predetermined, unalterable plan, should be grasped, although historians could follow both lines by assuming different levels of causation.[146] While admitting all such variables, however, the appeal to a moral order in Greco-Roman historiography still implied an idea of historical recurrence, an idea, that is, of repeated actualization of retributive principles.

These principles manifested themselves in distinctive types of situations, one might even say in dramatic situations.[147] The humbling of the arrogant, the

143. For such a list see Diodorus *Bib.* XVI,lxi,1–4 (on the various fates of those who outrage the Delphic Oracle). For theologizing about death see, e.g., Plutarch *Vit. Cat. Min.* lxviii,1f., Seneca *De tranquillitate animi* xvi,1–4, and cf. Herodotus *Hist.* I,31; Arrian *Anabasis* vii,17.

144. E.g., Polybius II,lxx,4–7. Polybius was favorable to Antigonus the Great, yet he did not elicit any particular significance from his nasty death on the battlefield.

145. Herodotus IV,79. Cf. also, e.g., Timaeus, Frgs. 19 (23), 119a, 155 (*FGH*, pt. IIIB, pp. 585, 634, 644); Xenophon *Anabasis* V,iii,13; and (as background) Theognis 197–208.

146. E.g., Herodotus I,46 (Justice), VII,10 (Fortune, Nemesis, and God); I,210, II,120, III,40, VII,10, 139, IX,100, etc. (the divine); I,91, III,108, IX,16 (destiny). On Thucydides, cf. F. M. Cornford, *Thucydides Mythistoricus*, London, 1907, ch. 6; on Polybius, see below, pt. 2(ii). For background examples, note how Isocrates (who doubted the existence of the gods: *Nicocles* xxvi) implies, on the one hand, that the Persians were punished for their offence against the gods, and on the other, that their downfall was due to a natural degeneracy (*Paneg.* cxlvii, cl ff.). According to another approach, the gods, though accepted as agents, were subject to a higher, inexorable set of laws: e.g., Homer *Iliad* XVI,433; Simonides in Plato *Leg.* V,741A; Aeschylus *Prometheus vinctus* 515–21; Herodotus I,91. On these principles of fate and destiny, though, one must remember the variety of terms used in classical literature (ἡ μοῖρα, ἡ πεπρωμένη, ἡ εἱμαρμένη, *fatum*, *vicis*, *retributum*, etc.), and the conventional appeal to them as a way of showing how historical protagonists were deluded or were unable to understand the moral laws governing affairs (esp. Herodotus VII,7, 18, 37, 52, 237, VIII,75, 99, 101).

147. Cf. Aeschylus *Persae* 1–154, Aristotle *Rhetorica* 1393a25ff., 1360a34–6, Cicero *De inventione* I,xix ff. as background. For classic instances of the dramatic situation in historiography, see Herodotus (below, and cf. S. Benardete, *Herodotean Enquiries*, The Hague, 1969, pp. 4, 209); Thucydides IV,18; Xenophon *Hellenika* V,iv,1; Poseidonius in Athenaeus *Deip.* X,439E, 542E; and on Polybius, see below, pt. 2(ii). On the confusion of history with rhetoric, cf. Polybius II,lvi,7–13, XII,xxiv–xxva (against Phylarchus and Timaeus); J. B. Bury, *Ancient Greek Historians*, London, 1909, pp. 124, 165ff., 209.

chastisement of the impious, the effectiveness of the wise, etc., were invariably integral to such situations. This being the case, interest rests not on the recurrence of particulars or of strikingly similar circumstances, but on the continuing reappearance of event-types, -shapes, and -patterns, and on the operative principles they betoken. The recurrence of these configurations, moreover, need not be represented as curves and alternations; it involves, rather, a complex interaction of forces which sees that moral behavior and attitudes have their fitting consequences. A Heraclitean oracle provides us with a suitable image: all existing things are likened to the stream of a river, and no one stepping into the river a second time can expect to find it the same.[148] In uttering this Heraclitus hardly abandoned his belief in the consistent preservation of cosmic balance, yet so many were the eddies, whirl-pools, and bypassed waters in the rushing river that talk of wavelike undulations hardly sufficed to account for its many-sided ferment. And so historians, although it is illusory to imagine them engaging in relentlessly impartial philosophical exercises with their narratives, sought to elicit the actualization of these principles where they chose, as they passed from career to career, from state to state.

It cannot be pretended, of course, that the historiographical tradition upholding belief in the moral order was without competitors or agnostics. Epicurean writers tended to denigrate retributive notions in their appeals to "mere chance,"[149] and one should remember such a restless soul as Tacitus, who, despite his references to divine chastisement, to the fitting exposure of crimes, and to the need "to confront evil words and deeds with the menace of posterity's reprobation," was nevertheless attracted to the Epicurean view that the gods remained aloof from mankind, unconcerned with the prosperous wicked and the suffering good.[150] But antiquity's defences of the moral order remain numerous and fascinating.

The moral order in Herodotus' work is especially worthy of our attention. His great history has its climax in the invasion of Hellas by the notorious Xerxes, whose defeat was largely accounted for in terms of a divinely ordained retribution. Xerxes was immoderate in good fortune, arrogant in his pretensions and his use of power, outrageous against the ways of Justice, and blind to fate. He produced an unnatural imbalance in the world by daring to lead his forces across the Hellespont to enslave Greece.[151] This significant case of Xerxes did not stand alone, of course; it was informed and prefigured by preceding, if less significant, events. Other kings, Croesus and Polycrates, for example, suffered for being overly fortunate, the former because he was too proud, the latter because destiny could not be evaded.[152] Divine retribution or the satisfaction of

148. Frgs. 41–2 (Bywater) = 218 (Kirk-Raven).

149. For the evidence in Polybius see below, pt. 2(ii).

150. *Annales* VI,22, *Historiae* IV,26, and cf. I,3, IV,26, *Ann.* III,65 (for the quotation), IV,1, XIV,5, XVI,16. On the theme of posterity's favor or retribution in medieval historiography see below, Chapter 4, sect. H.

151. Herodotus VII,10, 16, 24, 49–51, 140, 220, VIII,77, 109, 115–7, IX,16; cf. VII,8, 33f., 54–7.

152. I,34ff., 91, III,40–3, 120ff. and other examples; II,161, V,92, VII,158.

justice was instanced repeatedly—Croesus was defeated for his ambitious attempt to extend Lydian territories and for seeking revenge against Cyrus (I,73–91); Cambyses met with a bitter end for his uncontrolled outrages (III,13–68); there were fitting deaths for Oroetes the murderous Persian, Scylas the presumptuous Scythian, Pheretima the vengeful Egyptian, Aristagoras the unworthy Ionian, for the Spartan Cleomenes who committed a crime against Demaratus, and so on.[153] A man of geographical interests, Herodotus had a point to make about traditional boundaries. Whenever they were crossed with hostility—the Halys, the Araxes, the Nile, the Danube, the Hellespont—then acts of immoderateness had been performed and the established balance upset.[154] Such violations ultimately stand in marked contrast to the Greeks' indifference to territorial expansion (cf. V,49–51), and to their lawful restraint at the end of the Persian War in merely creating the conditions for Ionia's final liberation (VII,102–5, IX,77–80).

Herodotus also suggested that revenge frequently provided the awful motivation for political imbalance, or for invasion and war;[155] in fact, Darius' fury over the Athenian sack of Sardis (V,105), and Xerxes' effort to vindicate Persian power after Marathon (VII,8), fit within a longstanding pattern of "tit for tat" going back before the Trojan War (cf. I,1–5, II,112–130).[156] While Herodotus was conscious that revenge could mother crimes, he recognized as well that unrequited evildoing could accumulate in the hands of a person or nation, until it reached a turning point.[157]

When retribution resulted from any of these excesses, it was not merely effected by human will and reaction. The "appropriate punishment for evil" (*tisis*), the alterations of fortune, the eventual reestablishment of traditional (or natural) boundaries, as well as the flourishing and waning of régimes,[158] were all ultimately secured at a higher causal level. Events did not have a merely humanistic meaning, and we find Herodotus appealing to victorious Justice, to the providential divine, to punishment for evil as if it were a natural process, even to the old gods.[159] Of course he could afford to be enthusiastic about the final issue of the Persian Wars. It was different for his more disillusioned successor, Thucydides, who witnessed the subsequent struggles within Hellas, and who was

153. III,120–8, IV,76–9, 205, V,49–51, 124–6, VI,75–85. Cf. C. W. Fornara, *Herodotus: An Interpretative Essay*, Oxford, 1971, pp. 77–91.

154. See above, pt. 1(i); cf. I,28, 72 (Halys), 189 (Gyndes), II,16 (Nile Delta), IV,92ff. (Danube and Araxes), VII,30–8 (Hellespont), VIII,49f. (Greek isthmus) on Herodotean geographical conceptions.

155. Herodotus' adverse attitude toward war (e.g., I,88, VIII,3), even toward strife (*eris*) (I,82, V,88, VI,129, IX,33), contrasts with the position of Heraclitus.

156. Esp. I,2 (quotation); cf. R. Sealey, "Thucydides, Herodotus and the Causes of War" in *Classical Quarterly* N.S. VII, 1957, pp. 1–12.

157. I,34ff., II,124–34, VII,8ff.

158. Immerwahr, op. cit., pp. 153ff. The flourishing and waning of Lydia, Samos, and Egypt prefigure and inform the rise and belittling of Persia (I,28–95, II,124–182, III,39–60, 120–5 and passim).

159. II,120, III,108f., VI,117, IX,100; cf. Cochrane, op. cit., pp. 460ff.

forced to be far more sober about the essentially human, psychological nature of power conflict and social malaise.[160]

II. POLYBIUS: KEY LINES OF APPROACH

Herodotus, it is clear, believed that history reflected the recurrent operation of moral principles. By both his own explicit interpretation and his representation in key dialogues of the views of sage-like advisers (especially Croesus and Artabanus, who were understood to have learned the major lessons of history),[161] he suggested that different event-complexes could be connected and paralleled. Departing from the earlier annalistic-genealogical approach to recording the past, he used not only dialogues but preexisting *Novellen* (such as the story of Solon's conversation with Croesus about happiness in I,31–33) to endow his material with a universal character, and to raise questions about human life in general.[162]

The work of Polybius has much in common with the achievement of Herodotus. Polybius' *Historiae* are studded with ethically-pointed episodes, and they illustrate the recurrent operation of retributive principles. Like Herodotus, Polybius acknowledged a moral governance over human affairs, although his pragmatic bias made him more interested in causality at a mundane level and his concessions to voluntarism (as against determinism) were therefore greater.[163] With Herodotus one often feels that fate governs all and that human effort is merely its handmaiden; Polybius, despite his talk of nature and Fortune, gave more weight to human beings as fundamental historical agencies. His Fortune was never as inexorable as destiny, and men seem to have a greater chance of saving themselves from the adverse side of extra-anthropological forces. On the other hand, we must remember that Polybius saw human activity as bounded by a finite number of possibilities and played out within a recognizable ambit. Human affairs reflected classifiable situations and event-complexes. Despite their contextual individuality, the general forms with which these situations came to be endowed and the recognizable types of issues they involved were recurrent, leaving a basis on which one could learn from the past. Most of these situations had a strong ethical aspect, and when drawing attention to them in his narrative Polybius was only too willing to point the moral. Such didacticism was an essential part of his utilitarian outlook. Not only was there more than one kind of guide for rational action to be learned from history, but he understood ethical attitudes to be closely intertwined with political policy—a point manifest enough if one considers the dual connotations of the Greek term *aretē*

160. See below, sect. C, pt. 2, and cf. A. G. Woodhead, *Thucydides on the Nature of Power* (*Martin Classical Lectures* XXIV), Cambridge, Mass., 1970; P. Huart, *Le Vocabulaire de l'analyse psychologique dans l'oeuvre de Thucydide* (*Études et Commentaires* LXIX), Paris, 1968, pp. 9ff.

161. Esp. I,86–91, 207, III,14, 36 (Croesus), VII,10–2, 15–8, 46f., 50–3 (Artabanus).

162. Täubler, op. cit., pp. 57–65 for background (with special reference to Hellanikos and the Croesus *Novelle*).

163. Cf. Pédech, op. cit., pp. 54ff., 75ff.

(virtue; also excellence, valor) and the Latin *virtus* (virtue; also merit, strength). Polybius could convince himself more readily than a modern that in drawing morals he was imparting political wisdom to his readers.

Whether Polybius distorted the facts in his search for moral meaning in human affairs, or whether he simply highlighted what was already implicit in the events themselves, is a matter for debate. What is more relevant for us is that his preoccupations with moral lessons and retribution reflect an important type of recurrence thinking, and one which has not yet been properly recognized as part of a whole body of ideas. Perhaps, when "crime does not pay," we might be persuaded that history has repeated itself, but Polybius gives us reason to believe that this kind of approach to historical repetition can be filled out with some sophistication and intricacy. If the overall effect of his work was to show that justice was satisfied, we still have to say something about the variety of crimes, requitals, situations, and relevant causal explanations in the *Historiae*. Important matters to be raised here are his treatment of the hybristic cycle (and its relation to the role of fortune), as well as the ethical front to his accounts of defeat and death.

That the insolent were brought low was an old truth going back before Herodotus, and it was a convention Polybius was happy to retain and exemplify. Regulus, for instance, became too harsh in his moment of victory. He should have both corrected his behavior and distrusted fortune, and for his mistake in not doing so he paid dearly (I,xxxi,4–7, xxxiv,8, xxxv,1–10).[164] Prusias II of Bithynia, an effeminate man with unchecked passions, sacked temples not only in neighboring regions but in his own country, and in view of his arrogance and misdeeds (or "causes," as Polybius significantly called them), it "seemed like heavenly vengeance" when he lost his entire infantry (XXXII,xv,7–8, 13–14). To turn from individuals to states, Polybius remarked that the insolence of the Galatian Gauls had been quenched by the Romans in the cause of freedom (III,iii,5), and he foreshadowed forthcoming difficulties for the Aetolian confederation by placing a strongly pejorative stress on their insolence.[165] In these cases he was developing a common classical preconception that insolence (*hybris*) led to eventual punishment and nemesis. Taken as the simple complex: evil→requital, pride→fall, it is not easy to consider this preconception to be cyclical. Yet tied to the idea of fortune's wheel, as it often was, and so endowing that idea with an ethical content, this retributive model may be more justifiably referred to in terms of a hybristic cycle. Polybius, of course, was interested in an interconnection between the role of fortune and the operations of retributive principles, and it is important to observe how he achieved this, especially as he was playing with at least two apparently contradictory pictures of fortune, one which highlighted her capriciousness and another her function as a mistress of the moral order.

164. Against Walbank's later view (*Commentary*, vol. 1, p. 93, and cf. J. P. Balsdon, "Some Questions," p. 159 n. 2), but for his earlier conclusions ("Polybius, Philinus," p. 10). Cf. Diodorus *Bib.* XXIII,xv,1–6.

165. II,iv,6 (cf. Roveri, *Studi*, p. 129), IV,iii,5, 10–3, xvi,4, lxii,4f., IX,xxxv,6, XXX,xi,1–6.

The key issues here are exposed in an interesting passage in Bk. XV. Philip V and Antiochus the Great had committed shameful deeds against Ptolemy Philopator's infant son, and in commenting on the treaty between the Macedonian and the Seleucid in 203 BC Polybius wrote:

Who can look into this treaty, as into a mirror, without fancying that he sees reflected in it the image of all impiety toward God and all savagery toward men, as well as the unbounded covetousness of these two kings? But at the same time who among those who reasonably find fault with Fortune for her conduct of human affairs, will not be reconciled to her when he learns how she afterward made them pay the due penalty, and how she exhibited to their successors, as a warning for their edification, the exemplary chastisement she inflicted on these princes? For . . . she raised up against them the Romans, and very justly and properly visited them with the very evils which, contrary to all law, they had designed to bring on others. . . . (xx,4–6)

Here Polybius first alludes to the idea of Fortune as indifferent to morality, yet as enamored with change, an idea not foreign to some of his own procedures.[166] Not openly rejecting that conception, he went on to contend that what appeared at first to be unreasonable permissiveness on Fortune's part was *in the end* not so, that her superficial amorality actually laid the basis for, or preceded, actualization of the moral order.[167] He thus attempted to remove the conflict between Fortune's ethical neutrality and her providence (incidentally revealing yet another of his eclecticisms).[168]

This passage contains another important Polybian notion: that Fortune's support of Rome represented exemplary punishment of Rome's enemies, in this case the arrogance of Philip and Antiochus. Its ethical implications aside, the rise of the Roman dominion was unprecedented and defied reason. It was a product of Fortune as the incalculable. With these implications duly acknowledged, however, its occurrence said something both about Roman virtues and

166. See above, sect. A, pt. 1(ii), and IX,xxix,10, X,xxxvii,4, xl,6, XI,xix,5, XXXI,xxix,3 (in these cases *tautomaton* might have been used just as easily as *tychē*, as in III,xcvii,5, XV,xxix,5, XVIII,xii,2, XXII,iv,3, XXXI,xxv,10); cf. VI,xliii,3.

167. Cf. Seneca (adapting Epicurus) on Fortune as the *temporary* protector of evildoers (*Epist. mor.* XCVII,13f.). For Polybius, Fortune was no mere protector; she also meted out punishment.

168. Some writers considered that if a man was at the mercy of fortune it would be difficult to see how justice could be satisfied: e.g., Aeschines *On the Embassy* 118, 183; Seneca *Epist. mor.* XCVIII,1–6, and cf. VIII,3f., LXIII,7–11, CXIII,27f., *De tranq.* xvi,3; Fronto *De Eloquentia* I,9; cf. Pédech, op. cit., p. 74 n.105ff., pp. 331f. Certain Epicurean writers, according to Polybius, ascribed eventualities to chance on the supposition that there was no moral order: *Hist.* I,lxiii,9 (which does *not* contradict I,iv,1), X,ii,5, v,8, XVIII,xii,2, XXXII,viii,4. Polybius refers to chance in the works of these Epicureans as *automaton* or *tychē* either without the article or adverbially. Although it is true that there are times when Polybius referred to *tychē with* an article as the "blind chance" of Epicurean historiography (X,iii,7, vii,3, XXXI,xxx,3), it is clear that in these cases he attacked a false notion, one to which he himself did not subscribe (points overlooked by Walbank in his discussions: *Commentary*, vol. 1, pp. 16ff., vol. 2, pp. 194ff., 564; cf. Pédech, op. cit., pp. 343ff.). Polybius paid deference to these lines of approach in recognizing the incalculability of fortune's behavior, even her *prima facie* ethical neutrality, but he also felt bound to account for the alternative view of her as a mediator or moral governess. This alternative view was surely inherited: cf. Anaximenes of Lampsacus, Frg. 11b, sect. 15 (*FGH*, vol. 2A, p. 120); Theophrastus, Frg. 73 (Wimmer); Demetrius [see above, sect. A, pt. 2(ii), pt. 3(ii); cf. Pédech, p. 332]; Philinus [see above, sect. B, pt. 1(ii)].

about fitting retribution against peoples who lacked their victor's sense of honor and justice. In reviewing the discussions of the defeat of nations before Rome (or before Achaia, as in the earlier stages of the *Historiae*), it strikes one that all the peoples opposing these two "righteous" powers have moral guilt imputed to them. A curious mixture of bias and hindsight surrounds Polybius' analysis of the downfall of nations or rulers who were guilty of godlessness or lawlessness, and who paid for their deeds by defeat and therefore punishment. The desecration of sanctuaries, the shedding of innocent blood, bestial behavior, and the betrayal of pre-fixed arrangements form the major categories of outrage, and in their turn Illyrians, Gauls, minor Greek states which oppose Achaia, Aetolia, Sparta, the Carthaginians, the kings of Macedon, Egypt, and other Eastern nations are accused of one or another of these transgressions,[169] and each is requited for such deeds. For their aggressions against Rome, the Illyrians and Gauls suffer in defeat (II,xi–xii, and cf. I,vi,5–6, vii,5; III,iii,5, and cf. II,xx,7); the Mantineans, for their betrayal of Achaia, experienced the fitting enslavement of their males (II,lviii,4–10, 12); the savage Cynaetheans received a "deserved fate" at the hands of the Aetolians (IV,xix,13–xx,3). For their unscrupulous policies, quite unworthy of imitation, the Aetolians and the Spartans bore the greatest calamities (xxvii,8; cf. 1–10), especially through Philip and then through Rome; and Philip V himself, who rivalled even the Aetolians in his impieties (cf. V,xi,1), was eventually punished by Fortune or heaven after he declared war on the Romans (XXIII,x,2, 4, 12–15). Before Philip's kingdom fell, however, the Carthaginians had paid dearly in the Hannibalic War. In the words of Cornelius Scipio's speech after Zama, the gods had given victory to the defenders, not to the unjust aggressors or treaty-breakers, and Fortune had quite changed affairs since Hannibal's invasion of Italy (XV,viii,1–5, and cf. 9; xv,1).

Polybius applied this kind of interpretation to individuals as well as to states,[170] though the individuals concerned were frequently powerful representatives of groups. In many cases the moral worth of a society hinged on such representatives. The instance of Lysicus the Aetolian is memorable: after he was slain the Aetolians were able at last to live in concord,

> so great it seems is the power exercised by men's natures that not only armies and cities, but national groups, and in fact all the different peoples which compose the whole world, experience the extremities of either misfortune or prosperity, owing to the good or bad character of a single man. (XXXII,iv,2)

With individuals, of course, retribution most frequently took the form of an appropriate death. Justice was satisfied by the ugly death of evil men, as in the case of the ephors who unlawfully placed Lycurgus on the Spartan throne (IV,lxxxi,5), or of Apelles the Macedonian and others who, for their outrageously false charges against Aratus, were forced to commit suicide (IV,lxxxvii,

169. E.g., II,viii,13, xix,9, IV,xvii,10–2, xviii,10, xxv,4ff., xxxv,3f., lxii,2ff., V,ix,1–4, x,8, VII,xiv,3, XIII,xi,1ff., XV,i,7f., XXII,xvii,5, XXX,xxvi,8f.

170. And cf. I,lxxxiv,10, lxxviii–lxxxiv, XXXVI,xvii, XXXVIII,iii,7–11, for whole regions.

10–1, V,xxvii,5–9; cf. IV,lxxvi, lxxxii–vii). To the list we may add Agathocles, friend of Ptolemy Philopator, who had engaged in reckless and murderous intrigue (XV,xxvia,1–2); Scopas the Aetolian, who had perpetrated many of the Aetolian League's impious and lawless policies, and who had transferred his criminal activity to the Middle East (XVIII,liv,6–12, and cf. XIV,v,1; xiv,4; XV,xxva,15; XVI,xxxix,1–2, etc.); and Orophernes, king of Cappadocia, who lost both his kingdom and his life on account of his passion (XXXII,xi,1). Losses other than death, admittedly, could be experienced by the guilty, but the actualization of the same retributive principles was implied.[171]

In a variety of other ways the lives of individuals disclosed the workings of a moral order. Once, when discussing treachery, Polybius enunciated the rule that

> not a single man ever betrays a town or an army or a fort without being found out, but even if any be not detected at the actual moment, the progress of time discovers them all in the end. (XVIII,xv,7)

Here he skirted the difficulty of a seemingly inoperative moral order by making a standard qualification: on occasion one had to wait for justice to be satisfied. The obvious difficulty surrounding the idea of fitting deaths also drew a stock solution: the unfortunate deaths of valorous men were inspirational and glorious (cf. III,cxvi,9–13, XVI,ix,1–2, XXX,vii,3–4, XXXVIII,i,7). Still another loophole he accepted was that resort to violence by worthy men need not constitute impiety, but could be a work of correction and discipline meriting admiration (II,lvi,14–15).

For Polybius, therefore, the historian had the onerous task of locating the worthy and unworthy in human affairs. He had to interpret how the outcome of events was in keeping with, or causally connected with, given moral conditions. This work was not taken on simply for the sake of ethics, but mainly for the cause of political success; the lessons of history taught both goodness and effectiveness, for these were part and parcel of one and the same virtue.

## III. POLYBIUS ON THE SPECIAL CASE OF ROME

What of the remarkable accomplishments of Rome? According to Polybius, what is their full bearing on the recurrent operation of retributive principles? First we must reassert that régimes could collapse on account of their moral unworthiness, not just because of natural decay or reversed fortune. Not only were Carthage, Macedon, and Hellas punished when they were conquered by Rome, but Polybius considered long-past downfalls in this light as well. He evidently accepted traditional interpretations of Xerxes' failures and Alexander's achievements as retributions for Persian outrages (V,x,8; cf. XXXVIII,ii,1–5), and on two occasions he associated Sparta's loss of Greek hegemony with her overambitious aggressiveness (VI,xlviii,8, XXXVIII,ii,7). On the other hand, the

171. E.g., XIII,v,4–6, XXIII,x,12–6, XXXI,ix,1–4, XXXII,xv,1–14, XXXIII,vii,1–3.

Romans had achieved an unprecedented greatness where others had failed, and for Polybius that had much to do with their virtue.

Now he wished to insist that Rome came only very slowly to imperial overlordship,[172] that initially she had no designs for world but only for an Italian supremacy (VI,1,6), and that her search for greater power emerged from the necessity of defending herself against intense foreign aggression (I,xii,7, and cf. iii,10; lxiii,9; III,cxviii,9). We have noted how Polybius highlighted the condition of balance between Rome and Carthage during the First Punic War; it was part of his message in Bk. I to affirm that the Romans in Sicily were not there as aggrandizers (and there may be an implicit contrast here with Athenian aggression and the Sicilian Expedition).[173] This same theme was carried still further. Hannibal was characterized as the aggressor who invaded Italy (Bk. III), while Rome had to defend her very existence at Cannae (III,cxviii,5–6). Philip V was culpable in declaring war on Rome (cf. XXIII,x,2–4), while Rome was justified in condemning his outrages (XXII,xiii,6–xiv,9).

Rome was the "great exception" once again, this time from the ethical point of view. That assumption is nowhere more evident than in Polybius' treatment of Cornelius Scipio, whom he deemed comparable to Sparta's Lycurgus (cf. X,ii,9–13). Scipio had subjected the greater part of the world to Rome and could have obtained royal power anywhere he chose, but he excelled all others in "greatness of mind" and put loyalty to his country before the enticements of fortune (X,xl,7–9; cf. 6). According to Polybius, Scipio deserved admiration for his incredible foresight (cf. esp. X,v–xvii), but especially for his moderation in power, for he neither committed outrage nor succumbed to insolence (cf. XV,iv, 7–12, v,8, xvii,4, XXXI,xxv,8). In Polybius' treatment of the battle of Zama, the magnanimity of Scipio's Roman policy and the guilt of Carthage were heavily contrasted (XV,xvii,3–4, 6).[174] But in any case Scipio was a product of a virtuous polity. A just moderation dictated Rome's international dealings (cf. XVIII, xxxvi,5–xxxvii,12); there was a persistent adherence to duty among her soldiers (VI,xxxvii,12; liv,4–lv,5, and cf. I,xvii,1; III,lxxv,8; IX,iii,6; etc.); she had the ability to adapt and recover in times of vicissitude (esp. VI,ii,5–7, and cf. III,lxxxv,10; cxviii,9, etc.); and she was even the liberator of enslaved states, a rôle which, when Greece and Asia Minor were involved, recalled a time-honored cause from the time of the third Persian War (XXI,xxii,5–xxiii,12). Polybius was even prepared to condone Rome's exhaustive killing of the enemy (at least during the Hannibalic War), accepting it as a realistic means of inspiring terror (X,xv,4).

So the outstanding virtue of the Romans (their institutions included) made a vital contribution to their success. It could not be said that their achievement

172. In Zosimus *Historia nova* I,i,1. Was there inclusion of a statement about this slow development in the Polybian archeology?

173. Eisen, op. cit., pp. 156ff.; cf. Frg. XXVIII (157).

174. Also cf. I,lxxiv,1–3, II,vii,1–4, XV,xxi,1–4 (on non-Roman generals), X,xxxii,7–12 (on Marcellus).

was the product of blind chance (fortune as mere luck or coincidence); it was the result of merit and national purpose. Perhaps Fortune, as a rational, directing, even if unpredictable, governess, was their supporter, but Roman leaders had learned to be moderate under good fortune and to recover well in adversity.[175] On the other hand, it would be false to conclude that Polybius sided with the traditionalist patriotism which extolled Roman merit as supreme over fortune, and which opposed the way Grecizers ascribed Rome's imperial accomplishments to an incalculable force (cf. Chapter 4, sect. C). As usual, Polybius was eclectic, and it was no contradiction for him to acknowledge Roman merit before blind chance and at the same time to marvel at the ways of intelligent Fortune. Thus such apparently conflicting ideas as fortune, human purpose, and the overriding moral order of human affairs were loosely, but to Polybius' mind satisfactorily, accommodated to each other.

Here one may also reflect on Polybius' approach to boundaries and their violation. Certain passages remind one of Herodotus on such matters. Before Zama, for instance, Hannibal was made to salute Scipio:

> Would that neither the Romans had ever coveted any possessions outside Italy, nor the Carthaginians any outside Africa, for both these were very fine empires and empires of which it might be said on the whole that Nature herself had fixed their limits. (XV,vi,5)

Rome was exceptional, however, and because of Fortune's special permissions, because of Rome's superior institutions, because of the virtue of her men, she was granted what was unprecedented—"rule and mastery over the whole world" (cf. XXI,xvi,8). Polybius did not withhold an ethical justification for this special situation. If the Carthaginians, for example, had been the aggressors in crossing the Ebro, a crucial Iberian boundary, Rome, by contrast, was guiltless in traversing and acquiring control beyond it, in defence.[176] If Antiochus the Great had been the aggressor in Asia Minor (cf. esp. XXI,xiv,7), Rome was justified in a restrained entrance into Asia.[177] In fact, the offensive expansionism of the three major powers of Carthage, Macedonia,[178] and Seleucia was sufficient pretext to bring Rome well beyond Italy to Africa and Asia. From a moral point of view, then, Roman imperial activity was analogous to Alexander's chastisement of Persia (cf. V,x,8). But that was not Polybius' only way of looking at the boundary question. As a man with geographical interests, he gave a fascinating account of the Euxine Sea, contending that it would eventually be silted up and become a shallow fresh-water lake (VI,xlii,4, 6; cf. xl,5, 10). Was there a special reason for his preoccupation with this curious matter, as well as with the silting up of the Palus Maeotis (xl,8–9, xlii,4), or in other words with the geographical

175. Polybius would have concurred with Dio Cassius that Scipio, as the greatest exemplar of military virtue, "never trusted fortune unthinkingly for anything": *Hist. Rom.* XXI,xxvii,5; Polybius X,ii,5f., 13, iii,1, xxxiii,1–3, XV,xvi,6.; yet cf. Frg. XC (161).

176. III,vi,2f., xv,5, xxix; yet cf. III,xcvi,5.

177. XXI,xiv,3–7 (cf. Livy *Ab urbe* XXXVII,xxxv,5–7), xvi,8; cf. xi,2ff.

178. XXIII,x,3f.

point at which Europe and Asia almost met (cf. xliii,2)? Did he believe that even the processes of nature were denying Rome's world dominion to be a violation of established boundaries? That is a speculative but not unwarrantable suggestion, especially since Polybius was interested in natural as much as in purposive and suprahuman causes.

We must protest that the great moral exception of Rome did not deny the normative and recurrent processes of retribution. The same principles operated with worthy states as with unworthy ones, so that Roman virtue still formed part of the intricacy of moral reciprocities.[179] Moreover, Polybius understood virtue to be an important factor in the establishment of a great régime, while moral degeneration was crucial for its decline. If there had been a time when the great Macedonian monarchs Philip II, Alexander the Great, and Antigonus III had conspicuously avoided outrage against those whom they conquered (cf. V,ix,8–x,8), that was not true of the impious Philip V (x,9–xi,2), and thus the downfall of Macedon was commensurate with the ethical decline of her rulers.[180] This same notion of "change for the worse" was applied to Rome, though placed in the future. Polybius hinted that certain changes in his own day foreshadowed a more general Roman decay and collapse (see sect. A, pt. 2, ii). He scarcely managed to exonerate the Romans for appropriating the riches of Syracuse (IX,x,9–13), and toward the end of his work suggested that earlier Roman moderateness was disintegrating. Those who upheld the virtues associated with the Scipionic tradition were decreasing in number (cf. XVIII,xxxv, 1–2, 6, XXXI,xxv,5a–xxvi,10), and Rome's eventual conquest of Macedonia and Carthage carried new and disturbing implications for the future.

> For at first they had made war with every nation until they were victorious and until their adversaries had confessed that they must obey them and execute their orders. But they struck the first note of a new policy by their conduct to Perseus [Philip V's successor], in utterly exterminating the kingdom of Macedonia, and they had now completely revealed it by their decision concerning Carthage. For [at the beginning of the *Third* Punic War] the Carthaginians had been guilty of no immediate offence to Rome, but the Romans had treated them with irremediable severity, even though they had accepted all their conditions and consented to obey all their orders. (XXXVI,ix,6–8; cf. also XXXVIII,xx,3)

As with other great régimes which had been created by virtue but which overtested fortune, even though she was exceptional Rome would pay for her excesses. Polybius' view that Roman greatness was produced by both virtue and

179. In an interesting passage (V,lxxxviii,3) he indicated that although virtue and lack of virtue brought different measures of control over life, that was in accordance with the same reciprocal principles: "So great is the difference both to individuals and to states between carefulness and wisdom on the one hand and folly with negligence on the other, that in the latter case good fortune actually inflicts damage, while in the former disaster is the cause of profit." Cf. X,xxxiii,2–7; Frg. XXX (184).

180. Polybius' way of praising Hannibal is partly to explain the degree of his success: e.g., X,xxxiii,1–3, XV,xvi,1–5; cf. IX,xxii,1–10).

fortune was skirted by fatalism, by the foreboding that as Rome continued toward her end virtue would diminish and fortune hold sway.[181]

The defender of the moral order was inevitably didactic in his approach to events; history taught how men ought to behave and what were the recurrent consequences of evil and virtue. Before Polybius, however, various Hellenistic historians had taken the workings of retribution to absurd or quasi-mechanical lengths. Polybius himself is important for having such a relatively critical approach. He boldly attacked Timaeus for contriving punishments to suit the men he reckoned evil (XII,xiib,1–3) and insisted that Timaeus had made these men more guilty than either the facts or the nature of their deaths indicated (xiii,1–xv,7).[182] Against Phylarchus he protested that the historian must praise good conduct and not just dwell on evil and its consequences (II,lx,3, 6; cf. also II,lvi,3–5, lix). For his own part, Polybius strove to establish canons of interpretation which did justice to the available data, yet which were at the same time paradigmatic and instructive. If the facts did not seem to accord with his presuppositions about the moral order, he either suggested possible solutions or simply raised questions. One way of providing a solution to a difficulty was to put it in its proper context, or, as we have said before, to reckon with the fact that subsequent events put an entirely different complexion on earlier situations. Thus the reader might be stunned that the evil Perseus defeated the Romans while defending his throne (in 169 BC), but Polybius eagerly pointed out that the wrath of the gods was destined to fall on Macedonia (XXXVI,xvii,14–15).[183] Unlike some of his cruder predecessors, furthermore, Polybius did not insist on a one to one ratio between the crime of any protagonist and the recognizable punishment. He readily acknowledged that some men, such as Hermeias the Seleucid (V,lvi,13) and Agathocles, friend of Ptolemy Philopator (XV,xxxiii,6), died deaths not adequate to their evildoing. In these particular cases, nevertheless, he went out of his way to stress that the relatives and associates of these men perished with them (V,lvi,14–15, XV,xxxiii,7–13), so that the events still had moral intelligibility. Again, on one occasion he discussed a most unfortunate victim of treachery. Achaeus the Seleucid satrap had provided against every contingency and yet he failed to escape death. Polybius felt bound to extract a moral meaning from this awkward case:

> The event created a general feeling of pity and pardon for the victim, while his betrayers were universally condemned and detested. (VIII,xxx,9; cf. 1–8)

Polybius was therefore more cautious and subtle in his ethical interpretations than those before him. There were even times when he virtually admitted that

181. Cf. below, Chapter 4, sect. C for post-Polybian discussion of these issues; Kajanto, op. cit., pp. 92ff. for background.

182. See P. Pédech, "Introduction" to *Polybe: Histoire livre XII*, Paris, 1961, pp. xxii, xxxi, for discussion.

183. Polybius could have ascribed Perseus' momentary victory to fortune, i.e., if Diodorus reflects him as a source in *Bib.* XXX,x,1.

he did not have the answers (cf. XVI,xxxii,5 and XXXII,iv,3)! Perhaps he was not so "unflagging in his production of evidence for heavenly justice" as such a writer as Diodorus Siculus,[184] but that has much to do with his rather profound insistence that the ethical meaning of events should be interpreted as much as possible from "the reasons and purposes" of the doers, and not represented as if history was simply at the mercy of external, superhuman agencies (II,lvi,16; cf. 13–15).

Despite the complicated nature of Polybius' approach, it is hard to deny that to elicit the continual manifestation of moral governance was one important means of asserting that history repeated itself. While recognizing his interest in the considerable variety of human experiences,[185] one must return again and again to his presuppositions about the general face of events, about types of dramatic situations, and about governing principles. Polybius was probably trained as a rhetorician, and though placing truth before rhetorical embellishment (XII,xxva,5–xxvb, 4; cf. also II,lvi,10ff.), he had a feeling for incidents possessing universal and paradigmatic qualities (and thus having affinities with the rhetorician's stock of pertinent examples).[186] He did not write only to edify, but to affirm something of practical importance about the nature of history.

All the reciprocal models we have discussed, indeed, either carry utilitarian implications or simply presuppose that behind variety and particularity lie the typical and the similar. With Polybius above all, we find that they fall into a whole body of doctrine about historical recurrence which undergirds his work. In his writing we have seen how cyclic and reciprocal frames, moral teaching and political analysis, even a variety of causal explanations, have become interrelated in a complex, imaginative methodology.

## C. Other models of historical recurrence

There are some conceptions of historical repetition in classical historical thought which cannot be termed either cyclo-alternating or reciprocal. Chief among these are conventional *metabolē* theory, and the appeal to the permanent traits of human nature.

### *Conventional* metabolē *theory*

#### I. GENERAL

A widely-adopted approach to change in human affairs was probably born in Sophistic circles (Chapter 1, sect. C), and it was largely used to explain political change, especially the degeneration of governments. Descriptions and explanations of deterioration were couched in ethical terms, and a vocabulary of

184. R. Drews, "Diodorus and His Sources" in *American Journal of Philology* LXXXVIII, 1962, p. 385; see below, Chapter 4, sect. G. Diodorus developed Polybius' notion of renown and infamy in posterity as it was connected with the moral order: see, e.g., *Bib.* XIV,i,2f., XXIX,xviii.

185. E.g., I,i,1ff., xxxv,9f., III,iv, XII,xxvb,2f.

186. Pédech, *Méthode*, pp. 42f.

*metabolē* (change) gained currency. According to the *metabolē* theory the causes of erosion usually lay with rulers. It was they who turned an order of lawfulness and political responsibility into a régime of injustice, lawlessness, and depravity. The attitudes of unworthy rulers were frequently characterized in terms of arrogance, impiety, or greed. Deterioration in the form of civil disorder and faction fighting was often termed *stasis*.[187] This way of thinking, this gnomic combination of the moralistic and the phenomenological, has persisted even to our own day, although it has become intermixed with biblical and Christian beliefs about sin and injustice. As it presupposes typical factors and conditions in political decline, this is a form of recurrence thinking.

Doctrines emerged as to the typical forms of constitutional *metabolē*—from kingship to tyranny, aristocracy to oligarchy, popular government to mob rule (to recall our previous analyses in Chapter 1); and there was also talk about political changes as the result of plain boredom or the desire for change itself.[188] The recurrence of such changes, however, was not necessarily tied to cyclo-alternating or reciprocal processes. In the Polybian cycle of governments, admittedly, constitutional change was clearly understood as part of a cyclic movement, and there is no gainsaying that the emphasis on civic deterioration could be associated with the idea of natural decay and of an upset balance. As a notion of recurrence in its most basic form, however, nothing more was implied than that certain changes, separated in space and time, were similar and subject to the same kind of delineation. One should be wary of ascribing to the Greeks and Romans any doctrine of historical laws (as we find them in the writings of Comte or Marx or Hempel). Reference to rules, to general truths, or to the recognition of reappearing or recurrent general conditions is more appropriate.

## II. POLYBIUS

We have previously discussed how in his sixth book Polybius analyzed natural transformations from one constitution into another and placed constitutional changes in a set causal chain. In Bk. VI, however, he spent little time in justifying his thesis factually or in annotating it with reference to states and historical contexts. In any case, he probably lacked the relevant data to effect such a systematic "apology," although elsewhere in his work he did cite separate instances of constitutional change, mainly those belonging to the period 220–145 BC. Perhaps the changes were considered in parallel rather than linearly, but almost every case is significantly reconcilable with the *Anacyclōsis* or with the assumed relationship between internal processes of change and the fluctuations of external politics. To begin with kingship: he took pains to point out that where this constitutional form persisted it did so through the *natural* kingly qualities of the rulers.[189] Thus when Philip V underwent a moral change

187. Esp. Ryffel, op. cit., pp. 49, 70, 82, etc.

188. E.g., Polybius XXXI,xxv,1–8, XXXVI,xiii,3; cf. Plato *Leg.* VII,798C–D; Sallust *Catiline* XXXVII,1–3; Velleius Paterculus *Historiae Romanae* I,xvi,2–5.

189. E.g., VIII,x,10, xi,1, xxii,1, XXVIII,xxi,4f., xxii,5.

for the worse, he lost the good characteristics natural to a king (cf. X,xxvi,7–8, XIII,ii,1), and became a tyrant (cf. IV,lxxvii,4, V,xi,6, VII,xi,1, 10).

The change from kingship to tyranny, the most widely known form of political transformation, was hardly forgotten in the *Historiae* outside Bk. VI. Philip occupies most of the attention, and it is his change of habits and style of dress (cf. X,xxvi,1–4) which especially recalls the picture of royalty's degeneration in VI,vii,5, 7.[190] There are other cases (cf. II,xlvii,3, VIII,xxii,3, XIV,xii,3–6) of this transformation as a typical one. Even with Perseus' succession to Philip by hereditary right and with the former's apparent continuation of the Macedonian monarchy, Polybius seemed bent on avoiding a vitiation of his anacyclic theory. His solution was that tyrannies could quite easily become entrenched (XIII,vi,2; cf. VIII,xxxv,6), and also that at the beginning of their reigns men who later became tyrants often appeared to offer the hope of good things [so XV,xxiv,4 (xxiva,1) on Philip; XXV,iii,1–8, and cf. XXXVI,xvii,14, on Perseus].[191]

Outside the case of Rome, however, one looks in vain for an example of a state which undergoes a number, let alone a whole series, of transitions along the anacyclic path. In his narrative Polybius almost invariably mentioned one kind of shift at a time. Perhaps he referred to multiple political change in Spartan history from Cleomenes III to Nabis, yet the sequence of transitions only partially followed the cycle of governments. The external intervention of Antigonus Gonatas in Sparta's affairs complicated matters, and in this case Polybius was considering a rather special line of change—the degeneration of the Spartan *mixed* constitution into tyranny.[192] As for other individual changes in the *Historiae*, concrete examples of transformation from tyranny into aristocracy and from aristocracy into oligarchy are lacking (even within Bk. VI as it now stands). The replacement of oligarchy by democracy also seems to be forgotten.[193] Before he had settled on a theory of constitutional change, moreover, Polybius put Achaian democracy after the tyranny of Ogygus' sons (II,xli,5), and democracy in Greater Hellas after a period of *stasis*.[194]

However, when one examines mutations covered in the tail end of the anacyclic course, matters become different. In keeping with both his own theory and the Thucydidean diagnosis, he ascribed the dissolution of Athenian democracy, as well as the downfall of the Theban constitution (VI,xliv,3–6, 9), to the contentiousness of the populace. And in commenting on the Tarentine affairs of 213–212 BC Polybius came close to describing the multi-staged path from democracy to mob rule and on to the kingship:

190. Cf. XXIX,xiii,1f. on Genthius of Illyria also. That Polybius did not conceive Philip to change into a demagogue or "populist" (as against a tyrant), see D. Mendels, "Polybius, Philip V and the Socio-Economic Question in Greece" in *Ancient Society* VIII, 1977, pp. 167f.

191. Cf. XVIII,xxxiii,4–8, XXV,iii,1–4, discussed in sect. A, pt. 1(ii).

192. See Excursus 1.

193. It is possibly referred to in VII,x,1 (Messene).

194. The latter case could have been explained away by appealing to the unexpected (external) destruction of the Italian cities' leading citizens (II,xxxix,2; cf. 5f.).

Whenever freedom has long predominated, then there is a feeling of satiety toward the present conditions, and next comes a search for a despot [cf. VI,ix,9] who, once found, becomes a thing shortly hated again because the change is to the worse. (VIII,xxiv,2 [xxvi,2])

Here one discovers a picture of general constitutional decay which supplements the analysis of VI,lvii,6–9, with its sequence oligarchy/democracy/mob rule. On the other hand, a different principle of change was invoked. We find the idea of an insidious reaction to surfeit, a notion evident in earlier Greek reflections on society, which was also voiced nearer his own time.[195] Concerning mob rule, Polybius' handling of Cynaetha in 220 BC is interesting. He depicted Cynaetha as a state ruled by the mob, with "constant massacres, expulsions, robbery of goods, and confiscation of lands" (IV,xvii,4; cf. xx–xxii), thus using language reminiscent of the crucial passage in VI,ix,9 about the eve of complete constitutional breakdown.[196]

As Polybius took constitutional decay to be prevalent among states conquered by Rome, one justifiably expects references to mob rule, demagogy, *stasis*, and despotism to come more and more frequently from his pen. Take Molpagoras, demagogue of Cius: he flattered the populace, incited the mob against the rich, killed some of the latter, banished others whose property he confiscated and distributed among the people, and then speedily attained to "monarchic power" (VI,ix,6–9, XV,xxi,1–2).[197] Polybius also remarked on internal troubles in the democracies of Boeotia (XX,vi,3, vii,4, XXII,iv,1–3, XXVII,i,8–9), Aetolia (XXVIII,iv,13, XXX,xi,6; cf. XXI,xxxi,8–11), Achaia (XXIV,x,10), the rest of Greece (XV,xxi,3–8, XXII,vi,7; cf. XXXVIII,xii,5–6, xvi,7, xviii,7ff.), and, in accordance with the analysis in Bk. VI, Carthage.[198] The tendency toward decay within democracies is invariably connected with the unruliness of the masses, and a *stasis* results from factionalism and demagogic ambition.

In review, then: the constitutional mutations of the *Anacyclōsis* were occasionally isolated in the Polybian narrative. Not that they were individually elicited just to confirm anacyclic theory. *Metabolē* theory comprised an independent body of historical explanation, and when Polybius employed its ethical language—when he alluded, for example, to the excessive pride of the Tarentines, the greed of Molpagoras, the insolence of Hasdrubal[199]—he was using ideas of recurrence which stood in their own right, even if he desired to relate them with consistency to his natural cycle of governments, as well as to his belief in the repeated actualization of the moral order.

195. E.g., Herodotus *Hist.* VIII,77, Lucretius *Rer. nat.* V,170–3, 1412–5; cf. (on boredom and change for its own sake) above, sect. C, pt. 1(i). The notion of change being brought about by a succeeding generation (cf. Bk. VI) is distinguishable from, though hardly unrelated to, the above conception (cf. II,xxi,1f.).

196. Walbank, *Commentary*, vol. 1, p. 657.

197. I differ here from Walbank, "Spartan Ancestral Constitutions," pp. 304f.

198. See Chapter 1, sect. E, pt. 2; cf. XXXVI,vii,3–5, XXXVIII,viii,11–5.

199. VIII,xxiv,2a, XV,xxi,1b, XXXVIII,viii,13 and cf. XX,vi,2f.

### *The appeal to the permanent traits of human nature*

This second non-cyclical, non-reciprocal approach to historical recurrence has a renowned locus classicus. Toward the beginning of his history Thucydides boldly asserted that his creation was written to last forever. It was not just for the benefit of the immediate public but for any who wanted

> to understand clearly what has happened and what will happen, when, in accordance with human nature (or things), events like this and of this kind will occur again. (*Hist.* I,22[4])

By "human nature" Thucydides did not simply mean the personal characteristics and dispositions of men. In another famous passage, when analyzing the civil disorders which convulsed the Hellenic world, he contended that

> many calamities fell upon the cities on account of this *stasis*, as will always be the case while human nature is what it is, although whether the situation remains at rest or admits of variation depends on what is brought to hand by each change of events. (III,82 [2]; cf. also 84)

In this second passage "human nature" appears to denote general patterns of political behavior, and in fact Thucydides' interest in group psychology or human nature in general outweighed his concern for the inner personalities of individuals.[200] What, then, are we to make of these two significant quotations?

Even if he guarded himself against any position approaching the doctrine of exact repetition, Thucydides was surely affirming the recurrence of historical phenomena. History repeated itself because certain enduring factors governing group behavior continually reasserted themselves; as human nature does not change, even if its historical expressions vary, the same sorts of event-complexes can recur at any time. The central implication of his statements, then, is not so much that human nature is repeated as that event-types are. Such event-types were taken to recur because human intentions were executed and changing circumstances handled in characteristically typical ways—with self-interest, fear, suspicion, and so on.

But what did Thucydides mean when he contended that events like those in his own history would occur again? Was he referring to portentous situations between the last date treated in his *magnum opus* (411 BC) and the time it was ready for circulation? Or was he of the opinion that the particular conflict he was handling, or at any rate a conflict rather like it, would recur in the distant future? Did he assume, furthermore, that there were no recurrences to be sighted among the very historical events he took so many pains in recounting? We know he intended to carry his narrative as far as 404 BC; if he had been writing as late as that, or still later, would he have been in a position to forecast yet another major struggle, emerging this time out of the Greek fear of Spartan

200. Esp. *Hist.* I,88ff., II,48–54, III,36–49, 82–4, V,85–113, VI,61f., VII,71 and cf. I,76, IV,61, V,105. Note, however, C. N. Cochrane, *Thucydides and the Science of History*, London, 1929, p. 19.

domination?[201] It is not easy to offer answers to such questions with confidence. What remains important, however, is that he put a special premium on the study of human nature. Social behavior patterns and psychological characteristics were treated as separable phenomena, not just as reflections of a moral plan in history. After Thucydides, psychological observations became the stock-in-trade of the historian, and even if many of his successors were more interested in placing psychological responses within the context of the moral order, the appeal to the permanent traits of human nature merits independent consideration as a form of recurrence thinking. No notion of regular recurrence, though, seems entailed in Thucydides' position. If anything, it has its best analogy in diagnostic medicine, and without wishing to lend unreserved support to C. N. Cochrane's thesis of the relationship between the "scientific" historian Thucydides and the Hippocratic school,[202] I think it fair to assert that Thucydides' work is dotted throughout with what may be called case histories, useful for any unspecified and therefore relatively unpredictable time in the future.

In its special Thucydidean form this kind of recurrence thinking made little or no appearance in the pages of Polybius. However, in that he extracted practical lessons from history which he considered to be applicable for the future (cf. esp. IX,x,13, XII,xxvb,2–3, xxve,5–6),[203] in that he made general observations about human nature (about the psychology of men under stress, for instance,[204] or the animalization of men under certain extreme conditions),[205] and in that he presented patterns of social behavior paradigmatically,[206] he appealed both to the permanency of human nature and to the recurrence of characteristic behavior patterns. This was in keeping with his constitutional theory, for human motivations are distinguishable from naturo-biological operations in the *Anacyclōsis* even though they were bound up in the same process,[207] and it also remained in keeping with his approach to altered fortunes and the moral order, since these matters involved assessments of character.

The classical heritage, we may therefore reaffirm, contained a rich store of recurrence paradigms, and it is certainly false to generalize about them as cyclical when so much else remains. Polybius' history best illustrates the genuine

201. Cf. Diodorus *Bib.* XIV,vi,1–3 on the year 404 BC. Most commentators, however, refer the comment to the distant future: see, e.g., A. W. Gomme, *A Historical Commentary on Thucydides*, Oxford, 1945, vol. 1, pp. 149f. (mentioning the Second World War!); P. J. Fliess, *Thucydides and the Politics of Bi-Polarity*, Baton Rouge, 1966, passim (mentioning the Cold War!); cf. G. B. Grundy, *Thucydides and the History of His Age*, London, 1911, p. 8 (on historical cycles).

202. Cochrane, *Thucydides*, passim.

203. Cf. I,lxxi,7, II,iv,5, ix,6, lvi,9f., IV,xi,7f., xxxiv,2, etc., for cases not so connected with Thucydides' stance.

204. E.g., II,xxxv,8–10, IV, viii, xxi, XI,ii,10f., xxv,7, xxviii,2, XVI,x,2–4; cf. IV,xxx,4–6, xxxviii,10, xxi,6.

205. E.g., I,lxv,8, lxvii,6, lxxxi,7–10, II,xxx,4, X,xli,7, XIII,vii, XVI,xxiv,4, XXXII,iii,7; cf. VI,v,6–9, ix,9, xxi,6.

206. Cf. esp. Roveri, op. cit., pp. 112–40 for an excellent discussion.

207. See above, Chapter 1, sect. B, pt. 2 for the distinctions here; cf. K. E. Petzold's review of Eisen's *Polybiosinterpretationen* in *Gnomon* XLII, 1970, p. 389.

diversity of recurrence conceptions. At the risk of appealing to a notion of recurrence, one might rank his writings as a high point or maturation point of this kind of thinking, since he drew such a variety of ideas together. Moreover, although the *Historiae* hardly contain allusions to every known and every possible node of relevance, they reflect a distinctive Greco-Roman concern for putting intelligibility into historical change and thus equiping men for action.

We have found still more than this about classical historical thought. Especially (though not exclusively) in connection with ethics, appeals to recurrent configurations or operative principles afforded a way of disclosing "the meaning of history."[208] Images of recurrence, in the main, were used reflectively in historiography; events were colored by these images through hindsight more than by the judgment of immediate involvement. An historian would usually survey a broad complex, such as a great war or the emergence of a great power (happenings which have a certain "recognizability"), and he was then left to elicit the profiles, the special meanings and causal factors in particular events and situations within his chosen compass.

It is unsatisfactory to describe Greco-Roman historical thought as "humanistic," for the ancients could emphasize more than one principle of causality, and were commonly preoccupied with extra-human or even divine principles as the key to history. In this crucial respect Greco-Roman historiographical preconceptions were not dissimilar to those of the other intellectual tradition which has had such a decisive impact on Western thought—the biblical tradition. If we are accustomed to the forced Greek-cyclical/Judeo-Christian-linear dichotomy, it may well come as a surprise that in the biblical tradition as well, history was commonly endowed with intelligibility and theological significance in recurrence terms. Thus we may now turn both backward and sideways to the complex world of biblical and ancient Near Eastern literature.

## *Addendum:* Special cases of recurrence

There is a motley of Greco-Roman recurrence ideas which do not fit neatly into any of the previously-stated categories, but which form a miscellany concerned with very particular instances of recurrence. An historian may have perceived, for example, that two events possessed something special in common to warrant his own pointed comments, as did Florus (second century AD) when he noted that the assissination of Caesar by Brutus was like the earlier Brutus' expulsion of Tarquinius Superbus.[209] Again, an historian could describe one

208. K. Löwith, *Meaning in History*, Chicago, 1949, pp. 4–9, though he overcontrasts Greek and Christian approaches to uniqueness; for reappraisal cf., e.g., Herodotus *Hist.* I,60, VII,20, VIII,105, 135, IX,64, 78; Thucydides *Hist.* I,1(3), 21, 138, II,8, IV,40; Theopompus, Frg. 19 (*FGH*, pt. 2b, pp. 529f.); Polybius *Hist.* I,i,51, lxiii,4–8, lxxxviii,7, II,xxxv,2, xxxvii,6, III,ciii,4, cvii,9, VI,ii,3, VIII,ii,4, XIV,v,13f.

209. *Epitome* II,xvii,7. Also for parallel occurrences on the same date or day, see, e.g., Herodotus *Hist.* VII,166; Timaeus in Dionysius of Halicarnassus *Arch.* I,lxxiv,1; Ennius *Annales*, Frg. 501; and note Josephus *Bellum Judaicum* VI,267f. and cf. *Antiquities* XII,vii,6 on the destructions and desecrations of the Jerusalemite temple.

agent's behavior as a conscious imitation of the acts of another, like Theseus duplicating the labors of Hercules.[210] A related preoccupation here would be the historian's encouragement of his readers to emulate the noble deeds of the past,[211] and so effect recurrence by such reenactment. To take a third case, there might be at least two parallel sets of phenomena which teach the same lesson and which even share special similarities. Some of Plutarch's observations in the renowned lives may be noted. Not atypical of Plutarch are those lessons he drew from a comparison of Demetrius I and Mark Antony, when he concluded that "Both were insolent in prosperity, both abandoned themselves to luxuries and enjoyments," and so both "had only themselves to thank for their final disasters."[212] He occasionally became much more specific, however, as in a fascinating passage where he compared the careers of Demosthenes and Cicero:

> The divine power seems originally to have designed Demosthenes and Cicero upon the same plan, giving them many similarities in their natural characters, such as their passion for distinction and their love of liberty in civil life, and their want of courage in dangers and war, and at the same time also to have added many accidental resemblances. I think there can hardly be found two orators, who, from small and obscure beginnings, became so great and mighty; who both contested with kings and tyrants; both lost their daughters, were driven out of their country, and returned with honor; who, flying from thence again, were both seized upon by their enemies, and at last ended their lives with the liberty of their countrymen. (*Vit. Demosth.* iii,2–3)[213]

There remains concern here for overriding principles, yet at the same time the interest in striking resemblances between particular events and characters, and in resemblances elicited for their own sake, comes out very forcefully. Such parallels could be drawn between more normative event-complexes and biographical details, as when Thucydides subtly likened the Persian invasion of Hellas and the Athenian expedition to Sicily as two cases in which the diminishing of supplies was a crucial factor (*Hist.* VI,33[5–6]).

This miscellany does not merely include the obvious forms of parallelism. Two events may have some similarity although they are antithetical to each other, and recurrence may still be suggested. When Herodotus, for example, reported how Xerxes lashed the unpredictable Hellespont, the reader was meant immediately to be reminded of a similar act by Cyrus, who, on preparing for his victory over Babylon, "punished" the river Gyndes, which had drowned his horse, by rather sensibly dividing it into hundreds of passable channels (cf. *Hist.* I,189–90, VII,34–36). Again, an idea of historical repetition may be conveyed by depicting history's protagonists as special human types: for example, the comparable

210. Diodorus *Bib.* IV,lix,1; cf. I,ii,4, XII,ix,6, XVI,xliii,3; Plutarch *Vit. Thes.* xxix,3, *Vit.* (*Poplicola and Solon Compared*) i,1.

211. Plutarch *Vit. Tim.* i,1; Livy *Ab urbe* I,*proem.* 10, etc.; cf. (among the rhetoricians) Aspasia(?) in Plato *Menex.* 246D ff.; Isocrates *Paneg.* xii ff.; Aeschines *Contra Tim.* xxv–xxvi; etc.

212. *Vit.* (*Demetrius and Antony Compared*) iii,1ff.

213. Also *Vit.* (*Aristides and Marcus Cato Compared*) i,1. On relevant background to Plutarch's *Lives*, see D. A. Russell, "On Reading Plutarch's Lives" in *Greece and Rome* Ser. 2, XIII, 1966, pp. 144–9.

personality types in Herodotus, King Croesus who became adviser to Cyrus, the Artabanus who counselled Xerxes—the two mentors held to parallel values, and both were faced with the same kinds of situations (esp. I,207–8, VII,10, 16, 46–51). In Thucydides, Pericles (the ideal democratic politician) and Cleon (the demagogic bête noire) find their counterparts in the two different approaches of the Sicilian politicians Hermocrates and Athenagoras.[214] And in Xenophon one should note recurrent references to those good commanders who hold in common a concern for strong military discipline.[215]

Finally, there remains the complex area associated with such notions as restoration, renewal, rebirth, and the like.[216] Such conceptions could be integrated with cyclical frameworks—with doctrines of returning Ages, for instance—but they can be placed in greater isolation. When these ideas are taken as a separate bundle, of course, not all of them have real significance for us. Aristotle's assertions that Theramenes (at the end of the fifth century BC) wished to restore the old Solonian constitution in Athens (*Ath. pol.* xxiv), or Augustus' claim that he himself restored many of the customs of his ancestors (*Monumentum Ancyranum* viii), do not strictly disclose presuppositions or views about historical recurrence. On the other hand, occasional passages concerning restoration, renewal, reestablishment, etc., persuade us that the writer does harbor relevant preconceptions, as with Dio Cassius' (flor. 194–205 AD) claim that upon Julius Caesar's arrival in Rome (43 BC), "everything once done in the days of Sulla occurred also at this time,"[217] and with the contentions of "Vopiscus" (fourth century) that Augustus "restored" Rome's old greatness after a period of "wasting away" (*Vita Cari* III,1).

Some of these miscellaneous ideas find a place in Polybius. Certainly he was fascinated by parallelism or close similarity. He drew out the remarkable similarities between Epameinondas' march on Sparta and Hannibal's march on Rome, both of these strategies being unexpectedly thwarted when the moment of victory was nigh (IX,viii,1–ix,4). He paralleled Philip II and Alexander with Philip V and Perseus by contending that what each father had planned each son put into effect (XXII,xviii,10). And to take a horizontal rather than a linear case, he remarked on the extraordinary likenesses between those men who controlled the destinies of Carthage and Hellas at the moment of their ruin—Hasdrubal and Critolaus (XXXVIII,viii,14–15). In view of the connections forged between the Spartan and Roman polities in Bk. VI, it was natural that he should stress the close resemblances in the characters and principles of Cornelius Scipio Africanus and Lycurgus the legislator (X,ii,8), and he noted other such parallel sets

214. *Hist.* I,107, II,13, 22, 65, III,36–40, IV,21, 27ff., VI,32–40, 76–80, 99, etc.; cf. J. H. Finley, "The Unity of Thucydides' History" in *Athenian Studies* (*to W. S. Ferguson*), Cambridge, Mass., 1940, pp. 284–9.

215. See H. D. Westlake, *Essays on Greek Historians and Greek History*, Manchester, 1969, p. 207, for Xenophon on Hermocrates, Agesilaus, Teleutias, Ephicrates, and Jason.

216. Latin is replete with relevant verbs: *restauro*, *instauro*, *renovo*, *nascor*, *revirisco*, *reparo*, etc.

217. See *Hist. Rom.* XLVII,iii,2; cf. iii,1–v,1.

of political behavior (cf. XV,xxxv).[218] If he gives no example of any protagonist emulating a great man from the past, he clearly fosters the idea that "virtuous" deeds (in both the pragmatic and ethical senses) should be imitated, at least by the politically active.[219]

218. E.g., I,xxxi,4f., XVIII,xxxix,4, XXXVIII,viii,4.
219. E.g., II,lxi,3, X,xxi,4, XI,viii,7, XV,xxxvi,3f., XXII,xvi,3.

# Chapter 3

# Notions of Historical Recurrence in Luke and the Biblical Tradition

In editing documents from the period 336 BC–AD 337, Sir Ernest Barker compared the Polybian *Anacyclōsis* with chapter 7 of the contemporaneous Jewish tract Daniel. While admitting that the two writings shared "a scheme of world history, . . . a doctrine of change and a succession of epochs," Barker noted obvious differences. The anonymous author of Daniel certainly conceived external history as a succession of empires—four, to be specific—but he looked ahead to "the true end and consummation of history," the "divine cosmic event," rather than to the constant perpetuation of transitions "based on a principle." For the author of Daniel history itself has no "inner logic," and Barker considers his doctrine of succession to be "merely temporal," a doctrine which, being influenced by the Zoroastrian idea of fixed time periods, was "stamped on to historical vicissitudes rather than elicited from them."[1] As

1. Sir Ernest Barker (ed.), *From Alexander to Constantine: Passages and Documents Illustrating the History of Social and Political Ideas 336* BC–AD *337*, Oxford, 1956, p. 104; cf. p. 103. Daniel is almost unanimously dated to the late 160s BC.

Daniel was no piece of history-writing, this comparison is somewhat unfair, but at least it sets one thinking about the historical outlook of the monotheistic world behind our Western tradition. That world has not generally been celebrated for its ideas of historical recurrence, and one might well ask why we are considering the biblical heritage at all. Barker's allusions to succession and periodicity provide the first clues, but the detailed analysis of Jewish and early Christian historiography that follows will disclose many others.

We should begin with the admission that there exists a widely accepted contrast between the Greco-Roman cyclical and the Judeo-Christian linear approaches to time and history.[2] It is often contended that one great legacy of the Judeo-Christian tradition was the straight-line view of history, the view that history ran from Creation and God's first covenants with man to the future eschatological fulfillment of his promises. The "Greeks" or Greco-Roman ancients, by contrast, even when they write of catastrophes and cosmic conflagrations, are taken to acknowledge no such final and unrepeatable events. It is often supposed that theirs was a cyclic view of history, that they insisted on the eternal return of what had been before, while the Hebrews "thought the sequence of historical events" to be "a purposive movement towards a goal," something "non-recurrent, non-reversible and unique."[3] As we shall see, such a contrast should be eyed with caution. There also remains a related dichotomy between Hebrew linear thinking and non-Hebrew cyclicism, one created by those studying Near and Middle Eastern literature written prior to the movement of Hellenization. Yahwist rejection of nature worship and mythology, and of a time-view heavily influenced by belief in the annual and cyclical rejuvenation of the world order, has been highlighted by such leading writers as Mowinckel and Noth.[4] Their comparisons between biblical and "foreign"

2. E. Franck, *Philosophical Understanding and Religious Truth*, London, 1945, pp. 67ff.; A.-H. Chroust, "The Metaphysics of Time and History in Early Christian Thought" in *The New Scholasticism* XIX, 1945, pp. 329ff.; R. Niebuhr, *Faith and History*, New York, 1949, pp. 42ff.; K. Löwith, *Meaning in History*, pp. 4ff.; J. Baillie, *The Belief in Progress*, London, 1950, pp. 52ff.; T. Boman, *Das hebräische Denken in Vergleich mit dem griechischen*, Göttingen, 1954 edn. (ET, 1960), ch. 3; R. Bultmann, *History and Eschatology* (Gifford Lectures, 1955), Edinburgh, 1957, esp. pp. 5, 15; P. Tillich, *Systematic Theology*, London, 1964, vol. 3, pp. 374ff.; J. L. Russell, "Time in Christian Thought" in *The Voices of Time* (ed. Fraser), pp. 68f.; cf. C. Dawson, *Progress and Religion: An Historical Enquiry*, London, 1929, pp. 142ff.; J. MacMurray, *The Clue to History*, London, 1938, pp. 110f. For some qualifications see P. Vidal-Naquet, "Temps des dieux et temps des hommes: esai sur quelques aspects de l'expérience temporelle chez les grecs" in *Revue de l'Histoire des Religions* CLVII, 1960, pp. 55ff.; W. Eichrodt, "Heilserfahrung und Zeitverständnis im Alten Testament" in *Theologische Zeitschrift* XII, 1956, pp. 103ff. For some cogent criticisms of this contrast, see A. Funkenstein, *Heilsplan und natürliche Entwicklung: Gegenwartsbestimmung im Geschichtsdenken des Mittelalters*, Munich, 1965, p. 128 n. 24; A. Momigliano, "Time in Ancient Historiography" in *Quarto Contributa alla Storia degli Studi Classici e del Mondo Antico* (*Storia e Letteratura* CXV), Rome, 1969, pp. 13ff.; Ishanad Vempeny, *Inspiration in the Non-Biblical Scriptures*, Bangalore, 1973, pp. 135f., 175; G. A. Press, "History and the Development of the Idea of History in Antiquity" in *History and Theory* XVI, 1977, pp. 280ff.; cf. T. Driver, *The Sense of History in Greek and Shakespearean Drama*, New York, 1960, pp. 57f.; G. C. Starr, "Historical and Philosophical Time" in *History and Theory* VI, 1966, pp. 27f.

3. J. Barr, *Biblical Words for Time* (*Studies in Biblical Theology* XXXIII), London, 1962, p. 140.

4. S. Mowinckel, *He That Cometh* (ET), Oxford, 1959, pp. 151f.; M. Noth, "God, King and Nation" in *The Laws in the Pentateuch and Other Essays* (ET), Edinburgh, 1967, pp. 145–54, 164–7. On

conceptions concern a special and early context, yet they have strengthened the wedge between Greek and Hebrew views of history.

The real strength of this wedge, though, depends on Jewish eschatological ideas, and one should stress that expectations of an imminent end to history arose with post-Exilic Judaism, early Israelite historiography not being known either for its apocalypticism or for broad schematizations of world history. The concern of the Deuteronomic historian, for example, was to account for the circumstances facing Israel in his own day, at the time of the Babylonian exile (586 BC). Even the Chronicler, writing later during the restoration period, does not seem to look ahead to any conclusive occurrence, or to any "Day of Yahweh" with an eschatological complexion.[5] Now certainly anyone expecting an utterly decisive end to history would be precluded from speculating about the perpetual return of previous conditions,[6] but more limited teleologies—anticipations of a future restoration or establishment in power, for instance[7]—offer less support for a strong contrast between Hebrew and non-Hebrew conceptions. And even in the more apocalyptic positions, it must be realized that just because a given view of history may entail belief in the coming of an all-important end-time, it does not automatically follow that the view will be a non-cyclical one. The Zoroastrian picture of world (or cosmic) history is a case in point. Here the doctrine of the future final victory of Ahura Mazda over Ahriman is coupled with a notion of history's twelve successive Ages, each equal in length, and this notion Barker, for one, has no hesitation in calling cyclical.[8] Despite early Christian eschatology, moreover, Joachim Jeremias is happy to accept "for the New Testament the conception that world history proceeds in circular movements," since it contains so much talk of Ages (*aiōnes*).[9] Such comments as these naturally cast a shadow of doubt over a well-worn distinction.

On the other hand, there is some value in differentiating here between views of time or cosmic process and views of historical change. The ancient Hebrews

---

the "myth and ritual" or "pan-Babylonian" school (criticized by Noth for arguing that Hebrew attitudes under the monarchy were dominated by cyclical conceptions) see S. G. F. Brandon, "The Myth and Ritual Position Critically Considered" in *Myth, Ritual and Kingship: Essays on the Theory and Practice of Kingship in the Ancient Near East and Israel* (ed. S. H. Hooke), Oxford, 1958, pp. 284–8; H. Frankfort, *Kingship and the Gods: A Study of Ancient Near Eastern Religion as the Integration of Society and Nature* (An Oriental Institute Essay), Chicago, 1948, pp. 337ff.; Noth, loc. cit., pp. 149–72 [yet cf. his *History of Israel* (ET), London, 1960 edn., pp. 220f.]; G. von Rad, *The Message of the Prophets* (ET), London, 1968, pp. 83–8.

5. Mowinckel, op. cit., pp. 132f., 142–54; G. von Rad, *Message*, ch. 8, on the "Day of Yahweh" and its complicated history. On the two historians see below, sect. A, pt. 4, sect. B, pts. 1–2.

6. To that extent the arguments of O. Cullmann, in *Christ and Time: The Primitive Christian Conception of Time and History* (ET), London, 1962 edn., pp. 51–60, have to be taken seriously, and note the literature he cites.

7. E.g., 2 Sam. 7:13, 16 (carrying implications concerning the future reestablishment of monarchy); Hag. 2:6–9 (on the rebuilding of the temple).

8. Op. cit., p. 104. Pahlavi texts (trans. E. West), in *Sacred Books of the East* (ed. F. M. Müller), vol. 1, pt. 1 (Oxford, 1880), Bundahish, I, III, XXX, XXXIV; cf. H. Corbin, "Cyclical Time in Mazdaism and Ismailism" in *Man and Time: Papers from the Eranos Year Books*, London, 1958 (= *Eranos Jahrbücher* XX, 1951), pp. 115ff.

9. Cullmann, op. cit., p. 52; cf. J. Jeremias, *Jesus als Weltvollender*, Gütersloh, 1930, pp. 8ff.

and early Christians were clearly opposed to the belief in an eternal return. Admittedly, the Israelites participated in yearly festivals, and they could speak of the "return," the "coming around," or the "circuit" of seasons and natural periods.[10] But it is remarkable how they still managed to think historically when, for their immediate neighbors at any rate, human life was under the spell of "unhistorical, cyclically-oriented nature mythologies, and the magical ordinances of fate."[11] Furthermore, when late Jewish and early Christian thinkers came under the influence of Hellenistic philosophy, they refused to abandon themselves to the cyclical cosmologies and quasi-cosmological catastrophe theory of the time.[12] Such reactions against cyclic time and cosmology were bound to affect biblical historiography. After all, there are distinctive biblical attitudes toward key events and covenants in the past. The special achievements of heroes and rulers or the curiosity value of certain incidents counted far less for the monotheists of the Bible than the ways by which Yahweh had established a relationship with his people. To this extent at least, then, the Judeo-Christian-linear/Greek-cyclical contrast still has worth. We are going to maintain in this chapter, however, that paradigms of recurrence, including those of cycle and alternation, were certainly not foreign to Hebrew and early Christian interpretations of historical change.

To clarify important issues, it is useful to reflect on some recent arguments put forward by B. Albrektson. Surveying historiography in the ancient Near East, Albrektson is not prepared to ascribe any cyclical views to those Mesopotamian records so often compared with Old Testament histories. Putting aside the Babylonian New Year Festival and its parallels as of no real relevance to ancient attempts at interpreting historical events, he refuses to consider Mesopotamian notions of historical "undulations" (alternating fortunes, rise and fall, etc.) or schematizations into periods as cyclical notions.[13] One wonders, then, what he *would* consider to be a cyclical notion, and whether he would restrict it to an idea of exact cyclical repetition appealing to Stoic or neo-Pythagorean systems, or to views of history with the strong implication of an eternal return. My contention is that this unduly restrictive approach is not very useful.[14] As we have

10. Barr, op. cit., p. 141, on 2 Sam. 11:1; 1 Kings 20:22; Isa. 24:1; Job 1:5; and T. Boman, op. cit., p. 135, on Exod. 34:22; 1 Sam. 1:20; 2 Kings 20:26; 1 Chron. 20:1; 2 Chron. 24:23, 36:10; cf. also Ps. 104:29f. Cf. *ANET*, pp. 301ff. (on neo-Babylonian chronicles); see also above, Chapter 2, sect. A, pt. 2(i) (on Aristotle).

11. V. Hamp, "Geschichtsschreibung im Alten Testament" in *Speculum Historiale: Geschichte im Spiegel von Geschichtsschreibung und Geschichtsdeutung* (ed. C. Bauer, J. Boehm, M. Müller), Munich, 1965, p. 134.

12. Cf., e.g., G. W. Trompf, "The Conception of God in Hebrews 4:12–13" in *Studia Theologica* XXV, 1971, pp. 125ff. On Ecclesiastes and Origen as borderline cases, see below, sect. B, pt. 3, and Chapter 4, sect. F.

13. B. Albrektson, *History and the Gods: An Essay on the Idea of Historical Events as Divine Manifestations in the Ancient Near East and Israel* (*Coniectanea Biblica*, *OT. Ser. I*), London, 1967, pp. 93–5.

14. One might be tempted to level the same criticism against Barr, who, on quoting (pseudo-)Aristotle on "human things are a circle," denied that this statement reflected "a cyclic view of time," but averred that the writer was only making "a rather obvious judgement from the

shown, the minimal expectation from a cyclical view is simply the recurrence of the same stages of development, together with the idea of a return to an original set of general conditions. The exact or detailed repetition of events or characteristics is not a necessary prerequisite, and his approach does not square with ancient presuppositions rating alternative or undulatory conceptions as cyclical (so Chapter 2). Albrektson's position nicely demonstrates how definitions can affect interpretation, even though he is handling the same data available to others. Furthermore, his argument not only reflects weaknesses in the linear-cyclical contrast but also encourages us to reinforce our early claim that notions of historical recurrence are not exhausted by cyclical ideas (p. 1). Interestingly enough, Albrektson correctly argues that the search for law-like principles underlying historical events is "not in itself equivalent to a cyclic view of history,"[15] but draws the misleading conclusion that what he considers to be non-cyclical approaches are merely linear, when in fact at the very least, and without involving the label "cyclical" at all, they may well tell us something about the preoccupation with *recurring* historical phenomena.

On considering recurrence (rather than specifically cyclical) ideas, then, one is by no means left with that cut-and-dried issue bequeathed to us by Albrektson and other espousers of the linear-cyclical dichotomy.[16] The need for reevaluation applies no less to the later biblical material than to the earlier, and it is a central purpose of this chapter to establish this very point. In the early Christian work Luke-Acts (once described by Eduard Meyer as the greatest historiographical achievement between Polybius and Poseidonius),[17] there lies an impressive variety of recurrence ideas, many of which have their background in Hebraic as well as Hellenistic historical thought. The Israelite-Jewish books which are treated as background in the following pages, moreover, are those works we have the least difficulty in calling historical, and whose authors, far from showing disinterest in psychology or human achievements, can no longer be contrasted unfavorably with the famous Greek historians as creators of an inferior, theocratic quasi-history.[18]

---

fact that human realities come to be and pass away" (op. cit., pp. 140f.). Barr, however, (who seems to appeal to Pythagorean and Stoic standpoints as the paradigm cases of cyclicism on p. 140 n. 2) is discussing views of time and not of history (cf. p. 142), though how he can get away with contending on the one hand that Aristotle's statement "can hardly be called a cyclic view of time" and on the other that Qoheleth, who made "exactly the same point" (p. 141), reflects "in some sense a cyclic view of time" (p. 140), is beyond me. Cf. Boman, op. cit., pp. 122–37; E. von Dobschütz, "Zeit und Raum im Denken des Urchristentums" in *Journal of Biblical Literature* XLI, 1922, pp. 212ff., for related discussion.

15. Op. cit., p. 94 n. 87.

16. G. W. Trompf, "Notions of Historical Recurrence in Classical Hebrew Historiography" in *Vetus Testamentum* (forthcoming), on the views of both Albrektson and H. Gese ("Geschichtliches Denken im Alten Orient und im Alten Testament" in *Zeitschrift für Theologie und Kirche* LV, 1958, pp. 133f.).

17. E. Meyer, *Ursprung und Anfänge des Christentums*, Berlin, 1921, vol. 1, p. 2.

18. Against R. G. Collingwood, *The Idea of History*, Oxford, 1946, pp. 14–31; cf. J. Myres, *Herodotus, Father of History*, Oxford, 1953, pp. 60ff. For critical appraisals of classical Hebrew historiography, see L. Rost, *Die Überlieferung von der Thronnachfolge Davids*, Stuttgart, 1926,

## A. Luke-Acts and the reenactment of significant events

The Gospel of Luke and the book of Acts, conventionally ascribed to one of the traveling companions of Paul (cf. Col. 4:14; 2 Tim. 4:11), comprise two volumes of a famous (late-first-century?) New Testament work. I am arguing that these volumes have an important and interesting place in the history of recurrence ideas. They reflect notions which derive from both Hebraic and Greco-Roman traditions, leading us to look back into the Old Testament world while at the same time allowing us to continue our story forward from Polybius.

Luke-Acts has been described as the "burning issue" or "storm centre" of New Testament scholarship.[19] After prolonged discussion on Luke's reliability, as well as his special Christological and eschatological positions, there is now a pressing need to examine Luke's relationship to Israelite-Jewish and Greco-Roman historiography. One useful way of doing this is to trace notions of historical recurrence in his writing. Despite all the doubts surrounding the real authorship of Luke-Acts, as well as its date and provenance,[20] one can be more definite about Lukan presuppositions and intentions. The debate over Luke's status as theologian or historian notwithstanding, it may be fairly contended that Luke, before all other New Testament writers, saw himself to be writing history. Discussing the central section of the Gospel elsewhere, I have argued that Luke arranged and interpreted Jesus' teaching and activity so as to make plain the essence of his message and to show what kind of master Jesus was and the sort of teaching he delivered.[21] In this central section the Church's preaching

---

passim; G. von Rad, *The Problem of the Hexateuch and Other Essays* (= *Gesammelte Studien zum AT*) (ET), Edinburgh, 1966, pp. 176ff.; R. N. Whybray, *The Succession Narrative: A Study of II Sam. 9-20, I Kings 1 and 2* (*Studies in Biblical Theology* N.S. IX), London, 1968, passim; E. Meyer, *Geschichte des Altertums*, Berlin, 1921, pt. 1, vol. 1, pp. 227ff.; M. Noth, *Überlieferungsgeschichte Studien I, die sammelnden und bearbeitenden Geschichtswerke im Alten Testament*, Halle, 1957 edn., pp. 3ff., 110ff.; G. von Rad, *Old Testament Theology* (ET), Edinburgh, 1962, vol. 1, pp. 334–54; A. S. Kapelrud, "The Question of Authorship in the Ezra-Narrative: A Lexical Investigation" in *Skrifter utgitt av det Norske Videnskaps-Akademi*, Oslo, 1944, esp. pp. 95–7; Trompf, "Notions"; etc.

19. E. Käsemann, *Exegetische Versuche und Besinnungen*, Göttingen, 1960, vol. 1, p. 8; W. van Unnik, "Luke-Acts, a Storm Center of Contemporary Scholarship" in *Studies in Luke-Acts* (P. Schubert Festschrift) (ed. L. E. Keck and J. L. Martyn), London, 1968, p. 15.

20. On authorship (and reliability) questions see esp. F. J. Foakes Jackson and K. Lake, *The Beginnings of Christianity*, London, 1920–33, vol. 4; M. Dibelius, *Studies in the Acts of the Apostles* (ET), London, 1956, ch. 6; E. Haenchen, "Tradition und Komposition in der Apostelgeschichte" in *Zeitschrift für Theologie und Kirche* LIII, 1955, pp. 205ff.; "Das 'Wir' in der Apostelgeschichte und das Itinerar" in ibid., LVIII, 1961, pp. 329ff.; E. Trocmé, *Le Livre des Actes et l'histoire*, Paris, 1957; H. J. Cadbury, *The Making of Luke-Acts*, London, 1958 edn., pt. 1; *The Book of Acts in History*, London, 1955; R. Bultmann, "Zur Frage nach den Quellen der Apostelgeschichte" in *New Testament Essays* (T. W. Manson Festschrift) (ed. A. J. B. Higgins), Manchester, 1959, pp. 68ff.; J. Dupont, *Les Sources du Livre des Actes*, Bruges, 1960; C. K. Barrett, *Luke the Historian in Recent Study*, London, 1961; W. W. Gasque and R. P. Martin (eds.), *Apostolic History and the Gospel* (F. F. Bruce Festschrift), Exeter, 1970; cf. Gasque, *A History of the Criticism of the Book of Acts*, Manchester, 1969. On provenance see esp. Eusebius of Caesarea *Ecclesiastica historia* III,iv,6; cf. M. Wilcox, *The Semitisms of Acts*, Oxford, 1956, pp. 178f.

21. G. W. Trompf, "La Section médiane de l'Evangile de Luc: l'organisation des documents" in *Revue d'Histoire et de Philosophie Religieuses* LIII, 1973, p. 144.

(kerygma) was only allowed to persuade in terms of a "factual" narrative, and the same may be said of Luke-Acts as a whole. It is an important premise of the present study that Luke respected and criticized sources more like an historian than an evangelist, and that his primary concern was to demonstrate for inquirers what Jesus was really like as an historical personage, and how the Christian message spread rapidly beyond Galilee and Judea, eventually reaching the hub of the Roman Empire (see Excursus 2). However, this is not to deny that Luke was a believing historian, thoroughly sympathetic toward the chief protagonists of whom he wrote, and also a child of ancient, not modern, historiography. This meant that he inevitably brought theological presuppositions to bear on his picture of Jesus and the early Christians, and was hardly unconcerned to gauge the persuasive effect of his writings on the unconverted and suspicious. Now it is of paramount importance that among the theologically significant notions behind his account, or among the conceptions of historical change he brought to his task, there lie forms of recurrence thinking.

It has been rightly contended that in Acts one finds the Church reenacting the life, death, and resurrection of (Luke's) Christ, but this claim has so far been poorly or else overimaginatively defended. The general argument of M. D. Goulder, for example, fails to convince. According to his *Type and History in Acts*, certain cycles and patterned structures are evident in both Luke and Acts, and Goulder even sought to work out elaborate parallels, catena by catena, between the first and second volumes.[22] On the whole, he has foisted frameworks upon a Luke whose all too rich and complicated handiwork cannot sustain them, and in the end they appear more like the figments of Goulder's creative typologistic imagination than the ingredients of Lukan theology.[23]

## *Central cases of reenactment*

We begin our examination of Luke-Acts by considering some significant parallels between the two volumes, parallels which disclose Luke's interest in the reenactment of Jesus' life, death, and resurrection by the apostles and missionaries of the earliest Church, or, more generally, his interest in the reenactment of significant events (cf. p. 3). Placing them in the order most useful to us, the cases I have in mind are:

a. The deaths of Stephen and of Jesus.
b. The prison release of Peter and the resurrection appearance of Jesus.

22. London, 1964, pp. 34ff.; cf. pp. 16f., 22, 26, 40, 61, 72–4, 83f., 101, 138, etc.

23. Cf. the important review of Goulder's book by J. L. Houlden in *Journal of Theological Studies* XVII, 1966, pp. 143–5. My own detailed criticism would take more space than can be afforded here. It should be made clear here that R. Morgenthaler's attempts to account for frequent doubleting (*Zweigliedrigkeit*) in his *Die lukanische Geschichtsschreibung als Zeugnis*, Zurich, 1949, 2 vols., does not represent a thesis about historical recurrence (cf. my criticisms, "Section," p. 154), while the recent study by C. H. Talbert, *Literary Patterns, Theological Themes and the Genre of Luke-Acts* (*Society of Biblical Literature Monograph Series* XX), Missoula, 1974, does not seriously compete with (and could even complement) my approach (see below, sect. A, pt. 6).

c. The farewell speeches of Paul and Jesus.
d. The journeys of Paul and Jesus to Jerusalem.
e. The trials of Paul and Jesus.

a. The work of Stephen, his famous defence of Jesus' messiahship before the Sanhedrin, and his subsequent death, occupy two well-known chapters in Acts (6–7). Although Luke clearly distinguished between the ministries of Jesus and the Church, and wrote about the emergence of early Christian communities as a development in consequence of Jesus' work,[24] it is evident that he wished to portray Stephen's death and its circumstances as a reenactment of Christ's passion. Admittedly, Stephen was an individualistic teacher and figure for Luke, and his death as the first Christian martyr was a special one. On the other hand, Stephen's final words ("Lord Jesus, receive my spirit," "Lord, do not hold this sin against them": Acts 7:59–60) bear a remarkable correspondence to two important sayings of the crucified Jesus ("Father, forgive them, for they know not what they do," "Father, into your hands I commit my spirit": Luke 23:34, 46). Significantly, these two sayings are unique to the Lukan Gospel account, and to the rather independent Lukan passion narrative. It is noteworthy, too, that both Jesus and Stephen witness to the Son of Man before their passions (Luke 22:69, Acts 7:56), and Stephen's reference to this figure is the only such reference in Acts (and one of only three references outside the Four Gospels).[25] Furthermore, the same Jewish court tries both figures: both victims were "led" to the Sanhedrin (Luke 22:66 and ff.; cf. Mark 14:53, Matt. 26:57, Acts 6:12), and both were put to death outside the city.[26] Also, although Luke curiously omitted all mention of false witnesses at Jesus' trial, along with the accusation that Jesus intended to destroy the temple (cf. Mark 14:56–9), such witnesses accuse Stephen instead, and level a charge concerning his threat to the temple (Acts 6:13–14).[27] Besides this, Luke reported that both Jesus and Stephen were condemned as disturbers of the existing socio-political order, a quite independent view (Luke 23:2; Acts 6:14).

b. A comparison of the story of Peter's prison release in Acts 12 with the most basic resurrection traditions of Luke's Gospel [24:1–11 (and 12?), 36–43][28] supports this understanding of the Evangelist's approach. Imprisoned by Herod,

24. On Luke distinguishing the pre- and post-ascension situations, see Luke 22:69; Acts 7:56; H. J. Cadbury, "Acts and Eschatology" in *The Background of the New Testament and Its Eschatology* (ed. W. D. Davies and D. Daube), Cambridge, 1965, p. 305; H. Flender, *St. Luke: Theologian of Redemptive History* (ET), London, 1967, pp. 37ff.

25. Cf. Rev. 1:13, 14:14; and see R. Pesch, *Die Vision des Stephanus: Apg. 7,55-6 im Rahmen der Apostelgeschichte* (*Stuttgarter Bibelstudien XII*), Stuttgart, 1966, pp. 66f.

26. Cf. G. Stählin, *Die Apostelgeschichte* (*Das Neue Testament Deutsch V*), Göttingen, 1936, p. 114.

27. Also note that Jesus' prediction at Luke 21:5–37 is in public; yet cf. Mark 13:3; Matt. 24:3. Hence Luke omits reference to the false witnesses at Jesus' trial.

28. On the Emmaus narrative (24:13–35) as a Lukan insertion grafted on to the more received traditions: A. A. Ehrhardt, "The Disciples of Emmaus" in *New Testament Studies* X, 1963, pp. 182ff.; G. W. Trompf, "The First Resurrection Appearance and the Ending of Mark's Gospel" in ibid., XVIII, 1972, p. 325.

Peter had small hope of escape, for John the Baptist and the apostle James had already been executed by the Herodians (Luke 3:19–20, 9:9, Acts 12:1–2). Yet Peter was miraculously released, and this, significantly enough, at a time near the Passover (Acts 12:4, cf. Luke 22:1ff., 23:54)[29] and at the hands of an angel (Acts 12:7; cf. Luke 24:23; cf. 4)[30] Of course, the differences between the resurrection proper and Peter's release are evident enough, but we are not meant to miss similarities. The description of Peter's return is most intriguing. As with the resurrection, women are associated with his reappearance (Acts 12:12–13; cf. Luke 23:55–24:10, 22), yet as in the case of the tale of the women in Luke's version of the empty-tomb tradition, the claim of the maid Rhoda that Peter is free and at the door is not believed by the others (Acts 12:13–15; cf. Luke 24:11, but cf. Matt. 28:8, 10, 16, John 20:18). Only the actual appearance, which in each instance was terrifying (Acts 12:16; cf. Luke 24:36), proves Peter and Jesus to be humans in the flesh and not spiritual beings (Acts 12:15b; cf. Luke 24:36, 39). In assuring the company of his safe return, moreover, Peter gives a charge to "tell this to James and the brethren" (Acts 12:17b). The very presence of this charge is suggestive of the resurrection, though its form is closer to Jesus' post-resurrection commands in other Gospels than in Luke's.[31]

All these resurrection and appearance elements in Acts 12, then, claim due attention, all the more so when one realizes that after recording his escape Luke drew his account of Peter's career to a close (19b). Hence this act of deliverance came to repeat (to a degree Luke considered sufficient both for his readers and for his purposes as a historian) the events of Christ's all-important rising from the dead. Luke hardly wished to deny that the deeds of the apostles formed fresh, distinctive episodes in history, but for him many of their acts only acquired their full meaning through crucial events which preceded them. As we shall see, he was fundamentally preoccupied with the relatedness of historical events, and the existence of special connections between key incidents represented for him a form of authentication, confirming that the events he treated had a superior significance. The instancing of the Church's "reenactments" of Christ's life was the chief means by which this significance could be conveyed.

c. A third important example of Luke's interest in such reenactment can be found in Paul's farewell speech at Miletus (to the Ephesian elders) (Acts 20:17–35). This statement is no Pauline proclamation of Christ to the unconverted; it stands as Paul's warning of forthcoming trials both for himself and the Church, and it is his reflection upon his own ministry. Significantly enough,

29. Goulder, *Type*, pp. 43f.; and on the Evangelists' dating of the crucifixion see M. H. Shepherd, "Are Both the Synoptics and John Correct about the Date of Jesus' Death?" in *Journal of Biblical Literature* LXXX, 1961, pp. 123ff.

30. In appealing to the guards in Matthew's resurrection story as a parallel to Peter's guards, Goulder (op. cit., p. 44) reveals himself an incautious disciple of Austin Farrer [cf. "On Dispensing with Q" in *Studies in the Gospels* (ed. D. Nineham), Oxford, 1955, pp. 55ff.]. On prison as death, see, e.g., 1 Pet. 3:19, and on open gates as a release from death, Philostratus *The Life of Apollonius of Tyana* VIII,xxx. Acts 5:17–27 only prefigures and reinforces the approach in 12.

31. See Excursus 3, Exegetical Note A.

Paul here reminds his listeners of warnings issued by Jesus, and the reader is meant to recall Jesus' ministry. Not only that, but as Luke is alone among the Synoptists in recording a farewell discourse by Jesus at the Last Supper table (Luke 22:24–38),[32] and as he took Paul to be a central figure of his Church history, it is likely that Luke deliberately sought to organize a correspondence.[33] Like Jesus during his progress toward Jerusalem, Paul is ready to journey to the holy city (Acts 20:22; cf. Luke 9:51, 13:22, 33–34, 17:11, 18:31, 19:11).[34] Like Jesus, he foretells the dangers ahead of him (Acts 20:23; cf. Luke 9:22, 44, 17:25, 18:31–2); like Jesus, he is preparing to complete his work (or as with John the Baptist, "finish his course").[35] Like Jesus in the farewell discourse of Luke, Paul foretells betrayals and falling away in the Church (Acts 20:29–30; cf. Luke 22:21–2, 31–2),[36] reminds his listeners of his past trials (*peirasmoi* in both Acts 20:19 and Luke 22:28), and enjoins them to both sacrificial service and alertness.[37]

In Luke all the final references to Jesus' forthcoming suffering are confined to the supper context (Luke 22:15, 22, 37; yet cf. Mark 14:21, 41, 49, Matt. 26:24, 45, 56), and in that setting they are made much more explicit than in the other Synoptists.[38] It is interesting that Paul enacts the Lord's Supper not long before his farewell speech is delivered (cf. Acts 20:7, 11), and quite apart from this speech, when Paul is on the verge of reaching Jerusalem, he is taken to face the same decision Jesus faced in Gethsemane, whether to avoid or to accept great danger (21:10–14; cf. Luke 22:39–46). Paul and Jesus resolve to face their respective crises in a similar way, by asking God's will to be done (Luke 22:41 ≠ Mark, Matt., Acts 21:14b). Granted the special nature and circumstances of Paul's speech, the impression remains that Paul's preparations for his forthcoming ordeal reenact those made by Jesus before the crucifixion (cf. Acts 20:20–1, 25–27).

d. We may now turn to a fourth and still more important case, the journeys of Paul and Jesus to Jerusalem. It is well known, on the one hand, that Acts largely concentrates on the voyages and missionary career of Paul (13:1–21:17, 27–28), and on the other, that one of the most distinctive features of Luke is the "great omission," that is, Luke's departure from his key Markan source so as to portray Christ's great *journey* from Galilee to Jerusalem (9:51–19:58).[39]

32. Yet cf. Mark 14:26–31 ≠ Matt. 24:30–5. In presenting such a discourse, Luke has something in common with John (13:21–28:1).

33. See Excursus 3, Exegetical Note B.

34. Cf. also Acts 20:16, 21:11–4.

35. Acts 20:24; cf. Luke 13:32b for Jesus, Acts 13:25 for John.

36. Although Luke evidently inherited a warning against Peter in particular, which he preferred to use instead of the general warning to all the disciples (so Luke 22:31f. instead of Mark 14:26f.), he retained the less specific Markan element by using the plural *humas* in vs. 31 to cover all the apostles, while focusing on Peter in vss.32–4. Note also Acts 20:29, and cf. Luke 10:3.

37. Acts 20:31, 33–5, and cf. Luke 22:24–7, 35, 36, 40.

38. Luke 22:15, 22, yet cf. Mark 14:25 and Matt. 26:29.

39. Goulder insists, without any real justification, that Jesus undergoes two journeys in Luke, to match matters up with Paul's two main missionary expeditions (op. cit., pp. 135–9).

Without doubt, the "journey element" is one of the crucial unifying factors in the whole work Luke-Acts, and it is probable that Luke's special organization of material in this connection was governed by a characteristic concern to disclose reenactment and recurring profiles. One need not insist on anything like exact parallels to defend this point, but it was clearly important for Luke that there were corresponding event-complexes in the lives of Jesus and Paul. He turned Jesus into a traveler of some consequence engaged in something like a great missionary journey. This was a relatively easy and not entirely unhistorical thing to do, though certain incidents or portions in his central section do sit rather artificially in a travel narrative.[40] By doing this, of course, Paul's journeying comes to reenact Jesus', despite the enormous geographical differences. Their ministries of healing and of preaching God's kingdom bear a special relationship,[41] and when it is time for Paul to travel to Jerusalem for the culminating ordeal (Jerusalem really seems less perilous for him than other places, but Luke intended the events of Acts 21:27–26:32 and their consequences to be climactic),[42] the lineaments of recurrence become obvious. It may be objected, of course, that in Acts Paul journeyed not only to Jerusalem but eventually to Rome as well, and that this hardly compares well with the events of Jesus' passion and resurrection; yet Luke does conceive of these consummating events in his Gospel as a journey [so Luke 22:22 (*poreuetai*); cf. Mark 14:21 ≠ Matt. 26:24],[43] and he alone among the Evangelists placed a resurrection appearance in a journey context (Luke 24:13–35, though cf. pseudo-Mark 16:12), the account of this appearance bearing clear signs of Luke's style and imagination.[44]

e. Our last introductory example, a comparison of the trials of Jesus and Paul, conveys a similar impression. Although the trials of both figures preserve their uniqueness, and their outcomes are quite different, Luke nevertheless attempted to connect them. Most significant are certain peculiarities in the Lukan description of Jesus' trial. It is only in the third Gospel that Herod makes an appearance as a judge (Luke 23:6–12). Whereas the other Evangelists wrote of only two tribunals, a Jewish and a Roman, Luke added a third, and one cannot help wondering whether this third Herodian element, which is so sketchily treated and looks suspiciously secondary,[45] arose from Luke's effort to expose correspondences in the careers of Jesus and Paul. Interestingly, Paul was presented

40. E.g., 11:14ff. (cf. Mark 3:19bff.), 13:10–7, 14:1–24, 18:15–7 (cf. Mark 10:13–7). Mark wrote of Jesus' traveling (D. Gill, "Observations on the Lukan Travel Narrative and Some Related Passages" in *Harvard Theological Review* LXIII, 1970, p. 218), but Luke omitted Markan travel details which did not suit a journey from Galilee to Jerusalem (e.g., Mark 7:24–37).

41. On connections between the healing miracles in Luke and Acts see Excursus 3, Exegetical Note C. On preaching the Kingdom of God see Luke 4:43, 8:1, 9:11, 16:16; Acts 19:8, 20:25, 28:23, 31.

42. Cf. 21:31, 23:12ff., along with the space devoted to Paul's final Jerusalem visit and resulting imprisonment.

43. Gill, loc. cit., p. 215, and also on both Luke 22:22 and Acts 1:10f., see J. Navone, *Themes of St. Luke*, Rome, 1970, p. 67.

44. Pseudo-Mark probably follows Luke: G. W. Trompf, "The *Markusschluss* in Recent Research," in *Australian Biblical Review* XXI, 1973, pp. 20f.

45. Note the details of 23:11; cf. Mark 15:16–20.

before the judgment-seats of the Jews (Acts 23:1–10), the Romans (21:37–22:29, 24:1–23, 25:6–12), and the Herodians (25:23–26:32; cf. 23:35b). He was also the butt of a condemning crowd shouting "Away with him!" (21:36; cf. 22:22), a phrase Luke alone puts in the mouth of the hostile mob calling for Christ's crucifixion (Luke 23:18).[46] There were three distinct stages in the Roman trial of Paul (cf. Acts 21:33–40, 24:1–2, 25:6), just as there were, according to Luke's unique arrangement, in the case of Jesus (Luke 23:1, 13, 22),[47] and in addition, both Jesus and Paul were consciously portrayed as innocent, as victims of a Jewish hatred alien to the ways of Roman justice (cf. vs. 47b, yet cf. Mark 15:39b; Acts 26:32).[48] Though differences can hardly be neglected (Paul utters lengthy apologies at his trial, for example, while Jesus says little), intimations of reenactment are once again present.

There are similar cases of reenactment—the raising of Dorcas and the raising of Jairus' daughter, the healing of Simon's mother-in-law and the healing of Publius' father—which, although minor, show the same interests.[49] A consistent tie-up in the miracle tales of both books, however, can hardly be expected. Perhaps we could add to our list of reenactments certain miracle types such as the curing of paralysis,[50] or the fact that the early missionaries performed "signs and wonders" just as Jesus had done (Acts 14:3), but these stand as much looser parallels. The search for patterning in Luke-Acts, moreover, must have some reasonable limits imposed on it. Goulder, for one, has been quite unrestrained in such a search. He attempts to educe, for example, a cyclical series of "deaths and resurrections" from Jesus, through such early disciples as Stephen and Peter, to Paul (and including the imprisonment and miraculous release of Paul and Silas at Philippi).[51] As we have seen, however, Luke focused primarily on the *death* of Stephen, with no hint of resurrection; he concentrated on the resurrection characteristics of Peter's release, and expended no effort to parallel his prison cell with a garden tomb; he was interested in the elements of reenactment in Paul's trial, without wishing to pretend either that Paul's journey across the great sea to Rome, and the shipwreck, represented his death, or that his arrival at the last port of call amounted to his resurrection.[52] Moreover, to use the word "cycle" in connection with such examples is to use it inadvisedly.[53] In view of

46. Luke is closest to John (19:15) here; yet cf. Luke 23:21; Mark 15:13, 15; Matt. 26:22, 23.

47. Cf. Mark 15:1b–15; Matt. 27:11–26; John 18:28–19:16 (John again being closest to Luke).

48. Also Luke 19:47–22:2; Acts 21:17–28 (mounting troubles through their activities in the temple); Luke 19:47, 22:3–6; Acts 23:12–5 (Jewish plots laid against them). Cf. Talbert, op. cit., p. 17, for further discussion.

49. See Excursus 3, Exegetical Note C.

50. Luke 5:18–26, Acts 9:32–5; or the raising of dead youths: Luke 6:11–6 (om. Mark, Matt.), Acts 20:7–12; or the exorcism of demons which cry out concerning the Most High God: Luke 8:28b, Acts 16:17, and cf. Luke 4:34b, Acts 8:7. There are many other points of correspondence, some of which are noted by Talbert, op. cit., pp. 16–8, 23–7, 35f., 40, 44f., 51f., 57, 59, 61, 97f.

51. Goulder, op. cit., ch. 3.

52. Against ibid., pp. 36ff. Cf. C. F. Evans, "The Kerygma" in *Journal of Theological Studies* VII, 1956, p. 32.

53. Goulder gives the word no clear definition, apparently confusing historical with literary cycles (op. cit., pp. 16ff.). Incidentally, lectionary cycles (which also interest Goulder) have no real

distinctions already drawn, it would be more accurate to talk about notions of reenactment. This reenactment carries with it a sense of recurring event-shapes and profiles, since we have been concerned not only with similar actions but with parallel situations—deaths, journeys, trials—as well.

## *The question of typology*

It should be acknowledged that some scholars have understood Luke's methods and interests to be typological.[54] If we wish to define his historiographical framework more precisely, this view must be reckoned with. One must be cautious here about what is meant by typology and whether it can be clearly distinguished from a concern with reenactment. First let it be said that typology can be applied to a whole set of notions not readily assimilable to the idea of "repeated history." The great Flood, for instance, could be taken as a prefigurative symbol of Christ's redemptive passion and death;[55] we may also recall here how Paul conceived Adam as a type of "the one who was to come" (Rom. 5:14b), and how the Epistle of Barnabas saw Isaac as a type of Christ sacrificed (7:3). Such typological lines of thought, very Jewish in background, border on allegory,[56] and are distinguishable enough from Luke's general approach, for he was less concerned with symbolic relationships than with the more direct grasp of similarities and parallels between sets of historical happenings. In those typological illustrations just cited, moreover, there is an underlying emphasis on the prefiguration of Christ in earlier occurrences, whereas in Luke's writings happenings are so described as to recall prior deeds and events. One need not exclude Luke's methods from the compass of typology, perhaps, for certain brands of typological preoccupation evidently constitute forms of recurrence thinking. To suggest Christ to be a new David or a new Moses, for example, is to make at least a minimal claim that some past aspect of God's dealings with his people has been restored and reappropriated in the present. Nevertheless, Luke's rather special position requires isolating. It is unfortunate that recent debates about typology within the Bible have been overly concerned with the subtle differences between typology, allegory, and prophecy fulfillment,[57] and it has generally been assumed that an interest in historical repetition is foreign to

---

bearing on the present discussion: cf. L. Morris, *The New Testament and Jewish Lectionaries*, London, 1964, and works cited there.

54. E.g., Goulder, op. cit., ch. 1; C. F. Evans, "The Central Section of St. Luke's Gospel" in *Studies in the Gospels* (ed. Nineham), pp. 37ff.; G. W. H. Lampe (with K. J. Woollcombe), *Essays on Typology* (*Studies in Biblical Theology XXII*), London, 1957, p. 25.

55. T. Merton, *Bread in the Wilderness*, London, 1953, pp. 58f.; cf. (for background), Ambrose *De sacramentis* II,1; *De mysteriis* x, xxiv.

56. Allegory is usually distinguished from typology, however, although their merging is possible: cf. J. Barr, "Typology and Allegory" in his *Old and New in Interpretation: A Study of the Two Testaments* (Currie Lectures, 1964), London, 1966, pp. 103–117.

57. E.g., ibid., pp. 103–117 and ff.; Woollcombe in Lampe, op. cit., p. 42; Lampe, "Hermeneutics and Typology" in *London Quarterly and Holborn Review* N.S. XXXIII, 1965, pp. 17–25; though for more expansive approaches see O. Cullmann, *Salvation in History* (ET), London, 1965, pp. 132ff.; J. Strelan, *Search for Salvation*, Adelaide, 1977, ch. 4.

biblical and especially to New Testament literature. As a result, Luke's position in relation to other New Testament methods and interpretations has not been fully appreciated.

In recounting the deeds of Jesus and the early missionaries, Luke did not just wish to make fleeting yet pointed allusions to past parallels, as if to show his incomparable artistry in a series of subtle asides. Nor was he merely demonstrating how Jesus, even though he ultimately superseded them, embodied the major categories of the Old Testament heritage—lawgiver, king, prophet, and sage.[58] Furthermore, Luke was not interested in arranging his material as orderly *midrashim* or *pesherim* (commentary or interpretations) upon long sequences found in the scriptures,[59] nor was prophecy fulfillment for him only a way of authenticating Jesus or showing the ancient oracles to be right.[60] Luke was fundamentally interested in more directly historical connections, as an historian of the Hellenistic period. He wrote as though established historical events, which were for him divinely guided,[61] had their own inner relatedness, connections between events amounting to the virtual reenactment of special happenings or the repetition of an earlier stage of history in a later one, or even the recurrent operation of certain laws or principles. By the time Luke-Acts was written many connections between Jesus and the Old Testament and between the work of the Church and Jesus' ministry, had already been forged. Luke appears to have interpreted this inheritance under the influence of his historiographical assumptions. As with Polybius, these assumptions were bound to affect the reliability of his account.[62] But the main point is that he emerges as an historian comparable to Polybius (who, after all, managed to infuse a theological significance into his work), rather than as someone concerned to make a series of evangelistic and theological assertions in the form of a narrative.[63]

But to state the case thus is, once more, to look ahead to further analysis.

58. Cf. Matthew's approach: 5:1, 17–48 (lawgiver); 23–24 (prophet); 11:19b, 12:42b, 13:54 (sage).

59. Against Evans, "Central," pp. 42ff., on the running connections between Luke 10:1–18:14 and Deut. 1–26 (though in personal communications Professor Evans has since expressed serious reservations about this article), and against J. Drury, *Tradition and Design in Luke's Gospel: a Study in Early Christian Historiography*, London, 1976, pp. 43ff. and passim (though space prevents me from criticizing this new work). *Midrashim* were running commentaries on one text often presented in the light of others, connections thus being forged between beliefs (more than events) in different books; a *pesher*, as is illustrated by the famous Qumranite Habakkuk commentary, was an interpretation of an ancient text in the light of current events, and was usually intended to show how prophesied events had been actualized.

60. See below, pt. 5 (cf. Matt., John 19:24, 28).

61. Esp. Luke 22:22 (yet cf. Mark 14:21; Matt. 26:24); Acts 4:28, 17:24ff., and on the Holy Spirit as an agent in history see below, sect. B, pt. 4.

62. See Excursus 3, Exegetical Note D.

63. It is certainly unwarrantable to overstrain the distinction between the historian and the theologian in Luke's case, and some scholars insist on the compromise phrase "theologian of history": E. Lohse, "Lukas als Theologe der Heilsgeschichte" in *Evangelische Theologie* XIV, 1964, pp. 256ff.; K. M. Flender, op. cit., pp. 1ff.; R. Maddox, unpublished work-paper, F. Hahn's NT Seminar, Mainz, 1969–70 (with kind permission). However, it is Luke's self-understanding, or his conscious approach of a recognized literary rôle, that is crucial here.

## *Lukan geography*

Up to this point we have been concentrating on the obvious cases of reenactment in Luke-Acts, but there are other associated yet distinctive links between the two volumes. These are present in Luke's handling of geography. The peculiar geographical emphases and modifications in the Gospel have already been analyzed in detail by Hans Conzelmann, and they have been ascribed both to an ignorance of the Palestinian region and to theological preoccupations.[64] These kinds of explanations, however, are open to question, as I shall now seek to demonstrate.

As I see it, the clue to the Gospel's geography lies in Acts. In Acts 1:8 Jesus states that his followers will witness to him in "Jerusalem, in all Judea and Samaria, and to the end of the earth." Luke thus prepares his readers for remarkable developments to come. It does not follow, however, that the four areas mentioned above were treated in four separate stages of Acts. The preferable way of dividing the book is as follows:

1. The Jerusalem ministry of the disciples (Acts 1:12–8:1a).
2. Work in the regions immediately around Jerusalem (a kind of Palestinian or Levantine region) which includes Judea (with Caesarea), Samaria, (Galilee?), Syria, Phoenicia, and even Tarsus (the frontier?) (Acts 8:1b–12:25).
3. Missionary work abroad under Paul (13:1–21:16), including an interlude at Jerusalem to settle policy concerning the Gentile mission (15:4–29), and the eventual journey back to Jerusalem (20:1–21:16).
4. Events to do with Paul which occur mainly in Jerusalem and Caesarea but which eventually result in Paul's voyage to Rome and his settlement there (21:17–28:31).

Admittedly, scholars have suggested that brief summaries in the early parts of Acts (2:47, 6:7, 9:31, 12:24, and even 5:11–12) count for something in separating stages of development,[65] yet it is more sensible to take these as a way of covering events that remain unnarrated, just as Luke's generalizations about the disciples' "signs and wonders" imply the performance of more miracles than those described. The four sections outlined above speak for themselves, although the second remains somewhat controversial. It is an embarrassment to exegetes who set much store by the apparently programmatic statement of 1:8, or by summaries, since a mission to Samaria precedes any to Judea (cf. 8:5ff.) and because the summary of 9:31 hardly emerges as concluding a stage of geographical expansion.[66]

A close look at 8:1b–12:25 (the second section), reveals that Luke's attention fastened on the Levantine regions around Jerusalem and that he consciously projected an intermediate stage of missionary expansion before the wider work of Paul.[67] Perhaps he was historian enough not to paint an overly geometric

64. H. Conzelmann, *The Theology of St. Luke* (= *Die Mitte der Zeit*) (ET), London, 1960, pp. 18ff.

65. E.g., Goulder, op. cit., pp. 14ff., and note *RSV* paragraphing.

66. This verse marks the end of adverse conditions (largely created by Saul: 8:3), not the end of a stage of geographical spread (cf. 9:26–9, 30b, 32ff., 11:25).

67. 8:1b (as the preface), 5, 14b–5, 28, 40; 9:32, 36; 10:24; 12:17b (on the new work of Philip and

picture of the Church's growth, but his preconceptions clearly had their influence. Even when he inserted material at the end of this stage on James' martyrdom and Peter's imprisonment (12:1ff.), material which could have been directly linked with Jerusalem, he gave his accounts hardly any geographical definition. Herod seems to control extra-Jerusalemite regions (cf. 12:19b, 20b);[68] he does not imprison Peter within the city where haven can be found (12:10; cf. 4b); and he dies in Caesarea, resplendent before shouting Phoenicians (vss. 20–23). By the end of chapter 12 (vss. 24–25), then, the reader is confronted with a movement affecting the whole region to the far east of the Great (Mediterranean) Sea, and converting both Jews and non-Jews (cf. esp. 10, 11:19–20). The conditions are thus ripe for expansion to the west.

Having conceived the geographical pattern of Acts in this way, it is profitable to reflect on the geography of the Gospel. The Gospel also appears to fall into four sections:[69]

1. Background and introduction to Jesus' ministry, with a geographical emphasis on Jerusalem and Judea (Luke 1:1–3:13).
2. The Galilean ministry of Jesus, but taking in the regions immediately around Galilee, including Judea (3:15–9:56).[70]
3. Jesus' journey from Galilee to Jerusalem (9:51–19:44).[71]
4. Jesus in Jerusalem, his teaching there, the trial, crucifixion, resurrection, and ascension (19:41–24:53).

It will be obvious by now that the divisions of Luke suggest a parallelism of stage sets with Acts, although some analysis of the distinction between these four parts is required.

Concerning the first section (and I am assuming Luke 1–2 to be genuinely Lukan),[72] the prominence of Jerusalem and Judea should be recognized. Luke freely admitted Jesus' Galilean upbringing (2:39–40, 51–52; cf. 1:26, 2:4a, 4:22b, 24), but he did everything possible to relieve Jesus' background of cultural obscurity, and to focus the beginnings of his story on better-known geographical areas, especially on Jerusalem, cultural center of the Jewish religion, a place

Peter); 9:2, 10, 19b–22, 30b (the Damascan Christians and prospects at Tarsus, skillfully introduced with the persecutions of Saul). The importance of Jerusalem as a geographical center was not lost (8:14, 25; 9:26–9; 11:2–18, 27; 12:25), but it was the regions around Jerusalem which bore the real attention.

68. Did Luke confound (consciously or unconsciously) Herod Antipas with Herod Agrippa I? If so, this may explain their association with extra-Jerusalemite regions: cf. below, sect. C.

69. Against Conzelmann's threefold division (op. cit., pt. 1, sect. B); and W. C. Robinson's different fourfold division, following that of K. L. Schmidt (Robinson, *Der Weg des Herrn: Studien zur Geschichte und Eschatologie im Lukas Evangelium (Theologische Forschung XXXVI)*, Hamburg, 1964, pp. 23ff.

70. Luke 9:51–6 may be included in both sections or in either one; it is probably a transition piece from one stage to another.

71. Luke 19:41–4 may be included in both sections or either.

72. Cf. R. Laurentin, *Structure et théologie de Luc 1-11*, Paris, 1957; P. S. Minear, "Luke's Use of Birth Stories" in *Studies in Luke-Acts* (ed. Keck and Martyn), pp. 112–8; R. E. Brown, *The Birth of the Messiah: A Commentary on the Infancy Narratives in Matthew and Luke*, London, 1977, pp. 242ff.

steeped in history both ancient and recent.[73] The second section, covering Jesus' Galilean ministry, also reflects special Lukan stresses of a geographical and ethnological nature. Jesus does not travel far from the Galilean region (cf. Mark 7:24–31), yet he does visit nearby areas—the land of the Gerasenes (Luke 8:26–39), the "mixed" city of Bethsaida-Julius (9:10), even parts of Samaria (9:51–56; cf. Mark, Matt. 10:5) and Judea (4:44; cf. Mark 1:39).[74] Certainly the ministry, when it is not localized near the Sea of Galilee, is made to face to the south or east, and away from either the north or the seaboard (or, in other words, the future mission fields).[75] As for the third section, it was deliberately contrived as a journey to Jerusalem, without any specific geographical locations on the way (cf. 13:22, 17:11), except at the very beginning (9:51–56) and at the approach to Jerusalem, when geographical details suddenly acquire surprising detail (18:35, 19:1, 11, 29, 37, 41, 45). With the fourth section the special geographical features primarily concern Luke's emphasis on a longer period of Jesus's teaching in the temple (19:47, 20:1, 21:37a; cf. Mark 11:27–14:1, Matt. 21:14, 23, 26:1–5),[76] and his confining of the resurrection and ascension to Jerusalem or nearby (24:13, 35, 50–53; cf. Mark 14:28, 16:7, Matt. 28:7, 10, 16–20, John 21:1–23, Evang. Petr. 14:58–60).

Scholars usually explain such Lukan peculiarities in terms of Gospel comparison, referring to special sources, the relative inadequacy of Luke's geographical knowledge, and the theological factors motivating his modification of the Jesus tradition. This kind of approach has been fruitful, but as Luke and Acts form a single work it is imperative that these two volumes should also be viewed synoptically. The comparable division of each into four sections points to a more far-reaching explanation of the special characteristics of Luke, and one which comes to grips with the Evangelist's historiographical methodology. The great cultural centers which matter for his history figure prominently at the beginning and end of each volume, so that each has its geographical complements. In Luke the coming of Jesus has much to do with Jerusalem, the religious capital of Israel, and the comparable movement in Acts lies with Paul's return, after many travels, to Jerusalem, city of the mother Church, the consequence of this return being his last voyage to Rome, political capital of the world. In Luke, toward the end, Jesus spends some time within the complex of temple life, and the early Church at the beginning of Acts reenacts that special Lukan dimension of his ministry (Acts 2:46, 3:1, 8–9, 11, 4:1, 5:20–21, 25, 41; cf. Luke 24:53).[77]

73. Note 1:9, 39, 65b; 2:4, 22–38 (yet cf. Matt. 2:13–21), 41–51; 3:31b; 4:9–12 (yet cf. Matt. 4:5–7). So despite Conzelmann, op. cit., pp. 18ff.; cf. J. Dupont, *Die Versuchungen Jesu in der Wüste* (*Stuttgarter Bibelstudien XXXVII*) (GT), Stuttgart, 1969, pp. 64–6, on the temptation narratives; Polybius *Hist.* XVI,xxxix; Josephus *Antiq.*, esp. XVIII; Tacitus *Ann.* XII,54f., etc., on information available to literate Gentiles about Jerusalem or Judea.

74. Also Luke 23:5 and cf. 4:36f.; 5:17b; 6:17b; 7:17b; Acts 10:37. The harder reading of Luke 4:44 is to be preferred.

75. There is no reference to Caesarea-Philippi in Luke 9:18–22 (yet cf. Mark 8:27–39, Matt. 16:13–30), and note the omission of Mark 8:24–30 ≠ Matt. 15:21–8.

76. Though note Luke 22:53a ≠ Mark 14:49a ≠ Matt. 26:55b—all *kath' hēmeran.*

77. See also Acts 21:26; cf. Luke 2:22, 46, 19:45f., etc.

The second sections of the two volumes, moreover, correspond. Both suggest a limited expansion of activity foreshadowing the more extensive traveling to come; both show the good news to be preached in a mainly Jewish setting, yet still reaching beyond the Jews to the Gentiles (the centurion of Luke 7:2 and ff. and the centurion Cornelius in Acts 10:1ff. represent part of the Evangelist's efforts to force a connection),[78] and the mission activity beyond that of Jesus in both sections is focused primarily on the twelve (Luke 5:10, 6:12–16, 8:1b, 51b, 9:1–10; cf. 8:9–15, Acts 8:1b, 5, 14b, 26, 9:26, 32, 10:9–11:18, 11:22). Luke takes pains, nevertheless, to insure that there was no doubling-up of Jesus's regional ministry by the apostles: he mentions no apostolic mission to Galilee, apparently assuming that the area had already been handled (cf. Acts 9:31);[79] he has Jesus preach only to the villages of Samaria (Luke 9:52, 56) but has Philip in the city of Sebaste(?) (Acts 8:5, 9, 14; cf. 25b); and he faces Jesus's ministry away from the seaboard and northern centers tackled by the early Church (cf. Acts 8:40, 9:19bff., 32b, 36, 10:24, 11:19; cf. 21:3–4, 7, 28:3). Despite his establishing the differences, however, the regional ministries of Luke 4:14–9:56 and Acts 8:1b–12:25 are both limited developments (before the thrust toward Jerusalem in Luke; cf. Acts 10:37, 13:31; and toward the west and Rome in Acts). These thrusts, of course, were covered in the third sections, a parallel between the journeys and adventures in Luke and Acts being intended. Interestingly, the more far-reaching Gentile mission of Acts depends on the selection of non-apostolic evangelists (cf. 13:1–3), while Jesus' journey in Luke begins with the commission of the non-apostolic seventy(-two) (10:1–12, 17–20).[80] By introducing this larger assembly in the Gospel, Luke created the impression of a far wider group of disciples than had been suggested before,[81] and in this "central section" Jesus' teaching becomes increasingly directed beyond his immediate followers.[82]

In Luke-Acts, then, the Church comes to reenact Christ's activity by undergoing similar stages of development and by working in parallel geographical contexts. Thus, more broadly conceived colligations in Luke, and not key actions or incidents alone, are repeated in the second volume. While this could be regarded as the approach of a typological theologian, there seems less reason for saying that Christ's life is a prefigurement of apostolic Christianity than for

78. With the special emphasis on piety; yet cf. (on the centurion of the Gospels) Matt. 8:5ff., John 4:46ff.

79. Yet cf. Mark 16:7; Matt. 28:7, 10, 16–20; C. F. Evans, "I Will Go before You into Galilee" in *Journal of Theological Studies* N.S. V, 1954, pp. 11ff.; L. E. Elliott-Binns, *Galilean Christianity* (*Studies in Biblical Theology XVI*), London, 1956, ch. 4.

80. On the MSS diverging, see Trompf, "Section" p. 154. Cf. also J. J. von Allmen in *Vocabulary of the Bible* (ed. Allmen) (ET), London, 1958, pp. 285a–b (on Christ as gatherer of the twelve tribes paralleled with Paul as gatherer of the nations).

81. Numerous passages before the journey begins at 9:51ff. reflect the special position of the twelve (e.g., 4:38; 5:1–11, 27–32; 6:12–6; 8:1–12, 28ff., 49ff.). After 10:1–20, however, the word "disciples" represents a less confined group (11:1; 12:1, 22; 16:1ff.; 17:1ff., 22ff.; 18:1ff., 15; yet cf. 17:5; 18:31).

82. 10:25ff.; 11:15ff., 27ff., 37ff.; 12:13ff., 41ff., 54ff.; 13:1ff., 10ff., 22ff., 31ff.; 14:1ff., 15ff., 25ff.; 15:1ff.; 16:14ff.; 17:11ff.; 18:18ff., 35ff.; 19:1ff.

concluding that Luke was organized both volumes so as to disclose patterns of reenactment. Eliciting recurrences was the prerogative of the ancient historian, and the exercise of this prerogative does not come unnaturally from one who sought to introduce Christianity in the Greco-Roman world. His approach was at one with his efforts to relieve early Christianity of obscurity, to stress well-known Jerusalem and Judea, to cut a clear path through the technicalities of Jesus' debates with the lawyers, to avoid forging relationships between the Old Testament and the new way which were unintelligible to Gentile readers, and yet at the same time to highlight Christianity's special features as a cultural phenomenon which was universalist, superior to Judaism, and not politically subversive.[83]

## *Old Testament background*

One may well ask whether this kind of approach belongs to a recognizable historiographical tradition.[84] Ancient Israelite histories come to mind, since Luke made extensive use of Old Testament quotations, and scriptural phraseology underlies much of his narration. As notions of reenactment formed one important ideological basis for the great Israelite festivals,[85] it is only natural that they should have been transferred to and redeveloped in historiography. The great Deuteronomic history affords some important examples. In Joshua, for instance, the Jordan-crossing was consciously likened to the Exodus and the traversing of the Red Sea (Josh. 4:23, and see 6, 7, 21; cf. Deut. 6:20, Exod. 12:26–27), and Joshua came to possess the attributes of a second Moses.[86] We are meant to recognize, too, that the first Jordan-crossing was later reenacted by Elijah and Elisha, who both struck the waters with a mantle (2 Kings 2:8, 14). The interesting Captivity-Exodus motif also makes an appearance. This motif was present in prophetic works at the time of the Exile, when a disaster comparable to the Egyptian bondage had occurred.[87] It was rather subtly appropriated by the Deuteronomist (cf. Deut. 28:68), and he alone among biblical historians made the Egyptian experience a time of punishment for Israel (preceding deliverance), just like the exile to Babylon (cf. Jer. 16:14ff., 23:7f., Ezek. 20:5ff.).

Aside from these very obvious cases, and without elaborating on the well-known ground plan and basic theological standpoint of the Deuteronomist,

83. Trompf, "Section," pp. 146ff.; I. H. Marshall, "Tradition and Theology in Luke (Luke 8:5–15)" in *Tyndale Bulletin* XX, 1969, p. 73; cf. R. Banks, *Jesus and the Law* (*Society for New Testament Studies Monograph Series XXVIII*), Cambridge, 1975, p. 97ff., 180ff., and passim (for Luke's concentration on well-known legal matters). See below, sect. A, pt. 5, sect. B, pt. 4 on the relationship between the Testaments. Cf. Flender, op. cit., pp. 117ff.

84. The following section was based on Trompf, "Notions."

85. Esp. von Rad, *Message*, pp. 78ff. (the passover was a reenactment of an historical liberation, for example).

86. Josh. 4:5–7, 14, 5:15 (cf. Exod. 3:5), 24:25; cf. D. Daube, *The Exodus Pattern of the Bible* (*All Souls Studies II*), London, 1963, p. 11.

87. Esp. W. Zimmerli, "Le Nouvel 'Exode' dans le message des deux grands prophètes de l'Exile" in *Maqqél Shaqedh* (*W. Vischer Festschrift*), Montpellier, 1960, pp. 216ff.; cf. C. Chavasse, "The Suffering Servant and Moses" in *Church Quarterly Review* CLXV, 1964, pp. 162f.

there are other suggestions of reenactment which throw light on Lukan methods and assumptions. The Deuteronomist saw Moses, for example, not just as the dispenser of the Torah but as a prophet or "prophetic covenant mediator" who, despite his unique greatness (Deut. 34:10), was "the first in a series of prophets" (cf. 17:15–22). Thus "what Moses did in Deuteronomy so also did the prophets during the course of Israel's history," for, like him, they delivered the covenants and warnings of Yahweh.[88] Of all the prophets, Elijah is the one most strikingly presented as a new Moses, mediating a new covenant between Yahweh and his people from a mount, destroying his enemies with a curse, actually seeing God pass by, handing his work on to a successor, and being eventually taken up by God.[89] And there is another feature of interest partly connected with Moses, although it is better described as a special parallel between two stages of development, rather than a simple reenactment. According to the Deuteronomic frame, the wilderness wanderings bore unfavorable comparison with the actual possession of the land, because although Yahweh's commandments were delivered outside Canaan, the wilderness period was a time of grave disobedience.[90] When Joshua completed the work of Moses, however, Israel was obedient and worthy enough "to rest" before her enemies (using the verb *naḳah*).[91] A parallel seems to have been purposely drawn between this early situation and a later one under David and Solomon. Of the two monarchs, David was the great and seminal figure comparable to Moses, and was the recipient of a new covenant (2 Sam. 7:8–17), yet in his time there was great turbulence, both internal and external. It was only under his successor that the people were able "to rest" completely before their enemies, the temple then having been built.[92]

To elicit the reenactment of significant events, then, to suggest how a given figure or set of conditions recalled prior developments, was hardly foreign to Old Testament historiography, and such preoccupations do not stop short at the Deuteronomic historian.

The Chronicler's four volumes are also extremely pertinent. It is well known that his account of Israel's history from David to the Exile diverges somewhat from the Deuteronomic history, and the differences imply a good deal about special notions of recurrence in his work. Like the Deuteronomist, the Chronicler was not uninterested in paralleling the work of the great Israelite leaders. It

88. E. W. Nicholson, *Deuteronomy and Tradition*, Oxford, 1967, pp. 117f. (whence the quotations).

89. 1 Kings 18:30–40, 19:9–14, 16–21; 2 Kings 1:9–16, 2:1–15; cf. Deut. 3:21f., 4:10ff., 24:10b, 31:23, 34:9; cf. Exod., 19:16ff., 24:10, 33:11, 17–23 (J); Num. 14:26–34 (J?). Also see J. N. M. Wijngaards, *The Dramatization of Salvific History in the Deuteronomic Schools* (*Oudtestamentische Studien XVI*), Leiden, 1969, pp. 60–3.

90. Deut. 1:26f., 34f., 43–5, 2:14f., 32:51; Josh. 5:4–12.

91. Josh. 22:4, 23:1; cf. 11:23b, 14:15b, 21:44; Judg. 2:10.

92. 1 Kings 5:4, 8:56; cf. 4:25 (although note 2 Sam. 7:1, 11a on David's time). On the parallelism (without reference to "rest" theology, however), see G. Östborn, *Yahweh's Words and Deeds: A Preliminary Study into the Old Testament Representation of History* (*Uppsala Universitets Åarskrift VII*), Uppsala, 1951, p. 32.

has been recently argued, for example, that he "modelled the transition of rule from David to Solomon on that from Moses to Joshua."[93] But it is his handling of geography and general cultural atmosphere and his effort to expose similarities between certain event-complexes throughout his work that are of special relevance here.

Geographically, the Chronicler focused very heavily on Jerusalem. Apart from the fact that the northern kingdom and its centers gained so little of his consideration,[94] what happens in Jerusalem, where "Yahweh, the God of Israel, dwells forever" (cf. 1 Chron. 23:25),[95] represents his central preoccupation. For a post-Exilic writer the fate of the Jerusalem temple and its cult, and the restoration of community life in Jerusalem and Judea, were of crucial importance. There was a continuous story to be told from David's capture of "Jebus" (1 Chron. 11:4ff.) to the restoration period; within that story, the holy temple had first been built, eventually destroyed, and then rebuilt and restored—a point of great relevance to the idea of recurrence. According to the Chronicler, David was less a warrior and defender of his realm than a builder, architect, and cult organizer,[96] and Solomon was treated far less as one wise beyond compare than as a king building and ordering the temple.[97] Now in the books of Ezra and Nehemiah, significantly, we find an intense interest in the architectural history both of the Second Temple and of the restored Jerusalem, and it is an interest which noticeably complements the characteristic treatment in the earlier (?) volumes.[98]

The Chronicler apparently selected and organized his material to draw parallels between religious life under the righteous Judean monarchs and life under the restored community. To isolate the obvious ones: Not only were David and Solomon both concerned with building projects and temple officialdom, but the more meritorious of their successors had a degree of involvement also, an involvement which looked ahead to the restoration.[99] It is also noteworthy that the northern kingdom became a real defence hazard in 2 Chronicles just as the "province beyond the river" (= Samaria) was to the restored Judeans.[100]

93. H. G. M. Williamson, "The Accession of Solomon in the Books of Chronicles" in *Vetus Testamentum* XXVI, 1976, pp. 351ff.

94. Cf. 2 Chron. 10:1–19, 13:3–20, 16:1–6, 18, 20:35f., 25:17–24.

95. Though cf. R. E. Clements, *God and Temple*, Oxford, 1965, p. 128, on 2 Chron. 6:18, 21, etc.

96. 1 Chron. 13:1ff.; 14:1f. (≠ 2 Sam. 5:11f.); 15:1; 16:4ff., 37ff.; ch. 17; 21:18–22:19; ch. 28; 29:1–5; cf. von Rad, *OT Theology*, vol. 1, p. 351 (on David producing a "pattern" for Solomon like a "new Moses").

97. 2. Chron. 2:5–8:16; cf. 1 Kings, chs. 5–8; but note 2 Chron. 1:7–13, 9:1–12, and parallels.

98. Ezra and Nehemiah may have been produced before 1 and 2 Chronicles, or else were meant to have been read before the latter; cf. Goulder, unpublished typescript on the Chronicler, ch. 9, pp. 1ff. (by courtesy).

99. On Jehoida, Joash, Uzziah, Jotham, Hezekiah, Manasseh, Josiah: 2 Chron. 23:1–14, 24:5, 26:9, 27:3f., 32:5, 33:14, 34:8b–12a (only in Jehoida's and Josiah's cases are there parallels in 2 Kings).

100. 2 Chron. 11:5–12; 17:1; 25:7 (all om. 2 Kings); 16:1ff.; ch. 28; cf. Ezra, 4:9ff.; 5:3ff.; Neh. 2:9f., 4:1ff.; etc.

Material concerning the religious organization of the righteous kings of Judah, moreover, much of which is peculiar to the Chronicles, forged yet another connection between the pre- and post-Exilic situations,[101] and the priestly and Levitical duties were taken to be organized by monarchs—David, Solomon, and Hezekiah in particular—in a manner similar to restoration arrangements.[102] There are even signs that the Chronicler actually forced a post-Exilic Levitical organization on the kingly period (esp. 2 Chron. 23:2–11; cf. 2 Kings 11:4–10).[103] As for the form and content of religion in the two eras, his work suggests a variety of correspondences—in the form of temple dedications, for example (with their accompanying grand sacrifices), the keeping of the great feasts under righteous rulers, as well as purifications, exhortations, prayers, and psalms.[104]

The evidence overwhelmingly supports the view, then, that the material peculiar to Chronicles has been incorporated into those books because of their relatedness to the restoration scene. The events of the monarchical and (immediately) post-Exilic periods have been consciously paralleled. Nowhere is this more obvious than in the writer's treatment of the two important kings Hezekiah and Manasseh. The former reigned after a time of "captivity" (one afflicted on Ahaz by the Assyrians: 2 Chron. 28:20–22, 29:9, om. 2 Kings); he also performed a work of restoration with regard to the temple (29:3, 35b, om. 2 Kings), and was later forced to build up the broken walls of Jerusalem in defence against Sennacherib (32:5, om. 2 Kings). The latter actually experienced a "Babylonian exile," a punishment for his wickedness, but in his distress "he entreated the favor of Yahweh" and so humbled himself that God "brought him again to Jerusalem into his kingdom" (2 Chron. 33:12–13, om. 2 Kings). On his return Manasseh—significantly—built outer walls for Jerusalem (vs. 14a) and restored (*kūn*) Yahweh's altar in the temple (vs. 16).[105] Thus the actions of both kings foreshadow and are reenacted in the work of the restoration community. Such foreshadowing may perhaps be deemed a brand of typology, but one must guard against what has become the tyrannical propensity to uncover typological theology or literary motif without so much as a thought for specifically historiographical methods, techniques, and interests. Thus when the Chronicler, or even Luke, wished to suggest that older actions or activities were reenacted in more recent times, and when his description of earlier events was adjusted to strengthen the desired impression, he was writing historically by his lights. His

101. 2 Chron. 15:12–15; Ezra, 10:5b; Neh. 10:29 (oaths before Yahweh); 2 Chron. 17:7–9; 19:9f.; 34:30–2 (≠ 2 Kings 23:1–3); Neh. 8:1–4 (teaching and reading the Torah).

102. 1 Chron. ch. 15; 16:4; 2 Chron. 5:5–13; 7:6; 8:14f.; ch. 34. Cf. A. C. Welch, *The Work of the Chronicler: Its Purpose and Its Date* (Schweich Lectures, 1938), London, 1939, ch. 3; von Rad, *Theology*, vol. 1, pp. 351f.

103. Cf., however, W. Rudolph, *Chronikbücher* (*Handkommentar zum AT XXI*), Göttingen, 1955 edn., introd.; J. M. Myers, *I Chronicles and II Chronicles* (Anchor Bible), New York, 1965, vol. 1, pp. xlv ff.

104. For the references see Trompf, "Notions."

105. Parallel to Ezra 6:3, 9:7; Neh. 1:3bff., 9:27ff. On *kūn*, see G. Lisowsky, *Konkordanz zum hebräischen Alten Testament*, Stuttgart, 1958, p. 672.

disclosure of significances in events was integral to his historiographical enterprise, not just a passing theological reflection over and above his narrative.

Admittedly, one should be cautious here. It is all very well to write of parallelisms, correspondences, or even reenactment in the Chronicler's history, but was he really concerned with historical recurrence? Or were his chief concerns really rather different—to legitimate certain post-Exilic cultic offices (von Rad), or to illustrate religious continuity between the monarchical and restoration periods (Ackroyd), or to write a series of *midrashim* on the Hexateuch (Goulder)?[106] Certainly his sense of precedence and continuity cannot be denied, but why should one suppose that such a sense automatically excludes notions of historical repetition? We moderns, of course, tend to treat parallelism, foreshadowing, or pointed correspondence as a rather anemic variation of the recurrence idea, suggesting the loosest, least precise of repetitions. We may even want to argue that if we include parallelism and the like under the umbrella of recurrence, then the idea of historical recurrence has become too broad to be meaningful. But we cannot impose our logical distinctions on archaic minds which shared a different conceptual framework. The ancient historian usually worked out such connections, however allusively, with the utmost seriousness; they brought cohesion and deep significance to his narrative.

These sorts of connections shine through the Chronicler's arrangement of materials. G. Östborn, although he has been overeager to uncover patterns of cyclical thinking in the Old Testament, rightly noted that the Chronicler's general schema—a new and good order established under David and Solomon, in accordance with the law of Moses/disturbances of this order through the disobedience of kings/a new and good order established under Ezra and Nehemiah, in accordance with the law of Moses—also points in the direction which interests us.[107] And there remains the emphasis on two key figures at both the beginning and end of the whole narrative. David and Solomon are brought into closer relationship than in the Deuteronomic history (2 Chron. 22:6–23:1, 28:1–29:25; cf. 1 Kings 2:1–9), and the originally quite separate careers of Ezra and Nehemiah are telescoped together (esp. Neh. 8:9, and cf. Ezra 9–10, Neh. 9–10).[108] The Chronicler's unqualified approval of these four, in contrast to

106. Von Rad, *Theology*, vol. 1, p. 352, and cf. p. 330 n. 6; P. Ackroyd, "The Age of the Chronicler: The Great Reformers, 1" (Lecture to the Australian and New Zealand Society for Theological Studies, Melbourne, 17 August 1970); "History and Theology in the Writings of the Chronicler" in *Concordia Theological Monthly* XXXVIII, 1967, pp. 508ff.; "The Temple Vessels—A Continuity Theme" in *Studies in the Religion of Ancient Israel* (*Vetus Testamentum Supplement XXIII*), Leiden, 1972, pp. 166ff.; cf. *Continuity*, London, 1962; Goulder, "The Chronicler," op. cit., ch. 9.

107. Op. cit., p. 41; cf. pp. 36ff.

108. For background see D. N. Freeman, "The Chronology of Israel and the Ancient Near East" in *The Bible and the Ancient Near East* (W. F. Albright Festschrift) (ed. G. E. Wright), London, 1961, pp. 213ff.; H. H. Rowley, "Nehemiah's Mission and Its Background" in *Men and God: Studies in Old Testament History and Prophecy*, London, 1963, pp. 229ff. See also F. M. Cross, "A Reconstruction of the Judean Restoration" in *Journal of Biblical Literature* XCIV, 1975, p. 11

evident reservations about the other rulers in between, even the more righteous ones,[109] clearly calls for a reevaluation of his historiographical presuppositions. While we have yet to examine his approach to retribution, it may be affirmed that his redaction indicates an interest in recurrent patterns, both in the reenactment and foreshadowing of key religious practices and in a special paralleling of spiritual conditions under the united monarchy and the restoration community. For him, admittedly, history did not have its own inner, natural logic, for he tended to view events *sub specie aeternitatis*; but he understood the Lord of history to be revealing his providential activity in the configurations and eventualities he so carefully detected.

### *The reenactment of Old Testament events in Luke-Acts*

The redactions of the Old Testament historians and the connections they made between key events in Israel's history obviously form an important intellectual background to Luke-Acts. Luke was well acquainted with the Old Testament (LXX), and both his use of the text and his re-creation of ancient atmosphere surrounding the scriptures persuade one that he sought to forge links between the momentous happenings of recent times and the previous history of Israel. Was he merely trying to establish a certain continuity between the old and the new, or to indicate the fulfillment of ancient predictions in the events of the "last era," or to allude to the *typoi Christou* in the Hebrew writings? Or are we justified in pressing our earlier line of argument yet further and contending that Luke saw reenactment of the old in new times? Certainly he did not hesitate to admit Christianity's Jewish origins, and even if he stressed the Jewish rejection of Jesus (sect. B), he acknowledged Israelite-Christian continuity. It is true, too, that he interested himself in the fulfillment of ancient prophecy (cf. esp. Luke 4:21; Acts 2:15ff.), and what is conventionally deemed typology is not entirely absent from his work (cf. below). Luke's employment of the Old Testament and its atmosphere, however, was quite distinctive compared to other early Christian treatments. How is it to be characterized?

Five relevant features may be singled out:

1. Luke's implicit claim that all the law and the prophets refer to Jesus.
2. His special approach to scriptural fulfillment.
3. His attempts to forge links between the old and the new orders by suggesting the reenactment of certain events.
4. His paralleling of the general atmosphere of both orders.
5. His decidedly "typological" connections between the Old Testament and both Jesus and his Church.

First, the strongly Lukan references to the law and the prophets in Luke 24

---

for evidence from 1 Esdras and Josephus that Nehemiah's diary was added late as part of the final edition of the Chronicler's work.

109. See below, sect. B, pt. 2; cf. esp. 2 Chron. 19:2f., 20:33, 24:17ff., 32:25, 35:22b.

(vss.25–27, 44–45; cf. also Acts 26:22–23 and 28:23b) merit attention.[110] In 24:25 Jesus rebukes the two disciples on the Emmaus road for not believing *all* that the prophets had spoken. He then asks whether it was not necessary that Christ should suffer and enter into his glory (vs.26; cf. Mark 9:12b), and beginning from Moses and *all* the prophets, he explains or interprets to them *all* the scriptures about himself (vs.27). To the disciples not long afterward and by way of a reminder (cf. 18:31, 22:37), Jesus asserts that it has been necessary for *all* that was written about him in the law of Moses, the prophets, and the psalms to be fulfilled (*plērōthēnai*) (vs.44), and he then opens their minds to the holy writings (vs.46). The stress on the exhaustive witness of scripture is intriguing. Although Luke has selected Old Testament quotations throughout his work, he here appears to reject the search for purple passages to legitimate Christological claims. This apparent rejection implies that Christ did not fulfill the scriptures just by actualizing various proleptic visions (the number of which was limited in the Old Testament), and leads us to ask whether for Luke the events of the Old Testament could be fulfilled by being reenacted. The use of the verb *plērōthēnai* in 24:44 may perhaps at first seem to count against this alternative view, but we must probe further.

In the second feature, what did Luke understand by fulfillment of the scriptures, and how distinctive was that understanding? His use of *plēroun* and *plērōthēnai* (apart from instances where the meaning has nothing to do with fulfillment)[111] offers rather meager evidence for clarifying semantics. In three cases the verb indicates that a foretold state of affairs has come to pass (Luke 1:20, Acts 1:16, 3:18),[112] and on other occasions although Luke did not use that verb he implied that proleptic statements about the new Age were being realized.[113] Yet such popular phraseology as: "In order that the scriptures might be fulfilled" does not seem to have suited Luke as it did the other Evangelists.[114] Perhaps the best clue to a more characteristically Lukan understanding of fulfillment lies in Luke 22:16, where criteria are provided by synoptic parallels (cf. Luke 22:18 ≠ Mark 14:25 ≠ Matt. 26:29).[115] There *plērōthēnai* (om. Mark, Matt.) carries a definite sense of reenactment: the passover is now being kept, yet it will also be "fulfilled" in the kingdom, that is, it will be reenacted in a more complete and decisive way at a later stage. This passover itself was Christ's reenactment of a Mosaic institution, but a reenactment so as to give it a completeness and a newer significance which the earlier ordinance lacked.[116] The future meal in the kingdom, the eschatological banquet, will be both a reenactment and a final comple-

110. On Luke 24:25–7 and 44f. as Lukan theology, see Conzelmann, op. cit., p. 202.

111. Cf. Luke 2:40, 3:5; Acts 2:2, 28, 5:3, 28, 13:52.

112. Are the last two references based on pre-Lukan, Aramaic sources? Cf. G. D. Kilpatrick, *The Origins of the Gospel according to St. Matthew*, Oxford, 1946, p. 45; Wilcox, op. cit., p. 145 n. 8.

113. Luke 3:3–5, 7:27, 19:38, 20:17, 41–4; Acts 2:16–21, 25–8, 34f., 3:18, 4:25–8, 7:52b, 8:32–5.

114. See W. F. Moulton and A. S. Geden, *A Concordance to the Greek Testament*, Edinburgh, 1906 edn., p. 816.

115. In Luke 22:16, Luke has specially developed what he received in Mark 14:25.

116. On Luke linking the passovers of Moses and Christ see G. B. Caird, *Saint Luke* (The Pelican Gospel Commentaries), Harmondsworth, 1963, pp. 34f.

tion of the Last Supper. It is typical of Luke that atonement theology should be only vaguely if at all present in his account of the pre-crucifixion supper (cf. esp. Mark 14:24; Matt. 26:28); his chief concern was with stages of development—the original passover, Christ's new passover (located at a specific time before, and thus clearly distinct from, the time of the passion),[117] and the passover to come.

This approach to *plērōthēnai* in 22:16 enables us to give a constructive explanation for other strongly Lukan usages. At times the verb was utilized to convey the completion of an act or time span,[118] yet key passages make it evident that for Luke scripture could see fulfillment by a special and potent reenactment of Old Testament events. In Luke 9:31, at the scene of the Transfiguration, to take a most important example, Moses and Elijah appear and speak to Jesus about his *exodos* "which he was going to fulfill (*plēroun*) in Jerusalem" (om. Mark Matt.). By allusion, the scriptures, the book of Exodus in particular, come to refer to Jesus, and yet he actually reenacts the Exodus supersessively by journeying to Jerusalem and by overcoming the powers which temporarily bind him there. And in Luke the ascension or *analēmpsis* (cf. Luke 9:51a) represents the culmination of Christ's personal victory and the attainment of his glory; if the appearance of Moses on the mount points to the new exodus, the simultaneous appearance of Elijah looks to the ascension (so *symplērousthai* in 9:51a, and cf. LXX 2 Kings 2:9, 10, 11b).[119] Thus the Lukan Jesus comes to reenact two important high points in the Old Testament. The implications of fulfillment in ch. 9, moreover, are similar to those in 22:16 on the passover.

When one turns to that crucial passage in Luke 4 which introduces Jesus' Galilean ministry, this same sense of fulfillment emerges again. Jesus reads from the scroll at Isa. 61:1–2 (with 58:6b!), announcing that "today" this passage had been "fulfilled" (*peplērōtai*) (4:21). Luke evidently wished to stress Jesus' teaching more than his deeds in this context,[120] since it was the words of good news in the passage which were being fulfilled.[121] Yet neither Luke nor his readers would have denied that Isaiah himself, in uttering his oracle, had proclaimed this good news to the poor, to the prisoners, and to those waiting the Lord's acceptable year;[122] it was simply that Christ had also preached these things and that his

117. Hence the phrase "before I suffer": 22:15b, om. Mark, Matt. Cf. Matt. 27:15a, John 18:39.

118. Fulfillment in the other Gospels generally means prophecy fulfillment, yet for Luke on "completion" see Luke 7:1, 21:24; Acts 2:1, (*syn-*) 7:23, 30, 9:23, 12:25, 13:25, 14:26, 19:21, 24:27, (*ek-*) 21:26. On *telein*/*telesthēnai* see Luke 2:39, 12:50, 22:37; cf. 18:31.

119. Cf. *analēphthēnai*, *analambanomenon*, *anelēphthē* in these OT verses respectively. Luke clinches the connection by referring to this *analēmpsis* at the beginning of a passage reminiscent of an Elijah story (9:52–6; cf. 2 Kings, ch. 1) and by using a cognate expression for the ascension (Acts 1:11). On the *Elias-Christologie* in Luke here, see also K. Rengstorf, *Das Evangelium nach Lukas* (*Das Neue Testament Deutsch III*), Göttingen, 1962, p. 125.

120. Note how vss. 18f. condense the original to put an emphasis on acts of proclamation.

121. *Hē graphē* should be translated "the passage of scripture" as against *hai graphai*, "the scriptures"; cf. K. Lake and H. J. Cadbury, "The Acts of the Apostles: English Translation and Commentary" in *Beginnings* (ed. Foakes Jackson and Lake), pt. 1, vol. 4, p. 12.

122. Isa. 51:1ff. was treated by some Jewish writers as concerning the Messianic Age (H. L. Strack and P. Billerbeck, *Kommentar zum Neuen Testament aus Talmud und Midrasch*, Munich, 1924

proclamation was the final one, the one which completed the preaching of all God's messengers in Israel's past. Fulfillment here entails reenactment. It is thus significant that Jesus, through his additional remarks (in 4:25–27), is then likened to the prophets Elijah and Elisha, who were sent to others rather than to a disobedient Israel. Once more Jesus does what has been done previously, yet the consequences of *his* actions, by comparison, were all-decisive. Such evidence indicates, then, that Luke did not wish to confine the Old Testament witness about Christ and the last times to prophetic prediction, and that he fostered a special understanding of fulfillment based on the historical relatedness between one age and another. It is true that Luke connected the fulfillment of prophetic utterances with Jesus' suffering (Luke 18:31–34a, 22:37; Acts 3:17–18, 13:27, 29; cf. Luke 24:25–26; Acts 8:32–33), but on the other hand, we could hardly expect him to have fastened onto the very small number of prophecies about a suffering (even a resurrected!) Messiah in the name of *all* the prophets. One of his key emphases was that Jesus was in line with the ancient prophets, that like them (though as the final actor in the whole drama of Israel's history) he encountered, warned, and was put to death by the same rebellious people [cf. Luke 4:24–39, 11:49–51 (Matt. 23:34–36), 13:33–35, 20:9–18 (≠ Mark 12:1–12); Acts 7:52–53; cf. 28:25–27]. On the understanding that Jews still rebelled against God's commandments even when confronted with the Messiah, and that Jesus carried the corrective yet despised work of God's servants to a finale, then the whole of the law, prophets, and Bible refers to Christ.

The special sense of reenactment in Luke's approach to scripture fulfillment brings us to the third feature of his work worthy of examination, his attempt to forge links between the old order, the time of the law and the prophets (ending with John the Baptist), and the new Age of salvation (beginning with Jesus's baptism),[123] by suggesting the reenactment of certain events. We have covered some of the relevant ground already; it may be reiterated how for Luke Jesus repeated the deeds of Moses (in his passover and exodus) and of the great prophet Elijah (both in not being sent to his own at a time of crisis, and in his ascension). In some other respects Luke's Jesus appears as a new, though better, Moses. He authorizes twelve tribal representatives and seventy others to perform special tasks for him;[124] like Moses and Elijah he receives a special revelation on the mountain (and in the waters);[125] he is a great teacher of God's

edn., vol. 2, p. 146), but the prophet himself was not forgotten (cf. *Isaiah Targum*, ed. J. F. Stenning, Oxford, 1949, p. 172, *l*.3). A similar approach underlies Acts 13:32 (pre-Lukan?).

123. Luke 3:2–6, 16–8, 7:24–30, 16:16, 20:1–8; Acts 1:22, 13:24f., 19:3f. John seems to be placed midway between the two Ages (Luke 3, 7:26, 28; Acts 13:25a), and although Luke distinctively notes the completion of John's ministry before recounting Jesus' baptism and lineage (Luke 3:19, 21f., 23ff.; cf. Mark 1:9, 14; Matt. 3:13, 4:12; John 1:19ff., 3:22–4), the evidence does not warrant the fixed three-staged view of history educed by Conzelmann; see below, sect. C.

124. Luke 6:13–6, 9:1–6, 22:29f.; Num. 1:44, 11:16f., 24f. (though some might prefer the harder reading for Luke 10:1 and 17).

125. Luke 6:12, 9:30f., 35 (cf. 3:21f.); Exod. 19:20, 33:21–3 (cf. 14:21f.); 1 Kings 19:8, 11f. (cf. 2 Kings 2:8, 11b, 14b).

Word[126] (even if he is less a legislator in Luke than "the prophet like unto Moses" who was to come: cf. 7:16b, 26:19; Acts 3:22–23, 7:37).[127] and like Moses he performs "signs and wonders" only to face the rebelliousness of his own people (Acts 7:35–43, 52–3; cf. 2:22–23). As for the other prophets, we have already argued that Luke's Christ reenacts their careers as a whole, though the work of Jesus (and even John) represented a culmination point in Israel's history (Luke 11:32b, 7:26b, 28). It was not possible that a prophet should die "away from" (*exō*) Jerusalem (13:33), which may simply mean that none died clear of Jerusalem's influence,[128] but most probably means that Luke was simplifying matters unduly in his effort to convey the impression of reenactment (cf. Neh. 9:26). Even the special details of John's death are omitted in Luke (3:20, 7:19, 9:7b; Acts 7:5a; cf. Mark. 6:14–29), so that this general impression comes the more easily. Statements about imminent doom for the house of Israel, moreover, are more frequent and more widespread in Luke than in the other Gospels (cf. esp. 11:50, 13:35, 19:41–44, 21:6–24, 23:29–30; cf. Mark 13:2–23; Matt. 23:36–24:28), and thus Jesus emerges as a prophet of coming destruction like those of old, such as Jeremiah and Ezekiel, who predicted Jerusalem's earlier captivity and downfall.[129] Jesus' and John's call to repentance receives a sharper focus in Luke than with other Evangelists;[130] Luke therefore characterized Jesus's teaching as a recalling to God in line with the old prophetic message, but at a higher level and at the beginning of the last Age (cf. 7:28, 16:16). For Luke Jesus was "sent" as any prophet is.[131] Furthermore, he consciously fostered parallels between Jesus and both Elijah and Elisha. The miracle story cycles associated with these two figures were the most obvious biblical precedents for Gospel episodes,[132] and Luke has developed the connection variously with miracle stories and special utterances.[133] Like Elijah, Jesus is capable of calling down fire on his rejectors (but he declines!: Luke 9:52–56; cf. 2 Kings 1:10, 12), and in the same context hears an excuse from a potential disciple similar to one heard by Elijah from his eventual successor (Luke 9:61; cf. 1 Kings 19:20). The ascension clinched the parallelism. Perhaps Luke did not wish to identify Jesus

126. Luke 4:4, 8, 12, 5:14, 23, 30f., 33–5, 6:3–5, 9, 20–49, 10:26–37, 13:15–7, 14:4, 20:21–47 (with close exegesis revealing how little Luke was interested in Jesus as the interpreter of the Torah).

127. Background: Deut. 18:15; IQ Test. 5–8; Test. Benj. 9:2 (ιβς); 1 Macc. 14:41b.

128. Background: Neh. 9:26; 2 Chron. 24:21; Mart. Isa., etc.

129. Cf. Deut. 28:64; Jer. 8–22; Ezek. 4–8. Note Luke's significant use of the term *aichmalōtisthēsontai* in 21:24 (om. Mark, Matt.), a technical term recalling the earlier captivity of the Jews and the fall of Jerusalem; cf. LXX 2 Kings 24:14 (*aichmalōsias, aichmalōtisas*). As interesting background to Luke's approach here, see pseudo-Jonathan, Gen. 4:12, 14 (M. Ginsburger, ed., Berlin, 1903, p. 9), where the use of the term *galī* (om. MT) makes Cain the first man to be punished by exile.

130. Esp. 13:3, 5, 15:7, 10, 16:30, 26:47 (om. Mark, Matt.), 5:32b; cf. Mark 2:17; Matt. 9:13.

131. G. W. H. Lampe, "The Lucan Portrait of Christ" in *New Testament Studies* II, 1955–56, p. 169.

132. B. Lindars, "Elijah, Elisha and the Gospel Miracles" in *Miracles: Cambridge Studies in Their Philosophy and History* (ed. C. D. F. Moule), London, 1965, pp. 66–76.

133. See Excursus 3, Exegetical Note E.

with Elijah (that identification was actually reserved for John),[134] yet Jesus' words and deeds resurrect the greatest work of the prophets—their pronouncements of judgment, their call to "return" (*shūv*) from evil, and their miracles, which were, after all, recorded in the historical books forming part of "the Prophets" (*n$^e$bi'm*). To reiterate, *all* the prophets referred to him and were "fulfilled" through him.

We may now turn from Jesus to the early Christian communities. Luke wished to demonstrate that God's new instrument, the Church, encountered the same Israelite rebelliousness which not only Jesus but God's servants of old had met with. According to Stephen's protracted address, the same people who would not listen to Moses in the past did not heed the proclamations of the Church either (Acts 7:39–43, 51–53; cf. also Luke 16:31). For Luke, then (and this was hardly out of line with a key Old Testament theme), disobedience was a recurring phenomenon in Jewish history. At the end of Acts there lies a significant Isaianic quotation (from 6:9–10) which makes this very point as a finale to his volumes (28:26–27). Whereas Matthew places this oracle on the lips of Christ, treating it as a fulfillment of a predictive statement about the last times (cf. Matt. 13:13–15), Luke conveys the impression that both Isaiah's original listeners and the Jews of Paul's own day were "dull in heart," "heavy of hearing," and with "closed eyes."[135] In Paul's opinion the Holy Spirit was right in saying these words to their fathers (28:25b), and so the present disobedience is taken as a repetition, though a more guilt-incurring repetition, of former violations. Thus this passage of scripture is fulfilled in the special Lukan sense already discussed.

Other Old Testament references in Acts may be interpreted along similar lines. Luke wrote after the fall of Jerusalem, and as we have already suggested, he was also quite aware of the earlier ravaging of Jerusalem and the temple (at the hands of the Babylonians). In two quotations the two destructions of Jerusalem appear to be presupposed. When Stephen quotes from Amos 5:25–27, the prophet's predictive judgment is not that the disobedient, idol-worshipping Israelites will be "carried away beyond Damascus" (so LXX 5:27a), but "beyond Babylon" (Acts 7:43b).[136] By implication, then, there will be a second punishment for the Jews parallel to yet far more extreme than the Babylonian exile. When James quotes from three prophets (mainly from Amos 9:11–12) in Acts 15:16–18, the second fall of Jerusalem is assumed, and the second restoration, which is the eschatological restoration, is announced (cf. sect. C).[137] In Acts,

134. Luke 7:27 (cf. Mal. 3:1), yet note Mark 9:11; 13 ≠ Matt. 17:10–2, 11:14 (om. Luke). Some believed Elijah would restore the twelve tribes (Ecclus. 48:9f.); cf. Lampe, "Lucan Portrait," but there is no evidence that Luke was interested in this tradition.

135. Does Luke's special treatment of Isa. 6 throw some doubt on whether it formed part of early Christian *testimonia?* Cf. T. Holtz, *Untersuchungen über die alttestamentlichen Zitate bei Lukas* (*Texte und Untersuchungen zur Geschichte der altchristlichen Literatur CIV*), Berlin, 1968, pp. 35f.

136. Against the view that this was a "pointless alteration": W. L. Knox, *Some Hellenistic Elements in Primitive Christianity* (Schweich Lectures, 1942), London, 1944, pp. 14f.

137. This restoration belongs to the "time of the Gentiles" (vs. 17b, Luke 21:24b; yet cf. Mark

therefore, particularly in connection with Jewish disobedience and its consequences, Luke reflects his interest in historical recurrence as he specially understood it; without going beyond the permissions of evidence, the Church comes close to being the "righteous remnant" and the "new Israel" who, like the rebuffed holy ones of old, bears the true message of salvation.[138]

In two other ways Luke forged links between the old and new orders: by paralleling the general atmosphere of both orders, and by "typological" connections. We may comment briefly on each. Luke, proficient in Greek, was able to infuse a heavily biblical (or, if one prefers, Septuagintal) atmosphere into some parts of his work. There are both stylistic touches and whole scenes which were intended to invoke the Old Testament world. They indicate his working knowledge of the ancient scriptures, particularly of the historical works they contained, since Luke was, after all, writing a history which was meant to carry on the narrative of divinely-guided affairs to the climax of the last days.[139] In the main, the more archaic qualities in Luke's narrative are influenced by 1 Samuel–2 Kings, 1 Chronicles–Nehemiah. The career of Jesus and the acts of the apostles recalled the ancient historical accounts of God's champions, especially the prophets.[140] Both the beginning and end of Luke-Acts, moreover, have striking affinities with the opening and closing chapters of the great Old Testament histories. The *Magnificat* of Luke 1 and the genealogy of 3 have strong associations with the prayer of Hannah in 1 Samuel 2 and the genealogy of 1 Chronicles 1. One may also note the parallels both between the decree of Augustus (Luke 2:1) and the decree of Cyrus (Ezra 1:1b–4), and between the chronological procedures of Luke 1:5, 3:1–2 and Ezra 1:1a. And scholars have overlooked the similarity between the ending of Luke's work (Acts 28:30–31), and the conclusion to the Deuteronomic history at 2 Kings 25:27–30. Both Jehoiachin and Paul were captives away from their fatherland, and yet were allowed relative freedom and the economic means to live comfortably. The strange ending of Acts is no longer strange; it has the special touch of Old Testament history upon it.

There remains the Evangelist's more directly typological approach to the ancient scriptures. This concerns his appeal to traditional motifs and categories which were not developed in terms of reenactment, but by which he nevertheless characterized Jesus (and his Church). The most important of such categories was the Davidic-monarchical one, which related to Jewish expectations of the Messiah. It is admittedly true that once Jesus was raised and glorified his kingly power was unmistakably assured, and in his universal dominion the Davidic

13:20, Matt. 24:22). On Luke's historicization of the Little Apocalypse, see below, pt. 6, and sect. B, pt. 4.

138. Acts 2:43–7, 3:21, 4:24–31, 7:48f., 13:16–43, 15:15–21, 21:17–26, etc.; R. J. McKelvey, *The New Temple: The Church in the New Testament*, Oxford, 1969, pp. 86ff.; cf. P. Richardson, *Israel in the Apostolic Church* (*Society for New Testament Studies Monograph Series* X), Cambridge, 1969, pp. 31ff.

139. See Excursus 3, Exegetical Note F.

140. See Excursus 3, Exegetical Note G.

rule found restoration and reenactment, but on considering the "Jesus of history" Luke was only able to evince the reenactment of some of the most significant events of the Old Testament in a rather shadowy way.[141] It was not easy to depict the earthly Jesus in a monarchical rôle, like Simon Maccabeus, for example, whose rule was presented as a return to the ideal conditions of the Davidic-Solomonic era in 1 Macc. 14:4–15, 37–41.[142] Consequently, Luke's Davidic theme is less concerned with reenactment than with suggesting David and his kingdom to be the type and prefigurement of the glorified Christ and his dominion.[143] Furthermore, despite his special recapitulation of the old order,[144] Luke's Christ was ultimately a unique figure. We should put our study of recurrence notions in Luke into proper perspective by emphasizing that his Christ was the unique harbinger of final salvation, and the Church of Acts was bent on proclaiming this special saviorhood.[145] The genuine individuality of Jesus, however, was not in spite of, but because of, his reenactment of Old Testament word and deed. There are certainly theological stances in Luke-Acts, but we still rest on the position that they lie behind, rather than overcome or substitute for, Luke's conscious attempt to write a sympathetic narrative, to write a history which was meaningful in terms of his intellectual inheritance.

In review, Luke emerges as one preoccupied not only with interrelating events and situations within a first-century arena, but also with demonstrating connections between the old and new orders. Thus his protagonists, particularly Jesus, reenact the most significant events of the Old Testament, and the spiritual quality of their recent activity resuscitates what was outstanding in the Israelite past. In establishing these latter connections, Luke was deeply influenced by the Old Testament sacred histories; it was not just their contents which were important for him but the manner in which they, too, interrelated occurrences and circumstances from different periods and suggested instances of a later return to former conditions. It should be observed, moreover, how Luke's special approach to the Holy Spirit enabled him to reinforce the impression that the spiritual vitality of Israel's past great ones had recurred in his own time. Though the Spirit was manifest in greater fullness than ever before with the coming of

141. Luke 1:32f., 2:8 (cf. Rengstorf, op. cit., pp. 40f.), 3:22, 31b, 4:18a (cf. 2 Sam. 23:2), 27, 10:38, 19:38, 23:2f., 38; Acts 2:30f., 13:22f.; cf. (on Christos) Luke 4:41b, 9:20, 23:35b, 39b, 24:26, 46; Acts 2:36, 17:3, etc., and (on kingship through glorification), Acts 2:24f., 3:20f., 5:31, 10:42, 13:32–6, etc. A. R. C. Leaney surely exaggerated when claiming that Luke's Gospel concentrates mainly on the kingly aspects of Christ's work: *The Gospel according to St. Luke* (Black Commentaries), London, 1966 edn., pp. 34–7.

142. Also 9:21 (≠ 2 Sam. 1:19, 25) for the lament of Judas Maccabeus; cf. Goulder, *Type*, p. 12.

143. The typologies of Christ and the Teacher of Righteousness as the new or second Moses in Matthew and Qumranite literature thus carry a stronger implication of recurrence in this case: cf. W. D. Davies, *The Setting of the Sermon on the Mount*, Cambridge, 1964, pp. 25ff.; N. Wieder, "'The Law Interpreter' of the Dead Sea Scrolls: The Second Moses" in *Journal of Jewish Studies* IV, 1953, pp. 158ff.

144. Luke's approach foreshadows that of Irenaeus, though it is not to be confused with it: see below, Chapter 4, sect. D, pt. 2.

145. I. H. Marshall, *St. Luke: Historian and Theologian*, Exeter, 1970, chs. 4–8; cf. *The Gospel of Luke, a Commentary on the Greek Text*, London, 1978.

Jesus (Luke 1:35, 41, 3:22a, 4:1, 18, 10:21), and with the ongoing mission of the Church (Acts 2:4, 4:31, 8:17, 10:44, 11:15, 13:2, 9, 16:7, etc.; cf. Luke 11:13, 12:12), it had also been at work in Old Testament times (Acts 1:16, 4:25; cf. 17:25b, Luke 1:17). As usual the events of the new time reflect *both* reenactment and uniqueness.

### *Luke-Acts and the reenactment of significant events in Gentile history*

Naturally, Luke's interconnections between the old and the new would have been best appreciated and understood by those who had already pored over the pages of the Septuagint, but what of his Gentile readers? Luke was never so technical nor so Semitic in his approach that his work would have fallen on deaf ears among non-Jews. The links he disclosed between latter-day events and Israelite history, we should hasten to add, were through brief and not particularly subtle allusions. Yet a writer who presents himself as an historian and informer for a wider public, but who other expects his readers to bear with the Septuagintalisms of Luke 1–2 seems something of a paradox. It is surely worth inquiring how interested he was in the problems of his Gentile readers, and to what extent he accommodated himself to their non-Jewish understanding of history.

Luke never assumed the rôle of a theoretician in his work, one who expounded his view of historical processes in a series of parentheses. To that extent he was firmly entrenched in the Hebraic (and earliest Christian) rather than the Greco-Roman historical tradition. Yet his work seems like a circuitous voyage from one cultural milieu to another, and as the narrative continues Hellenistic readers would have felt more and more at home among details of Roman administration, pagan folklore, and the great cultural centers of the Empire. Put simply, the shift from Jerusalem to Athens and Rome was more a matter of interest to Gentiles (particularly Greeks and Romans, of course) than to Jews or inhabitants of the Middle East. Luke could have expanded on the local, Levantine and Syrian thrust of the Church, or considered missionary work east of Jordan and south of Gaza[146]—after all, there were other stories to be told, and we have no reason to believe that he was incapable of looking in other directions. But to depict a westward thrust was a very useful ploy for the benefit of readers living under the Roman aegis. In any case, the literary cohesion of Luke-Acts was facilitated by this approach.

The movement westward also nicely heightened the significance of recent developments, suggesting a workable pattern or contour. It was the apprehension of a clear shape acquired by a whole series of events which so commonly motivated the history-writing of the ancients and of many after them. A great war (so Herodotus, Thucydides), a process of decay (the Deuteronomist,

146. Acts 1:9f., 8:26ff. are indications that Luke could have been led in other directions. That he was unaware of Paul's early movements (in Arabia, Gal. 1:17) is demonstrated in Acts 9:23ff. Cf. also Eusebius *Eccles. hist.* I,xiii, IV,1ff.

Poseidonius: cf. Chapter 4), or "surprising new developments" (Polybius), were the most easily recognized configurations. It is important, moreover, to realize that biographies were in vogue in Luke's time and that they recounted the sometimes startling, sometimes edifying accomplishments of well-known personalities or "immortals."[147] In his day, too, the unparalleled imperial success of Rome was extolled. Polybius' history, naturally enough, was a popular one, and on reading how he held Fortune to have directed affairs toward Roman supremacy (*Hist.* I,iv,2), and how the great Scipio Africanus, out of magnanimity and loyalty to Rome, refused the opportunity of subjecting the whole world to himself (X,xl,7–9), one might well be pardoned for characterizing Polybius' general thesis as "the gospel of Rome." Certainly Luke and Polybius shared an interest in expansion and widening influence, in the breakdown of traditional geographical boundaries, and in the virtues required for achieving these things,[148] although they differed radically over the permanent consequences of the events they described. It is remarkable that Polybius could readily predict the fall of something so apparently immovable as the Roman Empire, and yet Luke could acclaim the final durability of a movement which had merely thrown confusion into diaspora synagogues and captured the attention of a few Roman officials!

Enough has been written to persuade us that Luke did not write exclusively under the influence of the biblical tradition. In fact, it has already been fairly popular to consider his work in connection with Greco-Roman histories, lives, and romance literature,[149] so much so that the relationship between Luke-Acts and Old Testament historiography, on which we have partly commented, has been neglected. The Hellenistic side of the coin, however, requires reexamination with questions of historical recurrence in mind. Knowledge of Israelite historiographical procedures is indispensable for grasping Luke's working assumptions and methodology, yet his procedures are not explicable wholly in such terms. Certainly the parallelisms of the Deuteronomist (between the two periods of "rest," for instance), or of the Chronicler (between the Davidic-Solomonic and restoration eras), bear comparison with his links between the Old Testament, Christ's life, and early Church history. Reenactments of special events (as in Josh. 4, 1 Kings 19, and 2 Kings 2) may certainly be likened to those we first elicited from Luke-Acts, and the Evangelist's geographical patterning is comparable to the Chronicler's top-heavy concentration on the destiny of Judah. If we have found "updating" in the Chronicler's work, we can also detect it in Luke's "farewell discourse" and in the Herodian trial of Jesus, as well as in

147. For the relevant literature see F. W. Walbank and D. A. Russell in *OCD*, s.v. "Roman Biography" (pp. 167f.); C. H. Talbert, "The Concept of Immortals in Mediterranean Antiquity" in *Journal of Biblical Literature* XCIV, 1975, pp. 419ff.

148. On Roman loyalty as virtue see above, Chapter 2, sect. B, pt. 2(iii); cf. Luke 12:8–12 (on vs. 10, Trompf, "Section," p. 148).

149. Since Cadbury, *Making*, pt. 2; Dibelius, op. cit., chs. 8–9. Cf. A. Ehrhardt, "The Construction and Purpose of the Acts of the Apostles" in *Studia Theologica* XII, 1958, pp. 45ff.; Barrett, op. cit., pp. 26ff.; E. Plümacher, *Lukas als hellenistischer Schriftsteller: Studien zur Apostelgeschichte* (*Studien zum Unwelt des Neuen Testaments* IX), Göttingen, 1972, ch. 1; Talbert, "Concept."

his referral of the visionary predictions of the Little Apocalypse to the fall of Jerusalem in 70 AD.[150] But the intensity with which Luke heightened history's significance by interconnections, reenactment, and the return of prior conditions suggests an eclectic tendency, a conscious effort to bridge the gap between the sensibilities of Jews and Gentiles by educing significances which were meaningful to both. We may well ask whether Ulrich Wilckens was not right when he broadened the sense of "Salvation History" and asserted that "the *Heilsgeschichte* of Luke is that of the Hellenistic historian."[151] Without dilating on difficult German terms, however, we may now consider Luke's approaches to historical recurrence, especially to reenactment, vis-à-vis Greco-Roman historiographical preconceptions.

Luke did not refer explicitly to the major events of Gentile history, but that was natural enough, for these events did not belong to the ethnic and religious tradition which lay behind Jesus and his first followers, and the history of "the nations" was much more diffuse than the story of God's people. However, concerned as he was with Gentile readers and, among other things, their suspicions toward Christianity, we should not be surprised to find subtle allusions to the great events and achievements of the pagan past.[152]

We may reflect first on imperial, and especially Roman, history. Judea was one of the far corners of the Roman empire. With striking speed, as Polybius had observed, the Roman standard had penetrated as far as Egypt and the Levant. Luke's was a comparable success story on a quite different plane. Christianity moved in the reverse direction, and the provinces first affected were those which Rome took last. When the crucial Hellespontine boundary had been crossed or bypassed, the missionary work extended to European centers riddled with history and past glory. Macedonia and its city of Philippi, the country and capital which were once the starting point of Alexander's great military expedition to the East and an important springboard for Roman intervention into Asia,[153] now actually "need" Paul (!) according to the divine vision (Acts 16:9; cf. 7–12). Athens, once a city of splendor and great learning, has the trivial speculations of its intellectuals (17:21), and its worship of gods made with hands (vs.29, and cf. 24–25), exposed by a message with a superior revelation. Corinth, the city whose destruction above all marked the real defeat of traditional Hellas

150. On the last matter see esp. C. H. Dodd, "The Fall of Jerusalem and the Abomination of Desolation" in *Journal of Roman Studies* XXXVII, 1957, pp. 47ff.; cf. R. Maddox, op. cit., pp. 4f.

151. "The Understanding of Revelation within the History of Primitive Christianity" in *Revelation as History* (ed. W. Pannenberg) (ET), London, 1969, p. 98.

152. When Josephus, in writing so voluminously about the unique Jewish traditions (*Adversus Apionem* II,164–6, *Antiq.* I,14, 20, III), briefly commented on the great variety of polities and constitutional changes (*metabolai*) experienced by the Jewish nation (I,14), and intruded Greek notions of early pastoralism, the growth of ethical consciousness, and political *metabolai* into his work (I,52f., 60f., 64–6, 69f., IV,223, V,132ff., 234, VI,83–5, XI,111–3, XIV,90f., XX,229f., etc.), he adopted a method and made accommodations in a way not very dissimilar to Luke's. On Luke allaying suspicion see esp. Cadbury, *Making*, pp. 308ff.

153. Cf. P. Lemerle, *Philippes et la Macédoine orientale à l'époque Chrétienne et Byzantine*, Paris, 1945, and see above, Chapter 2, sect. B, pts. 1(i) and 2(i) on the importance of the Hellespontine boundary.

and of the great Achaian League before Rome,[154] was the place in which God announced that he had "many men" (18:10b), and Rome, the imperial hub itself, came to hear the unhindered proclamation of the kingdom (28:28–31). It is not unfair to infer that Luke consciously likened Christian expansion to a conquest. He took extreme care not to identify the Romans as the opposition, yet there is opposition to missionary progress in Acts, and Luke concentrated mainly on the Jews, almost to the point of creating a stereotype, as those who persistently worked for the "defeat" of the Christians (see sect. B, pt. 4). Clearly a most powerful theme of Acts, however, is that whatever the obstacles, whether they were disturbing Jews, unruly mobs (14:11ff., 19:23ff.; cf. 7:54ff.), erring administrators (14:5, 16:19ff., 22:23ff.) or even natural disasters likely to be ascribed to the recalcitrant hand of fortune (27:14ff.), the Christians were ultimately (and in Paul's case invariably) successful.[155]

The "Way" was not reckoned as a substitute for the Roman *imperium*, of course, but its successes were, by implication, a replay of the Roman accomplishment on a different level. Christianity may not have been a political movement (and certainly not an insurrectionary one) according to Luke, but it had significance for all aspects of life, since the whole world would be judged by the coming Lord (Acts 10:42, 17:31).[156] It had to have the appearance of changing the world, therefore, and at this point in the history of the contemporary imperial monolith, nothing could be more convincing than the appeal to an ever-widening influence comparable to that of the momentous and much lauded Roman expansion. Such an appeal was not unJewish, for the Bible also looked to the universalization of God's direct rule. The sending of Yahweh's messengers to the nations had been prophesied in Isaiah 66 in a way that could be reckoned a brief summary of Acts, and Luke probably believed that the "time of the Gentiles" ended with a rebuilt temple in which the nations would participate (Acts 15:16–18; cf. Luke 22:24, Isa. 66:23).

As well as the imperial motif, there are other signs that Luke utilized very general patterns and renowned incidents of Greco-Roman history, and that he did so to soften the alien Jewishness of Christianity's earliest setting and to render events more congruous to the assumptions and historical reflections of literate Gentiles. Jesus did not come into the world unannounced; for non-Jewish readers the "portents and oracles" of Luke's opening chapters, the divine disclosures concerning the nativity, the virgin birth(?), would all have been persuasive of greatness.[157] This may be asserted despite the Septuagintalisms of

154. Polybius *Hist.* XXXIX,iii,3 = Plutarch *Vit. Philop.* xxi; Orosius *Historia adversus Paganos* V,3; cf. P. N. Ure and N. G. L. Hammond in *OCD*, s.v. "Corinth" (p. 290).

155. On Paul: 9:23ff., 29f.; 13:8–12, 45–8; 14:19–21; 16:25–34; 17:6ff., 32–4; 18:6–11; 19:28–20:1; 22:22–9; 25:6–12; 27:39–44; 28:4–6, 30–1. The picture painted by Luke of resilience in the face of great odds was an important, persuasive point for Greek and Roman readers.

156. This point is made in sermons for Gentile listeners, but cf. 2:30; 3:26; 7:52, 56; 13:33ff. for the Jews.

157. Esp. Herodotus *Hist.* I,108–20; Plutarch *Vit. Thes.* ii,1ff., *Numa Pomp.* iv,1ff., *Pericl.* iii,2ff.; Apollodorus *Bibliotheca* III,v,7; Philostratus *Life of Apoll. Tyana* I,5. On the virgin birth of

Luke 1–2, which would have had an effect similar to archaized Greek, a literary throwback becoming popular in the first century.[158] Details of Jesus' youthful genius, together with Luke's comments on what was customary at the time of his infancy and upbringing, fit well with preoccupations reflected in Hellenistic biographies.[159] Jesus was a wonderworker who "amazed" with his healing and teaching,[160] who effected *paradoxa* (events contrary to expectation: 5:26b; cf. Polybius!),[161] who, despite the Jewish context of his work, was recognizably an extraordinary instructor, disputant, and "Peripatetic,"[162] who enjoined his followers (as did Epictetus for one) to lead a simple and disciplined life,[163] who faced his destiny bravely and "stoically" (cf. 22:42–44, 67, 70, 23:3b, 9), whose death was a "spectacle" (cf. 23:48a),[164] whose return to life was decidedly miraculous in character (at least in terms of the Synoptic tradition: cf. 24:15–31, 36–42; cf. Mark 16, Matt. 28:9–10, 17), and whose ascension was given a concreteness suitable to the Hellenistic mentality (Acts 1:9, om. Mark, Matt., John).[165] No specific, well-known events of Greek or Roman history are mentioned, but Jesus has absorbed into himself what the Gentiles, in their writings and opinions, expected of human greatness: virtue and the criteria for divinization. This may not quite convince one of Luke's interest in reenactment and parallelism (as against his concern to be intelligible), but it remains true that the allusions become more specific at the climax of the Gospel story.

A well-known tradition about the founder of Rome, for instance, and about

---

Romulus and Remus cf. Plutarch *Vit. Romul.* iii,1ff.; Sextus Aurelius(?) *De viris illustribus urbis Romae* i,1; and on Luke's probable interest in Romulus see below.

158. Pausanias, Galen, Arrian, and Lucian are all noted for their tendency to archaize Greek.

159. See the stories of the young Moses, Samuel, and David for important biblical background here, yet note Plutarch *Vit. Thes.* v,1 (for example, "Ἔθους δὲ ὄντος . . . ).

160. Cf. esp. Philostratus *Apoll.*, esp. II, IV; Lucian *Alexander the False Prophet* 26ff.

161. Luke alone among the Evangelists uses this term, which was employed in Hellenistic historiography; see above, Chapter 2, sect. B, pt. 1(ii). On Josephus' more Jewish reactions to the idea of miracles as *paradoxa*, see G. MacRae, "Miracle in the *Antiquities* of Josephus" in *Miracles* (ed. Moule), pp. 136–8, and cf. J. M. Hull, *Hellenistic Magic and the Synoptic Tradition* (*Studies in Biblical Theology* N.S. XXVIII), London, 1974, ch. 6; P. J. Achtemeier, "The Lucan Perspective on the Miracles of Jesus: A Preliminary Sketch" in *Journal of Biblical Literature* XCIV, 1975, p. 556.

162. Cf. Diogenes Laertius *Vit. philos.* i,17, v,2; Philostratus I,18, II, III,1, 14, IV,5, etc.

163. Epictetus *Dissert.* III,xxii,2: "I wear a rough cloak now, and I shall wear it then; I sleep hard now, and I shall sleep so then. I will take to myself a wallet and staff, and I will begin to go about and beg, and to reprove everyone I meet with," etc. Significantly, Luke stresses the earliest, hardest mission charge three times: Luke 9:1–5 (≠ Mark, Matt.), 10:2–12, 22:35f. (om. Mark, Matt.), probably suggesting that early Christian rigor exceded that of competing philosophical schools. Note Luke's reference to Jesus as *epistatēs* in 5:5, 8:24, 45, 9:33, 49, 17:13 (om. Mark, Matt.); cf. *Die Inschriften von Priene* (ed. F. H. von Gaertringen) (*Inscriptiones Graecae* vol. 12, pt. 1), Berlin, 1906, no. 112, 73ff.

164. Yet cf. Mark, ch. 15; Matt., ch. 27; John, ch. 19. The term *theōria* here recalls references to unusual sights and eventualities in Greek histories, e.g., Herodotus *Hist.* I,30; Polybius *Hist.* I,ii,1, cf. i,6.

165. See below (on Romulus); Philostratus VIII,30f. (though note Gen. 5:24; Deut. 34:6; 2 Kings 2:11f.; 4 Ezra 14:49); cf. H. Schlier, "Jesu Himmelfahrt nach den Lukanischen Schriften" in *Besinnung auf das Neue Testament* (his *Exegetische Aufsätze und Vorträge II*), Freiburg, 1964, p. 228; Talbert, "Concept," pp. 435f.

events at the end of his reign may well lie behind Luke's account of Christ's death and resurrection. Romulus, so it was believed, died or disappeared when the "face of the sun was darkened, and the day turned to night"[166] (cf. Luke 23:44–45a, with its special reference to the darkened sun, om. Mark, Matt.). He was taken to heaven[167] (cf. Luke 23:43),[168] returned to meet a close friend, Julius Proculus, as he "was traveling on the road"[169] (cf. Luke 24:13–17), announced that he had originally come from and was returning to heaven[170] (cf. Luke 1:35, 24:26, Acts 1:9–11), and ordered Julius to tell the Romans "that, by the exercise of temperance and fortitude, they shall attain to the height of human power" (*dynamis*)[171] (cf. Luke 24:49b, Acts 1:8a on *dynamis* from on high). The parallels with Luke are hardly tenuous; it is quite plausible that Luke treated the end of Jesus' earthly career so as to recall a tale about significant events which Romans knew from childhood. That Luke himself believed the account of Romulus' ascension and return is unlikely, but he took contemporary beliefs into consideration, gearing his narrative to prove not just that Jesus' glorification reenacted the heavenly elevation of Rome's first king and founder but that Jesus outclassed him, as it were, in being the exalted king of the universe.

This kind of hidden polemic, this representation of events as subtle reenactments of widely acclaimed actions of greatness, surrounds the Lukan treatment of the crucifixion and its prelude. Luke was well aware that the two forms of dying most praiseworthy among Gentiles were death in battle and suicide conceived as liberation from the troublesome world.[172] An honorable man, moreover, was expected to kill himself if he failed in his duty (so Acts 16:27).[173] Luke was doubtless sensitive to the fact that the crucifixion was "utter foolishness" to the Gentiles (cf. 1 Cor. 1:23b): Jesus let himself fall into the hands of sinful men and let them kill him. Whereas, for example, Cato the Younger killed himself by the sword to avoid submission to Caesar's tyranny[174] and Socrates took hemlock after refusing the opportunity of unlawful escape,[175] Jesus, by contrast, allowed himself to be taken (Luke 22:47–53; cf. Mark, Matt.). Yet in that he was resigned to his "destiny" (22:22a; cf. Mark 14:21a ≠ Matt. 26:24a), he reenacted the heroism of the great Stoics, and faced his "fate" with immense courage

166. Plutarch *Vit. Romul.* xxvii,6.

167. Ibid., xxvii,7.

168. Cf. Cadbury, "Eschatology of Acts" in Davies and Daube (ed.), *Background*, p. 305, who wrongly supposes that Luke considered Jesus to have descended to Hades between his death and resurrection, despite the Evangelist's pointed use of the term *paradeisos* in 23:43b.

169. Plutarch *Vit. Romul.* xxviii,1; cf. Cicero *Re pub.* II,x,20, *Som. Scip.* vii,24; Livy *Ab urbe* I,xvi,5–8.

170. Plutarch *Vit. Romul.* xxviii,2.

171. Ibid.

172. Cf. esp. Seneca *Epist. mor.* XXIV,24f., XXX,15–7, *Ad Marciam de consolatione* xx,6ff.; Plutarch *Vit. Cat. Min.* lxvii,2, lxxi,1f., and notes below.

173. Cf. Plutarch *Vit. Brut.* xliii,5–7 (the case of Cassius Longinus), and note the analysis of Judas' death below, sect. B, pt. 4.

174. Plutarch *Vit. Cat. Min.* lxvii,1–lxx,6.

175. Diogenes Laertius *Vit. philos.* ii,42ff.; Xenophon *Apologia, finis*; Plato *Apologia*, esp. 36B–42.

(22:42–44; cf. Mark 14:36, Matt. 26:39, 42).[176] And Luke took pains to prove that the trial, mocking, crucifixion, and death of Christ were in the foreknown plan of the divine (cf. esp. 18:31b, 22:22a; Acts 4:28, 13:29), and that "it was necessary" for him to suffer before entering into his glory (Luke 24:26). On the one hand, therefore, a Gentile might protest his "righteous innocence" (23:47; cf. Mark 15:39βb ≠ Matt. 27:54βb), as one unjustly condemned like Socrates,[177] and still claim on the other that he died magnificently,[178] even if Jesus' release differed in kind from the deaths that the Gentiles traditionally held to be most meritorious. It is remarkable how Luke educated his Gentile readers to accept an execution on the most despicable of scaffoldings.

It is not unwarrantable to conclude, moreover, that the famous departure of the Stoic Cato Minor has had its impact on the writing of Luke 22. On the evening of his suicide at Utica, Cato went to a supper with his close friends, and the wine engendered an agreeable discourse on Stoic dogma, during which he made it plain that "as good men only are free, and wicked men slaves" he was about to end his life and find complete liberation.[179] His companions and servants became dejected; after walking with his friends outside, Cato eventually wished to perform the deed. His son and his servants were slow to respond to his requests for a sword, but at last he acquired one, and after some sleep, he stabbed himself.[180] When the news was out, according to Plutarch, the people of Utica acclaimed Cato as their "benefactor and savior," the only free and undefeated man.[181] In Luke Jesus also supped with his chosen companions and foreshadowed death inevitable for him during a discourse at table [22:16, 22, 36–37 (cf. Mark 14:21, 25, 27 ≠ Matt.); cf. 18:31–34]. His followers became confused and dejected [22:23 (om. Mark), 45βb (cf. Mark 14:40 and Matt. 26:43!)]. By this stage in Luke's account, many Gentile readers would have been as confused as the disciples themselves about Jesus' attitude to his own death. Luke skillfully, and with subtle apology, anticipated their reactions. In the supper discourse, Gentile assumptions about greatness are contrasted with Jesus' own understanding of the matter (Luke significantly transplanted a saying from another context in Mark to this new setting: 22:24–27, and cf. Mark 10:42–44 and above, pt. 1),[182] and there remained ambiguity as to what Jesus intended to

176. Plutarch *Vit. Brut.* lii,1–liii,5 (Brutus and Porcia); *Vit. Cic.* xlviii,1–4 (Cicero); Seneca *Epist. mor.* CII,26ff., etc., though cf. also 1 Sam. 31:4ff. (Saul); 1 Macc., 1–2; Josephus *Antiq.* XVIII,23, *Bell. jud.* I,58, II,151.

177. For evidence about an early association of Christ with Socrates see Lucian *Pereg.* 11; Justin Martyr, *Apologia* II,x,5.

178. With Luke there are no cries of anguish from the cross: cf. Mark 15:34 ≠ Matt. 27:46; John 19:28.

179. Plutarch *Vit. Cat. Min.* lxvii,1f.

180. lxviii,1–lxx,6.

181. lxxi,1.

182. Luke 22:24–30, significantly, sits rather artificially within vss.14–38; its insertion is to be accounted for not only in terms of the Gospel's structure (the paralleling of Jesus' and Paul's farewell discourses), but also of content. The same applies to the Emmaus story.

do with the two swords offered to him, if he was "to be reckoned among the criminals" [Luke 22:37b, and cf. Mark 15:28 (some MSS)]. Jesus made a crucial decision in a state of agony, as though his was the hardest of all courses of action (vss.41–4, yet cf. Mark ≠ Matt.). The issue becomes one of an inner contest in which Christ has to be reconciled with the divine decision to the exclusion of other alternatives, so that allowing himself to be taken, he neither committed himself to suicide nor to self-defence. His friends hardly responded ably to the hour of crisis (22:23, 45, 50, 55–62; cf. Mark 14:37ff., 47, 66ff., Matt. 26:40ff., 51, 69ff.), though Luke, with Gentile predispositions about manliness in mind, avoided highlighting the disciples' cowardice (yet cf. Mark 14:27, 49b–50 ≠ Matt. 26:31, 56, om. Luke).

Thus Jesus' death reenacted great deaths among the Gentiles, at least in a loose sense. In spite of appearances, the crucifixion did not clash with such deaths, but it transcended and was ultimately superior to any death. In Luke, to reiterate, little or no atonement value was attached to Christ's passion; his is the death of a great man, directly in line with the martyrdom of the prophets but also sufficiently in line with deaths of virtuous innocents. Even condemned by disobedient Jews, hanging upon a Gentile cross, his greatness is paradoxically supreme.[183] Luke was not unconcerned, then, with historical parallels from non-Israelite history. Admittedly, the pagan past could only remain on the fringe of his considerations (unless he had been prepared to wax theoretical), yet this was natural enough, since preserving former deeds did not have the same deep significance for Greeks and Romans as it did for Jews. Hence, from the non-Jewish tradition(s) Luke could only appeal to those renowned incidents, developments, and motifs which were in common parlance.

We have spoken more of Luke than of Acts in this connection, yet in Acts our impressions are further confirmed. In Hellenistic literature "the story of the traveling teacher and wonderworker was a favorite theme" from Diogenes Laertius to Philostratus.[184] Wilfred Knox has asserted that, for Luke, Paul's journeys may have been a "mere framework," not being "intended as a detailed itinerary,"[185] yet points of debate aside, the Evangelist may well have concentrated so heavily on a wondrous expedition in almost half of his second volume in order to invoke the great journeys of the pagan past. For Luke, surely, Paul was not merely in line with traveling teachers and thaumaturges; he was the brave apostle of the new and final Age in world history. But he was also an heroic figure (braving perilous paths like Theseus, suffering shipwreck like Ulysses (cf. Acts 28:3–6),[186] and as suggested already, the thrust of his missionary

183. On greatness in Luke see esp. Luke 1:32a, 7:16 (normative classical greatness), 9:48f., 22:24–7 (true, spiritual greatness).

184. E. Norden, *Agnostos Theos: Untersuchungen zur Formen-Geschichte religiöser Rede*, Stuttgart, 1923, pp. 34ff.; E. Rohde, *Der griechische Roman*, p. 327; W. Knox, op. cit., p. 13.

185. Ibid., p. 13.

186. For other instances of shipwreck adventure see, e.g., Dio Chrysostom, *Orat.* VII,2f.; Aristides *Hieroi logoi* II,65ff. (and see below n. 267). The voyaging from island to island (Acts 27:7f., 18, 28:1) suggests the atmosphere of the *Odyssey*.

enterprise recalled the penetration of great imperialisms and the heroic protagonists who made them possible.[187]

Perhaps it is natural to assume that the missionary enterprise of Acts is likened most of all to the broadcasting of a new philosophy. Like the philosophers, the disciples opposed superstition (8:9ff., 14:14ff., 17:23–24, 29, 19:26; cf. 15:20, 29); like the Pythagoreans, they practiced communism (4:34–5:11) and considered their master divine;[188] like Socrates, Paul was accused of "preaching strange gods" (17:18);[189] like Stoicism, Christianity was cosmopolitan and universalist (10:42, 14:15–17, 17:26ff.; cf. 2:5ff., etc.), and it preached a monotheism congruous with many eminent Greco-Roman spirits (esp. 17:24–29; cf. 14:15–17).[190] The Christians, however, were the harbingers of an entirely new historical era, and this era not only had consequences for people's beliefs, but was the culmination of world history, the periods of régimes and the boundaries of their habitations being in God's cognizance and plan (17:26–28; cf. 30–31).[191] Thus Gentile history acquires a background importance for Christianity's emergence,[192] even if the Jewish setting counted for more in terms of divine authentication. Both Jew and Gentile had to learn that God did not dwell in temples made with hands (7:48, 17:24–25), and that the new kingdom involved Jew and "Greek" together,[193] for the barriers of Jewish exclusivism were broken down (10:9–11:18, 15:12ff.; cf. Eph. 2:12–22), and the nations were no longer left to wander in their own ways (Acts 14:16, 17:30a, yet cf. Deut. 4:19b, 32:8–9). The new movement was unique, then, and recent events carried their own marks of providence, though they were countersigned by reenactments, patterns, and connections.[194]

## B. The recurrent actualization of retributive principles in Luke-Acts and the biblical tradition[195]

Reference to Lukan ideas of divine providence brings us back to those notions of reciprocity we examined in Greco-Roman histories (Chapter 2, sect. B). The

187. Cf. L. Pearson, *The Lost Histories of Alexander the Great* (*Philological Monographs* XX), Ohio, 1960, and (on Scipio Africanus), Polybius *Hist.* X,iv–xx.

188. Iamblichus *Vit. Pythag.* vi, xxviii; Porphyry *Vit. Pythag.* ii, xxviii, and on the divinization of Epicurus and Apollonius see Talbert, *Literary Patterns*, p. 126.

189. Cf. Xenophon *Memorab.* I,1ff.; H. Conzelmann, "The Address of Paul on the Areopagus" in Keck and Martyn (eds.), op. cit., p. 219.

190. Talbert argues that Luke's picture of Christians as doers of God's words conformed to Greco-Roman expectations of philosophical schools (op. cit., p. 91), Luke-Acts covering something akin to the "succession of philosophers" described by Sotion, the key (yet lost) source behind Diogenes Laertius (p. 133). These valuable points, however, do not commit us to Talbert's conclusion that Luke's work falls into the genre of "lives of the philosophers." Cf. also Talbert, "Shifting Sands: The Recent Study of the Gospel of Luke" in *Interpretation* XXX, 1976, pp. 387–9.

191. See above, Chapter 2, sect. B, pt. 2(i), on the importance of boundaries in Greek historiography; cf. Deut. 32:8f., Gen. 10 (P) for OT background.

192. As it did among apologists to come: e.g., pseudo-Justin *Hortatory Address* xv–xxi, xxxvii.

193. For *Hellēnes* to signify Gentiles in general see Acts 14:1, 19:10, 20:21 (cf. 1 Cor. 1:22–4).

194. E. Haenchen, *Die Apostelgeschichte* (*Kritisch-exegetischer Kommentar über das Neue Testament III*), Göttingen, 1965, pp. 86f.

195. The following two sections are based on Trompf, "Notions."

belief that retributive principles were continually operative in human life is writ large in biblical historiography, and this belief should now be analyzed.

## *The Deuteronomic historian*

It is significant that the Israelite-Jewish writers came closest to stating a cyclical (or alternation) view of history through interpreting the laws of rewards and punishments. Judges 2, as part of the Deuteronomic history, is a central case in point. There one finds a pattern of events which may be described either as a four-staged sequence capable of repetition or as an undulatory process. The generation of those who possessed the land had passed, and the Deuteronomist introduced the new period of the Judges. The new generation did not know Yahweh's past work for Israel, and they "did what was evil in the sight of Yahweh," "forsaking" him and "serving the Ba'als" and other gods. They provoked Yahweh's anger, so that

> *whenever* they marched out, Yahweh's hand was against them for evil, as he had warned and had sworn to them [cf. Deut. 28:15ff.], and they were in sore straits. (2:10–15, my italics)

Then Yahweh raised up Judges to save them, and although they did not listen nor obey God like their predecessors:

> *whenever* the Lord raised up Judges for them, the Lord was with the Judge, and saved them from their enemies all the days of the Judge,

because he was moved to pity by their groaning under oppression. But "*whenever* the Judge died they turned back and behaved worse than their fathers," and Yahweh in his anger said he would not drive out the nations left unconquered by Joshua, but let them test Israel (2:16–22).

Christopher North justifiably contended that the Deuteronomist (whose editorial work in these and subsequent passages is clear enough),[196] took the period of the Judges to be

> marked by a monotonously recurring cycle of Israelite apostasies from Yahweh, their oppressions at the hands of enemies, their sorrow for their perilous plight and their cries for deliverance, Yahweh's response in raising up Judges, the deliverances effected by the Judges, the periods of peace and order that followed, until at the death of the Judge the process was set in motion all over again.[197]

On the one hand, the four stages of defection, oppression, prayer (the importance of which becomes obvious after ch. 2), and deliverance[198] suggest a recurring sequence not unlike the *Anacyclōsis*, or else a more straightforward

196. On the redaction criticism of Judges see C. A. Simpson, *Composition of the Book of Judges*, Oxford, 1957, pp. 133ff.

197. C. North, *The Old Testament Interpretation of History* (Fernley Hartley Trust Lectures), London, 1946, pp. 96f.

198. For the sequence put in these terms see J. M. Myers in *The Interpreter's Bible* (ed. G. A. Buttrick et al.), New York, 1953, vol. 2, s.v. Judg. 2 (p. 701).

alternation between a low point (oppression brought on by disobedience) and a high point (liberation and security brought on by obedience under a Judge). This second frame is reminiscent of other Near Eastern theories in which "national" fortune and misfortune follow one another in undulatory succession.[199] The schema of Judges 2, however, remains uniquely Israelite, and it does not stand in its own right, either, but only as one of a number of ways in which retributive laws were manifested in Israelite history. Admittedly, the Deuteronomist applied the pattern of Judges 2 with fair consistency in subsequent chapters.[200] Israel was oppressed for her disobedience in succession by Mesopotamians, Moabites, Canaanites, Midianites, Ammonites, and Philistines,[201] and each time the Israelites cried to Yahweh, so that he gave them Othniel, Ehud, Deborah, Gideon, Jephthah, and Samson to gain victory and times of security.[202] This pattern was carried to the rule of Samuel, who was considered the last Judge.[203] With the defection of the sons of Gideon, of Eli (also one who "judged" Israel), and of Samuel,[204] the Deuteronomist reinforced the cyclo-alternating process with a theme about the repeated disobedience of "second-generation rulers." However, it is not strictly true that Judges 2 "states succinctly the Deuteronomic conception of history,"[205] for it merely approaches one aspect of it, and only speaks to a specific period of Israel's history. Certainly Judges makes those traditional distinctions between Israelite-Jewish and Greco-Roman views of history look simplistic, even though the notion of the *cyclos* can hardly be read into a chapter deriving from an ancient Near Eastern context. But to be overeager about cyclical thinking in Judges 2 would in any case be to miss the point that for this part of his account the Deuteronomist specially appropriates a current model to strengthen his more general thesis about the recurring operation of retributive principles in the Israelite past.[206] Besides, as we have already shown, notions of historical recurrence cannot be confined to cyclical notions. Either to exaggerate cyclical thinking in the Old Testament or to exclude it altogether (especially on principle!) is to ride roughshod over a vital distinction.[207]

199. M. G. Güterbock, "Die historische Tradition und ihre literische Gestaltung bei Babyloniern und Hethitern bis 1200 (pt. 1)" in *Zeitschrift für Assyriologie* XLII (N.F. 8), 1934, pp. 13ff.; E. A. Speiser, "Ancient Mesopotamia" in *The Idea of History in the Ancient Near East* (ed. R. C. Denton), New Haven, 1955, pp. 55f.; H. Gese, loc. cit., p. 134.

200. Problems exist with Judg. 3:31, 10:1–5, 12:8–15, and chs. 17–21, but they may well be secondary interpolations later than the Deuteronomic redaction: cf. Simpson, op. cit., pp. 142ff.

201. Judg. 3:8, 13f., 4:2, 6:1–6, 10:7–9 (the reference to the Philistines in 7b surely being post-Deuteronomic), 13:1.

202. 3:9–11, 15–30, 4:4–5:31, 6:11ff., 11:1ff., 13:2ff. The verb *shaqāt* and not *nāḳāh* is used for "rest" in 3:11, 30b, 5:31b.

203. 1 Sam. 2:22–31, 3:1, 4:1–5:2, 7:2 (a low point), 7:3–17 (a high point).

204. 4:18b; cf. 8:33–9:57; 1 Sam. 2:12–7, 34, 4:11, 8:1–3.

205. Myers in *Interpreter's Bible*, p. 107.

206. The Babylonian-Exilic provenance of the Deuteronomic history may help to explain the use of such a model. Cf. M. Noth, *Überlief. Studien*, pp. 96ff., 107ff.; P. Ackroyd, *Exile and Restoration: A Study of Hebrew Thought of the Sixth Century BC*, London, 1968, pp. 65ff.

207. Against Östborn, op. cit., pp. 60ff., cf. von Rad, *OT Theology*, vol. 1, p. 330, n. 6.

Within the Deuteronomic history, admittedly, the writer's belief in recurrent retribution is most vividly conveyed in Judges 2. Although the rest of the work lacks the symmetry of Judges, the Deuteronomist was remarkably consistent in proving for his readers that transgression (that is, disobedience against the law delivered to Moses, which prefaces the history in the form of Deuteronomy, and rejection of Yahweh's pronouncements uttered through the prophets) must needs be requited by God, and faithfulness, in turn, be rewarded. The cardinal message of his history, of course, is that the fall of Samaria (721 BC) and of Jerusalem (586 BC) and the exile in Babylon were divine punishments against a people whose persistent sin became too monstrous for serious disaster to be avoided. There was a sense in which an accumulation of transgression brought such extreme consequences, although he certainly took the heinous crimes of Jeroboam I of Israel in erecting golden calves at Bethel and Dan (1 Kings 12:25–31; cf. Deut. 5:7–10, 9:16), and of the Judean Manasseh in both building altars to false gods and shedding "much innocent blood" (2 Kings 21:2–9, 16; cf. Deut. 21:1–9, 12:23, 19:10, 13), to be of decisive importance for the eventual collapse of both the northern and southern kingdoms (2 Kings 17:21–23, 21:10–15, 23:26–27, 24:3–4).

Not only is it true that the Deuteronomist explains the momentous disasters befalling Israel and Judah in terms of retributive logic, but there is abundant evidence for his interest in the distribution of recompenses throughout the whole period under consideration. There are, to be sure, interesting variations on this important, if not central, theme. A recompense for good may come in terms of something so blessed as peace (as with Solomon, for example), yet it could also be found in something so grim as death (as in the case of Josiah, who was saved from worse troubles to come by being "gathered to his fathers").[208] Divine punishments, for their part, could be meted out immediately or relatively quickly, or else deferred until a much later time.[209] Without going into unnecessary detail, however, I simply wish to emphasize the pains the Deuteronomic writer took to illustrate the recurrent experience of appropriate recompenses and "the recurrent pattern of failure and grace," as Ackroyd puts it.[210] His efforts to interpret the past were intended to remind the Israel of his day that if she sought God here guilt would be absolved and her fortunes would alter.[211]

Significantly, retributive logic is used to explain large stages in Israel's history in such a way as to provide the real unity of the Deuteronomist's work. If the period of the Judges witnessed fluctuations, there were two great periods of

208. 1 Kings 3–10 (cf. 11); 2 Kings 22:20, 23:29f.

209. E.g., Josh. 12:2–26; 1 Kings 14:10, 21–2, 25–6, 15:29, 16:10, 22:34–5; 2 Kings 1:15–7, 9:30–7, 10:27, 32, 13:22f (not detained); 1 Sam. 2:34, 8:4–22; 1 Kings 11:39, 14:10–8; cf. Deut. 17:14–7 (detained).

210. Ackroyd, *Exile*, p. 74.

211. On the Deuteronomist's hope for the return of a righteous Judean monarch see M. Noth, "La Catastrophe de Jérusalem en l'an 587 avant Jésus-Christ et sa signification pour Israël" in *Revue d'Histoire et de Philosophie Religieuses* XXXIII, 1953, pp. 87ff.

righteousness: one under Joshua, when only Achan's sins marred the bright picture of success, and when the "whole land" was taken and the twelve tribes given settlement;[212] and the other under David. David conspicuously committed no outrage or sin of blood-guiltiness, and he was also forgiven for taking Bathsheba and for numbering Israel, even though a price was paid in each case.[213] While David's merits were being acknowledged, however, the Deuteronomist paid much attention to punishments befalling those who threatened so righteous a king—on Saul and later contenders for David's position.[214] Such requital came upon single individuals during David's reign, but in other times of general disobedience or of evil kings the whole populace experienced it. The Deuteronomist did not paint an idyllic picture of the wilderness wandering, to take a key example, but held it to be a rebellious period. When disobedient, the Israelites were defeated by enemies (Deut. 1:26, 43; cf. 19–46), and not until the warriors who transgressed had died off (2:14b–16) could progress be made (2:21, 33–36, 3:6). Even Moses was punished for his disbelief (32:48–52; cf. 2–13 [J], 27:12–14), and it was Joshua who was the hero of the almost transgressionless period of settlement which followed. As for post-Davidic times, Solomon's rule saw "rest" only as long as his faithfulness lasted (cf. 1 Kings 11:14–15), and deterioration in his reign foreshadowed the general decline treated in 1 Kings 12–2 Kings 25, when there was such great evil that only a great disaster could requite it.

Thus the Deuteronomist's work was a history of the recurring execution of appropriate recompenses, and Israel's past was viewed as though the same principles operated time and time again. Implicitly, the nature of rewards and punishments was in accordance with the degree of merit or of incurred guilt, but these operations were ultimately dependent on Yahweh and not upon natural or "mechanical" laws. The main point is, however, that the writer bequeathed an account of about six centuries in which history, in a special sense, repeated itself. His picture of the repeated acts of transgression against God's commandments, and the repeated consequences of such disobedience, his characterization of recurrent "event-shapes"—typical transgressions, typical warnings, fitting deaths and recompenses—all reflect a preoccupation with historical recurrence. There is, of course, no exact repetition, and the model of cyclo-alternating change in Judges 2 is only confined to one part of the history. Yet much of what we previously uncovered from Greco-Roman historiography on recurring principles in history and on lessons learned for the future from the past is present in a distinctively Hebraic form. The Deuteronomist almost certainly

212. Josh. 11:23 (yet cf. pre-Deuteronomic 13:1b), chs. 13–22, and on "rest" theology see above, sect. A, pt. 4.

213. 2 Sam. 12:9–18 (cf. chs. 15–18), 24:11–6; and (on avoidance of outrage), e.g., 1 Sam. 24:6, 25:26, 26:9–10, 29:6, 8f., 2 Sam. 4:11f., 9:3–8, 21:7; 1 Kings 2:31–3, 19:22b, 20:3b.

214. 1 Sam. 13:13–4, 15:19–23, 28, 35, 16:14, 19:5–10, 24:20; 28:3–17, 31:2ff.; 1 Sam. 26:16; 2 Sam. 3:30, 18:9–15; 1 Kings 2:31f.

assumed that event-patterns similar to those he recorded would happen in the future if the same kinds of transgressions and deeds were effected. By reviewing their checkered past the Israelites had much to learn for the future consolidation of their nation and their faith.

It remains true that the Hebrew language lacked conceptual tools to convey the idea of historical recurrence more lucidly,[215] but the genuine interest in repeated instances of retribution is undeniable, as is that concern to document the reenactment of events and reappropriation of former conditions. The otherwise eccentric Chevalier Bunsen was surely correct when he asserted that the Hebrews, just as much as the Greeks, had a clear perception of "the moral law ruling human affairs," holding "that the divine principle of truth and justice . . . will prevail."[216] But we can now go further. Like the Greeks, Hebrew historiographers exploited notions of historical recurrence; they adapted what they received to their ancient Near Eastern context. This is all the more confirmed by the development of retributive ideas in the Chronicler's work, which in 1–2 Chronicles overlaps with 2 Samuel–2 Kings.

## *The Chronicler*

Beside the Deuteronomic work the Chronicler's treatment of retribution looks crude and almost mechanical. We have already noted now he extolled the two periods of the united monarchy and the restoration. He idealized both David and Solomon: they were virtually without sin and in consequence were decisively supreme in war and prosperous at home. The time of restoration was also one of righteousness, with both Ezra and Nehemiah working assiduously to avoid transgression and thereby the punishments of the past.[217] The interim period, however, was tainted with evils which made the Exile inevitable. While he was far less severe on certain of the monarchs of Judah,[218] the Chronicler's post-Solomonic pre-Exilic history still remains one of repeated disobedience. Although Yahweh had persistently sent messengers to the kings, they kept despising them, and the priests and people had also acted unfaithfully, until no "remedy" was left (2 Chron. 37:14–16). Recurring disobedience marked the pre-

215. The verb *shūv*, which has much usage in OT historical books (cf. Lisowsky, op. cit., pp. 1408ff.), sometimes carried the sense of a return to a state of either righteousness or wickedness (for the former: Deut. 1:45, 4:20, 13:18, 30:2ff.; 1 Sam. 7:3; 1 Kings 8:33ff.; for the latter: Judg. 2:19, 8:33; 1 Kings 9:6), and occasionally meant "repeat" in a way that should interest us: e.g., 1 Kings 13:33; 2 Kings 21:3 (= 2 Chron. 23:3); 2 Chron. 19:4. But there was a general dearth of verbs denoting recurrence. *Shānāh* was confined to the immediate repetition of an act by one and the same person: e.g., 1 Sam. 26:8; 2 Sam. 20:10; 1 Kings 18:34, and for the use of *shūv* in this sense, 1 Sam. 3:5, 6; 1 Kings 19:6b; 2 Kings 1:11, 13. On *yāsaph* (which can also carry the sense of "doing again"), see F. Brown, S. R. Driver, C. A. Briggs, *A Hebrew and English Lexicon of the Old Testament*, Oxford, 1907, p. 415. As a result of this paucity, recourse to repetitious phrases ("he did evil [or right] in Yahweh's sight") or to *wᵉhāyāh* (Judg. 2:18f.) or *ʿōd*, was virtually inevitable.

216. C. C. J. von Bunsen, *Outlines of the Philosophy of Universal History*, London, 1854, vol. 1, pp. 5f.

217. Trompf, "Notions."

218. 2 Chron. 13:1ff., 27:1ff. (Abijah and Jotham); 17:1–20, chs. 29–32, 34–35 (Jehoshaphat, Hezekiah, Josiah), (cf. 19:1–3, 32:25, 35:22b) 14:1, 26:4 (Asa, Uzziah).

Davidic period also. The Chronicler provides an insight into his understanding of early stages of Israelite history in the famous prayer of Nehemiah (in Neh. 9). Although the Davidic-Solomonic era is not mentioned, Nehemiah reflects on the whole period from the patriarchs to the possession as a time of close relationship with Yahweh—the disobedience in the wilderness being glossed over quickly (9:16–19; cf. Deut. 1–2, etc.)—and within the restoration situation, Nehemiah sought a return to that relationship (vss.32–38). The times in between possession and restoration, however (though we may exclude the high point under David and Solomon), were disobedient and rebellious days. In a manner reminiscent of Judges 2, the prayer refers to the Israelites' rejection of both the law and the prophetic warnings, so that Yahweh gave them "into the hands of their enemies."

But in the time of their suffering they cried to thee and thou didst hear them from heaven; and according to thy great mercies thou didst give them saviors who saved them from the hands of their enemies. But after they came "to rest" (*noaḥ*)[219] they did evil again before thee, and thou didst abandon them to the hands of their enemies, . . . yet when they turned and cried to thee, thou didst hear them from heaven, and many times (*'ithim*) thou didst deliver them. (Neh. 9:26–28)

Once more Israel's disobedience heads a sequence, and is followed by defeat, supplication, and Yahweh's succor (vss.29–31). Hence an undulatory model makes its appearance, with national misfortune (caused by disobedience) and deliverance (due to reliance on Yahweh) succeeding each other in turn. We may therefore assume that, even accounting for the special period of "saviorhood" under David and Solomon, the Chronicler took not only the period of the Judges to be one of fluctuation (on the basis of Judges 2), but also the monarchical period as well, from Saul to Zedekiah.[220] What we anticipate from Judean *kingly* history, then, is an impression of alternation not strictly present in the Deuteronomic account. The Chronicler was admittedly bound to pay deference to the formal judgments of his major source as to the righteousness or wickedness of different monarchs, yet even in doing that he managed to create a more symmetrical pattern of alternation in comparison to that of his predecessor. For the purposes of simplification, the Deuteronomist's picture may be construed as in Diagram VI. The Chronicler modified these classifications in order to ease certain transitions from high points to low points, thus creating the effect of a zigzag line of development between two sets of general conditions. He both altered and added to his main source, and isolated different stages in the careers of certain kings along the way.[221] The overall result has been characterized in Diagram VII, and this diagram neatly shows how the Chronicler actually concerned himself with a process of historical recurrence.

219. The Chronicler places such rest indiscriminately in untroubled, righteous times under the Judges and Kings.

220. In this connection note the Chronicler's special emphasis on crying to Yahweh in distress in 2 Chron. 20:9, 29:8–10, 32:20ff., 33:12; cf. 6:24ff., 12:7.

221. For the fine details see Trompf, "Notions" (inset).

Diagram VI The Deuteronomic Picture of Monarchical Rule from Saul to Zedekiah (Judea)

| | | | | | | | | |
|---|---|---|---|---|---|---|---|---|
| *Good Kings:* | Saul(1)* | David<br>Solomon(1) | Asa<br>Jehoshaphat | Joash | Jotham | Hezekiah | Josiah | |
| | | | | Azariah<br>(=Uzziah) | | | | |
| *Evil Kings:* | Saul(2) | Solomon(2)<br>Rehoboam<br>Abijah | Jehoram<br>Ahaziah | Amaziah | Ahaz | Manasseh<br>Amon | Jehoahaz<br>Jehoiakim<br>Jehoiakin<br>Zedekiah | Exile |

*Bracketed numbers denote identifiable stages in certain kings' reigns.

Diagram VII The Chronicler's Picture of Monarchical Rule from Saul to Zedekiah (Judea)

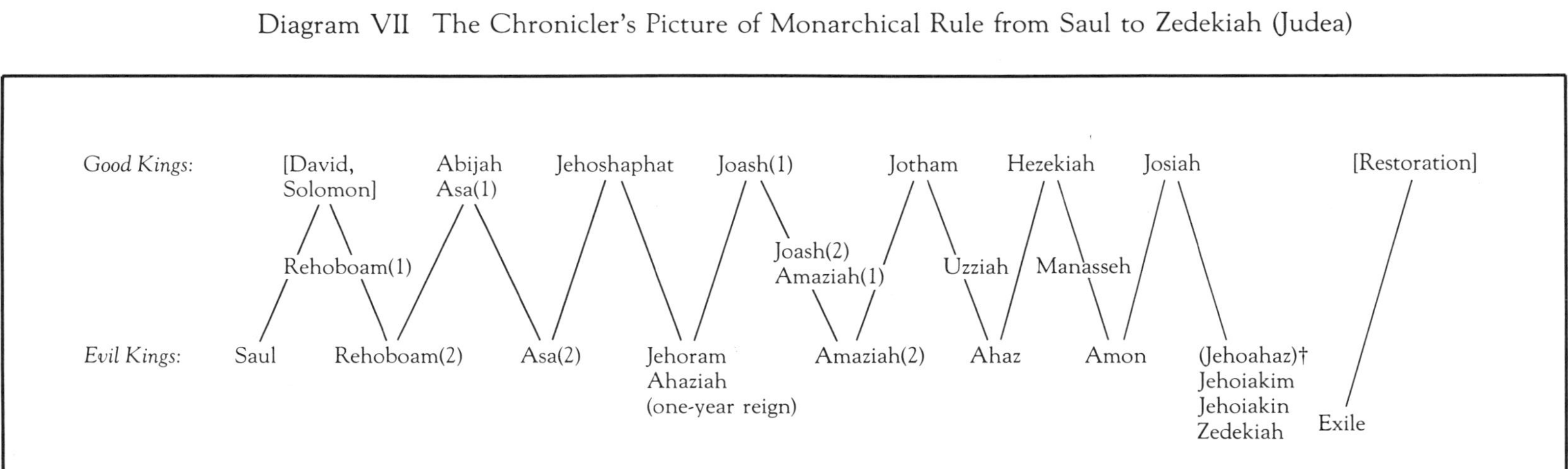


†The Chronicler does not inform us whether this king did evil or right before Yahweh.

This patterning was reinforced by the Chronicler's somewhat shallow analysis of retributive principles. Every illness, for instance, had to be accounted for in terms of requital, the violent deaths of kings (even that of Josiah) were seen as punishments, and every defeat was a sign of disobedience.[222] By contrast, material prosperity accompanied almost blameless rule (see above and cf. esp. 2 Chron. 17:5, 20:20 [om. 1 Kings] 32:27ff. [cf. 2 Kings 20:12ff.]); and except for the murder of the prophets, the violent deaths of those who did not deserve them were overlooked (cf. esp. 2 Kings 25:18–21 [om. 2 Chron.]). In the Chronicles, moreover, oracular activity manifests itself with greater regularity than with the Deuteronomic work.[223] In all, we find in this later history an eclectic intertwining of relevant themes—of reenactment, continuity, retribution, and alternation between two sets of general conditions.

Retributive beliefs were very old both in and near Israel, and they were bound to persist beyond the Exilic and restoration periods into later phases of Judaism's life. Aside from wisdom writers, apocalypticists, and midrashic commentators (who all had much to say about the consequences of sin and righteousness),[224] attention is drawn to late Jewish interpretations of retribution applied (in a straightforward manner) to significant historical events. Key writers illustrating the development of these notions to the time of Luke include the authors of 1–2 Maccabees, Flavius Josephus, and Philo Judaeus.

### *Later Jewish writing*

The brilliant successes of the Maccabean brothers, as commemorated in 1 Maccabees (ca. 120–100 BC), should be regarded in the light of Antiochus Epiphanes' great sin against the temple (1:54–59), and the zeal of Mattathias' house to purge Israel of Hellenes and of Israelites succumbing to Greek ways (cf. 2:20–29, 3:4–6, 8, 7:24, 9:73b, etc.). Significantly enough, warriors not true to the Maccabean cause met with military disaster (5:55–61) (Alcimus the anti-Hasmonean high priest dying a terrible death: 9:54–55, and cf. 7:12–14, 21–25, 9:1, 54), while the Maccabees themselves were able to build up Jerusalem (4:60, 10:11, 14:37, 16:23). In 2 Maccabees, by comparison, the disasters experienced by Israel before the emergence of the Hasmonean saviors were ascribed to her disobedience (6:12, 8:32), yet when the worst of the misfortunes befell her (with Antiochus' desecration and murders), the Israelites cried to the Lord in their oppressed state (8:2–4) and his anger was turned to pity (vs.5b). As a result, the oppressor died a hideous death (9:1ff., 28), and Judas Maccabeus won stupendous victories against the next Seleucid (8:24, 10:31, 11:11, 12:27–28, 13:15,

222. Ibid., for references.

223. 2 Chron. 12:7f., 13:5–12, 15:2–7, 16:7–9, 19:6f., 9–11, etc.; cf. von Rad, "The Levitical Sermon in *I* and *II Chronicles*" in his *The Problem*, pp. 267ff.

224. R. H. Pfeiffer, *History of New Testament Times, with an Introduction to the Apocrypha*, London, 1949, pp. 334ff., 377ff. (esp. on Ecclus.). For apocalypticists: e.g., Zeph. 2–3; Isa. 65:11f.; Dan. 7:26, and cf. 11:45; *IQH* 10; *IQW* 16; I En., 62:12, 90:18, 91:11; cf. Rev. 19:21, 20ff. *Midrashim*: e.g., *Gen. Rabba*, 49–50 (P. R. Weis, *Midrashic Selections II*, Semitic Studies Series, Leiden, 1955, p. vii). Cf. also Jth. 11:10 (with the heroine's deeds reenacting those of Jael and of other Judges, 4:9, 5:24; cf. 3:15ff.; Judg. 9:10, 13:15–8, 14:18, 16:16ff.

15:15–34). In this second work, Yahweh's act of deliverance ranks among similar acts of the past (cf. 8:19–20), the general situation being conceived of as another instance of the sequence defection/oppression/prayer/deliverance (as best reflected in Judges 2 and Nehemiah 9). Although the format of 1–2 Maccabees conformed slightly to Hellenistic tastes,[225] the understanding of God's justice behind historical events was still essentially Jewish. It is different with 4 Maccabees and with Josephus, both first century AD, into which Greco-Roman conceptions of the moral order had infiltrated. In the former, the cruel tyrant Antiochus Epiphanes suffers appropriate punishment through divine *pronoia* or providence (9:24, 17:21–22; cf. 18:5, 22), and he is never really victorious over the virtue and manliness of Israel's martyrs (17:23; chs. 9–13). As for Josephus' volumes, there one finds a rather more complex attempt at interrelating Greek and Hebraic notions of divine justice, an attempt requiring separate attention.

Josephus, while acknowledging with regret the recurrent suffering of the Jews under the Egyptians, Assyrians, Babylonians, Persians, Macedonians, and Romans (*Antiq.* XX,259–60), went so far as to contend that fortune (*tychē*) was on the side of imperial Rome in the Jewish War (XIX,77; cf. *Bell. Jud.* IV,622), and that inescapable fate (*chreōn*) had led the Jews to the destruction of 70 AD (V,355, 572, VI,314; cf. IV,622–3, VI,267–8). Whereas one can merely suppose that the author of 4 Maccabees saw both the wreaking of divine vengeance on Antiochus and the vindication of the martyr-heroes as typical sets of events exemplifying the providential order, Josephus treated Jewish history as a whole, and was even more open in his willingness to combine Hebrew and Gentile notions of recurrence. He traced the beginning of Israel's real misfortunes to Jeroboam I, who, after the great and prosperous reign of Solomon (cf. *Antiq.* VII,337–8), transgressed the Law with his golden heifers. If we interpret Josephus correctly, Jeroboam's sin was "the first of evils" which resulted in defeats and bondage that went on not just to the Babylonian exile (as the Deuteronomist had it), but to the fall of Jerusalem in 70 AD as well (VIII,229; cf. IX,282). Thus the event of 70 AD, ordained in advance by God, was a recurrence of the earlier destruction (in 586 BC) foretold by the prophets (*Bell. Jud.* VI,250, and cf. 109; *Antiq.* X,142, and cf. 139–141). In both cases the Jews were culpable (*Bell. Jud.* VI,110, and cf. V,572, VI,251, 314–5; *Antiq.* X,78–81, 103–4, 139, and cf. 183), and both destructions occurred on the same date (*Bell. Jud.* VI,250) so that Josephus marvelled at the "exactness of periodicity" (VI,268, and cf. also 2 Macc. 10:5). These preoccupations were not unJewish, and yet Josephus went quite a long way toward integrating the recurrence models and conceptions of two cultures.[226]

This conclusion is supported by his handling of fortune (*tychē*). It has already

225. E.g., 1 Macc. 3–4, 6, 10, 15; 2 Macc. 2:19–32, 15:37–9; cf. H. Cancik, *Mythische und historische Wahrheit: Interpretationen zu Texten der hethitischen, biblischen und griechischen Historiographie* (*Stuttgarter Biblestudien* XLVIII), Stuttgart, 1970, pp. 110ff.

226. Note also his Hellenistic-looking comments on the idea of learning from history in *Antiq.* VIII,418–20, and cf. I,3, although the basic lesson of history was that "those who follow the will of God and do not venture to break his excellent laws are offered felicity for their reward" (I,*pref.*).

been shown how the cyclical notion of fortune's wheel, of the unexpected tumbling of the oversuccessful, was used in Greek historiography to confirm the moral order (Chapter 2, sect. B). Josephus found it easy to take over this elementary idea. When discussing the situation after Solomon, he averred that "many times" (*pollakis*)[227] the causes of men's evil ways and lawlessness lay in the greatness of their affairs and in the improvement of their personal position (*Antiq.* VIII,251a). On account of their strength they become "unjust and impious" (carrying their subjects with them: 251b–252), and once such men act outrageously, they cannot elude their just punishment (cf. XI,274–5, I,14, 20). So Josephus rather neatly combined Gentile doctrines of both changing fortune and retributive justice with the Hebraic belief in the fall of the proud and the divine punishment of the transgressor. The Hebrews did, after all, have their counterpart to the notion of insolence (*hybris*): the prophets had raged against the overweening pride of both Israel's rulers (cf. esp. Isa. 2:12, 9:9, 13:11, 33:9, etc.; Jer. 13:9, 15–17, etc.) and Israel's enemies (Isa. 16:6; Jer. 48:29, 50:29–32, etc.); the Chronicler had noted more than once that a monarch's greatness was a prelude to his unfaithfulness or arrogance [2 Chron. 12:1, 26:16, 32:23–25; cf. 32:9–19 (2 Kings 18:17–35)]; and Ben Sirach, to take a wisdom writer from a later century, had philosophized about the downfall of proud rulers (Ecclus. 10:6–18). With the use of *hybris* and the verb *hybrizein* in the LXX[228] and the general permeation of Hellenistic ideas, the sort of conceptual link evident in Josephus was natural.

Not all men of Hellenistic sensibility were convinced of the existence of a moral order, of course, and we should make more than a passing reference to that fascinating document Ecclesiastes, written some three centuries earlier than Josephus by a much more questioning soul. For a Jew, the writer makes a remarkably extensive use of the cyclical conceptions of his day—both those used in his own cultural milieu to reflect on the processes of nature (Eccles. 1:4–11, 3:1–8), and those applied to human affairs by his "Greek" contemporaries (cf. 5:13–14, 7:14, 16–17, 11:9, 12:1ff.). Pessimistic in inclination, the original writer (whose position may be isolated from redactional layers)[229] not only insisted that prosperity could easily pass (11:6, and cf. 7:14),[230] and that wealth could quickly be lost in "a bad venture" (5:13–15) (so musing on the vicissitudes of fortune), but drew the more far-reaching conclusion that all human activity was ultimately futile since *miqrěh* (= misfortune rather than fate?)[231] and death come

227. This term, denoting recurrence, appears in Polybius *Hist.* VI,v,5, Plato *Leg.* III,676C.

228. Cf. E. Hatch and H. A. Redpath, *A Concordance to the Septuagint*, Oxford, 1897, vol. 3, pp. 1379–80.

229. R. B. Y. Scott, *Proverbs, Ecclesiastes* (The Anchor Bible), Garden City, 1956, pp. 197f. (on the non-Greek background to the pessimism); W. O. E. Oesterley and T. H. Robinson, *An Introduction to the Books of the Old Testament*, London, 1934, pp. 209ff. (on literary criticism).

230. Or else it has an ultimate futility about it (2:1–11), or cannot be fully enjoyed (6:1–13). Comments against those who accepted a "necessary" correlation between prosperity and righteousness?

231. Cf. O. Eissfeldt, *The Old Testament: An Introduction* (ET), London, 1965, p. 498. For a comparable mood see Marcus Aurelius *Medit.* IV,xxxii,1f.

to all (cf. 2:14, 3:19, 9:2, 3). Man must be moderate and astute in the days of his life,[232] and yet he lives in a world where there is really no moral order (3:16–22, 7:15, 8:12–14, 9:2–6), despite God's ultimacy (2:24b, 3:14a, 5:19b, 12:1–8). It is a world in which anything can happen unexpectedly either for good or ill (9:11–12, and cf. 11:6). By way of a climax, the treatise finishes with a majestic and poetic statement about the futile end of human toil and the death of all men (12:1–8). Ecclesiastes lies on the fringe of our investigations, however, because the writer dilates upon the human condition in general and not on man's history in particular. On the other hand, the work clearly shows that historical linearity was not the automatic drawcard of every Old Testament writer, and it reveals how the Greek concept of *cyclos* as applied to human things made its entrance into later Judaic thought. It is significant that the likely provenance of Ecclesiastes is Alexandria,[233] and if so, it provides important background to that ancient Jewish scholar who, before all other Jewish writers, had no compunction in appropriating Greek cyclical frames for the interpretation of historical events: I mean Philo Judaeus (ca. 30 BC–AD 45).

Philo could not only write about retribution as though the operations of the Jewish God and of *dikē* (justice) amounted to the same thing, but also of the divine lordship over history in terms of fortune (*tychē*) and of classically conceived *metabolē* (change).[234] Not only did he reckon with the breeding of arrogance among the prosperous (*Vit. Mos.* I,30, 160–1), he actually claimed that fortune moved human affairs "up and down" (*anō kai katō*) on the world's draughtboard, so that "many times" (*pollakis*) the lofty were pulled down and the lowly raised, even in the space of one day (I,31). For Philo, Fortune was an agency of God, the mediating *Logos* (Word, Reason) in its rôle as the distributor of all things and as preserver of "the immutable law of balance."[235] All levels of human life reflect this distributive activity: the biological processes, the unexpected and sudden loss of great wealth, even the overthrow of an empire (*De Iosepho* 128–9, 131–2). Because the world tends to maintain a certain equilibrium—as Heraclitus had taught—it was likened to an inclining from one side to the other (*rhopē*) (132, and cf. 139–140; *De Ios.* 144f.). All things moreover, "change into their opposites" (to elicit another Heraclitean doctrine which Philo even injected into the teaching of Moses), and this was supremely true of human things with all their instability (*Vit. Mos.* I,41). Thus human history became a matter of alternating distribution. The empires, which Philo enumerated from Egypt onward, move up and down in a "ceaseless flux" since "the divine *Logos*—which most people call fortune—dances circularly" from one nation to

232. 3:1–14a, 4:17–5:12, 7:1–7, 8:1, 9:15, 10:1–20, 11:10.

233. E. H. Plumptre, *Ecclesiastes* (Cambridge Bible Commentary), Cambridge, 1887, pp. 44ff., 228; Eissfeldt, op. cit., pp. 497ff.

234. On God and *dikē* see, e.g., *In Flaccum*, 115; *De vita Mosis* I,326; *De praemiis et poenis*, 29, 169; cf. E. R. Goodenough, *An Introduction to Philo Judaeus*, New York, 1962 edn., p. 45.

235. E. Bréhier, *Les Idées philosophiques et religieuses de Philon d'Alexandrie*, Paris, 1950, p. 89; cf. H. A. Wolfson, *Philo: Foundations of Religious Philosophy in Judaism, Christianity and Islam*, Cambridge, Mass., 1948, vol. 2, p. 422.

another.[236] Under such a dispensation, the whole world may be characterized as a democracy, since what some nation or city had once, others have now, and in time all share the benefits of fortune (*Immut.* 176b).[237] God is therefore Lord over the "general direction of human material affairs" even though every state "organized by men" was "the product of their fallen nature."[238] In general terms, Philo managed to theorize not merely about undulations, about the "upward and downward" tendencies in the career of his own or any ethnic group, but also about movements which, in space and time, were spread between peoples. In this respect, his succinct yet probing statements remain both unique in the ancient world and, in the history of recurrence ideas, extremely important.

Philo sought enthusiastically to accommodate much of Greek philosophy and political theory to his stock of essentially Jewish commitments. In his eclecticism he far excelled any of his Jewish or Christian contemporaries, Luke included. With regard to historical processes, his way of intertwining Greek ideas of political change with Jewish beliefs about Israel's uniqueness adds to this impression. On the one hand, he pictured the recurring rise and fall of human phenomena. Such alternations or cycles (and the two are interchangeable for Philo) represented a normative instability among nations. This instability was not simply perpetuated by the overriding law of distribution (Greek necessity/the Jewish idea of cosmic theocracy), but also by the recalcitrant wills of individuals (Greek *metabolē* theory/Jewish insistence on human responsibility for deeds). So Philo wrote not only of a "necessary" flux, but also of "kingdoms set among men, with wars and campaigns, and numberless evils which men ambitious for power inflict on their fellows" (*De Abrah.* 261).[239]

As for his concept of the rise and fall of peoples, this clearly owes much to Hellenistic notions of change, but not everything. Philo may have been the first Jewish writer to make so much of a "ceaseless flux" outside Israelite history, yet we must remember that biblical literature contains numerous references to the emergence and disappearance of certain foreign powers. Apart from assertions that Yahweh ruled over all historical events,[240] or that régimes were as impermanent as mere stubble before his tempest (cf. Isa. 40:23–24), one should note apocalyptic pictures of successive empires. If some apocalyptic works, such as Daniel, contained only a bare outline of how such empires rose and fell, others, such as the Egyptian Sibylline Oracles (III), openly ascribed their fall to God's retribution upon tyranny and outrage.[241] Interestingly, these notions of rise and fall, Philo's included, were not presented in *biological* terms. Philo's conception of recurrent instability among the Gentiles, then, had its basis in both tradi-

236. *Quod Deus immutabilis sit*, 176, and cf. 173–5; *De Ios.* 134–7; and on flux in Heraclitus' philosophy, see above, Chapter 2, sect. B, pt. 1(i).

237. For democracy still more theologically considered, see *De Abrahamo*, 242.

238. Goodenough, op. cit., p. 68.

239. Also *Vit. Mos.* I,160–1, *De Ios.* 56f.

240. E.g., Amos 9:7, Isa. 10:5–15, 44:1–7, 22ff.

241. Dan. 2:37–43, 7:2–8, 11:2–12:45 (yet cf. 4:33, 5:21f.), Sib. Or. III,182, 199–210.

On the other hand, despite Israel's own troubles Philo consistently contrasted the normative precariousness of Gentile politics with the soundness of Jewish statesmanship. Abraham rises above the inferior machinations of politics, Joseph possesses insight into the nature of human affairs, and Moses is both disciplined in prosperity and supremely perceptive in legislating for a polity.[242] Beside the wars, tyrannies, mishaps of fortune, and iniquities of the Gentiles he placed the "venerable and godlike" Torah—a symbol of permanence.[243] It had been unchanged by political turbulence, and for Philo it even came to incorporate within itself the cosmic laws of the philosophers, so that he could proceed to make the extraordinary claim that it was honored by all peoples (*Vit. Mos.* II,16–19).[244] Like Polybius, Philo distinguished the norm from a "great exception," and even claimed a special naturalness for Mosaic institutions, as Polybius had done for Roman constitutional development. In view of the diaspora, moreover, he placed weight upon the geographical spread of Jewish practices over the whole known world,[245] and thus joined Polybius and Luke in treating geographical breadth as a mark of heavenly approval.

If Judaism transcended the normative processes of recurrence and if Israel had received a revelation from the eternal heavens which cut across earthly discordance, Judaism also represented for Philo the religious focal point through which the whole of human history was to acquire its ultimate meaning. The cycles of history would not run on unceasingly; Philo was too Jewish to abandon the concept of a Messianic Age. In the end there would come a reign of peace in which Israel would find prosperity, the dispersed Jews would be reunited in their homeland, and those Gentiles who abandoned their own peculiar customs would avoid judgment and become obedient servants of God's law.[246] This is of great significance. Philo inherited a Judaism in which the expectations of the last Age of the Messiah had wide currency. In this respect he may be considered to be in a different position from the Deuteronomist or the Chronicler, who, despite the fact that certain eschatological-looking affirmations were uttered near their time, do not seem to have shared the opinion that all history, as against significant stages of history, reached a point of completion. Philo, even in committing himself to a rather loosely-formulated eschatology, was able to enunciate a cyclical view of normative historical events. Nothing could be more

242. *De Ios.* 107–50, esp. 142a, 148–50; *Vit. Mos.* I,32, 162; cf. 41; *De Abrah.* 217ff.

243. *Vit. Mos.* II,13f. (on Gentile societies); *De Ios.* 143, and cf. 145 (on *tarachē, ataxia, asapheia* among the nations). On Israel's vicissitudes see *Vit. Mos.* II,15 (but with no analysis of constitutional change as in Josephus).

244. Cf. ibid., II,21., 25ff. (on the widespread adoption of the Sabbath law, and respect for the LXX by Ptolemy Philadelphus).

245. *Legatio ad Gaium* xliv,349ff., and cf. Wolfson, op. cit., vol. 2, pp. 417–20. Philo was not so much influenced by Polybius as one who appealed to those familiar with the Polybian ideology.

246. Ibid., vol. 2, pp. 408–17 for references. Philo may have questioned the belief in the world's end: cf. *Doxographi Graeci* (ed. H. Diels, W. de Gruyter), Berlin, 1958, p. 107 n.1, and *Aet. mund.*; but this does not rule out the fact that his Messianic Age would bring an end to the patterns of the current historical order.

damaging to the case of anyone arguing that an eschatological outlook on history requires thoroughgoing linearity or, in turn, that a cyclical view requires an eternal process. While Philo's eschatology must reject the idea of an eternity of social and cosmic cycles, his interesting eclecticism still remains.

### *Luke*

Luke, like the Israelite-Jewish thinkers, concerned himself with the issue of retribution; in fact, it is one of his cardinal themes. There is much material in Luke-Acts on the Jewish repudiation of the kingdom of God. The rejections run in a long series from the time of Jesus' ministry up to Paul's encounter with the Jewish leaders at Rome.[247] As with the Deuteronomist, disobedience becomes almost monotonous, and sin seems piled on sin until the final and implicitly divine renunciation of Judaism (at Acts 20–8). Luke consciously paralleled the pattern of Jewish disobedience in his own time with the pattern in the Old Testament, according to which the Israelites would listen neither to their great lawgiver (cf. 7:35ff.) nor to the prophets (esp. 7:52, 28:25bff.). Expressions of man's alternating relationships with Yahweh, to be found in Old Testament histories (as in Judges 2 and Nehemiah 9), have also had their slight impact, especially in the speech of Stephen (Acts 7). Both in this speech and in Paul's sermon in the synagogue at Pisidian Antioch there is the suggestion that God repeatedly revealed himself to, and acted for, his people (7:2–3, 9–10, 30–33, 38, 45–47, 52, 13:17–22), and repeatedly established covenants for their future well-being (7:5, 34, and cf. 6–7; 13:23).[248]

In Stephen's interpretation of Israelite history, above all, the inner contradiction between Israel's reception of revelation and her transgressions becomes apparent. Here we are not far from the older pattern of successive obedience and disobedience, the good works of God's servants being consistently undermined by "resistance to the Holy Spirit" (cf. 7:52). The progress of the patriarchs was marred by the jealousy of Joseph's brothers (vss.9–10; cf. 3ff.), the promising upbringing of Moses by the earlier rejection of his people (vss.21–29), the Exodus by the idolatry in the wilderness (vss.38–43), and the eventual erection of the Temple by a wrong spiritual understanding (vss.44–50). If angels had once delivered the Torah, it was not kept (vs.53); the prophets were persecuted and killed (vs.52). The function of this speech, then, quite apart from questions of its pre-Lukan elements,[249] was to instance the accumulating guilt of the Jews in terms of their own religion and their own outstretched past, let alone in the light of recent events. Thus the patterns of the new history were essentially the same as the old. Perhaps Luke's approach was not so simplistic that he side-stepped Christianity's Jewish origin or failed to mention either conversions

247. It is unfair, incidentally, to single out diaspora Jews as Luke's chief *bêtes noires* (cf. Acts 7:9, 9:29b, 21:27) in the light of Acts 4–5, 23:12ff., and, of course, Luke in general.

248. Note, as more recent background than Judges or Nehemiah here, Ecclus. 44ff.; Ta'anith (Babylonian Talmud) ii,4; cf. *Zadokite doc.* (MSA) 1,3.

249. Cf. J. Munck, *Paul and the Salvation of Mankind* (ET), London, 1959, pp. 222–4. The non-Palestinian geography in this speech is less important for Luke here than for the original writer.

among the Jews or hindrances caused by Gentiles,[250] but there is a strong anti-Semitism nevertheless, and it may well owe more to Luke's historiographical predispositions than to the facts themselves.

It was with Paul's arrival in Rome that Luke chose to disclose God's rejection of the Jews in favor of the Gentiles (Acts 28:26–28). That is significant, for it was the Romans who destroyed the holy city of Judaism. Unlike Mark (and even Matthew?) Luke had concrete information about the fall of Jerusalem and the events of 68–70 AD (Luke 21:20, and cf. 24; 19:43, yet cf. Mark 13:14, Matt. 24:15). Certainly all the Synoptics quoted Jesus' saying that "not one stone [of the temple] would be left upon another" (Mark 13:2b ≠ Matt. 24:2 ≠ Luke 21:6),[251] yet only Luke was in a position to give real substance to that statement, to see that it was not just another "desolating sacrilege" (cf. Dan. 9:27b, 11:31; 1 Macc. 1:54), like the desecration of Epiphanes, but something far more disastrous (cf. esp. Luke 19:43–44, om. Mark, Matt.). Its only precedent lay in the calamity effected by Nebuchadnezzar. The coming event of horror, however, was no longer the symbol of the eschaton's eventual arrival, which was to occur after the gospel had been preached to all nations (cf. Mark 13:10, 14; Matt. 24:14, 15), but it was a thoroughly historical event, and a known one, which happened between the "time of witness" (Luke 21:13) (or, in other words, the period covered by Acts to ca. 63 AD)[252] and the "times of the Gentiles," still awaiting completion before the cosmic indications of the eschaton (Luke 21:24b, and cf. 25–38; Acts 15:16–17).[253]

This event of 70 AD was thus viewed by Luke less in terms of world crisis than as a specific occurrence in Israel's history which marked the fall of God's wrath upon the contumacious Jews (Luke 21:22, 23b). For Luke it is therefore another Babylonian captivity (though worse), and he used the biblical word for being "dragged into exile" to express its bitterness (see above, n. 129). The second fall, indeed, fulfilled the scriptures (Luke 21:22b; cf. *plēsthēnai*[254] om. Mark, Matt.), and by this Luke did not just mean prediction fulfillment. Pondering on his remodelled quotation of Amos in Acts 7:42–43, one is hardly unjustified in concluding that he expected 70 AD to see a fulfilling completion of what had already happened to the Jews centuries earlier. The devastation was not merely a recurrence, however. If Judah had once paid for her disobedience by exile, she now paid with real finality, because this time she rejected the *Christos* and his

250. Acts, 2:5, 41, 47, 4:36, 6:7, 11:19ff., 13:43, 14:4b, 17:4 (on Jewish converts); 16:22ff., 17:32, 19:24ff. (on Gentile hindrances).

251. On authenticity questions see W. G. Kümmel, *Promise and Fulfillment: The Eschatological Message of Jesus* (*Studies in Biblical Theology XXIII*) (ET), London, 1957, pp. 99ff.; L. Gaston, *No Stone on Another: Studies in the Significance of the Fall of Jerusalem in the Synoptic Gospels* (*Supplements to Novum Testamentum XXIII*), Leiden, 1970, chs. 1–2.

252. Following H. Metzger, *St. Paul's Journeys in the Greek Orient* (*Studies in Biblical Archaeology IV*) (ET), London, 1955, p. 73.

253. Also Conzelmann, *Theology*, p. 129; cf. pp. 125–35.

254. The verb is *pimplēmi*, which Luke usually employed to mean filling or completing a time period, but here it suggests fulfillment. On this special sense see W. F. Arndt and F. W. Gingrich, *A Greek-English Lexicon of the New Testament (and Other Early Christian Literature)*, Chicago, 1957, p. 663b; cf. Luke 1:20, DWΨ21.

messengers. The Christ himself foretold that the temple would be reduced to rubble (see Luke 21:6; cf. Acts 6:14a, verses which look ahead to a city levelled by Titus),[255] and Paul had pronounced an oracle of coming vengeance upon its high priesthood (so Acts 23:3, which foreshadows Ananias' assassination by bandits).[256] While Luke saw a parallel between the earlier and later destructions, then, the punishment of 70 AD was directly related to the recent coming of Jesus and whether he had been accepted or despised.

As I have suggested elsewhere, Luke organized the Jesus tradition, especially in the "central section" of the Gospel, to demonstrate the sort of teacher Jesus was, the essence of his teaching, and the kinds of situations he faced.[257] It is significant that out of the three areas he highlighted in the travel narrative—security, discipleship, and the retributive consequences of rejecting or accepting the divine intention—the last receives the most space. In any case, Luke acknowledges the retributive implications of Jesus' coming almost from the beginning. John the Baptist anticipates imminent judgment and wrath (Luke 3:7–9), and the mightier man he expects to follow him is a judgelike figure (3:16b–17). Other suggestions of retribution foreshadow the relevant material in the travel narrative,[258] but it is there that the real challenge to the "evil generation" intensifies, and the Jews, especially their leaders, are attacked for unbelief.[259] As recompense, Israel's house is forsaken (13:35, om. Mark, Matt.) (here the quotation from Jeremiah contributes to the parallel between the new situation and the events of 586 BC),[260] and the blood of all the murdered prophets requited (11:50 ≠ Matt. 23:35). With the Jerusalem ministry it becomes clearer that Jesus is not only the herald of a rendering of justice (*ekdikēsis*) which finds its concrete embodiment in the city's destruction; his work also foreshadows a far wider judgment associated with his Coming (*Parousia*), which for Luke, I maintain, was not far off.[261]

All these retributive ideas are more decidedly Jewish than Greco-Roman, even if they were hardly alien to prevailing Hellenistic mentalities. Luke, however, betrays a more eclectic bent in his handling of recompenses applied to individuals. Judas' death is an important case in point. Matthew may have related how Judas "repented," returned the blood money, and hanged himself in remorse (27:3–5), but Luke claimed that Judas bought a field from the reward of his injustice (*adikia*) and then unwittingly died a hideous death (Acts 1:18). As an instance of divine retribution, Luke's account would have been far more compelling for both Jews and Greeks, the Jews acknowledging its basis in biblical prophecy (2:16, 20), the Greeks seeing it foreshadowed in ancient "oracles"

255. Cf. Josephus, *Bell. Jud.* VII,1–4.
256. Josephus II,441f.
257. Trompf, "Section," pp. 143ff.; cf. B. Reicke, "Instruction and Discussion in the Travel Narrative" in *Studia Evangelica I* (*Texte und Untersuchungen LXXIII*), 1959, pp. 206ff. on alternating audiences (between the disciples and outsiders).
258. Esp. 4:29, 5:21, 30, 33, 6:2, 7f., 45–9, 7:31–5, 9:5, 10:10–2.
259. Trompf, "Section," pp. 147ff.
260. Jer. 22:5b, a prophecy unequivocally related to the earlier destruction.
261. See Excursus 3, Exegetical Note H.

and by Jesus himself (vs.20; cf. Luke 22:22b), and both intuiting it as a fitting end for the one who betrayed the Lord.[262] For another case we may turn to the death of Herod (Agrippa I) as recounted in Acts 12:20–23. In contrast to Luke, Josephus found much to admire in Agrippa (*Antiq.* XIX,328–342; cf. XVIII,144, XIX,300–11), and he tried to show that, although the king died so suddenly, he was consciously self-reproachful about the sin of omission which brought about his death (XIX,343–350; cf. XVIII,200). Luke, for his part, saw his sudden end as direct retribution upon an unrepentant king who persecuted the Christians and refused to give "the glory to God" (Acts 12:23; cf. 2–3). Luke's explanation was easier and more readily acceptable to Jew and Gentile alike. Admittedly, the language of retribution is heavily biblical (23b; cf. Josephus' "fate": *Antiq.* XIX,347), yet it may well be that the Evangelist deliberately blurred the distinction between the evil Herod of Luke and the evil Herod of his second volume, so that, at the very least, the hideous death of Acts 12 stood as a symbol of retribution against "Herodianism."[263] It is important, moreover, that no requital of any kind is actually effected in his Gospel, as distinct from Acts (note Luke 9:54), and that chastisement was reserved for the time between the resurrection and the eschaton. Here we may have alighted on one key motivation for Luke's writing of a second volume. What Jesus had warned about was becoming actualized, and those who rejected him had to face their deserts. In this sense the foretold doom of Ananias (in Acts 23:3) points to retribution upon the high priesthood which sentenced Jesus to death. Luke's relative indefiniteness about individual culpability, both at the crucifixion and at Stephen's martyrdom,[264] allowed him to suggest that the murder of Ananias stood as God's wrathful visitation upon the heads of the Jewish religion in general, a punishment sealed in 70 AD. Thus the reversals of fortune proclaimed at the onset of the Gospel in the *Magnificat* are shown to have been actualizing in the events of recent times.[265]

There are other instances of requitals for individuals in Acts—the cases of Ananias and Sapphira, Elymas, and the sons of Sceva, for example (Acts 5:1–11, 13:6–12, 19:13–17)—and again the sins and appropriate penalties have paradigmatic qualities. There is thus a theme in the book that the enemies of God's new ways must suffer penalties befitting their recalcitrance. Even Saul

262. To illustrate how Luke's treatment is more characteristically Greco-Roman than Jewish at this point, Matthew's comments on Judas' end may be compared to Polybius' description of the suicide by hanging of Archias the betrayer of Cyprus in *Hist.* XXXIII,v,2–4. Cf. also above, Chapter 2, sect. B, pt. 2(i) and (ii).

263. If Luke saw a distinction between Herod the king (Acts 12:1a) and Herod the tetrarch (Luke 3:19a, 9:7a; cf. 3:1), most of his readers, being ill-informed on Palestinian affairs, could have been excused for confusing the two. Did Luke wish to suggest that justice was satisfied (the murder of John and the mockery of Jesus being paid for by the events of Acts 12), and so blur the distinction between the two Herods? Cf. Acts 25:13, 23–6, 26:1f., 24ff. on naming Agrippa II; and on anti-Herodianism in the Gospels see H. Braunert, "Der römische Provinzialzensus und der Schätzungsbericht des Lukas Evangeliums" in *Historia* VI, 1957, pp. 192ff.

264. Significantly, Luke did not single out Caiaphas as the high-priestly culprit of Jesus' trial (Luke 22:66–71, yet cf. Matt. 26:57, 59–68; John 18:13f.), only once referring to him, and even then after Annas (a name hardly unlike Ananias!) in Luke 3:2.

265. See J. Drury, op. cit., esp. pp. 53f. on the "reversal of fortunes" theme in Luke.

pays for his sins as a persecutor, although along with Jesus and the other disciples he eventually came to suffer as an "innocent," thus representing a "great exception" in terms of divine retributive principles.[266] In showing at the end of his work how Paul survived shipwreck, in fact, Luke clinches his point about innocence, because for many of his Gentile readers it was obvious that a guilty man would have drowned.[267] Apropos of Christianity's uniqueness: certain manmade movements may have sprung up in the same part of the world during roughly the same time period, but they came at best to nothing, at worst to disastrous ends, and did so, as it were, recurrently. These movements included the insurrections of Theudas and of Judas the Galilean (cf. Acts 5:35–39),[268] as well as the Sicarii movement and one of their revolts under the "Egyptian" (21:38).[269] But Christianity was neither typical nor politically harmful; it was, as Gamaliel unwittingly admitted, "from God" (5:39). It may fairly be argued, moreover, that Luke appealed to the Holy Spirit as the special "agency of support" for Christianity, an agency comparable enough to personified providence, fate, or fortune to be intelligible to "Greeks," yet nearly enough indistinguishable from the "Spirit of the Lord" in the Old Testament to preserve continuity between new and former times.[270]

Luke, then, apparently shared with other ancient Mediterranean historians basic presuppositions about the recurring actualization of retributive principles in history. And he was happy to convince both Jew and Gentile: retribution in Luke-Acts is what was commonly expected of it in two major cultural heritages, and his work—dotted with identifiable and recurrent event-shapes and situations—was not so out of line with precedents in either Hebrew or Greco-Roman historiography as to be an unwanted compromise.

## C. Notions of Rise and Fall and of Successive Ages, Especially in Luke

Other elements in Luke's history corroborate his interest in recurrence, although they belong more decidedly to the Jewish than to any other tradition. I think of his assumptions about rise and fall and his understanding of Age theory. Concerning rise and fall, one should note the Lukan implication in the Aeropagus speech that divine Providence ruled over the *kairoi* of the nations, that is to say, the times in which they flourished (Acts 17:26b). Luke, however, was committed to a Judeo-Christian eschatological view that the world powers would eventually be supplanted by a divine rule. Although Luke tried to be

266. On background to New Testament ideas of innocent suffering see 2 Macc. 5:28, 7:32f., 37; 4 Macc. 1:11, 6:28ff.; cf. J. Downing, "Jesus and Martyrdom" in *Journal of Theological Studies* XIV, 1963, pp. 281–5. On Saul paying by blindness see Acts 9:8–9, 18.

267. G. Miles and G. W. Trompf, "Luke and Antiphon" in *Harvard Theological Review* LXIX, 1976, pp. 259ff.

268. Luke put them in the wrong historical order: Trocmé, op. cit., pp. 193f.

269. Cf. Josephus *Bell. Jud.* II,261ff.

270. On the Holy Spirit in *Luke-Acts* see Excursus 3, Exegetical Note I.

cautious with his Roman readers, the broad vision in Luke 21 sees all nations reduced to conflict and confusion before the final redemption (10, 12a, 25).[271] He therefore took the impermanence of manmade empires for granted; even the fall of the Jewish nation was objectified as a key illustration of socio-political transience. The issue of imperial fluctuation is perhaps secondary for Luke, and he has nothing so theoretical on this matter as Philo. However, something tantamount to a doctrine of rise and fall is implicit in his writings.

And what of Age theory? Like most Jewish and Christian writers of his time, Luke accepted the idea of two great Ages, "this Age" and "the [Messianic] Age to come" (Luke 18:30 ≠ Mark 10:30). For Luke the Messianic Age was still to come in fullness, even if it had already begun with Christ's ministry.[272] The completion of "this Age," moreover, saw a final generation from the Incarnation to the eschaton, a few men thus being privileged to see both the passing of the old order and the full arrival of the new.[273]

Referrals to successive Ages, naturally important in the history of recurrence ideas, came late in Jewish thought. It stands to reason that with the lengthening of known Israelite history, it became necessary to describe it in terms of stages. If the Deuteronomist had conceived such stages as marked off by "lifetimes" or "generations" (*dōrōth*) or by periods of obedience and disobedience, and if such writers as the "Priestly" redactor and the Chronicler also wrote of theologically significant epochs,[274] authors reflecting on Jewish history in a post-restoration context found it difficult to reduce chaos to order. Significantly, apocalyptic periodization was based on the "times" of those empires which had subjected Israel, from a given writer's own day back as far as Nebuchadnezzar, or even to ancient Egypt. As Barker rightly observes, this periodization was artificial and usually governed by special theological considerations, including the belief in the Age to come (an Age, incidentally, when original sinlessness would return).[275] The notion of an old and a new Age, which may well have had its place in Jesus' teaching, was quickly assimilated into Christian theology, and some early Christians were prepared to accept the more elaborate apocalyptic

271. Cf. Conzelmann, *Theology*, pp. 138ff.

272. The conventional dividing line between the two Ages was the time of the Messiah, when God's final rule would be ushered in (e.g., 1 En. 16:1b; 2 Bar. 69:4f., 83:7). The Messianic Age was to be preceded by crises, and (for most) its coming would make possible the resurrection of the dead (*Sanh.* ix,5, x,1; *Sotah* ix,5–*finis*). This dividing line continued to be drawn by the early Christians (e.g., Matt. 13:39f., 49, 24:3, 28:20; Mark 10:30f.; Luke 8:30; 1 Cor. 2:6–8, 3:8; Eph. 1:20f.; Heb. 6:5), yet because the Messiah had already come, a "realized eschatology" emerged, to use C. H. Dodd's phrase, whereby Jesus' first coming was at the "completion of the Ages" broadly conceived (e.g., Heb. 9:26; 1 Cor. 10:11b; Gal. 4:4).

273. On Conzelmann's thesis about Luke's three-staged view of history see Excursus 3, Exegetical Note J.

274. On the Deuteronomist see esp. Noth, *Überlief. Stud.*, pp. 23–6 (cf. above, sect. B, pt. 1); on P see esp. North, op. cit., pp. 110f.; on the Chronicler see above, sect. A, pt. 4, and sect. B, pt. 2.

275. Cf. D. S. Russell, *The Method and Message of Jewish Apocalyptic, 200 BC-AD 100*, London, 1964, pp. 224ff. (and on Barker see above, Chapter 3, introd.). On the theme of a recurrent struggle in which Yahweh the Creator overcomes Chaos see Jeremias, op. cit., pp. 204f.; N. L. A. Tidwell, "A Biblical Concept of Sin" in *Church Quarterly Review* CLXIII, 1962, pp. 416f.

frameworks.[276] Such ideas of succession, as we contended at the beginning of this chapter, were recurrence notions, even though the time lapses or imperial efflorescences were very roughly conceived.[277] Moreover, insofar as apocalyptic schemes presupposed that empires emerge, expand, and dissolve, or that great time intervals, even without a return to former eons, are repeated in their basic configurations, reference to "cyclo-alternating rise and fall" or to "periodic cycles" is admissible. That apocalyptic writers believed themselves to be living near the end of time did not prevent them from reflecting on the outstretched past in these terms.

What of Luke in this connection? While he acknowledged the two major Ages, Luke wrote of other time divisions only in terms of *geneai* (generations) (Acts 13:36, 15:21; cf. 8:3), *kairoi* (times of flourishing) (17:36; cf. 1:7, Luke 21:24) or *chronoi* (extensions of time) (Acts 3:21, 17:30; cf. 1:7). In one interesting passage (Luke 17:26–32), admittedly, he seems to have "Hellenized" a Jesus saying (better preserved in Matthew) so as to treat the eschaton as a final retributive disaster in line with great upheavals of the past, that is, with the Flood and with the destruction of Sodom. But his intriguing concessions here to Greek theory about recurrent catastrophes show no reference to inter-cataclysmic Ages. Philo (and Origen following him) treated these two renowned events as the biblical equivalents of "Greek" catastrophes, the first being a deluge and the second a conflagration.[278] These writers consciously diverged from pagan views, however, by contending that the two great upheavals demonstrated God's periodic punishment of evil men. It is precisely this element which is highlighted by Luke, as also by the author of 2 Peter, the latter prefacing the three major examples of retribution—the Flood, the destruction of Sodom and Gomorrah, and the Last Day—by a reference to the Fall of Angels (2:4–10).[279]

Again, in Acts 3:21, Luke has Peter foretell the "restoration of all things," but if recurrence is implied, it is not that of *palingenesia* (the cosmos recommenced) but the return to an original Eden-like perfection.[280] Moreover, there seems to

276. 2 Esdras and 1 Enoch, for example, experienced Christian redactions: cf. Eissfeldt, op. cit., pp. 620, 625.

277. On the emergence of empires see, e.g., Dan. 2:38–41, 7:3–8; 2 Esd. 11:1ff., 12:10ff.; Test Napht. 5,8; Sib. *Or.* 4:49–192; *Bahman Yast* i,3 (192) (West); 4QFrg. in J. T. Milik, "'Prière de Nabonide' et autres écrits d'un cycle de Daniel" in *Revue Biblique* LXIII, 1956, p. 411 n. 2). Cf. D. Flusser, "The Four Empires in the Fourth Sibyl and in the Book of Daniel" in *Israel Oriental Studies* II, 1972, pp. 148ff.; M. Hengel, *Judaism and Hellenism* (ET), Philadelphia, 1974, vol. 1, p. 182; J. J. Collins, "The Mythology of Holy War in Daniel and the Qumranite War Scroll" in *Vetus Testamentum* XXV, 1975, p. 602. On successive Ages see 1 Enoch 85:1–90:20; 2 Esd. 14:11f.; 4 Esd. 3:4ff. (on six Ages), 14:11 (on twelve Ages); 2 Bar. 53:5ff., 56–74 (on twelve periods alternating between good and evil: cf. A. C. B. Kolenkow, "An Introduction to II Bar. 53, 56–74: Structure and Substance," Harvard Doctoral thesis, Cambridge, Mass., 1971, ch. 2); Test. Abrah. 19; Ass. Moys. 1:2, 10:12 (cf. *Sanh.* 97b); Josephus *Bell. Jud.* II,374; and see below, Chapter 4, sect. D, pt. 2.

278. For background see Bk. Jub. 5:2b; Vita Adae et Evae, 49:3, cf. Plato, *Tim.*, 22c.

279. For further discussion see W. L. Knox, *St. Paul and the Church of the Gentiles*, Cambridge, 1939, p. 6 n. 2, and below, Chapter 4, sect. D, pt. 2, for Philo and Origen on catastrophe theory.

280. E. Dinkler, "The Idea of History in Earliest Christianity" in *Signum Crucis: Aufsätze zum Neuen Testament und zur christlichen Archaeologie*, Tübingen, 1967, p. 327. The term used is *apokatastasis* (Acts 3:21), which is a Stoic term for cosmic rejuvenation; cf. *Stoic. vet. frag.*, Frgs. 599, 625 (von Arnim, vol. 2, pp. 184, 190).

be no obviously cyclical element in his approach to periodicity. If the later Jewish Sibylline Oracles (III) could put the rise and fall of empires within the context of "the circling years of time" (158–60, 289, 563, 649, 728), and the writer of 2 Esdras speak of the biological senescence of the present order (14:10; cf. 11–12, 16; see even Heb. 8:13b), Luke, for his part, simply conveyed the impression of one great Age merging with another. In this, nevertheless, he was still betraying the hand of a Hellenistic historian. If Polybius saw that Rome's rise to supremacy was contemporaneous with the decline of opposing powers, Luke reckoned the breaking-in of God's kingdom to coincide with the downfall of the old elect, and with a troubled conclusion to the "times of the nations."

Like the Polybian *Historiae*, Luke's work is important for reflecting a large variety of recurrence notions and models, even if many of the individual conceptions received clearer definitions elsewhere in biblical and related literature. Like Polybius, too, Luke had eclectic tendencies. Although many of his historiographical presuppositions and methods derived from the Hebraic tradition, Luke went out of his way to accommodate Gentile tastes, like many writers in that tradition before him. On the other hand, Luke was concerned to bridge the conceptual boundaries between two quite different cultures, whereas Polybius' syncretism has to do with apparently conflicting lines of philosophical and historical thought within the world of the Hellenistic schools.

There are, however, significant differences between the approaches of Polybius and Luke. There is no theoretical statement about historical processes in Luke-Acts; unlike Polybius, Luke made known his ideas of recurrence through allusion, and particularly through the special organization of his material. Moreover, while cyclical and alternation ideas are the major component in Polybius' historical interpretation, for Luke the idea that incidents and stages are reenacted is primary. The cycles and alternations of the *Historiae* are conceived to be fairly regular and predictable (except in the case of fortune's wheel), whereas Luke's reenactments are either events which could happen at any time, or stages within sequences which reflect a divine plan.[281] One of Polybius' chief aims was to give explicit predictive guidance on human affairs, and the cycles of human life persuaded him that such an intention could be realized. The reenactment notions of Luke, however, are oriented far more toward the past than toward the future, and instead of bearing pragmatic implications they simply speak of God's purposes behind human activity. Again, although Polybius does not seem to have believed (any more than Luke) in the repetition of precisely the same event-conjunctions, he sensed that contours and event-complexes would recur in an apparently limitless future. Of Lukan reenactments, by contrast, we can posit no such reappearances, since he expected the eschaton to alter earthly existence so drastically.

281. The parallel "stages of development" in Luke-Acts (see sect. A, pt. 3) represent two sequences with four divisions, but each sequence cannot be termed a cycle except in the loosest sense, since the implication of any return to an original point of departure is so weak. The *recurrence* of "stages of development," then, best describes this aspect of Luke's interpretations.

This comparison of cycles and reenactments, however, does not give a complete picture. After all, cyclical conceptions (Age theory, rise and fall) have some airing in Luke-Acts, and Polybius appealed to notions of recurrence which did not presuppose regularity. Besides, the differences are very much less pronounced when one compares their approaches to retributive principles. In Hebrew historiography, the nearest thing to the formulation of historical laws came with the doctrine of recurrently actualized recompenses, and in such writers as the Deuteronomist and the Chronicler these recurrences teach men how they ought to behave in the future. Luke inherited this understanding of historical processes, and even though he looked forward to the Messianic Age he could still imply that men should continue to make similar spiritual preparations for the days ahead. In both Polybius and Luke, moreover, the workings of the moral order reveal divine or suprahuman causation. For monotheistic Luke, of course, God lay behind all the patterns of recurrence; the different levels of causality in Polybius' approach do not make their appearance in Luke. That is not to say that Luke cannot be regarded as "a genuinely classical historian," for the way he elicited paradigmatic incidents, the way he did not reproduce everything with "photographic fidelity" but displayed "only what is typical and significant,"[282] indicates otherwise.

If this comparison suggests anything wider, it is that of the two great traditions behind Western thought, the classical was not the exclusive bearer of recurrence ideas. Admittedly, the Jews and early Christians were averse to certain doctrines of cosmological recurrence. They would have accepted neither the eternity of the world nor the possibility of exact repetition.[283] But they had been influenced by cosmological cyclicism, for Middle Eastern astronomy lies behind their Age theory. In any case, we have not located a classical *historian* who believed in exact recurrence.[284] Biblical scholars have tended to contrast cyclical views in Greek philosophy with Judeo-Christian positions; they have not paid enough attention to the methods of Greco-Roman historiography. Above all, however, one has to reckon with the rich stock of conceptions we have just been analyzing. They stand together with Greco-Roman models and ideas as contributors to Western historical thought, though whether the two sets of ideas became assimilated or were held in relative separation requires our further investigation.

282. J. Rohde, *Rediscovering the Teaching of the Evangelists* (= *Die redaktionsgeschichtliche Methode*) (ET), London, 1968, p. 154 on the views of Dibelius.

283. Origen's interpretation of Ecclesiastes might suggest otherwise (*De principiis* I,iv,5, III,v,3; cf. I,vii,5), but it is not conclusive that Origen ascribed either of these views to the Preacher.

284. On middle-Stoic Poseidonius, however, see below, Chapter 4, sect. A.

# Chapter 4

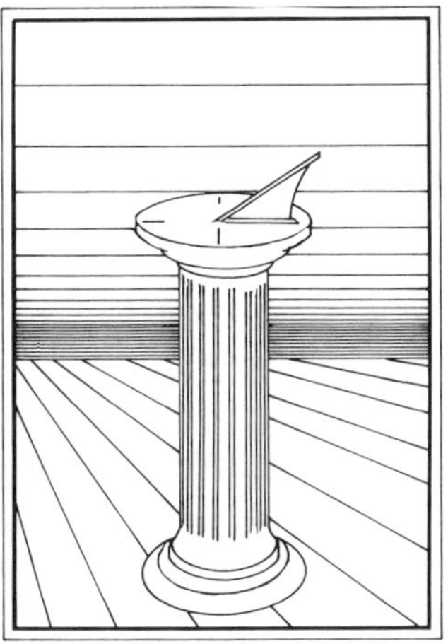

# From Later Antiquity to Early Renaissance

Despite Christianity's rôle as a "third genus" in the garden of Greek and Roman civilization, and despite the decisive victory of Christian theology over the older Hellenistic schools, there was an extensive synthesizing of biblical and Gentile ideas from the fourth century AD on. Much has been written about Greco-Roman influence on Christian thought, but there has been little work on the merging of historiographical preconceptions, models, and methods in the patristic and subsequent periods. The making of a sharp distinction between Christian linearity and classical cyclicism has undoubtedly hindered rather than facilitated careful investigation in this area. Yet if a study of New Testament and late Jewish literature shows certain weaknesses in this dichotomy, a look at subsequent developments reveals even more. In the patristic and medieval periods, the interrelationship between Greco-Roman and Middle Eastern ideas of recurrence becomes still more interesting and complex.

There were some notions of recurrence in both traditions (and I am resigned to calling these Greco-Roman and Judeo-Christian) which could be bound closely together. These included ideas of retribution, rise and fall, and Age succession. The more decidedly political, pragmatic concerns of Greco-Roman historiography, however, contrast dramatically with the greater concentration in Hebrew and early Christian writing on theological issues and on very broad questions about human existence. This contrast helped to set the tone for a dialectic between "secular" and "sacred" history, and certainly prevented the settlement of a uniform, integrated interpretation of history's processes and significance. Nevertheless, if we may generalize about the movement of historiographical ideas from the Augustan period to the early Renaissance, classical "pragmatism" and "secularism" were progressively overridden by the avowedly Christian search for theological meaning in history.[1] Christianity's triumph, however, hardly ended the preoccupation with historical repetition, and the fate of any particular recurrence idea was not determined simply by the supremacy of one ideology over another. Matters were complex, and we must turn to detail.

One may first ask what happened to the central models and conceptions which have held most of our attention so far—the Polybian cycle of governments and Luke's understanding of reenactment. Interestingly enough, both sets of ideas undergo a further development which neatly conforms to the conventional ancient/medieval/Renaissance schematization. The Polybian *Anacyclōsis* (together with the concern for variegated patterns of constitutional change) disappears from view after the emergence of a Caesarean non-Republican Roman dominion, only to return much later in the pages of Machiavelli's *Discorsi* (1513–1517). As for Luke's special understanding of reenactment, it became obscured behind medieval typology and allegory, only to make a reappearance with certain Reformation emphases on the return to primitive Christianity.

Let us take the fate of the *Anacyclōsis*. As Polybius' model was so elaborate, one would hardly expect a spate of would-be successors ready to apply that model to the facts. Certainly Cicero (106–43 BC), who knew the *Historiae* Bk. VI, was happy to write of "cycles and apparent recurrence in the changes and vicissitudes of public affairs" (*Re pub.* I,xxix,45; cf. II,xxv,45, III,xxiii,34), but in this general comment he seems much more flexible about constitutional cycles than the architect of the *Anacyclōsis*. Arius Didymus, Cicero's contemporary, seems to have accepted Polybius' six-constitution classification, yet he wrote only of the common degeneration of each "right constitution" into its "bad" counterpart, not of a fixed sequence of change.[2] Cicero himself was just as reserved, if

1. Using G. J. Holyoake's coinage loosely, "secularism" means here "the interpretation of affairs without (or with a minimum of) resort to theological explanations."

2. In Stobaeus *Anthol.* II,vii,26 (Arius using *ochlocratia* for degenerate democracy; cf. also Philo *De agricultura* 45). For a comparable six-part first-century classification (though with the term "oligarchy" replacing "aristocracy" and *dynasteia* replacing "oligarchy"), see Plutarch *De unius in republica dominatione*, 826E.

not more so, on this matter. The three simple, primary constitutions were liable to decline into their perverted forms,[3] but he was only prepared to suggest "what commonly happened" rather than to endorse any fixed course, and so he permitted a greater variety of change. Furthermore, he placed greater stress on the principle of "change into opposites"; linking it with notions of reversal and requited immoderateness, he generalized that "everything in excess (*nimia*) . . . is usually changed into its converse" (*Re pub.* I,xliv,68; cf. xlii,65). In this he once again showed his wariness of determinism; matters are stated so broadly that alternatives and exceptions in political change are covered. An eclectic in his own right, Cicero was not committed to the simplistic analyses of either Plato or Polybius, and he preferred to appeal to more popular, less restrictive models of recurrence.

Tullius Cicero certainly used cyclical language very loosely. Any cycle of constitutional change was confined to a simple process of *metabolē*, an alteration in which a constitution could either give way to its opposite form or "pay" for its imbalance.[4] Sensitive to the number of possible changes in these terms, he probably disagreed that the *Anacyclōsis* corresponded to realities, and it is not likely that he based his own history of the Roman constitution (in *Re pub.* II) on the stages in Polybius' lost "archeology." He declined to conceive of Rome's constitutional development as anything like an anacyclic process, and although he admitted that Rome had been born and grown to its maturity (see sect. B), he maintained that her state was eternal.[5] On the other hand, his views on Rome's mixed constitution are comparable to those of Polybius. Such a constitution could forestall decay and corruption, since this was what "commonly happened" with constitutions so "well-balanced" (*Re pub.* I,xlv,69). Moreover, if one understood the cyclical tendencies of constitutional change, Rome's stability could be indefinitely preserved, "every citizen being held in his own station" to maintain the balance.[6]

If Polybian frames of reference had only a slight impact on Cicero, matters were different with the author of the *Archaeologiae Romanae*, Dionysius of Halicarnassus (flor. 30–8 BC). Dionysius apparently wanted to demonstrate how Rome's constitutional history did in fact follow the normative anacyclic path of Polybius VI,iv–ix. He discarded Polybius' anthropology and subscribed to the current opinion that the Senate was an important institution as early as the monarchical period,[7] yet he nevertheless drew on the anacyclic zigzag in his record of major constitutional transformations from Romulus to the fall of the Decemvirate. From founder Romulus to Servius Tullius, Rome was ruled by

3. *Re pub.* I,xlv,69 (on "tyranny from kingship, factions from aristocracy, turbulence . . . from popular rule," so recalling the Polybian classification); cf. I,xxxii,48–xxxvi,56, xlii,65–xlv,69, II,xxix,51, xxxix,65.
4. Esp. I,xlvi,70, II,xxxix,65f.
5. Pöschl, *Römischer Staat*, pp. 99–105; cf. p. 83; *Re pub.* I,xlvi,70, II,xxxix,65f.
6. *Re pub.* II,xxv,45, and I,xlv,69 for the quotation.
7. E. Cary, "Introduction" to Dionysius *Roman Antiquities*, Cambridge, Mass., 1948, p. xxi; cf. *Archaeol.* II,xiv,1–4, VI,lxvi,3, etc.

kings (despite the creation of other nonmonarchical bodies); Tarquinius Superbus then converted the kingly polity into a tyranny. This, when overthrown, was replaced by an aristocracy, and despite the establishment of such nonaristocratic institutions as the dictator and the tribunes, the state remained in that form until the oligarchy of the Decemvirs.[8] Democratic-plebeian pressure then removed the oligarchs, but the subsequent constitutional settlement was not characterized as a democracy so much as a compromise between patrician and plebian elements in the state—a compromise that was to the advantage of the patrician (or senatorial) sector.[9]

Dionysius has idiosyncratic touches, yet the *Anacyclōsis* clearly lies behind his interpretations. Unlike Polybius, however, he placed the settling-down of a balanced polity *after* the oligarchic Decemvirs. Why? Because the failure of Polybius to use the Decemvirate interlude in support of anacyclic theory was so surprising? Or because it was not clear to Dionysius where oligarchy fitted into Polybius' analysis of Roman constitutional development? Both factors probably contributed. Polybius seems to have located oligarchy between the future decline of Rome's mixed constitution (*mixis*) and the emergence of democracy (see Chapter 1, sect. E), not as the prelude to a balanced constitutional order. Dionysius, for his part, put oligarchy in the past, and, living a century after Polybius, could analyze Roman decay differently. As a Greek he was certainly not committed to a doctrine of an eternal Rome (*Roma aeterna*). Since the fall of Carthage, he maintained, old Roman virtues and former times of internal order were eclipsed by rapacity among the people, by extravagance, and by the undermining of the constitution through those aspiring to tyrannical overlordship.[10] At the time when Gaius Gracchus took tribunician power (in 121 BC), the old constitutional harmony which had kept the citizens from mutual slaughter for 630 years was ended by "ceaseless slaying and banishment," and Dionysius characterized this disintegration in the same sort of language used by Plato and Polybius when they described complete constitutional breakdown.[11] It is hard to decide whether he took Rome's dissolution to be imminent or whether he simply forecast the eventual decay of what was, after all, just another human institution. The evident influence of anacyclic theory remains, although Dionysius' work is apparently the first and last application of Polybian theory in antiquity.

The cumbersome nature and artificiality of the *Anacyclōsis* was not, as we have already suggested, the sole explanation for its submersion. Another important cause lay with the end of the Roman Republic and the institution of an hereditary rule (*imperium*) from Julius Caesar onward. The consequences of Caesar's acquisition of supreme power presented an exception too great for older consti-

8. VI,i,1 (from monarchy to tyranny to aristocracy); cf. II,iv,1ff., IV,xli,1–4, etc. (and esp. XI,ii,1–iii,1 (the Decemvirate as oligarchy).

9. XI,i,6, xlvi,1, l,1–liii,3, lv,1–lxii,3.

10. II,xxxiv,2f. (cf. Polybius *Hist.* XXX,xxii,1–12), IV,xxiv,3, V,lx,2, lxxvii,4–6, XII,i–xii.

11. II,xi,2f.; cf. Polybius VI,ix,9; Plato *Resp.* VIII,566A.

tutional theory to continue standing. The exposition of the theory of constitutional change, of which the *Anacyclōsis* had been but one, albeit significant, expression, was left without a raison d'être. That does not mean that the entrenchment of the Principate brought on an intellectual crisis, as if cyclical and recurrence thinking became questionable and linear views acquired a new validity.[12] The old interest in the relationship between monarchy and tyranny still persisted, and for some the Principate was like a return to early Roman kingship.[13] However, the effect of long-term absolutism was to shift the issues of historical recurrence away from questions about instabilities and curving courses in constitutional history and onto questions about the life cycle of the whole state and about the rise and fall of whole empires. Constitutional variety lost importance; instead, new attention was given to absolutist monoliths both preceding and including Rome.[14]

What was the fate, then, of Luke's particular understanding of reenactment? The more obvious connections made in his work—between Jesus' journey and the Exodus, for example, and between the deaths of Jesus and Stephen—were picked up from time to time in patristic and medieval commentary, but in general his historical outlook was obscured behind new kinds of exegesis and theology. Elements of thinking akin to Luke's certainly manifested themselves: with writings of rabbinic Judaism, for instance (in which the deeds of Moses and the coming Messiah were sometimes paralleled,[15] Rome referred to as Edom, and the biblical *hagōyīm*—nations—updated to apply to contemporary powers),[16] or with such a Christian intellectual as Lactantius (ca. 240–ca. 320), who once averred that the Church was living in a second (though greater and nonlocalized) "Egyptian Captivity," awaiting a second Exodus.[17] But such elements were never drawn together to form a comprehensive understanding of history in terms of reenactment and fulfillment in the peculiarly Lukan sense.

Luke's original views suffered from typological and allegorical interpretations of the Scriptures, or even from exhortations to the imitation of Christ. In the Middle Ages there was a continuing interest in the relationship between the Old and New Testaments, of course, but the prevailing tendency was either to

12. Against R. Häussler, *Tacitus und das historische Bewusstsein* (*Bibliothek der klassischen Altertumswissenschaften N.S. II*), Heidelberg, 1965, pp. 180–3 and passim, whose thesis my subsequent pages call into question. Note A. Momigliano's critique of Häussler's book in *Quarto Contributo*, p. 41 n. 47.

13. Tacitus *Ann.* III,55ff., V,5ff., XV–XVI; Suetonius *De vitae Caesarum* (Tiberius, 49ff.; Nero, 27ff.; Galba, 12ff.), on tyranny. On the apparent return to the early monarchy, cf. [uncertain], *De vita et moribus imperatorum* (*Epitome de Caesaribus*) i,1; with Seneca, Florus, and Ammianus (see below, sect. B). Interest in three constitutions and their perversions was not dead even in the fourth century AD: cf. Sallustius *De deis et mundo* xi (Nock, p. lxxvii).

14. Cf. above, Chapter 2, sect. A, pt. 3(i). On preoccupation with Alexander's accomplishments (first century BC on) see Quintius Curtius *Hist. Alex. Mag. Maced.*; Plutarch *De Alexandri Magni fortuna et virtute*; Arrian *Anab.*; cf. L. Pearson, *Lost Histories*, pp. 1ff.

15. See J. Jeremias, "Μωυσῆς" in G. Kittel (ed.), *Theological Dictionary of the New Testament* (ET), Grand Rapids, 1967, vol. 4, p. 860, for a sound discussion of such parallels.

16. E.g., *Sanhedrin* (*Babylonian Talmud*, vol. 3, ed. I. Epstein, London, 1935), p. 52 and n. 8.

17. *Divinae institutiones* VII,xv (Migne, *PL*, vol. 6, cols. 284f.); cf. Matt. 2:15.

ransack the Old Testament for *prefiguring* types of Christ or to elicit allegorically- (more than historically-) conceived correspondences. Neither prefigurative nor allegorical Christian exegesis (emanating from the Antiochene and Alexandrian schools, respectively), nor yet the symbolist method of certain Western medieval schools, receives detailed consideration in this study, lying as they all do on the fringes of our discussion (cf. Chapter 2, sect. A, pt. 2).[18] Patristic and medieval ideas of imitation, moreover, though capable of being "educated" into a recurrence view (Chapter 2, Addendum; Chapter 5, sect. B, pt. 5), were predominantly expressed within the context of moral and spiritual encouragement.[19] Even if certain spiritual giants (such as St. Bernard and especially St. Francis) were extolled for walking in the footsteps of Jesus,[20] their achievements were not associated with a view of history as a complex story of reenactment. St. Francis' life became a recognized turning point of history in certain frameworks of medieval Age theory, but, as we shall see, the perspectives of Luke and Franciscan theologians were quite different (sect. D).[21] To be sure, we have discovered Luke to be a more unexpectedly canny writer than others have imagined, and one whose methods and basic ideas were extraordinarily difficult to reproduce. Post-biblical intellectual climates were just not suited to their development. Reenactment became "liturgicalized" in the sacraments and the ecclesiastical year, and a relatively nonhistorical hermeneutic prevailed, one which was influenced by classical philosophy and which generally put priority on the stable, eternal qualities of divine truth, as if the biblical books, whether old or new, expressed truths which were valid for all time.[22] As shall be shown, however, biblical notions of reenactment were not without importance for nurturing the idea of a "renaissance," and they were revived and adapted most interestingly by the Radical Reformers of the sixteenth century.

Although the Polybian *Anacyclōsis* and Lukan ideas of reenactment faded

18. R. P. C. Hanson, *Allegory and Event: A Study of the Sources and Significance of Origen's Interpretation of Scripture*, London, 1959, pt. 3; K. J. Woollcombe, "Patristic Typology" in *Essays on Typology*, pp. 69–75; R. L. Wilken, *Judaism and the Early Christian Mind: A Study of Cyril of Alexandria's Exegesis and Theology*, Yale, 1971, pp. 93–161; B. Smalley, *The Study of the Bible in the Middle Ages*, Oxford, 1952, pp. 83ff., 196ff. For classic examples of typology see John Chrysostom, *Homiliae in Joannem*, lxxxv, 1ff. (*PG*, vol. 59, cols. 459ff.), on Isaac as a type of Christ; Cyril of Jerusalem *Catechesis* xiv,20 (*PG*, vol. 33, col. 849) for Jonah as such; and in general, Ambrose *De sacr.* I,v,13–II,i,1 (patristic); Bonaventura *Collationes in Hexaemeron* XVI, 23–9 (medieval).

19. For biblical background see E. J. Tinsley, *The Imitation of God in Christ*, London, 1960; and for the best-known monument of imitationism, Thomas à Kempis *Imitatio Christi* (1418).

20. E.g., William of St. Thierry *Vita prima Bernardi* (ed. G. Webb and A. Walker, London, 1960), *proem.* (p. 9); *Actus beati Francisci et sociorum ejus* (ed. S. Sabatier, *Collection d'études et de documents*, Paris, 1902, vol. 4), i,1ff. Cf. G. G. Coulton, "The Story of St. Francis of Assisi" in Foakes Jackson and Lake (eds.), *Beginnings*, vol. 2, pp. 438ff.; D. Knowles and D. Obolensky, *The Christian Centuries*, London, 1969, vol. 3, p. 345.

21. See G. Leff, *Heresy in the Later Middle Ages: The Relation of Heterodoxy to Dissent c. 1250-c. 1450*, Manchester, 1967, vol. 1, pp. 54ff., pp. 124ff., the emulation of Christ through St. Francis' ideal (which was "firmly set within the sacramental life of the church," p. 58), being distinguished from the placing of St. Francis in a sequence of world Ages by theologians of history.

22. G. Dix, *The Shape of the Liturgy*, London, 1945 edn., pp. 243ff.; H. E. W. Turner, *The Pattern of Christian Truth: A Study in the Relations between Orthodoxy and Heresy in the Early Church* (Bampton Lectures, 1954), London, 1954, pp. 442–70.

from the scene for some time, simpler conceptions of historical recurrence continued to enjoy a rôle in historiography, and some have even persisted to this day. Admittedly, we have long been asked to believe that Christianity effected a decisive triumph for historical linearity over cyclical modes of thought, and certainly the Judeo-Christian understanding of history excluded any doctrine of eternal recurrence, whether of worlds or inter-cataclysmic periods. Theologians as far removed in sensibility as Origen and Augustine are renowned for having remonstrated against Stoic world cycles or the doctrine of man's eternity.[23] But that only tells one part of a complicated story. Cyclical conceptions, some of which we detected in biblical literature, do have a place in Christian interpretations of history from the patristic period to the Reformation. Moreover, we must remember that we are dealing with notions of historical recurrence in general and not with cyclical views in particular; our broader approach should constrain us against belaboring the distinction between these two great traditions.

## A. Beliefs about the decay of Rome

From the time of Polybius onward, the question of whether the greatness of the Roman empire would dissipate became increasingly important for historians. Cato the Censor and Dionysius were among the earliest to treat the matter. They shared the view held by Polybius that new luxuries had an adverse effect on Rome's virtues and institutions.[24] The idea of Roman deterioration (*degeneratio*), however, was more complex than one might suspect. Middle Stoics such as Poseidonius and Seneca, for instance, placed it in the wider context of a three-staged cosmic cycle. The universe was undergoing the cycle's third phase—one of decline—and for Poseidonius Roman decline was part of a worldwide abandonment to the passions.[25] Poseidonius was also among those arguing that dissipation of the old Roman virtues followed the removal of the Carthaginian threat. This was a line taken up by Diodorus Siculus (flor. 60–21 BC) and Florus (flor. 120–130 AD), although none of these writers developed the external/internal theme which had interested Polybius, a theme to be picked up again and developed by Machiavelli much later (see Chapter 5, sect. B, pt. 2).[26]

23. Origen *Contra Celsum* IV,67f., V,20f., and cf. IV,12; Augustine *De civitate Dei* XII,10–13.

24. Cato in Plutarch *Cat. Mai.* xix,3; cf. above (on Dionysius), and Chapter 2, sect. A, pt. 2(ii) (on Polybius).

25. Seneca *Epist. mor.* XV,4–6, 35–8, and cf. 10b ff. (on views of both Poseidonius and Seneca); Poseidonius, Frgs., 5, 18, 24, 27, 36 and cf. 4, 6, 9, 35 (*FGH*, vol. 2A); Athenaeus *Deip.* VI,273D–275A; and for a sound discussion see G. Verbeke, "Les Stoïciens et le progrès de l'histoire" in *Revue Philosophique de Louvain* LXII, 1964, pp. 12, 15, 18, 20–7. On Poseidonius as the first historian of cosmic *degeneratio* see K. Reinhardt, "Philosophy and History among the Greeks" in *Greece and Rome* XXIII (N.S. 1), 1954, p. 85; cf. *Poseidonius*, Munich, 1921; G. Pfligersdorffer, *Studien zu Poseidonius* (*Österreichische Akademie der Wissenschaften: Philos.-hist. Klasse* CCXXXII/5), Vienna, 1959, pp. 85ff.; against L. Edelstein, *Idea of Progress*, ch. 4 (who evades the distinction between moral and technological progress in Seneca and Poseidonius).

26. On Diodorus and Florus see below, sect. C; cf. Valerius Maximus *Factorum et dictorum memorabilium* IX,i,3; Dio Cassius *Hist. Rom.* II,viii; Livy *Ab urbe* III,x,8, VII,i,7, X,vi,3, etc.; Sextus

Concentrated as they are on the decline of a single political society (or on world decay generally conceived), these preoccupations have limited relevance to our investigations. Yet the notion of Roman decline naturally became linked with the past decay of other great régimes. To place Rome's career in line with previous imperial achievements required information about the great empires of the distant past. Although the Greeks had some acquaintance with the emergence of Egypt, Assyria, Media, and Persia (through the writings of Herodotus and Ctesias: Chapter 2, sect. A, pt. 3), and although Alexander's conquests suggested a developing imperial lineage, especially in the Middle East, it was apparently not until after Sulla's time that Roman readers became interested in the ancient Orient or began to see the significance of an imperial succession in which Rome had taken a latter-day position.[27] Certainly, the obscure Aemilius Sura and the poet Ennius (239–169 BC) both implied that Rome was a true successor of former world powers,[28] but it was only with a greater spread of Middle Eastern ideas that succession theory gained wide currency at Rome. Antiquarian accounts of Eastern lands (Diodorus Siculus on ancient Egypt, for instance, or Josephus' *Jewish Antiquities*) had their impact, and a most crucial ideological acquisition was the belief in four world-monarchies followed by an eternal fifth (a belief that may well have derived from anti-Hellenistic Persian sources rather than from Daniel).[29]

Notions of the successive emergence and dissipation of empires could be variously manipulated, and writers as far apart as Appian (b. 116 AD) and the poet Claudian (d. 404 AD) were equally unprepared to assert that the fifth monarchy of Rome would decline like the others.[30] But pessimists were certainly about, some even anti-imperialistic in bent. Dionysius, while praising Rome at the expense of her inferior predecessors—Assyria, Media, Persia, and Macedonia

---

Aurelius Victor (4th century AD) *Historiae abbreviatae* (*Liber de Caesaribus*) xiv,5. On the Gracchi as the culprits see Dionysius *Arch.* II,xi,2f.; cf. Diodorus *Bib.* XXXIV/V,v,1–x,1, xxviiia,1–xxix,1, xxxiii,5f.; Florus *Epitome* I,xlvii,8 (both cautious about offering favorable opinions); Sallust *Bellum Iugurthinum* xli,1–xlii,5; cf. *Bell. Cat.* ii,6, v,1, x,2–5; xxxvii f. (cynical about nobles and populism alike); Valerius Maximus *Fact. dict. mem.* IV,i,8 (pro-Gracchi). On *degeneratio* theory in Roman historians see esp. Livy *Ab urbe* I,*proem.*, IV,iv,12, VI,i,2 (cf. D. W. Packard, *A Concordance to Livy*, Cambridge, Mass., 1968, s.v. "more maiorum" and "more antiquo"; P. G. Walsh, *Livy: His Historical Aims and Methods*, Cambridge, 1961, pp. 10–19; W. Liebeschuetz, "The Religious Position of Livy's History" in *Journal of Roman Studies* LVII, 1967, p. 55); cf. Sallust *Bell. Cat.* ii,1–6, *Bell. Iug.* xli,9; Cicero *Re. pub.* II,ii,4–xxiii,43, *De officiis* II,viii; Tacitus *Germania*, *Ann.* I,3 (yet cf. III,55); and (on Seneca, Lucan, and Juvenal), Cochrane, *Christianity and Classical Culture*, pp. 162f. For an interesting but slight development of the internal/external theme, see Tacitus, *Agricola*, 11–12 on the Gauls and Britons.

27. J. B. Swain, "The Theory of the Four Monarchies: Opposition History under the Roman Empire" in *Classical Philology* XXXV, 1940, pp. 1–13.

28. Aemilius Sura in Velleius Paterculus *Hist. Rom.* I,vi,6 gloss, listing the Assyrians (with their first king Ninus), the Medes, Persians, Macedonians, and Romans as the great races holding power. For Ennius see *Annales*, Frg. 501 (Vahlen).

29. E. Meyer, *Ursprunge*, vol. 2, pp. 189ff.; Swain, loc. cit., pp. 8f.; M. Hengel, *Judaism*, vol. 1, pp. 182f.; cf. *Dinkard*, ix,8; *Bahman-Yašt*, i,3 (192) (West).

30. Appian *Hist. Rom.*, *proem.*, I,8ff.; Claudian *De consulate Stilichonis* iii,159–66 (only Claudian hailing Rome as eternal); cf. Plutarch *De fortuna Romanorum* 317F; and on Claudius Ptolemaeus (2nd century AD), E. Bernheim, *Lehrbuch der historischen Methode*, Leipzig, 1908, p. 74.

(*Arch.* I,i,2–4)—nevertheless anticipated her eventual decay (see above). He thus implied the idea of recurring decay in the history of world empires, an idea developed by Diodorus Siculus and by a man most unpopular among the Romans, Pompeius Trogus (flor. 30 BC–10 AD). Diodorus, as we shall show, placed the altering fortunes and moral degeneration of late Republican Rome within the context of the great movements of rise and fall (sects. C, G). Trogus, for his part, wrote a history from Ninus, the first Assyrian king, to Augustus, arranging his books around the four great empires of Assyria, Persia, Macedon, and Rome, with other great régimes as satellites. Trogus deemed all four great empires unworthy and overaggressive, and in consciously representing Rome as the fourth world power and monarchy, he apparently believed that she was to go the way of the ruined monoliths before her, a preferable, fifth kingdom being yet to come.[31]

These men of foreboding, however, wrote centuries before anything like the actual dissolution of the Roman empire. Later historians, by contrast, could be less prophetic and more diagnostic about Roman decline.[32] One, the proto-Gibbon Zosimus (late fifth century), a man in a quite different context from Diodorus or Trogus, and well situated to see the writing on the wall, formulated an even more coherent theory of rise and fall which included Rome. Zosimus lacked intellectual flair, and his pragmatic approach to such big questions looks somewhat pale beside the imposing edifice of alternative explanations for Roman decline in *De civitate Dei*, the great monument of a Christian near-contemporary. However, it was Zosimus' claim that if Polybius had shown how Rome in a short time attained to its greatness, he was in a position to show how rapidly it decayed.[33] In introducing his *Historia nova* he asserted that empires fell through internal division and disunity. Thus while the Greeks had been a match for the Persian giant at Artemisium, Salamis, and Plataea (480–79 BC) (I,ii,3), their power was drained through the contest for hegemony between Athens and Sparta, allowing Philip of Macedonia to seize Hellas at the battle of Chaeronia (iii,1–2). Under Alexander, the Macedonian empire expanded enormously, but at his death it too became politically divided, and was therefore too weak to withstand the forces of Rome (iv,1–v,1). In the case of each empire, growth resulted from consolidation against an enemy, and Rome herself, in response to that fearful threat posed at Cannae, rose to be a great power within fifty-three years.[34] With world dominion, however, her aristocracy was replaced by a monarchy, which in turn tended to decay into tyranny (v,2–3). After Augustus, good laws alternated with tyrannical ones (vii,1).

Proceeding on, Zosimus told a tale of an empire which became a battleground between contestants for power in the eastern and western sectors, of an empire

31. Swain, loc. cit., pp. 15–8.

32. So Justinus (3rd century), abbreviator of Trogus; and for Aurelius Victor on the decay of a civilization see W. den Boer, *Some Minor Roman Historians*, Leiden, 1972, pp. 93ff.

33. *Historia nova* I,lvii,1.

34. I,i,1; cf. (on the other empires) II,ii,3, iii,2, iv,1. Zosimus considered himself to be developing Polybius' line of interpretation: see above, Chapter 2, sect. A, pt. 3(i) and (ii).

sapped of its internal virtue through the impieties of Christianity.[35] Outside powers were fast acquiring the advantage. In Rome's decay history was repeating itself, not in its details but in its general movements, and Zosimus was ready to develop an ethico-theological side to his analysis. He insisted that a "certain divine providence" ruled affairs, and that it both effected appropriate retributions and controlled those movements of destiny or *Moira* which, connected with astral orbits, brought all periods of efflorescence to an end.[36] In the decline of Rome, therefore, he saw both the reappearance of a general event-shape and the recurrent actualization of moral principles (so cf. sect. G).

## B. The body-state analogy applied to Rome

One might suppose that the continuance of outside pressure and internal turbulence intensified the expectancy of Rome's downfall. Yet to refer to Rome as "the eternal city" was commonplace as early as the fourth century AD,[37] and Rome's very durability could allay pessimism. If some continued to dilate upon the decay or overturning of all things, the extraordinary and prolonged history of the Principate engendered modifications to traditional recurrence views. One model of recurrence, probably of ancient origin, has an important bearing on the tension between pessimism and optimism in the Roman empire. We name it "the body-state analogy."[38] Perhaps it is no more than a special version of the biological principle applied to history, but it is detachable and appears much more in Roman than in mainstream Hellenistic writing.[39] If the common terms appertaining to the biological principle were genesis, growth, acme, and decay, those belonging to the body-state analogy were more specifically human, and even psychological, in connotation: birth, infancy, childhood, youth, maturity, and senescence. When Cicero asserted that he would describe the Roman state at its birth and in its times of growth, adulthood, and robustness,[40] he was developing traditional biological language into an analogy between the life cycle of an individual and developments undergone by political societies.[41]

Nearly a century later Seneca applied the analogy more rigorously. Rome's infancy he placed with Romulus, and her boyhood he put under the subsequent kings.[42] Her growth (*adulescentia*) ran from the banishment of Tarquinius to the

35. II,viii–xxxiv (esp. xxix,3f., xxxi,1–3), xli–ix, IV,xxix–xxxiv, lix ff., V,lix,1ff.

36. Esp. I,i,2 (on providence), II,vi–vii. Cf. F. Paschoud, "Introduction" in *Zosime: Histoire nouvelle*, Paris, 1971, p. lxiii (his recent *Cinq Études sur Zosime*, Paris, 1976, being unavailable to me); A. Momigliano, *Polybius between the English and the Turks* (The Seventh J. L. Myres Memorial Lecture), Oxford, 1974, p. 5.

37. E.g., Ammianus Marcellinus *Rerum gestarum libri* XIV,vi,1, XXVIII,i,1, XXIX,vi,17. As background see Tibullus *Carmina* II,v,23.

38. In German scholarship the term *Lebensaltervergleich* is current.

39. For its possible background in Dicaearchus, though, and then Varro, see R. Häussler, "Vom Ursprung und Wandel des Lebensaltervergleichs" in *Hermes* XCII, 1964, pp. 322–5.

40. *Re pub.* II,i,3; cf. V (in Augustine *Civ. Dei* II,21).

41. On the comparable but different analogy between the body and the whole cosmos used by Stoics and Christians, see below, sect. D, pt. 3.

42. In Lactantius *Div. inst.* VII,xv (*PL*, vol. 6, cols. 788f.). There is a correspondence here with the early, naturalistic phase of *general* human development: cf. *Epist. mor.* XC,6.

end of the Punic Wars, when the state was "confirmed in its manly strength." In stretching herself over the whole world, however, Rome abused her strength: the state made ready its own destruction and entered "its first old age." This period evidently involved the civil strife which arose before the establishment of emperorship, while the imperial rule itself was taken not only as further agedness, but as reversion, a revolving back to a second infancy (*quasi ad alteram infantiam revoluta*).[43] This second childhood should probably be located at Augustus' reign.[44]

It is unlikely that Seneca used this model to express a hope for Roman rejuvenation; certainly Christian Lactantius did not interpret him this way later on,[45] and it makes sense that a Stoic who mused over worldwide decay would refer to a second childhood only with irony. A century later, however, the epitomizer Florus certainly appealed to the idea of a genuine revivification of Rome after temporary senescence. The breakdown of Florus' body-state analogy is close to Seneca's. Roman childhood (*infantia*) (there is no mention of boyhood) ran from Romulus to the downfall of the kingship, and her *adulescentia* from the consulships of Junius Brutus and Collatinus Tarquinius (the post-monarchical founders of the Republic) to the time of the Second Punic War. But Florus has a longer history on his hands. Between this war and the death of Augustus he placed Rome's manhood or robust maturity, and after Augustus came old age.[46] Under the rule of Trajan, however, old age was averted, and as if restored, her prime of life flourished once more (*quasi reddita iuventute reviruit*: *Epit.* I,*proem*.8). Here is a rather less cynical approach to the imperial destiny and one important in the history of ideas. What are its implications?

For an abbreviator, Florus' understanding of Roman history is remarkably complex and not unoriginal. First, he subscribed to a theory of decline. Rome's newly-found interest in Asia, after the fall of Carthage and the Numantine War, formed the key turning point in her history.[47] Up to the point when the subjugation of Africa, Macedonia, Sicily, and Spain had been completed, the people of Rome had been "fine, superior, pious, inviolate, and magnificent" [I,xxxiv (19,1; cf. 2)], and despite her momentary setbacks Rome's path from Romulus to the war against Numantia was one of steady growth.[48] Up to the Numantine war, the body-state analogy and a more widesweeping moral interpretation of Roman history could be mutually accommodated, but from then on

43. In Lactantius VII,xv (col. 789).

44. *Dialog.* XI,xii,3–5; cf. VI,ii,3f., xv,1–3, X,iii,2f.; its beginning with the Gracchi? (cf. VI,xvi,3f., X,vi,1), or just before Julius Caesar? (*Epist. mor.* XCVII,2–10).

45. *Div. inst.* VII,xv (cols. 789f.). But what was the original context? And was it written during his exile of AD 41? After all, Seneca had his moments of pro-Caesarean ebullience (e.g., *De clementia* I,i–iv).

46. *Epit.* I,*proem*.,4–8; cf. I,ii,1 (1st Age), xvii,i,22,1, 25,9 (2nd), xviii,1, xlvii,1 (3rd). His choice of the term *robusta* recalls Cicero.

47. I,xxxiv,19,1–3 (cf. 18,1ff.), xlvii,8. Den Boer takes Florus to place the turning point at 130 BC: "Florus und die römische Geschichte" in *Mnemosyne: Bibliotheca Classica Batava* (Ser. IV) XVIII, Facs. 4, 1965, p. 374.

48. I,vii,3, xii,1, xvii,22,1, 25,9, xviii,23, xxii,31, 43, xxiii,1. The point about moral degeneration derives from Livy: cf. *Ab urbe* XXXIX,vi,7.

complications arose. In the middle of Florus' third stage of "young manhood," conditions of moral defect manifested themselves. These not only involved internal disorders and civil war, from the Gracchan revolutions to the contest between Pompey and Caesar [cf. I,xxxiv (19,3–4) xlvii,5], but also a zenith of Roman military might [xxxiv (19,3)]. This zenith was in fact an excess (*nimia felicitas*)[49] and it inevitably brought domestic strife and ruin to the state (xlvii, 3–13; cf. II,xiii,8). Florus skillfully wove together the theme of a change in fortune, the biological model (including its acme of psycho-physical development), and the popular idea of a Roman degeneration after the Gracchi. On the other hand, although he reckoned further victories from the Numantine War to Pharsalia as immoderateness, and as an arming for self-destruction (cf. II,xiii,2), he still generalized about the third stage of Roman history as manhood (*iuventus*). The first half of this stage was one of moral worth, and the whole stage ended with the great *pax Augusta* (II,xxxiv,64; cf. xxxiii,54, xxxiv,61ff.), so Florus was still able to assert that the "manly" empire spread peace throughout the known world (I,*proem.*,7). In a sense the Augustan Age (*saeculum*)[50] marked a reversion to the standards of better days—evils and extravagances being checked—and Augustus, in founding the new rule, appeared like a second Romulus (II,xxxiv, 65–66). Following Augustus, however, from Tiberius to Nerva, came senescence.

Yet how did Florus view his own time, and in what sense was the reign of Trajan a form of historical recurrence? What, too, of Hadrian, Trajan's successor, under whom Florus was writing? We must first acknowledge that Trajan's reign was not described as a second infancy but as renewed manhood (*iuventus*). That thought contrasts with the pessimism of Seneca, who probably understood Rome's second childhood as a prelude to real senility. Florus was implying that Rome could actually recover her vigorous manhood even after a period of agedness. Thus he was not far from the view of Rome as the eternal city, and he emerges as a virile nationalist, convinced that the period of old age, and not Rome's entire career, was but a temporary affair.[51] As Paul Jal has shown, Florus joined voices with those other writers who had acclaimed Trajan to be the restorer of imperial energy.[52] For Florus, Trajan overcame indolence or *inertia* (which was reckoned a key evil in the post-Augustan empire by certain Stoicizers), and the reign of Hadrian, pacifistic though it was, carried on the renewed Roman "manhood" in Trajan's tradition.[53] Rome, it appears, had not succumbed to the ordinary processes of the life cycle. She had experienced a kind of recurrence by which the norms of biological change had been eluded.

49. *Felicitas* is synonymous with *eutychia* or good fortune in this and similar contexts, and when personified was identical with the goddess *Fortuna*.

50. A departure from Florus' normal use of *aetas* for a stage in the life cycle of Rome.

51. Den Boer, "Florus," pp. 386f.

52. P. Jal, "Nature et signification politique de l'oeuvre de Florus" in *Revue des Études Latines* XLIII, 1965, pp. 372–4 (on Pliny the Younger's *Panegyricus* and Tacitus' *Annales*). Sextus Aurelius Victor picks up this theme in the fourth century (*Hist. abbrev.* xiii,6).

53. Jal, loc. cit., pp. 371f., 375ff.; cf. Florus I,*proem.* 8 (the books on Trajan's and perhaps Hadrian's reigns not being extant).

Seneca had stuck with the original conception of bodily processes; his form of recurrence had been the return of monarchy, which he associated with childhood. Florus, however, with a curious eclecticism, an optimism that departed from the middle Stoic philosophy of history, had made harmony possible between Rome's prolonged endurance and her experience of a natural, "organic," development. One might be tempted to infer that this harmonizing derived from a spiral model, as if Rome's cyclical development had reached a higher plane; but it was the empire's unusual forestallment of inevitable decay which is the basis for Florus' approach, not a doctrine of spiraling progress.

In the second half of the fourth century Ammianus Marcellinus, a pagan who wrote history under an empire fast becoming Christian, took these harmonizing tendencies somewhat further. He evidently held that talk about an eternal city did not conflict either with the use of the body-state analogy or current notions of degeneration. The phrase *Roma aeterna* comes frequently from his pen,[54] yet in vividly describing the luxury, gluttony, and loss of old virtues among Romans he still appealed to the image of the life cycle (*Rerum gestarum* XIV,vi,3–6).[55] Rome had undergone childhood (*pueritia*), a period of wars with immediate neighbors.[56] Her adulthood consisted of overseas expansions, and in old age she entered a quieter time, one during which, like a thrifty, wise, and wealthy parent, she entrusted her patrimony to the Caesars (4–5). Interestingly, Ammianus wrote neither of a second infancy nor of a revitalized manhood. He simply commented:

> Although for some time the tribes [of Rome] have been inactive, . . . yet the composure of Numa Pompilius' time has returned (*Pompiliani redierit securitas temporis*), except that throughout all the parts and regions of the earth, Rome is looked up to as mistress and queen. Everywhere the white hair of the senators and their authority are revered and the name of the Roman people respected and honored. (XIV,vi,6)

We have come some way from Seneca and Florus, although some of the latter's eclectic tendencies seem carried to their logical conclusions. Rome's old age (*senium*) brought a certain declining and slackness[57]—thus far Ammianus made concessions to *degeneratio* theory—but this old age meant stability and venerableness. Ammianus so stated his position that he combined the idea of the world's eternity with the middle Stoic vision of history. And what of his invocation of King Numa? To return to the conditions of Numa's reign was perhaps like a return to childhood (since the early monarchs belonged to this stage), and Ammianus might seem to be implying that Roman growth had begun again,

54. *Rer. gest.* XIV,vi,1–3, and references in n. 37 above. On background in Roman literature of the later empire see G. B. Ladner, *The Idea of Reform: Its Impact on Christian Thought and Action in the Age of the Fathers*, Cambridge, Mass., 1959, p. 18.

55. Cf. XIV,vi,7–vii,1 and see below (no books before the 14th having survived).

56. For 300 years (4). For this and the large tallies of Florus (cf. *Epit.* I,*proem.*, 5f.), along with the historical inaccuracies they incurred, see Häussler, "Ursprung," pp. 318f.

57. Cf. *discessit* in vi,4; *otiosae* in vi,6 (a term for inactivity evidently chosen to replace *inertia* or *desidia*).

perhaps on a new plane, with Augustus its second Romulus and his successors like the good Roman kings. However, it sufficed for Ammianus to imagine an enduring old age. Rome now possessed a glorious and permanent empire, one "destined to live so long as men shall exist" (XIV,vi,3), and this appeal to an enduring old age was a convenient (and not unprecedented)[58] way of preserving the unmodified version of the life-cycle model. By recalling Numa, besides, he could still educe a kind of recurrence in his own time.

The seriousness with which these authors took the body-state analogy may startle us, but to put such general meanings upon the events of the past was a perennial, even responsible, concern of historians. The march of events naturally affected the meanings put upon them, and both the special contexts in which authors were writing, as well as their differing presuppositions, fostered a variety of interpretative pictures. Seneca, for example, was naturally more pessimistic in the earlier, more uncertain days of the Principate, whereas by his day Ammianus was more ready to see a parallelism between the ancient line of Roman kings and later imperial lineages. It was not just optimism which allowed Ammianus to perceive this parallelism; he believed he saw it in the facts, as did Florus when he connected the two key periods of youthful imperial expansion under the Republic and Trajan. However, all these altered perspectives involved more than just one recurrence frame. We have been concentrating on the body-state analogy, but behind it there still lies the conventional biological principle with its three stations.[59] What the analogy allowed historians to do was to integrate biological imagery with alternative tools for interpreting Roman history, with the doctrine of *degeneratio*, for instance, or of imperial rise and fall. Even "historical optimism" as reflected in Florus and Ammianus was tied in with the model of a life cycle. We could claim, in fact, that a tension we first located in Polybius (Chapter 2, sect. B), between the praise of Rome as the most natural and excellent of empires (and therefore "the great exception"), and the resigned acceptance of her inevitable future decay recurs in the compromises and disagreements of later historians.[60] Yet another frame of interpretation, of course, was fortune's wheel. Not only could this conception be tied into the paradigm of a life cycle but it too could be integrated with a variety of other recurrence ideas and its continuing history after Polybius' time thus deserves consideration.

## C. The Roman Principate and fortune's wheel

After Polybius, though not simply because of him, Romans found it more respectable to ascribe their state's achievements to fortune as well as virtue.[61] For

58. On this loophole see Martial *Epigrammata* VI,3(3f.); "Vopiscus," *Vita Cari* III,1ff. (see also below); cf. Prudentius (a contemporary of Ammianus) *Contra Symmachum* II,309–323 (and below, sect. D, pt. 2).

59. In Seneca *iuventus* (manhood/age of military service) is clearly the zenith; in Florus and Ammianus the last stage competes with it.

60. Florus *Epit.* I,xxxiv,2, 13f. (cf. Plutarch and Ammianus, below, sect. B), on Rome as exceptional.

61. E.g., Cicero *Re pub.* II,xii,30; Dionysius *Arch.* I,iv,2; and on the later idea of a pact between *virtus* and *fortuna*, Florus I,*proem.*,2; Ammianus XIV,vi,3; cf. Plutarch *Fort. Rom.* 317C.

lovers and respecters of traditional *virtus*, however, the popularly conceived, unpredictable, even malicious Fortune was no satisfactory explanation for the Roman triumph.[62] Polybius and Dionysius, Greeks sensitive to Roman values, severely criticized those of their Greek-writing predecessors who had appealed to "mere chance" or luck in great events. Against the Epicureans Polybius had injected moral meaning into Fortune's ways. The ravine between *fortuna* and *virtus*, he suggested, could be bridged (see Chapter 2, sect. B). Not all the Latins took the cue, of course. If some treated Fortune as a morally defensible goddess, most saw her only as capricious.[63] Be that as it may, there came a natural and important coalescence of the Hellenistic and the Roman Fortune. *Fortuna* had originally mostly to do with individual destiny and with a special form of protection accruing to the state, but she was soon elevated to be an arbiter of greater magnitude.[64] Her new rôle in the Roman context was acquired during the decline and fall of the Republic, and the question soon arose as to how the emergence and persistence of the Roman Principate was related to fortune's normative fluctuations. Even Polybius had agreed that Fortune would not smile on Rome forever, and subsequent views of degeneration reinforced such a stance. On the other hand, Polybius had entertained the view that Fortune's treatment of Rome had been unique, that she had permitted Rome alone to succeed to world dominion. That was a point to be seized on by the optimists.

Perhaps the most famous statement about both the work of Fortune and the accomplishments of Rome was made by Plutarch, probably during his sojourn in the capital (ca. 70s AD), in *De fortuna Romanorum*. Plutarch was much more a rhetorician than an historian in this piece (and his exuberance can be traced to a desire to please Roman ears),[65] yet he made some important distinctions

62. Esp. Livy, XX,liv,10f., lxi,13–5, XXVI,xli,9; cf. III,lviii,4, V,xix,8, XVIII,xlvi,14f., XXX, xxx,10, XXXIII,xxxiii,8; and for discussion see H. Tränkle, *Livius und Polybios*, Basel and Stuttgart, 1977, pp. 97f.; cf. G. Stübler, *Die Religiosität des Livius (Tübinger Beitrage zur Altertumswissenschaft XXV)*, Stuttgart, 1941, pp. 108–13; I. Kajanto, *God and Fate in Livy*, pp. 34, 62, 92–5; C. P. T. Naudé, "*Fortuna* in Ammianus Marcellinus" in *Acta Classica*, VII, 1964, pp. 75f. Cf. also Chapter 2, sect. B, pt. 2(ii).

63. As morally defensible: Polybius (see above, Chapter 2, sect. B, pt. 2); Dionysius *Arch.* I,iv,2 (yet cf. II,xvii,3f.); Diodorus (below); Plutarch *De fortuna* 976ff., etc. Livy concurred with difficulty: cf. Kajanto, op. cit., pp. 63–100; Walsh, op. cit., pp. 55–9. On fortune's fickleness see Seneca and Poseidonius (Chapter 2, sect. B, pt. 2); Cicero *De amicitia* liv, *De offic.* I,vi,19, *Consolatio* in Lactantius *Div. inst.* III,xxvii; Curtius *Hist. Alex. Mag. Maced.* III,ii,17, viii,20, 39, xi,23, xii,19–21, xiii,12, etc.; Pliny the Elder *Naturalis historia* II,22; Tacitus *Ann.* VI,22; Sallust *Bell. Cat.* viii,1–5, li,25 (cf. R. Syme, *Sallust*, Berkeley and Los Angeles, 1964, pp. 242f., 245–8); etc.

64. On religious background see W. Otto in *RECA*, vol. 7(1), pp. 12ff. s.v. "Fortuna"; K. Kerenyi, *Die griechische-orientalische Romanliteratur*, Tübingen, 1927, pp. 12, 18, 32, 131, 180, 186, 199, 242; A. J. Festugière, *Personal Religion among the Greeks*, Berkeley and Los Angeles, 1954, pp. 73ff.; J. Ferguson, *The Religions of the Roman Empire*, Ithaca, 1970, ch. 5; and on *fortuna* as the protective force behind the state see esp. Naudé, loc. cit., pp. 77ff. The whole question of the relationship or apparent contradiction between the ideas of fate or necessity and fortune, and the implications of such a relationship for historiography, represents a vast and complex area for discussion. I have considered some pertinent issues in Chapter 2, sect. B, pt. 2(ii) and Chapter 4, sect. A, but other references should be noted along the way (esp. in sect. G, and in Chapter 5, sect. B, pt. 2).

65. *Fort. Rom.* 318D, 319B, E, 320A–322C, 323E–328C (on Rome specially blessed and chosen by fortune), 316C, E, 317C (with recognition of *aretē* = *virtus*).

nevertheless. He was struck by Rome's durability (316D). Whereas Fortune's support of previous empires had been temporary, she made an exception of Rome (314F–318A, 324B). Now what were the marks of this exception? Not just succor in times of adversity, nor simply the achievement of world dominion in such a marvellously short space of time, but rather the creation by Fortune of a singularly different set of conditions—for Rome's special benefit. The normative situation under Fortune's hegemony was "the turning, drifting, and changing of all peoples continuously" (317B), a general process of recurring change. Rome, however, was endowed with an exception to this cycle. She had actually acquired the supreme dominion for which others had striven in vain,[66] and increasing in strength and vastness, her "unfaltering dominion was brought within an orderly and single cycle of peace" (317C)—a cycle of self-perpetuation.

For Plutarch this statement was quite extreme. In other works he sought to justify Fortune's ways as ethically defensible, as operations which both curbed excess or insolence and tested human resilience.[67] That was as approach very characteristic of the Cynics—though it had the favor of others as well—and it appears in Plutarch's more definitely historiographical writings.[68] But in the above oration the deeds of Fortune tend to be disconnected from the moral condition of men. Usually such a dissociation led to a stress on Fortune's incalculable whims, a stress adding little new to the continuing history of fortune's wheel. More interest lies, however, with views concerning the moral appropriateness of Fortune's ways, or in other words, with developments of the more complex approach we located earlier in Polybius. According to that position, Fortune's operations made some ethical sense; she recurrently supported those whom she considered worthy, or who were resilient under her blows; she turned against those who took too much advantage of her in their immoderateness, even if she was ultimately free to change conditions as she willed. Her moral overlordship and her incalculability were intertwined. In his oration Plutarch did not depart radically from this line. For some ultimately incomprehensible reason, perhaps, Fortune had created a special cycle, so that in Rome's case other cyclical processes could be forestalled. Part of the Polybian explanation for Rome's situation, we will remember, lay with the natural emergence of the mixed constitution and with the virtues of Roman discipline, yet Plutarch, by contrast, focused on the supreme rôle of Fortune. Nevertheless, he hardly avoided giving the impression that the Romans deserved their lot, so that Fortune's unpredictable actions still remained morally congruous.

Plutarch justified Fortune's ways with some optimism for the future of the Roman Principate. Others could be backward-looking. Diodorus Siculus deserves some comment. Writing his world history in the century before Plutarch, Dio-

66. 317B; cf. 326A–C (on Alexander's prospects and fortune); Trogus in Justin *Epit.* XII,xiii,1.

67. *De consol. Apoll.* 102E–103F; cf. Dio Chrysostom *Orat.* LXIII-LXV.

68. On cynicism in Rome under the early Principate see D. R. Dudley, *A History of Cynicism from Diogenes to the Sixth Century*, London, 1938, pp. 119ff. Dio Chrysostom, who considered himself a Cynic, taught Favorinus, Plutarch's closest philosophical companion.

dorus conceived the passage of great events to be a continual process of alteration between prosperity and adversity. His views are popularist: they reflect some of the syncretistic tendencies of his day. If Philo, for example, that exponent of Hellenized Judaism, had conceived fortune to shift through time, moving the empires "up and down" (Chapter 3), Diodorus had a comparable picture:

> Human life, as if some god were at the helm, moves in a cycle through good and evil alternately (*enallax*)[69] for all time. (*Biblioth.* XVII,lix,6)

> The divine power sees that fair and ugly conditions, good and evil, succeed one another in turn. (XXXIV/V,xviii)

Like Philo, Diodorus made no distinction between the cyclical and alternating moments of history, and like Philo, Diodorus identified Fortune (*tychē*) with Providence (*pronoia*) and both with the divine.[70] If Fortune still remains forever shifting and fickle, and always willing to alter the balance,[71] no blind impersonality remains in her character, and she leans

> toward what is morally fitting, to involve those who have contrived any injustice against others in the same hardships themselves. (XXXVII,xvii)

Changes in personal fortune occupy most of his attention, but Diodorus also conceived *tychē* to govern the great régimes (although these powers were still dependent upon the skills and attitudes of individuals).[72] What, then, of Rome? Certainly she was a great exception. Like any other dominion, however, she was bound to experience (and ultimately crumble before) the vicissitudes of fortune. An unalterable Necessity governed all, even if Diodorus was not so fatalistic as to deny that virtue (*aretē*) could postpone adverse change.[73] According to this interpretation, the remarkable growth of the Roman empire had the support of Fortune as the providential overlord (cf. esp. XXVI,xxiv,2, XXXI,iv). The Romans succeeded, moreover, because they were more virtuous than their arrogant enemies (XXVIII,iii), especially in being so moderate in great prosperity (cf. XXXI,iv, vi). After Rome had defeated her enemies, however, the situation altered quite dramatically from an ethical viewpoint. Not only was Roman imperialism more severe (cf. XXXII,iv,4–5), but with no external threat, civil disorder broke out (XXXIV/V,xxxiii,5–6). Furthermore, this most powerful people were given over to a soft, undisciplined way of life, with excessive love of wealth (XXXVII,iii,2, xxx,1–2), and when they were plunged into the disaster of

69. Note Polybius' more limited use of the term *enallax* with reference to *tychē*: *Hist.* I,lxxxvi,7, IX,xxi.

70. Esp. XX,xiii,3, XXXIV/V,ii,47, and see below, sect. G.

71. XXXI,xii; cf. XI,lxxi,5, XIII,xxi,5, XIV,xx,3, lxxvi,1–4, XVIII,xli,6, xlii,1, XX,xxxiii,3, XXIV,xiii,1, XXVI,vi,2, xvi,1, XXVII,xv,3, etc. Note XVII,xlvii,6, lix,7, etc., for the formula "the unexpectedness of fortune."

72. E.g., XIII,xxi (Athens); XXVI,xx (Syracuse); XXXI,x (Persia/Macedon); cf. XXVI,xxiv,2 (Rome vs. Carthage).

73. Fate, fortune, providence, and the divine are indistinguishable in Diodorus: e.g., XVII,cxvi, 1–4, XXXIV/V,ii,24b.

civil war, the remnant of the virtuous Romans was murdered (ii,14, xxix,1–5, esp. 5; cf. v–vi). Thus

> in the days of old, the Romans, by adhering to the best laws and customs, little by little became so powerful that they acquired the greatest and most splendid empire known to history. But in more recent times, when most nations had already been subjugated in war so there was a long period of peace, the ancient practices gave way at Rome to pernicious tendencies. (iii,1)

Under the surveillance of Fortune or Providence, it was Rome's turn to face the possibility of decline.

Espousers of the theory of Roman degeneration would have concurred. Diodorus, of course, had not confined his study to Rome; he had treated her changed circumstances as one, albeit special, illustration of moral governance throughout all history.[74] For many of the pessimists, this simply meant that Rome's decay could be placed in a wider perspective. On the other hand, when they reflected on the awful collapse of the Republic, some writers found it more difficult than did Diodorus to extract ethical meaning from the passage of events. They pictured Fortune as amoral, cruel, and difficult to bear.[75] Livy, for one, tended to waver between two approaches. Caught between popular Hellenistic ideas about Fortune's caprice and the justifications of Polybius, and nurturing his own special brand of pessimism, he achieved a vague compromise in which Fortune's moral neutrality and her retributive activity, and her support of and malice against Rome, play their different parts.[76] And in keeping with his theory of degeneration, the divine, supportive activity of Fortune was stuffed mainly into the first decade of his huge chronology.[77] As Livy's case illustrates, the longevity of the empire had not yet had its full impact on historiography.[78] When it did, however, writers were forced to reconsider which way the wheel had turned. By the second century there was a tendency to annotate and analyze the changes of fortune *within* the history of a Rome whose extinction could not be foreseen, or who had far outdistanced her predecessors and rivals. Of most interest here are the *Epitome* of Florus, to which we must return, and the work of "Flavius Vopiscus," a biographer writing almost two centuries after Florus, very early in the fourth century.[79]

74. XXXVIII/IX,v (*finis*) (with comments below, sect. G); cf. XXXII,xxiv.

75. See n. 63 above.

76. Kajanto, op. cit., pp. 63–100; cf. (on the extent to which Livy's usages are Greek), H. Erskell, *Augustus, Felicitas, Fortuna: lateinische Wortstudien*, Göteborg, 1952, pp. 171ff.

77. Kajanto, op. cit., pp. 99f.; cf. p. 63.

78. Note also Curtius' cautious hopes in *Hist. Alex.* X,ix,6, that the Roman empire, "provided divine jealousy be absent, will continue in the good times of this our Age, hopefully forever, at any rate for very many years."

79. Note also Dio Cassius, *Hist.* V,xxi,2, VIII,xxxvi,25, IX,xxxix,3, XXI,lxx,5, XLIV,xxvii,3f., XXXIX,xv,1–3 (on the alterations of fortune, mainly intrinsic to human affairs and not supervised by higher principles, affecting the individual lives of the great *Romans*); cf. VIII,xxxvi,12f., XXI,lxx,4–9, XXXVII,xx,3, etc. (on Rome and her heroes representing the "great exception"); Marcus Aurelius *Medit.* IV,xxxii,1–xxxiii, and cf. xlviii,2 (on the passing of *Roman* régimes and cultures).

Florus inherited more than one stock interpretation of Roman history. Among the options there lay the doctrine (stemming from Polybius but fully articulated by Diodorus) that the changed habits of the Romans and their harsher imperialistic policies had put fortune "to the test." Florus appropriated this doctrine in his own way. Superficially, in his *Epitome*, the height of Rome's good fortune and the acme of her "youthful" power run together, and he reinforced this impression when in Bk. I he recounted the victories of Rome up to those of Pompey and Caesar (40s BC) (xxxv–xlv). For Florus, on the other hand, the special dispensations of Fortune had been curtailed after the Numantine War (133 BC) (cf. I,xxxv,1).[80] It had been by their own *virtus*, though with the help of *fortuna* and the gods, that the Romans had achieved genuine greatness,[81] but they exceeded the limits allowed by Fortune's permissions, only to discover that "fortune, after all, was so much more powerful than virtue!" (II,xvii,11).[82] This theme was also explored in terms of territorial boundaries. Before the Numantine turning point Rome's imperial expansion across preestablished boundary lines could be condoned, even acclaimed as a positive work of Fortune (I,xxiv,1–3; cf. 13–14); but when immoderateness was evident it required asking whether Rome should have grasped even beyond Italy, let alone to have passed from Europe into Asia (I,xlvii,6–7). According to Bk. II, the dissensions which began with the Gracchan revolutions and continued to Julius Caesar's day were the product of "too much well-being," since Fortune could not but envy so apparently inviolable a power (II,xiii,1, 8). But declining morality, brutalities under Marius and Sulla, and the vices of Pompey, Caesar, and Antony afforded good ethical reasons for her altered disposition.[83] Fortune was adverse from ca. 130 BC (though that did not bring the loss of world hegemony), and she remained that way until the change for the best under Augustus, who ended civil war and beat off external threats (II,xxi,(12),1–3; cf. xxii–xxxiii). We have lost the later portions of Florus' work, but it can safely be inferred that he took Rome to experience two further turns of fortune—one adverse, the other favorable. If one combines his body-state analogy with his interpretation of changing fortune, a model of recurrent rotation in Roman history emerges (Diagram VIII). Moreover, he implied the probability of Rome's further endurance, and thus future experience of similar alternations.

Florus' position foreshadows the much more elaborate yet comparable analysis of Rome's career by "Vopiscus." In his biography of the emperor Carus and his sons,[84] "Vopiscus" contended that the Roman state was by turns "raised up

80. Although individuals could be favored by fortune after this curtailment: cf. I,xi,21, xlv,1 (Pompey and Caesar).

81. I,*proem.*,2, iii,9, vii,1–3, xviii,8, 22, xxii,20, xxii,30–1, etc.

82. Cf. Curtius *Hist. Alex.* III,xii,19–21, on drawing too much on fortune's favors only to meet with serious repercussions later.

83. II,ix,12–25, xiii,2, 9–14, xviii,2, xx,2, xxi,1. Because Pompey had benefited from too much fortune before Pharsalia, he lost to Caesar (I,x,21, II,xiii,35, 45, 51); Caesar, who had worried about his "excess of prosperity," was eventually assassinated (79, 94f.). On Octavius and Antony see xiv,5, xxi(11),1, 3, 10; cf. (in general) xiii,78.

84. On the problematic authorship of the *Scriptores historiae Augustae* see P. White, "The

Diagram VIII Patterns of Recurrence in Florus' *Epitome*

| | | | |
|---|---|---|---|
| Romulus to the end of the Numantine War (ca. 130 BC) | Support of *Fortuna* | Infancy to manhood (first stage) | |
| From ca. 130 BC to the end of the Civil Wars | Adverse fortune | Manhood (second stage) | Territorial expansion |
| From Octavius' successful campaigns to the *Pax Augusta* | Good fortune | The transition from manhood to old age (= full manhood? cf. I, *proem.*,7–8) | |
| Tiberius to Nerva | [Adverse fortune][1] | Old age | Imperial *inertia* |
| Trajan, [Hadrian][2] | [Good fortune][3] | Renewed manhood | [Territorial expansion][3] |

[Bracketed sections indicate safe inferences.]

1. The comment by Florus in II,xiii,8 that "the cause of these disasters [the Civil Wars], as with all such things, is an excess of good fortune" suggests Florus to be foreshadowing conclusions drawn outside Bks. I and II. We may surmise that the internal dissensions after the experience of too much well-being (made inevitable by Augustus' achievements) were treated as part of a time in which fortune was adverse to Rome.
2. See above, sect. B.
3. Territorial expansion under Trajan—the annexation of Dacia, Armenia, parts of Numidia and Parthia, etc.—was well-known, and must surely have come under the heading of fortune's favors.

and thrown down by diverse commotions" (*variis vel erecta motibus vel adflicta: Vit. Cari* I,2). He appealed to the body-state analogy, at first rather idiosyncratically—stating that Rome had suffered all the changes that human life may suffer in the case of a single mortal[85]—but also conventionally, conveying the impression that Rome reached old age in the civil wars before being restored by Augustus (cf. Seneca). His analysis, however, was dominated by an interest in alternating fortune, and may best be represented as in Diagram IX (see II,1–III,8). With "Vopiscus" there is no suggestion of an overall Roman wane (though he hints at moral decline).[86] Leaving other empires unmentioned, he simply utilized

Authorship of the *Historia Augusta*" in *Journal of Roman Studies* LVII, 1967, pp. 115ff.; R. J. B. Syme, *Ammianus and the Historia Augusta*, Oxford, 1968, pp. 178ff.

85. I.e., "thriving," "growing up," "waxing," "losing strength"; cf. II,4, 5, III,1.

86. The emperors from Diocletian to Galerius do not appear in his initial analysis, but cf. XVIII,3–5 (and on his favorableness toward Diocletian, XIII,1f., XV,6, XVIII,3ff.

## Diagram IX Vopiscus and Changing Fortunes in Roman History

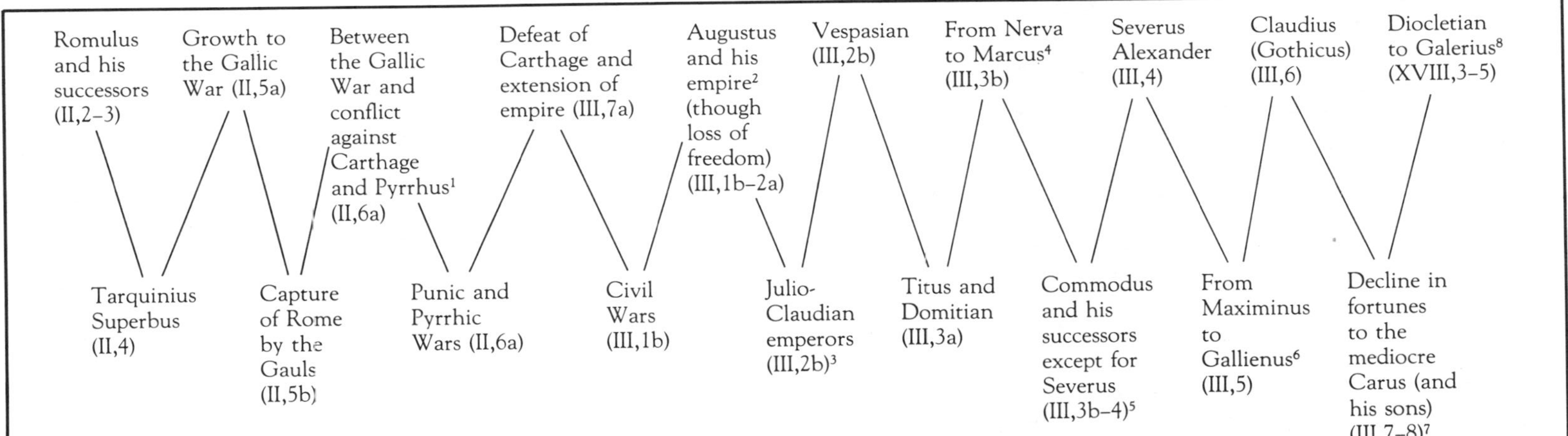

Changing Fortune in Roman history

1. The Punic Wars are taken as a period of calamity (partly following a line laid down in Polybius *Hist.* III,cxvii,1ff.; Livy *Ab urbe* XXII,liv,10–11, XXIII,xxii,1, xxiv,6, XXV,xxxviii,10, etc. on the withdrawal of fortune's support of Rome), with no reference to the idea of internal strength under the pressure of adversity (see Chapter 2, sect. B, pt. 1(ii); Chapter 4, sect. A).
2. "per Augusta deinde reparata."
3. "Tot Nerones" refers to the line of *Tiberius* Claudius Nero—Tiberius, Caligula, Claudius, Nero, and then Galba, Otho, Vitellius.
4. I.e., Nerva, Trajan, Hadrian, Antoninus, Pius, Marcus Aurelius.
5. The successors of Commodus being Pertinax, Didius Julianus [Severus], Caracalla, Geta, Macrinus, Elagabalos.
6. So, Gordian I and II, Balbinus, Pupienus, Gordian III, Philip, Decius, Trebonianus, Aemilianus, Valerianus, Gallienus (these last two being referred to in III,5).
7. Aurelian, Tacitus (both referred to in III,7), Florianus, Probus (cf. III,7); with the sons of Carus being Carinus and Numerian. Vopiscus disliked Carinus (cf. XV,7–XVI,7, XVIII,1), and could only see misfortune in Numerian's career (see XI,1–XII,1). Note also the general summary of the Carians' reigns in XX,1ff., although Vopiscus described Carus as a "good ruler" in IX,4.
8. I.e., Diocletian, Maximian, Constantius, Galerius.

the model of fortune's wheel for one continuing imperial history. His treatment nicely illustrates how recurrence conceptions could alter with the remarkable longevity of the Principate. The empire persisted; in "Vopiscus" history became the history of her recurrent vicissitudes.

We could go on indefinitely. Roman historians, we have seen, joined the Greeks in considering Fortune as an arbiter of human affairs. Moreover, the belief in Fortune's providential overlordship became steadily entrenched among them, though it had to be accommodated to a resigned acceptance of her mutability. If Livy had struggled to intertwine the two outlooks on fortune, the older problems were hardly alive by the time of Ammianus Marcellinus,[87] and it was eventually possible for a Christian historian such as Procopius (sixth century) to attribute the responsibility of events "to God and Fortune at the same time, and apparently without seeing any contradiction in it."[88] By Procopius' day Fortune the capricious, the Epicureans' blind chance, was outlawed; but the same great empire held on to its existence, and thus Fortune, taken as divine and as responsible for the feats of Rome, still lingered in the minds of men.

## D. Age theory from later antiquity to the early Renaissance

### *Later pagan views*

Almost all the conceptions we have just examined—the body-state analogy, models of growth and decay, of changing fortune, and the like—fall within the ambit of cyclical thinking. Other modes of thought may also be justifiably placed in this category, although with greater caution. I have doctrines of successive Ages (cf. Chapter 2, sect. A, pt. 3) in mind.

Both classical catastrophe theory and the Stoic doctrine of periodic cosmic dissolution were still being aired as late as the fifth century AD, although the two positions were often integrated into a neo-Pythagorean solution (Chapters 1–2).[89] Whatever the dominant school of thought, world history had to receive

87. Naudé, loc. cit., pp. 77–88; P. M. Camus, *Ammien Marcellin: témoins des courants culturels et religieux à la fin du IVe siècle*, Paris, 1967, pp. 176–86.

88. M. A. Elferink, "ΤΥΧΗ et Dieu chez Procope de Césarée" in *Acta Classica* X, 1967, p. 133 (and see below, sect. G).

89. On the survival of "classical" catastrophe theory see, e.g., Alexander of Aphrodisias *In Aristotelis meteorologicorum libros commentaria* I,89,*ll.*11–15, 90,*ll.*12–7, and cf. IV,126 (M. Hayduck, ed., *Comm. Arist. Graec.*, vol. 3, pt. 2, pp. 60–2, 181) (3rd century AD); Proclus *In Timaeum* 36D; Olympiodorus *In Aristotelis meteora commentaria* I,xiv,26, II,ii,31, and cf. I,vi,13 (G. Stüve, ed., *Comm. Arist. Graec.*, vol. 12, pt. 2, pp. 119, 143, and cf. p. 56) (both 5th century). On restating the Aristotelian doctrine of recurrence in form rather than number see, e.g., Simplicius *Aristotelis physicorum* V,4 (227b21) (H. Diels, ed., *Comm. Arist. Graec.*, vol. 10, p. 886, *ll.*3–6, 19–20) (6th century), and cf. Cicero *Somn. Scip.* vii,23. On the persistence of Stoic doctrines of cosmic conflagration, cf., e.g., Augustine *Civ. Dei.* XII,13; Sallustius in Nock, p. lxii; Latin Asclepius in *Corpus Hermetica* III,26a (Nock and Festugière edn., vol. 2, p. 331); Chalcidius *Platonis Timaeus* clxviii (Wroebel edn.); Nemesius *De natura hominis* xxxviii (*PG*, vol. 40, cols. 757–60). On neo-Pythagorean solutions see "Ocellus Lucanus" (see above, Chapter 1, sect. A; Chapter 2, sect. B, pt. 3); Eudemus, Frg. 88 (Wehrli, vol. 8, p. 41); Porphyry *Vit. Pythag.* xix; Synesius *De providentia* (cf. *PG*, vol. 66, col. 1277); Origen *Contra Celsum* V,21; cf. Plutarch *De fato* 569A–B (on Plato

some intelligible demarcations; from the first century BC on, Greek and Roman intellectuals show an increasing concern to divide it into stages and epochs. The ancient means of making such divisions—the Hesiodic Ages, models of a Great Year or of successive human generations—were still available, but new tendencies and new forms of syncretism manifested themselves.

Of growing importance was the belief in a "sympathetic" connection between the movements of the heavenly bodies and changes in terrestrial affairs.[90] Continuing Roman interest in predictive prophecy and portent, the westward spread of oriental astrologies, and the Poseidonian doctrine of "sympathy" among all parts of the universe were all symptomatic of this tendency. In fact, Poseidonius "had opened up the possibility of a single, readily intelligible principle or Intelligent Mind which ordered and brought into unison all the various aspects of the cosmos."[91] As a result, an astronomical basis for historical periodization became available and could be referred to as a means of harmonizing or supplanting older, apparently contradictory, positions. These new astronomical models provided the opportunity for synthesis and compromise between classical theories about regional cataclysms, for example, which did not accord with the Stoic picture of an ever-recurring cosmic cycle, and between these two views and beliefs about successive Ages. Catastrophes were readily connectable with heavenly movements. As Plato himself had admitted, such upheavals could be caused by planetary deviation (*Tim.* 22D). Probably under the influence of the Babylonian Berossus, Stoics felt less inhibited than their older representatives in speculating about the intermediate stages of world history, whether inter-cataclysmic or periodic in a more historical sense.[92] For others, moreover, nothing precluded the probability that the Ages of Hesiod were based on planetary periodicity.[93] In one fascinating product of syncretism, four metal Ages of world history saw the successive dominance of the four elements and of the four influences of Saturn, Jupiter, Neptune, and Pluto.[94]

The referral to astronomical principles, however, was not only a means of harmonization. More significantly still, it enabled the reckoning of large time

---

transformed into a neo-Pythagorean teaching that there was an exact recurrence of all things after the Great Year had been completed). On the neo-Pythagorean revival in the Latin West during the reign of Theodosius I see Ladner, op. cit., pp. 18f.

90. Esp. note Poseidonius in Strabo *Geographia* III,v,8; Plutarch *Platonicae quaestiones* ii,9, 13; Eusebius *Praeparatio evangelica* xv,40, and cf. pseudo-Aristotle *De mundo* v–vi.

91. W. L. Knox, *Saint Paul*, pp. 63f.; cf. F. Cumont, *Oriental Religions in Roman Paganism* (ET), New York, 1911, cf. 7; F. A. Yates, *Giordano Bruno and the Hermetic Tradition*, London, 1964, pp. 45ff.

92. Seneca *Nat. quaest.* III,xxix,1 (on world dissolution in two stages, the first being a deluge, which had passed), and cf. Cicero *Somn. Scip.* vii,23, *De nat. deor.* II,xlvi,118; (lost *Hortensius* (did it refer to the Great Winter and Summer of Aristotle's *Protrepticus*? cf. Censorinus *De die natal.* XVIII,11); Celsus in Origen, *Contr. Cels.* I,19, IV,67.

93. Plato had suggested a connection between the end of the Age of Kronos and heavenly movement in *Politicus* 271D–C, but see Hyginus *Poetica astronomica* II,xxv (1st centuries BC/AD), and Firmicus, above, Chapter 2, sect. B, pt. 3(i).

94. Nigidius Figulus (a Pythagorean of the 1st century BC) *De diis* iv; cf. K. F. Smith, "Ages of the World (Greek and Roman)" in *ERE*, vol. 1, p. 198b and 199b. In contrast to Hesiod, the Cumaean Sibyl referred to four rather than five Ages.

stages to be dissociated from momentous physical occurrences such as conflagrations or floods. As a result, although undoubted attention was given to such vast periods of time as the Great Year (variously computed) or the major Zoroastrian cycles,[95] there was also increased interest in shorter time stages more relevant to the ken of the historian than to that of the cosmologist.[96] I think primarily of that intriguing unit the *saeculum*, which, deriving from Etruscan lore, came to be interpreted as a period of just over 100 years,[97] and which took an important place in speculations about the destiny of Rome. *Saeculum*, of course, figures as an alternative expression for an "Age" (*aetas*, *aevum*), and in its barest form *saeculum* theory amounted to little more than a doctrine of successive time lapses, or even the sequence of stages within a Great Year. But it was susceptible to some interesting developments. Seneca, for instance, used the term *saecula* of the stages in Rome's "bodily" transformations, and he propagated the view that the life cycle of a state consisted of five human generations or, significantly, *saecula*.[98] Others were interested in the transition from one *saeculum* to another, assuming a coincidence between some special planetary position and a momentous happening on earth. Cicero placed such a transition—possibly the beginning of a Great Year—at the time when Romulus ascended into heaven and the sun was eclipsed (*Somn. Scip.* vii,24).[99] Some interpreted the civil-war period as a *saeculum* of woe brought to a conclusion by Octavius. The *Pax Augusta*, it was held, marked a transition from one passing Age (which required correction) to another of a new and special nature.[100] Virgil's optimistic musings in the *Fourth Eclogue* come to mind, with his combination of the Hesiodic frame and the great line of *saecula* (cf. *ll.* 4–5).[101] According to Etruscan lore (as distinct from *Works and Days*) there were at least nine Ages, and more than one writer took the period of the civil wars as the last in the series.[102] Evidently sharing this opinion, Virgil considered that both the

95. Varro collected various Hellenistic estimates of the Great Year's length: in Censorinus XXI,3, and cf. Cicero *Somn. Scip.* vii,24. For Zoroastrian cyclical conceptions at Rome see Dio Chrysostom *Orat.* XXXVI,42, and cf. Plutarch *De Iside et Osiride* 47ff. On the appearance of the Phoenix and the Sothic period (or Egyptian Great Year) see R. van den Broek, *The Myth of the Phoenix according to Classical and Early Christian Traditions* (*Études Préliminaires aux Religions Orientales dans l'Empire Romain XXIV*), Leiden, 1972, pp. 67–76, 98–108.

96. Varro in Censorinus XX,12–XXI,2 (distinguishing recent historical man from the shadowy personages of ancient and antediluvian times); Cicero *Somn. Scip.* vii,24 (on how, even by his own time, one-twentieth of the Great Year had passed).

97. I.e., the age of the oldest in the community at the time of the state's foundation, the length of the next *saeculum* being determined by the age of the oldest person living when that time lapse had passed: cf. Varro in Censorinus XVII,5f., 9–11.

98. In Lactantius *Div. inst.* VII,xv (*PL*, vol. 6, col. 788); cf. Rose, loc. cit., p. 139.

99. See Chapter 3, sect. A, pt. 6, for Luke connecting the ascensions of Romulus and Jesus. Did Luke imply that Jesus' death marked the end and beginning of a Great Year? Cf. (on a Great Year in the biblical tradition) 1 Enoch 16:1, 18:16, 21:6.

100. Livy, Frg. 56 (from *Ab urbe* CXXXVI) in Censorinus XVII,10; Florus *Epit.* II,xiv,5–8.

101. Cf. also Florus II,xxxiv,65.

102. Diodorus Siculus *Bib.* XXXVIII/IX,v; Lucan *Pharsalia* vii,387 (following Housman's emendation); cf. Juvenal *Satires* xiii,28 (here the Age of the Principate being but a continuation of the Ages of decline). Like Plato, the Etruscans took each successive Age to be worse (and of less concern to the gods): Diodorus *Bib.* XXXVIII/IX,v.

Hesiodic generations and the (Etruscan) *saecula* had run their courses, only to be renewed.[103] Others were rather more cavalier with such concepts. Florus is a later writer with a different approach. He divided Rome's third bodily stage or *aetas* into two century-long periods, calling the first Golden (since it saw the subjugation of Africa, Macedonia, Sicily, and Spain) and the second Iron, with its terrible civil wars (*Epit.* I,xxxiv(19),1–3; cf. xlvii,2–3).[104] There were other interpretations. The revived Golden Age (whether as *aetas* or *saeculum*) was placed in the reigns of Augustus' successors (those of Caligula and Nero for two)[105] and for those who were disappointed at developments under the Principate, less optimistic epithets from the same stock of ideas were applied.[106]

What remains crucial about the appeal to *saecula* is that key contemporary historical events and not just distant, momentous physical changes came to give substance to Age theory, even though wider perspectives were not submerged. Moreover, the recurrence of *saecula* usually entailed more than the mere succession of bare temporal structures; it could involve the renewal of whole epochal sequences, or, less dramatically, the return of general conditions associated with any stage in a preestablished sequence of Ages. Oftimes, though, it was simply the signs of a transition between *saecula*, rather than general conditions internal to them, which mattered. According to Zosimus, to take a late (fifth-century) example, the end of an "Age, which the Romans call *sekoula*, could be marked by disease, famines, and decay" (as happened during Diocletian's reign), and could also witness war, strange portents, and divine retributive intervention.[107] In this version of recurring *saecula* the catastrophic indications of a passage from one large time lapse to another remain rooted in "real" historical events. One is reminded of the efforts of both Dicaearchus and Polybius to rank such disturbances as war, famine, and disease with the more widely acknowledged upheavals by flood and fire (Chapter 1, sect. A).

By Zosimus' time, nevertheless, more unhistorical preoccupations with astronomy and its periodizations were winning the day.[108] The endless but computable journeys of the heavenly bodies provided the key to man's past and future, and thus the planets dictated the dimensions of an Age. It was not surprising that a

103. On Virgil's neo-Pythagoreanism here, see J. Carcopino, *Virgile et le mystère de la quatrième églogue*, Paris, 1930, pp. 30–105, and on his Age theory in the *Aeneid* by comparison, see G. Miles, "Glorious Peace: the Values and Motivation of Virgil's Aeneas" in *California Studies in Classical Antiquity* IX, 1976, pp. 159f.

104. Cf. B. Gatz, *Weltalter, Goldene Zeit und sinnverwandte Vorstellungen* (*Spudasmata* XVI), Hildesheim, 1967, p. 105.

105. E.g., Philo *Leg. ad Gaium* II,3 (Caligula); Seneca *Apocol.* IV,1 (Nero); Martial *Epigr.* IV,3 (Domitian); Anonymous in Spatianus *Pescennius Niger* (*Script. hist. Aug.*) XII,6; Symmachus *Orationes* iii,9 (Gratian). Coins for Hadrian in 121/2 bore the symbol of the Phoenix and the legend *saeculum aureum* (van den Broek, op. cit., p. 105). For further related references, Gatz, op. cit., pp. 138–40, and for imitations of Virgil's optimism see above, Chapter 2, sect. A, pt. 3(i).

106. E.g., Anonymous in Suetonius *Tiberius* lix; Ablabius in Sidonius *Epist.* V,viii,2.

107. *Hist. nov.* II,i,1, and cf. 2, 3, iii,2f. Cf. (on portents), e.g., Livy, Frg. 68; Florus *Epit.* II,xvii,5–9; Silius Italicus *Punica* IX,1ff.

108. Cumont, op. cit., pp. 178ff.; Nock, prolegomena to Sallustius, *Concerning the Gods and the Universe*, Cambridge, 1926, p. lxxii. Cf. also Macrobius *Saturnalia*, esp. I,xvii–xxii; *Commentarii in somnium Scipionis* I,xix,19, 27.

model so all-encompassing and self-contained as that of Firmicus Maternus should make its appearance. According to Firmicus, the five Ages of man (now too Romanized to be recognizably Hesiodic) and the movements of the five planets combined to produce a sequence of eons which recurred forever.[109] So, also, the basis was laid for our common century, a workable unit perhaps, but a mere extrapolation of time which, even in our own day, so often obfuscates the interpretation of human things.

But the history of Age theory was not only a pagan history.

## *Patristic writers*

The idea of successive Ages had infiltrated into Judeo-Christian circles by way of apocalyptic literature. On the other hand, both Jew and early Christian tended to react against mythopoeically-conceived schematizations and against astral determinism. If the clue to Zoroastrian successionism lay in the protracted Mazda-Ahriman conflict, Jewish writers appealed to eons in connection with their own (sacred) national history and the emergence of the great Near Eastern empires. Ancient catastrophes, moreover, such as the Flood and Sodom's destruction, spoke of God's personal control over history and his concern to destroy evil, rather than of planetary influences.[110] However, Jewish and early Christian thinking was certainly affected by cyclical conceptions of historical recurrence, and this was so in the areas concerned with the emergence and disappearance of empires and with the classification of human history into Ages or epochs. The point can be nicely illustrated from the writings of the Church Fathers.

It has been established that models of rise and fall, as well as Age schematization, were not foreign to biblical literature, and it was from a Middle Eastern stock of ideas that patristic speculations about history gathered most momentum. Already within biblical writings there was a convergence of traditions (Chapter 3, sect. B), and if diaspora Jews like Philo or Christian converts like Luke could not go untouched by Hellenism, this is no less true of most early Church Fathers, who, bred in the world of Gentile beliefs, were forced to write in the philosophical language of the doubters they sought to convince.

At this point, however, an old shibboleth emerges: the rigid dichotomy between "Greek" and "biblical" views of time and history. Scholars in the field of patristic studies have quite naturally been led to accept this dichotomy, and not

109. *Mathesis* III,i,11–5, and cf. above, Chapter 2, sect. B, pt. 3(i). The system of seven Ages corresponding with seven cosmic epochs dominated by seven planets was a variant more influential in the east of the empire: F. Cumont, "La Fin du monde chez les mages occidentaux" in *Revue de l'Histoire des Religions* XLII, 1931, p. 48.

110. See Chapter 3, sect. C, and Origen *Contr. Cels.* IV,11f., 20f.; cf. Tertullian *Apologia* xviii,3; Lactantius *Div. inst.*, II,xi; Eusebius, *Hist. eccles.* I,ii,19ff., and below. For background, see J. J. Collins, *The Sibylline Oracles of Egyptian Judaism* (*Society of Biblical Literature Dissertation Ser. XIII*), Missoula, 1974, pp. 101ff.; E. L. Eisenstein, "Clio and Chronos: An Essay on the Making and Breaking of History-Book Time" in *History and Theory* VI, 1966, pp. 40, 47f.

without reason, since many Fathers made a mockery of cyclicism (especially Stoic versions of it), and not the least among the mockers was St. Augustine.[111] More than one modern scholar has highlighted a contrast between the Greek view of time "as above all cyclical or circular, returning perpetually on itself, self-enclosed, under the influence of astronomical movements which command and regulate its course by necessity," and the Christian view of time as "irreversible," "neither external nor infinite in its duration," proceeding in a straight line from creation to the eschaton in accordance with the divine plan of salvation.[112] This way of stating the case does have substance. Insofar as this contrast makes clear that an ultimately directionless history was repugnant to any orthodox Christian committed to *creatio ex nihilo* and the Last Judgment, and insofar as it elucidates the Christian rejection of astral fatalism, of melancholia toward the perpetual and necessary round of all things,[113] it has validity. This contrast also points out the "contempt for history" in Greek philosophy, in which the events of human affairs, considered ever-moving, ever-becoming, and recurring, had little significance of their own "apart from the world of intelligible essences" set against them. That contempt differs radically from the Christians' stress on the historical rootedness of their faith.[114] However, when scholars so confuse cosmological and historical conceptions that all linearity is removed from Greco-Roman historiography and all cyclical conceptions from early Christian interpretations of world history, neat distinction has stretched the facts. When Gilles Quispel wrote that

> whereas Herodotus, the first important historian among the Greeks, spoke of a cycle of human events, the last great historian of ancient times [Augustine] leads his readers from the *falsus circuitus* to the *trames recti itineris*, the straight line of history,[115]

he missed two basic points. First, compared to Empedoclean, Stoic, or neo-Pythagorean cyclical theory, Herodotus' narrative concerned historical movements over a limited period of time, and this (together with his understanding of retributive principles) makes his position relatively innocuous even if not conducive to a Christian outlook. Second, although Augustine condemned the "false circuit" of cosmology, he nevertheless subscribed to a doctrine of imperial rise and fall and of the successive Ages of human history.

111. *Civ. Dei.* XII,13; cf. Origen *De principiis* II,iii,4, *Contr. Cels.* V,20f.; Tatian iii; Eusebius *Theophaneia* II,21; Nemesius *De natura hominis* 38; etc.

112. H. C. Puech, "Gnosis and Time" in *Man and Time: Eranos Yearbooks*, pp. 39, 46; cf. Cochrane, *Christianity and Classical Culture*, pp. 483f.; Löwith, *Meaning*, pp. 160ff.; G. Quispel, "Time and History in Patristic Christianity" in *Man and Time*, pp. 95–8; R. Bainton, "Ideas of History in Patristic Christianity" in *Early and Mediaeval Christianity*, London, 1965, pp. 8f.

113. Note Marcus Aurelius *Medit.* IV,xxxii–xxxiii, X,xxxiv, XII,xxx,ii; cf. Puech, loc. cit., p. 45; E. R. Dodds, *Pagan and Christian in an Age of Anxiety*, Cambridge, 1965, chs. 1–2.

114. H. E. W. Turner, op. cit., pp. 424f.; R. G. Collingwood, *Idea of History*, pp. 20–5, and cf. esp. Celsus in Origen *Contr. Cels.* IV,58ff.; Plotinus *Enneads* VI,ix,8; Olympiodorus, *Commentary on Phaedo* (W. Norin, ed., Leipzig, 1913), p. 192, *ll.*4–6; p. 195, *l.*27–p. 196, *l.*9; p. 197, *ll.*4f.; p. 236, *ll.*9ff.

115. Loc. cit., p. 98; cf. F. Châtelet, "Le Temps de l'histoire et l'évolution de la fonction d'histoire" in *Journal de Psychologie (Normale et Pathologique)* LIII, 1956, pp. 365–72.

Certainly the Fathers almost invariably dissociated historical patterns from planetary movement, and history's course was always referred to the will of the personal Creator.[116] For them the ultimate meaning of history no longer resided with recurring conjunctions of physical or human events, but with unique, unrepeatable acts, with Creation, the atoning crucifixion, and the eschaton. This outlook lessened "the grip of the past"; it undercut the assumption that it was recurrent, normative event-complexes which constituted history's essential message for man, and it gave hope to those bowed in resignation to a predetermined or unforeseeable future.[117] Yet the story would not be complete were we to overlook the fact that notions of generation and corruption, of bodily processes, changing fortunes, Age succession, rise and fall—all of them cyclical notions—could be absorbed into Christian historiography and Christian philosophies of history. Neither would the tale be told if we failed to note how "pragmatic" Christian historians found lessons for the future in their own day just as their pagan predecessors had done,[118] and how even the most theologically-inclined, in characterizing the vicissitudes of the "Earthly City," could appeal to pagan recurrence models. And what if we extend our search beyond cyclical thinking to historical recurrence in its broader aspects? As we shall see, Christians made no mean use of their Greco-Roman heritage.

Admittedly, their special touches were distinctive enough. The Christians drew many of their facts from the biblical past, and to the extent that they divorced historical processes from the extra-historical and the mythopoeic, they furthered the historicization of recurrence thinking. Such historicization did not spring in a direct line from the neo-Pythagorean anti-Stoic insistence on one endless world history. It was more the historians' historicization, the confining of recurring patterns within one circumscribed history, the beginning of which was known from the Bible, not unknown like the shadowy eons of Plato's *Laws*, and the first stages of which devolved around men, not around the gods.[119] It is

116. Origen, who of all the early Fathers was most susceptible to developing this sympathetic principle, since he propounded a doctrine of the "rise and fall of souls" (see above, sect. F), was cautious about the connections between metempsychosis, fatalism, and the eternity of the world: cf. *Commentaria in Matthaeum* XIII,i [ed. E. Benz, E. Klostermann, L. Früchtel, *Origenes Werke*, vol. 2 (1935), in *Die griechischen christlichen Schriftstellen*, ed. O. Stählin, Berlin, 1899, p. 176, *ll*.5–15]; Pamphilius *Apologia* (for Origen) x [ed. Benz et al., vol. 12 (1941), p. 9, *ll*.43–50]. One Eastern theologian, however, is famous for his concessions to astral fatalism. I refer to Bardesanes (3rd century), who is reputed to have said, among other things, that "Christ was born at the hour of Jupiter, died at the hour of Mars, and was resurrected again at the hour of Jupiter": in Gregory bar Hebraeus, *Concerning Christological Heresies* (in *Patrologia Orientalis*, ed. F. Graffin and F. Nau, Paris, 1903ff., vol. 31, p. 256); cf. Bardesanes *Coniunctiones astrorum* (in *Patrologia Syriaca*, ed. R. Graffin, Paris, 1894–96, vol. 2, pp. 614ff.), and the MS on Fate, published as *Le Livre des lois des pays* (ed. F. Nau), Paris, 1931.

117. B. A. van Groningen, *In the Grip of the Past: Essay on an Aspect of Greek Thought* (*Philosophia Antiqua VI*), Leiden, 1953, passim and pp. 109–20.

118. E.g., Procopius *Huper tōn polemōn* I,i–ii (cf. Thucydides *Hist.* I,22), and on medieval historiography see below, sect. H.

119. Against S. Toulmin and J. Goodfield, who miss this point about historicization, when arguing that Christians lost a sense of enormous lengths of time (*The Discovery of Time*, Harmondsworth, 1967, pp. 67ff.). Origen seems to have compromised with Plato's profound sense

also justifiable to contend that the Christian attack on pagan cosmology tended to place a restraint upon cyclical thinking in general. But we are still compelled to agree that cyclical models were not excluded from Christian historical thought. It was not heterodox for a writer such as Lactantius to accept the commonplace that human affairs and lives experienced generation and decay;[120] or for Basil to agree with Theognis that God inclines the scale to men "now one way and now another," so that they experience alternation between prosperity and adversity;[121] or for Prudentius to employ the body-state analogy in explaining Rome's late reception of Christianity.[122] Such cyclical conceptions, however, are nowhere near as prominent in patristic and medieval thought as ideas about the Ages of man and the successive emergence of great empires.

As we have seen, doctrines of successive Ages were not confined to the Middle East, yet the Fathers, committed to the primacy of scripture, leaned heavily toward the schematizations of Daniel and other apocalyptic writings, and to the New Testament treatment of the "new *aiōn*." In the first century AD, the idea of the millennium gained currency. According to the Christian Apocalypse (20:4ff.; cf. 2 En. 33:1; 2 Esd. 7:28), Christ and his martyrs would reign over the earth for a thousand years before the final defeat of Satan, the cosmic transformation, and the descent of the heavenly Jerusalem. For apocalypticists, a thousand years was "a day in God's sight" (cf. Ps. 90:4; Bk. Jub. 4:29–30; 2 En. 32:1; 2 Pet. 3:8), and for many it was significant that Adam's lifetime fell just short of a thousand years.[123] With the circulation of such beliefs, coupled with expectations of a final millennium, there emerged very early in Christian literature the model of world history as a Great Week, divisible into at least six millennial days, with a final (eschatological) day of rest (Epist. Barn. xv,3–8).[124]

---

of distant time by presupposing many other Ages before the *aiōn* of this world (*De princ.* II,iii,5); and for some background in Jewish thought, note (from the Babylonian Talmud) *Pesahim* 54a; *Shabbath* 88b; *Hagigah* 13b, 14b, and also *Genesis Rabba* 1, and cf. E. Adler, "Ages of the World (Jewish)" in *ERE*, vol. 1, p. 203a). On orthodox Christian criticism of pagan antediluvianism and the astrological calculations of the "Chaldaeans" see, e.g., Julius Africanus *Chronographia* (Frgs.) (PG, vol. 10, col. 65a); Lactantius *Div. inst.* VII,xiv (*PL*, vol. 6, cols. 780b–781a).

120. *Div. inst.* II,xi (cols. 315a, 361a); yet cf. Origen *Contr. Cels.* IV,60 (against Celsus' conclusion that continual generation and corruption bespeak the ultimate indestructibility of matter and the universe); Gregory of Nyssa *De hominis opificio* III–XXI (on mortality as an *essential* characteristic of humanity being pushed in the background by the Christian view of personal immortality).

121. *Homily* xxii (background in Theognis 157); cf. Tertullian *Apol.* xxvi,1 (on imperial rise and fall within an ordained "body of time"); *De Pallio* ii,1 (*Corpus Christianorum, Series Latina*, Turnhout, 1953ff., vol. 2, p. 735) (hereafter *CCSL*) (on alternation between unity and discord as a natural process).

122. *Contra Symmachum* II,309–323, surely an optimistic passage in the tradition of Florus and Ammianus, despite his expectations of an ultimate End. So G. Boas, *Essays on Primitivism and Related Ideas in the Middle Ages* (*Contributions to the History of Primitivism*), Baltimore, 1948, p. 184; and against L. G. Patterson, *God and History in Early Christian Thought* (*Studies in Patristic Thought*), London, 1967, p. 91.

123. Background: Gen. 5:5; Bk. Jub. 4:29f.; cf. Justin Martyr *Dialogus* lxxxi; Irenaus *Adversus Haereses* V,xxiii,2; Lactantius *Div. inst.* VII,xiv.

124. Background in rabbinics: *Sanh.* 97a; cf. W. Bacher, *Agada der Tannaiten*, Strasbourg, 1884, vol. 1, pp. 133ff.; E. Adler, loc. cit., p. 204a. Early Christian models: Julius Africanus *Chron.* I,1;

The first attempts to apply this model to the facts were not uniform, even if based on the obvious stages of Israelite history, but one account came to acquire renown and recognition above all. It appears in the last pages of St. Augustine's *De civitate Dei.* The first great day or *aetas* was from Adam to the Flood, the second from the Flood to Abraham, the third from Abraham to David, the fourth from David to the Babylonian captivity, the fifth from the Exile to Christ, the present time seeing the sixth Age, and the future a seventh (and an eighth!) (XXII,30).[125] A tidy vision indeed; and it nicely reflected both Christian soteriology and basic Christian expectations of history. But what has it to do with the idea of history repeating itself? Was it in any sense employed as a model of historical recurrence, or is it safer to concur with the kind of interpretation summed up in Roland Bainton's neat phrase: "not cycles but successive creations"?[126]

Let us clarify the issues. It must be conceded that the Christians' conception of history, and even of the eons comprising it, was progressionist. Events were moving toward a perfect end. Thus numerous patristic writers could invoke the Great Week to arouse hope in the coming fulfillment of God's ancient promises, such as those to Abraham.[127] It not only bears remarking that the dividing of history into stages did not automatically produce an interest in recurrent patterns, but also that some Fathers sought to accommodate the history of salvation to Greco-Roman pictures of mankind's natural history.[128] As Amos Funkenstein has ably shown,[129] such writers as Irenaeus, Tertullian, Eusebius, and Augustine believed that the unfolding of God's plan, with the eventual emergence of Christ's Church, meant progress, not degeneration or recurrence.[130] Let me qualify my position still more circumspectly: in some of the following pages I am intent on documenting the survival of recurrence ideas during the Middle Ages, not on proving that they formed a dominant patristic

---

Hippolytus *Commentaria in Danielem* (*Fragmenta*) iv (*PG*, vol. 10, col. 645A); cf. (on the idea of a final millennium) Papias in Eusebius *Eccles. hist.* III,xxxix,12; Justin *Dial.* lxxxi.

125. Cf. *De Genesi contra Manichaeos* I,23, *De catechizandis rudibus* xxii,39, *De Trinitate* IV,iv,7. For background on Ages identified by key biblical personages: 4 Ezra 3:45; Theophilus of Antioch *Ad Autolycum* iii,28. For background on the eighth great day: Irenaeus *Adv. Haer.* V,xxiii,2 (following Côtelier's reading; cf. J. Daniélou, "La Typologie millénariste de la semaine dans le Christianisme primitif" in *Vigiliae Christianae* II, 1948, p. 10); Tertullian *De anima* xxxvii; and for the relative originality of Augustine's model see F. E. Robbins, *The Hexaemeral Literature*, Chicago, 1912, p. 72.

126. "Ideas of History," p. 8.

127. E.g., Tertullian *Adversus Marcionem* III,24; Gregory of Elvire *Tractatus Origenis* viii (Battifol, p. 95); St. Ephraim of Nisibis *Commentarius in Genesim* i; Aphraates *Demonstratio* II,14 (the three Eastern theologians being of the 4th century).

128. E.g., Julius Africanus *Chron.*, Frgs. (*PG*, vol. 10, cols. 63ff.); Eusebius (ed. Jerome) *Chronicorum* (A. Schoene, ed., Frankfurt, 1875, vol. 1, cols. 71–131); and later (6th century), Joannis Malalas *Chronographia* III, para. 74Aff. and passim (ed. L. Dindorf in *Corpus scriptorum historiae Byzantinae*, Bonn, 1831, pp. 61ff.) (henceforth *CSHB*).

129. Cf. A. Funkenstein, *Heilsplan und natürliche Entwicklung*, ch. 1, pts. 2–4.

130. E.g., Irenaeus *Adv. Haer.* IV,xxxv,1–xxxviii,4, lxiii,3; Tertullian *De Pallio* ii,1, 7, *Apol.* xlviii,10f.; Eusebius *Hist. eccles.* I,ii; Augustine *Civ. Dei.* IV,7, XVIII,1; cf. Funkenstein, op. cit., pp. 19ff.

and medieval theme. Even if they were almost always pressed into the service of a basically linear perspective, that does not prevent one from writing their history. The persistence of these ideas, even though in a secondary rôle, is a proper subject of history, and hardly unimportant background for the development of recurrence ideas in post-medieval Western thought.

The adoption of the Great Week schema and of Age theory did engender certain ideas which we may fairly rank among the manifold forms of recurrence thinking. Both Irenaeus and Lactantius, for instance, taught that the first (and fallen) man Adam virtually occupied the first millennium, while Christ, the perfect man, was given rule over the sixth.[131] Other conceptions were less typological. Augustine, who took the first Age beyond Adam to the Flood, detected a symmetrical pattern of generations (and not of years!)[132] over the first five Ages. The first two Ages were each ten generations in length, and the next three (following Matt. 1:17) fourteen generations (*Civit. Dei* XX,30). Such a pattern may seem of little import to us moderns, but for many medieval thinkers it spelled divine control over the whole world.[133] Perhaps the recurrence of generation figures may seem incidental to this suggestion, but it was nevertheless present and was susceptible to some interesting and relevant elaborations, as when Orosius, an Age-theorist influential upon medievals, contended that Abraham was born on the 25th of December in the forty-third year of the reign of the ancient Assyrian king Ninus,[134] and that Christ was born on the same date in the forty-second year of the Roman Principate.[135]

We could argue, admittedly, that there were many events covered by the Great Week which belonged to the future. In part at least, it was "a survey of history in future form,"[136] and so seems to lie on the fringe of our investigations, like theories of cosmological recurrence. If we are reminded here that our primary concern is with recurrences elicited from the past, however, it remains true that only the more daring and chiliastic of Christians were specific about events

131. *Adv. Haer.* V,xxxiii,1f. (*PG*, vol. 7, col. 1185b) (Adam and Christ both dying on a Friday); cf. III,xxxii,1, IV,lv,1, and (on Irenaus' theology of "recapitulation") III,xix, V,xxxiii,2). Lactantius *Div. inst.* VII,xiv (Adam being created on the sixth day, and Christ appearing in the sixth millennial day).

132. Discovering patterns in accordance with years was made difficult by divergences in figures for the age-length of biblical personages given in the LXX and MT. The LXX, for example, places Noah 1,000 years after Adam. Problems raised by using single millennia, though, were circumvented by some writers appealing to double millennia, e.g., *Sanhed.* (*Bab. Tal.*) 97a (on three double millennia: of chaos, Torah, and the Messiah).

133. E.g., Gregory of Tours *Decem libros historiarum* I,iv, vii, xii, xv–xvi (6th century); Bede *De temporibus liber* XVI (*PL*, vol. 90, col. 288) (8th century); Rhabanus Maurus *Liber de computo* xcvi (*PL*, vol. 107, cols. 726b–727a (9th century). For Jewish background see, e.g., *Pirqe Aboth* v,2; *Genesis Rabba* xix,7ff.; and on successive generations expressing the "cyclical reality of the cosmos" in antiquity, see E. Voegelin, *Order and History* (vol. 4: *The Ecumenic Age*), Baton Rouge, 1974, pp. 85ff.

134. See above, sect. A (on Sura, Trogus); cf. Thallus in Lactantius *Epitome institutionum Divinarum* xxiv (on Belus, Ninus' father); Eusebius *Chron.* (Schoene, col. 53).

135. Orosius *Historia* VII,2 (*PL*, vol. 31, col. 1064); cf. Gregory of Tours I,vii, xviii.

136. Terms from E. Hennecke in his *New Testament Apocrypha* (ed. W. Schneemelcher) (ET), London, 1965, p. 584.

to come.[137] And while Age schematization certainly encouraged thinking about recurrence in eschatological terms, with hopes of a "new Exodus" or with the vision of a path "from God to God" through history as a totality,[138] the complete story is surprisingly more complex. Take, for instance, Christian appeals to a returning Golden Age. Clearly the earliest instances of this notion in Judeo-Christian literature were millenarian, the Golden Age being identified with the divine eschatological rule.[139] But there were later shifts away from a purely futurist outlook. In this connection, Lactantius is most interesting.[140]

Lactantius was affected by the eschatology of Sibylline literature and also was the inheritor of a Great Week schema. Combining these with anticipations of a Golden Age, he contended that, in the seventh millennium, the rule of Saturn would return (*Div. inst.* VII,ii, xxiv). That had been no primeval or mythopoeic reign, however, for Lactantius used all his powers to prove that Saturn was a post-diluvian monarch, a friend and contemporary of Belus (the father of King Ninus),[141] and that he had been a king before mankind abandoned itself to polytheism and idolatry.[142] His had been a reign of gold and of monotheism, followed by the "miserable and disastrous" *saeculum* of iron, in which false religion prevailed and in which there lived but seven wise men.[143] From the Age of iron, history had undergone degeneration down to the present (cf. VII,xv). Lactantius was rewriting world history, apparently modifying the Age theories of Hesiod, Plato, the middle Stoics, and the Sibyls to suit a new case.[144] Now Lactantius

137. F. L. Griffith, "Ages of the World (Christian)" in *ERE*, vol. 1, p. 191a; N. Cohn, *The Pursuit of the Millennium*, London, 1957, pp. 8–12 and passim.

138. For the last idea (in Augustine's theology of history) see G. E. Cairns, *Philosophies*, p. 255; and on the new Exodus see above, Introduction.

139. E.g., according to the Sibyl Tiburtina: cf. Cohn, op. cit., pp. 15f.

140. On Lactantius' knowledge of the relevant literature see *Div. inst.* VII,xxiv. To enrich my discussion below, I have been unfortunate in not procuring the very recent colloquium *Lactance et son temps* (*Collection Théologie Historique XCVIII*), Paris, 1978.

141. *Epit.* xxiv, *Div. inst.* I,xiii. Cf. Justin *Hist.* xliii,1; Thallus in Lactantius *Epit.* xxiv; Augustine *Civ. Dei* XVIII,15.

142. *Epit.* xxv; *Div. inst.* V,v; cf. II,xiv on an antediluvian pre-Noahic Age before Saturn. Lactantius was not the first to historicize the Golden Age so strongly or to treat it as a "social era": cf. Seneca *Epist. mor.* XC,4ff.; A. T. Y. Serra, "The Idea of Man and World History from Seneca to Orosius and Saint Isidore of Seville" in *Journal of World History* VI, 1961, p. 702.

143. *Div. inst.* VI,i (*PL*, vol. 6, cols. 449a–450b).

144. Hesiod's five Ages, except for the fourth, were associated with metals, as were the four Ages of the Cumaean Sibyl and Ovid (gold, silver, bronze, and iron). Lactantius mentioned only two metal Ages, his position being closer to Plato (and Platonic emphases behind Ovid) in distinguishing the ancient Age of Kronos = Saturn from the present Age of Zeus = Jupiter (cf. above, Chapter 1, sect. A). Lactantius, however, most definitely demythologized Saturn and Jupiter as (Greek) kings of the decidedly historical past, appealing to the testimony of the Erythraean Sibyl: *Div. inst.* I,xiv (cols. 191a–192a). Lactantius' picture of the Saturnian Age corresponds to the first Stoic Age under the law of nature, but the Age of the Seven Sages, instead of representing a zenith (cf. Seneca XC,35ff.), becomes a calamitous Iron Age with only seven men in its favor. In the final analysis, we must admit that Lactantius used a four-part schema, but it was one unique to him. We find its closest parallel in Bede on the four Ages of the Sun, in his *Sibyllinorum verborum interpretatio* (*PL*, vol. 90, col. 1182b–c), where the first generation (*generatio*) of men are described as "plain, pure, loving liberty, and truthful," the second as "living splendidly, increasing in numbers" ($\neq$ Lactantius' antediluvian and Saturnian Ages). With the third generation, "men rise up against

knew of the seven-day schema, but he neither documented it from biblical history, as did Augustine, nor interwove it carefully into his more classically-derived model. His seven great days were millennia, the sixth not yet being completed (VII,xiv), but the length of each of these days was dependent upon the movements of the seven planets and—selling out somewhat to astrology—he simply comments that these "differing and unequal" movements "are believed to cause the varieties of circumstances and times."[145] That was a cautious statement, and deliberately so. It was vague as well, since the millennial stages could not be readily justified by known historical facts. Lactantius certainly noted Adam's millennium (the interval which Augustine replaced by his first ten generations) and, following a line most clearly seen in Hippolytus, he implied that the sixth millennium was nearing completion[146] (a position which the anti-chiliastic Augustine found distasteful).[147] On the other hand, Lactantius looked to his other framework when considering the Incarnation of Christ. Here his historicization of the Golden Age becomes still more interesting, for he claimed not only that the conditions of Saturn's Age would return in the last millennium, but that the *species* (appearance? image? semblance?) of this Golden Age had already returned (*rediit*), and justice already seen restoration (*reddita*) in the coming of Christ. As a result of this coming, there was once more the "pious religious worship of the one God"—at least among a few.[148] The Golden Age had been substantially, though not completely, de-eschatologized—or at least, it was both present and future.

Lactantius' musings are something of a landmark in Christian thought. If the great Virgil had once announced the return of the Golden Age under Augustus, later (and non-Christian) interpreters had either pushed the Age further on into others' reigns (pt. 1), or had been happy to conclude that there was no exact recurrence at Augustus' time, but only the restoration of similar conditions.[149] It was not unnatural, then, that classical rhetoric should soon combine with Christian anticipation. For, Christian hopes of a future Age of Gold notwithstanding, an inspired vision of the Incarnation and of the new Christian order

---

men, with many fights within Rome" (≠ Lactantius' Iron Age), and with the fourth, men reject Christ (≠ the Age after the Incarnation, though for Lactantius the coming of Christ began to reactualize the conditions for a Golden Age).

145. VII,xiv (col. 782a). Cf. Bardesanes *Coniunct. astr.* (*Patr. Syr.* vol. 2, pp. 161ff.), on the 6,000 years of world history and planetary movement.

146. VII,xiv (col. 781a); Hippolytus *Comm. in Daniel.* iv (PG, vol. 10, col. 655); cf. Daniélou, loc. cit., pp. 12f.

147. Augustine took the *beginning* of the sixth Age to be marked by the Incarnation, and although contending that history was not yet 6,000 years old (*Civ. Dei*, XVII,40), he avoided talk of millennia and stressed the unknowability of the final Age's duration: cf. *De gen. con. Manich.* I,24; Cohn, op. cit., p. 14; E. Lewalter, "Eschatologie und Weltgeschichte in der Gedankwelt Augustins" in *Zeitschrift für Kirchengeschichte* LIII, 1934, pp. 1ff.

148. V,vii (col. 570a). In his concern to convert the pagans, Lactantius seems to have forgotten about Israelite history!

149. E.g., Servius *Commentarius in Virgilium* (*in Bucolica, Georgica et Aeneidem*), Strasbourg, 1468 (Melb. Pub. Libr.), p. 7, col. 2, p. 8, col. 1, and for other references to *aureum saeculum* in Servius, see J. F. Mountford and J. T. Schultz, *Index rerum et nominum in scholiis Servii et Aelii Donati tractatorum*, New York, 1930, p. 152.

could be ascribed to Virgil and men could continue to attest the return of the Golden Age with the reigns of later, faithful protectors they admired. Claims of such a return came to be made of rulers as widely separated as Theodosius the Great in the fourth century (by Claudian), Charlemagne in the eighth (Modoin), Henry VII in the fourteenth (Dante), and Pope Julius II in the sixteenth (Giles of Viterbo).[150]

It is evident, then, that although early Christian outlines of history's Ages were framed with soteriology and the Last Things in mind, they contained important elements of recurrence. Moreover, to speak of "successive creations" cannot dispel our previous conclusions that Age theory represents one form of recurrence, in fact of cyclical, thinking (even when Ages are conceived in the barest forms). It is hardly insignificant that Irenaeus should refer to the Great Week and its inner proportions as cycles,[151] or that Lactantius should take each millennium (connected as each was to planetary revolutions) to be a *circulus*.[152] And the ninth-century Byzantine chronographer Syncellus, even when he treated time sequences in the Bible which bore no symmetrical relationship, had no compunction in referring to them as *cycloi*.[153]

## *Medieval writers*

Augustine's Great Week model (outlined briefly in the last pages of *De civitate Dei*) had a long history through the Middle Ages. That it lasted longer than those schemes which confined world history to 6000–7000 years was due partly to the eminence of Augustine himself (at least in the West), but above all to its relative flexibility.[154] The length of the sixth Age was left unspecified, Christ's nativity was placed near its beginning rather than its end, and chiliasm was decried. Augustine's strictures did not bridle all, perhaps,[155] but his open-ended framework provided a basic standard for medieval Age theory, and it held on even to the Reformation. The model often appears in theological writings, yet it

150. Claudian *In Rufinum* I,50ff. (in *Claudii Claudiani carmina*, ed. J. Koch, Leipzig, 1893, p. 12); [also, on Constantine, Lactantius(?), *Oratio ad Santos*; cf. E. Barker, *From Alexander to Constantine*, p. 218]; Modoin, in *MGH*, *Poetae*, vol. 1, p. 390, *ll*.24–7; Dante *Epistolae* VII,1; cf. *De monarchia* I,xi (with a similar conception in Plutarch, below, pt. 3); for Giles of Viterbo see Chapter 5, sect. B, pt. 4. Cf. also Cohn, op. cit., ch. 5, on hopes for a returning Holy Roman Emperor.

151. *Adv. Haer.* V,xxiii,2: *secundum autem circulum et cursum dierum*; *secundum hunc circulum dierum*.

152. *Div. inst.* VII,xiv (col. 782a).

153. *Chronographia* (in *CSHB*, para. 16D, p. 29).

154. The belief that the 6,000th year of history and the Age of Sabbath Rest were relatively near (the sixth millennium having preceded the Incarnation by hundreds of years), was not only in the *Epistle of Barnabas* (xv,4f.), Irenaeus (*Adv. Haer.* V,xxviii,3), Hippolytus and Lactantius (see above), but also in Clement of Alexandria (in J. Malalas, *Chron.*, Bk. X *CSHB*, p. 228). Such authorities influenced Byzantine chronological speculations decisively: V. Grumel, *La Chronologie* (*Traité d'Études Byzantines I*), Paris, 1958, p. 3 and passim; A. Vasiliev, "Mediaeval Ideas of the End of the World" in *Byzantion* XVI, 1942–3, pp. 462ff.

155. Cf. Cohn, op. cit., pp. 13ff. and passim; Griffith, loc. cit., p. 191a.

is also found in annals and other historiographical works as background material,[156] and it even seeped through to the histories of the Byzantine East.[157]

There were also adaptations of the Augustinian norm, and some are important in the history of the recurrence idea. Augustine himself presented a more elaborate account of the Great Week. In this second version, each *aetas* is not only associated with seven creative Days (cf. Gen. 1), but with stages of the bodily life cycle as well. Appropriating the body-cosmos analogy of the Stoics and the body-state analogy of the Roman historians, he reinterpreted world history for a new intellectual cause. Antediluvian times were represented as the infancy of the whole breed of men (*infantia universi saeculi*); from the Flood to Abraham came mankind's boyhood (*pueritia*), for we remember our childhood, not our infancy; from Abraham to David, youth (*adolescentia*), when a people of God were "begotten"; from David to the Exile, mankind's prime (*iuventus*), the kingly period; and from the Exile to the Incarnation, old age (*senectus*), "an Age weakened and broken." In the sixth Age humanity approached the end of its life, with the temple devastated, but a special situation arose, as when in a man's old age a new man is born who lives spiritually.[158] How skillfully has Augustine turned Roman ideas about rejuvenation into a new theology! On the surface, perhaps, this elaboration looks like the body-state analogy applied to biblical as against Roman history, but it was world history was actually being envisaged,

156. For theological literature see esp. Eugyppius *Thesaurus* lvii (*PL*, vol. 62, col. 668); Isidore of Seville *Etymologiae* V,xxxviii–ix (vol. 82, cols. 223f.); Julian of Toledo *De comprabatione aetatis sextae* III (vol. 96, col. 569c–d); Bede *De temp. lib.* xvi (vol. 90, col. 288); Alcuin *Disputatio puerorum* (vol. 101, col. 1112); Rabanus Maurus *Commentaria in Genesim* I,x (vol. 107, col. 469b); *Lib. de comp.* xcvi (vol. 107, cols. 726–8); Honoré d'Autun *De imagine mundis* II,lxxv (vol. 172, col. 156c–d); Peter Abelard *Expositio in hexaemeron* (*Moralitas*) (vol. 178, col. 772a–d); Rupert of Deutz *In librum Ecclesiastes* i (vol. 168, col. 1200b–c); Hugh of St. Victor *De scripturis et scriptoribus sacris* xvii (vol. 175, col. 24); Bonaventura *Collat. in hex.* XV,12–8; Henry of Cossey *Super Apocalypsim* (Bodelian Lib. MS, Oxford, Laud Misc. 85) [all the above being in chronological order, 5th–14th centuries, and only d'Autun, Abelard, and Bonaventura among them using the body-history (or state) analogy along with the Great Week model]. On Philipp van Haveng, Joachim, et al., see below, and note that Taio (7th century) had a special version involving the Great Hours rather than the Great Week: *Sententiae* III,iv (*PL*, vol. 80, cols. 854a–855b). For historiography see esp. Gregory of Tours *Dec. lib. hist.* I,i–xvii; Ado of Vienne *Chronicon in aetates sex divisum* (*PL*, vol. 123, cols. 23ff.); Marianus Scotus *Chronicon* I,xi–xxi (abbrev. in *PL*, vol. 147, cols. 623b–624a; cf. *Germanicarum rerum quatuor celebrioses vetustioresque chronographi*, Basel, 1559) (the above being 6th–11th centuries). On Bede's interest in the Great Week Schema as an historian see C. W. Jones, "Bede as Early Mediaeval Historian" in *Medievalia et Humanistica* VI, 1946, p. 32; and on historians following the stages of biblical history suggested by Augustine (and Eusebius-Jerome) without extracting a Great Week model, see esp. Sigebertus of Gembloux *Chronica* (*PL*, vol. 160, cols. 57ff.); Otto of Freising *Chronicon seu historia de Duabus civitate* I–II; Matthew Paris *Chronica majora* I (these being 12th–13th centuries). On the division of historical works into seven books (as suggested by the Great Week), see, e.g., Orosius *Hist.* I–VII; Ranulf Higden *Polychronicon* i,26 (cf. J. Taylor, *The "Universal Chronicle" of Ranulf Higden* Oxford, 1966, p. 36); and on Brunetto Latini's *Il Tesoro* (1268), cf. F. J. Carmody, "Latin Sources of Brunetto Latini's World History" in *Speculum* XI, 1936, pp. 359ff.

157. E.g., Ducas *Historia Byzantina* I (*CSHB*, pp. 10–2, para. 1A, 2A, 2D, 3A). Significantly, Ducas wrote his history from 1204, the year of the Latin occupation of the East.

158. *De Gen. con. Manich.* I,23 (*PL*, vol. 34, cols. 190–3, esp. 192).

or better, the history of those theologically significant events which ultimately mattered for mankind's destiny.[159]

In this elaboration, however, rejuvenation implies recurrence only in the sense that the old spiritual vitality of God's city had been reacquired in the Church at a time when Israel had fallen and Rome declined.[160] Clearly the Augustinian framework has various implications: it impinges, among other things, on medieval ideas of imperial rise and fall and the logic of retribution in history—which are yet to be discussed. While we still focus on Age theory, though, it is helpful to note not only how many theologians made use of this model, but also the limits of its adaptability as time went on, and its diminishing usefulness during the High Middle Ages. For those who were intensely interested in the progress of the Church rather than in secular affairs, the long-standing body-state analogy could not be easily transformed into a body-church analogy. For an ecclesiastic to speak of the senility, let alone the demise, of the Church was hardly to appear as a man of faith! Thus in the sixth century Gregory the Great listed three Ages of the Church as boyhood, youth, and maturity, with no others.[161]

Many writers may have prefaced their reflections on world history with Augustine's framework, but when it became a matter of relating the model to the ongoing, complex turbulences of the post-antique world, the task was very difficult. Rare are the authors who tried to do this with a genuine interest in ideas of recurrence,[162] although there is one minor twelfth-century figure, Philipp van Haveng, who merits attention. Forced to put the unsatisfying language of the life cycle aside, Philipp transformed Augustine's less elaborate schema into one with an "undulation from periods of good to periods of evil and back."[163] Considering the great and composite idol of Dan. 2:32–35, he linked each of its substances to one of the seven Ages of the world,[164] and dilated on the relative merits of each Age (see Diagram X). Overly allegorical and lacking inner consistency, his picture nevertheless shows a creative departure from the

159. R. L. P. Milburn, *Early Christian Interpretations of History* (Bampton Lectures, 1952), London, 1954, pp. 76–88; cf. J. Chaux-Ruy, *Saint Augustin: temps et histoire*, Paris, 1956, chs. 5–6.

160. Concerning secular or terrestrial history, Augustine made noticeably little of the Roman high point under Augustus at the time of the Nativity (*Civ. Dei* XVIII, 46); he dwelt, rather, on the inevitable decay to befall the empire: W. Rehm, *Untergang*, pp. 22–7. On the other hand, the sixth Age, though senescent and witness to the downfall of the Jews, contains within it the Incarnation and the growth of God's City *qua* Church; *De Gen. con. Manich.* I,23 (col. 192). On the complex development of Augustine's ideas about world history, see F. E. Cranz, "The Development of Augustine's Ideas on Society before the Donatist Controversy" in *Harvard Theological Review* LVIII, 1954, pp. 255ff.; Funkenstein, op. cit., pp. 37ff.

161. *Expositio in librum Iob, sive moralium libri XXV* i,12, 19 (*PL*, vol. 76, col. 108). For the use of the life-cycle analogy to convey the progress of spiritual knowledge, see, e.g., Tertullian *De virginibus velandis* I; and (much later) John of Salisbury (12th century) *Historia pontificalis, prolog.* 2.

162. In passing, note the Age theory of Anselm of Havelberg: *Dialogi* I,5f. (*PL*, vol. 188, cols. 1147a–1149b), with the sixth Age (of the Holy Spirit, and of the present) being one of renewal.

163. G. Boas, op. cit., p. 181; cf. Philipp's *De somno regis Nabuchodoser* (*PL*, vol. 203, cols. 586–8).

164. Augustine's eighth Age was only infrequently referred to in medieval literature: e.g., Rabanus Maurus *Lib. de comp.* xcvi (*PL*, vol. 107, col. 728a).

## Diagram X Age Theory in Philipp van Haveng

| Ages | Metal Parts of the Image | Qualities of each Age |
|---|---|---|
| 1. Adam to Noah | Gold (head) | GOOD (glorious and excellent, knowing only the natural law to love God and man) |
| 2. Noah to Abraham | Silver (breast and arms)[1] | BAD (because of its evil, it received the Deluge)[2] |
| 3. Abraham to Moses (modifying the Augustinian scheme)[3] | Bronze (stomach, thighs)[4] | GOOD (an Age of "patience and fortitude," of the patriarchs' faith)[5] |
| 4. Moses to David (modifying the Augustinian scheme)[3] | Iron (legs) | GOOD (with illustrious men) |
| 5. David to the Advent (modifying the Augustinian scheme)[6] | Mud and Clay, trying to be conjoined with Iron (feet) | BAD (no concord between Gentiles and Jews) |
| 6. Advent to the end of the apostolic mission | The shattering of the statue by a stone | GOOD (the preaching of the Gospel) |
| 7. The time of the AntiChrist | (feet of Iron and Clay again!) (Iron = strong Church, yet Clay = eschatological troubles) | BAD (great tribulation) |

1. Philipp separated the symbolic significance of the breast and arms, and though the latter belongs to the silver part of the image he applied the arms to the third Age of Abraham to Moses.
2. He seems to be in difficulties here! He fastens onto events at the beginning of this Age; thus the punishment for its evil is, curiously, at its commencement.
3. In Augustine's primary model, Moses is not mentioned and the third Age runs to David; in Philipp's schema the Exile is omitted.
4. Philipp considered the bronze stomach to symbolize the men of that time lapse which ran from Moses to apostolic times, i.e., from the third to the sixth Age.
5. This Age must be taken to include Abraham's wanderings, while the second Age is probably meant to end at his calling.
6. Philipp here may be thinking more about the latter half of this *aetas* rather than the former, which saw the continuation of the Davidic monarchy. It is probable that this Age begins with David's death, however, and that Philipp understood most of the post-Davidic kings to be compromisers with Gentile ways, and thus creators of tension within Judaism.

Augustinian standard,[165] and reflects an attempt, however unwitting and obscure, to write a special pattern of recurrence into Salvation History. The Ages have been tied in with what we shall soon find to be a popular medieval conception (though with a classical background), that history consists of vicissitude, or of fluctuations between favorable and adverse conditions.

Philipp was not tampering with the most momentous doctrines of the Christian faith, perhaps, for interest in the Ages of the world was relatively peripheral in medieval theology. On the other hand, by the end of the twelfth century the traditional Augustinian frame had so outlived its usefulness that new questioning and attempts at reinterpretation brought the theology of history, as a debatable issue, closer to the center of the stage. The figure chiefly responsible for this shift was the theologian of the *Spiritualis intellectus*, the breakaway Calabrian ascetic Joachino di Fiore (ca. 1132–1202).

Like most theologians of his day, Joachim was not concerned with history for its own sake; yet if his deepest desire was to comprehend the mystery of the Trinity,[166] he thought he saw his hopes being realized by using an historical exegesis. Joachim, as is well known, divided world history into three periods, the three *statūs* or great Stages of the Father, Son, and Holy Spirit. This triad of history was certainly not a fresh discovery, it has a background not only in ancient literature but in medieval theology as well.[167] What is not always realized, too, is that his schema was a serious modification, rather than a replacement, of the Augustinian seven-Age model. With the triadic framework, moreover, he propagated the idea of a "providential progress toward an historical *eschaton*,"[168] and Joachim certainly held this view more convincingly than Augustine: he firmly located future eschatological happenings in the known historical order.[169] Joachim, then, historicized eschatology. If under the first dis-

165. On the relative fossilization of Augustinian theological yardsticks by Carolingian times, see H. von Schubert, *Geschichte der christlichen Kirche im Frühmittelalter*, Tübingen, 1921, pp. 447ff.

166. M. Reeves, *The Influence of Prophecy in the Late Middle Ages: A Study in Joachimism*, Oxford, 1969, pp. 23–6, 30.

167. For rather distant background see Varro in Censorinus *Die natal.* XXI,1ff. (see above, Section D, n. 96); Gal. 3:23–9; Rom. 4:9ff.; *Sanhedrin* (*Bab. Tal.*) 97a; *Avoda Zara* 9a; *Seder Eliahu Rabba* (ed. M. Friedmann, Jerusalem, 1960 edn.) 6; *Pesiqta*, in S. R. Driver and A. Neubauer (eds.), *The Fifty-third Chapter of Isaiah according to the Jewish Interpreters* (*I: Texts*), Oxford, 1876, p. 11. Cf. Marcellus of Ancyra, Frgs. 67, 71, 117, 121 (Klostermann edn.), on "economic Trinitarianism." On Trinitarian modalism in medieval theology, i.e., doctrines of three successive revelations, the third being associated with the outpouring of the Spirit, see P. Lehmann, "Mittelalter und Küchenlatein" in *Historische Zeitschrift* CXXXVII, 1928, p. 204 (though Rupert of Deutz, important here, is not discussed). On the Age of the Spirit in Anselm of Havelberg, see n. 162 above, and note also Aquinas' more static conception of the angelic order as an Age or *aevum* between time and eternity: cf. F. H. Brabant, *Time and Eternity in Christian Thought* (Bampton Lectures, 1936), London, 1937, p. 37.

168. Löwith, op. cit., p. 146; cf. W. Kamlah, *Apokalypse und Geschichtstheologie: die mittelalterliche Auslegung der Apokalypse vor Joachim von Fiore* (*Historische Studien CCLXXXV*), Berlin, 1935, esp. pt. 3, chs. 3 and 4, for background.

169. For Augustine the *civitas Dei* was only realizable upon the genuine "death" of the known historical order. *Mors seculi* was the phrase used by Augustinians to refer to the end of the sixth Age; see, e.g., Bede *De temp.* xvi (PL, vol. 107, col. 1112d); Rabanus Maurus *Lib. de comp.* xcvi (vol. 107, col. 728a). Cf. T. E. Mommsen, "St. Augustine and the Christian Idea of Progress: The

pensation of the Father, God's faithful ones had been slaves to the Law, and if under the second or "clerical order" they were more nearly, though incompletely, spiritual, the passage of history prefigured a new, free, deinstitutionalized and imminent Age of the Spirit. How much easier was it for an Italian monk to make such a claim in the twelfth century than for an African bishop who had just heard disturbing news about Alaric's sack of Rome in 410! However, it has not been enough stressed that within Joachim's treatment of known past history, quite apart from his anticipations of a "contemplative order" to come, there is an evident interest in recurring as well as in linear patterns. History progressed stage by stage as if along a pathway,[170] but that did not mean that certain stages or substages failed to share common elements, authenticating God's providence.

Joachim did not dispense with the Great Week model, but he divided the sixth Age into six smaller periods (*etatulae*) and is reported to have taken his own times to be at the end of the fifth *etatula*.[171] The first five grand Ages ran, as conventionally, from Adam to Christ, and beginning from Abraham they also formed the stage (*status*) of the Father. The real problem, which arose with the present Age, was quite naturally a pressing one for an exploratory mind in the twelfth century. The last hopes of a 6000-year-old historical order were dying after 1000 AD,[172] and the sixth Age of the Augustinian scheme was already top-heavy with momentous events, including the establishment of the Roman curia's "plenitude of power." Old ideas were crying out for readjustment and Joachim met the challenge. His ultimate optimism toward future temporal events was hardly Augustinian, and the same may be said of his approach to the "middle stage" of history. The traditional picture of Christian phenomena at the end of history was reoriented, Christ's coming being placed more in the center of world events than toward their culminating point. This is true for Joachim, however, much more in the sense that the present Age (either *aetas* or *status*) was "the Son's Age" and much less in the sense that Christ's first coming was in the middle of chronological time (*die Mitte der Zeit*), to use Conzelmann's (false) characterization of Lukan theology.[173] In any case, this new perspective, together with Joachim's extensive historicization of eschatology,[174] suggested

Background of *The City of God*" in his *Medieval and Renaissance Studies* (ed. E. F. Rice, Jr.), Ithaca, 1959, pp. 265ff.

170. Cf. Joachim's important diagram in *Concordia Novi ac Veteris Testamenti* II,1 (Venice, 1519 edn., reissued Frankfurt, 1964, p. 14, cols. 3f.).

171. Robert of Auxerre in *MGH*, *Scriptores*, vol. 26, pp. 148f.; cf. Joachim *Concord.* III,1 (p. 25, col. 1); Reeves, op. cit., pp. 40f.

172. It was under serious questioning in the West as early as the ninth century: Rabanus Maurus, *Enarrationem in epistolas Beati Pauli* xxv,1 (*PL*, vol. 112, col. 657d). Cf. n.154 above.

173. Against O. Köhler, "Der Neue Äon" in *Saeculum* XII, 1961, pp. 188–90, who places too much emphasis on the connection between Joachim's basic schema and the BC/AD interests of the chronologists.

174. Joachim was not very specific about coming "political" events in the Last Age, but at least he refers to the conversion of the Jews (cf. Reeves, op. cit., pp. 6, 47). Could we expect more details? The seventh Age is to be without the political institutions of the old order—unless monasteries are to remain—and the shift from a (Hebrew) synagogal to a (Christian) clerical order foreshadowed this. For background on the idea of this shift see John Scotus Erigena (see F. L. Griffith, loc. cit., p. 191a); Rupert of Deutz *In librum Ecclesiastes commentarius* (*PL*, vol. 168, col. 1200c).

ways of reconceptualizing historical periodization in keeping with the changing scene. One may even claim that it was a seminal development behind the now ever-present distinction between ancient, medieval, and modern times. Joachim's stage of the Son, for instance, was something of a theological prototype of the secular, cultural concept of an *intermedia aetas*. When Petrarch emerges in the Trecento, extolling antiquity, lamenting post-Roman times, and occasionally anticipating a coming Age of Gold, we might almost be persuaded that he appropriated a Joachite framework for new purposes, and that his projected Age of Gold is the secular paradigm of Joachim's "contemplative order."[175]

Joachim may seem a medieval with modern implications, but there are a great many traditional qualities about his work. What gives him a special flavor is his historical exegesis; and the elaborate patterns he extracted from the biblical and ecclesiastical past are of particular interest to us. The future Age of the Spirit set aside, he elicited recurrences from both within and between the first two (definitely historical) stages of the Father and the Son.[176] To begin with, because Joachim held orthodox views about the procession of the Holy Spirit and the begetting of the Son, he attempted to detect the operations of the three Persons within each *status*. Here the rôle of historical personages becomes important. The first *status* strictly began with Abraham, from the second *aetas*, and seeing the establishment of the *Ordo conjugatorum* (the union of God's people under the Law), it ended at the Incarnation. But it had its proleptic representative in Adam, the first man.[177] The second *status*, occupying the sixth *aetas*, witnesses the *Ordo clericorum* (the dispensation of the Church), but again, Joachim locates the real commencement of this order as far back as Isaiah in the *status* of the Father. The third *status*, occupying the last Age, will be the time of the last order, the *Ordo monachorum* (monastic piety) but, in keeping with the doctrine of the double procession of the Holy Spirit, it has two precursory representatives, Elisha and Benedict in the *statūs* of the Father and the Son, respectively.[178]

Not only do we discover an element of recurrence in the sense that with each great Stage one finds the apparent incubation of the next, as Norman Cohn has so neatly put it,[179] but striking parallels are extracted at least from the first two. Elisha, who marks the beginning of the third Stage, lived twenty-three generations from Adam (following Matthew's genealogy of the *Ordo clericorum*), yet Isaiah, who marks the beginning of the second *status*, can also be said to live twenty-three generations after Adam (according to Luke's genealogy of the *Ordo monachorum*).[180] From Abraham to Christ, and from Christ to the projected

175. On Age theory from Joachim to Petrarch, see Excursus 4.

176. Joachim's forms of recurrence thinking led M. V. Bloomfield to write, not inaccurately, about his combinations of "cycle and pattern": "Joachim of Flora: A Critical Study of his Canon, Teachings, Sources, Biography and Influence" in *Traditio* XIII, 1957, p. 268.

177. That the Trinity is considered in relative detachment from the Creation here (e.g., from speculation about the *Logos*), further testifies to Joachim's historicizing tendencies.

178. Esp. *Concord.* II,1 (p. 8, col. 4; p. 9, cols. 1,4; p. 10, col. 1).

179. *Op. cit.*, p. 101 (this element looking ahead to one of Marx's models).

180. *Concord.* II,1 (p. 11, col. 3; cf. cols. 1f.).

beginning of the last *status*, lie two intervals each spanning forty-two generations, and the same number of generations separated the two important figures of Elisha and Benedict.[181] Elijah (whose relationship with Elisha symbolized for Joachim the procession of the Holy Spirit from the Son) returns to history as John the Baptist, to effect the formal beginning of the second *status*.[182] There were other, similar recurrences besides, once again conveyed through parallels between history's great Stages. Seven persecutions against God's ancient people, for instance, were followed by seven against the Church;[183] Jewish kings and synagogues were paralleled by Christian emperors and churches.[184] Within the first *status*, to take another case, Joachim also detected the alternating influence of the Son and the Spirit as embodied in the seven great prophets and the seven great kings of the Old Testament.[185] And so Joachim proceeded, demonstrating that significant events and characteristics in one great Stage had counterparts in another, recurrences which impressed a divine stamp on salvation history.

There is a danger in casting Joachim as one mainly concerned with historical recurrences, when he is so much better known for his allegory and for a kind of figurative exegesis which is only of marginal interest to us here.[186] Yet although he had certainly not divested himself of theological superstructures, his methods and enthusiasms nevertheless show some genuine interest in the facts of historiography and their special relationships. Perhaps the Joachites who followed clung to their divine numbers and quaint theological models, but they could also produce some important insights. Batholomew of Pisa's division of history into seven Ages BC and seven AD, for example,[187] reflects a greater appreciation of general configurations of Western history from the fall of Rome to the supremacy of *Respublica Christiana*. His detailed identification of the Ages by the

181. II,1 (p. 11, col. 4 to p. 12, col. 2). Out of keeping with the tables of II,1 (p. 11, col. 3 to p. 12, col. 1), Joachim argues for three sets of time lapses, 21 generations in length (Adam to Jacob, to Isaiah, to Christ), in IV (p. 43, col. 3). Cf. II,3 (pp. 17f., cols. 3ff.).

182. Esp. *Tractatus super quatuor Evangelica* (Fonti per la Storia d'Italia, Istituto Storico Italiano, Rome, 1930), p. 23, *l*.21 to p. 24, *l*.16 (a case of special translation, not metempsychosis). For background see Matt. 11:10, 14; Luke 7:27; Tertullian *De anima* xxxv.

183. *Concord.* I (p. 5, cols. 2–4); cf. *Expositio prophetiae anonymae Romae repertae anno 1184* (MS Ant., 322), fol. 150c (OT persecutions: Egyptians/Midianites/other nations/Assyrians/Chaldeans/Medes and Persians/Greeks; and against the Church: Jews/Pagans/Arians/Goths/Vandals/Alemani/Lombards). Joachim departed from Eusebius' model of five or ten persecutions (*Martyrs of Palestine* I,1ff., IX,1ff.; cf. Sulpicius Severus *Sacrae historiae* II,33; *Vita S. Martini* xxxiii; Orosius *Hist.* VII,26f., and (on the East) J. Moreau, "Observations sur l'ΥΠΟΜΝΗΣΤΙΚΟΝ ΒΙΒΛΙΟΝ 'ΙΩΣΗΠΠΤΟΥ" in *Byzantion* XXV–XXVII, 1955–57, pp. 263–7), though his manner of eliciting parallels between the Testaments is not dissimilar to Orosius'.

184. Reeves, op. cit., p. 303. Rome was founded at the time of king Uzziah and of Isaiah, at the beginning of the second *status* (*Concord.* II,1, col. 3), coming to an end as an empire, along with the *Ordo clericorum*, once the third *status* was ushered in.

185. *Concord.* III,1 (p. 17, col. 1).

186. E.g. (on the allegorical relationships developed between Abraham and Zechariah, Sarah and Elizabeth, Isaac and John), II,1 (p. 8, col. 1); *Tract. quat. evang.*, p. 24, *l*.27 to p. 25, *l*.22. Many other examples could be given.

187. *De conformitate vitae beatae Francisci ad vitam Dominis Jesu* (*Analecta Franciscana* IV, 1906), pp. 75–8.

names of their key historical representatives developed an old theme in a manner much more suggestive of recurrence, with his impressive trio of Adam, Christ, and St. Francis.[188] And in their hopes for an imperial savior, whether a Hohenstaufen or Charlemagne *redivivus*, later Joachites became more specific in their historicization of the Last Things.[189] More impressive developments, however, came with the humanists.

### *Early humanism*

In the pages of a fascinating letter by the early humanist Coluccio Salutati (1331–1406) one finds a quite new perspective on traditional Age theory. His position is a development of lines already suggested in late medieval thought, although Salutati also addressed himself to new problems posed by a resurgent interest in the classics. Writing to Zonari (Chancellor of Bologna), he sought to rebuff the charge that Virgil's widely acclaimed *Fourth Eclogue* contained heretical cyclical notions contrary to the doctrine of Christian salvation.[190] Salutati contended that ideas close to Virgil's could be found in the oracles of the Cumaean Sibyl and in Ecclesiastes.[191] In defending a cyclical view of history, however, he subscribed neither to Stoicism nor to neo-Pythagoreanism—though the distinction between these two would have passed him by. He readily admitted that "nothing returns in precisely the same form," yet somewhat analogously to nature, human affairs had a certain periodicity and "every day," he insisted, "we see some image of the past renewed."[192]

The extraordinary thing is that instead of justifying this view from classical historiography Salutati attempted to placate his opponent by resorting to the Great Week model.[193] He accepted the basic Augustinian framework of seven Ages, but his modifications, though small, are highly significant. The beginning of each Age was marked by "miraculous creations" and the end by notable slaughters, so that Salutati's picture of world history is marked by a certain *alternatio*[194] (see Diagram XI). Historical processes were cyclical enough for the defence of Virgil, at least for the Virgil who announced the return of general

188. The fourteen Ages or "Seals" and their special representatives are: Adam-Noah (Adam)/Noah-Abraham (Noah)/Abraham-Moses (Abraham)/Exodus (Moses)/David-Elijah (David)/Elijah-Exile (Elijah)/Exile-Maccabees (Simon)/Onias the last of the old, the Incarnation denoting a new order in the middle of history/John the Baptist-Pentecost (Christ)/Pentecost-Nero (Paul)/Nero-Constantine (St. Antony)/Constantine-Benedict (St. Laurence)/Barbarian Invasions (St. Benedict)/Age of Frederick II (1206) (St. Francis). For background on the naming of key figures see, e.g., Irenaeus *Adv. Haer.* IV,lviii,1f., 9 (5 Ages); Berengaudus, *Expositio super septem visiones libri Apocalypsis* (*PL*, vol. 17, cols. 934ff.); Otto of Freising *Chron. hist. Duab. civ.* VIII,14 (7 Ages).

189. Reeves, op. cit., pp. 302–392; cf. pp. 170, 302, 327, 385 esp.

190. *Epistolae*, 5 May 1379 (in E. Emerton, *Humanism and Tyranny: Studies in the Italian Trecento*, Cambridge, 1925, pp. 300–4).

191. Ibid., pp. 303f.

192. P. 305. He quoted Eccles. 1:10 (on p. 304), the passage Augustine claimed had been misused by Origen: *Civ. Dei* XII,13; cf. Origen *Contr. Cels.* IV,12.

193. Domenico Silvestri, asked by Salutati to write to Zonari earlier, had been rather too contentious on this issue: cf. B. L. Ullmann, *The Humanism of Coluccio Salutati* (*Medioevo e Umanesimo IV*), Padua, 1963, p. 54.

194. *Epist.* (Emerton, p. 306).

Diagram XI Salutati's Age Theory

| Ages | Miracles | Slaughters |
|---|---|---|
| 1. Adam to Noah | Creation of Man | The Deluge |
| 2. Noah to Abraham | The preservation of Noah | Sodom and Gomorrah |
| 3. Abraham to David | The preservation of Lot before Abraham's journey | Saul's death (= Gilboa) |
| 4. David to the Exile | Preservation of David from Saul's fury | The Babylonian exile |
| 5. Exile to Incarnation | Preservation of Daniel and the three children | Slaughter of the Innocents, Roman Civil Wars[1] |
| 6. Incarnation to Judgment | The New Man, Christ, created | Final conflagration |

1. The only entrance of secular history into the schema.

conditions, the Virgil of Servius and the medievals, if not for the neo-Pythagorean who anticipated the veritable recurrence of Achilles and Troy. Of supreme importance here is that the Great Week model comes to confirm rather than to weaken the case for historical cyclicism. It is Salutati who demonstrates so clearly why a cyclical view of history, or one which conceives of cyclical movements within a history delimited by Creation and the End, was neither logically nor ideologically incompatible with the Christian world view. We must insist, however, that he merely articulated what was already inherent in Christian interpretations of history. Only the self-honesty and antiauthoritarianism of an early Renaissance humanist could dispel all those old anxieties about philosophers "gyrating in a maze."

Notions of successive Ages and certain subsidiary ideas of recurrence, then, were carried on in the Christian theology of history. Although stemming mainly from biblical literature, patristic and medieval Age theory was enriched by related classical conceptions of the "metal" Ages, for instance, the *saeculum*, the body-state analogy, even a special language of circularity—and it is thus a witness to the intersecting of recurrence ideas from two traditions. This is not meant to gloss over the limits of the integration nor the distinctive qualities of Christian speculation on these matters. The cyclical side of Christian Age theory was not frequently stressed, the idea of any eternal recurrence of eons was considered anathema, and both biblical imagery and typological hermeneutics often had a heavy influence. Even with Salutati's picture we have these same Christian characteristics, although he was more undaunted than his predecessors in espousing a cyclical view of history.

## E. The rise, fall, and succession of empires: Patristic and medieval themes

According to Daniel, four kingdoms (probably the Chaldean, Median, Persian, and Greek) emerged on earth one after another. Under the influence of biblical apocalypticism, the early Christians naturally became interested in this imperial succession as a key to world history.[195] One of the earliest commentators was the Roman Hippolytus (ca. 170–ca. 236). In the four beasts of the sea from Dan. 7:3–8 and in the multi-metallic image of Dan. 2:36–45 he saw the four great monarchies of Babylon, Media-Persia, Greece, and, most significantly, Rome. And he looked to a final imperishable kingdom to come.[196]

Now some pagan historians had already accepted a scheme of four impermanent world monarchies, with an eternal fifth to come (sect. A). Christian writers, implacably opposed to a pagan empire, were happy to reinforce a pre-existing school of "opposition history,"[197] and they relied above all on Daniel to give their position a divine validity. It was of course Jerome's *Commentarii in Danielem* which came to represent the most authoritative exegesis for medieval writers. Though it expanded earlier and simpler interpretations and removed some of their punch with too much detail,[198] the central doctrine remained. Human history since Abraham (whose lifetime marked the foundation of the Assyrian or first Babylonian régime) experienced the successive emergence of four world empires. Jerome did not dilate on conceptions of rise and fall or growth and decay, yet the assumption of a recurring emergence and waning of great dynasties was built into this schema, and this is most evident in his explicit anticipations of Rome's collapse.[199] His line reflects the weight of his biblical learning: rise and fall have far less to do with the curve of the biological principle than the plain fragility and recurrent dissipation of all human things.

This kind of exegesis on Daniel had an extensive history through the Middle Ages.[200] One early modification of the schema bears attention: it is connected with Augustine, and it further highlights that thorny problem of distinguishing between succession and recurrence. As early as the second century BC, the poet Ennius had suggested that Rome was founded in the year of Assyria's downfall,[201] and this notion was probably reproduced in the pages of Varro.[202]

195. For waning interest in history among the Jewish rabbis (mainly because it had degenerated into a succession of pagan empires), see J. Neusner, "The Religious Uses of History: Judaism in First-Century AD Palestine and Third-Century Babylonia" in *History and Theory* V, 1966, p. 171.

196. *Comm. in Dan.* (Frgs.) I, III. Hippolytus may have treated the four world empires in close conjunction with the Great Week model (IV), but it is a popular misconception to see these frameworks sitting together throughout the medieval period (for they are not that compatible).

197. Swain, loc. cit., pp. 18ff. Cf. esp. Justin *Hist.* xxix,2, xxx,3f., xxxiv,1, 3, etc.

198. I,ii,31/5 (*CCSL*, vol. 75A, p. 794, *ll.*388–401) on Dan. 2; and II,vii,4–7a (pp. 839–42) on Dan. 7.

199. Esp. *Epistulae* CXXVII,3, 12.

200. For the many references see H. H. Rowley, *Darius the Mede and the Four World Empires in the Book of Daniel*, Oxford, 1935, pp. 74–6.

201. *Ann.*, Frg. 501 (Vahlen), the year being estimated as 880 BC.

202. In Augustine *Civ. Dei* XVIII,22; cf. Swain, loc. cit., p. 14.

Augustine exploited it with refreshing vigor. He not only implied that Rome was the true dynastic heir of the first great empire (a view which doubtless preceded him),[203] but he also referred to Rome as the "second Babylon" and to Babylon as the "first Rome."[204] He thus simplified the older four-part schema into two, both Babylons representing the Earthly City (*Civitas terrana*) from post-diluvian times until his own day. This city, Augustine insisted, was built immediately after the Deluge. It was not raised by Semiramis, King Ninus' mother, as Trogus had claimed; nor was it merely a very old Assyrian city, after Orosius.[205] Semiramis may have repaired it (*Civ. Dei* XVIII,2), but its true beginnings were in the tower of Babel (= Babylon), and its originators were "the wicked" (XVI,11). Babylon eventually took the form of the Assyrian empire, lasting until the reign of the Judean Hezekiah. It endured just short of a millennium, and, most significantly of all, collapsed at the very time when Romulus founded Rome (XVIII,22).

On the one hand, then, Augustine disclosed the continuity of the Earthly City, yet on the other he taught the parallel rise and dissolution of the two Babylons. The relative tension between ideas of progression and repetition recalls the Chronicler (see Chapter 3). In Augustine's case, however, we are not dealing with one cultural tradition, but with a special kind of succession—both a transmission of power and the recurrence of broadly conceived phenomena. Recurrent rise and fall was reinforced by Augustine's stress on "the mutability of the human estate" (e.g., XVII,13). By this second idea he meant to stress not history's infinite variety but its frequent turns of fortune, its vicissitudes, of which the rise and fall of great empires was the choicest example. That was a view which became very popular in the medieval centuries.

The tension between progressionism and the idea of recurrence was sharpened in subsequent world-monarchy theory. Following his north African mentor, Orosius (early fifth century) contended that there had been two great empires, the Assyrian and the Roman, one collapsing and the other originating during the same "reign." Orosius, however, played more mysteriously with chronology. He noted, for instance, that between the first year of Ninus' reign and the restoration of Babylon by Semiramis, and between the first year of the reign of Procas, Assyria's last king, and the time when Romulus founded Rome, there were two parallel time intervals, each sixty-four years in length (*Hist.* II,2). With a characteristically patristic approach, Orosius labored the recurrence of specified time intervals. He took the two great satellite empires of Macedonia and Carthage to have each lasted seven hundred years. The great power of Babylon, by contrast, if one calculated its duration from its origins to its conquest by Cyrus, lasted twice that length, and a similar estimate seems to have been given

203. *Civ. Dei* XVIII,22, 27, etc.

204. XVIII,2, 22. Of some (often overplayed) background importance is 1 Pet. 5:13, Rev. 14:8, 16:19.

205. Trogus in Justin *Hist.* I,2; Orosius *Hist.* II,2. On Augustine's implicit criticism of Orosius (*Civ. Dei* XI–XXII being written after the latter's *Historia*), and on Orosius' unAugustinian tendencies, cf. T. E. Mommsen, "Orosius and Augustine" in op. cit., pp. 329ff.

to the life span of Rome. Rome, according to Orosius, was almost extinguished by fire during the 700th year of its existence (53 BC?), that is, halfway through its career. It was also seriously afflicted by the Goths in the same year of its existence as that of Babylon when laid waste by the Medes, and a comparable doom to Babylon's was not far off.[206]

For Orosius, all these facts made it "clearer that God is the one ruler of Ages, kingdoms, and places." God's providence was certainly reflected in history's continuity, especially in the transference of rôles and properties from one empire to another, the secondary régimes included. On the other hand, it was also confirmed by patterns of recurrence, by duplicated time lapses too remarkable to be coincidental, and by the repeated appearance and dissolution of the great states.

It was in fact Orosius' representation of the two supreme and two "guardian" empires, as well as his account of the imperial inheritance, which formed the basis for what is known as medieval *translatio* theory. The intellectual background to this set of ideas is quite complex. For certain Fathers, especially for the Latins Tertullian and Augustine, Rome was wickedness incarnate, a phenomenon to be swept away by God; for such writers as Origen and Jerome it was no more than a tool for making salvation available to countless men.[207] Others contemplated the promise of a Christianized empire, and they weakened the strong stance on eschatology and Roman degeneration. The transition is nicely illustrated by Lactantius. While persecuted by Diocletian, Lactantius quoted gloomy verses from the Sibylline books, Seneca, and pseudo-Hydaspes without compunction, and prophesied the return of world domination to the Orient.[208] On Constantine's rise to power in 312 his tune changed, and he prefaced a later work with rhetorical phrases about a great restoration and a divine victory for the servants of God, even about "perpetual peace."[209]

His contemporary, Eusebius of Caesarea, waxed even more enthusiastic about the new situation. If the Incarnation had once coincided with the *Pax Romana*, a "close parallel between the victory of Christian monotheism and the growth of the Roman Monarchy" had now become clear.[210] For Eusebius, indeed, Constantine's reign was the Golden Age returned. After the Flood, which was the last of many great "cataclysms and conflagrations" inflicted upon wicked mankind long floundering in bestiality and polyarchic disorder, the first monarchical empire—that of Assyria—emerged. Out of this empire the righteous Abra-

206. *Hist.* II,1, VII,2. The two secondary empires of Macedonia and Carthage arose from the north and south, while Assyria and Rome sprang from the east and west (I,1f.). The first two came as "protectors and guardians" while supremacy was being transferred to the Romans, these two being "accepted by the power of time, not [as with Assyria and Rome] by the law of inheritance" (II,1).

207. Cf. Rehm, op. cit., pp. 20–6 (other minor figures of pertinence being Melito of Sardis, Arnobius, and Minucius Felix).

208. *Div. inst.* VII,xv; cf. *De ira Dei* xxiii.

209. *De mortibus persecutorum* i, and cf. lii; Eusebius *Hist. eccles.* X,iv,72.

210. Mommsen, "St. Augustine" in op. cit., p. 283; cf. Eusebius *Hist.* X.

ham had been called. He was a practitioner of the "true religion" later obscured by Mosaic legalism. Now, due to the Incarnation, patriarchal spirituality had revived under Constantine—a "second Abraham"—though its effects were obviously far broader, and its context, within the last empire, different. "The essence of Eusebius' view was that the clock had been put back, that history was repeating itself," even if his ideas of recurrence were not those to suit neo-Pythagoreans or Stoics, since "now the 'bright intellectual daylight' had dawned and there was no night to follow."[211] Hopes for the Church's terrestrial future, then, did not discourage either Lactantius or Eusebius from appealing to notions often presumed to have been the exclusive province of their pagan adversaries.

These tendencies toward de-eschatologization were hardly without influence. Orosius, for one, felt the need to match Augustinian pessimism with hopes about the empire's future. "We are placed in the last time," he certainly admitted,[212] but he also believed that general human conditions were better with the steady Christianization of the Roman world (*Hist.* IV,12, V,1–2, 11, VII,35, etc.). He could afford to be less optimistic than Eusebius, however; since Constantine there had been persecutors and not just Christians at the helm of the empire, and despite the great reign of Theodosius I the possibility of further difficulties for the Church (and with the barbarian pressures, for the empire) was still present. In the main, Orosius was resigned to writing the history of vicissitudes, of "ups and downs" in affairs, with the eschaton as the only end of great moment. That was a position which took a grip on the medievals. It held on even when all Western rulers were avowedly Christian, because it linked biblical assumptions about temporal instabilities with continuing expectations of the Last Time.

Whether pessimistic or optimistic, patristic ideas of world history usually reflected intense interest in the city and empire of Rome. As conqueror of "the whole world," Rome had erected the last great imperial monolith. Yet the *caput mundi* and the Western empire actually experienced a fall in 476. A shock indeed! and there was still no evidence of the world's end. For those in the Eastern empire, of course, at least after the partition of 395, this thought-provoking eventuality had a ready-made explanation. The Byzantine emperor was accepted as "King of the Romans" and his city as "new Rome" or just as "Rome."[213] In the West adjustments did not come so easily, although the doctrine of Rome as the last empire was not abandoned,[214] and it even gathered

211. *Hist. eccles.* I,ii,19–23, iv,5ff.; D. S. Wallace-Hadrill, *Eusebius of Caesarea*, London, 1960, p. 183, and cf. pp. 169, 173–8, 182–4; Funkenstein, op. cit., pp. 31ff.

212. Rehm, op. cit., p. 28 (the world being at that time 5,618 years old, the notion of the six millennia of history had a greater hold over Orosious than Augustine).

213. W. Hammer, "The Concept of the New or Second Rome in the Middle Ages" in *Speculum* XIX, 1944, pp. 51f.

214. *Quandiu stat Colisaeus, stat et Roma/Quando cadet Colisaeus, cadet et Roma/Qando cadet Roma, cadet et mundus*: pseudo-Bede *Excerptiones patrum, collectanea flores ex diversis, quaestiones et parabolae* (*PL*, vol. 94, col. 543).

a new momentum after the "dark ages." As early as the *Chronica* of Marianus Scotus in the ninth century the idea of an imperial translation from the old Rome to the northern Frankish dominion makes its appearance.[215] The decisive factor in giving feasibility and logical force to the doctrine of transferral of rule was, of course, the crowning of Charlemagne as Holy Roman Emperor in 800. Aachen became the new Rome, as subsequently did Ottonian Trier.[216] The translation of the Roman empire, it was at last contended, passed successively from the Franks to the Germans,[217] high medieval and later theorists viewing Byzantium as the imperial custodian between the fall of pagan Rome and 800.[218] As Walter Rehm cogently argues, old patristic notions of degeneration had been transformed into a doctrine of continuity in European history, and although eschatology was still in the background, the vision of this continuity suggested the possibility of "newness" in the historical order, of a new Rome and a new European unity.[219] These shifts force one to ask whether older notions of rise and fall had slowly become modified into a more definitely successionist viewpoint to which no sense of historical recurrence appertains. The effect of Christian progressionism admitted, however, it cannot be proven that the idea of imperial rise and fall was either consciously modified or suppressed.

Perhaps the figure most usefully studied in an effort to clarify some of the key issues here is Otto of Freising (ca. 1110–1158), a man of royal blood and Cistercian training, bishop from 1138 on, participant in the Second Crusade, and famed author of the *Gesta Friderici* on the deeds of Frederick Barbarossa. In Otto's *Chronicon* on the "two cities," which was a universal chronicle beginning as far back as Adam and finishing as far forward as the mid-twelfth century, one discovers the same tensions of thought just discussed. Otto retained the "pessimism" toward history of one accepting the imminence of the eschaton (cf. *Chron.* II,13 *finis*),[220] but at the same time he claimed that the City of God had now progressed to the point of almost exterminating the City of Earth, history virtually becoming the history of the Church (V,*prolog.*)[221] Otto espoused the

215. W. Goez, *Translatio Imperii: ein Beitrag zur Geschichte des Geschichtsdenken und der politischen Theorien im Mittelalter und der frühen Neuzeit*, Tübingen, 1958, pp. 194ff.

216. On Aachen see Modoin, MGH, *Poet.*, vol. 1, p. 390 (esp. vss.24–7); Angilbertus, MGH, *Script.*, vol. 2, p. 395 (cf. *Poet.*, vol. 1, p. 368). On Trier see Anonymous, *Vita S. Deicoli* in MGH, *Script.*, vol. 15, pt. 2, p. 676; Anonymous, *Gesta Treverorum*, MGH, *Script.*, vol. 8, p. 135. Cf. Hammer, loc. cit., pp. 56–9 for other texts.

217. Esp. Otto of Freising *Chron. hist. duab. civ.* VI,24. In the following analysis I used the edition of C. Urstisius in *Germaniae historicorum illustrium*, Frankfurt, 1670, pp. 1–194, Hofmeister's edition not being available to me.

218. Otto IV,5, V; cf. Rodulfus Glaber *Historiarum sui temporis libri quinque* I,ii f., iv,16, and on Andreas of Regensburg (15th century), see H. Brack, "Bayerische Geschichtsverständnis im 15 Jahrhundert" in *Speculum Historiale* (ed. Bauer et al.), pp. 337f.

219. Op. cit., pp. 28f.

220. Along with other near-contemporaries such as St. Bernard (cf. Otto's *Gesta Frid.* I,37), Bernhard of Moles, Gualterus Mapes, Walter von der Vogelweide, Ekkehard of Aura, and Engelbert of Admont.

221. This progress was from Augustus to the present, Arianism and the disobedience of "Jews and Gentiles (= Muslims)" amounting only to passing setbacks. On hopes for future progress, see *Gesta* I,29, 44 (on the Second Crusade).

theory of translation of power from the old Rome to the Franks and the Germans, so that he could still hold Rome to be the last of four great empires (following the Assyro-Babylonian, the Medo-Persian, and the Macedonian, but not the Carthaginian, régimes).[222] The new Christian empire, however, illustrated the further diminution rather than the strengthening of the Earthly City.[223] The waning of the empire, then, exemplified the recurrent and inevitable fate befalling manmade institutions, whereas the progress of the Church reflected God's eternal strength and foreshadowed his ultimate victory. Otto held, in fact, that the Church, though not perfect, was a mixed state (*civitas permixta*) through which heaven intermingled with earth. In other words, it was the "great exception," the "mixed polity," enabling the Holy Roman Empire to forestall the decay natural to manmade institutions.[224]

On the nature of imperial succession in particular, lineal and recurrence notions present themselves in Otto's work without contradiction. He asserted, for example, that Rome succeeded Babylon as a son succeeds his father, and he thus took over the Augustinian view that when Babylon fell, Rome was born. Using both the body-state analogy and Orosius' idea of guardianship, he contended that the Persians and Greeks each protected and guided the Romans in turn, until, reaching "robust age," the Romans threw off the yoke of their teachers and claimed their inheritance (II,27). Again, in Rome's "extreme old age" the kingdom of the Franks was just commencing (IV,31 *finis*, 32), and at this stage the Eastern empire of Constantinople was the temporary custodian of the dominion which the Franks inherited through Charlemagne (V,31). Now there is an undeniable concern for directionalism in all this. Events form a procession heading toward a desirable end. On the other hand, the use of organic language invokes another way of thinking, and in his long story Otto did not fail to bring out recurrences.

In the first place, Otto paralleled stages and outstanding points in the careers of the two great empires of Assyro-Babylonia and Rome. The origin and dissipation of these régimes were similar: they both began to subjugate neighbors soon after their foundations, and they both reached a zenith, only to be very gradually brought low. In the processes of their degeneration, the taking over of the earlier empire by the Medes was just like the passing of the Roman rule to Constantine (IV,31). Before being brought low, both empires were "dishonored," the first by Artabus and the second by Alaric (IV,21; cf. 31),[225] and they were eventually "possessed" by foreigners, the former by Cyrus the Persian and the latter by Odovocar the barbarian (IV,31; cf. 30). The translations of power subsequent to these possessions were also paralleled (though in this

222. *Chron.* I,6ff., II,1ff., 25ff., 40ff.; cf. his letter to Rainhald, trans. by C. C. Mierow, "Introduction" to *The Two Cities: A Chronicle of Universal History to the Year 1146 AD by Otto, Biship of Freising* (ed. A. P. Evans and C. Knapp) (Records of Civilization), New York, 1928, pp. 29f.

223. *Chron.* IV,5, V,*prolog*.

224. For detailed discussion see Funkenstein, op. cit., pp. 97–100.

225. The reference to Alaric's dishonoring of Rome salvages the historical detail of Augustine's *De civitate Dei* from irrelevance.

case recurrence was more "horizontal" than "vertical"), for Otto claimed that Baghdad, an old center of the Turkish empire, was a part of ancient Babylon, just as medieval Rome was a part of the old one, and that Ecbatana, the newer royal city in the East, was comparable to the Carolingian Aachen (VI,3). The careers of the great empires, then, disclosed parallel configurations, and the patterns of their rise, fall, and changing fortunes were all within the divine plan.

A second way in which Otto educed historical recurrences was through repeatedly emphasizing the mutability of human affairs (*mutatio rerum*). The passing of empires was the grandest illustration of this changeableness, but it was also shown in the altered fortunes of great men,[226] and in recurring troubles which inflict themselves on any state.[227] Otto was happy to call the changing of fortune a *rotatus rerum*,[228] and to describe vicissitudes as *alterna mutatione* after the manner of the sea ("which is now lifted up by the increases that replenish it, now lowered by natural loss and waste" [II,51; cf. VI,*prolog.*]). Such up-and-down or overturning movements, Christian variants of fortune's wheel, lay at the heart of the historical process. Along with other medieval theologians, Otto denied that men were citizens of any "continuing city" (cf. Heb. 13:14), contrasting the everlasting stability of God and his city with a pageant of temporal flux.

To conclude, then. If the suspicion of philosophical cyclicism was endemic to patristic and medieval Christianity, that did not mean complete abandonment of ancient forms of pattern-making. There are enough views concerning successive Ages and recurrent rise and wane to permit the generalization that certain cyclical notions were firmly imbedded in Christian ways of doing and interpreting history. Expressions of mutability in medieval historiography confirm this judgment. In the West, for example, Orosius had no compunction in describing the troubles of mankind as "cycles of war" (*bellorum orbes*) (*Hist.* III,2), nor was Otto alone in likening historical change to tidal oscillations.[229] In the East, where politics admitted of less variation, historical change was often conceived in terms of the successive troubles affecting the Byzantine empire.[230] Why should it sound surprising, then, that the eminent Michael Psellus (ca. 1019–ca. 1078), philosopher, historian, and secretary of state to two Byzantine emperors, should blithely write of the empire's troubles as "irregular cyclical processes" (*anomalous anakuklēseis*), or as successive barbarian assaults which were deflected "like the waves of the sea" (*Chronographia* VI,72)?[231] And explicit

226. *Chron.* II,14 (on the death of Cyrus), 25 *finis* (on that of Alexander).

227. II,43 *finis*–44, 51 (on Rome from the Jugurthine War to Caesar).

228. II,25 (chapter heading); cf. VI,31 (on *mutatio* and *rotatio* as virtually synonymous).

229. Background: Philo *Quod Deus immut.* 175f.; Augustine *Civ. Dei* XIX,7; Orosius *Hist.* VI,14; cf., much later, Giovanni Colonna *Mare historiarum ab orbe condita ac sancti Galli regis Ludovici IX temporare* (14th century).

230. E.g., Procopius *Hup. polem.* I,iii,1ff., III,i,1f., V,i,9ff. (a determinative work); cf. (in the West) Augustine *Civ. Dei* XVII,13.

231. Also on recurrent troubles for the Church, see the literature on successive persecutions cited in n. 183 above; cf. (with more general statements) John Chrysostom *De providentia Dei* XVI,1–4; and XIV,2–16; Theodore Metochites *Historiae Romanae* in *Operum ex recensione, J. Meursi*

references to cycles illustrate how classical molds of recurrence informed medieval historiography, without denying that the Christian positions remain ideologically distinctive, and that notions of rise and fall, as well as political alternation, had already existed in the biblical tradition.

Not that our account of the penetration of cyclical ideas is complete. We have yet to deal more fully with the notion of fortune's wheel, which was tied in with doctrines of retribution (sect. G), and there are other special cases to consider.

## F. Special cases of cyclical thinking: Origen, Gemisthius Plethon, Nicephorus Gregoras

As we have already indicated, ideas of cosmic return had next to no Christian supporters. Perhaps some Christian intellectuals held terrestrial events to be determined by heavenly movement,[232] but the doctrine of an eternal recurrence based on planetary periodicity was decried. In the medieval West astrology may have been popular, but not as the basis for a philosophy of history,[233] and the doctrines of eternal return were touched on only rarely and superficially.[234] There were two important Eastern figures, nevertheless, who strove to come to terms with classical cosmologies—the patristic writer Origen (ca. 185–ca. 254), and Gemisthius Plethon (ca. 1355–ca. 1450), a neo-pagan from the end of the period under discussion. Both committed themselves to the doctrine of metempsychosis and a system of cosmic Ages. Origen the Christian, however, was sensitive about what the Bible did not permit. His theology allowed for numerous historical orders (*aiōnes*) both before and after the present one (a view based on Eccles. 1:8ff.; 2 Cor. 4:18; Eph. 2:7),[235] and he contended that throughout all Ages human souls rose and fell in a purificatory process which ended with union with God.[236] All such developments, however, lay between

(ed. J. Lami), Florence, 1746, vol. 7, pp. 791f., in the East; Augustine *Div. Dei* XVIII,52, in the West. Background: Josephus *Antiq.* XX,259f. With these writers, trouble or persecution has been abstracted into sets of conditions which recur; they are not merely listing like phenomena (e.g., as in Heb. 11 or Sidonius *Epistularum* V,vii,6).

232. E.g., among patristic writers, Lactantius *Div. inst.* VII,xiv (cols. 780ff.); Bardesanes *Coniunct. astr.* (pp. 161ff.); among medievals, Dante *Convivio* XIV,11; G. Villani *Chroniche Fiorentine* I,60, II,2; and among early moderns, Flavio Biondo *Historiarum ab inclinato Romanorum Decades* (1483), Basel, 1531 edn., p. 392.

233. Cf. T. O. Wendel, *The Mediaeval Attitude toward Astrology* (*Yale Studies in English* LX), New Haven, 1968; W.-E. Peuckert, *Astrologie*, Stuttgart, 1960, vol. 1, pp. 169ff.

234. E.g., Siger of Brabant *De aeternitate mundi* iii (cf. also Dante *Paradiso* XXXIII,137ff.), but Siger (some of whose works are admittedly lost) said next to nothing about historical processes except that the ancients lost all knowledge of former cycles. Probably he accepted Aristotelian catastrophe theory.

235. These Ages are not intercataclysmic periods (for these in Origen, see above, Chapter 3, sect. C; Chapter 4, sect. D, pt. 2), but eons beyond the known historical order (i.e., before Adam? certainly after "the end of the Age"); *De princ.* I,vi,2, 3, II,iii,5, III,v,3; cf. I,iv,5, vi,3, II,iii,5, III,v,3, on the biblical bases in Eccles. 1:9f.; Isa. 65:17; Acts 13:21; 2 Cor. and Ephes.

236. III,i,23, 24, vi,1ff. Cf. M. Gaster, "Transmigration (Jewish)" in *ERE*, vol. 12, p. 437a (on Samaritans).

the Creation and the Last Things.[237] Plethon, by contrast, adopted a Pythagorean position, which he claimed was shared by Zoroaster and Plato. Affirming the world's everlastingness, he maintained that for all eternity "the very same cycles of time, lives, and events" would recur.[238] All events, he held, were determined by the divine planets,[239] and after every human life cycle the soul passed into a new body.[240] Plethon's cyclical theory, therefore, was naked and unashamed.

Unfortunately, however, it is difficult to assess the relevance of Plethon's views for historiography. *On the Laws*, his most important tract, is in tatters. We have one interesting clue, though. He referred to two men called Hercules, one the son of Amphitryon and the other of Alcmene, as the same soul. Two Bacchuses were treated likewise and he also implied that Zoroaster and Plato were one *psychē*.[241] Despite his broadly cosmological preoccupations, these brief allusions to famous personages recall the musing of a man much more interesting in the history of historical thought, one Nicephorus Gregoras (1295–ca. 1359), a leading scholar of the fourteenth-century Byzantine Renaissance.

Nicephorus had once reflected on how historical occurrences were continually different, yet frequently similar. Rather more interested in the similarities, he argued that it was quite natural if "resemblances should sometimes present themselves in the diversified unrolling of events."[242] Perhaps matter is indeterminate, he wrote, but certain "mathematical relations," signs of a governing Intelligence, consistently "find themselves," and even if they are products of different sets of conditions they come to resemble each other.[243] More significantly, these conjunctions of events "reappear cyclically many times in a similar manner, and are periodically produced in identical effects."[244] For Nicephorus, reference to such recurring cycles was not heretical. Be that as it may, the last, more momentous, part of this sentence finds him in deeper water, for Nicephorus appears to have allowed for the recurrence of identical conditions! This Pythagorean element did not fit easily with his treatment of repetitions in more general terms. But he defended it from history nevertheless:

237. I,vi,1f., III,v,1, vi,1ff.; cf. II,i,3, IV,iv,1.

238. *Nomōn syngraphēs* III (Alexandre, ed., **ΠΛΗΘΩΝΟΣ; ΝΟΜΩΝ ΣΥΓΓΡΑΦΗΣ**: *Pléthon, Traité des lois*, Paris, 1858), p. 256, and cf. pp. 252, 256.

239. *Nomōn* III,xxxi (pp. 120ff.), and cf. II,vi (p. 66). On the significance of Plethon's determinism in the history of thought see F. Masai, *Pléthon et le platonisme de Mistra*, Paris, 1956, pp. 98–100, and cf. p. 98 n. 1.

240. III (p. 258), an argument against those (Christian) "sophists" who promised heavenly rewards.

241. III (pp. 252, 254, 256) (it was significant for him that Zoroaster and Plato were separated by just over 5,000 years). On the issue of two men named Hercules see H. J. Rose and C. M. Robertson in *OCD*, pp. 498f., s.v. "Hercules."

242. *Epistulae* LX (to Maximus, ca. 1330–40), in *Correspondance de Nicéphore Grégoras*, ed. R. Guilland (Collection Byzantine), Paris, 1927, p. 203, *ll.*4–6, (this being avowedly on Plutarch's authority).

243. *Epis.* LX (p. 203; cf. pp. 203–5), and cf. LIII (to Pepagomene, ca. 1330–40) (p. 199).

244. **ΚΑΙ ΠΟΛΛΑΚΙΣ** ἐφ' ἑαυτοὺς **ΑΝΑΚΥΚΛΟΥΜΕΝΟΥΣ ΟΜΟΙΩΣ** καὶ **ΚΑΤΑ ΠΕΡΙΟΔΟΥΣ** ξυμπίπτειν τὴν γένεσιν εἰς **ΤΑΥΤΟΤΗΤΑ** προξενοῦντας, LX (p. 203). My emphasis.

There existed, we know, two Hercules, one in Egypt and the other in Boeotia; they carried the same name and there was no difference between one and the other. Their exploits, the proof of their wisdom, were identical. Of the two men under the name of Perseus, one, it is said, fought a war against the Gorgons, dwelt in Atlantis and strenthened the Atlantids' invincible power; the other was from Macedonia, and he combatted the Romans, effecting astounding victories against them. There were two Scipios, both very powerful at Rome; the one acquired glory from devastating Africa almost in its entirety, the other from his razing of the great African metropolis, Carthage, much later.[245]

Nicephorus, however, was in logical difficulties. How could there be exact recurrence of any given event without the exact repetition of all its causal antecedents and subsequent effects? Identical conditions could only recur, he acknowledged, alongside of and even integrated with different or new sets of conditions. The two Perseuses, for instance, inhabited different lands and performed distinguishable if similar deeds.

Such compromise with Greek cosmology, then, had its awkwardness. In a later letter Nicephorus managed to arrive at a more sophisticated position when discussing history as the work of a divine embroiderer or weaver. To use this illustration of a woven cloth, especially material in the making, clarifies his case with striking brilliance. On a piece of cloth one may observe "identical effects" in various parts of its complex patterning, yet the precise locations of these effects differ. Thus in history there may be a continual overthrowing of resemblance by uniqueness or distinctiveness, yet at the same time conditions are persistently reuniting in characteristic ways, so that sometimes "there are produced harmonies of identity."[246]

Nicephorus is an important figure, and we shall return to him below. His manner of reckoning with both the particular and general, the unique and the recurrent, in historical development is highly captivating. On the philosophy of history, however, he said too little, although one is probably justified in claiming him to be the most intellectually rewarding of the cyclical thinkers of the West between Hellenistic times and the Renaissance.

## G. Principles of retribution from later antiquity to the early Renaissance

Nicephorus also espoused a doctrine of divine rewards and punishments in history, and at this point we may conveniently turn to reciprocal ideas of recurrence, and to that important area concerned with the moral order.

245. LX (p. 203). On the two Hercules, see above; on the first Perseus, cf. Hesiod *Theog.* 274–81; *Buckle of Hercules* 216–31; and on the second, Polybius *Hist.* XXV,iii,XXXVI,xvii, and above, Chapter 2, sect. C, pt. 1(ii). The two Scipios, presumably, were Africanus and Aemilianus.

246. CLII (to Matthew Cantacuzenus, ca. 1340–50) (p. 239). Nicephorus added another image: among individuals, blood and facial features may reflect remarkable similarities, yet character development will produce differences.

The idea of a recurrently actualized moral order found ready acceptance among Christian writers. It had a basis both in the tradition of the holy scriptures and in that of the Greco-Roman culture of Mediterranean converts. More than either Age theory or doctrines of rise and fall, it pointed to a supernatural overlordship. Even if the names of the key agencies conveyed some divergent implications (*tychē* and Yahweh are very different!) there were crucial points of intersection, particularly in the appeal to divine *pronoia* or *providentia.* And if there had been more than one reciprocal paradigm among the pagans, the invocation of retributive principles steadily acquired its greatest popularity even before the Christian empire.

We may go back as far as Diodorus (first century BC). Of all Polybius' successors, he was the most thoroughgoing in his attempt to trace the recurrent operation of retributive principles in world history.[247] He was, however, a popularizer. Rather unsubtle, he could not sustain the different levels of causal explanation managed by his great predecessor, and too eager to justify the works of Justice, he frequently misrepresented his sources.[248] Yet his straightforward approach remains instructive. History's eventualities, it seems, were consistently prone to be "morally fitting" (sect. C), so that changes of fortune and circumstance usually had moral explanations. To take the case of a nation, Diodorus suggested that Athens suffered the Sicilian disaster because of her extreme arrogance (cf. *Biblioth.* XIII,xxi,1–xxiv,6). The Carthaginians, moreover, lost Sicily for similar reasons (cf. esp. XIV,lxxvii,4), and whereas Sparta and Macedonia collapsed for lack of virtue (XV,xix,4, 1, 1–2, XVIII,xlii,2, XXVIII,vii; cf. XXI, viii,2), Philip II and the Romans had had their moments of glory for possessing it (XVI,i,4–6, xxxviii,2, lx,4, lxiv,3, XXVII,iii *finis*). What Diodorus considered to be virtue (*aretē*) and its absence was standard. Moderation was a priceless asset and excess abhorrent. If Athens had failed to be humble herself to fortune and had initiated an unjust war (XIII,xxi,2–5), men could learn a better lesson from the Sicilian Gelon, who prospered by being "so clement amid constant excess" (xxii,6; cf. 4–5). Piety, as against its opposite, was another imperative. Retribution came consistently to those who flouted the gods or pillaged sacred shrines, to men like Philomenus the Phocian, Antiochus Epiphanes, and the tribune Aulus.[249]

The teaching that immoderateness incurred trouble or punishment was a common theme of later antiquity.[250] Diodorus is unique only in illustrating the

247. Against A. A. de Miranda, "La Irreligiosidad de Polibio" in *Emerita* XXIV, 1965, p. 60, who argued that Polybius' outlook on the moral order was not taken with seriousness after him. For very recent debate over Polybius' personal religious position, see P. Pédech, "Les Idées religieuses de Polybe étude sur la religion de l'élite gréco-romaine au II$^{e}$ siècle av. J.C." in *Revue de l'Histoire des Religions*, CLXVII, 1965, pp. 35ff., and A. J. L. van Hooff, "Polybius' Reason and Religion; the Relations between Polybius' Causal Thinking and his Attitude towards Religion in the *Studies of History*" in *Klio*, LXIX, 1977, pp. 101ff. (my own position being a *via media* between the views of these two scholars).

248. R. Drews, "Diodorus," pp. 383–92.

249. E.g., XIV, i,2, VI,xiv,3–5, lxi,1f., XXIX,xv, XXXVI,xiii,1–3.

250. Historiographers: e.g., Poseidonius in Athenaeus *Deip.* X,439e, XII,542b, 549d–e;

truth so painstakingly, and in such a way as to convey the impression of recurrently operative principles. His doctrine of requited arrogance, moreover, complemented his treatment of fortune (*tychē*). Though the alternating shifts of fortune seem morally neutral and certainly unexpected, a supernatural providence lies behind all. As already hinted, even empires rise if they possess virtue (for fortune/providence will support them!) and fall for lack of it.[251] Though they did not appeal to fortune, the Church Fathers would have been impressed. It is interesting how serious-minded pagans and early Christians sometimes talked the same language while drawing different conclusions. That there was a correspondence between moral behavior and "consequences," moreover, was defended by various historians of Rome. Livy, for example, had ascribed Roman decline to the corresponding decline in ancient virtues, while later pagans laid the blame for Rome's troubles at the feet of the sacrilegious Christians.[252] The same sorts of general assumptions, already extant in biblical literature, appeared in Christian historiography, though we must reckon with different contexts and important intellectual shifts.

In times of bloody persecution, Christians could afford to question a moral order *within history*. After all, certain biblical writers had been uneasy about it (see Jer. 12:1; Ps. 73:3 on the prosperity of the wicked; cf. John 9:2–3, Job);[253] and there were also some non-Christian moralists who were sensitive about relevant discrepancies bypassed by the popularizers. Divine vengeance seemed to be frequently delayed, for instance, and innocent victims often died before they could see retribution fall on those who afflicted them.[254] Questioning souls were justifiably troubled. The dogmas that in the event of delayed punishment the evildoer would suffer either inward torture in life or notoriety in death, and that those who suffered undeservedly would be honored in posterity,[255] came to be seen as flimsy rationalizations. Naturally enough, the belief in *other-worldly*

---

Dionysius *Arch.* XX,x,2; Dio Cassius *Hist.* I,v,4, IV,xvii,2, V,xxi,2; Plutarch *Vit.* (*Alcibiades and Coriolanus Compared*) iii,1ff., (*Pelopidas*) xxxv,2ff., (*Caius Marius*) xxiii,1, (*Demetrius and Antony Compared*) iii,1ff.; Florus *Epit.* I,vii(13),1–3, xvi(21), xviii,29f.; Ammianus *Rer. gest.* XIV,i,1, 3, XXVI,viii,13; "Vopiscus" *Vit. Car.* VIII,1–3, IX,1–3, XII,2f., et al. Moralists: e.g., Seneca *Epist. mor.* XCVII,13f.; Cicero *De offic.* III,v; Plutarch *Consol. Apoll.* 105B; Marcus Aurelius *Medit.* XII,5; Athenaeus *Deip.* XII,523c ff.; Julian *Epist.* xlii (388c); *Against the Galileans* 161A–171D, et al.

251. See above, sect. C; cf. XIII,xxiii,3, XVIII,liii,2, 4, lix,5. On the hybristic cycles see esp. XXVII,vi,2, xi,3,xv,2, XXIII,xv,10, and cf. XIII,xxv,1f., xxii,6–8.

252. Livy *Ab urbe* I,*proem.*11; Zosimus *Hist. nov.* II,viii, xlix, IV,xl; Julian *Ag. Galil.* 193C ff.; *Epist.* x, xxii, lxxxi; Eutropius *Breviarum ab urbe condita* X,16f. (on how the Christian Jovian dishonored Rome); Ammianus XXXI,xii,9–xiii,13, XV,vii,6–10 [though Ammianus was fair toward the Christian and critical of Julian's policy: cf. K. Rosen, *Studien zur Darstellungskunst und Glaubwürdigkeit des Ammianus Marcellinus*, Bonn, 1970, pp. 132ff.; R. C. Brockley, *Ammianus Marcellinus: A Study of His Historiography and Political Thought* (*Collection Latomus CXLI*), Brussels, 1975, pp. 168ff.]. Overall, cf. A. Momigliano, "Pagan and Christian Historiography in the Fourth Century AD" in his *The Conflict between Paganism and Christianity in the Fourth Century*, Oxford, 1963, esp. p. 81.

253. Subsequent redaction of Job tends to obscure the original poet's penetrating critique: cf. S. Terrien, "The Book of Job" in *The Interpreter's Bible*, vol. 3, pp. 878a–1902a.

254. Esp. Plutarch *De sera numinis vindicta* 548C–549D.

255. Diodorus XVI,lxi,1–4, and cf. Cicero *Pro Sestio* lxvii,40. Background: Theognis 315–8.

rewards and punishments received a greater airing in later antiquity, increasingly so the more there was intellectual interchange between pagan and Christian.[256] It is fair to assert that Christian beliefs about heaven and hell provided more intellectually satisfying solutions to the problems of the moral order than those offered by pagans, who often added a blind fatalism to their face-saving explanations. That is an interesting sidelight to the history of Christianity's rise to ideological supremacy. But we must not forget the two main lines of thought among Christians. For Luke and for the great Old Testament histories, the moral order was reflected within history, although even within Luke-Acts speculations about the afterlife and the eschaton had broadened the perspective. From as early as Nero's day, on the other hand, a key problem for Christians was the agony of the martyrs, and doctrines of both other-worldly recompenses and imminent judgment endowed such tribulations with ethical meaning. However, the line of thought concentrating on the known historical order was attractive for those who sought a more direct rapprochement with pagan historiography, and it was also quite naturally resurgent when anti-Christian persecution diminished.

Lactantius merits consideration here. In his *De mortibus persecutorum* (318?), written under Constantine the Great, he placed a strong—almost pagan?[257]—emphasis on the correspondence between moral action and consequence within history. He demonstrated how consistently those emperors and imperial pretenders who had persecuted or opposed the Christians died horrible deaths, "the adversaries of God always receiving wages worthy of their crime" (v). Lactantius' methods, then, expose his unmistakably anti-pagan commitments; the pre-Constantinian emperors were veritable criminals paying for their evils.[258] Unlike Eutropius, he could hardly deem such unbelievers "worthy to be enrolled among the gods," and unlike Zosimus he took the arrogance of the emperors and not the sacrilege of the Christians to be the cause of the empire's troubles.[259] In a persuasive fashion he turned popular pagan historiographical assumptions to the service of the Christian God, who propelled the recurring operation of retributive principles.[260] This God not only effected requital against

256. Cicero *Somn. Scip.* vii,25 (for some influential thoughts, cf. Macrobius *Commentarii in Somn. Scip.*); M. P. Nilsson, *Geschichte der griechischen Religion* (*Handbuch der Altertumswissenschaft V,2*), Munich, 1924, vol. 2, esp. pp. 220ff. On the questioning of traditional views of the moral order see, e.g., Plutarch *Ser. num.* 548Bff., *Vit.* (*Pelopidas and Marcellus Compared*), ii,1–iii,4, and in John Chrysostom *De provid.* IX,5 (cf. G. Soury, "Le Problème de la providence et Plutarque" in *Revue des Études Grecques* LVIII, 1945, pp. 163ff.); Aurelius IX,2; Sallustius (Nock, p. lxxv)—although evidence for popular pagan belief in a moral order and divine retribution goes as far forward as the sixth century AD: B. P. Grenfell and A. S. Hunt (eds.), *Greek Papyri*, Oxford, 1896, vol. 2, p. 84.

257. Cf. Cochrane, *Christianity and Classical Culture*, pp. 218ff.

258. So ii (Nero); iii (Domitian); iv (Decius); v (Valerian); vi (Aurelian); xvii (Diocletian, his long reign lasting "for as long as he did not defile his hands with the blood of the just," ix); xxiv; xxxiii (Galerius Maximian); xxvi (Severus); xxviii, xxx (Maximian Herculius, whose flight from Rome is parallel to that of Tarquinius Superbus); xliv–1 (Maximin).

259. Eutropius *Brev.* IX,28, X,2, 8, 18 (even Christians Constantine and Jovian being so enrolled!); Zosimus III–IV; cf. Lactantius *Mort. pers.*, e.g., vii, ix on his *hybris* theme.

260. I.e., they are not natural, but are the results of God's will: cf. xxxi.

the persecutors, but rewarded the innocent by the restoration of his Church under Constantine.[261] The delay of this victory was ascribed to divine patience:[262] the divine Being has no shadow of capriciousness about him. Lactantius' position heralds the mainstream Christian position on *fortuna*: the element of caprice is removed from providentialism, so that a positively ethical monotheism takes over.[263] Punishments of the persecutors were thus viewed as a series of "great and remarkable examples from which posterity might learn that there is but one God" (*Mort. Pers.* i).

Eusebius was one important contemporary of Lactantius who agreed that history was teaching men the truth of monotheism. He was less interested in recurrent instances of retribution, however, than in the plan of salvation which made world Christianization possible under Constantine.[264] It was he above all who challenged the old pessimistic-eschatological approach to salvation history. The Eusebian vision lost its clarity on Constantine's death, with the resurgence of paganism, the Arian schism, and a furthering of the split between East and West. When Eusebius' avowed continuator Socrates (ca. 380–450) wrote his account of these new, disturbing events,[265] reciprocal paradigms made a reappearance. Socrates adopted the view that the empire was providentially supported only when there was a right relationship between Church and State—an interesting jump.

> The mischiefs of the State and the troubles of the Church have been inseparably connected. . . . They have either arisen together or immediately succeeded one another, . . . so that I cannot believe this invariable interchange is merely fortuitous, but am persuaded that it proceeds from our iniquities, and that these evils are inflicted on us as merited chastisements.[266]

Thus Socrates openly adopted the principle of *do ut des* (give and be given to). History proved that the empire would be protected if Christian emperors upheld orthodoxy—an apologetic line against those who were pointing the finger at the *homoousios* party.[267] This was an approach still current in the East two centuries

261. See i, xxiv *finis*, xxxiv, xlviii, lii; cf. xviii, xliv, *De ira Dei* xvi, *Div. inst.* V,xxii–xxiv.

262. *De ira Dei* xx, *Div. inst.* II,xvii.

263. On Lactantius' "annihilation" of fortune, see *De falsa sapientia philosophorum* III,xxviii, xxix (*PL*, vol. 6, cols. 437f., 440–2), and cf. Augustine, later, *Civ. Dei* IV,18 (*PL*, vol. 41, cols. 196f.). As a result, Western medieval appeals to *fortuna* were not common in writing. In the sixth century Boethius partly salvaged Fortune from theological suspicion, but he concentrated on her effect on private affairs rather than on history: *Philosophiae consolationis* (ed. R. Peiper, Leipzig, 1871), II,*pr.*ii,27ff., iii,36f., etc. (yet cf. II,*pr.*ii,32A, on the falls of Perseus and Croesus). For Boethius, moreover, the element of chance in life is only motion and change on the rim of the great wheel which has God as its center, and Christian prudence can overcome fortune's caprice (IV,*pr.* vi,21ff.). See also below, Chapter 5, sect. B, pt. 2.

264. *Hist. eccles.* X; cf. II,x,1, III,iv,2ff., v,2, vi,28–vii,1, 8ff., VII,xvi,3f.

265. *Hist. eccles.* II,1ff., III,1ff., IV,1ff.

266. Ibid., V,*proem.*

267. I,16, 18, 34, V,10, VI,6, VII,20, 23. The members of the *homoousios* party were the champions of orthodoxy, defending the doctrine that the pre-existent Christ as the divine Logos was of "one essential being" with the Father (and not a created, second divinity, as the Arians taught).

later, as is instanced by the Church historian Evagrius (536–600), who insisted that "earthquakes, pestilence, and other disasters" in the empire were expressions of God's wrath against heresy and disobedience.[268]

In the West, comparable interpretations were applied to post-Constantinian developments by Orosius. The pagans, as is well known from Augustine's *De civitate Dei*, had blamed the Christians for Alaric's sack of Rome. That imputation in itself reflected assumptions about historical retribution or the religious principle of *do ut des*. Orosius responded to the challenge not by denying the premises like Augustine, but by working out their logic in Christian terms. His analyses of events from Constantine to Honorius (*Hist.* VII,28–43) are especially interesting. In Bk. VII he

> set forth what persecutions of the Christians have been carried out and what retributions have followed, aside from the fact that all men are prone to sin and are accordingly punished individually. (VI,22 *finis*)

Constantine, according to Orosius, had reversed the old order, and yet not all his successors imitated him; taking one at a time, the historian proved that "divine judgment ever keeps watch for a twofold purpose," to assist those who hope in the Church and to punish those who condemn it (36 *finis*). Evil Constantine II, Constans, Julian the Apostate, Valero the Arian, as well as both the defecting Mascezel and Radagaisus the Goth, all paid for their sins with horrific deaths,[269] while the orthodox emperors did not.[270] Even Jovian, whom Eutropius castigated for being the first emperor ever to cede Roman territory to an enemy,[271] and who in fact died a ghastly death, received Orosius' quiet sympathy (31). On coming to the barbarian incursions into Italy, and their assaults on the city of Rome, Orosius sought to hoist the pagans with their own petard. Through the barbarians God was punishing the blasphemous city for all her past (and to some extent persistent) evils; eventualities would have been far worse had it not been for the presence of Christians in Rome, who were protected by God (37, 39). The pagans were thus mistaken in accusing the Christians (cf. 37), just as they were mistaken earlier in believing that Roman *virtus* and not God saved Rome from Hannibal, for it was God who had done that, meting out only a partial punishment to the city because of the faithful Romans to come (IV,17). Orosius, then, wrote history like his pagan predecessors, yet with the biblical God as the divine governor. Joining Lactantius and Socrates, he produced a type of "official history" of momentous political events, but with a Christian interpretation to counter tenaciously-held pagan alternatives.

268. *Hist. eccles.* II,13, IV,8, 29 (this being a counterblast against Zosimus: cf. III,40ff.). Eventually Western events became too disorderly for Easterners to include in their histories: cf. Sozomen *Hist. eccles.* III,7, VII,10; G. Downey, "The Perspective of the Early Church Historians" in *Greek, Roman and Byzantine Studies* VI, 1965, p. 66.

269. *Hist.* VII,29, 30 *finis*, 33, 36, 37, and, on Stilicho and Eucherius, 38.

270. VII,28 *finis* (Constantine); 32 *finis* (Valentinian); 34 *finis* (Gratian, the case of an innocent man's death requiring requital); 35 *finis* (Theodosius the Great).

271. *Brev.* X,17.

Such late patristic treatments of the moral order seem a far cry from the subtleties of Polybius. Though simplistic, however, these approaches expose the recurrence element in retributive thinking even more starkly than the pages of the Polybian *Historiae*. The idea of historical recurrence, they also confirm, is hardly foreign to Christian historiography.

In the West, on the other hand, there were men whose understanding of history followed a contrary train of thought. If, due to the stable succession of the Byzantine kingdom, Easterners tended to assess historical developments in terms of each emperor's reign, or historical fluctuations in the light of each emperor's moral and spiritual worth, in the West the onthrust of the barbarians, coupled with some of the peculiarities of Latin theology, made for a different outlook. Under the thoroughly pagan circumstances of the late second century, Tertullian could only foresee judgment upon iniquitous Rome;[272] in the uncertainties of immediately post-Constantinian times, Cyprian saw the sorry world in old age awaiting its Judge.[273] Such gloominess persisted in the thinking of Augustine and his Gallic contemporary Salvianus (ca. 400–ca. 480), who became only too conscious of the great barbarian threat to the empire. Both held up the threat of damnation against Rome, and their sense of an imminent Judgment cut right across any hopeful talk about alternations between good and bad among the emperors. Salvianus went so far as to argue that except for certain Romans who were true to the faith, "the others are all or almost all more guilty than the barbarians, and more criminal in their lives."[274]

Now to the extent that Augustine and Salvianus saw the trouble of the empire as "punishment fitting the crime," they accorded with the older representation of retributive principles.[275] Yet in the early parts of *De civitate Dei* Augustine succeeded in launching a highly sophisticated onslaught against the pagan interpretation of retributive principles, against the notions that Rome's past successes had been due to virtuous adherence to traditional religion and that the deaths of her past great ones had been "fitting."[276] His appeal to a heavenly city both in and beyond this world vitiated the rather outworn doctrine that the moral order worked itself out purely within history.[277] Augustine's whole approach to grace, moreover, was alien to that more "official" Christian philosophy of history found in Socrates or Orosius.[278] If Augustine had requested

272. *Apologia* xx, xxii,1; xli,1, etc.

273. *Ad Demetrianum* ii–iv.

274. *De gubernatione Dei* IV,13. The seeds of the idea of a "new barbarism" (cf. Vico, Brooks Adams, later) may be found in Salvianus.

275. In fact, Augustine was not only prepared to blame paganism for calamities in Roman history, but even contended that "if these [pagan] gods . . . were unknown . . . and [the true God] alone was known and worshipped with sincere faith and virtue, [the Romans] would have received a better kingdom here . . . and might receive an eternal kingdom hereafter" (*Civ. Dei* IV,28, and cf. II,4–13; III,1; and L. G. Patterson, op. cit., pp. 121f.).

276. *Civ. Dei* I,7f., 14, 22, III, V,25, etc.; cf. Mommsen, "Orosius" in op. cit., pp. 335ff.; J. Chaux-Ruy, op. cit., pp. 71ff.; H. von Campenhausen, "Augustine and the Fall of Rome" in *Tradition and Life in the Church* (ET), London, 1968, pp. 201ff.

277. *Civ. Dei* XI,1, XVIII,1ff., 46ff.

278. Mommsen, "St. Augustine" in op. cit., pp. 281–98. Cf. Arnobius of Sicca *Adversus gentes*

Orosius to demonstrate how wars, diseases, sorrows, and famine had been with men always, not just in the present time, he was uneasy about his friend's rather naïve applications of retributive logic.[279] Admittedly, Orosius acknowledged extraterrestrial judgment for individuals, but he still had not achieved what Augustine prized so vehemently—the freeing of God from limiting assumptions about rewards and punishments in history. As for Salvianus, he made the somewhat "aristocratic" view of reciprocity between action and consequence look positively genteel, even irrelevant, since he saw no immediate hope for his contemporaries even if they did repent.[280]

When those dark and unsettling days of the barbarian invasions in the West were over, however, Orosius' more simplistic view of providential history came back with a vengeance, although it was more confined in its applications. Medievals said much about how "cruel tyrants always came to wretched ends," as John of Salisbury put it,[281] yet much less about the recurring actualization of the moral order in general. Even the rule about tyrants, which was reinforced by such great intellects as Aquinas and Marsilius of Padua, became more a dogmatic "given" about requited sin than an historical maxim to be consistently defended by facts.[282] Not that medieval historiography bridled methodical documentation; it was just that an opposing philosophy of history no longer presented itself, and there was thus little demand for Christian writers to engage in a stage-by-stage interpretation of divine distributions. There is no shortage of medieval allusions to retribution—to the requited wicked and the rewarded beneficent—but affirming history's moral order became less a matter of instancing recurrent operations than of simply reminding the reader of God's providence. In a comparable way, notions of changing fortune and of history's alternations were absorbed into a dogmatic contrast between divine immutability and human vicissitudes.

Within the Byzantine historiographical tradition, both a sense of "Roman continuity" and a stronger concern to maintain the classical tradition fostered approaches to the moral order of more interest to our theme. In important histories by Procopius (sixth century), and especially by Psellus (eleventh century) and Nicephorus Gregoras (fourteenth century), various reigns were evaluated in terms of divine retributive principles. According to Procopius, who betrayed a residual pagan fatalism, God foresaw and determined all; even

---

I,1–23 (*PL*, vol. 5, cols. 714ff.), for an earlier, 4th-century African critique of conventional retributive logic.

279. So Orosius *Hist.*, *prolog.*

280. *Gub. Dei*, esp. VIII,3f.

281. *Policraticus* VIII,18 (cf. Cicero *De offic.* II,vii, as background). Also, on miraculous retribution in medieval hagiography, see K. Thomas, *Religion and the Decline of Magic*, Harmondsworth, 1971, p. 51.

282. E.g. (in the West), Bede *Hist. eccles. gentis Anglorum* III,1f., IV,26, 29f.; Nithard *Histoire des fils de Louis le Pieux* II,8–10; Eadmer *Historia novorum in Anglia* 184; Otto of Freising *Chron. hist. duab. civ.* II,14, III,7, 10–IV,19; John of Salisbury *Historia pontificalis* vii,15f. et al. (the above 8th–12th centuries). The teaching of Aquinas and Marsilius on tyranny is discussed below, Chapter 5, sect. A, pts. 1, 6.

occurrences without any apparent rational explanation—such as the unexpected capture of the Gothic kings Theodatus and Vittigis by the unfortunate Belisarius—could be recognized by hindsight as part of his preordained purposes.[283] Psellus, striving for a middle ground between dry annalism and ebullient rhetoric (cf. *Chron.* VI,73), left the impression that the successes, failures, and deaths of each emperor he treated were connected with the moral worth of their rules.[284]

Gregoras was a more complicated thinker; he deserves to be considered in conjunction with his theoretical mentor, Theodoros Metochites (d. 1332). Both scholars sought to amalgamate the idea of recurring retributive principles governed by God and the ancient notion of fortune's constantly turning wheel. They maintained that the moral order was worked out within history. The other-worldly Judgment (the Judgment which John Chrysostom had once reckoned both the final resting-ground of Christian theodicy and the solution to the problem of innocent suffering) was pushed into the background.[285] Interested in the revival of Hellenism,[286] both also adopted a deterministic outlook on affairs, one which was guaranteed to disturb any anti-fatalistic theologian.[287] Their determinism entailed concession to the idea that seemingly impersonal factors governed the movements of history. It thus represented a reaction against the traditional Christian stress on the active, personal intervention of God in events, especially significant events. Yet neither writer abandoned his belief in providence (*pronoia*); it was just that their interpretation of it was not strictly orthodox.[288] With Metochites, deterministic tendencies show up most clearly in his treatment of fortune (*tychē*). History is conceived as a theater (*theatron*) in which one can view the constant changing of fortunes among both individuals and states. History is never still (*astasia*); like Philo, Metochites described its movements as "up and down," and like Plutarch he wrote of how fortune turned, drifted, and changed within history.[289] Gregoras, by compari-

283. *Anecdota* iv,42–5; cf. iii,30ff., and, for other cases, M. Elferink, loc. cit., pp. 111ff.

284. *Chron.* I,37 and cf. 29, 31, 34 (Basil II), II,10 (Constantine VIII, though the sense of retribution is weak), III,15, 26 (Romanus III), V,14 (Michael IV), 24 (Augusta); yet cf. VI,16.

285. Chrysostom *De provid.* XXIV,1–8.

286. See S. Runciman, *The Last Byzantine Renaissance* (Wiles Lectures, 1968), Cambridge, 1970, pp. 94–7.

287. On background to emphasis on the freedom of moral choice (as against the moral fatalism of certain pagans) esp. in Origen, John Chrysostom, and Theodoret, see H. G. Beck, *Theodoros Metochites: die Krise des byzantinischen Weltbildes im 14.Jahrhundert*, Munich, 1952, pp. 96–9.

288. For perspective, cf. M. Elferink, loc. cit., pp. 111ff. (on Procopius); J. Hussey, "Michael Psellus, the Byzantine Historian" in *Speculum* X, 1935, p. 88 (on Psellus); O. Veh, "Der Geschichtsschreiber Agathias von Myrina" in *Wissenschaftliche Beilage zum Jahresbericht 1953 des Gymnasiums Christian-Ernestinum*, Beirut, 1954, p. 26 (on Agathias, Procopius' continuator).

289. On the world as theater see Beck, op. cit., pp. 106f. On (including change into opposites), **ΘΕΟΔΩΡΟΥ ΤΟΥ ΜΕΤΟΧΙΤΟΥ**, Ὑπομνηματισμοὶ καὶ Σημειώσεις γνωμικαί (*Memorials and Sententious Observations*) *Theodori Metochitae Miscellanea Philosophica et Historica Graeca* (ed. C. G. Muller and T. Kiessling), Leipzig, 1821, pp. 197, 572f., etc., and on constantly changing fortune, see ibid., *logia* 67, 87, 115–7, 119. On Metochites admiration for Plutarch see *log.* 71; cf. also *Specimina Operum Theodori Metochiae qua inscribuntur* **ʽΥΠΟΜΝΗΜΑΤΙΣΜΟΙ ΚΑΙ ΣΗΜΕΙΩΣΕΙΣ ΓΝΩΜΙΚΑΙ** (ed. J. Bloch), Copenhagen, 1790, p. 131.

son, placed a rather unpopular stress on connections between heavenly movements and momentous terrestrial events.[290] Changes above portended changes below: an eclipse of the sun in 1267, for example, announced victory against Byzantium by the Turks, as well as internal dissension, and one in 1342 represented a sign of the impending evils of the usurpation and abhorrent Hesychasticism of John VI Cantacuzenus.[291]

Both Byzantines, however, still identified these apparently inevitable processes with providence, or God's control of the universe. Recurring fluctuations and alternations between prosperity and calamity not only conformed to what was willed by God but illustrated the continuing operation of his retributive principles. If it is part of the preordained nature of things that any man cannot "remain very long at the height of success,"[292] eventualities are nevertheless connected with the moral condition of history's protagonists. According to Metochites, providence gave prosperity to the good and punishment to the wicked,[293] and although human affairs were forever changing, those who were moderate in good fortune could expect success or well-being (*eupragia*) not given to the insolent,[294] while empires too proud and power-seeking, such as Athens and Carthage, justly fell before more moderate régimes.[295] No man could expect permanent happiness, perhaps, nor any nation permanent success, but as a general rule providence worked for the overall good of mankind.[296] Applying some of his mentor's doctrines to his *Byzantinae historiae*, Nicephorus both defended the moral order and warned of fortune's caprices. The impious and evil were punished by divine retribution, visited by a kind of Christianized nemesis.[297] Even Byzantium as a whole received punishment for its impiety in the crisis of 1345, when the Hesychastic Cantacuzenus failed to forestall the Turkish threat.[298] Changes in fortune, moreover, were inevitable. Even such a moderate ruler as Philip of Macedon could not reign without his supremacy being threatened, and régimes, even if they were as worthy as was Rome, could not retain control over their territories forever. Fortune's wheel ran again,[299] then, though her acts were bound to be morally fitting; if Fortune was at all

290. *Byzantinae historiae*, esp. I,1(4–5) (*PG*, vol. 148, cols. 120b–121a); cf. also R. Guilland, *Essai sur Nicéphore Grégoras: l'homme et l'oeuvre*, Paris, 1926, pp. 230f. For background see Beck, op. cit., pp. 98–100; I. Ševčenko, *Etudes sur la polémique entre Théodore Métochite et Nicéphore Choumnos*, Brussels, 1962 (on the East); see above, sect. F (on the West).

291. *Byz. hist.* IV,viii,2(108–9) (*PG*, vol. 148, col. 245b–c); XII,xv,2 (623–4) (col. 841a–c), and cf. IX,xv,4(385) (col. 573a); xii,2f.(455) (col. 649a–b) (the eclipse being connected with a change of succession); xiii,2(458) (col. 653a–b); xiv,1(460) (col. 656b–c); XI,iii,1(535–6) (col. 737a–b).

292. Guilland, op. cit., p. 235.

293. *Hypomnēmatismoi*, *log.* 66, and cf. Beck, op. cit., p. 109.

294. *Hypomn.*, esp. *log.* 56, and cf. 52.

295. *Log.* 104–9, and cf. Bloch edn., pp. 150–60.

296. *Log.* 118f.

297. Guilland, op. cit., pp. 234–6, and cf. *Byz. hist.* XI,viii,1(549) (vol. 148, col. 753a) on the death of Basil Trebizond; XIII,iii,1–3(647) (cols. 859ff.) on Cantacuzenus' death; XXIX,ix(241) (vol. 149, col. 210) on the torture of Palamas; cf. also IV,ii,1f.(83–4) (cols. 212–3); VII,iv,1–3(224–7) (cols. 385–7); VIII,iii,1f.(293–4) (cols. 467–70); IX,ii,2(399–400) (col. 585); XXII,iv(1054–55) (cols. 1332–4).

298. Ibid., XV,ii,6(752–3) (vol. 148, cols. 989–92).

299. E.g., IV,iii,1f.(89–91) (cols. 221a–223b).

distinguishable from God, she stood as a vaguely personified symbol of human instability.

Thus in Metochites and Nicephorus we detect some interesting developments. Key classical notions of recurrence were intensively reapplied, but they came to form a new version (rather than a rejection) of the ongoing Christian teaching about earthly uncertainties, and about God's ultimate control of affairs both within and beyond the historical order. These transitions of thought are vividly reflected in some of Nicephorus' letters on providence and historical repetition. In his simile of history as an embroidered or woven cloth (sect. F), Nicephorus was trying to formulate a succinct statement about both the overall impact and the particular details of the past. What struck him as the mark of providential governance was the fact that, together with history's recurrent resemblances, there was a continuing freshness and rich diversity as well. The great providence "has mixed everything up so that it surpasses our intelligence"; it is, "as it were, like a *cyceōn*," a word which suggests a special planetary conjunction, or a cyclone of wind, or even the maturing of cheese, but which reaches beyond these as a verbal intuition of the whole historical process. History had its cyclical side, its generations and corruptions as in nature, its "alternating movements of succession, never interrupting in appearance or disappearance"; yet at the same time it threw up an unfathomable and ever-confusing mutability.[300]

Nicephorus and Metochites foreshadow some of those important intellectual shifts which mark the classic Renaissance of western Europe. Their deterministic tendencies herald the thoroughgoing Hellenism and fatalism of Plethon, who was a seminal figure behind the Platonic revival of Quattrocento Italy.[301] Their free appeal to fortune anticipates a similar license among Western (and not necessarily impious!) humanists.[302] Furthermore, they stressed the utility of history and attempted to reinvigorate Christian historiography with Hellenistic modes of interpretation. These latter characteristics introduce us to two important approaches to recurrence which are neither cyclical nor reciprocal, and with which we may profitably conclude this chapter.

## H. History's lessons for future behavior

In recognizing the principles governing affairs, these Byzantines contended, men could act more effectively in the future and make the most preferable moral choices. Despite Nicephorus' musings on a second Hercules and a second

300. *Epist.* LX (to Maximus) (Guilland edn., p. 205), for the first quotation. Guilland translates *cyceōn* as maturation or special conjunction (pp. 78f. n.1), but in *Epist.* XIX the term is discussed in connection with wind as a destructive force, the notion of a whirling process implied. *Cyceōn* can also mean the mixing of a drink! Cf. *Epist.* LX (pp. 203–5), on mutability (p. 205), CLII,9 (p. 239) on *genesis* and *phthora*, and 9 (p.239) for the second quotation.

301. Beck, op. cit., pp. 126–31; K. M. Setton, "The Byzantine Background to the Italian Renaissance" in *Proceedings of the American Philosophical Society* C, 1956, pp. 72–6; A. Vacalopoulos, "The Exodus of Scholars from Byzantium in the Fifteenth Century" in *Journal of World History* X, 1967, pp. 470ff.; P. Sherrard, *The Greek East and the Latin West: A Study of the Christian Tradition*, London, 1959, pp. 120ff.

302. See below, Chapter 5, sect. B, pt. 2.

Perseus, however, their general pictures of recurrence did not focus on the return of identical conditions so much as on history's *hypodeigmata* (patterns), its shapes, its examples of *hybris* (insolence) requited, its fallen empires, and so on.[303] The varying fortunes of great Greeks and Romans amply illustrated these patterns, and students were not merely expected to admire or condemn such men but to grasp the practical value of historical study for present and future contingencies.[304]

The fact remains that both Metochites and Nicephorus reacted against a well-entrenched contemplative approach to history, according to which the past was to be studied so that the worthy might receive praise and the wicked blame. This line had its roots in the prologues of Diodorus and Livy,[305] but whereas the former related this idea to the recurring actualization of the moral order and the latter filled his history with exemplars intended to possess some practical civic (as well as moral) value, medieval writers (both Eastern and Western) tended to adopt this approach with neither historical recurrence nor political pragmatism in view. History became more a spectacle, displaying *mutatio rerum*, replete with notable deeds both valorous and ignoble, and often saying something about the nature of God. If it had something practical to offer it was in showing what constituted moral virtues and their opposites.[306] Ethics, perhaps, is not impractical, yet such Byzantines as Metochites and Nicephorus, and many Quattrocento humanists besides, lamented their predecessors' lack of concern for the political usefulness of the past. For them, history's theater-like spectacle came to have practical significance. In depressed Byzantium, naturally enough, the two Hellenists' emphasis was more on the need to recognize preordained tendencies; in the turbulence of Italian city-state politics history acquired more immediate pragmatic value, providing the guidelines for active involvement in civic affairs.[307]

In Greek historical theory, as we have argued (Chapter 2), the theme of history as a guide to action bound a great variety of recurrence notions together. "If ever again men find themselves in a like situation," wrote Lucian in paraphrasing Thucydides, "their knowledge of what has already happened will

303. E.g., *Byz. hist.* XII,i,4(576) (PG, vol. 148, cols. 781–4), and cf. above sects. F, G *finis* on variety; Metochites *Hypomn.*, *log.* 87–91, 112, 117, etc. on *hypodeigmata.*

304. Beck, op. cit., pp. 102, 112.

305. Diodorus *Bib.* I,i,1, 3, 4; Livy *Ab urbe* I,*proem.*, 10–12.

306. In the East: e.g., Procopius *Anec.* i,10; Agathias (*CSHB*, p. 134, para. 21); Attaliates (*CSHB*, *prefat. epist.*); Nicetas Acominate (*CSHB*, p. 4); Gregory of Cyprus *Elogii*, and cf. J. F. Boissonade (ed.), *Anecdota Graeca*, Paris, 1829ff., vol. 1, p. 360; Pachymer (*CSHB*, vol. 1, p. 12); Cantacuzenus (*CSHB*, vol. 1, pp. 8f.). In the West: e.g., William of Tyre, *Historia rerum in partibus, transmarins gestarum, pref.*; John Froissart *Chronique* I; Enguerrand of Montrelet *Chronique*, *prolog.*, I,xxxix; G. de Nogent *Histoire des Croisades, prolog.* For perspective see Funkenstein, op. cit., pp. 70ff.

307. D. J. Wilcox, *The Development of Florentine Humanist Historiography in the Fifteenth Century* (*Harvard Historical Studies LXXXII*), Cambridge, Mass., 1969, pp. 36ff. (on Leonardo Bruni's acceptance of Polybian utilitarianism); M. Gilmore, *Humanists and Jurists: Six Studies in the Renaissance*, Cambridge, Mass., 1963, ch. 1; C. Trinkaus, "A Humanist's Image of Humanism: The Inaugural Orations of Bartolomeo della Fonte" in *Studies in the Renaissance* VII, 1960, pp. 101–5; W. H. Woodward, *Vittorino da Feltre and Other Humanist Educators*, Cambridge, 1897, p. 124.

enable them to act wisely."[308] In Roman historical thought appeals to *exempla* were more typical, yet to cite outstanding examples of civic valor or "test cases" of the past was both to encourage imitation of the good and to pass down the benefit of others' experience.[309] *Exempla* were hardly foreign to medieval histories: in these histories we can certainly isolate the propensity to classify men, behavior, and situations into types.[310] Even if their sights were dogmatic, medievals still assumed that human affairs threw up the typical along with the variable. However, it was in those renascences of fourteenth-century Byzantium and Quattrocento Italy that ancient pragmatism was reengaged. In general terms, it was reasserted that the study of past behavior equipped the statesman to gauge others' motives and act with foresight; yet men were often enjoined not just to feel their way from one relatively similar set of circumstances to another, but to acquire a knowledge of recurrent event-shapes, or even to imitate the deeds of ancient worthies (Chapter 5).

## I. Notions of cultural rebirth or renaissance

Very famous expressions of cultural rebirth were voiced by the early Italian humanists, first in those claims by Boccaccio and Bruni that Dante and his intellectual achievements had dispelled old darkness with new light,[311] and then with the stark Petrarchan contrast between glorious Roman antiquity and the dark Middle Age (sect. D, pt. 3). Such asseverations herald the popular fifteenth- and sixteenth-century view that moderns had revivified the spirit of antiquity so long deadened.[312] One should recognize, however, that although such notions of rebirth seem grounded in the changes of the time, they nevertheless possess a long and fascinating background history.

Laying aside religious notions of a second birth, of resurrection, and even of revitalized and reformed spirituality, we may concentrate on the subject of cultural recurrence. Different trajectories of thought lie behind the idea that the genius and vitality of a former culture could be rekindled in a later one. We can

308. *Hist. Syngr.* xlii; cf. Thucydides *Hist.* I,22; Polybius (above, Chapter 2, sect. C, pt. 2 and addend.); Procopius *Bella* I,1f.

309. E.g., Polybius *Hist.* VI,liv,6–lv,4 (on the Roman story of Horatius Cocles); Cicero *De oratione* ii,26, *Orationes* 120, *De offic.* III,4; and cf. R. Rambeau, *Cicéron et l'histoire romaine* (*Collection d'Études Latines: Series Scientifique XXVIII*), Paris, 1953, pp. 25–54. Also note Augustus in Suetonius *Aug.* xxviii,1f., and on Livy and Ammianus, W. Liebeschuetz, loc. cit., p. 45; Brockley, op. cit., pp. 161ff.

310. J. Taylor, op. cit., pp. 40, 46; R. Newald, *Nachleben des antiken Geistes im Abendland bis Beginn des Humanismus: ein Überschau*, Tübingen, 1960, p. 300.

311. *Earliest Lives of Dante* (by Boccaccio, Bruni, and Villani) (ed. J. R. Smith), New York, 1901, pp. 9ff., 81ff.

312. H. Weisinger, "The Self-Awareness of the Renaissance as a Criterion of the Renaissance" in *Papers of the Michigan Academy* XXIX, 1944, pp. 561ff.; "The Renaissance Theory of the Reaction against the Middle Ages as a Cause of the Renaissance" in *Speculum* XX, 1945, pp. 461ff.; cf. W. K. Ferguson, *The Renaissance in Historical Thought: Five Centuries of Interpretation*, Cambridge, Mass., 1948, pp. 9–28; F. Simone, "La Coscienza della Rinascità negli Humanisti" in *La Rinascità* II, 1939, pp. 838ff., III, 1940, pp. 163ff.

go back as far as Aristotle; more than once he dilated on the periodic emergence, disappearance, and re-emergence of ideas and techniques,[313] and he applied the biological principle to the history of artistic achievement, notably to Attic tragedy.[314] His disciple Dicaearchus produced the *Bios Hellados*, a study of what was tantamount to Hellenic civilization in all its manifold aspects. Transcending age-old differences between Dorian, Ionian, and Thracian, Dicaearchus conceived Greek manners and culture as a self-contained set of phenomena forming a giant life cycle.[315] Broader conceptions like this naturally appealed to those Romans who visualized two great efflorescences of human civilization—Hellas and Rome—succeeding one another. The Roman cultural achievement, it was maintained, was not inferior to the Greek one; there were many common elements in institutional and intellectual life, and Rome flourished after Hellas had succumbed to a general state of senescence.[316]

The notion of great men representing given civilizations is also seminal for the idea of cultural rebirth. Aristotle considered Zoroaster and Plato as pinnacles of intellectual achievement from two separate cultural contexts 5,000 years apart.[317] Later moralists singled out men of comparable stature among both the Greeks and the Romans. Plutarch's *Parallel Lives* are obviously crucial here.[318] Not only do they contain illustrations of special and striking recurrence (as with his comparison of Demosthenes and Cicero; Chapter 2 Addendum), and not just instances of an actualized moral order, but they also parallel two great civilizations through a comparison of individuals. Not that Plutarch underrated dissimilarities between the personalities he placed side by side, and he was also capable of admitting glaring contextual differences: of Titus Falmininus and Philopoemen he once significantly commented, "The former was assisted by the power of a flourishing Rome, and the latter flourished under a declining Greece."[319] The richness and variety of his subject matter conceded, he still achieved a significant set of general parallels which reached beyond the person-

313. *Meteorol.* 339b, *De caelo* 270b16, *Metaphys.* 1074b1–14, *Polit.* 1329b25; cf. Jaeger, *Aristotle*, pp. 128ff., and for a later, Stoic expression of this idea, Marcus Aurelius *Medit.* V,xxxii.

314. Declaring it had declined from Euripides to his own day: *Poetica* IV,1449a14–5; cf. K. von Fritz, *Aristotle's Contribution to the Practice and Theory of Historiography* (Howison Lecture, 1957), Berkeley and Los Angeles, 1958, pp. 121f.

315. F. Wehrli (ed.), *Schul. Arist.*, vol. 1, pp. 47ff.

316. Cf. e.g., Dionysius of Halicarnassus' hope for an Atticist revival in the Roman world (*Peri tōn Archaiōn Rhētorōn*, 2: εἴτε θεοῦ τινος ἄρξαντος εἴτε φυσικῆς περίοδου τὴν ἀρχαίαν τάξιν ἀνακυκλούσης), and Velleius Paterculus' opinion that under both Greece and Rome special literary achievements, such as tragedy, philosophy, and oratory, only flourished over a short period (*Hist. Rom.* I,xvi,1–xvii,7). On paralleling institutions from both cultures see, e.g., Cicero *Re pub.* II,xxxiii,58; Dionysius *Arch.* V,lxxiii,3 (on tribuneship and dictatorship), and concerning Roman civilization and Greek senescence see, e.g., Cicero *Re pub.* I,xxxvii,58; Sallust *Catil.* li,28–34; cf. Augustine, *Div. Dei* II,21.

317. Frg. 6 (R$^2$8, 29, R$^3$6, 34, W.6), and cf. Jaeger, op. cit., pp. 133ff.

318. Valerius Maximus' lives were mainly Roman, though with an occasional Hellenistic example, as in *Fact. dict. mem.* VI,ix. Cf. also Cornelius Nepos *De excellentibus ducibus exterarum gentium*; Aelianus *Varia historia*; Plutarch *Consol. Apoll.* 119D. For a general introduction to Plutarchan biography see A. Wardman, *Plutarch's Lives*, Berkeley and Los Angeles, 1974 (his emphases being different from, though not contradictory to, mine).

319. *Vit.* (*Philopoemen and Flaminius Compared*) ii,1.

alities themselves to the careers of two esteemed civilizations. Hellas (or parts of it) and Rome had their comparable founders (Theseus and Romulus), their religiously inspired legislators (Lycurgus and Numa), their early opponents of tyranny (Solon and Publicola), their men of turbulence (Alcibiades and Coriolanus), and their men of supreme moral and civic virtue (Aristides and Marcus Cato). With regard to military giants, Roman generals operating before the downfall of Carthage and before imperialism to the east were paralleled with the great Athenian commanders, and the generals of the declining Republic with the warriors from Sparta and Thebes. The military succession of Sulla by Pompey, for instance, was explicitly likened to that of Lysander by Agesilaus.[320] And it was natural for Alexander and Julius Caesar, who each marked the end of earlier non-absolutist orders, to be placed side by side.[321] Beyond that, parallels begin to wear thin; in all, however, the total vision of two remarkable flourishings of civilization remains. Along with his sense of continuity in Greek and Roman history, Plutarch implied not only that Rome had gone much the same way as Greece—a sobering thought—but that men had and could reappropriate the virtues and achievements of former days. An older and preferable order of things, then, could be restored.

Although Plutarch's vision held its own, the new post-Republican developments and the Principate's continuing durability engendered a greater concern for Rome in her own right. If the work of Augustus and other emperors suggested the return of the Golden Age, Augustus and, at a much later stage, Aurelian also figured as agents of *restoratio*.[322] In the course of time parallels and recurrences were drawn from within the specifically Roman tradition,[323] and under a later, more decadent Rome rhetors propagated the idea of *Roma renascens*, of Rome periodically rejuvenated.[324] All these conceptions lie at the root of still later talk about rebirth and renovation, and they did not remain the exclusive property of pagan minds, but were imbibed by the new spiritual conquerors as well.

The theme of Rome reborn did not go untouched by Christians such as Claudian and Prudentius, together with others involved in the classicist revival in Theodosian days.[325] The views of these men foreshadowed sixth-century Christian attempts to refurbish the city of Rome with its ancient learning and splendor—attempts surrounding the papal court[326]—and they form an important background to the interesting reassessment of historical trends by such men as the pro-Gothic Senator Cassiodorus (ca. 485–ca. 580), who contended

320. (*Agesilaus and Pompey Compared*) i,3.

321. No chapter of comparison survives, yet cf. *Vit. Alex.* i,1.

322. Augustus *Monum. Ancyr.* viii, with Aurelian earning the title *Restitutor orbis*.

323. See above, sect. B. For an immediate example see Ammianus *Rer. gest.* XXI,xiii,17–9 (Trajan and Sebastius being likened to Scipio and Valens).

324. E.g., Claudian *De bello Gildonico* 17–27, 204ff. (Koch, pp. 38f., 44ff.); Novatian *Aeneads* cxi.

325. Claudian *Bell. Gild.* 17–27, 208ff. (pp. 38f., 44ff.); Prudentius *Contra Symmachum* I,54ff., II,656ff.; Rutulius Namatianus *De reditu suo e Roma in Galliam Narbonensem* I,137ff.; cf. Ladner, op. cit., p. 17 n. 5, pp. 251ff.

326. F. Heer, *The Intellectual History of Europe* (ET), London, 1966, pp. 35f.; J. von Schlosser, *Die Kunstliteratur*, Vienna, 1924, p. 34.

that, despite a "middle age of sin" and a "decay in spiritual discipline" (between Theodosius the Great and the hopeful reign of Theodoric), all was not lost, since the power for the Roman world to be reborn, a kind of pagan *renascibilitas*, was being experienced once more.[327] Such integration of recurrence and continuity, such intertwining of Roman imperialist ideology and Christian hope, shows how complex is the background history to the concept of "the Renaissance"! The concept, it should be stressed again, is not one-sidedly pagan but bears evidence of a confluence of ideas from both Greco-Roman and Judeo-Christian traditions.

We can turn at this point to the so-called "Carolingian renaissance" of eighth- and ninth-century Francia, after the more turbulent days of the barbarian migrations. One should appreciate the sense in which the Carolingians saw themselves as part of a Christian order, with its spiritual heritage in the faith of the Old and New Testaments; yet one should reckon with the resurgent idea of a new Roman order, of an empire succeeding to ancient Rome and preserving a *Western* imperial tradition. In short, there was a *holy, Roman* Empire. Alongside this dual sense of continuity were conceptions of rebirth and renovation. The ravages of the barbarians had created a definite line of demarcation between the old and the new, so seriously damaged was the empire and civilization of the Caesars.[328] For certain Franks, then, the reign of Charlemagne and even that of Charles the Bald represented the restoration of a former stability and the reappropriation of a lost culture. "Renewed, Golden Rome is reborn to the world," wrote Modoin, while Alcuin mused over the building of a new Athens in Francia and others referred to Aachen as a second Rome.[329] In this context, of course, the cultural distinctions between classical, Hellenistic, and Roman were quite blurred, assimilated as they were into one great former order of things which found its supreme expression in the rule of the Caesars.[330] On the other hand, a return to the biblical order was also sought-after. The new Christian king was as much "the King of Israel" and "David's royal son" (to demythologize Theodulf of Orléan's famous hymn) as Christ himself, and as Christ's king he was the new David, ruling over the new Israel, the "City of God," the "Whole body of the faithful."[331] Even Charlemagne himself conceived of his reign as Davidic, and alluded to his son Louis as Solomon.[332] In all these efforts to forge

327. Heer, op. cit., pp. 26f. (the Latin term denoting rebirth in the context of theology: cf. John 2:3).

328. G. W. Trompf, "The Concept of the Carolingian Renaissance" in *Journal of the History of Ideas* XXXIV, 1973, pp. 3ff., for detailed discussion.

329. Modoin in *MGH, Poet.*, vol. 1, p. 390, *ll.*24–7, and above, sect. D, pt. 2; Alcuin, *MGH, Poet.*, vol. 2, no. 170, p. 279, and above, sect. E; cf. Heiric of Auxerre, *MGH, Poet.*, vol. 3, p. 429 (on Charles the Bald's reign), and H. Fichtenau, *The Carolingian Empire* (ET) (*Studies in Mediaeval History IX*), Oxford, 1963, pp. 83ff.

330. E. Panofsky, *Renaissance and Renascences in Western Art: Text (Figura X)*, Copenhagen, 1960, pp. 46f.; Fichtenau, op. cit., pp. 83–5.

331. Trompf, "Concept," p. 24 and n. 96. On depictions of the emperor as the new David in Count Vivien's Bible and the Gospels of Lothair, cf. J. Beckwith, *Early Mediaeval Art: Carolingian, Ottonian, Romanesque*, London, 1964, pp. 56–60.

332. J. M. Wallace-Hadrill, "The *Via Regia* of the Carolingian Age" in *Trends in Mediaeval Political Thought: Essays* (ed. B. Smalley), Oxford, 1965, p. 26.

links with what were preferable times, then, the idea of restored conditions, of *renovatio*, was of paramount importance.[333]

From the Carolingian period onward, as we might expect, writers thought about a new and better Christian order before they thought about the pagan past. Notions with important implications for the idea of cultural rebirth still held on—ideas of a second Rome or a new David, interpretations of specific events as new reenactments of ancient deeds,[334] for example—and there were concerted bursts of cultural activity and renewed acquaintance with the classics (especially in the twelfth century) to suggest the idea of a cultural reawakening. But medieval thinkers pressed pagans to the service of the faith, and while their culture was self-sufficient, no one yearned for the rebirth of antiquity. True, nostalgia for the greatness of the old Rome came quite early in the West,[335] but it was the early humanists' downgrading of post-Roman times, their assertions that these times were barbaric or now played out, and their evocation of ancient greats—pagan ones not least—into the pages of their writings, which produced the mature renaissance idea. The Quattrocento humanists' sense of discontinuity, for example, stands in marked contrast to the doctrine of *translatio studii*, according to which knowledge passed *per successum* from Paradise through the great custodians of culture—the Hebrews, the Egyptians, the Athenians, and Romans—finally coming to rest at Paris.[336] For many humanists the line of the great tradition had virtually been broken, only to be reforged in modern times.

Humanist outlooks could vary, however. Only a few joined forces with Plethon to turn back the clock, to prove that Julian the Apostate was right after all. The more impressive students of history simply underlined the new cultural and political vitality of the Italian cities. Flavio Biondo (1392–1463), for one, had his conservative streak. Though maintaining that the Latins had no historians between Orosius and himself, and though on the verge of conceptualizing a Middle Age,[337] he still harbored residual sympathies for the doctrine of

333. F. Heer, "Die 'Renaissance'-Ideologie im frühen Mittelalter" in *Mitteilungen des Instituts für Österreichische Geschichtsforschung* LVII, 1949, pp. 31ff., 80; cf. W. Ullmann, *The Carolingian Renaissance and the Idea of Kingship* (Birkbeck Lectures, 1968–69), London, 1969, pp. 138f. on the significance of Charlemagne's royal seal.

334. As, for example, when Dante heralded Henry VII as the leader of a new Exodus and of a new victory over the Philistines (*Epist.* V,1, VII,8), or when A. de la Vigne likened Charles VIII's invasion of Italy in 1494 to the struggle to free the Holy Land. On Florence as a second Rome and Pisa a second Carthage see L. Bruni Aretino, *Historiarum Florentini populi* (ed. E. Santini and E. de Pierro in *Rerum Italicarum scriptores*, Città di Castello, 1926, vol. 19, pt. 3), Bk. I, pp. 3, *ll.*10–12, Bk. XII, p. 285, *l.*27; cf. IV, p. 80, *l.*12ff.); and for the analogy drawn in the East between Byzantines and ancient Greeks, Turks and ancient Persians, see, e.g., Nicephorus *Epist.* XLVII (pp. 168f.).

335. On Hildebertus of Lavardin (1056–1133) see Rehm, op. cit., p. 32.

336. Inaugurated by Notker the Stammerer (ca. 885), this doctrine eventually received its grandest statement at the hands of Jean Gerson: E. Gilson, *La Philosophie au Moyen Âge des origines patristiques à la fin du XIV$^{e}$ siècle*, Paris, 1947 edn., pp. 193f., and cf. Funkenstein, op. cit., pp. 96f. (on those representing the *progress* of knowledge by this *translatio*). For background in classical ideas about recurring clusters of knowledgeable, skillful men see Tacitus *Dialogus de oratoribus*; Velleius Paterculus *Hist. Rom.* I,xvi ff., and cf. C. J. Glacken, *Traces on the Rhodian Shore*, Berkeley and Los Angeles, 1976 edn., pp. 444f.

337. Cf. *Scritti inediti e rari di Biondo Flavio* (ed. B. Nogara, in *Studi e Testi* XLVIII, 1927), pp. 148–68.

imperial translation when he wrote of the new and eternal empire of Christianity.[338] Along with Leonardo Bruni Aretino (1369–1444), though, Biondo held that the Italian cities of his own time were reestablishing the glory of fallen Rome, and his own consciously classical style was reinforcement to his claims.[339] Bruni, by treating Dante as a turning point in Italian culture and by considering the rise of the Italian city-states as a return to the government of free institutions which characterized Republican Rome, was first to crystallize the idea of a revived antiquity in terms of the great movements of European history. Concerning cultural change, moreover, both Biondo and Bruni held the opinion, which stems largely from Petrarch and which continued into the sixteenth century, that between antiquity and recent times Europe had been lost in barbarian darkness.[340] It was left to painters, sculptors, architects, antiquarians, rhetoricians, neo-Platonic philosophers, and other theoreticians of history and culture who came after them to actualize and expand what these two had sensed imperfectly about social and intellectual change. Whatever the emphases of their successors, whether they highlight the revival of pagan or of Christian antiquity, whether they put more weight on the return of former conditions or on the unique achievements of their own times, the sense of retrieval, of regaining lost dimensions in life, was all-pervasive.

Conceived in its simplest form, the idea of renaissance entails the belief that a given set of (approved) general conditions constitutes the revival of a former set which had in the interim been considered defunct or dying (see Introduction). Although enriched by cyclical lines of thought (by the idea of successive civilizations, decomposition followed by rebirth, the Golden Age returned, etc.), it falls into a separate category, and its history reflects a complex interlacing of classical and Christian threads.

Christian doctrine had its great triumph. Its victory was not so complete, however, that medieval historiography remained unaffected by non-biblical notions of historical recurrence. A rich stock of paradigms from the Hellenistic world had already entered the Judeo-Christian tradition before the Bible was completed, and though often modified, they continued to provide useful means of interpreting historical tendencies. It is unfair to conclude that they were more in use when men sensed the decrepitude of a civilization,[341] and even if theories

338. L. C. Baldeschi, *Studio critico sulle Opere di Flavio Biondo*, Macerata, 1895, p. 8; D. Hay, "Flavio Biondo and the Middle Ages" in *Proceedings of the British Academy* XLV, 1959, p. 109.

339. *Decades*, p. 30 (Biondo taking the beginning of his history as the fall of Rome); cf. Bruni, *Hist.*, Bk. I, pp. 7, *l.*36–13, *l.*29; pp. 13, *l.*30–16, *l.*34; pp. 16, *l.*35–22, *l.*26; pp. 22, *l.*27–Bk. II, p. 27, *l.*10; pp. 27ff., *ll.*11ff., on the five periods of Italian history, and cf. below, Chapter 5, introd. On Petrarch as background here, see E. Fueter, *Geschichte der neueren Historiographie*, Munich, 1911, pp. 2f.

340. On Biondo and Bruni, with Petrarch and Villani, see W. K. Ferguson, op. cit., pp. 18–25; cf. (in general) Weisinger, "Renaissance Theory."

341. Even if we were to confine ourselves to the cyclical paradigm, there is little justification from this period for C. van Doren's judgment that cyclical theories of history are decay theories in disguise: *The Idea of Progress*, New York, 1967, p. 174 (cf. above, sect. B, on Florus, sects. F, G, on Nicephorus).

of cosmic recurrence were outlawed by theologians, the cycles, the alternations, reciprocities, and renascences of human life were still elicited. Not that old Hellenisms were left unsubdued: any cyclical theory as elaborately conceived as the Polybian *Anacyclōsis* is absent from medieval literature; we see less of the biological principle; the wheel of fortune was often veiled behind the doctrine of terrestrial flux; and the "utilitarian" axis of Greco-Roman historical investigation was sacrificed upon the altar of a loftier spirituality. Despite Byzantine forerunners, such as Nicephorus and Metochites, it was only writers of the classical Renaissance who reapplied the cycles of nature and fortune and tried to recapture the lost pragmatism of the ancients. During the early sixteenth century the Polybian cycle of governments makes a dramatic reappearance in the pages of Machiavelli.

# Chapter 5

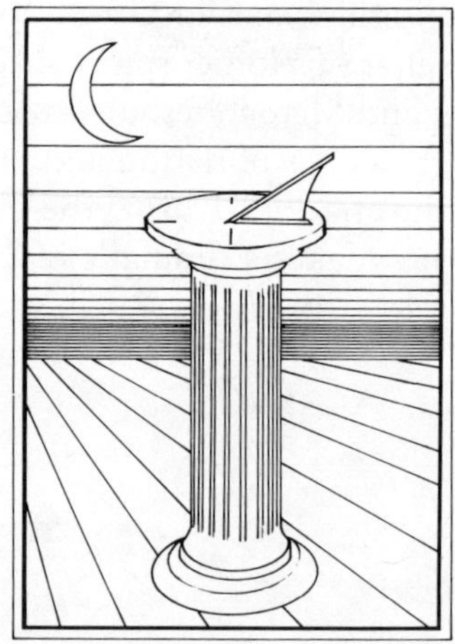

# Machiavelli, the Renaissance, and the Reformation

It has been claimed that historians and other writers of the classic Renaissance reverted to a cyclical rather than a lineal approach to history.[1] Our previous treatment of some of the Quattrocento humanists might at first sight seem to justify such an assertion, but one should be careful in generalizing about so rich an intellectual scene. What, in any case, could be meant by such a claimed reversion? A return to Stoic or neo-Pythagorean positions? Few intellectuals of

1. J. A. Mazzeo, *Renaissance and Revolution: The Remaking of European Thought*, London, 1965, pp. 7f., 41–3, 296; cf. E. H. Harbison, *Christianity and History: Essays*, Princeton, 1964, esp. pp. 275f. Although eliciting a variety of views from the literature, H. Weisinger argues that "the assumption about the course of human history which is most widely held in the Renaissance is the cyclical or tide theory": "Ideas of History during the Renaissance" in *Journal of the History of Ideas* VI, 1945, pp. 415ff. For recent work on Renaissance ideas of progress, though, cf. W. W. Ungar, "Modern Views on the Origins of the Idea of Progress" in ibid., XXVIII, 1967, pp. 55f.; A. B. Ferguson, "'By Little and Little': The Early Tudor Humanists on the Development of Man" in *Florilegium Historiale: Essays Presented to Wallace K. Ferguson* (ed. J. G. Rowe, W. H. Stockdale), Toronto, 1971, pp. 126ff.

the fifteenth and sixteenth century toyed with such views.[2] An application of cyclical models drawn from classical and Hellenistic historiography? That certainly would be closer to the mark. As we shall see, Niccolò Machiavelli (1469–1527) revived the Polybian *Anacyclōsis*, and many were the Renaissance appeals to the turning wheel of fortune and to the rise and wane of empires. But extravagant claims are to be avoided: Joseph Mazzeo's comments on some of Leonardo Bruni's views are a case in point. He contended that Bruni was thinking cyclically because he divided Italian history into five periods and because he argued that the last one (from the new republics to his own time) was the only period of Italian *libertas* after the time of Roman republicanism.[3] Yet talk of large periods was something few medieval writers were averse to: why should Bruni's attitude toward recent developments suggest anything more than the non-cyclical idea of cultural rebirth? This case nicely illustrates the necessity of distinguishing among different paradigms of recurrence before drawing snap conclusions. To put too much under the umbrella of "cyclical thought," for instance, instead of coming to terms with the wider ramifications of recurrence thinking, is overly facile. If by a reversion to cyclical views scholars like Mazzeo mean a reappropriation of Greco-Roman ideas of recurrence, then a rich collection of ancient non-cyclical paradigms has to be accounted for. One has also to gauge the continuing influence of medieval ideas on fifteenth- and sixteenth-century historical thought, and to appreciate that cyclical notions were not entirely absent from medieval approaches to world history. By way of generalization, the most we can say about the fifteenth and sixteenth centuries at this stage is that there was a revived interest both in the pragmatic implication of the lessons of history and in a wider variety of recurrent *casi*, as Machiavelli called them—repeated configurations, event-complexes, conditions, and the like.[4]

## A. Machiavelli and the cycle of governments

Of all the exponents of historical recurrence in the fifteenth and sixteenth centuries, Machiavelli, Florentine emissary and bureaucrat, stands out both for the range of ideas he exploited and for the profundity with which he developed and

2. Note Machiavelli, in the lighthearted prologue to *Clizia*: "If into the world the same men should come back just as the same events come back (*i medesimi casi*), a hundred years would not pass before we should find here the very same things" (*Opere*, ed. N. Conti, Florence, 1818ff., vol. 6, p. 136). Despite a better edition of the *Opere* by M. Bonfantini (*La Letteratura Italiana: Storia e Testi XXIX*, Milan, 1963), Conti's edition will be cited (in parantheses) hereafter, since its pagination enables an easier location of passages. On Renaissance Pythagoreanism, note Johann Reuchlin (1455–1522), who in his *De arte cabalistica* (1517) claimed to be Pythagoras reborn; cf. L. Spitz, *The Religious Renaissance of the German Humanists*, Cambridge, Mass., 1963, p. 67 and cf. ch. 4. Also, Cabalistic, Hermetic, and Pythagorean views about psychic transmigration figure in the thought of Giordano Bruno (1548–1600): cf. V. Spampanato, *Vita di Giordano Bruno, con documenti editi e inediti*, Messina, 1921, Documenti Veneti, xi,711, xii,720; F. Yates, *Giordano Bruno*.

3. Op. cit., p. 41, and on Bruni see above, Chapter 4, sect. I. The new republics are dated from ca. 1250 on.

4. Cf. Machiavelli *Discorsi sopra la Prima Deca di Tito Livio* III,43 (Conti, vol. 4, p. 259), on the famous statement that contemporary events had appropriate parallels in ancient times.

applied them. For the most part, Machiavelli concerned himself with political change and with the means of stabilizing polities; he was thus led to history, especially to the history of the greatest empire he knew, Rome, and to the history of Florence, his own famous city. In analyzing Roman and Florentine affairs he presented some of the best-known models of historical recurrence of his time. His most famous statement, in the *Discorsi* on Titus Livy (1519) (I,2), concerned the cycle of governments, and most probably derived from Polybius Bk. VI. It seems a useful starting point from which to examine both Machiavelli's own views and the idea of historical recurrence among his contemporaries. It is enlightening, however, to examine this cycle in conjunction with another crucial model found in his *Istorie Fiorentine* (1527) V,1.

## *Models in the* Discorsi *I,2 and the* Istorie *V,1*

With the *Discorsi* I,2 we return to themes we left off earlier; like Polybius, Machiavelli submitted that states pass through a cycle of constitutional stages. Although there are doubts about his access to a Latin translation of the *Historiae* Bk. VI,[5] it is not very likely that Machiavelli could have produced his scheme without having read either the appropriate passage from Polybius or a paraphrase of it. That is not to say, however, that the Florentine did not modify his source; careful exegetical work is required to gauge the degree of Machiavelli's dependence. It is surprising that a detailed exposition of *Discorsi* I,2 in these terms has not yet, to my knowledge, been forthcoming, but this may be due not only to uncertainties surrounding the accessibility of Polybius VI,v–ix, but also to the fact that it has been far from clear what relevance Machiavelli's "cycle of government" model has for the rest of his complicated—and oftimes disorganized—political analyses.

In the relevant chapter Machiavelli observed that some writers distinguished three kinds of states: the monarchical, the aristocratic, and the democratic (*Principato, Ottimati, Popolare*). Others had claimed, however, that these three worthy constitutional forms had evil counterparts, since monarchy could become tyrannical (*tirannico*), aristocracy become oligarchic (*stato di pochi*), and democracy dissolute (*licenzioso*).[6] For the first triad Machiavelli probably thought of such ancients as Herodotus and Xenophon;[7] as for the second, he wrote that more than one writer was involved, yet since he shows no acquaintance with Plato's *Politicus*, and since Aristotle's constitutional categories do not

5. Machiavelli had virtually no Greek. Florentine libraries probably lacked copies of the *Historiae* in Latin until 1520, yet for a brilliant (if speculative) account of how Machiavelli conceivably became acquainted with Polybius VI,v–xi, see J. H. Hexter, "Seyssel, Machiavelli and Polybius VI, the Mystery of the Missing Translation" in *Studies in the Renaissance* III, 1956, pp. 75ff. (yet for a rather adverse critique see J. H. Whitfield, *Discourses on Machiavelli*, Cambridge, 1969, pp. 191ff.).

6. (Vol. 3, pp. 235f.).

7. Cf. "some writers," a loose translation of Polybius VI,iii,5a? or was he deliberately vague in order to include medieval writers in the list? That he read Xenophon: *Disc.* II,13 (vol. 4, p. 51), III,22 (pp. 209, 211), cf. II,2 (p. 16), and Herodotus (or Herodotus behind Diodorus?): II,12, III,6.

fit in neatly with his vocabulary, Polybius was probably foremost in his mind.[8] After all, Machiavelli was about to embark on a careful analysis of Roman constitutional history; what piece of ancient theoretical writing could have served as a better preface to his theses? Just like Polybius, Machiavelli first introduced the six simple constitutional forms with a brief sketch of the zigzag line from monarchy to a degenerate democracy, and then went on to elaborate the cycle of governments.[9] Like Polybius again, he came to contrast the impermanence of simple constitutions with the durability of those combining monarchiacal, aristocratic, and popular elements into a mixture (*mista*).[10] Polybius, then, was undoubtedly his key source, though he was by no means a slavish dependent.

With Machiavelli's more highly-wrought model, the world and its inhabitants have a definite beginning. All talk of cataclysm is dropped (at this point).[11] On the other hand, his picture of early human life is derived far less from medieval theology than classical "anthropology." By suggesting that *caso* (chance, not fortune) gave birth to different forms of government, and that the world's original inhabitants were few in number and dispersed like beasts, Machiavelli even appears to owe something to Epicurean Lucretius.[12] However, his comments remain in accord with Polybius, who placed a greater stress than Lucretius on parallels between animal behavior and the herdlike groups which emerged after a catastrophe.[13] In any case, the Polybian *Anacyclōsis* was of decisive importance for what followed. In the primitive situation men gathered around the strongest and bravest; but they came to learn what justice is, and began looking to the wise and just rather than to men of physical prowess. Hereditary princedom became established. The heirs, however, did not possess their forebears' virtues, and tyranny soon arose. High-minded citizens, as conspirators themselves and as catalysts for a popular reaction, overthrew the hated régime and created an aristocracy. Soon it was their children who became

8. Aristotle writing of the degeneration of "polity" in "democracy": see above, Chapter 1, sect. D. Besides, Machiavelli probably took Aristotle to be the father of the simple tripartite distinction—monarchy, aristocracy, polity—which was used by medievals in his name: e.g., Thomas Aquinas *De regimine principum* I (d'Entrèves edn., p. 8); Marsilius of Padua *Defensor pacis* I,ix,9, xvii,2. Cicero was not Machiavelli's source for the sixfold classification, *De re publica* being lost to European intellectuals between the early Middle Ages and 1820. Machiavelli strangely (or coincidentally) concurs over the brevity of any simple constitutional form's existence (vol. 3, p. 236; *Re pub.* I,xliv,68 *finis*), but accessible fragments in Augustine (whom Machiavelli did not read anyway!) do not contain this point. Cf. H. Hagentahl, *Augustine and the Latin Classics* (*Studia Graeca et Latina Gothorburgensia XX, 1*), Göteborg, 1967, vol. 1; *Testimonia*, p. 543.

9. (Vol. 3, pp. 235f.); cf. Polybius VI,iii,5–iv,13.

10. (Pp. 238f.); cf. Polybius VI,ix,10–x,14.

11. Though cf. below, sect. B, pt. 1.

12. Lucretius *De rer. nat.* V,925–1104; cf. L. Strauss, *Thoughts on Machiavelli*, Glencoe, Ill., 1958, p. 201. Lucretius' work was one of the more remarkable "finds" of Renaissance humanism: R. R. Bolgar, *The Classical Heritage and Its Beneficiaries*, Cambridge, 1958, pp. 262–4; R. Sabbadini, *Le Scoperte dei Codici Latini e Greci ne' Secolo XIV e XV*, Florence, 1905, pp. 11f., 23–7.

13. *Hist.* VI,v,6–9; yet cf. Lucretius V,943–72, where the stress is on primitive man's *relationship* with the beasts.

overambitious and violent, and the resulting oligarchy suffered a fate similar to that of tyranny, only this time it was the whole people who seized the reins of power. Yet the popular stage was also short-lived: after a generation

it soon ran into that kind of license (*licenza*) which injured both public and private interests. Everyone lived for himself, and a thousand acts of injustice were daily committed, so that, constrained by necessity (*necessità*) or directed by some good man (*buono uomo*), in order to evade such *licenza*, the community returned anew to the government of a prince, and from this went back again step by step toward a state of license in the same manner and from the same causes already indicated.[14]

Up to this last passage Machiavelli was following Polybius with some care, but he deviated from his source in his treatment of degenerate democracy and its aftermath. Polybius had postulated three stages from democracy to the complete collapse of political society: the emergence of corrupting demagogues within democracy, the institution of ochlocracy or mob rule once the masses have found a leader, and the return to brutishness, with its accompanying search for a "master and a monarch" (*Hist.* VI,ix,5–9). Machiavelli concurred that democracies degenerated into license, but he declined to reproduce the Polybian stages because he evidently did not accept the idea that a state reverts to conditions of savagery before the whole cycle of governments begins afresh. His *licenza* clearly stands for ochlocracy, but the state does not thereafter subside into bestiality; it is rescued from license by a reversion to the government of a *principe* (prince). On the surface of things, moreover, this last rule is that of a good, wise, and just *principe*, not the physically powerful leader of a human herd.[15] Machiavelli, it appears, sought to replace a weak link in Polybius' anacyclic chain, presumably because he did not see how both a decline into bestiality and the reemergence of a primitive monarch could be squared with the known facts. He took the cyclical model to cover constitutional changes only, and not the dissolution of whole political societies by natural (as against external) means. Machiavelli hence declined to adopt the Platonic-Polybian sequence of mob rule followed by a beastlike tyranny or savage monarchy.[16]

14. (Vol. 3, p. 238), M. Lerner's translation in part. Note Machiavelli's typical recurrence terminology: "si *ritorna di nuova* al principato," "e da quello di *grado in grado si riviene* verso la licenza, ne' modi e per le cagione dette."

15. The primitive monarch in Machiavelli's model is not referred to by the term *principe*, but as the "one who is strongest and bravest"; he is a man who leads the people like a herdsman before they elect a prince, choosing him "not out of preference for the strongest but because he was most prudent and most just" (vol. 3, p. 238). Concerning Polybius' leader or *prostatēs*, it is probable that for Machiavelli he is the "certain man" (*alcuno*) who leads the people's cause against oligarchy, a man for whom there is no equivalent, at least in this context, in Polybius. I hold that this represents a conscious modification.

16. Curiously, in the very same chapter Machiavelli goes on to assert that Solon's "popular government" did not have the same longevity as Lycurgus' constitution (cf. Polybius VI,xliii–l) and that it was quickly replaced by a tyranny (even though subsequently restored): *Disc.* I,2 (vol. 3, p. 239). This sequence hardly fits his cycle of governments, so how are we to explain it? Surely not as a case of a democracy lapsing into license, with a *principe* to follow. Most probably, as I will show later, Machiavelli considered Solonic democracy not as a simple constitution but as a democrat-

Now it should be clearly understood that Machiavelli called the recurring sequence of governments a *cerchio*, a circle in which governments "rotate" (*girando*).[17] What is more, he made three important comments about the process as a whole. First, as we have seen, he stressed the rapidity of the changes (*mutazioni*) involved, or the liability of all simple constitutions to decay quickly. Second, he maintained that states seldom remain on their feet long enough to experience all the changes of one whole cycle of governments. Perhaps, by nestling under the protection of some neighboring overlord state, a political society could "revolve indefinitely through the cycle," but the life courses of most states were cut short. They could be cut short, we may infer, not only by intervention or conquest from without, but also by internal dissension (cf. Polybius *Hist.* VI,lvii,2); states could fall into distress, and left without "counsel or power," they could no longer remain "on their feet."[18] Third, Machiavelli generalized about the zigzag sequence as a procession "toward conditions of license." It is well known that he was frequently preoccupied with the issue of decay—Italian decay especially[19]—and he envisaged the cycle of governments to be both moving toward and ending in the worst form of inner decay. The "ruin" (*rovina*) of the state intrigued him. Ruin could occur at any point in the cycle, perhaps, either by "foreign intervention or by civil discord," but the term most expressive of a complete internal collapse was license, the rule of each individual for himself and the absence of any political effectiveness.[20] The shadow of license hangs over his whole cycle somewhat as the awful condition of non-polity hangs over the Polybian *Anacyclōsis*. Along with the Polybian zigzag line, then, comes a stepwise movement toward utter disorder. This suggestion of *degeneratio*, indeed, substitutes for the conspicuous absence of the biological analogy in the *Discorsi* I,2. To relate the notions of growth, acme, and decay to the cycle of governments had been a difficult enough task for Polybius; yet on Machiavelli's new reading of the cycle, with no reference to the recurring conditions of non-polity and with a heavier stress on overall decay, the possibility of an effective relationship seems never to have presented itself.

These, in brief, are the basic characteristics of Machiavelli's best-known cyclical model. The model deserves still further analysis, and the questions we asked of the Polybian position may also be asked about it: whether, for example, any specified state was understood to have passed through the whole cycle, or whether a mixed constitution was conceived as the best means of forestalling the cyclical process. Before going further, however, it will pay to reflect upon

ically-inclined *republic*, which is worthy of being compared to the complex Lycurgan polity, and which does not fall within the ambit of the cycle in I,2.

17. (Vol. 3, p. 238). Governments in this case = *repubbliche* = civic societies in a general sense.

18. (P. 238) for all quotations.

19. F. Chabod, *Machiavelli and the Renaissance* (ET), London, 1958, pp. 79ff., 95ff.

20. *Istorie Fiorentine* I,5 (vol. 1, p. 9) for the quotations; cf. *Disc.* I,6 (vol. 3, p. 523). Machiavelli did credit oligarchy with some effectiveness: cf. *Il Principe* v,2 (vol. 4, p. 289); and even tyranny—ibid., xiv (p. 327), *Disc.* I,29 (vol. 3, p. 313)—but tyranny could easily bring *rovina* on a state: I,29 (p. 296), and was associated with *licenza* in I,2 (p. 23). Cf. also below, pt. 4.

Machiavelli's other important statement of recurrence in the *Istorie* Bk. V. There one finds what is basically an alternation model, with hints of the biological analogy beneath the surface. About to analyze the vicissitudes of Florentine and Italian politics between 1434 and 1494, he dilated on the recurrent oscillation between "order" and "disorder" within states:

For the nature of mundane affairs not allowing them to continue in a firm course, when states have arrived at their greatest perfection (*ultima perfezione*), they soon begin to decline (*scendino*). In the same manner, having been reduced by disorder and sunk to their utmost state of depression (*all'ultima bassezza*), unable to descend lower, they, of necessity, reascend, and thus from good they gradually decline to evil and from evil mount up to good.

Accounting for this oscillation, he argued that *virtù* (valor and political effectiveness) produces peace, peace brings idleness (*ozio*), idleness disorder, and disorder *rovina*. In turn, from *rovina* springs order, from order *virtù*, and from this, glory and good fortune (p. 125).[21]

This second model is distinctive in both its applications and its conception, even if it is quite complementary to the cycle of the *Discorsi*. To begin with its application: this model embraces political change in the broadest terms. All kinds of states, those with or without provinces or agglomerate territories, fall under its rubric. It involves states, moreover, in both their external and internal relations; although wider political conditions might be partly dependent on constitutional factors, this model does not tie the tendencies toward either ruin or good fortune to internal considerations alone. It is even possible, as Machiavelli himself suggested, that the whole cycle of governments might be experienced by a *subjugated* state; it was also possible for a state to attain supreme power externally while under an unworthy form of constitution, or to suffer unmitigated failure under a worthy one. That, of course, is not to deny points of intersection between the two models. The cycle of governments moved toward the low point of license; it was therefore conceivable that this license, which was certainly a form of disorder, coincided with an indeed brought on a state of utter ruin. Possibly, too, a state might achieve its zenith under a good constitution, even one of the three worthy constitutions of the *cerchio*! The second framework clearly subsumes the first, however, and for this reason one may declare it to be more basic for Machiavelli's interpretations of political change.

In conception the models have much in common. The *Discorsi* cycle has an element of alternating movement, with its fluctuation between "good" and "vicious" constitutions. The second frame may be deemed cyclical, with its stage-by-stage rise and descent and its reversion to an original point of depar-

21. Cf. *Disc.* I,4 (p. 243) on good government being only rarely unaccompanied by good fortune; I,11 (pp. 271f.) on good, religiously-based laws bringing good fortune.

ture. In both models, Machiavelli was preoccupied with decay and with the speed of change; he was interested in the overall tendency toward *licenza* in the *Discorsi* cycle, and with the implications of his broader model for the decline of valor in Italy.[22] On the other hand, the process of the *Istorie* V,1 boasts a clearcut zenith which the cycle of governments lacks, and even hints at the biological analogy.[23] Furthermore, although Machiavelli admitted that either sequence could be broken or distorted (the first cycle by external pressures, the second by "some extraordinary force," as he loosely put it),[24] the process in the *Discorsi* I,2 is clearly more fragile and is the less likely of the two event-complexes to be fully realized.[25] Again, the *Istorie* model is more distinctly Machiavellian. Behind it, perhaps, lie ancient and medieval notions of changing fortune, rise, decay, and vicissitude, yet Machiavelli has endowed it with much more of his own character and vocabulary than he did his version of the *Anacyclōsis*.

Examining the models together, one common characteristic may be seen which deserves a special note. Neither succession of events was viewed as the result of "natural processes." The constitutional *cerchio* is nowhere said to follow a course "according to nature," and although the second frame seems tinged with the biological analogy, nature still makes no appearance. What may we infer from this? Nature (*physis*) was a key concept in Polybian anacyclic theory; why should Machiavelli pass it by? Did he have an alternative idea? One which immediately suggests itself is *necessità*, a term used in connection with both models.[26] But Machiavelli's "necessity" does not mean some inexorable fate, but the weight of given (and manmade!) circumstances which demand a response, whether sufficient or inadequate.[27] Necessity certainly impels people to act, even if it is never the equivalent of such action, and while reason may not induce men to act, necessity certainly will.[28] This being the case, was necessity Machiavelli's substitute for *physis* or *natura*? Not convincingly. There is more to account for. As one constantly entering "the ancient courts of ancient men,"[29] Machiavelli was capable of combining more than one classical line of explanation in his approach to historical complexity. Necessity features only as a background force in his two major cyclical models; at different points in the cycles circumstances arise which call for decision and action, and *necessità* describes these circum-

22. Cf. *Ist.* V,1 (vol. 2, pp. 126f.).

23. His first model suggests three zeniths—monarchy, aristocracy, and democracy—yet the second requires the interpreter to select the uppermost point of political life and achievement prior to the declination toward ruin. Considerations other than purely constitutional ones would affect his selection.

24. (Vol. 2, p. 126).

25. That the *Discorsi* is no mere provisional statement, as orientation rather than doctrine, see below, pt. 2.

26. *Ist.* V,1 (p. 125), the passage being quoted at length above; *Disc.* I,2 (vol. 3, p. 238) on the constraints of necessity made obvious by the breakdown of popular government.

27. Appeals to necessity in *Il Principe* are well known: ii,2, 5, 11, 12, etc.

28. *Disc.* I,6 (vol. 3, p. 253); cf. I,3 (p. 244).

29. To quote *Lettere*, 10 Dec. 1513 (vol. 10, p. 168).

stances. By contrast, significantly, a more positive causal rôle is ascribed to human nature and motivation.

Now Machiavelli's views on human nature smack quite strongly of Thucydides (Chapter 2, sect. C). Human nature was remarkably stable, steady enough for rules of political behavior to be formulated. "Whoever considers the past and the present" (we find early in the *Discorsi*),

> will readily observe that all cities and all peoples are and ever have been animated by the same desires and the same passions; so that is is easy, by diligent study of the past, to foresee what is likely to happen in the future in any republic, and to apply those remedies that were used by the ancients, or not finding any that were employed by them, to devise new ones from the similarity of events. (I,39)[30]

Human nature being what it is, as Thucydides maintained, there will be future recurrences of present event-complexes; Machiavelli neatly coupled that doctrine with the more overtly pragmatic (even Polybian!) concern for remedying social ills through lessons from the past. It is this understanding of men and action which fills out the rationale of his two important cyclical frameworks. Humans respond to circumstances in a regular way. In their worthier responses tyrants are removed, or order is retrieved in the face of civic dissolution.[31] More commonly, however, the rule is corruption, with private ambition placed before the commonweal. Within the first cycle the powerful often become tyrannical, oligarchic, or licentious; within the second men tend to lose the *virtù* which once gave their state its greatness, and they become idle and disorderly. Machiavelli's models lack a "natural process" element, then, because his concentration was centered upon human motivation. This does not mean that deterministic-looking features make no appearance, however; men's deeds conform to regularities (*regole*) and there remains necessity, or decision-involving situations, which induce typical responses. Machiavelli qualified the cycle of governments more overtly than Polybius, and he also formulated his broader cycle, with its greater capacity to accommodate historical variations, yet he still insisted on the recurrence of event-patterns and on the constancy of the principles which made such recurrence possible. Admittedly, those principles are neither supernatural nor extrahuman, but principles there are. History remains the domain of human action, and in both key models the dynamics of historical repetition lie in the interplay between characteristic circumstances, responsibilities or pressures, and characteristic reactions. Although his eclecticism remains apparent, Machiavelli thus transformed ancient preconceptions into a persuasively fresh understanding of the human condition.

30. (Vol. 3, p. 338). Cf. Thucydides *Hist.* I,22(4), III,82(2); Polybius Vi,x, and cf. iii,2f., iv,12f., ix,10–14. On the stability of human nature through history see *Disc.* I,*proem.* (vol. 3, p. 22), I,3 (p. 241), 42 (p. 347), etc.; and on Machiavelli's use of Thucydides, II,2 (vol. 4, pp. 16f.), 10 (p. 44), 12 (p. 47), III,16 (p. 192).

31. Removing a tyrant meant acting out of necessity: cf. I,3 (vol. 3, p. 241), on such *necessità* in connection with the removal of Tarquinius Superbus.

## *Machiavelli on* Corpi Misti *and the constitutional history of Rome*

It is interesting that the absence of *natura* from Machiavelli's recurrence theory may be partly due to the fact that the term had such a wide usage among scholastics and theologians, both of whom he held in disfavor.[32] On the other hand, when once generalizing about mixed bodies (*corpi misti*), that is, "republics and religious sects," Machiavelli alluded to something like divine ordinance or even Aristotle's entelechy:

> All things of this world have a limit to their existence;[33] but those only run the whole course generally ordained by heaven (*dal cielo*) that do not allow their body to become disorganized, but keep it unchanged in the manner ordained. (*Disc.* III,1)

The theological touch may well come from dealing with religious groups as mixed bodies, but it is significant that Machiavelli took republics—as *miste*—to be superior to simple constitutions. The constitutions of Sparta and Rome, for instance, were much more durable for having an effective balance of power elements. May we assume, then, that states with complex constitutions, particularly republics, do not succumb to the rapid changes of his governmental cycle, even if they must eventually descend to some *ultima bassezza*?

Rome is the test case. Momentarily reverting to Polybius, we may recall that he forged a direct link between the anacyclic process and the natural development of Rome's polity. On the surface, that connection augured contradiction, but a closer examination made sense of his position. On the other hand, his views became intelligible only through a careful reconstruction of fragmentary evidence (Chapter 1, sect. E), and Machiavelli, lacking our materials, can hardly be expected to have offered an identical interpretation. In any case, Roman political history had been mediated to him by Livy and other post-Polybian authors, and he also declined to reproduce Polybius' emphasis on nature. How, then, did he understand the course of Rome's internal development, which is a favorite subject in the *Discorsi*?

After elaborating on his cycle of constitutions, Machiavelli made a brief comparison between Sparta and Rome (*Disc*, I,2). *Qua* constitution, the Spartan achievement was the better one, owing to Lycurgus' special foresight (cf. Polybius VI,l,21). Rome took longer to arrive at a state of good fortune, yet it did so neither through legislation nor through natural processes. Polybius had written of "many trials and troubles" in this connection (VI,x,14), while Machiavelli, having read his Livy as well, appealed to the accidental benefits of a disunion between senate and people, as well as to the background favor of *fortuna*.[34] And

32. See *Disc.* I,11–5 (pp. 269ff.); cf. Polybius VI,lvi,6ff., on Machiavelli's "shocking" utilitarian approach to religion. That he knew about equations of God and Nature, cf. *Ist.* IV,16 (vol. 2, p. 88).

33. Once again overt reference to biological or natural change and decay is conspicuously absent; yet cf. Polybius on *phthora* and *metabolē* in *Hist.* lvii,1.

34. (Vol. 3, pp. 238–40). ". . . So many unexpected events happened, on account of the disunion between the plebeians and the Senate, that what an organizer had not done, was done by chance (*caso*)" (p. 239); and p. 240 on fortune's favor. Cf., however, Polybius VI,ix,13f., x,12f.

once the Romans attained to their mixed constitution, we may presume, it then became a matter of keeping it "unchanged in the manner ordained."

Machiavelli was under no illusions, however, as to the difficulties of either securing or preserving the Roman stability. That he idealized Rome's government less than Polybius and Cicero, for instance, is even implied in his disinclination to describe its course as natural, and in his willingness to ascribe to fortune a rôle in Rome's internal politics.[35] Machiavelli's own context is all-important here. He knew only too well how the old Rome had declined and had fallen, and although prepared to admit that in Rome there were "more virtues than ever have been seen in any other republic" (*Disc.* I,i), her numerous faults could not be overlooked.[36] Livy's monument, for which the *Discorsi* was intended as a commentary, was a key factor behind this aspect of Machiavelli's realism. He could concur with Polybius that Rome had graduated toward a state of constitutional perfection. "Her first institutions," he could assert,

> were doubtless defective, but they were not in conflict with the principles that might bring her to perfection. (I,2)

On the other hand, there was Roman decline and Livian *degeneratio* theory to be reckoned with. Following Livy, he held that the Romans were less corrupt as a people while the Republican institutions were coming into being and when the government was less adequate. Their old virtues were gradually lost after the state's internal organization was settled and as the empire grew to its height.[37]

Accounting for these preconceptions, then, how do we characterize Machiavelli's picture of Rome's constitutional career? To begin with, her internal development had a zenith, this being attained when the conditions "for free public life" had been created (*Disc.* I,2). Her early course, therefore, ran toward *libertà*. The kingship founded by Romulus did not provide all the essentials for liberty, but these were acquired when the nobles and the people each gained a share of power in turn. The emergence and collapse of Roman kingship were in accord with earlier stages in the *Discorsi* cycle, but after the fall of the Tarquins there came an important departure. Because Romulus had already issued laws well suited for free public life (so Livy),[38] the Roman constitution quickly became complex, experiencing neither the rule of the few nor that of the many in simple form. Once consuls replaced the kings,[39] the government possessed a combination of two power elements—those of the (monarchical) consulate and the (aristocratic) senate. Then

35. Cicero referred to fortune's support more in afterthought: *Re pub.* II,xvi,30.

36. E.g., I,2, 28f., 32, 58, II,3 (on virtues), I,6, 35, II,*proem.* (on defects).

37. I,17 (vol. 3, p. 289), 18 (pp. 291–3), 47 (p. 355), II,8 (vol. 4, p. 36), III,1 (p. 131), III,25 (p. 242), and below.

38. *Ab urbe* I,viiiff. Also on Romulus' creation of the senate see Sextus Aurelius(?) *De viris illustribus* ii,10 (Cicero not being available).

39. His comment on driving the name and not the power of kings from Rome, I,2 (p. 240), refers back to the hatred of one-man rule in a post-tyrannical situation (p. 238).

it remained only for the people to be given power; this came with the insolence of the Roman nobility which . . . caused the people to rise against them, . . . the Tribunes of the People then being created. (*Disc.* I,2)

Now how are we to understand this passage from a two-pronged to a three-pronged constitution? Was it a transition from aristocracy through oligarchy to democracy, and thus part of an alternation between worthy and vicious constitutions? Certainly Machiavelli wished his readers to be convinced that Rome's pathway did somehow conform to the cycle of governments.

Authority passed in turn to kings, to the nobles, and to the people, and by the same degrees and for the same reasons discoursed above [in the outline of the cycle]. (p. 240)

Yet in the time between the expulsion of the Tarquins and the creation of tribunician power the cycle was not followed in its normal form. This was a period of "many disorders, clamors, and risks of scandal," a time of conflict between nobles and people which, for Machiavelli, set the tone for political agitations throughout the republic's life.[40] In Rome's path toward liberty, regal and aristocratic powers were never entirely abolished, so that on the institution of the tribuneship Rome was no mere democracy, but a republic with a balance of three power factors.

The stages in the Machiavellian account of Rome's *corso*, it may be noted, differed from those in Polybius. In our own analysis of the *Historiae* Bk. VI we established the Polybian sequence thus:[41]

"monarchy"
kingship
tyranny
aristocracy
*mixis*—(with growth, acme, decline)
oligarchy
democracy
ochlocracy
"monarchy"

Machiavelli's solution, affected by Livy, was different:

founder (there is no reference to Romulus as a "primitive" monarch)

kings

tyranny

consuls and senate as two settled power elements, with the people and the nobles in conflict, and with evidence of the latter's insolence

tribunician offices giving the people a voice

"perfect" *mista*

40. See *Disc.* I,4f. (pp. 242ff.) on Rome; and on a similar conflict in Florence see below.
41. See Diagram IV.

More follows, yet at this point we may comment on the ascending thrust of his sequence. The stages derive mainly from Livy, but they are presented to conform to the *Anacyclōsis*. Livy made no reference to the aristocratic oppression of the plebians prior to the establishment of the tribuneship,[42] yet Machiavelli made a point of the nobles' *insolenza*, probably because he held that, in its special way, Rome had experienced an oligarchy before the people acquired their voice.[43] Again, Livy nowhere contended that Rome had achieved constitutional perfection when the people obtained their measure of power; treating "the secession of the plebeians" he he simply went on to relate other troubles for Rome, both external and internal.[44] In Polybius, by comparison, there was a process of growth toward an acme—the Roman *mixis*—and it was up to Machiavelli to decide when this most admirable of constitutions had been achieved. In conformity with his view of accumulative development, Machiavelli placed the acquisition of a triadic mixed government after the establishment of the tribunician offices.[45] Significantly, his chapter on the creation of "the Tribunes of the People" follows immediately upon the *Discorsi* I,2. It was that creation which confirmed Rome as a republic or a "mixed body"; and this point granted, he could dig back historically to the foundations of Rome (I,9–34), and then forward toward the rise of the Principate (I,35ff.).[46]

In review, then, Rome reached perfection by not only experiencing kings and a tyrant, but also aristocrats who in turn became oligarchic, as well as the "democratic" plebeian activities which produced the tribunes. All these experiences, moreover, in their accumulative effect, contributed to the full stature of Roman republicanism.[47] What follows? What was the fate of the Republic, and

42. Interestingly, Cicero did not refer to such oppression, but only to the nobles' excess of power *via* the senate and consular office: *Re pub.* II,xxxii,56–xxxiv,59.

43. Placing a Roman oligarchy at this stage was not in Dionysius, let alone Livy. Dionysius (partly used by Machiavelli) interpreted the Decemvirs as oligarchic, but not the aristocracy before the creation of tribunes (see Chapter 4, introd.). On aristocratic insolence in Polybius, however, note *Hist.* VI,viii,5.

44. *Ab urbe* II,xxxiii–liii, etc.

45. Fascinatingly, the "accumulative" view of Polybius' archeology propounded by von Fritz (*Theory of the Mixed Constitution*, pp. 126ff., 434ff.) is truer for Machiavelli than Polybius (cf. above, Chapter 1, sect. E, pt. 2). To help account for Machiavelli's views, note that the passage which dated the beginning of the Roman *mixis* to the time of Xerxes' invasion and the Roman constitutional zenith to the time of the Second Punic War was probably not accessible to Machiavelli; cf. Moore, *Manuscript Tradition*, pp. 43ff., 171 (modern scholars inserting Exc. Vat., p. 372, M.25.30 H between Cod. Urb. fols. 60 and 66).

46. Reference to the creation of the tribunes being significantly omitted between I,34 and 35. Given a continuous commentary on Livy in *Disc.* I, that is where we would expect to find such a reference.

47. Machiavelli also took Romulus to be in a special sense the founder of the Roman *Republic* and a figure comparable to Lycurgus. He may not have intended to institute a republic, but he and his successors made laws which "looked forward" to the conditions of liberty: *Disc.* I,2 (vol. 3, p. 239); and (following Livy) Machiavelli considered Romulus the founder of the senate: I,9 (vol. 3, p. 263; Livy I,viii ff.). In that light he could even argue that creating the tribunes meant "a reversion to the original principles" (*ritirarono . . . verso il suo principio*) of the Roman constitution, and not the last stage in its growth to perfection: cf. *Disc.* III,1 (vol. 4, p. 129).

did Rome return to the path of the *Discorsi* cycle? For that matter, did her experience conform to the broader socio-political movement of the *Istorie* V,I?

At one point Machiavelli wrote about the insolence and intimidating actions of the tribunes, even prefacing his remarks by affirming that every human institution has an inherent evil (*Disc.* III,1). We need not suppose, however, that their excesses were equated with the license which followed upon democracy. Even though their untoward behavior had proleptic significance, and even though a gradual, long-term decline in morality was presupposed here,[48] Machiavelli located *licenza* where classical theory had generally put it—from the time of the Gracchi in the second century BC. Internal conflict over the agrarian reform issue

> led to violence and bloodshed beyond all bounds or precedent. So that, the magistrates being unable to check these disturbances, and neither party having any confidence in the public authorities, they both resorted to private remedies, and each of the factions began to look for a chief capable of defending them against the other. (*Disc.* I,37)[49]

In this "turmoil and disorder" the people looked to Marius, and in turn to Sulla, Pompey, and then, of course, to Caesar, who became "the first tyrant" in Rome (37). Now the picture of this lawlessness and the resort to private passions is clearly reminiscent of Machiavelli's description of license in the *Discorsi* I,2.[50] This time, too, the Polybian idea that mob rule produced demagogy and subsequently a "despot" or a "tyrant" (in Plato's sense) has some look in. In the troublesome aftermath of the agrarian laws, the populace bestowed favors on their champions, and as was typical with corrupt republics, the leading men "were more desirous of pleasing the masses than of promoting the general good" (I,37, II,22).[51] On the other hand, Machiavelli nowhere implied that when the Republic gave way to the Principate Rome sank into a condition of bestiality or nonpolity. Remaining true to his own modification of the *Anacyclōsis*, he showed that license was followed by reversion to one-man rule. This modification may well have been dictated by the facts of the Roman past in the first place. Polybius did not foresee the emergence of the emperors; Machiavelli, by contrast, had the whole course of Roman history before his eyes. The *Anacyclōsis* was tailored to suit the facts.

Rome, therefore, passed through at least one complete cycle of governments. In the establishment of a republic the *cerchio* had been forestalled and a peak in civic life achieved, but from the Gracchan period on she declined back into the

48. III,1 (pp. 130f.), where Rome's moral degeneration is traced as far back as Regulus; cf. Polybius I,xxviii ff., Livy XVII,*summ*.

49. (Vol. 3, p. 333); cf. III,24 (vol. 4, p. 213).

50. Cf. also II,22 (vol. 4, p. 86). "In quiet times, excellent men in corrupt republics, as a result of envy and other ambitious reasons, are looked on as enemies; hence the people follow either someone who through general self-deception is thought good, or someone put forward by men interested in what they can get from the public."

51. (Vol. 3, pp. 333f.); cf. Polybius VI,ix,6–8.

anacyclic path.[52] There remain, however, vexed questions about the Principate, which in the East, at least, lasted over a thousand years. To begin with, if Machiavelli named Julius Caesar as the first in a series of tyrants, he was also happy to call him *principe*,[53] a term, incidentally, which best accords with his account of the *Discorsi* cycle. And what of the long line of emperors? It is not clear whether they could be classified into "kings and tyrants" (cf. *Disc.* I,10),[54] but they were all *principi*,[55] and to that extent were comparable to the monarchs of England or France.[56] The continuity of ancient emperors and medieval kings obviously presented a problem in relation to his fast-moving cycle of governments, yet Machiavelli's apparent solution lay in a distinction between monarchs who inherited kingdoms and those who did not.[57] If kingships remained hereditary, ruin would surely come, since bad sons would replace worthy fathers, and the reinvigoration which came with fresh pretenders would be stifled. Although Rome remained in decline under the Principate (that is, vis-à-vis her republican peak), changes in dynastic lines preserved some health in the state, and it was also true that Rome's new *principato* marked a recovery after the disorder of license.[58]

All these constitutional changes, from Romulus to the Caesars, were placed within a wider context. Rome also experienced the cyclo-alternating process between order and disorder, good fortune and ruin. The pinnacle of her success came under the Republic; not only did she preserve a republican order for about three hundred years (even if with difficulty), but between the plebeian secession and the Gracchi she acquired a great empire, and was blessed both with rulers of *virtù* and fortune's favor. Now Rome's height as an empire was located where most classical authors placed it—after the defeat of Carthage, Macedonia, and Antiochus the Great (*Disc.* II,1).[59] A languor came on after Antiochus' defeat, when the number of virtuous men decreased, military commands were imprudently distributed, and agrarian troubles arose.[60] What were the further stages in the decline? Did Machiavelli believe that when the Republic collapsed into

52. I,37 (pp. 332f., and cf. pp. 333f.), and see Livy LVIII–IX *summ.*

53. *Princ.* xvi,3f.

54. "All emperors who succeeded to the empire through heredity, except Titus, were bad; those through adoption were all good, as were those five from Nerva to Marcus; and when the empire was left to heirs, it returned to a state of ruin" (vol. 3, p. 267).

55. *Princ.* xix,8ff.

56. A point important for the development of constitutional theory in the north: see, e.g., F. Raab, *The English Face of Machiavelli*, London, 1964, chs. 1–2.

57. In *Disc.* I,10 (just quoted), the distinction is between *eredità* and *adozione*; in *Il Principe* it is between hereditary rule and those who take over power when a given line has no successors or is overcome (esp. iii,3f.).

58. For important background see Plutarch *Vit.* (*Dion and Brutus Compared*), ii,1ff. (where Caesar's rule is considered the needed remedy for Rome's maladies); cf. C. P. Jones, *Plutarch and Rome*, Oxford, 1971, p. 101. In addition, Machiavelli could have found the idea of a reversion to *regnum* (as against primitive monarchy) in Sextus Aurelius Victor *Vit. et morib. imper.* i,1.

59. (Vol. 4, p. 13).

60. Virtue flourished up to Aemilius Paullus' day (flor. 168 BC): III,16,25 (vol. 4, pp. 194, 217); cf. L. J. Walker (ed.), *The Discourses of Niccolò Machiavelli*, London, 1950, vol. 2, p. 178 on Plutarch and Aurelius Victor as his sources for Aemilius. Also *Disc.* III,1 (p. 131), 16, 24 (pp. 194, 213–5).

conditions of license, the whole Roman state had descended to a low point of ruin and disorder? In Rome's case, in other words, did the end points of his two major cycles coincide?

The Florentine, unfortunately, does not answer our questions. Either Rome passed through one general moment, the Principate simply representing further, though prolonged, decay, with the Romans' "ancient valor" and their religious spirit now dissipated,[61] or else she experienced two cycles, the first ending in the civil wars and disorder of the first century BC, and the second covering the rise and fall of the Caesars' empire, from Julius to the utter ruin of the barbarian invasions.[62] The first alternative suits Machiavelli's republican bias, his apparent assumption that Roman history was basically the history of the Republic. The second possibility, however, can hardly be ruled out. Although Machiavelli described how a whole state could sink into *rovina*, this ruin did not necessarily mark complete destruction, but only an "utmost state of depression" from which ascent might begin again. In either case, the conception that human societies pass alternately between widely separated points of prominence and depression still remains.

## *The recurrent lapse of republics into tyranny: Rome*

Machiavelli left another major model of recurrence which was connected with constitutional history in general and Roman history in particular. Republics, as possessors of complex constitutions, were involved in a special *mutazione di stato*: the recurrent change from liberty to tyranny and vice versa.[63]

Roman republican history from the plebeian secession to the Caesars, we may assert, was conceived as a succession of breakdowns or near-breakdowns into tyrannies, each lapse being followed by the reacquisition of an essential republicanism. In Machiavelli's view, republics had a dangerous propensity toward turning into tyrannies, just as kingdoms often did,[64] and this could be illustrated by the case of Rome. Instead of reckoning the Decemvirate an oligarchy,[65] for example, he wrote of it as the tyranny of Appius Claudius and his supporters (cf. I,40,[66] III,26). From Appius he looked back to the attempt of Spurius Cassius to seize power, and interpreted it as a tendency toward the tyrannical (III,8).[67] He even gazed back as far as Tarquinius Superbus, as if the Republic, in a special sense created by Romulus and Numa, had first suffered at

61. II,8 (p. 36); cf. I,11 (vol. 3, p. 272); Rehm, *Untergang Roms*, pp. 54ff. In I,10 he does suggest that between Nero and Marcus Aurelius conditions improved over what existed just before and after.

62. *Ist.* I,1 (vol. 1, p. 2), on "the overthrow of so great an empire" and the multitudes "joining forces to bring about its ruin."

63. So *Disc.* III,3 (vol. 4, p. 135): "from republic to tyranny or from tyranny to republic"; III,7 (p. 166): "from free government to tyranny, and the opposite"; cf. 8 (pp. 169f.); 49 (p. 267).

64. I,10 (vol. 3, p. 265); cf. I,46 (p. 354), 58 (p. 386), III,8 (vol. 4, pp. 167, 169f.).

65. As did Dionysius and (according to Taeger's erroneous interpretation) Polybius: see above, Chapter 1, sect. E, pt. 2; Chapter 4, introd.

66. Two references to tyranny (vol. 3, pp. 343, 344).

67. (Vol. 4, p. 167): the people refused "to open Spurius the road to tyranny."

*his* tyrannical hands.[68] Looking forward, he alighted on the pretensions of Spurius Maelius and Manlius Capitolinus (III,28),[69] on the still later attempts at tyranny by Marius and Sulla (III,24; cf. I,37),[70] as well as those of Pompey and Caesar, the latter being the "first tyrant" in a series. Brutus and Cassius tried valiantly to restore the Republic and so to liberate Rome from this last tyranny, but they failed (III,6, in vol. 4, pp. 142–3). On earlier occasions Rome had been able to overcome such slides into tyranny by removing the usurper and by restoring her ancient form of government (I,45), thus returning to the "true path" (III,28). But by Caesar's time the Republic had become too decidedly corrupted. If the Romans had long succeeded in bringing their "mixed body" back to its "ordained" path, the Principate eventually dashed all hopes of that possibility.

Thus Machiavelli infused another model of recurrence into his interpretation of constitutional history. From our Diagram XII it appears as an alternation between liberty and tyranny, though one could also deem it a form of *metabolē* theory, since we are dealing here with the propensity of one constitution to change into another. The basis for this new model presumably lay in earlier analyses of Roman history. Livy himself had already implied that Appius Claudius was a tyrant,[71] and he wrote suggestively of other relevant figures covered in the *Discorsi*.[72] By Machiavelli's time, in any case, the contrast between republicanism and tyranny was a well-entrenched commonplace in political theory. Aquinas had written that "the degeneration of government into tyranny is no less frequent under a government ruled by more than one person than under a monarchy; in fact, it is probably more frequent,"[73] and within the Florentine political tradition Salutati had already used the examples of Spurius Maelius and Manlius Capitolinus as would-be tyrants, men who conspired against *libertas*.[74] Medieval scholars, of course, had invariably referred to corrupt kings as tyrants, and more recently pro-republicans had so labelled the up-and-coming Italian despots, particularly the notorious Giangaleazzo Visconti, who had posed such a threat to the free civic life of the early Quattrocento.[75] Machiavelli took up these threads and developed a model for political

68. III,8 (pp. 166f.); cf. I,9 (vol. 3, p. 263), 11 (pp. 271f.), 58 (pp. 385f.).

69. (Vol. 4, pp. 223–4), especially on how Spurius nearly ruined (*rovinare*) the Republic.

70. Sulla and Marius raised up armies "against the public good" (vol. 4, p. 215), emerging following the *licenza* depicted above in pt. 2 *finis*. Cf. also *Ist.* II,2 (vol. 1, p. 64).

71. *Ab urbe* III,xxxvi,2, 5, xxxvii.

72. E.g., IV,xiii,1–xvi,8 on Spurius Maelius. Cicero listed Tarquinius Superbus, Spurius Cassius, and Spurius Maelius together in *De amicitia* viii,28.

73. *De reg. princ.* v (d'Entrèves, p. 25).

74. *De tyranno* ii (Emerton, pp. 80f.; cf. 88f. where the combined reference to Tarquinius Superbus, the Decemvirs, and Nero implies that the Decemvirs represented a tyranny also).

75. H. Baron, *The Crisis of the Early Italian Renaissance*, Princeton, 1955, vol. 1, pt. 1; *Humanistic and Political Literature in Florence and Venice at the Beginning of the Quattrocento*, Cambridge, Mass., 1955, pp. 38ff.; D. J. Wilcox, *Development*, pp. 138ff. Such a despotic one-man rule Savonarola evidently had in mind when defending liberty against tyranny in *Trattato circa il Reggimento e Governo della Città di Firenze* (1498), III,3 (Firpo edn., pp. 47–53), a stance of background importance for Machiavelli; cf. Whitfield, op. cit., pp. 33f.

## Diagram XII Machiavelli on Roman Constitutional Change

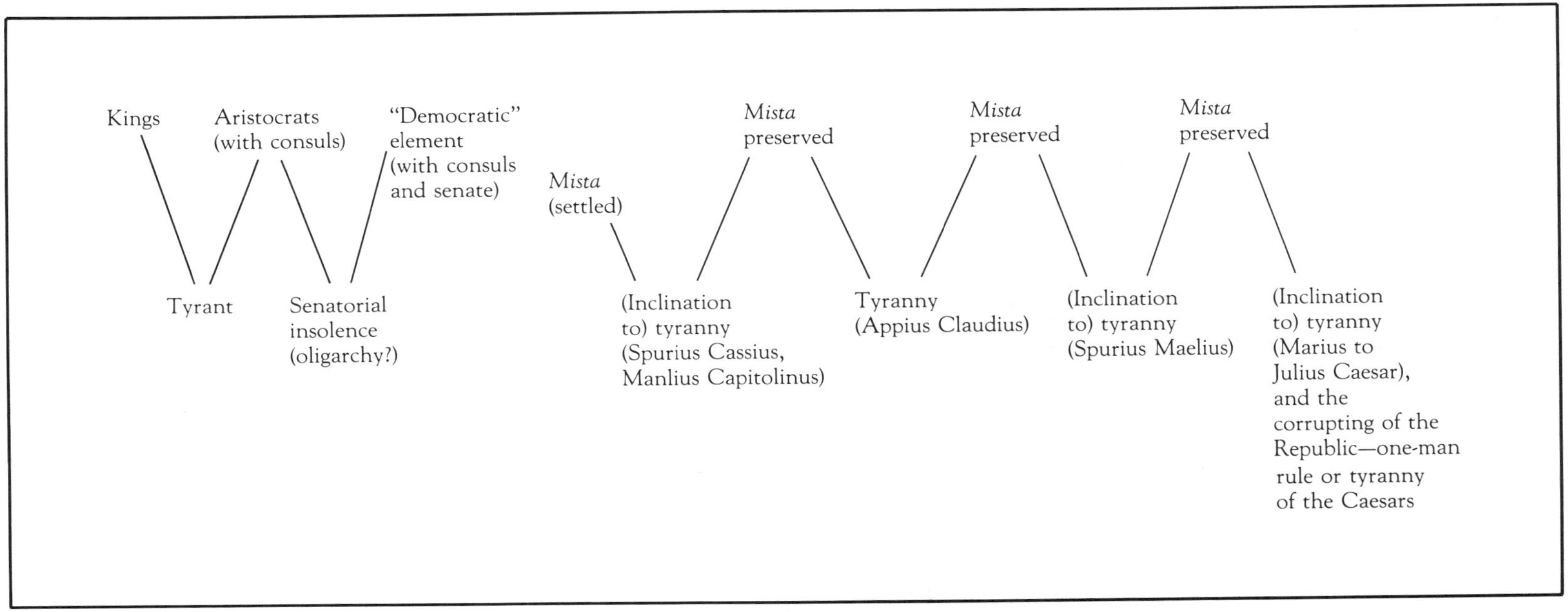

Kings

Tyrant

Aristocrats
(with consuls)

Senatorial
insolence
(oligarchy?)

"Democratic"
element
(with consuls
and senate)

*Mista*
(settled)

(Inclination
to) tyranny
(Spurius Cassius,
Manlius Capitolinus)

*Mista*
preserved

Tyranny
(Appius Claudius)

*Mista*
preserved

(Inclination
to) tyranny
(Spurius Maelius)

*Mista*
preserved

(Inclination
to) tyranny
(Marius to
Julius Caesar),
and the
corrupting of the
Republic—one-man
rule or tyranny
of the Caesars

change within republics. This model was not strictly integral to his first *cerchio*, and it is not even justifiable to call it cyclical, but it is certainly a model of historical recurrence with its own niche in his theory of change.

### *Reciprocal change within unstable republics: Florence*

Machiavelli called states other than Rome *repubbliche*, and the one he spent the most time documenting was his own beloved city-state. Florence, however, was understood to be a republic with glaring deficiencies; she merited only an unfavorable comparison with Rome. In fact, with all her vicissitudes of constitutional changes (after 1215), it could be claimed that she "never really experienced republican government."[76] Unlike Rome, she did not enjoy liberty from her beginnings, but only after a long period of servitude under ancient Rome and the medieval emperors. Thus old, bad institutions came to be mixed with newer, more preferable ones, while turbulence and divisions among the Florentines produced a harmful factiousness, rather than new laws or military valor.[77] Florence, then, was a republic of a degenerate ilk, and we may infer that, in Machiavelli's mind, her internal changes differed somewhat from Rome's. More like Athens, her power elements were not balanced evenly enough to prevent her from inclining toward unmixed constitutional forms.[78]

Assuming Florence to be a republic,[79] at least after 1215, one expects to meet the idea of republics recurrently breaking down into tyrannies and near-tyrannies, and this is just what one finds. Corso Donati pretended to *tirannide* in 1304, for instance, but met with disaster.[80] The republic gave extraordinary powers to Jacopo Gabrielli (in 1340) and the Duke of Athens (in 1342), and in each case found tyrannies on its hands, the tyrants being removed in their turn by popularly supported conspiracies.[81] Machiavelli described the members of the 1378 Ciompi revolt as tyrannical,[82] and also the citizens who caused the factionalism of the 1240s and the early 1290s.[83] To that extent, then, and since

76. *Disc.* I,49 (vol. 3, p. 360); cf. *Discorso sopra il Riformare lo Stato di Firenze* (vol. 5, p. 7).

77. *Disc.* I,49 (vol. 3, p. 360); *Ist.* II,2 (vol. 1, p. 65), 5 (pp. 69f.); cf. Bk. I, on servitude under the Romans; *Disc.* I,4 (vol. 3, p. 243), 8 (p. 260), 49 (p. 360), *Ist.* III,1 (vol. 2, p. 5), VII,1 (p. 263), on mixing institutions, factions, etc.

78. If in *Disc.* I,2 Athens was named a "popular government" (above, pt. 1), elsewhere Machiavelli called her a republic: I,28 (vol. 3, p. 309), 58 (p. 385). As the former her historical course did not follow the cycle of governments, but as the latter she could be understood as a republic susceptible to tyranny (that of the Peisistratidae, for instance). Republics, moreover, could be weighted in different directions—toward *lo stato popolare* as in Athens' case, aristocracy, or princedom: *Disc. rif. stat. Fir.* (vol. 5, p. 8); *Ist.* III,1 (vol. 2, pp. 5–7).

79. One cannot detect the *Discorsi* cycle in the *Istorie* except by supposing that the period of servitude under the emperors, the struggle between nobility and people, the period following the people's victory over the nobles, and the period of the Medici represent the sequence monarchy/aristocracy/democracy/monarchy. The book divisions of the *Istorie* (thus: I/II/III–IV/V–VIII) lend some support to this line, but I think it tenuous.

80. *Ist.* II,21 (vol. 1, pp. 91f.), 22 (p. 95); cf. II,7ff. (pp. 71ff.).

81. II,32 (pp. 110f.), 34–8 (pp. 117, 119, 121, 123ff.), III,1 (vol. 2, p. 7), 16 (p. 43); cf. also II,29ff. (vol. 1, pp. 104ff.) on Castruccio.

82. III,16 (vol. 2, p. 43), 20 (pp. 46f.), IV,9 (p. 78).

83. II,9 (vol. 1, p. 75), III,25 (vol. 2, p. 57), IV,2 (p. 69).

her republic "corrected" itself in each case, the Florentine and Roman cases were comparable. Once again, the tyrannies were not necessarily focused on individuals. On the other hand, Florence was a more poorly-constituted republic than Rome. She inclined too much toward *lo stato popolare* (cf. *Ist.* III,1), and for this reason was susceptible to another kind of change. In his preface to the *Istorie* IV, Machiavelli waxed theoretical about this other tendency:

> Republican governments, *more especially those imperfectly organized*, frequently change their rulers and the form of their institutions; yet not between liberty and servitude, as many suppose, but between servitude and license. (vol. 2, p. 67)[84]

Florence, then, not only experienced a struggle between tyranny and liberty, but dual tendencies toward both tyranny and license. In this poorly-constituted city-state, "only the name of liberty was in any estimation," and neither the nobles (as the main force making for servitude), nor the people (as the chief ministers of license), "chose to subject themselves to the magistrates or the law" (p. 67). The impression left is something like a beam-balance (cf. above, Chapter 2, sect. B), whereby the state can be tipped either way, toward the harsh or unbeneficial rule of the powerful, on the one hand, or toward extreme factiousness, the rule of "each man for himself," on the other. That the balance tips alternately is certainly implied in the *Istorie* IV,1, but in view of the complexities of Machiavelli's Florentine history, it is sufficient to stress the recurrent tendency to change either way. With the absence of "excellent laws" and institutions, the restoration of a balanced constitution was difficult and the pull toward disorder more likely.

Weak republics, however, do not always remain lost in servitude or factiousness. "When," Machiavelli insisted, "a good, wise, and powerful citizen appears, which is but seldom," ordinances may be established which offset contending dispositions and produce "a government called *libera*, with its institutions firm and secure" (pp. 67–8). This is interesting. Tyranny and license take weak republics toward utter ruin, yet the suggestion here is that a savior can redeem such a state. The savior seems to stand alone. We have come to another thorny area of Machiavellian studies, and one pertinent to the study of his recurrence ideas—the rôle of the prince.

## The Prince *and constitutional history*

Within the life of republics, princes evidently arose when license threatened the state. To take the Roman case: although Julius Caesar illustrated the recurrent lapse of republicanism into tyranny, he also headed a series of *principi*, rulers who arose once the republic had collapsed with factional fighting. Florentine politics exemplified both types of change more fully. If the city was a prey to tyranny, those times of turbulence, when her government remained

84. Machiavelli here dissociates his position from that of the early humanists who seemed to him to parallel Rome and Florence as great republics recurrently threatened by tyranny. Cf. also (p. 68).

wholly at the mercy of the people, saw the rising possibility of princedom as well.[85] It was following bitter feuding between the Medici, Rinaldo degli Albizzi, and Neri di Gino Capponi, that Cosimo de' Medici so took the reins of government that he convinced Machiavelli he was "prince in his own country."[86] The resurgence of popularism in Cosimo's closing years gave Luca Pitti the opportunity of virtual princedom,[87] and Lorenzo I rose to power in the wake of severe internal disruptions within Florence.[88] Outside the *Istorie*, Machiavelli commented on events after the death of Lorenzo I in a consistent vein. He admitted that Soderini's government (under which he served for thirteen years) was far from being a true republic, and that, together with internal disorders, the establishment of a *Gonfaloniere di Giustizia* for life (in 1509) opened the door to a princedom—to the return of the Medici.[89] Thus important developments in his own time, especially the outstanding rule of the Medicean house, conformed to a rule of constitutional change, and this rule of thumb was meant to develop rather than contradict his previous theoretical analyses. Florence stood as a good specimen of weak republicanism and its consequences.

Machiavelli, however, did not forget other Italian powers. In the *Istorie* this pattern, of republican breakdown into license and the resulting establishment of a princedom, is also documented from Milanese history.[90] He showed that between 1447 and the death of Filippo Visconti to the rise of Lodovico "il Moro" in 1480 Milan passed alternately between a badly-organized republic and the rule of a *principe*.[91] As with Florence, Milan fell into the hands of a prince on more than one occasion. Such badly ordered *miste*, then, suffered from the

85. For an early case (Andrea Strozzi, 1343), see II,29 (vol. 1, p. 105); and note Rinaldi degli Albizzi's (contrived?) 1400 speech concerning the possibility of a prince arising if the power of the people became excessive: ". . . then Florence would be governed either by chance, according to the will of the crowd, so that one party would live without restraint and the other in danger, or the city would be under the domination of one man who would make himself *principe*," IV,9 (vol. 2, p. 78) (a passage with some very Machiavellian touches!).

86. VII,5 (p. 269); cf. IV,26 (pp. 105ff.), 27 (p. 109), VI,23 (p. 230); *Disc.* I,17 (vol. 3, p. 287).

87. *Ist.* VII,4ff. (vol. 2, pp. 267ff.).

88. VII,13–9 and ff. (pp. 282ff.); cf. 5 (p. 269), VIII,33 (vol. 3, pp. 62–72); *Disc. rif.* (vol. 5, pp. 7–16).

89. *Disc. rif.* (pp. 8–9; cf. 9–11 on Lorenzo II's rule as a princely interlude). *Disc.* I,7 (vol. 3, p. 256), III,3 (vol. 4, pp. 135f.) for unfavorable comments against Soderini (one of Machiavelli's epigrams also assigning him to Limbo), I,52 (vol. 3, pp. 365f.), III,9 (vol. 4, p. 172) for a less critical evaluation.

90. On the decline of republics into tyrannies, cf. *Ist.* IV,24 (vol. 2, p. 103), VII,25 (p. 304), on both Lucca and Prato.

91. Upon Filippo Visconti's death the Milanese restored republican government. The people were afraid Francesco Sforza would seize control, and in this context he stood for tyranny: VI,13 (p. 213), 17ff. (pp. 218ff.), 19f. (pp. 223f.). However, Machiavelli emphasized the factiousness of the Milanese (how could they "keep themselves *liberi*?" Cosimo is made to ask), and the republic is pictured as breaking down into utter misery, due to the rise of the lower orders, so that Sforza enters Milan in 1450, not as a tyrant but as a prince: 23f. (pp. 231–4); cf. *Disc.* I,17 (vol. 3, pp. 289f.), *Disc. rif.* (vol. 5, p. 13). His successor, Galeazzo Maria, "proved licentious and cruel" (= tyrannical) and was slain in a resurgence of republicanism based on Cola Montano's ideology: *Ist.* VII,32 (vol. 2, pp. 316f.). The pattern was not dissimilar to that of Florence: Lorenzo I/the incompetent Piero/republic revived (1494–1512)/return of the Medici.

effects of license as much as tyranny, finding it hard to maintain an even keel between the two or to follow the correct path. Princedom was an important compensating factor, since it arose in the wake of factional fighting, and its emergence in the life of "defective republics" needed to be accounted for. Not that princely rule was the automatic guarantor of true liberty, however; that only came with a ruler especially endowed with the wisdom, goodness, and power to turn disorder into order.

This kind of interpretation allows us to say something briefly about the famous *Il Principe*, the tract written at a time when Soderini's republic had fallen, the Spanish had restored the Medicean house, and Machiavelli had been sent into exile. To begin with, the term *principe* was quite broad in its connotations. In relation to the true conditions of republican liberty, for instance, a prince could represent the tyrannical;[92] in the face of great inner turbulence, to take the other extreme, he could, if he were the right man, be the agent for placing a republic on a steady footing. Or his rôle could be conceived as lying somewhere between these two poles: as one outcome of constitutional changes within defective republics, or even as a would-be *buono uomo* who was seeking to put the state on an even keel but whose success was only temporary.[93] Again, a princedom could stand at the beginning and end of the constitutional cycle, or simply rate as an hereditary monarchy (for "principalities and republics" were the two ubiquitous forms of government in Machiavelli's own day).[94]

For the Florentine, then, a prince may arise in different contexts within constitutional history, and his rôle and associations differ in accordance with those contexts. Thus if one is to make sense of *Il Principe*, dedicated as it was to Lorenzo II, one has to understand how Machiavelli estimated Florence's situation in 1512. Now, that is not easy. Not only does he fail to insist in this work that Lorenzo's rule was a typical consequence of corrupt republicanism, the recommencement of a *cerchio*, the means by which the Florentine state could be brought back to its original principles,[95] or that it was merely the product of foreign intervention or some such other alternative, but the fact is that he was as concerned about what might happen (even what might be hoped for) as about what had already taken place. In *Il Principe*, moreover, his view was Italian as much as it was narrowly Florentine. We find ourselves waiting for a

92. E.g., Caesar or the Medici: *Ist.* VIII,1 (vol. 3, p. 6), 11 (p. 26).

93. Note *Disc.* I,11 (vol. 3, p. 272), 17 (p. 290), on *principi* whose work of reform is undone after their deaths; cf. also *Ist.* IV,1. Cosimo and Lorenzo I seem to fit into this category: *Disc.* III,1 (vol. 4, p. 128); *Ist.* VII,1–4 (vol. 2, pp. 261ff.), VIII,36 *finis* (vol. 3, p. 72); cf. *Disc.* I,55 (vol. 3, p. 376).

94. He was once so loose in language as to say that no constitution ever existed which could not be called either *repubblica* or *principato*: *Princ.* i (vol. 4, p. 275) (and for the background of this distinction in humanist rhetoric, see J. A. Pocock, *The Machiavellian Moment: Florentine Political Thought and the Atlantic Republican Tradition*, Princeton, 1975, pp. 50ff.).

95. On the *buono uomo* as the sagacious legislator bringing the republic back to its original principles, see *Disc.* I,9 (vol. 3, p. 262), 18 (p. 294). He could be a prince: I,2 (p. 238), 58 (p. 386). For further discussion see Pocock, op. cit., pp. 204f.

precise location of "the Prince" in his analyses of political change and historical recurrence, but the possibilities of 1513 were too open, the situation too transitional, the circumstances of Machiavelli's writing themselves too unsettled to provide a ready answer (see Excursus 5). It suffices to affirm that the appearance of a one-man rule at this juncture in Florentine history was certainly in keeping with his theories of constitutional change. This was true whether Lorenzo hastened the ruin of the state or whether he was a great "man of spirit and virtue"[96] who could remove the barbarian threat from the Italian peninsula. Lorenzo was installed in power after Soderini's inadequate republic collapsed; such republics bore either tyrants or princes, and on rare occasions—a sanguine thought for Machiavelli—a good, wise, and powerful source of "redemption."

Lorenzo II died in June of 1519. By that time Machiavelli was well enmeshed in pro-republican activities. And if he had once believed Lorenzo to be the potential *buono uomo* of his dreams, a new possibility now lay with a younger Medici, Pope Leo X, to whom he addressed his 1520 *Discorso* on Florentine reform. From Leo he requested not a monarchy but a *mista*, an evenly balanced tripartite constitution with Leo as its monarchical element. It was in the power of this most influential of men, a *buono uomo* likened to Romulus (vol. 5, p. 23), to put Florence on her feet. In the *Discorso* Machiavelli did not fail to appeal to a model of recurring change. Referring more to ideals than to tragic realities, he contended that:

> No firm government can be devised if it is not either a true princedom or a true republic, because all the constitutions between these two are defective. The reason is entirely evident—because the princedom has just one path to dissolution, that is to descend toward the republic. And similarly the republic has just one path toward being dissolved, that is, to rise toward princedom. Governments of a middle sort [e.g., Florence or Milan] have two ways: they can rise toward the princedom or descend toward the republic. From this comes their lack of firmness. (p. 13)

Machiavelli here acknowledged that true republics were not the only kind of stable, durable governments. Longlasting monarchies were evident in his day.[97] His interests, though, centered on the ordering of his own city-state, which had been accustomed to equality rather than autocracy (pp. 13–4). The key rôle of the legislator in this Florentine context was to forestall change, that is, to vitiate those recurrent processes which either weaken the republic or bring on its ruin. The secret of modern legislation was to gauge how and why constitutions were recurrently transformed into one form or another, and to devise means of containing the processes of change.[98]

96. On the alternatives see *Disc.* II,29 (vol. 4, pp. 113f.); cf. I,57 (vol. 3, p. 386).

97. Did Machiavelli explain why certain principalities—the Caesars, the French kings—continue in existence when, according to *Disc.* I,2 they should be replaced by minority rules? Without any assurance, three explanations are possible: monarchies were preserved when successors gained thrones by adoption rather than heredity (see above, pt. 2); men in power brought the constitution back to original principles, thus forestalling tyranny: cf. *Disc.* III,1 (vol. 4, p. 132); monarchies can be mixed constitutions: cf., e.g., *Disc. rif.* (vol. 5, p. 15), and see below, pt. 6 (on the theory of the French mixed constitution, surely known to Machiavelli).

98. Cf. *Disc.* I,9 (vol. 3, p. 264), 18 (pp. 294f.), on Cleomenes restoring the Lycurgan constitution

By these processes, of course, I mean those major ones already elicited from the Machiavellian *corpus*. We have isolated at least three key models of recurring constitutional change, and although in varying degrees they owe something to earlier theory, they all betray his special interpretative touches. The cycle of the *Discorsi* I,2 is the most theoretical and complex. It might seem formal and unrelated to the rest of his work, even "literally so unMachiavellian," as J. H. Hexter puts it,[99] that it does not seem to invite scholarly attention. But we have shown that although Machiavelli did not indicate the relevance of this scheme for contemporary politics, he revived the great anacyclic model of Polybius, consciously modified it, and applied the results to the important case of Rome. A second frame, outlined most clearly in the *Discorsi* III,3 and 7, covered the recurrent breakdown of republics into tyranny, a breakdown implicit in Livy, recognized in medieval and early Renaissance political writing, but only consciously developed as a recurrent pattern of constitutional change by Machiavelli. He applied it to the test case of Rome, but also documented it from the lives of more defective republics in modern Italy. In a third framework, expressed in the preface to the *Istorie* Bk. IV, he elaborated upon the lack of firmness within weak republics, leaving his conception of a wavering movement between servitude (under tyrants) and *licenza* (with the consequent emergence of one-man rule). The histories of Florence and Milan (and we may include, I think, Florentine affairs between 1492 and 1527) provided the basis for this sophisticated and highly intriguing line of interpretation. Finally, lying behind all and being much less a model of constitutional change, lay the general sociopolitical alternation of the *Istorie* V,1, the alternation between zenith and depression. Ancient Rome passed through one, perhaps two, such broad movements, and finally fell to the barbarians. Machiavelli also applied this last frame to the contemporary scene, although he made little differentiation between Italy and particular city-states such as Florence. He concurred with Bruni in connecting a revival of ancient republicanism with the emergence of the new Italian cities, and it was a crucial point for him that these cities had kept out the northern barbarians for so long.[100] Ruin would befall Florence in particular and Italy in general if the new barbarian threat could not be checked. This fourth model, embracing so much more than the others, and based on those traditional notions of fluctuation, rise and fall, which died so hard, was the setting in which all the other processes could operate. As the most fundamental of Machiavelli's recurrence paradigms, it accounted for changes by external as much as by internal means.

We possess here, then, a cluster of interpretative frames. A cycle of governments, a regular *metabolē* from one constitutional form to another, a reciprocal

---

at a time of Spartan corruption; I,10 (vol. 3, p. 268), 19 (p. 297), on how Caesar should have imitated Romulus, to bring the state back to original principles.

99. Loc. cit., p. 75.

100. *Ist.* V,1 (vol. 2, p. 126); cf. Bruni *Hist.* Bk. II (pp. 27ff.). In so interpreting the evidence, I dispute J. Mazzeo's contentions that for Machiavelli "the repetition of history will always be retrograde" or a descending series of cycles (*Renaissance and Seventeenth Century Studies*, New York and London, 1964, p. 150).

relationship between pressures within the state, a cyclo-alternating pattern of rise and descent—all are indicative of the vital rôle of recurrence thinking in Machiavelli's political theory. And none of these rules of thumb (*regole*) involves God or nature. Fortune, as we shall see, had its sphere, but the dominant thrust is that of human response before changing circumstances. The mystique of "underlying principles of change," so apparent in Polybius, has been replaced by an intense awareness that man is the only genuine subject of history, the one who produces circumstances either by active will or by default, who creates institutions yet corrupts them, and who is the key agent behind recurrent change and process.

One is struck, moreover, by the anti-eschatological axis of Machiavelli's historical thought. He did not expect an ultimate end to the present historical order; his attention centered on a continuing process and on the human factors which engendered it. As a political reformer, too, he reflected on original principles rather than on long-term goals (though concern for the former is not so unbiblical!), so that unsatisfactory political conditions could be removed by reverting to what had been preferable in the past. Nor did he truckle to the anti-historical tendencies of ancient philosophy or medieval theology. His models were not framed to elevate transitory human affairs to the realm of eternal intelligibility; he was not a "substantialist," and he therefore did not believe that events were important "chiefly for the light they throw on the eternal and substantial entities of which they are mere accidents."[101] He was not seeking a "sacred model" as were the theologians.[102] Historical patterns and recurrences were *in* the events, not "educated" by them; they were taken to be empirically grounded, not traditional truths suiting "the common intelligence." Not that he altogether escaped from philosophical or even theological assumptions, but he intended to arrive at his rules of thumb along empirical lines. All the models we have discussed (even his version of the *Anacyclōsis*, in which he was least successful in evading an anti-historical tendency) are monumental illustrations of his efforts to generalize from observation, and to be a man of science before a philosopher. Once the rules of change were grasped, then, one either conformed to or controlled the processes in accordance with one's preferred ends.[103]

## *Theories of constitutional change before and after Machiavelli*

Interest in patterns of constitutional change, as we have seen, was not absent from medieval and early Renaissance thought. However, it was generally limited in purview, focusing on the breakdown of kingship or of *libertas* into tyranny. Even Aquinas, when commenting on the three kinds of change outlined in

101. Collingwood, *Idea of History*, pp. 42f.; cf. pp. 20ff.

102. G. S. Rousseau, "The *Discoursi* [*sic*] of Machiavelli: History and Theory" in *Journal of World History* IX, 1965, p. 160.

103. Cf. ibid., p. 157 (cf. p. 156 n. 59), where, however, Rousseau goes too far in assuming that Machiavelli hoped legislators or governments would encourage the processes of recurrence (once they knew the set paths, and even if the next phase were bad).

Aristotle's *Nicomachean Ethics* Bk. VIII, declined to explore their applications to the contemporary scene.[104] In the East, a pragmatic concern for institutional life shows up in Metochites' writing. He discussed the tendencies of aristocracy and democracy to degenerate,[105] and examined the comparative merits of Rome and Carthage as mixed constitutions, ascribing the latter's weakness to the absence of a monarchical element.[106] This element, possessed by Rome, was the state's salvation, and Metochites promptly defended the existing monarchical system, despite the danger of tyranny.[107] In the end, though, he did not formulate a doctrine of recurring political transformations; his object, rather, was to extol kingship, the constitutional order so prevalent and so unquestionable in his day.

With the increasing circulation of classical historical texts, however, speculation on constitutional change was bound to reassert itself, even under kingships. Claude Seyssel (ca. 1450–1520), for instance, a contemporary of Machiavelli's, appears to have employed Polybius Bk. VI in defence of the French (mixed) monarchy. Referring to the three simple worthy constitutions, he argued that monarchy was the best, provided that the ruler possessed sufficient experience and desired to rule justly, while aristocracy inclined to oligarchy and democracy to a state of turbulence.[108] All unmixed constitutions, in fact, "eventually worsen due to continual growth," so that one form frequently arises from another.[109]

Seyssel appealed to the case of Rome, although his analysis of Roman constitutional history was hardly pure Polybius. For Seyssel, Rome experienced monarchical, aristocratic and democratic phases, and these were placed with the early kings, the Decemvirs, and with subsequent popular movements (a line taken by Dionysius: Chapter 4, introd.). Rather inconsistently, however, he claimed that the Romans "were for a long time governed by the consuls and the senate under the authority of the people," and thus they were ruled by a mixed form of government. The weakness in the mixture, significantly, lay with the third component: the people were responsible for "civil dissensions," until the state, passing the point of its virility and having acquired the best empire ever gained by a popular state, experienced a return to monarchy.[110] As with Machiavelli, then, the emergence of the Principate had to be incorporated into

104. *Decem libros Ethicorum Aristotelis ad Nicomachum expositio* 1672 ff. (ed. R. M. Spiazzi, Rome, 1949, pp. 442ff.); cf. also C. Martin, "Some Mediaeval Commentaries on Aristotle's *Politics*" in *History* N.S. XXXVI, 1951, pp. 29ff.

105. *Hypomnēmatismoi*, *log.* 96ff. (where he also comments upon the 14th-century Italian city-states as popular, unstable, and tending to change). Cf. also Nicephorus Gregoras on the Thessalonican Zealot ochlocracy: *Byz. hist.* XVI,ii(796) (Migne, *PG*, vol. 148, col. 1045); cf. E. Barker (ed.), *Social and Political Thought in Byzantium: From Justinian I to the Last Palaeologus*, Oxford, 1957, pp. 192f.

106. *Hypmn.*, *log.* 104.

107. *Log.* 101–3.

108. *La* [*Grant*] *Monarchie de France* (*et deux autres fragments politiques*) (ed. J. Poujol, Bibliothèque Elzevirienne *Études et Documents*, Paris, 1961), I,1 (pp. 103f.).

109. I,1 (p. 104).

110. I,2 (pp. 104–7).

Seyssel's analysis and so cover Polybius' ignorance of future contingencies. Seyssel also appropriated the post-Polybian body-state analogy, insisting that the passage from Romulus to the last Caesars was one from infancy to decrepitude.[111] His approach, in review, was muddled if interesting, a hodgepodge of classicisms made all the more unconvincing for being a defence of Louis XI's monarchy as a skillfully devised power balance.[112] His Italian contemporary far surpassed him in penetrating historical analysis, in systematizing facts, in formulating both adequate generalizations and coherent theory.[113]

And after Machiavelli? As a theorist of recurring constitutional processes, the Florentine had no real successors. When Francesco Guicciardini (1483–1540) commented on the *Discorsi* I,2 in 1531, he strangely avoided all discussion of his predecessor's recurrence theory,[114] although he did state his own opinion that the three major simple constitutions tended to lapse into tyranny, a mixed government best forestalling such decline.[115] If Guicciardini accepted the traditional contrast between liberty and tyranny, he was nevertheless more sensitive than Machiavelli over variety and contingency in human affairs, and thus was doubtful about any fixed course of constitutional change. Admittedly, he happily framed a rule that bloody factiousness among a free people invariably led to tyranny,[116] and other great advocates of the *mista*, such as Seyssel and Paolo Paruta, would have concurred.[117] But nothing so complex as Machiavelli's models, nor any statement of recurrence so theoretical as the Florentine's, remains in their work, not even in the writing of Donato Giannotti, at one time a frequenter of the Rucellai Gardens, who, though actually mentioning Polybius Bk. VI by name, asserted that *all* states incline to one of the three simple forms— monarchy, aristocracy, or democracy. These three were not placed in a six-part sequence, nor did each have specified vicious counterparts; it was just that each pure type could be corrupted by the excessive power of its own special

111. I,3 (pp. 107f.).

112. I.e., a balance among the nobility, middle men, and poor, and between the king and the institutions checking his power: II,6–19 (pp. 113ff.); cf. W. F. Church, *Constitutional Thought in Sixteenth Century France: A Study in the Evolution of Ideas* (*Harvard Historical Studies* XLVII), Cambridge, Mass., 1969, ch. 1.

113. That Machiavelli and Seyssel made contact through Lascaris, see Hexter, loc. cit., pp. 84ff. J. W. Allen, in his *History of Political Thought in the Sixteenth Century*, London, 1957 edn., p. 275, thought (erroneously) that Machiavelli influenced Seyssel.

114. *Considerazione intorno ai Discorsi del Machiavelli sopra la prima deca di Tito Livio* (1531) I,2 (cf. C. Grayson, ed., *Francesco Guicciardini: Selected Writings*, London, 1965, pp. 63ff.). Also V. de Caprariis' edn. of the *Opere* (*La Letteratura Italiana: Storia e Testi* XXX), Milan, 1961, was used, but it lacked some chapters of this work.

115. *Consid.* I,2 (Grayson, pp. 64, 65, 66), 10 (p. 78), 28 (p. 93) where the Decemvirs, interestingly, are considered a tyranny, II,24 (pp. 123f.) on lapses into tyranny; cf. I,2 (p. 63), 5 (pp. 70f.) on mixed government forestalling decline.

116. *Consid.* II,24 (p. 123); cf. I,2 (p. 66), 5 (p. 71), 58 (p. 104) for his distaste for "democracy."

117. Cf. Allen, op. cit., pp. 62ff. Though doubting the usefulness of Machiavelli's *cerchio* for understanding Roman history, Paruta documented Roman decline with the sequence mixed government/aristocracy/oligarchy/tyranny in his *Discorsi* (*Opere*, ed. F. le Monnier, Florence, 1852, vol. 2, pp. 101–3); cf. also Jean Bodin, *Methodus ad facilem historiarum cognitionem* (1566) (ET, ed. B. Reynolds, New York, 1966, pp. 183f.).

virtue, and thus each fall prey to tyranny.[118] It was an age of too much diversity and turbulence to admit of anything but the most general rules, and given both popular human rhetoric and the facts of despotic rules in Italy, Giannotti chose to describe all that debased the pure forms as tyranny.

In France, Jean Bodin (1529/30–1596), the most renowned political theorist after Machiavelli, hardly fulfilled the rôle of successor. If anything, his great statement on the variations of constitutional change virtually rang the death knell of the cycle of governments as viable historico-political theory. In the fourth book of his work *De la République*, Bodin listed a whole series of possible constitutional mutations, showing a multitude of combinations by which simple forms, worthy or defective, could change into each other. Any sense of a fixed series was replaced by a decisive (Aristotelian) emphasis on variability, change between any two of the six governmental types being possible.[119] In a very general way, perhaps, Bodin seems to outline something like a constitutional cycle or even what has been called a spiral.[120] After stressing such great variety, he proferred a potted world history of constitutions. The earliest governments were those of violent tyrants such as Nimrud (= Ninus), but their successors became either despots or kings.[121] With abuse of kingly power or the failure of a royal line, aristocracies became established, though without popular consent, and these existed simultaneously with monarchies.[122] Many such aristocracies and kingships, he wrote, eventually turned into popular governments, as with Athens and Rome,

> and since that time, people have discovered by the experience of many centuries that monarchy is a more stable, a more desirable, and a more durable form of commonwealth than either aristocracy or democracy,

the best monarchies now so prevalent "throughout the world" being the hereditary ones.[123] Rome, commencing with Romulus, passing through stages which were royal, tyrannical, aristocratic, oligarchic, popular, and ochlocratic, and

118. *Della Repubblica Fiorentina* (*Opere*, ed. G. Rosini, Pisa, vol. 2, pp. 13–7); cf. also E. Rawson, *The Spartan Tradition in European Thought*, Oxford, 1969, p. 145. On the place of the *governo misto* in Giannotti's thought, see esp. Pocock, op. cit., pp. 297ff., and Cf. F. Gilbert, "The Date of the Composition of Contarini's and Giannotti's Books on Venice" in *Studies in the Renaissance* XIV, 1967, p. 183.

119. *Six Livres de la République (avec l'apologie de R. Herpin)*, Paris, 1583 (Aalen, 1961 facs.), Bk. IV, p. 507 (to quote the whole passage would be tedious, though the best way to make the point); cf. *Methodus* (pp. 201–5, 212, 217ff.).

120. Häussler, *Tacitus*, pp. 72, 85.

121. This is quite consistent with Polybius; that Bodin knew his work, cf. R. Chauviré, *Jean Bodin, auteur de la République*, Paris, 1914, pp. 181ff.

122. The impact of Plato's *Laws*? Note esp. *Leg.* III,681D where aristocracy *or* kingship follows upon the earliest one-man rule; see above, Chapter 1, sect. D.

123. *République* IV, pp. 510–2 for the whole analysis, 512 for the quotation. Bodin considered early medieval rules (e.g., Merovingian, Carolingian) as aristocratic, thus foreshadowing the way Vico paralleled early Roman and barbarian institutions: cf. B. Croce, *The Philosophy of Giambattista Vico* (ET), New York, 1913, p. 218.

finally acquiring the hereditary monarchy which lasted to 1453,[124] encapsulated mankind's general political history. There is certainly an admission in this survey that societies have reverted to a monarchical order, and to that extent we have here an acknowledgment of recurrence. But that Bodin imagined himself to be depicting a constitutional cycle, or a grand movement of history which was liable to be repeated again, even if at some higher level, does not seem either likely or susceptible of proof. His outline of world history was deliberately flexible to account for varieties of change. He redeemed *metabolē* theory, the study of particular kinds of constitutional change, from the pitfalls of cyclicism. A fixed cycle of governments was too simplistic for Bodin: of all political theorists, be he ever so incoherent a philosopher, he did more than anyone to hasten the death of overcoherent constitutional theory.[125]

## B. Sixteenth-century themes

As with the Polybian *Anacyclōsis*, we have given separate treatment to Machiavelli's constitutional theory. A wealth of other recurrence paradigms from the sixteenth century, however, still remains before us, and we must attempt to endow this material with a semblance of order—a challenging task, since this period is renowned for its intellectual turmoil. On the one hand, humanism and the classical revival produced a more intense intermingling of the Greco-Roman and Judeo-Christian inheritances. On the other hand, the theological pull of the Reformation was away from the dangers of paganism and worldliness, leading thinkers to extract their truths about history more rigorously from the Christian tradition, the Bible included. However, if we continue first with the syncretisms of the Renaissance, these problems and these issues will be better sharpened and analyzed.

### *Natural processes, rise and fall*

Machiavelli certainly appealed to frames of recurrences traditionally associated with the ways of *natura*, but as we have stressed, it was *human* nature rather than nature itself which gripped him. His approach to continual change bears this out. When he acknowledged that "the affairs of the world shift so much,"[126] for example, he was not simply repeating a maxim of ancient philosophy, that all things come into being and pass away. Change was primarily change of purpose and reaction before altered circumstances, and the circumstances themselves were mainly products of will and passion.[127]

124. *Rép.* IV, p. 510: royal/tyrannical/aristocratic/popular; yet in *Methodus* (pp. 236f.): the early kingship/tyranny of the Tarquins/rule of the optimates and patricians/oligarchy of the Decemvirs/lawful and moderate rule of the people/ochlocratic anarchy of the turbulent plebeians (Gracchi to Sulla).

125. See also Excursus 6, pt. 1.

126. *Princ.* x,3 (vol. 4, p. 312).

127. Cf. *Disc.* II,*proem.* (p. 6), III,27 (p. 221); cf. I,5 (vol. 3, p. 247), III,49 (vol. 4, p. 267); and see below, pt. 2, on fortune.

Naturalistic interests are even subdued in Machiavelli's brief glance at catastrophe theory (in the *Discorsi* II,5). On surmising how the records of time came to be destroyed, he suggested two causes: first, the acts of men, and second, catastrophes such as pestilence, famine, or flood, produced from heaven. He implied that great disasters recurrently befell the human race, but only regionally (as men like Plato and Polybius held), and that this was because nature (periodically?) underwent spontaneous purgation when there was an "accumulation of superfluous matter," or in other words, overpopulation. The world had to relieve itself before such a necessity. These brief comments recall Platonic-Aristotelian views on cataclysms and even the Stoic doctrine of cosmic conflagration;[128] in fact, Machiavelli was less interested in natural factors behind catastrophes than supernatural ones. Such disasters were referred to heaven or God, and he took the Christian line (going back to the Fathers and even to Luke) that they were designed to chastise men, so that they might "become better and live with more convenience."[129] In this whole chapter, moreover, he remained more concerned with human powers of destruction than the supernatural ones. That human beings could demolish former civilizations fascinated him, and he pondered on the labors of the Christians who had eliminated the vestiges of pagan antiquity, and on the fact that the Romans annulled all but the memory of the ancient Tuscans (II,5, on pp. 29–30, 31). The stages of Italian civilization (ancient Tuscans/Roman/later Italian) were thus bounded by essentially human efforts at destruction, not by natural disaster.

Naturalism is also absent from Machiavelli's account of rise and fall. As has already been suggested, he preferred to write of ascent and descent, with little more than a hint of biological growth, acme, and decay. This organismic language, however, showed up with interesting variations in other writers. Guicciardini, for instance, mused on the natural mortality of all cities and states, as if they experienced life cycles,[130] and argued that varieties and changes in human affairs were natural and not supernatural.[131] Polydore Vergil (1470–1555), Italian author of the *Anglica historia* (1513), combined a muted version of *translatio* theory with the life-cycle idea. He referred to a succession of the "British" by the Norman "empires" within English history, taking the Danish and Norman incursions to represent pangs of old age for the "British" order, and the coming of the Normans as a renewal of the country's manhood.[132] Again, Bodin was all but truistic about the "birth, growth, flourishing, decadence, and ruin" of commonwealths, which slowly develop to perfection but which, because of the uncertainty and changeableness of human things, do

128. (Pp. 29–31); cf. above, Chapter 1, sect. A, though, unlike Plato and Aristotle, Machiavelli gave the world a beginning.

129. (P. 31); cf. *Ist.* 34 (vol. 2, pp. 252–4) on the 1456 whirlwind. For background in Luke, Philo, and the Fathers, see above, Chapter 3, sect. C.

130. *Ricordi* (final redact.) 189 (Grayson, p. 47); cf. 160 (p. 41). For Seyssel's body-state analogy, see *Grant monarch.* I,3 (p. 108).

131. *Ricordi* 33 (p. 14); cf. 123 (p. 33).

132. *Ang. hist.*, Basel, 1546 edn., pp. 62, 108 (*ll.*13–26), 499 (*l.*27).

not remain that way for long.[133] Unlike Guicciardini, however, both Polydore and Bodin believed such developments to be governed by the infinite wisdom of God. For the latter there were "eternal laws of nature," and the paths of empires, which "seem to proceed in a circle," were actually under "the influence of the celestial bodies, which produce a continual vicissitude of generation and corruption."[134] Opposed to the apocalyptic four-monarchy doctrine based on Daniel,[135] he reasserted the biological cycle in its full force, but as a motion controlled by God, who knew the secret numbers and time lengths for every natural course.[136]

The suggestion in Bodin that earthly affairs were in flux and in a state to be contrasted with the divine stability was a commonly restated theme in Reformation Europe.[137] However, his special and humanistic interest in biological cycles and their planetary influences is more distinctive, and was developed by a contemporary, Louis Le Roy (d. 1577), who had probably read both Machiavelli and Bodin's famous *Methodus*. According to Le Roy's *De la Vicissitude ou variété des choses en l'univers* (1575), the whole cosmos, including historical phenomena within it, is conceived as subject to natural motions—to generation, change, and corruption.[138] As with Bodin, the planets influence earthly affairs and a cyclical image of the political "growth and decay" was consciously substituted for the Danielic schema of four world empires.[139] His approach to rise and fall is nicely illustrated by his modification of a passage in Machiavelli on the translation of empires. The Florentine, characteristically, asserted that "human affairs are in a state of perpetual movement, always either ascending or descending." He then went on to comment on the succession of former powers:

> Reflecting upon the course of human affairs, I think that, as a whole, the world continues to remain very much in the same condition, the good balancing the evil; but the good and evil change (*variare*) from one country to another, as we learn from the history of those ancient kingdoms that differed from each other in manners, while the world at large remained the same. The only difference being, that all the *virtù* that first found a place in Assyria was thence transferred (*collocò*) to Media, and afterwards to Persia, and from there it came (*venne*) to Italy and Rome. (*Disc.* II,*proem.*)

For Machiavelli, then, political success depended upon special human qualities

133. *Rép.* IV, pp. 503f.

134. *Methodus* (p. 302) for the first two quotations; Church, op. cit., p. 213 n. 51, for the third.

135. *Methodus* (pp. 291ff., 301).

136. (Pp. 233ff.) on "changes in states correlated with numbers." In this section Bodin also concerned himself with individuals, maintaining that people recurrently died when they attained years which were multiples of seven or nine ("unless nature is checked by the divine will") (p. 226).

137. Weisinger (loc. cit.) made much of Fulke Greville (1554–1628) in this connection. Cf. his "Treatise on Monarchy," stanzas 105f., in *The Remains* (ed. G. A. Wilkes), London, 1965, p. 61.

138. *De la Vicissitude*, esp. I–IV (ed. B. W. Bates, Princeton Texts in Literature and the History of Thought, Princeton, 1944); cf. W. L. Gundersheimer, *The Life and Works of Louis le Roy (Travaux d'Humanisme et Renaissance LXXXII)*, Geneva, 1966, pp. 97ff.

139. Ibid., pp. 96f., 104.

of effectiveness (or classical virtue);[140] once this was dissipated in those who maintained a political society, their power would fall to those who had it. On Le Roy's part, however, there was a strong implication that translation was affected by a cosmic process ultimately beyond human control, and the natural cycle of growth and decay was an essential part of that process. "Virtue and vice fly by turns, passing from land to land, and ruling more in one time than another," and when virtue traversed the empires from Assyria to Rome, she did so through "a continual vicissitude of generation and corruption," eventually plummeting the world into a cycle of darkness.[141] In the case of the biological principle, therefore, the reversion to a classical way of thinking is more pronounced in Le Roy than in Machiavelli, and the former seems to have consciously employed the principle as a counter to Christian dogmatism and to the shallow yet persisting condemnation of *falsi circuitūs*. On the other hand, the Frenchman had not abandoned Christianity; he was not unhappy to perceive providence behind earthly instability or to believe in a Last Judgment. Like Salutati two centuries previously, he openly sought to establish the point that linear and cyclical views were not incompatible. He did this both by mitigating the distasteful apocalypticisms of the era, and by reinvolving an old gnome, which had not gone unused by Christians, that all human things burgeon and die.[142]

Neither Bodin nor Le Roy forgot that history entailed more than politics. Both wrote of general cultural history, and each was optimistic about the progress in arts, letters, and institutional life in their own time.[143] Le Roy's position is especially interesting, since he wrote so much about cultural recurrence as a natural process.[144] He maintained that past civilizations attained their peak through a concurrence of arts and letters, sometimes embodied in single individuals, such as Scipio Africanus and Charlemagne, who combined learning with military valor. The signs of cultural decay, on the other hand, included not only a waning of skill in arms and letters, but also a decline in morals and political responsibility (which are sapped by excessive love of liberty and religious dissension). Utter devastation was brought on by war and barbarism, until, as Aristotle had contended,[145] it was restored and reappropriated at a later time.[146] From cycle to cycle, however, there could be a progressive accumu-

140. Pocock, op. cit., pp. 157ff., Machiavelli making the quality of virtue hinge on the citizen's possession and command of arms more decidedly than most extant ancient writers.

141. *Les Politiques d'Aristote*, Paris, 1567, pp. 380f. and p. 267.

142. In integrating pagan and Christian views in this way, Gundersheimer maintains, Le Roy anticipates Vico as an exponent of "providential control over the cyclical course of history" (op. cit., p. 102).

143. Bodin *Methodus* (pp. 296ff.); Le Roy *Vicissitude* III, XI (both their stances representing important background to the seventeenth-century *Querelle* between ancients and moderns.

144. Cf. also Bodin *Methodus* (p. 302).

145. Le Roy correctly associates Aristotle's name with cultural recurrence: see above, Chapter 4, sect. I.

146. *Considération sur l'histoire françoise et universelle*, Paris, 1567, pp. 7–9; *Vicissitude* III (Bates, p.

lation of technique and wisdom. Every age had something to contribute and transmit to succeeding generations, and it was coincidences of military and intellectual accomplishment—the ages of Sesostris,[147] Ninus, Cyrus, Alexander, Augustus, the Saracens, and present times—that recurrently gave the greatest impetus to mankind's accumulating knowledge.[148] The more linear outlook, however (which certainly countered any theory of progressive degeneration), was interlocked with the cyclical one, and Le Roy persisted with his naturalism, as if, like Giorgio Vasari and the classical tradition behind him, he held that even the arts could grow, reach maturity, and decline into old age.[149]

Machiavelli appears rather idiosyncratic, then, for playing down a paradigm so prominent in other distinguished works of historical theory. Yet the biological principle was not invariably appealed to by those who were theorizing about rise and fall in the sixteenth century. The four-world-monarchy doctrine (as well as the Great Week schema), for example, still persisted, despite modifications.[150] And in some cases the modifications are of real interest, particularly in their accentuation of recurrence. Expounding his special version of *translatio* theory, for instance, the German Wimpfeling (1450–1528) ascribed a very great antiquity to the German empire, contending that it once warded off the Persians and Alexander, as well as Rome. Thus when Charlemagne, a German, was crowned Holy Roman Emperor, the imperial dignity was providentially restored to the Germany whence it first came.[151]

Bernt Rothmann (ca. 1495–1535), an "Anabaptist" theologian enmeshed in the 1535 Münster fiasco, makes for intriguing reading. He depicted history as a series of falls and restorations; viz., the bondage in Egypt and the return to

19). On the confluence of arts and letters Le Roy differs with Machiavelli's view that "literary excellence is subsequent in time to that of distinction in arms": *Ist.* V,1 (vol. 2, p. 127), and even Estienne Pasquier's view that when states "begin to grow and reach their maturity, it happens that culture begins to be appreciated and then, with the decline of the state, culture also declines," *Lettre* V, to the Chevalier de Montereau, in *Oeuvres* (Trévoux edn.), Amsterdam, 1723, vol. 2, pp. 9f.; cf. G. Huppert, *The Idea of Perfect History: Historical Erudition and Historical Philosophy in Renaissance France*, Urbana, 1970, pp. 42f.

147. In referring to Sesostris, an ancient (and mythical) pharoah (cf. Herodotus *Hist.* II,102–11), Le Roy looks beyond even Ninus.

148. With Sesostris and Ninus (no information); Cyrus (Pythagoras and Thales); Alexander (Plato, Euripides, Demosthenes, and Aristotle); Augustus (Horace, Ovid, Julius Caesar as historiographer, Pompey as a man of culture: cf. Plutarch *Vit. Pomp.* i,2ff.); Saracens (Averroes, Avicenna, Abenzoar); and with modern times, new experts in geography, warfare, languages, etc. Cf. *Le Timée de Platon*, Paris, 1551, fol. iir; *Le Sympose de Platon*, Paris, 1558, fol. 129r°; *De L'Origine, antiquité, progrès, excellence et utilité de l'art politique*, Paris, 1567, fol. 4r°; *Considération*, pp. 6ff.

149. Although Vasari (1511–1575) considered such a cycle to have been completed through the whole of Greco-Roman antiquity, with a similar cycle being undergone in his own time and with mannerism an index to decadence: *La Vite de più eccellenti Architetti, Pittori, et Scultori Italiani da Cimabue insino a temp nostri*, Florence, 1550, *pref.*; cf. von Schlosser, *Kunstliteratur*, pp. 227–80. On writers still closer to Le Roy on the rise and depletion of the arts, see, e.g., Gabriel Harvey, *Letter Book of Gabriel Harvey* (ed. E. J. L. Scott), London, 1884, pp. 85–7; Pasquier, *Lettre* V (p. 10).

150. See Excursus 6, pt. 2.

151. *Epitoma rerum Germanicarum* (1505); cf. B. R. Reynolds, "Latin Historiography: A Survey, 1400–1600" in *Studies in the Renaissance* II, 1955, pp. 31f.

Canaan, the Babylonian exile and the subsequent restoration, the fall of early Christianity (which decayed into institutionalism and false doctrine), and the final restoration which began with Erasmus, Luther, and Zwingli, and reached its height in the Münster program of a new Zion.[152] Both Rothmann's and Wimpfeling's interpretations show the free rewriting of history to legitimize political and religious causes in a turbulent period, and both illustrate how the mystique of recurrence could be used as a divine stamp of authenticity. They also demonstrate, however, that it was not just the revival of neat Greco-Roman paradigms which motivated men to cast their eyes over the great sea of the past. In any case, even if the biological principle was used more extensively in historical interpretation during the sixteenth century, we often find a mélange of ideas, medieval notions of earthly vicissitude and imperial succession continuing to have some appeal.

## *Feints of fortune and rules of reciprocity*

Unlike Bodin, Le Roy, and still more theologically-inclined historiographers in the sixteenth century, Machiavelli conceded little to supernaturalism. And yet, as is well known, he frequently appealed to *fortuna*. It was a concept from antiquity with which he was prepared to contend, one which had survived through the Middle Ages, though often intermingled with assertions about human vicissitudes and toppling tyrants.[153] Of course, past views on fortune varied, so that Machiavelli also had to make sense of a complex inheritance. Was Fortune the agency of mere caprice or was she some quasi-divine mistress directing the course of events toward just ends? He felt obliged to face these questions, to allot some credible rôle to the uncertainty factor in affairs, without vitiating his understanding of human action and response.

*Fortuna*, putting it most generally, produced constant variation. Thus

> Fortune shows her power a good deal, and because she is variable, republics and states often vary. (*Disc.* II,30)

> A republic . . . which relies more upon the chances (*impeti*) of fortune than upon the

152. *Restitution rechter und gesunder christlicher Lehre* (1534) (ed. A. Knaake, Halle, 1888, p. 17). The Münster program, of course, did not last long.

153. On *fortuna* in Western medieval historiography and literature, see A. Doren, "Fortuna im Mittelalter und in der Renaissance" in *Vortraege der Bibliothek Warburg* II, pt. 1, 1922–3, pp. 71ff.; M. R. Patch, "The Tradition of the Goddess Fortuna" in *Smith College Studies in Modern Languages* III, 1922, pp. 186ff.; *The Goddess Fortuna in Medieval Literature*, Cambridge, Mass., 1927. In medieval historiography, to choose the most pertinent examples, note Richard de Templo(?), *Peregrinorum et gesta itinerarium regis Ricardis* ii,45 (ed. W. Stubbs, *Chronicles and Memorials of the Reign of Richard I*, London, 1864, vol. 1), on *fortuna* aiding the brave though she wreak her splean on whomsoever she pleases; Hugo of Fleury *Chronicon* (ed. B. Rottendorf, Münster, 1636, p. 7), on *virtus* contending against *fortuna*. For early Renaissance connections between fortune and temporal flux see, e.g., Boccaccio *Vita di Dante* (Smith, pp. 20, 26, 63, and cf. p. 29); *De casibus virorum illustrium* (1544); Bruni *Vita di Dante* (Smith, p. 95); Poggio Bracciolini *Historia Fiorentina* (ed. L. Muratori), Milan, 1731, esp. 316D, 408B, and cf. 313D, 344B; G. Dati *L'Istoria di Firenze dal 1380 al 1405* (ed. L. Pratesi), Norcia, 1904, pp. 11, 39, 54, 76. Later, cf. B. Castiglione, *Il Cortegano, pref. aut.*; Vasari, *Vite*, *pref.*

*virtù* of her citizens, will experience all the vicissitudes which fortune brings. (*Disc.* III,31)

A prince who bases himself entirely on *fortuna* is ruined when she changes, while he is happy whose mode of procedure accords with the need of the times. (*Princ.* xxv,4)

These passages reflect Machiavelli's main emphases, which were more upon the adversities of fortune than upon her favors. *Fortuna* was a vivid image both for a future neglected by foresight and for altered circumstances which arise when men have not anticipated future contingencies. These circumstances may even go under the names of *vicissitudine* and *necessità.*[154] In one sense, of course, unforeseen eventualities were usually the product of human activity itself, but Machiavelli was prepared to appropriate a classical device and to extrapolate the uncertainty factor in terms of a suprahuman agency. How literally one should take some of his allusions is difficult to say. Fortune is usually personified, someone to be "negotiated with."[155] On the other hand, she is rarely so elevated as to appear as the arbiter of history's inevitable destiny. Instead of *substituting* for a collective exercise of human wills she seems to *summarize* them, though to appeal to her was to admit that something incalculable lay beyond and above the maelstrom of human activities.

In any case, to invoke *fortuna* was also a convenient way of isolating the requirements of *virtù* and of showing how men have responded to good or ill. A man (usually a ruler) of resilience can either check the motions of fortune when adverse,[156] or make the most of an opportune situation when fortune is favorable or enamoured of his boldness.[157] In short, success or felicity ensue when *virtù* and *fortuna* are suitably combined (an observable truth, not just a concession to the *virtus* and *fortuna* of Latin historiography). Among other things, such a marriage helped explain the success of Rome and the great Medici, and it would also account for the future effectiveness of "the prince."[158] However, historical episodes could bear these two potent agencies for change in varying proportions. In the Roman Republic, for example, virtue outweighed and controlled Fortune so that Rome marched to her heights even though Fortune had sorely tested her.[159]

The point here is that Fortune will often offer her favors and then withdraw

154. For background on fortune and necessity taken together, e.g., Plutarch *Vit. Caii Marii* xxiii,1, on these two as "that power which permits no great success to bring pure and unmixed enjoyment, but diversifies life with a blending of evil and good." This matches Machiavelli's brand of realism.

155. *Princ.* xxv,9 (vol. 4, p. 367) on negotiation; but on the idea of a necessary changeability, *Disc.* II,30 (pp. 118f.); *Ist.* VII,17, 18 (vol. 2, pp. 291f.), VIII,33, 34 (vol. 3, pp. 64f.).

156. *Princ.* xxv,1–8 (vol. 4, pp. 364–8); *Disc.* III,31 (pp. 229f.), 39 (pp. 247f.); cf. II,30 (pp. 118f.).

157. *Princ.* xxv,4–6, 9 (pp. 365f., 367f.), *Disc.* I,2 (vol. 3, p. 240), II,29 (vol. 4, p. 114), *Ist.* IV,5 (vol. 2, p. 73), VI,6 (pp. 203, 206).

158. *Disc.* I,4 (vol. 3, pp. 242f.), 20 (p. 298), II,1 (vol. 4, pp. 9–13), on Rome; *Ist.* VII,5 (vol. 2, p. 271), VIII,36 (vol. 3, p. 71), on the Medici; *Princ.* iii,8 (vol. 4, p. 287), xxv,7 (p. 372); *Disc.* II,29 (p. 115) on the prince. For Pasquier's reflections on the French monarchy in comparable terms, see Huppert, op. cit., pp. 42f.

159. *Disc.* II,1 (p. 13), III,9 (p. 171), 31 (pp. 229f.).

them, so that the real test comes in adversity when, unless men are properly equipped, they can be brought to their downfall. In cases of personal vicissitude, Machiavelli maintained that men rarely rose from "small fortune" to a high position of influence through force or fraud, although he admitted that success was easiest when *fortuna* supported human artfulness. On the other hand, he insisted that Fortune applied herself with almost irresistible strength to bring about the downfall of a great man.[160] Thus both good fortune and adversity placed demands on *virtù*, the former requiring a will to power and the latter adaptability, the one bringing the danger of insolence, and the other, despondency.[161] Whatever the eventualities, however, they could be prepared for as future possibilities revealed by the past, for history contained its lessons for present and future situations.[162] If the knowledge of constitutional processes equipped the legislator, the recognition of vicissitude was just as important. Turns of fortune, indeed, were integral to Machiavelli's conception of political change, since states could rise to the heights of good fortune or be lost in the shifts of party strife.

Fortune, we must reaffirm, does not necessarily conjure up the image of a wheel-like movement or alternation between two conditions; its operations can also be viewed as a part of the processes of reciprocity which go to make up a moral order. It is true that Machiavelli often wrote as though her fickleness was ordained and necessary, yet his Fortune was hardly blind or fickle, and at times her work could be identified with the work of God.[163] Can it be said, then, that Machiavelli's *fortuna* maintained a moral order? Some references suggest that she requited wickedness and turned against the proud,[164] but he also once remarked how "she often holds the good under her feet and exalts the wicked."[165] Generally speaking, it is remarkable how he "secularized" or "politicized" traditional notions of a moral order, making the outcome of events due less to a suprahuman agency than to the *virtù* or ineffectiveness of men themselves. In discussing the consequences of *insolenza* (= *hybris*), for example, he concerned himself not with overriding principles of justice or nemesis but with the vehement human reactions which insolence could produce in others.[166] Again, when he advised moderation it was for purely pragmatic reasons;[167] and when he described the evils which befell those misusing their

160. II,13 (p. 50), 29 (p. 113), III,37 (p. 306).

161. As in the case of Venice: III,31 (p. 231); and concerning individuals see *Di Fortuna* (vol. 7, pp. 75f.). Cf. R. M. Crawford, "*Per Quale Iddio*": *Machiavelli's Second Thoughts* (Australian Humanities Research Council Lecture, 1966), Sydney, 1967, p. 18; Pocock, op. cit., pp. 157ff.

162. *Disc.* II,30 (p. 228), III,31 (pp. 229ff.); *Princ.* xxv,1–4 (pp. 364ff.).

163. *Ist.* VII,21 (vol. 2, pp. 297f.), VIII,19 (vol. 3, pp. 40f.); *Princ.* xxv, 1 (Vol. 4, pp. 364f.); *Disc.* II,29 (pp. 113f.), and n. 162 above.

164. *Disc.* III,31 (p. 231ff.); *Ist.* II,29 (vol. 1, p. 107).

165. *Capitolo di Fortuna* (vol. 7, p. 72).

166. *Disc.* I,4 (vol. 3, p. 247), III,11 (vol. 4, p. 178); *Ist.* II,11 (vol. 1, p. 77), IV,2 (vol. 2, p. 69). At VIII,23 (vol. 3, p. 48) he might have appealed to a concept like Nemesis to explain the nasty death of Roberto da Rumini, but he did not.

167. *Disc.* III,19 (vol. 4, p. 143), 21 (p. 204f.); *Princ.* xv–xix (pp. 328ff.); *Ist.* III,23 (vol. 2, pp. 54f.).

power, he did not write of them in terms of divine retribution, but as the appropriate outcome of politically inept or unsustained courses of action.[168]

In a few cases there is a mixture of interpretative models; *fortuna*, he once declared,

> caused the hope of victory to operate so powerfully upon Niccolò Piccinino [the Milanese *condottiero*] and made assume such a tone of unbounded *insolenza*

that Francesco Sforza declined to support his projects.[169] But the more essential Machiavelli was the one who was fascinated by the effectiveness or ineffectiveness, the wisdom or foolishness of given policies or courses of action, and who sought to propose principles for right procedures. Concern for the recurrent actualization of retributive principles was replaced by humanistic concentration on the recurrent success or failure of action-types. In Machiavelli, moreover, the nature of men's deaths did not carry the same sort of significance often endowed upon it by the ancients. Death could say something about political failure, or about ruthless control required by necessity, but how men met their ends was not connected with a doctrine of a moral order. All this is not to deny the importance of *fortuna*. Men, it seemed, could only act within the bounds of her (negotiable) permissions.[170] But whether men succeeded or failed (or whether they died in pleasant or unpleasant circumstances) was chiefly attributable to them, to their adaptability and perseverance, to their astuteness or want of it.

The Machiavellian approach to fortune and the moral order was somewhat individualistic and atypical in its time. It may be contrasted with two extremes, the more Epicurean position, which stressed fortune's caprice and threw doubt on Divinity, and the more popular providentialist outlook. Of the doubters Guicciardini is the most interesting; not only did he take the enormously influential *fortuna* to be quite unpredictable and uncontrollable,[171] but he radically questioned the idea of a moral order. Unsure as he was about men's ability to predict the outcome of events with accuracy,[172] he was unhappier still about traditionalist appeals to fortune's wheel and retributive principles. To relate but a single course of Fortune's movements to a given individual's career was inadequate:

> One may be fortunate in one matter and not in another. I have been lucky with some gains . . . but in others unlucky. I have had things with difficulty when I wanted them; the same things when I no longer sought them have pursued me. (*Ricordi* 85)

168. *Disc.* III,6 (vol. 4, p. 143), on the end of tyrants; *Princ.* viii,6 (vol. 4, pp. 304–6) on Oliverotto; *Ist.* II,37 (vol. 1, p. 129) on the Duke of Athens, IV,33 (vol. 2, p. 122) on Rinaldo degli Albizzi, VI,6 (pp. 242–4), on Stefano Porcari.

169. *Ist.* VI,4 (pp. 198f.).

170. *Disc.* II,29 (vol. 4, pp. 114f.), 30 (pp. 188f.); *Princ.* xxv,1f. (pp. 364f.); and on God, esp. *Ist.* VI,34 (vol. 2, pp. 252ff.).

171. Esp. *Ricordi*, 30, 31 (Grayson, p. 13), 108 (p. 29), 161 (p. 41); cf. 20 (p. 10). Giovanni Pontano held similar attitudes to fortune, yet thinking more specifically of war: cf. *Actius* in *I Dialoghi di Giovanni Pontano* (ed. C. Previtera, Florence, 1943), p. 220, *ll.*9ff.

172. *Ricordi* 6 (p. 7), 23 (p. 11), 58, 61 (p. 19), 71 (p. 22), 81 (p. 24); yet cf. 67 (p. 21), and n. 171 above.

He acknowledged that good fortune could be man's greatest enemy because it caused him to become wicked, frivolous, or insolent (164), but he left this admission as an observation about human nature rather than about history's ordered patterns. He also considered the proposition that God left no virtue unrewarded and no sin unpunished in this world, not just in the next. Taking up the popular opinion that ill-gotten wealth was never allowed by God to pass to a third heir, he insisted both that there were many examples to the contrary, and that it was inevitable in any case that poverty should eventually succeed riches (*Ricordi* 33). To the maxim "God helped a man because he was good, another came to grief because he was wicked," he answered that the very opposite can happen (a point most acceptable to Augustine!) and that divine decisions were quite unfathomable.[173]

In some ways Guicciardini joins Machiavelli as an index to certain shifts and currents among Italian intellectuals. Both, that is, wrote more about the powers of fortune than of God, and they were less concerned with the moral order of history than with the effective ordering of one's actions and the state. Yet many of their contemporaries made less of a distinction between God and *fortuna* than one might suppose, and most continued to defend a providential order. Wrote Vasari:

> Fortune, when she has brought men to the top of the wheel, either for amusement or because she repents, usually turns them to the bottom;

yet on showing how this was true in the case of ancient Rome, he made no clear distinction between fortune and heaven.[174] And if an element of antique fatalism remains strong in the classically-oriented Vasari, others were more eager to merge the pagan and the Christian. According to Polydore Vergil, men might often seem to be at the mercy of fortune's inconstant ways,[175] but any concessions to the possibility of a morally meaningless order could be matched by instances of retributive justice. He elicited some important examples of fitting punishment from English history—against Queen Margaret, Henry VI, Richard III, and so forth.[176] He treated these requitals as recurring actualizations of God's retributive principles. Such justice was effected in accordance with Exodus 34:7, God visiting "the iniquity of the fathers upon the children and the children's children to the third and fourth generations,"[177] Biblico-Christian approaches to retribution, then, which we have identified in such writers as the Deuteronomist, Luke, and Orosius, still persisted, and in a northern milieu

173. *Ricordi* 92 (p. 26), and cf. 123, 125 (p. 33) on his agnosticism, even if he referred to God as an agent who could offset *fortuna*, and remained Catholic (Grayson, p. xvii).

174. *Vite, pref.*

175. *Ang. hist.*, p. 134, *l*.39, p. 149, *l*.23, p. 355, *l*.38, p. 495, *l*.46, p. 531, *l*.17.

176. Against Hlothere (p. 66); Lord Suffolk (p. 498); Margaret (p. 528); Buckingham (p. 553); Hastings (p. 543); Henry VI (pp. 509, 531); Edward IV's children (pp. 524, 547); Richard III (pp. 558, 564). Cf. D. Hay, *Polydore Vergil: Renaissance Historian and Man of Letters*, Oxford, 1952, pp. 142–4.

177. *Ang. hist.*, p. 66, *l*.33.

Vergil's work could even be said to be overly classical. In most English history-writing at the time, a moral order was commonly accepted. Some writers not only understood history to contain "morally significant sequences of crime and punishment," but also saw its sequences as rhythmic, or as a register of those rewarded and those punished.[178] "The metaphor of history as a wheel or circle," moreover, "occurs a thousand times" in Tudor and Elizabethan literature, but accompanying such images was a strong denial that events were produced by "chance or fickle fortune."[179] These Christian writers upheld a "moral contour of events," as Herschel Baker calls it, though it is significant that they could delineate this contour in cyclical or recurrence and not just in linear terms. Baker cogently argues that their works frequently "exemplify, and often explicate, the notion that history is not a string of inconsequential episodes but an intelligible design where repetition and recurrence provided the key to explanation."[180] Le Roy would have agreed heartily, and Salutati before him. For all the old, irrepressible fears of Stoic gyrations, these men insisted that cyclical thinking was not unChristian, and no denial of Beginning and End.

The model of fortune's turning wheel, then, although it could stand in its own right as a cyclical paradigm of change, was often incorporated within the reciprocities of the moral order. The vigor with which some of the sixteenth-century English writers pressed Fortune into the service of the moral order is reminiscent of Polybius, and especially Diodorus (Chapter 2, sect. B, Chapter 4, sect. G). These Elizabethans were much bolder than their medieval predecessors in stressing the circularity of Fortune's movements (and in hypostatizing her), while they repudiated southern, neo-Epicurean pictures of an utterly capricious Fortune with men at the mercy of her morally meaningless ways.[181]

If the Elizabethans had recaptured some of the Polybian balance between the incalculable and the providential, or between the cycles of fortune and the reciprocities of justice, Machiavelli effected a comparable retrieval in the more specific but important area of internal and external relations. In this case, it is not the moral order but regularities emerging from inter-state politics which are involved. We remember how the model of a shifting balance permeates Polybius I on the first Punic War (cf. Diagram V). Machiavelli's interpretation of order and disorder, war and peace, invokes a comparable paradigm, although in his case it is regulable human reactions rather than the arbitrations of Fortune which maintain the pattern of reciprocity. He enunciated a key rule in this connection: peace produced idleness and idleness leads to disorder (*Ist.* V,1). Rome,

178. E.g., (Thomas) *Cooper's Chronicle*, London, 1560, sig. a2$^r$–a2$^v$; Sir Walter Raleigh, *History of the World*, esp. II,xxi,6 (in *Works*, Oxford, 1829 edn., vol. 4, p. 613), cf. C. F. T. Brooke, "Sir Walter Raleigh as Poet and Philosopher" in *English Literary History* V, 1938, p. 104.

179. H. Baker, *The Race of Time: Three Lectures on Renaissance Historiography*, Toronto, 1967, pp. 64f.

180. Ibid., pp. 63, 64.

181. For the more providentialist approach to fortune among Italian intellectuals, however, see H. A. E. van Gelder, *The Two Reformations in the Sixteenth Century: A Study of Religious Aspects and Consequences of Renaissance and Humanism*, The Hague, 1961, pp. 44ff.

for example, was so continually successful abroad that consequent respite brought idleness and disorder one after another, thus heralding her ruin (*Disc.* I,6). With all their victories, moreover, the Romans bestowed the consulate on candidates according to favor rather than merit, and so her army's ancient discipline was eventually lost.[182] Matters were similar for Florence; internal dissension was more likely when she was not threatened externally.[183] And there was a second, matching formula: internal instability was prone to ease when a state faced an external danger or some great *necessità*. With a threat to the state's existence, people tend to unite, provided they are not so corrupt as to make this impossible.[184]

To the principles of unity in adversity and disunity in tranquility, still another may be added: that states are best equipped to succeed in war if there is stability at home. The most praiseworthy state, of course, succeeded in both external and internal spheres. Idleness was avoided at home by keeping the citizens continually occupied, and security maintained not only in warding off outside threats, but in effectively pursuing an aggressive foreign policy.[185] On the other hand, as it was very difficult to unite people in secure times, a state could benefit by prolonged but controlled internal divisions. Machiavelli was not thinking of factiousness here, which was purely destructive, but of the healthy competition in the Roman state between nobles and people, a contest regulated to keep civic life on the move and to contribute to the empire.[186] This idea was not out of keeping with the reciprocal principles suggested by the first two rules of thumb; for as the course of simple constitutions could be forestalled (by a *mista*), so too could the processes of internal-external relations. Machiavelli never forgot about social engineering, and he was eager to draw out the practical implications of his theory.

That outside pressure could engender political success and idleness cause destruction was a doctrine not unknown among successors of Polybius nor among medieval thinkers.[187] It is important, however, that Machiavelli treated these principles as recurrently actualized, and as embodied in identifiable event-shapes which keep on emerging in human affairs. That, and the complex levels of his analysis, particularly recall Polybius. Like Polybius, moreover, Machiavelli attempted to interrelate his images and his lines of interpretation. If near-contemporaries contemplated alternating states in history—between war

182. (Vol. 3, pp. 251, 253), I,18 (p. 293), II,8 (vol. 4, p. 36), III,16 (p. 194).

183. *Ist.* II,12 (vol. 1, pp. 79f.), III,29 (vol. 2, p. 66), IV,15 (pp. 87f.), VI,38 *finis* (pp. 259f.), VII,23 (pp. 299f.), 25 (pp. 302f.), 29 (p. 308).

184. *Disc.* I,3 (vol. 3, pp. 241f.), II,25 (vol. 4, p. 102); *Ist.* IV,30 (vol. 2, pp. 117f.), V,1 (pp. 26f.), VII,12 (vol. 2, p. 282); cf. *Disc.* I,1.

185. *Disc.* III,31 (vol. 4, pp. 229ff.); *Ist.* V,31 (vol. 2, p. 180), VIII,36 (vol. 3, pp. 68f.).

186. *Disc.* I,4 (vol. 3, pp. 242ff.); cf. III,21 (vol. 4, p. 230), on Rome's special political life preventing her from being despondent in defeat and insolent in victory.

187. On the ancients see above, Chapter 2, sect. B, pt. 2(ii), Chapter 4, sect. A; and on the medievals see esp. the *Chronica de origine civitatis* and Villani's *Chroniche*; N. Rubenstein, "The Beginnings of Political Thought in Florence" in *Journal of the Warburg and Courtauld Institutes* VI, 1942, pp. 198ff., and cf. Rousseau, loc. cit., p. 148 n. 27.

and peace (Erasmus)[188] or between periods of worthy achievement and those brought low by indolence, pleasure, and luxury (Nicolò Contarini)[189]—Machiavelli envisaged a cluster of such principles which all impinged on each other in a complex (though not always articulated) set of reciprocal relationships. Internal matters, for example, could be affected by processes of constitutional change, by the moral condition of the people, by the caliber of state leaders and the degree to which they might place their trust in *fortuna*. The external arena, again, could be influenced by the relative valor of the armies, the relative degree of *virtù* in different states, the relative power of people to recover from misfortune or to resist corruption in times of success. What happened in both spheres, of course, depended primarily on the facts of war and peace, and it is the alternate existence of these two sets of conditions which justified Machiavelli's special rules of reciprocity.

Did the Renaissance witness other such statements of reciprocal principles? One writer comes to mind, but his conceptions and intellectual dispositions are rather different. I think of Philippe de Commynes and his claims about the beneficial rivalry between the princes of Europe. In the main, Commynes was an orthodox defender of providence, for which he found "recurring evidence," especially in God's punishments upon evil kings.[190] Yet one of his more interesting contentions was that, to quell the insolence and engender "fear and humility" among peoples, God had provided each ruler and state with "its contrary" (*Mém.* V,18, 19). Such opposites operated at different levels, between nations (such as France and England), between city-states (such as Venice and Florence), between dynastic houses (such as Aragon and Anjou), and between principalities (as in Germany).[191] Commynes even guessed that a similar system of contraries applied in the other continents of Asia and Africa (18). On his reading of historical tendencies, men are continually inclined to do violence to each other, so that God provides constraints through both his retributive justice and the contraries, the presence of these reciprocal principles being illustrated by the events of European history. In holding this view Commynes appears to be less ethnocentric than Machiavelli, but such is not generally the case. Besides, in the former's work the processes of history are just as much

188. *Dulce bellum inexpertus*, on "ages rising to their flourishing state subverted by the fury of one tempest, the storm of war"; cf. "Extracts from Erasmus on the Subject of War" in *Tracts on Moral and Religious Subjects* (Society of Friends), London, 1829, vol. 1, p. 156.

189. N. Cozzi, *Il Doge Nicolò Contarini: ricerche sul Patriziato Veneziano agli inizi del Seicento*, Venice, 1958, p. 309; W. J. Bouwsma, *Venice and the Defense of Republican Liberty: Renaissance Values in the Age of the Counter-Reformation*, Berkeley and Los Angeles, 1968, p. 562.

190. M. P. Gilmore, "Freedom and Determinism in Renaissance Historians" in *Studies in the Renaissance* III, 1956, p. 56; cf. de Commynes, *Mémoires* (ed. J. Calmette), esp. V,20 (vol. 2, pp. 230ff.), and cf. V,19 (pp. 223f., 227f.), on various cases of retribution; and see H. O. Taylor, *The French Mind* (*Thought and Expression in the Sixteenth Century*, 1920, Bk. 3), New York, 1962, pp. 26–32, for a more general picture.

191. On the national level also: England vs. Scotland; Spain vs. Portugal. On the city-state level also: Siena, Pisa, and Genoa vs. Florence; Genoa vs. her smaller neighbors. At the dynastic level also: Visconti vs. Orléans; Austria vs. Bavaria. Cf. *Mém.* V,18 (pp. 208–10).

divine as human, whereas the latter achieved a secularization of medieval conceptions still lurking behind Commynes' writings, and he minimized the rôle of fortune in internal-external relations. Although the ancient Greek idea of change into contraries may have influenced Commynes' position, he nevertheless modified that idea quite radically and integrated it with Christian providentialism. Once again it is Machiavelli who shows himself to be the impressive reviver of ancient, particularly Polybian, notions of recurrence, yet with an original mind. Commonly, however, we find in the sixteenth century syncretistic tendencies: Fortune upholds the moral order, and classically-derived models of recurrence are used to reinforce a providentialist view.

## *Other Renaissance themes, especially concerning human nature and the utility of history*

While pagan ideas were being revived, then, they were susceptible to transmutation. Yet again, while medieval themes continued to press their claims, they were often tailored to suit the changing predilections and circumstances of the time. We are surveying a complex panorama; at best we can keep distinguishing the various paradigms of recurrence and the spheres to which they appertain, and we can also grasp a certain polarity between more thoroughgoing revivalists of pagan antiquity and those who concentrated on purifying the Christian heritage. Both the richness and the tension can be helpfully, if inadequately, summed up in the terms "Renaissance" and "Reformation," and to conclude this work we may explore those themes which best disclose the different ingredients of the sixteenth-century crucible.

As a means of both supplementing and gathering up the threads already pursued, we may now reflect on uniformitarian ideas of the Renaissance, appeals to the permanent traits of human nature. These may conveniently be treated with beliefs about the pragmatic value of historical study. The notion that history can teach lessons for the future was a binding theme in the recurrence thinking of the Greco-Roman ancients, and it was of equal consequence for the new champions of the *studia humanitatis.*

It is natural to return to Machiavelli, who made two renowned statements about human nature and history's practical implications for future action.

> Whoever considers the past and the present will readily observe that all cities and all peoples are and ever have been animated by the same desires and the same passions; so that it is easy, by diligent study of the past, to foresee what is likely to happen in the future in any republic, and to apply those remedies that were used by the ancients, or, not finding any that were employed by them, to devise new ones from the similarity of events. (*Disc.* I,39)

And again:

> Wise men say, and not without reason, that whoever wishes to foresee the future must consult the past, for all human events always have their own counterpart, (or resemblance) in ancient (or earlier) times. This arises from the fact that they are produced by

men who have been, and ever will be, animated by the same passions and thus they must, of necessity, have the same results. (*Disc.* III,43)

The Thucydidean claim that history repeats itself because human nature does not change, and the ancient "pragmatism" we have taken to be most cogently expressed in Polybius, are interlocked in these passages. They confirm our case, moreover, that human motivation and action form the key causal factor in Machiavelli's recurrence theory when generally conceived. If human nature remains the same (and for him men are prone to evil and corruption),[192] then the past may be ransacked for similar situations and patterns, and in the future one may expect resemblances to past events. History's resemblances include all the patterns, sequences, contours, and actualized principles we have already elicited from his writings, as well as a wide range of more isolated parallels varying in their sharpness and significance. It goes without saying that Machiavelli's very awareness of the many forms of historical recurrence adds to his importance in our story. He also envisaged a whole spectrum of similarities, ranging from striking likenesses between highly specific events to loose parallels between broadly conceived event-complexes.

The implications of Machiavelli's context are crucial; he reflected upon a long history of humankind stretching from his own day back to Moses and ancient Egypt. His advantage over the ancient historiographers was a decided one! He had much more material from which to derive generalizations, and the two enormous blocks of human history—"ancient times" and more recent times—were just waiting to be compared, for it was not as if the movements of the heavenly bodies had somehow forged a great gulf of dissimilarity between them (cf. *Disc.* I,*proem.*). Lying behind Machiavelli's sweeping vision was his deeply imbedded pragmatism. To know man and his past was to know how to act. To account for the (generally evil) nature of men, to be acquainted with their basic passions and love of novelty,[193] to avoid past errors, to imitate policies and deeds which had formerly had good effect,[194] to acquire both a wide political experience and a general familiarity with history,[195] was to be equipped for politics. Recurrence is therefore of immediate political significance, perhaps even more for a Florentine exile who could still rally support for a practicable republican cause in his own city than for an Achaian historiographer discoursing to foreign minds and wandering in alien lands.

No one among Machiavelli's contemporaries was as adventurous or as sophisticated as he in handling recurrence conceptions. Machiavelli had brought an enormous variety of ideas and paradigms into a working compatibility, and one

192. Esp. *Disc.* I,*proem.* (vol. 3, p. 227), 3 (p. 241), 42 (p. 347); cf. also A. Bonadeo, *Corruption, Conflict and Power in the Works and Times of Niccolò Machiavelli* (*University of California Publications in Modern Philology CVIII*), Berkeley and Los Angeles, 1973, for background.

193. *Disc.* I,3 (p. 241), III,21 (vol. 4, p. 204).

194. E.g., II,27 (p. 106), on avoidance; I,*prolog.* (vol. 3, pp. 228f., p. 231), 5 (pp. 246f.), 6 (pp. 252f.), 7 (p. 257), 10 (p. 267), 22 (p. 300), III,31 (vol. 4, p. 232); cf. *Arte della Guerra* 37 (vol. 5, p. 250), and below, pt. 5, on imitation.

195. Esp. *Disc.* I,*pref.* (vol. 3, p. 225), *prolog.* (p. 227).

can even conclude that his syncretisms are more convincing than those in Polybius. Whereas the latter had worked with three levels of causation—the supernatural, the natural, and the purposive[196]—Machiavelli fastened onto human will and response as the overriding factor. And his accounts of the different processes of recurrence were not only molded around the assumption that it was men and not metaphysical principles which made history, but that human nature was stable and that men's limitations and possibilities were so regulable that one could frame scientific maxims about human behavior and prescribe remedies for social ills. However, others were far from being persuaded by such far-reaching conclusions.

Guicciardini, who subjected the *Discorsi* to a detailed examination, is worth considering. He was quite prepared to rest on very general statements of uniformitarianism and statements which carried the implications of historical recurrence. In the *Ricordi* he wrote:

> Everything which was in the past and is now will be in the future, but the names change, and the outward appearance of things, so that anyone who lacks perspicacity does not recognize them and cannot draw conclusions or form any opinion from what he observes. (76)

And again:

> Past things throw light on things to come, for the world was ever of the same sort and all that which is and will be has been in other times, and the old things return with different names and colors. (336)[197]

Yet these claims for recurrence are much more restrained than Machiavelli's.[198] On the one hand, then, he was admirably critical of more doctrinaire approaches, while on the other he admitted the viability of an unpretentious, loosely-formulated conception of recurring situations and event-shapes, given the delimited possibilities for human behavior.[199] In making this concession, however, he still opposed using Rome as an instructive model for his contemporaries (*Ric.* 110)[200] and was suspicious both of predictions by logical inference from the past and of fixed rules which supposedly governed world affairs.[201] Moreover, on human nature he was unexpectedly opposed to Machiavelli, for

196. See above, Chapter 2, sect. A, pt. 2(ii).

197. 1528 edn., quoted in J. W. Allen, op. cit., p. 486.

198. The view that things always remain the same is really one (rather innocuous) form of a general doctrine of recurrence, and Weisinger belabors the differences (loc. cit., pp. 426–9).

199. Jacopo Corbinelli (b. 1534), historian of the French civil war, was an important author who came down on the side of Guicciardini and against Machiavelli on the doctrine of continuing sameness: cf. *Avvertimenti* CXXIII (on *Ricordi* 76), discussed in G. Procacci, *Studi sulla Fortuna del Machiavelli*, Rome, 1965, p. 177.

200. (Grayson, p. 30); cf. *Consid.* I,4 (p. 69), 49 (p. 103).

201. *Ric.* 6 (p. 7): "It is a great error to speak of public affairs indiscriminately and absolutely . . . because nearly everything has distinctness and exception due to differing circumstances." On prediction see 23 (p. 11), 58 (p. 19), 81 (p. 24), 114 (p. 31), 182 (p. 46); yet cf. 67 (p. 21) on military foreknowledge, and esp. 71 (p. 22), on the foreseeability of decline, yet with caution over predicting the time of events.

his stress on sameness had more to do with similar situations than with permanent character traits. He insisted that men's natures varied (*Ric.* 61), implicitly criticizing his predecessor for neglecting temperamental differences and individuality in people. And if he himself was to say anything lawlike about human nature, it was not that all men leaned toward evil but that they "inclined more to good" (134; cf. *Consid.* I,3). Machiavelli's estimate was distasteful to the aristocrat and to one whose responsibilities made him optimistic about the future of Italy.[202]

There were others who, although they did not address themselves to the Machiavellian enterprise, engaged in a far less ambitious program to disclose both the nature of man and the keys to effective behavior from the pages of history. M. P. Gilmore has argued that Erasmus held human nature to have remained substantially unchanged, and that "the same accidents could happen to individuals as to peoples again and again."[203] Integral to this view, of course, was the prevalent humanist assumption that the past instructed the present and future.[204] Erasmus was one among many who dilated on the exemplary truths of history and harbored the general assumption that it contained paradigms, patterns, or exemplars which could shape men's response to perennially-recurring situations.[205] If some still held up these exemplars for mere contemplation, most humanists were affected by a resurgent pragmatism which came to be as important in the sphere of religious belief and practice as in that of civic life.[206]

With Machiavelli, of course, the case for instructive history was most boldly stated. He reinforced his claims for historical repetition from the particular as well as from general principles and rules. It was possible, though most unusual, for almost exact recurrence to occur.[207] On rare occasions, "similar remedies could avail," but it was difficult to get a concurrence of similar circumstances.[208]

202. That Guicciardini, unlike Machiavelli, believed that "all men are by nature inclined to good more than evil" [134 (p. 35); cf. *Consid.* I,3 (pp. 66f.)] seems inconsistent with his skepticism about the benefits of popular rule. Interestingly, Machiavelli's more consistent position and his heightened awareness of the real and the ruthless bring him closer than Guicciardini to the Protestant Reformers.

203. M. P. Gilmore, "Fides et Eruditio: Erasmus and the Study of History" in *Teachers of History: Essays in Honor of Laurence Bradford Packard* (ed. M. S. Hughes), Ithaca, 1954, p. 16.

204. Ibid., pp. 12–22.

205. To paraphrase H. Baker (*Race of Time*, p. 16).

206. In France, note Seyssel, *Grant Mon.* (pp. 103ff.); Robert Gaguin (1433–1501), *Compendium de origine et gestis Francorum*, Paris, 1495 (the author seeking *exempla* from French rather than classical history); cf. Montaigne *Essais* III,8. In England, Sir Thomas North's version of *Plutarch's Lives of the Noble Grecians and Romans*, London, 1895–6 edn., vol. 1, pp. 7–11; Raleigh, op. cit., vol. 2, p. vi; Sir Francis Bacon, *The Advancement of Learning*, in *Works* (ed. J. Spedding, R. L. Ellis, D. D. Heath), London, 1857–74, vol. 6, pp. 327, 359; Thomas Beard, *The Theatre of God's Judgements*, London, 1597, sig. A3$^r$, etc. Cf. also W. H. Greenleaf, *Order, Empiricism and Politics: Two Traditions of English Political Thought 1500-1700*, London, 1964, pp. 95ff., 109–11.

207. E.g., in *Ist.* V (vol. 2, p. 132), he comments that, with bloodshed, the proscriptions under Cosimo could have resembled (*avrebbe . . . renduto similitudine*) those of Sulla and Octavius (so recalling Dio Cassius *Hist. Rom.* XLVII,iii,2; cf. above, Chapter 2 *addend.*). In *Ist.* VIII,15 (vol. 3, p. 32) Machiavelli notes how the Florentines routed the papal forces on the same field where Hannibal routed the Romans.

208. *Disc.* I,32 (vol. 3, p. 320): *Simili cagioni accaggiono rade volte* (*cagioni* here meaning a series of causes producing a situation).

On the whole, history leaves us mostly with relative similarities. How striking was the similarity, or how inclusive the model, was never philosophized upon with precision but was often left to the empathy of the reader. Some of his minor parallels are cases in point. In one interesting passage he likened the fates of Sparta and Venice. Both were endowed with excellent and comparable institutions, but once they made outside conquests they quickly fell.[209] That instance of parallelism has a definiteness which many others lack; nevertheless, even his crudest similitudes—on the comparable rôle of the geographical factor in the success of Tyre, Athens, and Venice, for example, or on Moses and the barbarians as "new occupants"[210]—all contribute to his total picture. Parallels, *exempla*, and precedents were common features of humanist writings, and the new intellectuals eagerly ransacked the documents of Greece and Rome to encourage the circulation of worthy deeds and revive the active life of civic virtue.[211]

## *New Age theory for a new world*

With later fifteenth- and sixteenth-century humanism, the enthusiasm for antiquity reborn went on undaunted. "Le Temps Revient," ran the device of Lorenzo il Magnifico, and affirmations that the Golden Age or the Platonic World Year had returned were not uncommon.[212] Such flamboyancy continued to make its presence felt in elegant letters until religious war rendered it too sedate and the *Querelle* between ancient and modern pricked its bubble. Preoccupation with historical recurrence, then, was an indication both of the revival of ancient pagan interests and of Renaissance optimism. Yet not everybody yearned for the lost days of Pericles and Scipio. There were still more elevated souls who pondered upon ancient Galilee and the distant heroes who had created the Christian world. They, too, in their new world of learning, reform, and exploration, often dreamt of a rebirth.

The sixteenth century witnessed fresh and often heated discussion of sacred history. Older interpretations of Daniel's visions were still in circulation, but if they were not muted by new theology they were placed aside as moribund

209. *Disc.* I,6 (p. 252); cf. I,5 (p. 245), 6 (p. 249).

210. II,27 (vol. 4, p. 107); cf. I,1 (vol. 3, p. 230) on the seafaring peoples, II,8 (vol. 4, pp. 36f.) on Moses and the barbarians. For other examples of similarities see I,55 (vol. 3, p. 374), 58 (p. 385), II,2 (vol. 4, p. 15), 4 (p. 23); *Princ.* vi,3f. (pp. 291ff.), viii,2, 4–6 (pp. 303ff.), xxxvi,3 (p. 369).

211. Classical *exempla*, however, were not the exclusive source of inspiration. For other kinds in Machiavelli, see esp. P. E. Bondanella, *Machiavelli and the Renaissance Art of History*, Detroit, 1973, chs. 4–6; cf. H. Butterfield, *The Statecraft of Machiavelli*, London, 1940, pp. 28ff.; L. Olschki, *Machiavelli the Scientist*, Berkeley and Los Angeles, 1945, pp. 43f.; J. Mazzeo, *Renaissance*, pp. 127f., 149f. In other writers, a war could be likened to a Crusade (e.g., André de la Vigne on Charles VIII's invasion of Italy), or a desperate situation to a biblical catastrophe (e.g., Luther's *De captivitate Babylonica* of 1520).

212. On Lorenzo's testament and the Platonic World Year, see P. O. Kristeller, *Studies in Renaissance Thought and Letters*, Rome, 1956, pp. 304ff.; on the Golden Age, e.g., A. M. Brown, "The Humanist Portrait of Cosimo de' Medici, Pater Patriae" in *Journal of the Warburg and Courtauld Institutes* XXIV, 1961, pp. 200f., 212; E. M. Gombrich, "Renaissance and Golden Age" in ibid., pp. 306–9; not to forget Giorgione's painting, "The Golden Age," Tasso's *Aminta* of 1573, van Vives' *In Eclogam IV*, *Allegoria*, and their like.

dogma. Humanists and Reformers were either more consciously relevant with their Age theories, or else they sought to liberate the study of the Church from world-historical schematizations altogether. The conventional four-monarchy scheme and the Great Week came to suffer its severest blow by the pen of the early Reformer Philipp Melanchthon (1497–1560). Ecclesiastical history, he insisted, should be considered in scholarship as but one, albeit important, branch of general history. As part of the human past, Church history could not be ensnared within imposed, inviolable frameworks that went forever unquestioned by the secular historian. It was the history of people, and people, furthermore, who had constantly erred and strayed into sin.[213] Such a clearing of the ground was one symptom of reform, and one sign among many others that in the sixteenth century theologians of history, not just humanists or neo-pagans, were reconsidering questions of historical recurrence.

It is helpful to hark back to Machiavelli for a moment, particularly to his observations on the return to original principles. Not only "mixed bodies" should frequently return to their original principles, if they were not following their ordained course, but religious sects (*sette*) as well (*Disc.* III,1). Temporarily waiving his discussion of Rome, he dilated on religious questions:

> Now with regard to sects we shall see that revivals (*rinnuovazioni*) are equally necessary, and the best proof of this is furnished by our own, which would have been entirely lost had it not been brought back (*ritirata*) to its first principles by St. Francis and St. Dominic, for by their voluntary poverty and with the example of Christ's life they revived (*ridussono*) the religious spirit in the minds of men, where it had almost become extinguished. (1)

Such renewals preserved the Catholic Church, just as comparable movements strengthened régimes. Furthermore, they saw the reappropriation of former conditions—though these are left only vaguely delineated—and Machiavelli even bordered on the idea of recurrent revivals in Church history, the example of Jesus being recaptured in the lives of his latter-day followers. Yet Machiavelli himself was no practical revivalist of religion. As a dispassionate observer, he was interested in attempts at renewal from a phenomenological point of view. Other spirits, of course, were less objective, with intensely zealous concern for renewal.[214]

213. A. Klempt, *Die Säkularisierung der universalhistorischen Auffassung: zum Wandel des Geschichtsdenken im 16. und 17. Jahrhundert* (*Göttingen Bausteine zum Geschichtswissenschaft XXXI*), Göttingen, 1960, pt. 1; cf. A. Sperl, *Melanchthon zwischen Humanismus und Reformation* (*Forschungen zur Geschichte und Lehre des Protestantismus, Ser.3, XV*), Munich, 1959, pp. 85–8. The attack on the Danielic schema was facilitated by new classifications of the types of history: e.g., Bodin *Methodus* (p. 15), on human, natural, and divine history; Francis Bacon, *Advancement*, in *Works*, op. cit., vol. 6, p. 183, on natural, civil, ecclesiastical, and literary history; and D. Wheare, *The Method and Order of Reading Both Civil and Ecclesiastical Histories* (ed. E. Bohun), London, 1685, p. 16, on divine, natural, political, and ecclesiastical history.

214. On hopes for ecclesiastical reform and renewal before Machiavelli, cf., e.g., A. Hyman, *The Christian Renaissance: A History of the "Devotio Moderna,"* Hamden, Connecticut, 1965 edn., esp. p. 303; H. A. Obermann (ed.), *Forerunners of the Reformation: The Shape of Late Mediaeval Thought*, London, 1967, passim; D. Weinstein, "Millenarism in a Civic Setting: The Savonarola Movement

It is well known that the Reformers took the true doctrines and spirit of Christianity to have been marred by medieval Catholicism. They were determined to prove that the hierarchical structure of the Church and the temporal power of the Pope represented denial of biblical Christianity. Catholic sacramental doctrines, moreover, were deemed largely false, or without sufficient basis in scripture. The important debate about justification (though simmering down somewhat after 1541) had everything to do with the radical Lutheran reappraisal of the sacramental system. Integral to their approach, of course, was the contention that true Christianity ought to be (and was being) brought back to its original foundations. This is true even though the Reformers did not view their work as just another chapter in the history of revivalism, but as something which belonged to a decisive moment in man's life and which was even pregnant with eschatological significance.

Did the Reformers maintain, then, that the changes in northern Europe brought a recurrence of former conditions and the return of an earlier purity and simplicity? The question is awkward. We may begin with Luther's view of Church history. At points the Reformation meant for him the dawning of a new Age, the last of three Ages in Church history. The first was "a kind of 'Golden Age'"—the period of the early Church—and it ended somewhere between Phocas and Boniface III (i.e., ca. 602–7); the second was the "Dark Age" of the Papacy, when "the simplicity and purity of the early Church was corrupted."[215] The third phase began with the Reformation, but it had its precursors—in Jean Gerson, for instance, curber of Papal pretensions, and "the first whom our Lord God began to enlighten in this last Age of the world."[216] However, we are oversimplifying matters, for there are other sides to Luther. He likened the world to a creaking old house on the verge of falling down, for it was now hurrying toward the Judgment Day.[217] Besides, Luther could envisage the whole of history as a scene of degeneration; the antediluvian Golden Age had never been recaptured, and his own era, which witnessed the third, final, and most terrible persecution of the faithful, was the most despicable of them all.[218] One side to Luther's theology, therefore, played down the restorative achievements of the Reformation, and his tripartite Age theory, though not unlike the schemae of Joachim, or better still Petrarch,[219] was moderated by his eschatology. When Luther's Age theory appeared in Calvin, by contrast, it had

---

in Florence" in S. L. Thrupp (ed.), *Millennial Dreams in Action: Essays in Comparative Study (Comparative Studies in Society and History Supplement II)*, The Hague, 1962, pp. 187ff.

215. Luther, *Werke: kritische Gesamtausgabe* (ed. J. C. F. Knaake et al.), Weimar, 1883ff., vol. 11, p. 36, and cf. E. Seeberg, *Gottfried Arnold: die Wissenschaft und die Mystik seiner Zeit*, Meerane, 1923, p. 435; and (for most of the quotations), Harbinson, op. cit., p. 278.

216. Quoted in E. Schäfer, *Luther als Kirchenhistoriker*, Gütersloh, 1897, p. 447.

217. *Werke*, vol. 34, pt. 2, p. 461, and cf. vol. 15, p. 32, vol. 45, pp. 336ff. Cf. also J. M. Tonkin, "Luther's Interpretation of Secular Reality" in *The Journal of Religious History* VI, 1970, pp. 136–40.

218. J. M. Headley, *Luther's View of Church History (Yale Publications in Religion VI)*, New Haven, 1963, pp. 122f., 143–53; M. Preuss, *Die Vorstellungen von Antichrist im späteren Mittelalter, bei Luther und der konfessionellen Polemik*, Leipzig, 1906, p. 87.

219. See Excursus 4; cf. below on the background to Guillaume Postel's tripartite model.

stronger recurrence overtones. Calvin was less apocalyptic in his views about the third Age; the world was waiting to be conquered by the Gospel and renovated through its power.[220] But not even Calvin, let alone Luther, believed that the clock could be turned back. Massive deinstitutionalization to restore the conditions of the earliest Church was impossible, and they who taught so were in error.

There were, it is well known, people who did teach so. Yet first we must place the idea of a reformed, restored, or renewed Church in a broader perspective. The Reformation, one should insist, was as much a product and part of the Renaissance as it was a reaction against it. Humanism not only fostered a conscious revival of ancient pagan ideas but also led to attempts at rediscovering Christian Antiquity, especially by such northern scholars as Erasmus, Lefèvre d'Étaples, and their associates. These men were engaged in editing and understanding patristic as well as biblical texts,[221] and they were involved in a movement of cultural rebirth in the north which lacked the decidedly pagan associations of Botticelli's *Primavera* and Ficino's Platonic philosophy. The scholarly redemption of Christian antiquity was fuel to the Reformers' fire. For them, it proved how much real Christianity had been submerged under heavy scholasticism.

Yet severance from the Mother Church was not everybody's solution to the recovery of a lost order. The notion of an ecclesiastical Golden Age, for example, was widely current among Renaissance Catholics. Both Virgil's *Fourth Eclogue* and the important pseudo-Clementine literature placed this Age in apostolic times,[222] and such men as Cajetan (founder of the Theatines) longed for "the Golden Age of the primitive Church" to return, and for the Church to be restored "according to antiquity."[223] Yet the time of Jesus and the Acts was not the only one reflected upon. If Erasmus, for example, had his more optimistic moments, the Golden Age he projected was probably best anticipated in the patristic period, when, just as in his own time, there was some concord between theology and the search for *bonae litterae*, and a great struggle against the winds of heresy.[224]

A different and even more enthralling development of this old theme is to be found in the strange writings of Giles of Viterbo (1467–1532), Prior General of

220. Commenting on Luke 17:20, in *Opera* (ed. G. Baum et al.) (*Corpus Reformatorum XXXV*), Berlin, 1863–1900, vol. 45, p. 425; and on Acts 15:9, in vol. 49, p. 346. Cf. Harbinson, op. cit., p. 281, and on Zwingli's adoption of the tripartite Age theory, A. Baur, *Zwingli's Theologie*, Halle, 1885–89, vol. 2, p. 68 and n.

221. L. Bouyer, *Erasmus and the Humanist Experiment* (ET), London, 1959, ch. 12; E. F. Rice, Jr., "The Humanist Idea of Christian Antiquity: Lefèvre D'Étaples and His Circle" in *French Humanism 1470-1600* (ed. W. L. Gundersheimer), London, 1969, pp. 163ff.

222. Esp. pseudo-Clementine *Epistle IV*.

223. Cf. P. Sarpi, *Istorie del Concilio Tridentino*, London, 1619, vol. 1, p. 34, vol. 3, p. 332. Cajetan (1480–1547) held a view opposed by Diego Lainez, S.J. (1512–1565) who considered the modern Church an improvement over the ancient (vol. 2, p. 108, vol. 3, pp. 230f.).

224. P. G. Bietenholz, *History and Biography in the Work of Erasmus of Rotterdam* (*Travaux d'Humanisme et Renaissance LXXXVII*), Geneva, 1966, pp. 28–46; cf. Gilmore, "Fides," pp. 23f.

the prestigious Augustinians, and a man who probably greeted young Luther on his visit to Rome in 1510–1.[225] Giles was vitally concerned to work for Church reform, dreaming as he did of a widespread renewal of poverty and sanctity suggestive of Joachim's third *status*. His understanding of history, moreover, reinforced the grounds of his hopes. Having been appointed General under Julius II, Giles delivered a protracted address before the Pope, openly asserting that Julius' Pontificate witnessed the fulfillment of that spiritual Golden Age associated with the sanctifying work of Christ. Early on, he mentioned history's four great Ages—those of Lucifer, Adam, Janus, and Christ—and claimed that, in varying degrees of quality and time, each Age, or at least the last three, experienced the flourishing of the golden life, a life lived in accordance with the demands of reason and religion.[226] In the second part of his oration he proceeded to show that the reign of Manuel of Portugal, which coincided with Julius' primacy, represented a new revival of the golden life, and (in the light of Hispano-Portuguese expansion) a fulfillment of biblical prophecies about the spread of Christianity.[227] He also conjured up a special parallelism between the present Age of Christ (as it was being consummated in the sixteenth century) and the third Age of Janus, the Age of the ancient Etrurian king who was placed before Belus and Saturnus at a point just after the Deluge.[228] He made much of the idea, moreover, that the Vatican hill, on which the new basilica of St. Peter stood so splendidly, was Etruscan and deeply significant for Etruria.[229] Such rhetoric may seem quite idiosyncratic, yet Giles employed Age theory rather refreshingly to say something about spiritual, and not simply cultural, rebirth.

When Leo X was elected to the Papacy, he persisted with these themes, and was even more enthusiastic in his use of recurrence images. In the *Historia XX saeculorum* (ca. 1513), he tried to combine two protean teachings—the four-world-monarchy doctrine and the theory of "metal" Ages—with his own idea of world Ages recurring in groups of ten.[230] There were ten Ages before and ten after the *true* Golden Age [which ran from Christ to Pope Silvester (314–335)], and if the first block of eons suffered a progressive degeneration up to the Incarnation, there had also been continual decay in spiritual life after it. Now, however, in the tenth Age after Christ, a new Age of Gold was beginning, this time, by Leo's hopeful rule, with accompanying signs of world conversion (marked by the Pope's friendly treatment of the Jews) and with the expansion of

225. J. W. O'Malley, *Giles of Viterbo on Church and Reform: A Study in Renaissance Thought* (*Studies in Mediaeval and Reformation Thought* V), Leiden, 1968, pp. 4ff.

226. *De Ecclesiae Incremento* (1507) (the Evora Latin MS, ed. J. W. O'Malley, in *Traditio* XXV, 1969), I,1–II,1 (fols. $4^{r}$–$43^{v}$, pp. 280–310), and on the golden life see esp. I,2 (fols. $8^{v}$–$9^{v}$, pp. 283f.), 3 (fol. $11^{r}$, p. 286, fols. $13^{r-v}$, pp. 287f., fols. $16^{v}$–$18^{r}$, pp. 309f.), II,2 (fols. $47^{r}$–$51^{v}$, pp. 312–6).

227. *Proem.* (fol. $1^{v}$, p. 279), I,1 (fol. $5^{r}$, pp. 280f.), 3 (fol. $11(a)^{r}$, p. 286, fol. $23^{v}$, p. 295), II,1 (fol. $43^{r}$, pp. 309f.), 2 (fols. $54^{v}$–$54(a)^{v}$, pp. 318f.).

228. I,3 (fol. $11^{v}$, p. 285).

229. I,3 (fol. $11(a)^{r-v}$, p. 286, fol. $23^{v}$, p. 295), 4 (fol. $28^{v}$, pp. 298f.), II,2 (fol. $54^{r}$, p. 318), 4 (fols. $70^{v}$–$72^{r}$, pp. 331f.).

230. His interest in ten Ages has a Cabalistic background: O'Malley, op. cit., pp. 103–8.

Christianity overseas.[231] According to this approach, the translation of empires from the Middle East to Rome belonged more to the pre-incarnational dispensation, while the significant movements after Christ were the migration of the Church into Europe and the virtual succession of the old Roman empire by the Roman Church.[232] On the same Vatican hill, moreover, Janus had once founded the ancient and pure religion of the Etruscans, before it was desecrated by the pagans, while Peter, the other keybearer, founded the Roman Church before that long interval of spiritual decline.[233] Now the great St. Peter's had been raised there, a crucial symbol of cultural efflorescence and of the Church's bright future. Intriguingly, Giles had no disdain for this great monument, yet it was the ideal of hard primitivism, of the poverty and destitution of the early "Golden" Church, which he continued to hold up to his contemporaries.[234]

For all his inconsistency and curious interests, and despite the fact that his dreams were fast made illusions by tumultuous events,[235] Giles made an impressive effort to fill out a Christian philosophy of history in terms of cycles and recurrence. He did not deny the eschaton, either (though history might experience another set of tenfold Ages before it came),[236] and for him the End was a time when all things returned to the fount of their being.[237] But the present was his all-important preoccupation; it bore such encouraging signs, and to proclaim them was to encourage the golden life and the genuine reform for which he yearned.

On the surface Giles presents himself as a latter-day medieval mind, unwilling to discard structures and methods dear to a long line of ecclesiastical predecessors. In lowering vessels into the variety of wells available to sixteenth-century scholarship, however, he was in fact an exploratory thinker bent on tendering an Age theory which was relevant to current situations. His method remained deductive in the sense that, like Age theorists before him, he sought to erect frameworks into which all historical events, including those quite unknown to him at the time, should fit. On the other hand, he played with a variety of models and images, and the very range of these and their sources of inspiration are an index to his flexibility and to his awareness of new developments and recently-discovered facts. His unusual adventures in ideas actually

231. *Hist.* fols. 1$^{r}$–17$^{r}$ (on OT period), fols. 21$^{v}$, 38$^{v}$, 47$^{v}$, 52$^{v}$, 56$^{r}$ (Church history). On Christ's Golden Age to Silvester: *De Eccles.* I,4 (fols. 27$^{v}$–28$^{v}$, pp. 298f., fols. 41$^{v}$–43$^{v}$, pp. 308–10), and on Leo X, *Hist.* fol. 316$^{v}$; cf. O'Malley, *Giles of Viterbo*, pp. 112ff.

232. *Hist.* fol. 20$^{r-v}$; cf. *Scechina e Libellus de Litterus Hebraicus* (1530) (ed. F. Secret), Rome, 1959, vol. 1, pp. 189ff. (on the succession of world empires); *Hist.* fol. 24$^{r}$ (on *translatio* in Church history); fols. 5$^{v}$, 20$^{r-v}$, 183$^{v}$, 189$^{v}$–190$^{r}$ (on the Church as the successor to the Roman Empire).

233. *Hist.* fols. 7$^{r}$ ff.; cf. (as background) Livy *Ab urbe* I,xix,2, VIII,ix,6; Matt. 16:19.

234. Cf. *Historia* (Codex Latinus 502) fols. 33$^{r-v}$, 35$^{r-v}$, 37$^{r}$; *Scechina*, vol. 1, pp. 165f.; *Hist.* (*XX Saec.*) fols. 194$^{r}$ ff., 245$^{v}$ ff.

235. Without abandoning his views about a new Golden Age, though, Giles wrote later about God's punishment of his wicked people ("the new Israel" at the hands of Charles V, the "new Cyrus," who sacked Rome in 1527, and Suleiman, who assaulted Vienna (*Scechina*, vol. 1, pp. 69, 98, 104f., 116, 155, 158–61; *Hist.* fols. 245$^{v}$–249$^{r}$.

236. *Scechina*, vol. 1, pp. 101, 180, 199; *Hist.* fol. 268$^{v}$, 321$^{v}$, and cf. 25$^{v}$.

237. *Scechina*, vol. 2, pp. 279f. (quoting Virgil's fourth *Eclogue*); *Hist.* fols. 14$^{v}$, 30$^{r}$, 306$^{r}$.

provide us with a helpful introduction to the most complex Age theory of the sixteenth century, that of the eccentric Norman theologian Guillaume Postel (1510–1581), a man like Giles in his concern to retain a universal perspective yet to reinterpret history in the light of modern change and newly-acquired information about the past.

Postel, unorthodox Jesuit, translator of the *Zohar*, researcher in the Holy Land, even early modern feminist, is probably better known for his apocalyptic expectation of "the restitution of all things" than for his abstruse explications of former Ages. *Restitutio omnium*, however, is itself a recurrence notion, "the general pattern of history" in his work being "one of return through a vast circle," toward the recovery of an original order and unity.[238] For the first time women became an important issue in the history of recurrence ideas, since Postel envisaged that the relationship between the male and female principles would be reperfected at the Eden-like End, Joanna the Venetian Virgin, his spiritual mother (from 1551 on), heralding the new spiritual advent of Christ.[239] Lest one think this great circle shades into mythic time at its beginning and completion, however, it should be recognized how Postel tried to reconstruct the distant past as an historian, and how, like Joachim, he imagined the *concordia mundi*, the social, linguistic, and religious unity to come, being realized in the world of time.

Following the Lactantian tradition (and interest in both Lactantius himself and his approach to the pagan deities stayed alive during the Middle Ages),[240] Postel identified the Golden Age with the time of Noah, his wife Naoma, and their family, and the massive repopulation of the earth after the Flood. Demythologizing, not just Saturn, but all major gods and goddesses of Greco-Roman antiquity, he held time to have obscured the fact that their names were all alternative titles for Noah and the "mother of the world," who had ruled in the Golden age of world unity. The path from Adam to Noah was little more than a prelude to this Age, although in appealing to a well-known analogy, both Adam and Noah belonged to the infancy of mankind's salvation history, before the Law was given to Moses in its youth. In intriguing fashion Postel interwove the language of the life cycle into the model of the Great Week (especially the Talmudic version of it as three successive double millennia), and into Paul's progressive, triadic representation of humanity "before the Law," "under the Law," and "under Grace."[241] To be under Grace, at the stage of maturity, however, did not mean a restoration of the pure Abrahamic religion before the Law, as

238. W. J. Bouwsma, *Concordia Mundi: The Career and Thought of Guillaume Postel (1510-1581)*, Cambridge, Mass., 1957, p. 281. On Augustine as background, see G. W. Trompf, "The Future of Macro-Historical Ideas" in *Soundings* VIII, 1979 (in press); cf. above Chapter 4, sect. D, pt. 2.

239. Bouwsma, *Concordia*, p. 276; cf. pp. 16–9.

240. E.g., note the writings of Stephanus Baluzius, Joannis Columbus, Toinardus Aurelianensis, Gisbertus Cuperus, Paulus Baudrus, etc. (*PL*, vol. 7, cols. 297ff., 389ff., 433ff., 463ff., 587ff., 839ff.); cf. J. Seznec, *La Survivance des dieux antiques*, London, 1940, pp. 13ff.

241. In the main I am indebted here to the excellent analysis of Bouwsma, *Concordia*, pp. 252ff., 283. For background in the Talmud and Paul, see above, Chapter 4, ns. 132, 167, cf. Excursus 4.

we saw it did for Eusebius, but it was a step toward the true end of mankind's spiritual career, this end entailing the return—as a kind of second childhood—to the Adamic and Noachian order beyond Abraham.[242]

In Postel's writings there were really only two great Golden Ages—those marked by a complete unity at the first and at the last—yet, in Lactantian vein again, he conceded to the remarkable emergence of the Christian empire the marks of a Golden Age in the middle of time. The place of early Christianity within the context of world history made it virtually impossible to find in its achievements a true parallel with his two great times of concord, but Postel argued that the succession of the four renowned world monarchies, each progressively worse than the other, lasted only until Constantine, who, as a descendant of the righteous Japheth rather than of evil Ham, took the *imperium* and recaptured something of Noah's earthly paradise. In addition, Postel treated the centuries between Noah and the victory of the Church and between this victory and the eschaton as interim periods, sad sequels to the Ages of Gold. If wicked Rome spelt the very reversal of the Noachic state, the rise of Islam was the comparable catastrophe in the Christian world; though just as Christ's first coming under the Roman Dominion foreshadowed the Constantinian Age, so the attainments of scholastic philosophy, in part made possible by Muslim thinkers, anticipated the final unity to come.[243] God ruled over his world, meting out his rewards and punishments as he willed, for these patterns were not natural nor products of an impersonal necessity, but the hallmarks of his providence and love.

In Postel, so late in the day, Age theory may be said to have reached a climax, or to have been temporarily recuperated by an agile master who gathered up the various reins of this tradition to drive it into the arena for its last moment of glory. Postel knew the European vision of the world was changing; hence he endeavored to incorporate the four continents in his purview. Columbus may have sailed to the Americas, but in recasting Greek catastrophe theory to suit his new perspective, Postel depicted Japheth's Italian descendants colonizing *Atlanticus* (= America) in *post*-diluvian times.[244] And Postel did not fail to account for the popular macro-historical conceptions of his day. With a Polybius-like syncretism he asserted the opening up of a new era of learning after "the dark Ages" (following the humanists), the overall progress of knowledge and science (in keeping with views to be crystallized later by Le Roy), the rôle of Jesus in the center of history (following Joachim), the emergence of a new spiritual order (along with Joachites and Reformers), even together with the clouds of darkness which presaged such a dawn.[245] Postel's view of history (which is too difficult to represent diagrammatically) is rich in texture indeed; it is testimony to the fact that Age theory, though apparently without the immediate practical

242. On Eusebius, see above, Chapter 4, sect. E. In Postel I suspect Samaritan influences here.
243. For the above analysis I rely heavily on Bouwsma, *Concordia*, esp. pp. 259–63.
244. Ibid., p. 258; cf. p. 272.
245. On Postel's pessimism and optimism, see esp. ibid., pp. 274, 286ff.

use of Machiavellian rules of thumb, could still provide some basis for one's orientation in human affairs, some good reason to pursue worthwhile goals. Postel was the last great figure in the long story of "classical" Christian Age theory, and surely he was its most complex, able, and relevant exponent.

## *The reenactment of significant events and other Reformation themes*

Invocations of the Golden Age rarely involved the belief in exact or near-exact recurrence, especially when they fell from the lips of Churchmen. Postel's special position notwithstanding, they were usually just forms of "Renaissance" enthusiasm. What was lost had been and could be reborn, but reborn into a quite different historical scene and under a different dispensation. This sense of proportion was retained by the leading Protestant Reformers when they reflected on the momentous events which shook Europe from 1520 on. There is no gainsaying their sense of historical direction, their acknowledgment that reform meant no simple reappropriation of primitive Christianity. Luther did not wish to see New Testament Christianity in isolation from the dogmatic decisions of the first six Councils, which he was ready to accept.[246] It is thus false to conclude that his program of revitalization had biblical patterns alone in mind. His conciliarism and his doctrine of the Christian magistrate owe something to post-biblical developments, and his sense of continuity and history dissuaded him from thoroughgoing "primitivism," even if he accepted the "early Church" as "a tentative norm."[247] Now it was, of course, precisely over questions of the historical boundaries of primitive Christianity that essential differences between the Reformers and more "left-wing" theological figures became exposed; we may turn to the Anabaptists, who, among all the voices of the Reformation, have the greatest importance in the study of recurrence ideas.

Admittedly, Anabaptism has been notoriously difficult to define, but few would now deny that a mainstream "orthodox" Anabaptist position can be identified.[248] Despite remaining differences, what was common to all Anabaptist groups was the firm acceptance of primitive Christianity as New Testament Christianity, as well as a conviction that the early Church of the Bible, particularly as reflected in Acts, should be the model of the Church in the sixteenth century. They insisted that the Reformed view of the nature and structure of the Church was not governed wholly by scriptural considerations. Conrad Grebel (d. 1526), a seminal figure, felt that Lutheranism "compromised" with the world in failing to imitate apostolic patterns.[249] If the Reformers claimed that the scriptures were the final authority in matters of doctrine and order, then why had they failed to reproduce New Testament Christianity? Grebel was a good

246. W. Elert, *The Structure of Lutheranism* (ET), St. Louis, 1962, pp. 185f., 205, 219–27, 285f.
247. Headley, op. cit., ch. 4.
248. G. H. Williams, *The Radical Reformation*, Philadelphia, 1962, esp. chs. 6–9, 14, 16–8, 26, 32.
249. H. S. Bender, "Grebel, Conrad" in *The Mennonite Encyclopedia* (ed. H. S. Bender et al.), Pennsylvania, 1955–7, vol. 2, p. 573.

spokesman for a typical Anabaptist point: that there should be obedience "only to the Gospel of the Word of God,"[250] and since apostolic Christianity was *in* the Word of God, it *was* that Word. The Anabaptists, indeed, believed that they themselves were re-creating in their own time the past Church they idealized. They worshipped and operated in groups smaller and more intimate than the large congregations of most European cities, and all trace of distinctive ecclesiastical dress or hierarchical order disappeared from their ranks. They took with utmost seriousness the Great Commission (cf. Matt. 28:18–20) to preach to all and to baptize in the Trinity's name;[251] they sought to return baptism and the Lord's Supper to their original form and significance;[252] many of them were prepared to practice, and to their minds to restore, the life of communalism which Luke had associated with the earliest Jerusalem Church (cf. Acts 2:44–5, 4:34–5);[253] and they extolled the idea of a purified body of believers constituting the true Church, the Elect of God, separated from (even if evangelizing in) the sinful world.[254] It was above all in these last views about election and an untainted Church (whose members were to adhere to strict personal rules for the purity of their lives, and from which waverers could be excluded by a "ban")[255] that the Anabaptists revealed their aspiration to reestablish the conditions of the earliest Church, right down to the fine details.

Their adamancy, of course, brought them into conflict with the Reformers. Concerning the purity of the Church, the Reformers insisted that it was both proper and inevitable for believer and unbeliever to mingle in their congregations, the wheat and the tares growing up together until the Judgment day.[256] For the Anabaptists, the apostolic model of the Church was a body of saints, a model they believed to be amply illustrated, significantly enough, in the book of Acts (esp. 1–7). The Reformers not only accepted a *Volkeskirche*, as Luther termed it, but they also expatiated on the applicability of the old Law for those not living under the Gospel. The Anabaptists focused more on their own relation to the Law, either subordinating it more completely to the new covenant, or in some instances treating the two covenants as one. On the one hand, the true Church owed allegiance to the new Law of Faith, and the life of the whole

250. To use the terms of Michael Sattler, from *The Trial and Martyrdom of Michael Sattler* translated in G. H. Williams and A. M. Mergal (eds.), *Spiritual and Anabaptist Writers* (*Library of Christian Classics XXV*), London, 1957, p. 140.

251. F. Littell, *The Origins of Sectarian Protestantism*, New York, 1964, pp. 111–7; cf. the "Schleitheim Confession," *conclus.* in *Baptist Confessions of Faith* (ed. W. L. Lumpkin), Philadelphia, 1959, pp. 30f.

252. Cf. esp. J. Loserth, *Balthaser Hübmaier*, Brno, 1893, p. 122; cf. "Schleitheim Confession," i, iii (Lumpkin, pp. 25, 26).

253. E.g., Pieter Ridemann, *Confession of Faith* (ET) (ed. K. E. Hasenberg), London, 1950, passim; Anonymous, "Mein Eifer tut mich dringen" in *Lieder der hutterischen Brüder*, Scottdale, 1914, p. 596; cf. Williams, op. cit., pp. 124ff., 144ff., 229ff.

254. Littell, op. cit., pp. 117ff.; cf. "Schleitheim Confession," iv (Lumpkin, p. 26).

255. "Schleitheim Confession," ii (p. 25); cf. Matt. 18:15–7.

256. R. H. Bainton, "Religious Liberty and the Parable of the Tares" in *Early Medieval Christianity*, pp. 106–21.

Christian community was to be lived above and apart from the old Law.[257] That was the normative position. On the other hand, it was proclaimed by the more eccentric Jacob van Campen that all written in the Old Testament could already be found in the New, and would take place "either spiritually or literally."[258] The consequences of this latter approach are vividly illustrated in the case of Rothmann, court preacher at Münster (1535), who, taking the Old and New Testaments as a single unit, sought to establish both the throne of David and "true Christian Government" in Westphalia.[259] Such unusual views aside, it was nevertheless the idea of the New Testament Church which provided the basis for the mainstream Anabaptist reform program.

One should add to this account of Anabaptist primitivism some comments about their martyrological and eschatological views, as well as their attitudes toward the state. Although his case may be a little overstated, Ethelbert Stauffer has cogently argued for an "Anabaptist theology of martyrdom,"[260] which involved a vital connection between the martyrs of the early Church and the thousands of persecuted Anabaptists. At one level there was simply recognition of a close similarity and a spiritual bond between the new sufferers and those scourged in early times. Thielman van Braght may have written up his famous history of martyrdom as a continuing story from the New Testament to the sixteenth century,[261] yet from his account of specific Anabaptist deaths we may note the frequent connection between the present and "primitive" situations. "I go the way of the prophets" (cf. Luke 13:33), the Dutch woman martyr, Anneken of Rotterdam, was taken to say, "the path of the Master and the Apostles."[262] On a different plane, one finds a sharpened awareness of an end-time. The martyr is understood to stand at the center of a battle between two eons: such biblical words as:

> They will lay hands on you and persecute you, delivering you up to the synagogues and prisons, and you will be brought before kings and governors for my name's sake. This will be a time for you to bear testimony (Luke 21:12ff.),

especially within the context of Christ's forewarnings about the world's end,[263]

257. Anonymous (Swiss Brethren), "Two Kinds of Obedience" (ET) in H. E. Fosdick (ed.), *Great Voices of the Reformation*, New York, 1957, pp. 296–9.

258. C. W. Neff, "Hofmann, Melchior" in *Mennon. Encycl.*, vol. 2, pp. 783ff.; N. van der Zijpp, "Jacob van Campen" in ibid., vol. 3, p. 60 (whence the quotation).

259. Cohn, *Pursuit*, pp. 298f., cf. B. Rothmann, *Restitution*, esp. p. 104.

260. E. Stauffer, "The Anabaptist Theology of Martyrdom" in *Mennonite Quarterly Review* XIX, 1945, pp. 179ff. H. S. Bender has criticized Stauffer's use of the term *theology* in this connection.

261. In translation, *The Bloody Theater or Martyr's Mirror* (ed. E. B. Underhill, for *Hanserd Knollys Society*), London, 1850, 2 vols.

262. Quoted from *Met Offer* in Stauffer, loc. cit., p. 195. Note also the interest in the ten stages of persecution in the early Church recorded by Eusebius in *Die älteste Chronik der hutterischen Brüder* (ed. A. J. F. Zieglschmid), Philadelphia, 1944, pp. 32f.

263. Cf. Mark 13, Matt. 24, Luke 21. I quote Luke because he emphasized and gave a tighter delineation to the persecution element. On the notion of the two eons see R. Friedmann, "Theology of Martyrdom" in *Mennon. Encycl.*, vol. 3, p. 520.

became immediately appropriate, and endowed present events with eschatological significance.

With the eschaton held to be nigh, the Anabaptists clearly held the present to be an utterly unique time; yet they thereby recaptured some of the real urgency of New Testament Christianity, and they still saw before them the real possibility of restoring the true Church. What is more, they sensed that the persecutors were being, or were about to be, divinely punished. For many of them, in fact, a "great battle was being fought between God and his enemies," which was

> best observed in the struggle between the prophets and martyrs of the Old Testament, then in Christ and his cross and resurrection, and finally in the martyrs of the Christian Church,[264]

and so out of the biblical past figures arose which characterized the eschatological nature of the present. Cain became the prototype of present sin; Vienna (a place of many Anabaptist executions) became the new Sodom; the Catholic emperor Ferdinand of Austria the new Pharaoh; and Philip II of Spain the new Antiochus Epiphanes.[265] Along with these parallels came the retributive notion that if past tyrants could not avoid God's vengeance, the new ones would not escape either.[266]

What of Anabaptists on the State? That is certainly a key question in the discussion. It has falsely been claimed that they denied the State any right to exist,[267] yet they certainly radicalized the separation of Church and State to the point of disputing the latter's power to extract taxes or military service from the members of Christ's saintly (and pacifistic) body.[268] Inevitable conflict with their would-be governors and the Magisterial Reformers resulted, but again they defended their position by reference to the pattern of the primitive Church. This Church was generally defined as the New Testament one, of course, and that says still more, for it was also understood to be a pre-Constantinian Church, and thus one which was in no way institutionally confused with the State. A line of demarcation at Constantine is important. Luther's tentative division of Church history into three Ages was hardly unconducive to the Anabaptist views, because the idea that the time of the primitive Church was followed by a period in which the original ideal had been betrayed, and that then apostolic patterns had returned, was central to, even if not always explicit in, their position. In dialogue with Reformed preachers at Bern in 1538, their members argued that the true Church had ceased for a time, but that they were giving it a new beginning, and insisted that theirs was not a new Church but a restoration

264. H. S. Bender, "Eschatology" in ibid., vol. 2, p. 247.

265. See *Älteste Chronik*, pp. 160, 236f. (on Vienna and Philip); *Ausband* (the Anabaptist hymnal), pp. 236, 380–3, 663 ("Cain and Ferdinand"); cf. Stauffer, loc. cit., p. 195.

266. Cf. *Älteste Chronik*, p. 239; T. van Braght, op. cit., vol. 1, esp. pp. 230f. (on 2 Macc. see above, Chapter 3, sect. B, pt. 3).

267. As J. W. Allen contends: op. cit., pp. 41f.

268. Esp. "Schleitheim Confession," vi (subsects. 2–4), and cf. vii.

of the one established by Christ.[269] The Hutterite Chronicle placed the end of the early Church at Constantine because, despite the Emperor's good intentions, the disease of craft and violence crept in and "the Cross was conquered and forged to the sword."[270] Though some pushed the "fall of the Church" a little later,[271] Anabaptist interpretations were almost exclusively governed by the vital imperative to conform to New Testament patterns. This tendency was rather unfortunate for them, perhaps, in that they could be easily associated with the extremist (especially anti-Trinitarian) thinkers who located the fall in the pronouncements of Nicaea (325) under Constantine,[272] whereas the Magisterial Reformers had felt bound to push decline at least beyond the crucial decision of Chalcedon (451). However, another line of argument served to dispel these associations: this was the acceptance of Hegesippus' assertion (as reproduced by Eusebius) that the Church was a pure and undefiled Virgin until Simon, son of Clopas, the last man alive to see and hear Jesus, was put to death.[273] Anabaptists, then, did not hesitate to employ extra-biblical material which confirmed their interpretation of New Testament Church life and organization,[274] and most of it was designed to point to conditions which were now being restored.

Having considered the stated lines of division between the First and Second Ages, however, what of that between the Second and Third? "The marks of the Fallen Church," as Littell calls them, were above all the union between Church and State, the limitations imposed upon individual conscience by the State Church, warfare in Christendom, infant baptism, and external religion,[275] and these evils persisted into the sixteenth century. For some Anabaptists, such as the Münsterites, no true Church existed during this middle period, but others spoke of a dispersed remnant of the persecuted faithful, Jan Hus being commonly named among them.[276] As for the Third Age, its emergence came with

269. *Acta des Gesprächs (Inn der Staat Bern)* (1538), Goshen College Library MS, pp. 34, 49, 52; cf. also F. J. Wray, "The Anabaptist Doctrine of the Restitution of the Church" in *Mennonite Quarterly Review* XXVIII, 1954, pp. 187f.

270. *Älteste Chronik*, p. 34; cf. also F. Meyer, *Der Kirchenbegriff der Schwärmer*, Leipzig, 1939, pp. 13–5.

271. Menno Simons placed the beginning of the decline early, but putting its completion at Innocent I's edict in 407 which made infant baptism compulsory: C. Krahn, *Menno Simons (1496-1561)*, Karlsruhe, 1936, p. 136.

272. Esp. Michael Servetus (1511–1553), *Christianismi Restitutio*, Vienna, 1553 (Frankfurt, 1966 facs.), Bk. I, pp. 24ff.; cf. W. E. Morse, *A History of Unitarianism*, Cambridge, Mass., 1945, vol. 1, pp. 142f.

273. Eusebius *Eccles. hist.* III,xxxii,7, and cf. 3–6; Littell, op. cit., pp. 63, 183 n. 51.

274. Williams, op. cit., p. 820, discusses some of the material used. It includes Eusebius, pseudo-Clementine *Epistle IV*, Philo on the Therapeutae (*De vita contemplativa*), the Shepherd of Hermas, and the apocryphal Gospel of Nicodemus. Cf. also C.-P. Clasen, *Anabaptism: A Social History, 1525-1618*, Ithaca, 1972, pp. 120, 184f., 193, on the appeal to Joachite ideas, even to Plato and Pythagoras.

275. Op. cit., pp. 64–76; cf. "The Anabaptist Theology of Missions" in *Mennonite Quarterly Review* XXI, 1947, pp. 10f. (on the breakdown of true missionary activity after Constantine).

276. K. W. Bouterwek, "Zur Wiedertäufer-Literatur I" in *Zeitschrift des bergischen Geschichtsvereins* III, 1864, esp. p. 304 (on Münsterite views); *Älteste Chronik*, pp. 35ff. (on the dispersion view).

the restitution of the true Church, the rebuilding of God's temple, as David Joris (ca. 1501–1556) put it,[277] though some were prepared to acknowledge that its precursors included not only men like Wycliff and Hus, but Luther and Zwingli as well.[278]

It is more accurate to speak of the Anabaptists as "restitutionists" than Reformers; that highlights their desperate effort to restore the Church's apostolic pattern, though restitution did not just mean "given a new lease of spiritual life" and *restitutio* was not deferred to some future date (as it was with Servetus).[279] The reestablishment of Christ's Church was a conscious remodelling attempted on the supposition that a return to apostolic conditions was within the grasp of sixteenth-century men and women. It was a process in the here and now which meant living and worshipping just as the early Christians had done, and dying like Jesus and his followers. Anabaptists actually understood and wrote about one another as engaged in this enterprise. They were articulating, then, a notion of historical recurrence, a belief which to their opponents seemed like the denial of time and of change. Their doctrine of *restitutio*, moreover, is especially important in connection with Lukan and other biblical ideas of reenactment. Both eschatological and linear lines of thought persist in their writings, as with Luke, yet the consciousness of their members living and dying like the characters of the Church's Golden Age is strikingly akin to Luke's picture of the early Church reenacting Christ's life, and of Christ reenacting the most crucial events of the Old Testament (cf. Chapter 3, pt. A). Within Anabaptism, moreover, the reenactment of Old Testament ways and events was not forgotten; their innocent suffering was associated with the ordeals of the prophets and faithful Israelites, as well as with the early Christians. It is interesting to note that the Hutterites, in abandoning city life for the wilds of Moravia, thought of themselves as escaping from an "Egyptian" captivity, establishing a levitical priesthood of communalism, and receiving manna (in the form of their new Church) in the wilderness.[280] This sense of reenactment was perhaps less concerned with the repetition of events than the reliving of conditions, but in theological reflection both were interwoven.

With the Anabaptists the idea of imitation, especially *imitatio Christi*, was very intense, and with them it acquired a special degree of historicization. It has been common, and not unwarrantable, to take the Anabaptists as a late medieval rather than a Reformation phenomenon, for the way they organized themselves

277. *'T Wonder-boeck*, Deventer, 1542, fols. 59f. His three-Age schema was probably influenced by Joachim, the Reformers, and some of the same sources important for Postel (cf. above, pt. 4). In Joris' framework, each Age was introduced by a David—David, Christ, and Joris himself! Cf. R. M. Bainton, *David Joris: Wiedertäufer und Kämpfer für Toleranz im 16. Jahrhundert* (*Archiv für Reformationsgeschichte VI*), Leipzig, 1937, p. 30.

278. Wray, loc. cit., pp. 192f.; cf. Williams, op. cit., p. 683, on the theology of history in Caspar Braitmichel's *Chronicle*.

279. Wray, loc. cit., p. 193, on Servetus' projected date of 1583 (according to his *Christ. restitutio* of 1553).

280. P. J. Klassen, *The Economics of Anabaptism, 1525-1560*, The Hague, 1964, p. 67, and cf. pp. 68ff.; R. Friedmann, "The Communism of the Hutterite Brethren" in *Archiv für Reformationsgeschichte* XLVI, 1955, pp. 202ff.

has affinities with the "heresy" movements of the Middle Ages or with the new medieval orders.[281] The radicals' stress on imitation appears as a development of an ongoing theme running through St. Francis, Thomas à Kempis, and on. Yet these radicals actually went so far as to consider themselves the true Church restored and not just a new movement; their imitation was not so much a new venture in piety, updated to suit the ascetic fervor of the day, but a vigorous effort to regain ancient conditions assumed to be beyond man's grasp. Jesus was imitated as an historical personage, yet that in fact greatly increased the paradigmatic importance of those very early saints who worked with and for him.[282] One lacks real proof, but this historicized "imitationism" probably owed something to the current idea of a recoverable antiquity or to a more sharpened awareness of historical reality which the new scholarly hermeneutic had fostered. There was also the related notion—which was very strong in Machiavelli[283]—that the ancients, placed correctly in historical context, ought to be imitated. For both Machiavelli and the Anabaptists, circumstances and the human condition had not changed so substantially as to make the reproduction of past worthy deeds or the reappropriation of better conditions a mere romantic fantasy.

If one may speak of two great "trajectories" in Western thought—the Greco-Roman and the Judeo-Christian—it can also be said that they were never more adapted to each other nor yet in such sharpened tension as in the sixteenth century. From one perspective, the Renaissance is a point of consummation in the history of interrelationships. If later biblical writers had begun the process of matching and synthesizing Greco-Roman paradigms of recurrence with those from their own tradition, the Renaissance completed it. The cycles and recurrences of classical antiquity often entered the discourse of the new historiography as though the pagan-Christian debate over time had never existed. That was not simply because of humanist attempts to reclaim antiquity; despite the special bridles of Christian theology, the whole history of recurrence ideas from the first century to the early Renaissance saw the withering away of a linear-cyclical, or better still, a linear-recurrence dichotomy. As a consequence, there was not only a revival of classical ideas of recurrence during the sixteenth century, but also the continued development and modification of medieval conceptions, conceptions which were commonly integrated with the ancient ones. Admittedly, the more recent notions were rather susceptible to replacement in an age of anti-Gothic sentiment; both the Great Week model and the four-monarchy theory fell into serious disrepute. But, as we have seen, it was not only medieval ideas of recurrence which could be threatened by historiographical criticism.

281. Cohn, op. cit., pp. 307ff.

282. See K. R. Davis, *Anabaptism and Asceticism: A Study in Intellectual Origins*, Scottdale, 1974, p. 137, though he overemphasizes the holy imitation of the historical Jesus in particular.

283. *Disc.* I,*proem.* (vol. 3, p. 228), I,5 (p. 228), 8 (pp. 268f.), 19 (p. 297), II,4 (vol. 4, p. 28), 6 (p. 39), 23 (p. 91), III,5 (p. 139), 22 (p. 209); *Princ.* vi,1 (p. 291).

From another viewpoint, one perceives intellectual discontinuity and even conflict between the two traditions in the era of Machiavelli and the Reformers. To begin with, if the humanists sought to recover antiquity in a broad sense, the biblicists of the Reformation wanted it in a much narrower sense. The intellectually tolerant were appalled at the bigotry of religious purists, while to the zealous the broad road was anathema. Furthermore, the emphases and preoccupations of the two "schools of opinion" could be noticeably divergent. There is a difference, above all, in the humanist concern for convenient generalizations about change and the theologians' interest in the divine purpose. We detected this same point of contrast in a comparison of Polybius and Luke: in the sixteenth century it emerges most sharply in Machiavellian theory and Anabaptist theology. Although there was a concern in both for effective action in the future, Machiavelli scanned the past for recurrences so as to uncover politically useful regularities, while the Anabaptists sought to disclose, and above all to act out, the divine plan. The differences are clear when one considers Machiavelli's cycle of governments and Anabaptist notions of reenactment. We are at a loss to know how these two sets of ideas could ever be related to each other. Obscured in the special imbroglio of *mediaevalia*, these ancient conceptions made their dramatic reappearance in the writings of Machiavelli and the radical Reformation respectively, yet they still remain in stark separation. The history of ideas is never so tidy that it furnishes its own work of art, or its own inbuilt symmetries!

An apt means of bringing this long historical analysis to a close would be to glance briefly at a late-sixteenth-century figure who succeeded in bringing some classical and biblical recurrence conceptions together in a rather unusual way, and whose work saw the attempted interweaving of threads which had hitherto remained in separation. I refer to the important Venetian historian and canonist Paolo Sarpi (1552–1623), and particularly to his *Istoria del Concilio Tridentino*, a vast work produced early in the seventeenth century, but which had its subject matter and its inspiration in much earlier years.[284] Sarpi was a nationalist who was as independent in his attitudes toward the Reformation and Counter-reformation as Venice herself, with her love of *libertà*, her anomalous Patriarchate, her fear of papal domination, her bargains with Protestantism. A Servite, Sarpi mixed his criticism of the northern Reformers with obvious respect and was highly condemnatory of Trent.[285] Moreover, he combined southern humanism with his antiestablishment theology in a remarkably balanced way, treating his history as a purely human study, with a reluctance to appeal to providence as a causal factor although he displayed a deep, theologically-grounded sympathy for the past history and future hope of the Church.[286]

284. Sarpi had begun this work at least by 1612. It was first published, in England, in 1619.

285. See *Istorie*, esp. vol. 1, pp. 20–6, 397f. (on Luther), vol. 2, pp. 192f. (Calvin), 301 (Beza); yet cf. vol. 1, pp. 71, 111, 135, vol. 3, pp. 396f. On Tridentine despotism, vol. 2, p. 438; and the Tridentine failure to understand Protestantism, vol. 1, p. 305 and below. On Sarpi's career and rôle in Venetian diplomacy see F. A. Yates, "Paolo Sarpi's 'History of the Council of Trent'" in *Journal of the Warburg and Courtauld Institutes* VII, 1944, pp. 123ff.

286. *Ist.* vol. 1, pp. 95f., vol. 2, p. 185; cf. W. J. Bouwsma, *Venice*, pp. 593ff.

The interesting thing about Sarpi is that he came so close to fusing the two major recurrence concepts which have just occupied so much of our attention—the cycle of governments and the return to the conditions of the primitive Church. Sarpi agreed with the general claim of Protestantism that the Church had declined since antiquity, but his position was idiosyncratic. On the one hand, he did not completely idealize the earliest Church, since he possessed an essentially neo-Platonic view of ideals and truth as timeless and not placeable historically, and because he held that the most ancient Church could hardly serve as a model for details, particularly on the two most basic sacraments.[287] On the other hand, he assumed that the Church had declined from the New Testament model, and declined virtually from the very beginning. This model, then, represented the summit of institutional perfection,[288] and despite his ambivalence, there emerged from his pen a hope of restoring the Church's original excellence. Institutional life was uppermost in his mind when he wrote:

It is very necessary that, just as we [Christians] have arrived by stages at this profundity of misery, so we must ascend through the same stages to return to that summit of perfection on which the holy Church once existed. This cannot be done without knowing what the administration of temporal things was in the beginning, and how that good governance was lost.[289]

A cyclical element emerges from this fascinating passage, and one is reminded of Machiavelli's comments in the *Istorie* V,1 about the inevitable path upward after the lowest point had been reached. Above all, our curiosity is captured by the idea that set stages of decline are repeated, presumably in the reverse order, so that an ascent may be made to better things.

In the pronouncements of Trent, Sarpi found the veritable low point of known Church history. For him, the most influential of the Tridentine ecclesiastics had turned their backs on the ancient Church and deluded themselves into believing that "the truth was now better known."[290] Of still more interest, Trent brought to a head all those tendencies which were turning the Church from a polity into a tyranny.[291] The slow process of the Church's decline was toward an extreme centralization. It is in analyzing this process that Sarpi appealed to constitutional models, contending that the earliest stage of the Church's institutional life was "popular" (presbyteries), while the second was "aristocratic" (bishops), and the third stage monarchical, with the subjection of the episcopates to the Pope.[292] Each stage was "incubated" in the preceding—a feature

287. *Ist.* vol. 2, pp. 388f.; cf. vol. 2, p. 453.
288. Vol. 3, p. 55.
289. *Trattato delle Materie Beneficiare* in *Scritti Giurisdizionalistici* (ed. G. Gambarin), Bari, 1958, p. 64.
290. *Ist.* vol. 2, pp. 416, 501, and cf. p. 108; vol. 3, pp. 230f., and cf. Bouwsma, *Venice*, p. 602 (whence the quotation).
291. Esp. *Ist.* vol. 1, pp. 217f., and cf. pp. 55, 78f.; vol. 3, pp. 47–53, 232; cf. his *Sopra l'Officio dell'Inquisizione*, in *Scritti Giurisd.*, pp. 176f.
292. On the whole process from "democracy" to tyranny, see *Ist.* vol. 1, pp. 350–2, vol. 3, p. 54; *Trattato* pp. 31, 41. In the "popular" stage, "councils" of presbyteries formed *local* ecclesiastical

reminiscent of Joachim's "elements" (*initia*)—until that final phase in the sixteenth century, when the papal monarchy had been converted into an open tyranny. Paolo Sarpi, then, laid out a whole sequence of ecclesiastical decay in constitutional terms, and evidently believed that a return to good governance was possible only by experiencing the same stages in reverse order, a difficult passage he could expect only in the remote future.[293]

In short, Sarpi stands at the end of our chosen time scale as a fascinating watershed figure. He was undeniably preoccupied with the kinds of patterns which had intrigued Machiavelli and others, and like the Florentine he sought to perceive the lawlike in the apparently irregular motions of the past.[294] The same sorts of basic socio-political questions confronted him:

> [H]ow does a republic degenerate into a principate? is such a transformation to be avoided or desired? can it be reversed? what is a tyrant and how does he behave? can he be restrained? The novelty of Sarpi's thought lies in the fact that he puts these questions to the Church.[295]

What emerges is his strange model of ecclesiastical history, combining into one the notion of rise and fall, a modified cycle of governments, even the idea of an eventual return to the Church's Golden Age, and the reappropriation of biblical Christianity. How fitting to conclude with such a thinker: with him it is as though the acorn has dropped from the great tree. From one object we can reflect on the entanglements, the vastness, and the richness of our whole enterprise; Sarpi's intellectual preoccupations and his relative eclecticism speak of many longstanding themes, while the individualistic and exploratory qualities of his mind look ahead to those subsequent giants who theorized about historical recurrence, to Vico, Lasaulx, Spengler, Toynbee.

---

aristocracies (the aristocratic element foreshadowing the next phase); in the "aristocratic" stage, monarchical episcopates ruled over separate areas (the monarchical element looking to the following step).

293. Letter to Groslot, 25 Sept. 1612, in *Paolo Sarpi: Lettere di Protestanti* (ed. M. O. Busnelli), Bari, 1931, vol. 1, p. 243; cf. *Trattato* p. 64.

294. *Pensiero* cxxxvi (in *Opere*, Helmstadt-Vienna, 1761ff., vol. 1).

295. W. J. Bouwsma, *Venice*, p. 608.

# Reflections

We have come to the point where we are not only able to question sweeping generalizations about Western views of history, but to reflect on our reassessment of these views on a still more theoretical plane. We have sought to undermine the well-known yet superannuated linear-cyclical dichotomy, and to explode the false popular opinion that recurrence views of history have been endemic to paganism but mortifying to monotheists. As Hannah Arendt nicely put it, St. Augustine may have claimed uniqueness for one or two events, but not for any others,[1] and medieval Christians could no more escape noticing the recurrent ups and downs of human affairs than could Philo the ancient Jew. The complexities of the case have been stated; but to ask what ought to have been the case may be a quite different question. Is the idea of historical recurrence, for example, an asset to the Judeo-Christian tradition? Would it not be fair to assert that the varieties of this idea were kept alive in the West because paganism, however, much transmuted, survived? In reflecting upon the thought of Origen, or Lactantius, or Gregoras, one is certainly tempted to answer yes to this last query, even though the persistence of Greco-Roman themes was to be the inevitable result of Christianity's adaptation to a Gentile world. In pondering on the special benefits of recurrence notions, however, it bears recalling what has been argued in the third chapter—that these ideas are actually found in the Bible, the most sacred if misused tome of Western culture. Interestingly, modern Christian scholars are still running away from the *falsi circuitūs* of the classical philosophers without having any precise ideas as to the theories from which they flee, or without even realizing that reputable Christian authorities from Orosius to Lasaulx were happy to refer to the cycles of history. The late Reinhold Niebuhr stands alone among the better-known twentieth-century theologians as one appropriating the broad notion of historical recurrence for theological purposes, and so in part confirming that it belongs to the rich stock of conceptions the West has inherited from the Bible and not just the other traditions of antiquity.[2] I consider it worth defending Niebuhr's enterprise with the reassurance that Jew and Christian have little to fear from ideas of historical (as against cosmological) recurrence, and that indeed they ought to acquaint themselves with these ideas if they intend to go on giving meaning to life.

It is strange how, in exposing the weaknesses of one dichotomy by traversing many centuries of "old Western" thought, we find ourselves, at this late stage,

1. "The Concept of History" in *Between Past and Future: Six Exercises in Political Thought*, London, 1961, p. 66.
2. *The Structures of Nations and Empires: A Study of the Recurring Patterns and Problems of the Political Order in Relation to the Unique Problems of the Nuclear Age*, New York, 1959.

confronted by another. Within the language of modern political theory one can find a differentiation between the "Christian" appraisal of history or human affairs and "modern" views. In this context what is called Christian is (rather unfavorably) contrasted with the modern political style (and its Greco-Roman foundations). As John Pocock states it, whereas "the Christian doctrine of salvation ultimately made the historical vision possible, for centuries it operated to deny that possibility." Greek and Roman intellects, with their doctrines of cyclical recurrence, might not have expected anything new to happen, yet they still left "room for the acute study of political and military happenings, and the actions of men." Such study was evidently not important for the monotheists, for although they preached about God's redemptive process through history, they tended to push "the meaning of actions . . . outside time," seeking only to establish their relation with the eternal.[3] According to this approach, the Christian view of history (virtually another name for the apocalyptic view) lacks that expansive freedom to deal with the real world which marks the participatory spirit of early modern Italian republicanism and the empiricism of Machiavelli. This is a boldly stated thesis and not one to be passed off lightly. It justifies the importance we have attached to the sixteenth century, and we could begin to support it by recalling the differences between Polybius and Luke, Machiavelli and Postel. On the other hand, there is enough in this book to convince one that the Christian view is too variegated and complex to fit such a mold; and although the conception of a path from creation to eschaton is fundamental, the Christian view plainly cannot be reduced to apocalypticism. It has many avenues which are too often left unexplored, and an interest in politics and history's *utilitas* are to be found along the way. The observant Guicciardini may be accepted as a Christian thinker along with the millennialist Savonarola, and the emergence of so-called modern views of history derives from the ongoing dialogue between the Greco-Roman and Judeo-Christian traditions, not from the dramatic (and too often mythologized) reappropriation of one at the expense of the other. The history of recurrence ideas through the Western tradition as a whole is an index to the continuities of macro-historical consciousness, warning us not to overstress apparently revolutionary breaks with the past. We can labor the deductive method of the medieval scholastics, for example, to the point of forgetfulness about medieval historiography, or about those who modified Age theory because the observable data demanded it; and we can extol the empiricism of Machiavelli without fully appreciating his heavy dependence on ancient models and principles.

While so reflecting, some will have been frustrated by my failure to discuss much more radically secularist approaches to history. Marx, of course, belongs to a subsequent volume, but I here anticipate irritation among certain Marxists who will wish me to have rooted Western ideas more firmly in socio-economic soil. Let me say that I have little quarrel with the Marxian view (most clearly enunciated by Plekhanov) which holds given ideas to be the product of both

3. *The Machiavellian Moment*, p. 31 and passim.

antecedent ideas and the circumstances to which the given ideas respond. That is precisely why I have tried to balance a sense of continuity with the admission that altered historical circumstances bring ideological readjustment. Unlike most mainstream Marxists, however, I hold that ideas can have "a life of their own," that they are quite capable of being seriously rethought, reflected upon, written down, under very divergent circumstances and social conditions. I also believe that, although the ideas in this history were expressed by the educated and not the socially deprived, they were more than often protest ideas, used to affirm that desirable change had or should come, or was coming. These ideas still remain the serviceable tools of dissent, more useful for the future, I suspect, than any doctrine of unqualified progress which projects a secular perfection, or a goal beyond all need of basic change and reform. Considering the omens for tomorrow, Marxists, too, will need to incorporate the idea of recurrence—perhaps dressed in a new vocabulary—into their system.[4]

Finally, I should reaffirm the view stated in the preface that there is one fundamental idea—that history somehow repeats itself—underlying the great variety of paradigms we have been eliciting. That such writers as Polybius, Luke, Gregoras, and Machiavelli have figured so prominently in the foregoing pages is because they drew on a rich stock of paradigms, their works thus reflecting a similar quality of awareness, a general apprehension of the human past as an arena in which certain types of situations, problems, characters, and styles make their reappearances. The uniqueness of events was not thereby denied—Hannibal's victory at Cannae or Cesare Borgia's conquest of the Romagna did not lose all the distinctiveness of their time and context—but special events or developments were endowed with universality, and so given an important place in the world of meaning. Virtually all the thinkers we have considered were intent on educing universal significance from the events they interpreted; even if the art of doing this was at times indistinguishable from that of a dramatist, philosopher, or theologian (rôles which in any case the learned were entitled to take), the interpreter of history could not hope to be relevant or to attract attention if his work had no point, no moral or advice. This is partly what is meant by Benedetto Croce's famous distinction between history and chronicle, although I doubt whether much of the medieval chronicling he thereby implicitly denigrated was left unplaced by its authors in the theater of providence. Certainly, paradigms of recurrence were not the only means by which to say something significant or useful, but in their capacity to interlock with such important (if apparently contradictory) ideas as progress, degeneration, fortune, necessity, and providence, they formed the tissue of a basic conception which lies close to the heartbeat of Western culture, and which goes back in its origins, with those ancient myths of eternal return, to the primal substructure of civilization itself.

4. That this has already been happening in China, cf., e.g., G. W. Skinner and E. A. Winckler, "Compliance Succession in Rural Communist China: A Cyclical Theory" in *A Sociological Reader on Complex Organizations* (ed. A. Etzioni), New York, 1969 edn., pp. 410ff.

# Excursus I

# Polybius on the Constitution of Sparta and Its Decline

1) It was convenient for Polybius to declare the Roman, Spartan, and Carthaginian constitutions to contain monarchical, aristocratic, and democratic elements. Admiration for the constitutions of Sparta and Carthage could be considered "traditional" by this time; they were (together with the Cretan polity, which Polybius vehemently withdrew from all comparisons, in VI,xlvii,6) the mixed constitutions meriting examination alongside Rome [xlvii,9, and cf. Aristotle *Polit.* 1269a29–1273b27; Isocrates *Nicocles* xxiv; Archytas of Tarentum in Stobaeus, Frg. 138 (Hense, vol. 4, pp. 85ff.)]. Yet Polybius, whose approach teaches us much about the shallowness of Hellenistic political theory, put popularism before careful qualification. In the instance of Sparta, the whole constitution was ascribed to Lycurgus (a late, post-fourth-century understanding: note Plato *Leg.* III,691D–E, 692A, yet cf. Plutarch *Vita Lycurgi* v,6–8; *De unius in republica dominatione, populari statu, et paucorum imperio* 827A–B), and Polybius chose to neglect the office of the ephors, mentioning only the people as the third power element (VI,x,8f.), presumably to expose a neat correspondence between Sparta and both Carthage and Rome (see li,1f., 6; cf. xi,12b; xiv,1–12, xv,9, xvi,1–xvii,9; and note also how the rôle of the tribunes, as against the Roman assemblies, is not highlighted: xvi,4). In the case of Carthage, kings were mentioned (li,2a), but whether the reference is to the Carthaginian *suffetes* or to military generals is not made clear (cf. Aristotle *Polit.* 1272b37–8). With both Sparta and Carthage there was no attempt by Polybius to isolate any complicating factor. If Plato could write of the tyrannical features of the Spartan ephorate (*Leg.* IV,712D), Aristotle of the predominantly oligarchic characteristics of the Carthaginian *politeia* (*Polit.* 1273a21–b24), and Archytas of Tarentum of a more complicated division of powers (in Stobaeus, Frg. 138), Polybius was too busy trying to draw parallels. As for his analysis of the Roman constitution, his claims about the power of the commons went too far (the senate being virtually supreme in his time), and his general approach was governed by the desire to view all three mixed polities within the theoretical, triadic model which had

become so popular in Hellenistic political writing. The "fashion-setting" *Tripolitikos* of Dicaearchus seems to have been the last word in the political theory of the fourth century, and yet "a barren formula," as Ernest Barker puts it. The "tripolity is only a mechanism, a doctrinaire mechanism at that," and it "never existed" ("Greek Political Thought and Theory in the Fourth Century" in *The Cambridge Ancient History*, Cambridge, 1927, vol. 5, p. 534). Cf., on other inadequacies in the Polybian analysis of the Roman constitution, von Fritz, op. cit., ch. 7; A. H. M. Jones, *A History of Rome through the Fifth Century* (Vol. 1, *The Republic*), London, 1968, pp. 176ff.

2) According to Polybius, the Lycurgan constitution of Sparta remained more or less intact until the battle of Leuctra (371 BC), but then *tychē* turned against the Spartans (i.e., they failed internationally), and over and above (but not because of) that, their *politeia* degenerated within.

> The Lacedaemonians enjoyed a most excellent constitution, and had been a most extensive power from the time of the legislation of Lycurgus to that of the battle of Leuctra. But after that event their fortune took an opposite turn, and their polity grew worse and worse. . . . (IV,lxxxi,12, and see also I,ii,3)

At the end of all the "internal distress and civic discord" (*stasis*) Polybius placed the rule of Cleomenes, who "*entirely* subverted the ancient constitution" (lxxxi,14), and who, by abolishing the ephorate, turned Sparta's traditional kingship (part of the *mixis*) into a tyranny (II,xlvii,3, and cf. IX,xxiii,3, xxix,8, xxxvi,4, XXIII,xi,4–5). Almost nothing was said by Polybius about Cleomenes' "Lycurgan" social reforms (cf. Plutarch *Vit. Cleom.* vi,1, x,1ff., yet cf. Polyb. *Hist.* IV,lxxi,2), and it was only after the intervention of Antigonus Gonatus that the *patrion politeuma* (ancestral constitution) was restored (II,lxx,1; cf. IX,xxxvi,4), although this restoration was short-lived and was followed by the one-man rules of Lycurgus and Nabis (IV,lxxxi,1, 13, etc.). What happened to Polybius' theory of constitutional change in this treatment? If Rome's career as examined in Bk. VI is to be taken as a guide, one would hardly expect a *mixis* to degenerate into a tyranny, so much as to slide through oligarchy, democracy, and mob rule to more complete dissolution (cf. esp. VI,lvii). Are we to assume that Polybius narrated the history of Hellas in the third century without realizing that his references to political *metabolai* in Sparta were in blatant disagreement with the theory of Bk. VI? If we are not willing to make that assumption, there are only two possible solutions left. The first is to suppose that Polybius, who mentioned the "rise and decline" of Lacedaemonia before coming to write Bk. VI (so IV,lxxxi,14), thought of as Cleomenes as a "Platonic" tyrant, the autocratic ruler who ends the process of constitutional decline and who later appears as the "*monarchos* figure" (Chapter 1, sect. C). At least two facts support this view; first, Cleomenes' rule was associated with policies to please the masses, "the hope of allotments and redivision of lands" (IV,lxxxi,2). Revolutionary land programs Polybius (quite conservatively) linked with demagogy or the emergence of a *monarchos* both in Bk. VI (ix,9) and elsewhere (XV,xxi,2) (cf. Chapter

1, sect. C). Second, Polybius at one point referred to Sparta's constitution, after the ephorate had been removed by Cleomenes, as a *monarchia* (XXIII,xi,4). On this reading the ultimate internal degeneration came with Cleomenes' constitutionally subversive monarchy (or, in Platonic terms, "tyranny"; cf. II,xlvii,3), and it came following a long period of discord, possibly of degenerate democratic tendencies under the influence of the ephorate, which Polybius did not consider to be a part of the original Lycurgan constitution (*Hist.* VI,x,1ff.) and which he treated as part of the traditional power grouping within Sparta's polity (cf. Plato *Leg.* III,692A; Aristotle *Politica* 1313a25; Plutarch *Vita Lycurg.* vii,1, *Moralia* 779E). On the other hand, Polybius certianly knew that Cleomenes *inherited* the Spartan kingship, and that he united his city-state in a war against Achaia and Macedonia (II,xlvi,7ff., etc.). Both crucial facts seem to count against the idea of Cleomenes as a "*monarchos* figure." Before exploring the implications of post-Cleomenic events in Polybius, we may state the alternative solution. The historian claimed that of all the paths of constitutional development, the Roman one was the *most* natural (VI,iv,13, ix,13; cf. x,12–13), and this being the case, it does not follow that for the Polybian scheme to be consistent, the Spartan *mixis* had to decline along the same line of change envisaged for Rome. In Sparta's case, it was sufficient to say that Cleomenes brought the ancient constitution to an end, and that it was reestablished (with the aid of Antigonus) only after Cleomenes had been defeated at Sellasia in 222 BC and had fled to Egypt. With either solution this second *metabolē* was effected *from the outside* and was thus not *kata physin* (natural). As for subsequent events, the first solution would see Lycurgus as king (cf. IV,lxxxi,1) and his successor as tyrant, whereas the second merely views these reigns as a resubversion of the ancient constitution—the use of the traditional Spartan *basileia* for a tyranny. The latter is the most sensible interpretation of II,xlvii,3 (cf. IV,lxxxi,13 on Nabis, and see Livy *Ab urbe condita* XXXIV,xxvi,14 (= Polybius, probably) on Lycurgus the tyrant; cf. V. Ehrenberg, "Sparta" in *RECA*, vol. IIIA, col. 1436). Polybius points out, incidentally, that the rulers he was prepared to dub tyrants never permitted such a name to be used of themselves (IV,lxxxi,13). This latter approach therefore accepts that the deviation from old stabilities became even worse after Cleomenes, and that following Cheilon's attempted revolution under Lycurgus (IV,lxxxi,1–10), there was an "extreme low" with the tyranny of Nabis (13–14). In conclusion, then, we may say that the former interpretation is certainly more interesting, extending as it does the range of *metabolai* (decay of the ancestral constitution/*monarchos* = Platonic tyranny/foreign intervention to restore the ancestral constitution/kingship/tyranny, but compared to the latter it is forced and less convincing. Once again Polybius seems to be dealing with one kind of *metabolē*, in this case the subversion of the *mixis* by a tyrant. That is a change which he notes to have happened twice in Sparta, yet which nevertheless seems of little significance for him. Ironically enough, as it is shown in Chapter 5, pt. 3, that was the kind of mutation which was of crucial importance in the interpretation of constitutional histories by Niccolò Machiavelli in the sixteenth century. We may also conclude that Polybius does not appear to have adjusted his account of Sparta's constitutional history to suit anacyclic theory, nor does it seem likely, as B. Shimron has tenuously argued, that Polybius suppressed all mention of Cleomenes' "Lycurgan" social reforms because, in the light of the Cleomenic War, they did not suit his contentions (in Bk. VI) that the Lycurgan *politeia* was unsuited for an aggressive foreign policy. (Cf. VI,xlix,1–l,5; see B. Shrimron, "Polybius and the Reforms of Cleomenes III" in *Historia* XIII, 1964, esp. pp. 152–3, and for an effective criticism, F. W. Walbank, "The Spartan Ancestral Constitution," loc. cit., esp. pp. 303–6.)

# Excursus 2

# Luke as Hellenistic Historian: Background Comments

Luke sought to present a *diēgēsis* (narrative), or an orderly account of *pragmata*; it was based on material handed down by "eye-witnesses" and "servants of the word," and was meant to be accurate (Luke 1:2–4). [One may assume his reference to others' narratives (Luke 1:1) allows us to apply the term *diēgēsis* to his own work. Cf. esp. W. Grundmann, *Das Evangelium nach Lukas* (*Theologisches Handkommentar zum Neuen Testament III*), Berlin, 1961, p. 1, and for the use of this term in classical historiography, see, for example, Polybius *Hist.* III,xxxvi,4. Note also his references to tradition and oral sources in vs.2, and to his intended "orderly account" in vs.3. The appeal to reliable authorities is reminiscent of classical historiography: cf. esp. the prologue of Dio Cassius' *Hist. Rom.* I,2–3, which is quite comparable to Luke's. On dedications, see below.] That Luke achieved accuracy is debatable; that his purpose was to be an historian is almost undeniable. He "treated" his subject, "informed" his readers, and was not obviously kerygmatic in pose, certainly not in the way that both John and Matthew were. [Cf. ἐποιησάμην περὶ πάντων (Acts 1:1), ἵνα ἐπιγνῷς περὶ ὧν κατηχήθης λόγων . . . (Luke 1:4). The interpretation of κατηχέω (in its passive aorist form) could be crucial, since if catechetical teaching is referred to here, then it might be suggested that the work was written for Christians, albeit newly-fledged ones. But that is not automatically required by the verb's usage in this way: cf. D. A. Wittenbach, *Lexicon Plutarcheum*, Oxford, 1830, vol. 2, s.v. κατηχέω. The author of John openly claimed to have written that men might "believe Jesus was the Christ, the Son of God" (20:30), while Matthew systematically pinpointed Jesus' fulfillment of ancient prophecy (1:22–3, 2;5–6, 15, 17–18, 23, 3:3, 4:14–15, 13:35, 21:4–5, 27:9–10, etc.; only in Luke 3:4 does Luke come close to Matthew's methods).] Although his characters confess Jesus as Christ, and although they preach not only prophecy fulfillment but a whole message of salvation, Luke simply takes for himself the guise of a narrator. [The liberty he took to insist that the resurrection was "factually proveable" (cf. τεκμηρίοις: Acts 1:3) was natural enough. On *tekmērion* in classical historiography, see esp. Thucydides *Hist.* I,1(5) and (12), 20, 21, 132, II,15 etc.] He attempted a "life of Christ" as distinct from making a statement of "the good news" (cf. Mark 1:1), and even if one is bound to ask serious questions about whether there were ideological changes within early Christianity to make such historical reflection possible, the simple points remain that Luke believed he had the sources to effect a narrative, that he possessed the requisite inside information and experience to write his two volumes, and that he knew of someone wishing to be informed. [For the view that such a work as Luke-Acts (which included, after all, a "church history") could only be envisaged once the Parousia was understood to be delayed, see esp. H. Conzelmann, *The Theology of St. Luke* (= *Die Mitte der Zeit*) (ET), London, 1960, pp. 95ff.; J. Rohde, *Rediscovering the Teaching of the Evangelists* (*Die redaktionsgeschichtliche Methode*) (ET), London, 1968, pp. 167–178.] In terms of classical historiography, moreover, Luke's work, executed in reasonably polished Greek, could be reckoned nonfictional, useful, and complying with the conventional canons of history-writing. If the prologues of each volume indicate anything more, it is that Luke-Acts was not directed just to early Christians, but was intended as a work of history for the "open market." [See esp. Dibelius, *Studies*, pp. 123ff.; cf. C. D. F. Moule, "The Intention of the Evangelists" in *NT Essays* (ed. Higgins), pp. 167–8. See also Polybius *Hist.* II,i,1; Diodorus Siculus, *Bib.* II,i, III,i; Josephus *Contra Apionem* I,i, II,1; cf. Artemidorus *Onirocriticus* II,*proem.*] Those prologues also place limits upon the idea of Luke as a creative theological writer comparable to the other Evangelists and NT thinkers. But we must tread cautiously here, especially because recent redaction-criticism has called us to consider Luke as a theologian in his own right. [Of recent monographs, Conzelmann, op. cit. (see pp. 12ff.); H. Flender, *St. Luke: Theologian of Redemptive History* (ET), London, 1967, pts. 2–3; and I. H. Marshall, *Luke: Historian and Theologian*, Exeter, 1970, esp. chs. 2–4, are crucial. See also the contributions to L. E. Keck and J. L. Martyn (eds.), *Studies in Luke-Acts*, London, 1968, pt. 2.] Certainly Luke was sensitive over current incredulities toward Christianity (Acts 26:24–32; cf. 17:32), and he made use of much material, Mark included, which many scholars would call more proclamatory than historical, or material which had not been preserved with the interests of historians or antiquarians in mind, but for sermons and catechesis in the young proselytizing churches. [For background on the study of the Jesus tradition, see M. Dibelius, *From Tradition to Gospel* (= *Die Formgeschichte des Evangeliums*) (ET), London, 1934, esp. pp. 25ff., etc.; R. Bultmann, *History of the Synoptic Tradition* (ET), London, 1963, esp. pp. 322ff. On Mark, and on the relative freedom with which other Evangelists presented the living *Kyrios*, see esp. J. M. Robinson, *The Problem of History in Mark* (*Studies in Biblical Theology XXI*), London, 1957, esp. pp. 54ff.; G. Barth, *Tradition and Interpretation in Matthew* (with G. Bornkamm and M. J. Held) (ET), London, 1963, pp. 95–124, etc.; C. H. Dodd, *Historical Tradition in the Fourth Gospel*, Cambridge, 1963, introd.; F. W. Beare, "Sayings of the Risen Lord in the Gospel Tradition" in *Christian History and Interpretation* (ed. W. R. Farmer et al.), Cambridge, 1967, pp. 159ff., etc. The status of Q is still in doubt. Was it a narrative work? Cf. V. Taylor, "The Original Order of Q" in *NT Essays* (ed. Higgins), pp. 246ff. In contrast to these writers, Luke most definitely takes Jesus (who is still for him the exalted, ever present *Kyrios*) in the past tense (so Flender, op. cit., p. 42, for discussion, and for background in ancient Christology).] Even if the presence of the prologues might deter us from expecting from Luke any radical, fabricating redactionism of such received material, no one would deny, in the light of synoptic and redaction-critical studies, that Luke has changed the tradition about Jesus (cf. Rohde, op. cit., ch. 5, for the consensus view). The case, however, must be stated clearly. On the one hand, Luke handled his sources like an historian rather than an evangelist. In the Gospel his modifications and adaptations were governed by a desire to characterize Jesus as an historical personage, rather than by any concern to erect a kerygmatically-oriented Christology. On the other hand, Luke wrote in support of Christ and the Christians, and his theological preconceptions are still detectable. As we can see from Chapter 3, moreover, his historical work was not to be written without an attempt to elicit patterns and truths which gave meaning to the sequence of events being examined, these attempts being so common in histories both Israelite-Jewish and Greco-Roman (cf. esp. Chapter 2, sect. B, pt. 2; Chapter 3, sect. B; Chapter 4, sect. G, mainly on the moral order in history). Such patterns and truths constitute Luke's presuppositional understanding of historical processes, that is, his working assumptions as one coming to the task of writing history. In this connection, incidentally, it is not warrantable to conclude that Luke drew a distinction between *Geschichte* (general, normative history) and *Heilsgeschichte* ("salvation-history" of Jesus and his Church) [so, against Cullmann's generalizations about the NT *Weltanschauung*, in op. cit., pts. 2–3, cf. E. Lohse, "Lukas als Theologe der Heilsgeschichte" in *Evangelische Theologie* XIV, 1964, pp. 256ff.]. One key reason why he wrote his narrative was that he believed Christianity—and its founder—had become the new and vital factor in the history of the *oikoumenē*, the world which was then ruled politically by the one supreme power of Rome. [The editorial introductions of Luke 2:1–2, 3:1 are important in this respect, as are the small "Pentecost" for the Roman Cornelius (Acts 10:44ff.), and the divine preparation of Paul for his journey to the political hub of the world (cf. 23:11). Luke was interested in the relationship of Christianity to the destiny of the whole world (8 out of 15 NT usages of *oikoumenē* belong to him, and cf. below, Chapter 3, sect. A, pt. 6). The inclusion of material with a non-Christian origin in Acts (e.g., 12:20–23, 17:14–6), supports this conclusion: cf. Dibelius, op. cit., esp. pp. 19–20.] We can assume, then, that Luke was doing theology only insofar as he skillfully organized "historical" materials of great significance, wrote with persuasive sympathy about the early Christians, and revealed, by both procedures, his preconceptions about the nature of history. He did not preach his theological views, but his presentation of events and of inherited traditions enables us to gauge his position. These comments apply as readily to

Acts as they do to Luke, and even if we have less corroborative evidence to check on the limits of the author's creativity in the second volume, it remains true that he emerged more an historian in Acts than in the Gospel, tracing as he does the beginnings and outward thrust of the Church. [The bulk of Luke is given over to the reporting of Jesus' teaching and *logia*, whereas most of Acts recounts key incidents and developments in the early Church, interspersed with longish sermons and proclamations, which fulfill a role in this volume not dissimilar to speeches in classical histories, and which reflect a mixture of Luke's creative and reconstructive imagination and his use of sources. (For seminal literature on the speeches, see E. Norden, *Agnostos Theos: Untersuchungen zur Formen-Geschichte Religiöser Rede*, Stuttgart, 1923, esp. pp. 3–21; C. H. Dodd, *The Apostolic Preaching and Its Developments*, London, 1944 edn., ch. 1; Dibelius, op. cit., pp. 138ff.; U. Wilckens, *Die Missionsreden der Apostelgeschichte: form- und traditionsgeschichtliche Untersuchungen, wissenschaftliche Monographien zum Alten und Neuen Testament V*, Neukirchen, 1961; Wilcox, op. cit., esp. pp. 158ff.; E. Schweizer, "Concerning the Speeches in Acts" in Keck and Martyn, eds., op. cit., pp. 208ff., etc.) In the Acts, moreover, not only is the narration more extensive, but Luke shows a more convincing knowledge of topography, of local color, customs, and politics. The geographical vagueness in the Gospel (cf. Conzelmann, op. cit., pt. 1) should be contrasted with the details given concerning Paul's journeys, esp. in Acts 13:13–14, 14, 16:6–15, 17:1, 18:18–23, 21:1–8, 27–28. In the story of Paul's sea voyage from Caesarea to Rome, the sense of reality attains its greatest height (27:1–28:16), even though there is some question here of whether the rich language derives from Luke's (or Paul's) own experience or from maritime tales familiar to the Evangelist (cf. W. L. Knox, *Some Hellenistic Elements in Primitive Christianity* [Schweich Lectures, 1942], London, 1944, pp. 12ff.; E. Plümacher, *Lukas als hellenistischer Schriftsteller: Studien zur Apostelgeschichte, Studien zur Umwelt des Neuen Testaments IX*, Göttingen, 1972, pp. 14–15 and n. 43).] Acts may have more than a modicum of fabulosity, of course, but it is our contention that one should first come to Luke's work there on the supposition that he was before all else "informing inquirors" as to the varieties of situations in which the early Christians found themselves, the sorts of messages they conveyed, the sorts of "signs and wonders" they performed, and, still more, the different kinds of people who joined "the Way." (Here I am merely extending the arguments I have already put forward in "Section médiane," loc. cit., pp. 143ff.)

# Excursus 3

# Exegetical Notes on Luke

A) The charge in Acts 12:17b runs: "Tell this to James and to the brethren (*adelphoi*)." Post-resurrection charges to "tell the *adelphoi*" appear in Matthew (28:10) and John (20:17) (cf. my discussion in "The First Resurrection Appearance," p. 322), and I have put forward the argument that Matthew's "Go and tell my brethren" derives from the original (but now lost) ending of Mark (ibid., pp. 322–4; cf. Trompf, "The *Markusschluss* in Recent Research" in *Australian Biblican Review* XXI, 1973, p. 16). In Luke, on the other hand, there is no such command, the order to remain in Jerusalem (24:49; Acts 1:4) being the only comparable bidding (on geographical issues here, concerning Galilee and Jerusalem, see esp. E. Lohmeyer, *Galiläa und Jerusalem*, Göttingen, 1936, passim, and cf. R. H. Lightfoot, *Locality and Doctrine in the Gospels*, London, 1938, esp. pp. 72ff.). There is at least one tradition which grants James the brother of Jesus an encounter with the risen *Kyrios* after an appearance to the brethren (1 Cor. 15:6–7a), but it is not reflected in the Gospels. Could it be argued that Acts 12:17b subtly alludes to this tradition? The phraseology probably derives from the original *Markusschluss*, although whether a reference to James lay in that ending remains problematical. [In "The First Resurrection," p. 322, I have argued that only the charge to tell the "brethren" lay in the Markan original, and that Mark merely alluded to a future appearance to James in a very vague way (cf. Mark 15:40, 16:1); but it is also possible that Luke's ἀπαγγείλατε **'ΙΑΚΩΒΩ ΚΑΙ** τοῖς ἀδελφοῖς ταῦτα derives from Mark's lost ending. In that case Paul's list (Cephas/the twelve/five hundred brethren/James/all the apostles) would tally extremely well with Mark's foreshadowing of an appearance to the disciples and Peter/James and the brethren, although Paul made no mention of an appearance to women, and there seems no possibility of reconstructing any allusion to Paul's last listed appearance from the original *Markusschluss*.] To speculate, then: Luke could have deliberately transposed an inherited post-resurrection charge to a later point in his story. He could have had more than one reason for doing this, moreover. Perhaps the naming of James was one way of indicating a change of leadership in the early Jerusalem Church (on leadership questions, see E. Schweizer, *Gemeindeordnung im Neuen Testament*, Zurich, 1959, sects. i ff.), and what is even more likely, perhaps he wished to make a point about the authority issue in the early Church. One should be reminded that in the Gospel he went out of his way to deny the first appearance to the three women (Mark 15:40, and cf. 6,3; Matt. 27:56, and cf. 13,55; cf. Trompf, "First Resurrection" pp. 308–13), and that he cleverly gave the priority to Peter, even though he had no story as confirmation (24:34; cf. 1 Cor. 15:5a). One of the key reasons for the insertion of the heavily Lukan Emmaus-road story was to make the point that Simon was the first recipient of such a momentous blessing. A skillful polemic against an alternative position suggests itself. In the "ecclesiastical politics" of early Christianity, the first appearance credited to Mary the Lord's mother (along with the other women) was probably connected with a later appearance to James, so giving grounds for the claim that special authority was given to Jesus' family (cf. Hegesippus in Eusebius *Eccles. hist.* III,xi, xx,6, xxxii,6; and see E. Stauffer, "Zum Kalifat des Jacobus" in *Zeitschrift für Religions- und Geistesgeschichte* IV, 1952, pp. 193ff.). Luke was pro-Petrine on the authority issue, and wished to highlight the original importance of the Apostles (Luke 24:33; Acts 1:2b–3, 6ff.), so that this later reference to James and the brethren is probably indicative of his views on Church leadership. Even though his approach subordinated the role of Jesus' family, however, we are not required to believe that Luke denied an appearance to James, but in view of his treatment of the women at the empty tomb, that possibility should not be ruled out. All this, furthermore, does not detract from Luke's stance as an historian; he still believed himself to be representing facts accurately, though some of his fine points here would have only been appreciated by members of the Church.

B) Luke appears to have interlocked two separate but related sayings from Mark in Luke 22:24–7. Mark 9:34f. and 10:42–4 thus become one, though Luke retains something of the pericope Mark 9:33–7 in Luke 9:46–8. In any case, neither saying from Mark is from a Last Supper context, both being shifted there by Luke. Luke 22:28–30 may be "treated" by Luke, yet seems derived from the so-called Q tradition (cf. Matt. 19:28, though Matthew, significantly, does not present it in a Last Supper context). Luke 22:31–4 closely relates to Mark's foreshadowing of Peter's denial: cf. Mark 14:27–31 ≠ Matt. 26:31–5, but Luke seems to have special material (of importance! see sect. A, pt. 6) which he has interwoven with his Markan source. That vs. 32 (at least) is pre-Lukan is suggested by parallels with John 17:15, 21:15–7, but concerning 35–8 scholarship moves in the dark because there are no parallels. 35f. may appear to look back to the mission charge given to the disciples in 9:3 ≠ Mark 6:8, and yet the list "purse, bag, sandals," rather than "staff, bag, bread, money," belongs not to the Apostles' mission but that of the seventy (-two) in Luke 10:4! The Isaianic quotation, although it probably reflects on the suggestive Mark 14:49b, is characteristically Lukan (cf. 24:26f., 46; Acts 8:32f., etc.). It could be contended that 22:36b, 38 look ahead to vss.49–51, yet the offering of weapons on Olivet and the ambiguous answer of Christ ("It is enough") have an interesting parallel in Slavonic Josephus (*Bell. Jud.* II, between 174 and 175). On the whole, the conclusion that Luke constructed Luke 22:24–38 out of pre-Lukan material, which did not originally belong to a Last Supper context, is warranted. He organized his material for special reasons. One, we are suggesting, is that he strove to make the whole passage complementary to Paul's farewell speech in Acts 20:18–35; for another, see sect. A, pt. 6.

C) a) The raising of Dorcas in Acts 9:36–43 is very reminiscent of the raising of Jairus' daughter in Luke 8:40–42, 49–56. Both healers are entreated to come as a matter of urgency (Luke 8:41, yet cf. 49; Acts 9:38); on arriving both have to contend with despairing mourning parties (Luke 8:52–3; Acts 9:39b–40a); both limit the number involved in the healing (Luke 8:51; Acts 9:40a); both call the dead ones to "resurrection" (Luke 8:54–5; Acts 9:40b–41). There could have been, in fact, some confusion between these two stories in the early development of Christian tradition. The Aramaic phrase Ταλιθα κουμ (= טְלִיתָא קוּם ) (cf. 5:41a) could easily, among those to whom Aramaic was unintelligible, become confused with a name; so Ταβειθα ἀνάστηθι (Acts 9:40b). This, along with other less specific parallels between the two *Novellen* as they have been bequeathed to us in the NT, suggests the possibility either of early confusion or of derivation from a common proto-tradition. In any case, however, there are signs that Luke endeavored to make them more parallel than they would have been in the forms in which he himself inherited them. Luke 8:40–56 derives from Mark 5:21–43. In his account of the healing of Jairus' daughter, Luke differs from his source in two remarkable respects. Whereas Mark tells how Jesus allowed only three disciples to follow him, proceeding from the scene where the news about the girl's death was received to the house (so Mark 5:37 in 35–38), Luke shows Jesus to have permitted no one but the three disciples and the parents *into the house* (8:51). Second, whereas in Mark Jesus "put the mourners outside" (5:40a), according to Luke (and in apparent contradiction to Jesus' disallowance) there were mourners at or near the scene of the healing, perhaps even in the house (8:52–53, although see 56a where only the parents are amazed). According to Luke, Jesus stops the mourners by orders to cease weeping, they laugh in scorn, and then seem to drop out of the picture. In Acts 9, on the other hand, Peter is called by believers (vs.38a; cf. 41b), and yet what appears to be a merely sorrowful group of spectators at the scene of Dorcas' death turns into a more discouraging one, since Peter "puts them out" (vs.40a; cf. Mark 5:40a, ἐκβάλλω being a strong word of expulsion for Luke: cf. Luke 4:29, 9:40, 49, 11:14–20, 19:45, 20:15; Acts 7:58, 13:50). Peter then heals Dorcas and shows her alive to the saints and widows. The riddle of Luke's methodology here is solved if we suppose that the tradition about Dorcas' healing had, when he received it, no elements of tension within it, but that the widows were reported to have "stood beside him" (vs.39) while he healed her. Luke may well have derived the feature of sending the discouragers outside (and the minimization of those involved in the healing) from Mark 5, and thus drew the stories of Dorcas and Jairus' daughter closer together, though without making them virtually the same story. In Luke 8:51–56, the minimization of participants and the contention against the mourners are both confined to the scene of the house (cf.

Mark, yet ≠ Acts 9:39), and thus again there is a subtle change of his material to effect the parallel, though once more without allowing the stories to become identical or confused. This interpretation satisfies redaction-critical considerations, and Luke's otherwise unaccountable changes in tradition.

b) Another interesting case involves the relationship between the healing of Simon's mother-in-law in Luke 4:38–39 and the healing of Publius' father in Acts 28:7–8. Quite apart from the familial associations of both, these are two fever cases (Luke 4:38b; Acts 28:8a), and each miracle is followed by the arrival of a whole group of people bringing their ailments (Luke 4:40–41a; Acts 28:9). It is fascinating that Acts 28:7–9 is the only NT complex comparable to Mark 1:29–34 ≠ Matt. 8:14–17 ≠ Luke 4:38–41 (very brief miracle story/consequent general healing activity), also that Luke apparently decided to retain in his Gospel this reference to the cure of Simon's wife's mother (and thus the second of Jesus' miracles) even though he had not yet introduced Peter! (so cf. Luke 5:1–11; cf. Mark 1:16–20, 29–34). [Concerning the miracle in Luke 5, the best Luke can do is to blot out all reference to Andrew, James, and John in vs.38, yet cf. Mark 1:29! so he must have been aware of the difficulties. The retention was not simply due to the fact that he wished to preserve the integrity of the Markan complex 1:21–39, but because this whole complex was useful both in introducing the healing ministry of Jesus (exorcism/cure/general statement) and in looking ahead to the disciples' healing ministries in Acts. Luke supplanted Mark 1:16–20 by his vss.1–11 because he mistook a story about the resurrection (or discipleship?) (cf. John 21:1–8, Evan. Pet. 14:58–60) to be a story about calling. Note the incongruity of 'Επιστάτα in Luke 5:5 and the Κύριε in 8b, and for further discussion, see esp. R. Pesch, *Der reiche Fischfang, Luke v;1-11 (Jo.xxi; 1-14); Wundergeschichte, Berufungserzählung, Erscheinungsbericht* (*Kommentare und Beiträge zum Alten und Neuen Testament*) Düsseldorf, 1969.]

These two cases of parallelism [i.e., a) and b)] should not come as a surprise. It was natural that Jesus' most dramatic miracle in the Synoptic tradition (and one so readily associated with the resurrection: cf. Luke 8:55b, 24:42–43) should have its counterpart in the work of the disciples, and whereas the small incident in Luke 4:38–41 forms part of Luke's introduction to the healing ministry of Jesus, Acts 28:7–9 represents the "conclusion" to the healing ministry of the disciples.

D) Luke's reliability is a secondary question, yet it should be noted that although there are indications of his rather free reshaping of tradition material, as his treatment of Jesus' farewell discourse, trial, crucifixion, and first resurrection appearance well illustrate, it is difficult to understand this remolding in terms of any kerygmatic theology; it is rather to be understood as the result of a view of history with theological implications. In Luke, the trial before Herod has no special, novel Christological significance; its inclusion may have been motivated by an inference that, because Jesus was a Galilean, he had to be tried by Herod Antipas (so F. C. Grant, *The Gospels: The Origin and Growth*, London, 1957, p. 137), but Luke's concern for parallelism remains the more cogent explanation.

His crucifixion narrative may well derive from a special source (note Luke 23:27–31, 39–43), but it should be noted that the two sayings ("Father, forgive them . . . ," vs. 34 and "Father, into your hands . . . ," vs.46), crucial to our understanding of Lukan parallelism between Christ and Stephen, both appear in *Markan* contexts, and therefore may well be inserted into them (so vss.32–8 ≠ Mark 15:22–32; and vss.44–49 ≠ Mark 15:33–41). Moreover, although one might suspect special theological considerations to lie behind 23:26–31, 46, 47b, it remains true that three points of Markan *theology* have disappeared from Luke's account. Ps. 22 is no longer uttered (cf. Mark 15:34), the rending of the temple veil accompanies the great darkness rather than Jesus' atoning death (Luke 23:45b, and cf. Mark 15:37–8), and the centurion affirms Jesus to be δίκαιος, not υἱὸς θεοῦ (cf. Mark 15:39b). In all, Luke softened the agony of the crucifixion: vs.34 replaces Mark's Ελλωι Ελλωι in 15:34; and vs.46 (cf. Ps. 31:5) replaces Mark's ἀφεὶς φωνὴν μεγάλην in 15:37. Luke placed greater stress on Jesus' innocence (vss.39–43, 47b, and cf. 4, 15, 22), and seems to take his suffering as a patiently borne necessity before his all-important resurrection and glorification. On the first resurrection appearance, Luke was probably driven less by theological than by other considerations, either the desire to be true to the tradition that gave Peter priority [1 Cor. 15:5 (+ original *Markusschluss*?); cf. Evan. Pt. 14:58–60], or else to bolster a "pro-Petrine" position in the mêlée of early controversies about leadership and authority in the early Church. As for Jesus' farewell discourse, not only do special considerations need accounting for (so above, Chapter 3, sect. A, pt. 1) but it has to be asked whether both "preludes" to the "passions" of Jesus and Paul represent special pieces reflecting Luke's organization of inherited tradition, or whether they were shaped to parallel each other with considerable freedom. Paul's speech in Acts 20 could well go back to an original (cf. Stählin, op. cit., pp. 267ff.), but it is difficult to decide. Like John, Luke may well have gained information that Jesus discoursed at the Last Supper, yet he may well have been forced to decide for himself which *logia* belonged to that context. For detailed discussion, see esp. A. Vööbus, *The Prelude to the Lukan Passion Narrative: Tradition-, Redaction-, Cult-, Motif-Historical and Source-Critical Studies* (*Papers of the Estonian Theological Society in Exile V*), Stockholm, 1968, p. 136 and passim.

Were some of the traditions he received about Stephen, Peter, and Paul already in a characteristic mold that recalled the Jesus tradition? It may well be that form-critics can effectively demonstrate this to be the case; but the redaction-critical point of Luke's exploitation, organization and adjustment of his materials still stands.

E) I discuss the connection between Jesus and both Elijah and Elisha made in Luke 4 in sect. A, pt. 5 (of Chapter 3). To this we may add:

a) The bringing of two young people to life: 7:11–7, 8:49–56, and cf. 1 Kings 17:17–24 (the women of Zarepheth and Nain both being widows, and the phrase "And he gave him to his mother" in Luke 7:15 recalling both 1 Kings 17:23 and 2 Kings 4:36); 2 Kings 4:32–7.

b) The healing of lepers (Luke 5:12–5, 17:12–9, and cf. 2 Kings 5:1–27) [= the one leprosy healing story in the Old Testament, Luke's reference to the faith of a Samaritan "foreigner" (rather than of the Jews) in Luke 17:16–8 (om. Mark, Matt.) recalling the case of Naaman the Syrian; cf. Luke 4:27!].

c) The feeding of a multitude (Luke 9:10–17, and cf. 2 Kings 4:42–4). Luke placed the scene of this feeding near βηθσαϊδα (9:10, yet cf. Mark 6:32, Matt. 14:13). Why? He was bound more strongly to his Markan source than to the briefer account of the feeding in 2 Kings, and yet Mark was evidently not interested in the appropriate Old Testament *Novelle*, so to effect a connection Luke mentioned a place-name reminiscent of βαιθαρίσα, a "foreign" city referred to in LXX 2 Kings 4:42a at the beginning of the relevant story. Also, on utterances, note Luke's adoption of "What have you to do with me?" in exorcism healing stories derived from Mark (Luke 4:34 ≠ Mark 1:24; Luke 8:28 ≠ Mark 5:7; cf. 1 Kings 17:18).

F) Luke seems to have used liturgical, homiletic, and polemical documents already saturated with Septuagintal expressions. The poetry of Luke 1–2, e.g., may well derive from early Jewish-Christian liturgies; cf. esp. Minear, loc. cit., pp. 116ff. Also, on the probability of sources behind Acts 7:2–53 and 13:16–41, see esp. A. von Harnack, *The Acts of the Apostles* (ET), London, 1909, pp. 219ff., 245ff.; C. H. Dodd, *The Apostolic Preaching*, ch. 1; M. Wilcox, op. cit., esp. pp. 171ff., etc. On the nature of the letter in Acts 15:23–29, note the opposing views of J. C. Hurd, *The Origin of I Corinthians*, London, 1965, pp. 240ff., and J. C. O'Neill, *The Theology of Acts*, London, 1961, pp. 94ff. On the other hand, there are clear indications that Luke was himself capable of archaicizing or of Semiticizing language for the sake of atmosphere: cf. esp. H. D. F. Sparks, "The Semitisms of the Acts" in *The Journal of Theological Studies* N.S. I, 1950, pp. 21ff.; Drury, op. cit., pp. 185f., and I am also indebted here to an unpublished paper on Septuagintalisms in Luke 1–2 by L. Murchison (Canberra, 1970).

On scenes as well as expressions recalling the Old Testament world, note first the strong biblicism of the infancy narratives in Luke 1–2. This is a world of oracular rhetoric reminiscent of the Old Testament (1:14–17, 32–34, 68–79, 2:29–32, 33b–35; cf. Judg. 5, 2 Sam. 2:18–26, 22:1–23:7), of signs and wonders delivered by angels (1:11–20, 26–38, 2:8–15; cf. Gen. 18–19, Judg. 6:11–24, 2 Kings 1:3, etc.), of barren women giving birth (1:7, 13, 18, 44; cf. Gen. 18:9–15, 1 Sam. 1:1–20, etc.), and of longstanding Jewish tradition (1:5, 8–9, 23, 59, 2:21–24, 39, 42; cf. Gen. 17:9–14, Exod. 13:1ff., Lev. 12:7–8, etc.). Mary's prayer of thanksgiving parallels the praise of Hannah at the beginning of the books of Samuel (1:46–55, 1 Sam. 2:1–10), and the young Jesus in the temple recalls the young Samuel, dedicated to God (2:52, and cf. 41–51; 1 Sam. 2:26, and cf. 1:22–28, 3:2–21). In more general terms, the coming of Jesus meant for Luke the special outpouring of the Spirit, the return of the *Shekhinah* and the Holy Spirit of prophecy, which, according to a strong tradition, were not to be found in the second temple, and according to some had either been withdrawn from Israel or not made present in their fullness. [Zech. 14 was commonly understood to be a prophecy of the returned *Shekhinah*; and on biblical and rabbinical attitudes to the withdrawal of the Presence and the Spirit (of prophecy), note esp. Ezek. 11:16, Jer. 24:4–7, *Targum to Haggai* 1:8, *Yer Ta'an* 65a (and cf. 4 Ezra 7:112, to take a Jewish writing roughly contemporaneous to Luke [for its date, see O. Eissfeldt, *The Old Testament: An Introduction* (ET), London, 1965, p. 626]). See also S. Schechter (ed.), *Documents of the Jewish Sectaries* (ET), Cambridge, 1910, vol. 1, pp. 223ff., and J. Bowman, *The Gospel of St. Mark: The New Christian Jewish Passover Haggadah* (*Studia Post-Biblica VIII*), Leiden, 1965, pp. 59ff.] It was important for Luke to give the new set of events the impress of what was greatest in the old. The old is still reenacted in the new, even if it supersedes it and produces dramatically different results.

G) To enumerate pertinent examples:

i) The career proper of Jesus is prefaced by a genealogy reaching as far back as Adam (Luke 3:23–37, and cf. 1 Chron. 1:1ff., yet cf. Matt. 1:1–17). Matthew has his genealogy run from Abraham to Jesus (cf. 1:2), and he is preoccupied with the genealogical symmetry of the fourteen generations of Jesus' line on both sides of the Babylonian exile (vs.17). Matthew appears to follow the presentation of genealogies as laid down in Gen. 5:6–28, 10:1, 15, 21 (using ἐγέννησεν), whereas Luke, significantly enough, seems to adopt a method close to that of 1 Chron. 1–3 (using υἱὸς: cf. Luke 3:23, 1 Chron. 1:3, 6, 7, 8, etc., though with τοῦ rather than the καὶ favored in Chronicles). In the cases of both Matthew and Luke, however, the method of presentation may have been a matter of inheritance; what is of most significance is that Luke adopted a list going as far back as Adam.

ii) Among the miracle stories, which frequently recall the Elijah-Elisha cycles, there are final injunctions derived from solemn benedictions in the Deuteronomic work (Luke 7:50b, 8:48b, yet cf. Mark 5:34b, Matt. 9:22b, cf. LXX 1 Sam. 1:17, 20:42). We may also note other short sayings in Luke associated with Old Testament history: cf. 4:34, 8:28 (1 Kings 17:18), and perhaps 9:61 (1 Kings 19:20), 20:4βb (2 Kings 4:29b), 12:14 (Exod. 2:14; cf. Acts 7:35).

iii) Jesus' pronouncements of woe and coming judgment are dispersed throughout the narrative (as with the historical books of the *n*[e]*bi'im*), rather than collected together (cf. Matt. 23–25). [Note Luke 6:24–26 (cf. Matt.) 10:10–1, along with the oracles against Israel's forsaken house, above, Chapter 3, sect. B, pt. 4.]

iv) Jesus and his disciples are depicted as teachers in the temple and in the synagogues, apparently after the fashion of an Old Testament model, such as Ezra [Luke 4:16–30, 44 (cf. Mark 1:29, 39), 6:6 (cf. Mark 3:1; noting Luke's διδάσκειν), 13:10 (cf. Mark, Matt.), 20:1, 21:37–8 (cf. Mark, Matt.) (though see above, Chapter 3, sect. A, pt. 3), Acts 2:46, 3:1ff., 5:12ff., 6:9, 9:20, 13:14, 43, 14:1, 15:21, 17:1–2, 18:4, 19:8, 24:12; cf. Ezra 8:3, 8, 2 Chron. 17:7–9, 19:9–10, 34:30–32].

v) Jesus and his disciples conform to a frame of prayerful piety reminiscent of the Chronicler's Judaism: Luke 3:21 (cf. Mark 1:9–10), 5:16 (cf. Mark 1:45), 6:12

(cf. Mark 3:13), 9:18 (cf. Mark 8:27), 9:28b–29 (cf. Mark 9:2b), 9:21–22 (≠ Matt. 11:25–27), 11:1 (cf. Matt. 6:7–9, yet note Mark 1:35b), 11:2–4 (≠ Matt. 6:9–13), 22:41 (≠ Mark 14:35), 22:44 (cf. Mark 14:39), Acts 1:24–25, 4:24–30, 6:6, 8:15, 10:9, 11:5, 12:12b, 13:3, 14:23, 20:36, 21:5b, 22:17. On prayer and fasting note Acts 13:3, 14:23, yet cf. Luke 5:33 (cf. Mark 2:18a). From the Old Testament, cf. 2 Sam. 7:18–29 ≠ 1 Chron. 17:16–27, 1 Kings 8:23–53 ≠ 2 Chron. 6:13–42, 2 Kings 19: 15–19, 20:2–3, 2 Chron. 30:18–19, 32:24, Ezra 9:6–15, Neh. 2:5–11, etc. On devoutness, cf. also Acts 2:5, 8:2, 10:2, 13:43, etc.

vi) The early Church cries in its affliction. Cf. Acts 4:24–30 and see 12:12b, 16:25 and in the Old Testament, see esp. Judg. 3:9, 15, 4:3, etc., 1 Kings 19:15–19, 20:2–3, etc., and see Chapter 3, sect. B, pts. 1–3.

vii) It possesses prophets among its members (Acts 11:27–28, 13:1, 15:32, 21:9, 10–13, cf. Luke 11:49). (The prophets, men of God, or seers in 1 Sam.–2 Kings and Chronicles play a central rôle as agents of Yahweh's words and will.) Barr (in *Old and New*, p. 136) intelligently noted the Old Testament atmosphere and "throwback" surrounding Acts 11:28, 21:10ff. There are priests to be noted also: 4:36, 6:7.

viii) Its leaders are given space to recall the mighty deeds of Yahweh in Israel's past (Acts 3:24, 7:2–50, 13:16–23; cf. esp. Josh. 24:2–13, 1 Sam. 12:6–18, Neh. 3:6–31), and they receive signs for their callings similar to those received by God's servants of old [Acts 9:3, 18, 10:10–22, 22:17–18, even 7:56; cf. Exod. 3:2–6 (cf. 4:11), 1 Sam. 3:2–18, 1 Kings 19:5–7, Ezek. 1:28b, Dan. 8:17]. [When Josephus wrote of Daniel's vision in Dan. 8:15–17, he left a scene quite similar to Luke's account of the Damascus road incident in 9:3 (cf. *Antiq.* X, 269). Note also the parallel between Acts 9:6 (cf. 22:10) and LXX Ezek. 3:22; cf. C. Mackay, "Ezekiel in the New Testament" in *Church Quarterly Review* CLXII, 1961, p. 11.]

ix) Its leaders bear the awesome responsibility of calling the people back to God (Acts 20:26–27; cf. Ezek. 3:18, 33:3–4), and undergo like trials. [The reminiscence of Ezekiel has been neglected here: Ezekiel wrote against the princes of Israel as "shepherds" (cf. 34:5), and accused them both of being "wolves" (22:27) and of neglecting the "sheep" (34:8). So note the statement "After my departure fierce *wolves* will come in among you not sparing the *flock*" in Acts 20:29 straight after verses 26–27 (with their background in Ezekiel).] Concerning the trials of God's servants, note esp. Jer. 38, Dan. 6 (cf. Acts 12, 16, etc.) on imprisonment; and on the shipwreck scene, compare Acts 27:18ff. with Jon. 1:4ff. (Was it part of Luke's intention to make Paul a more obedient and sensible servant than Jonah? Cf. Jon. 1:5 with Acts 27:18, 22, 30ff.)

x) There are several other features of Luke's work with the atmospheric ring of the great Old Testament histories about them. For example: the holy temple retains much of its traditional significance (Luke 1:9, 21, 2:27, 37, 46, 18:10, 19:45–6, 20:1, 21:37; Acts 2:46, 3:1, 5:20–21, 21:26–29, 22:17–18); there is a frequency of speech and dialogue not so common in Greco-Roman historiography yet typical of a book like 2 Samuel; the reference to official correspondence (Acts 15:23–29, 21:25, 23:25–30; cf. Ezra 4:11–22, 5:7–17, 7:12–26; 2 Chron.

21:12–15, 32:17), and the fulfillment of prophecy within the historical work itself [cf. Luke 1:20 and 64, 2:35 and ch. 23, 3:16b and 24:49b, 13:35 and 19:38; Acts 1:8 (with 11:16) and 2:2ff.; Luke 12:11 and Acts 18:6ff., 21:33–26:29; Luke 21:16b and Acts 7:60b, 12:2; Luke 21:18 and Acts 27:34, 39; cf. 18:10, and see 1 Kings 2:27; 13:2 and 2 Kings 23:16; 1 Kings 21:21–24 and 2 Kings 9:36; 2 Chron. 36:21 and 22, etc.]. As with Old Testament history, moreover, the Lord (= Yahweh) is frequently the agent in events (Acts 2:47b, 9:10, 18:9, 23:11; cf. 11:24, etc.), cf., e.g., Exod. 4:21, 7:3, etc., Josh. 11:20, Judg. 2:15, 16, 3:9, 13, 15; 1 Sam. 26:19; 2 Sam. 17:14, 24:1, 1 Kings 12:15, etc., and on most of these verses, W. Eichrodt, *Theology of the Old Testament* (ET), London, 1961–65, vol. 2, p. 178; cf. also Judg. 13:24, 2 Sam. 6:11; the "word of the Lord" is heard (Acts 5:31, 13:48, 19:10, 20; cf. esp. 1 Kings 12:22, 13:1, 2 Chron. 30:12, etc.); the "angel of the Lord smites" [Acts 12:23; cf. 2 Kings 19:35 (close verbal parallel), 1 Chron. 21:7–16]; the "hand of the Lord" is upon his ministers (Luke 1:66, Acts 11:21, and cf. 13:11): cf. 1 Kings 18:46, Ezra 7:6b, 9b, 28b, etc.

H) I have a suspicion that very close work needs to be done on Luke's understanding of the Last Judgment, but this awaits a future project. On the *Parousia*, note esp. Luke 21:34–6, 22:29–30; cf. 12:40, 17:26, 19:13–27. I do not concur with Conzelmann (*Theology*, pp. 131f.) that the *Parousia* is deferred indefinitely. Even if the final events are not quite so near as expected (Luke 17:22–5, 19:11, 21:9; Acts 1:6f.), God would soon be vindicating his elect (Luke 18:7f.), and all the major happenings of the eschaton would transpire within a generation of Christ's ministry (22:32; cf. 9:27). Even Christ's first coming was an eschatological event; cf. 11:20, 17:21; Acts 2:17Aa (with Luke's editorial introduction of "in the last days," om. LXX); and see G. Klein, "Die Prüfung der Zeit (Lukas 12, 54–56)" in *Zeitschrift für Theologie und Kirche* LXI, 1964, pp. 375–8. Jerusalem's fall, moreover, was a turning point in the last stages of world history, even if also viewed as a chastisement belonging very much to the (ancient) historian's history (for which see Luke 20:16 ≠ Matt. 12:9). Neither the first coming, nor 70 AD, however, is to be confused with the *Parousia*.

I) Concerning the Holy Spirit in Luke's work, we should note that, especially in Acts, the Holy Spirit's activity has everything to do with the momentous breaking-in of the last times (cf. 2:17), and with Jesus' attainment of his glory (Luke 24:49; Acts 1:8, 2:3f.). But the Spirit also controls the direction of historical events: 9:31, 13:4, 16:6f. (an important example), 19:21, 20:22; cf. 8:39, 15:28, 19:1, along with 28:4b on *dikē*). Luke's special stress here was less suited to Jewish than to "Greek" notions of mediation in history, whereas other approaches—the reference to Philip being gathered up and relocated by the "Spirit of the Lord" like Ezekiel, for instance (8:39; Ezek. 3:12, 11:24), and divine oracles with the words "thus saith the Spirit!" (cf. Acts 21:11)—appeal more to the Hebraic tradition. In general, cf. C. K. Barrett, *The Holy Spirit and the Gospel Tradition*, London, 1947, pt. II; J. K. Parratt, "The Holy Spirit and Baptism" in *Expository Times* LXXXII, 1971, pp. 234f.; F. F. Bruce, "The Holy Spirit in the Acts of the Apostles" in *Interpretation* XXVII, 1973, pp. 166ff.; and (for the purposes of comparing Luke and Paul) B. Lindars, "The Holy Spirit in Romans" in *Church Quarterly Review* CLXI, 1966, pp. 416–9.

J) Conzelmann's thesis that Luke understood Christ's work to be in "die Mitte der Zeit" and that he had a three-stage view of history (Luke 20:35, om. Mark, Matt.; 9:27; 21:32) must be seriously questioned. According to Conzelmann, the first of Luke's three stages is the time of the Law and the prophets, lasting until John the Baptist (cf. 16:16). The second, middle, stage was that of Jesus' earthly work, which had a definite starting point (the annunciation and birth) and a definite end (the ascension: cf. Mark, Matt., John, though note the Lukan-influenced longer ending of Mark). The third stage was the time of the Church or the apostolic deeds. Although Conzelmann perceives Luke's stress on the suddenness of the *Parousia*, he underestimates the Evangelist's expectation of an imminent end to the known order (op. cit., esp. p. 132, cf. above, Chapter 3, sect. B, pt. 4). He also forced a distinction between the "Satan-free" period of Jesus' lifetime and the difficult period of the Church's expansion [cf. S. Brown, *Apostasy and Perseverance in the Theology of Luke* (*Analecta Biblica XXXVI*), Rome, 1969, pp. 6ff.], and put too much weight on the isolated verse Luke 16:16, which in context has to do with the new demands of the Kingdom that Jewish rejectors are unable to meet (cf. 16:17–31; Trompf, "Section," pp. 151f.). W. J. Harrington's acceptance of Conzelmann's thesis (in *The Gospel according to St. Luke*, London, 1968, pp. 19f.), and his view that, whereas the Jews put the midpoint of time with the coming Messiah, Luke placed it with Jesus' first coming, distorts both the Jewish and the Lukan positions. Neither Luke nor the Jews were concerned with special midpoints.

# Excursus 4

# Age Theory and Periodization from Joachim to the Early Humanists

The more exploratory forms of post-Joachimite Age theory are of interest. Bonaventura (1221–1274), who was to some extent influenced by Joachimism, felt no inhibition about expounding Age schematizations different from the Great Week schema, and although some of his models were heavily allegorized, he presented some with five, four, and three stages. The five Ages in *Collationes in Hexaemeron* XV,19 (based on the five summonses in the parable of the hired laborers as expounded by Gregory the Great in *Homil. in Evangel.* xix,1) ran from Adam's creation to the Fall, to Noah, to Moses, to Christ, and, fifth, to the End. In *Collat.* XIV,12–5 the four orders of time—*tempus ante legem* or *naturae* (best embodied in the act of Creation and the lives of the Patriarchs), *tempus legis* (under Moses and his successors), *tempus prophetiae* (from Samuel on), and *tempus gratiae* (NT times)—are reminiscent of the triadic framework we found in Eusebius, which has its background in Gal. 3:15ff. and the Babylonian Talmud (see Chapter 4, n. 167). According to Bonaventura, each of these four times contained three mysteries: cf. Reeves, *Prophecy*, pp. 179f. (and on successions of four Ages elsewhere in medieval literature, see H. H. Glunz, *Die Literarästhetik des europäischen Mittelalters, Wolfram-Rosenroman-Chaucer-Dante*, Frankfurt, 1963 edn., pp. 583ff.). In *Collat.* XV,20 one finds three orders, Nature, Scripture, and Grace, a picture probably deriving from Ambrose (cf. *Epistolae* lxxiii) or Augustine (*Epist.* clvii), but also owing something to the older triadic framework just mentioned. Concurring with Joachim, Bonaventura placed the eschatological events firmly within history, even suggesting that the seventh Age of the Augustinian model ran simultaneously ("as a repose of the soul after Christ's passion") with the sixth: *Collat.* XV,18; cf. Joachim *Expositio in Apocalypsim*, Venice, 1527 edn., p. 9; Vincent de Beauvais *Speculum historiale* XXX,40). Bonaventura also concurred with Joachim in supposing that the final Age would be prefaced by a period of tribulation.

Peter John Olivi, a Joachimist apocalypticist writing early in the fourteenth century, adopted the Great Week model but transformed it to suit his own purposes. Jesus stands firmly in the center of history, the first three Ages (Adam to Noah/the time of the patriarchs/the Mosaic order) lying before him; but the new element in Olivi's work has mostly to do with reenactment, for he gives both Jesus and St. Francis as doors to new Ages. Jesus struggled against Mosaic legalism to usher in the fourth Age, which ran (and progressed) to Charlemagne. The fifth Age from Charlemagne to the thirteenth century (and in a sense beyond?) was one of decline, but St. Francis, like Jesus, was the crucial figure in the victory of the new over the old. At times one gains the impression that Olivi directly transferred Christ's mantle to St. Francis, and yet the latter is also described as the second Elias (or another John the Baptist) heralding Christ's coming again. Here we have the idea of reenactment (of a life in general), in any case, and the notion of undulation is also implicit in his Age theory, with the decline and progress on either side of history's twin heroes. Cf. esp. G. Leff, *Heresy*, vol. 1, pp. 124ff., for an introduction to Olivi.

Such theologically-oriented pictures had a lessened attraction for those who came to find the disciplines of scholasticism too logically cut-and-dried or disagreeable beside newer literary and historical sensibilities. Although the notion of a *medium aevum* between antiquity and recent times neither received full expression nor gained wide currency until the seventeenth century (cf. H. Spangenberg, "Die Perioden der Weltgeschichte" in *Historische Zeitschrift* CXXVII, 1923, pp. 10ff.), we should remember that in the Trecento Petrarch made that renowned distinction between ancient (*antiqua*) times (history to the adoption of Christianity by the Roman emperors) and modern (*nova*) times (from then on until his own day): *Epistolae de rebus familiaribus* VI,2 (ed. J. Fracassetti), Florence, 1859; cf. T. E. Mommsen, "Petrarch's Conception of the 'Dark Ages'" in *Medieval and Renaissance Studies*, p. 127. In the succeeding century, moreover, the phrase "Middle Ages," as used of post-Roman times, obtained some limited usage (Lehmann, "Mittelalter," pp. 200–6). With Petrarch and his sympathizers, historical divisions were based on cultural rather than on theological considerations. With them the strange passage to a secularized Age theory was virtually traversed, though the persistence of old conceptions to the Reformation should be acknowledged, as well as important traditional Christian conceptions which continued to inform the humanist periodizations.

On exponents of the classic Great Week Model during the Renaissance, see, e.g., A. Pierozzi, *Chronicon Universale*, Nuremburg, 1484, (cf. W. K. Ferguson, *The Renaissance in Historical Thought: Five Centuries of Interpretation*, Cambridge, Mass., 1948, p. 16); Sabellicus (Marcantonio Coccio) *Rhapsodie historiarum enneadeum ab orbe condito ad annum salutis humane 1504*, Venice, 1484ff. (cf. G. Falco, *La Polemica sul Medio Evo*, Turin, 1933, p. 30). For other Christian conceptions in early humanist periodizations, note how Flavio Biondo (1392–1463) gathered the "Middle Ages" into a millennium (415–1415), even if one divisible into two periods of unequal length: *Historiarum ab inclinato Romanorum imperio decades* (1483), Basel, 1531 edn., p. 393; and how Petrarch, with his contrast between antiquity and ignoble post-Roman times (cf. *Epist. de reb. famil.* XX,8) had hopes for a *restoratio* of the ancient Roman republic, but with a Christian face (cf. E. H. Wilkins, *Life of Petrarch*, Chicago, 1961, ch. 12). On the case of Salutati, see sect. D, pt. 4 (of Chapter 4); and for the new Age theory of the high Renaissance and Reformation, see Chapter 5, sect. B, pt. 4, and Excursus 6, 2b.

# Excursus 5

# Notes on Machiavelli's *Il Principe*

*Il Principe* was written at a moment of great crisis, both personal and general. 1512 saw the greatest of all tragedies fall upon both Italy and Florence. Significantly, Machiavelli brought his *Istorie* to a close at 1492 with the comment that:

> Soon after the death of Lorenzo, those evil plants began to germinate, which in a little time ruined (*rovinarono*) Italy, and continue to keep her that way. (VIII,36, *finis*, in vol. 3, p. 72)

That *rovina* entailed the collapse of the Florentine government in particular, through Spanish intervention, cf. *Disc.*, esp. I,7 (vol. 3, pp. 256–7); *Disc. Rif. Stat. Fir.* (vol. 5, p. 9). It is essential for an understanding of Machiavelli's approach to these troubled times that we account for the way he distinguished the fate of Italy from the fate of Florence, and at the same time appreciate how he interrelated them. When the moment of tragedy came, Machiavelli found himself thinking about national issues just as much as about the future of Florence. And his national consciousness is most intense in *Il Principe*. It has cooled off somewhat in the two Discourses of 1517–19 and 1520, presumably because by then Machiavelli viewed the general aftermath of 1512 with greater resignation. With regard to Florence in particular, there is no reason to suppose that the man who wrote *Il Principe*, who was the same person to be dubbed "Soderini's man" and to write a *Discorso* on reforming the Florentine *mista*, had abandoned his republican ideals. Certainly it was written to a Florentine prince, a Medici; yet Florence was not the only or even the primary concern of that little work. We would do well to heed J. H. Whitfield's healthy reminder that the last chapter of *Il Principe* was no mere afterthought (*Discourses on Machiavelli*; pp. 26–28). This chapter contains not only a final, crucial appeal to Lorenzo II to liberate all Italy from barbarian overlordship, but also his pointed acknowledgment that a Medici occupied such a vital position in Italy as the Pontificate: cf. xxvi,3 (vol. 4, p. 369). Read at its face value, moreover, much in *Il Principe* constitutes advice to a prince who is expected to conquer and subject territories not formerly his own. On this last point, those scholars taking the bulk of the treatise to be a general manual for princely rule (e.g., A. H. Gilbert,

*Machiavelli's Prince and Its Forerunners: The Prince as a Typical Book "De Regimine Principum,"* Durham, N.C., 1938, passim) should grasp the connection between the whole work and the concluding hope that Lorenzo could liberate Italy (with the expectation that no Italian, i.e., no Lombard, no Neapolitan, no Roman, etc., would withhold allegiance) [xxvi,7: "la Italia vegga dopo tanto tempo apparire uno suo redentore," "quale Italiano gli negherebbe l'ossequio?" etc. (p. 371) (texts vary here)]. And they should acknowledge all that soliciting about occupation, colonization, maintenance of control over peoples who have experienced another kind of rule and their own laws, and about the kind of soldiery and policies requisite for effecting such enterprises (v–viii, xii–xiii, etc.). It has to be taken with due seriousness that when Machiavelli wrote of the possibility and need of *uno nuovo principe* in Italy, he was expressing the hope that Lorenzo was in a position to become what is often referred to as a "new monarch," a ruler with as effective a territorial control as Louis XI or Charles VIII, Maximilian I or Charles V: see xxvi,1 (p. 368); cf. iii,1 (p. 277). Machiavelli operated in the courts of foreign kings; he felt equipped to offer guidance on the institution of such a principality. Hence the combination of hard-headed practical advice and soft-headed nationalism. Perhaps his hoped-for prince in this pamphlet emerges as a special case in terms of constitutional changes, since he was not treated from a purely Florentine point of view. But there remains a tie-up with the rest of Machiavellian theory.

For Machiavelli, the conquest of Italy by Spain meant the *rovina* of the Italian peninsula and not just of Florence (xxvi,1 *finis*, on p. 368, and see the last indented quotation). In terms of the cycle in the *Istorie* V,1, Italy's affairs had reached *all'ultima bassezza*, and in that light it was time to think about an ascent to better things. Moreover, in considering Florence and other city-states (except perhaps Venice) as political and constitutional entities which had failed in the crises of 1494 and 1512, his thoughts naturally turned to the *buono uomo* of his political theory, to the man who would follow the example of the great founder-statesmen and raise up a strong, consolidated state. From the constitutional point of view, men such as Romulus and Lycurgus were the best examples, as his *Discorsi* suggest, but when he was concentrating more on the creation of a state of considerable territorial proportions, as he was in *Il Principe*, initiators such as Moses, Cyrus, and Theseus automatically came to mind [so ibid., xxvi,2; cf. vi,3, where Romulus is also mentioned, and cf. also *Disc. Riform.* in vol. 5, p. 23. The case of Romulus is very important: see *Disc.* I,9 (vol. 3, pp. 291ff.); cf. W. Winiarski, "Niccolò Machiavelli, 1469–1527" in *History of Political Philosophy* (ed. L. Strauss and J. Cropsey), Chicago, 1963, pp. 268–9)]. To look at his position in this way is not to transform him into a prefigurer of modern nationalism, but to take him as one nostalgic about ancient glories and stabilities, and as aware of the secrets of the contemporary foreigners' success. The peculiarities of the Italian situation in 1512 induced in Machiavelli a brash, almost desperate statement of general policy, one which by hindsight we would call unrealistic, and one which was rather out of keeping with the overly cautious foreign politics of his contemporary republican colleagues (cf. F. Gilbert, "Florentine Political Assumptions in the Period of Savonarola and Soderini" in *Journal Warburg and Courtauld Institutes* XX, 1957, pp. 187ff.; cf. *Machiavelli and Guicciardini; Politics and History in Sixteenth Century Florence*, Princeton, 1965, pp. 105–200). When Machiavelli put pen to paper, however, he is unlikely to have felt there was any guarantee of Lorenzo being persuaded of his opinions, let alone being convinced that an exile should be reinstated and reemployed by the state. Machiavelli was not *that* unrealistic. He knew his manual might not be used for the *redenzione* of Italy; but it would still be of service to any individual ruler seeking a strong control over his estate.

Whatever Lorenzo's potential or policies, his presence in Florence confirmed rather than vitiated Machiavelli's theory of constitutional *mutazione*, even if some uncertainty surrounded the extent to which the Pope or Lorenzo was in control of Florentine affairs. It does not appear, however, that Machiavelli considered the restoration of the Medici as part of the cyclical process of constitutional change outlined in the *Discorsi* I,2, for if that were the case, Lorenzo's rule should have been preceded by *licenza*, a descriptive term Machiavelli never used of the Florentine republic of 1494–1512. On the other hand, whereas one would expect him to write about the governments he worked under with a natural sympathy and loyalty, and whereas one would anticipate him to be favorable to Soderini's order as a type of *mista*—for the installation of Soderini as *Gonfaloniere a Vita* might seem to represent the addition of a monarchical element to the aristocratic and democratic institutions already existent in the state—one finds him very critical of the pre-1512 republic and its leaders, even declaring it to be "entirely defective and remote from a true republic": cf. *Disc. Rif.* (p. 9); and on leaders of the Republic, 1494–1512, cf. esp. *Princ.* vi,6–7 (vol. 4, p. 293), *Disc.* I,7 (vol. 3, pp. 256–7), 45 (p. 351), 52 (pp. 365ff.), etc. [If Soderini as *Gonfaloniere* for life represented the monarchical element, the popular Great Council and Eighty created by the Savonarolan government represented the democratic aspect, and the councils with more prescribed membership, associated with and including the *Signoria*, represented the aristocratic side. Granted this, however, Machiavelli's policies for a *mista* were quite idiosyncratic, at least in the *Discorso sopra il Riformare*. There he proposed a *Signoria* of 65 (with the *Gonfaloniere* holding only a short-term post), a Council of 200 (for the "middle men" of Florence) and popular councils. Superimposed over the whole was the monarchical power of Pope Leo X (*Disc. Rif.* in vol. 5, pp. 15–17; cf. Donato Gianotti, who took a *Gonfaloniere a Vita* to be a necessary prerequisite for a *mista*).] Outside his potential rôle as *uno buono uomo*, then, Lorenzo's rule was that of a prince (or maybe a tyrant) who had arisen in a corrupt republic. That is how Machiavelli came to look at Lorenzo in the *Discorso* of 1520 (cf. pp. 10–11), and in *Il Principe* in 1512 he had to reckon with the possibility that Lorenzo was nothing but such a ruler, despite his higher hopes. One other way of looking at the *mutazione* of 1512–3, of course, was to accept it not as part of an internal process, but as something foisted upon Florence *ab externo*, in which case consistency with his theories of constitutional change ceases to be of real relevance, because patterns of internal transformation were broken. But it is also true and important that 1512–3 could be looked at from that other quite different perspective. Florence, along with the rest of Italy, had failed to stave off the barbarians and preserve its own life; thus here was one of those turning points which called for a return to original principles and the spirit and virtue of a good man. The Florentine people, moreover, were generally corrupt, and they required a new director. *Il Principe* was certainly written first and foremost to a potential "good man," one who may even resort to ruthlessness and apparent tyranny if his work was to be done effectively; yet to reiterate, it was so written in order to be of value to one who might put Florence on the more "conventional" pathways of princedom or tyranny. That is part of the brilliance of *Il Principe* and a key reason why it has remained a hotbed of controversy for so long. Claims about the book's purpose have rarely been entirely wrong, but have almost always been unwarrantably exclusivist, confining its purport to one emphasis or another. Assessing the Florentine and Italian situation from San Casciano was not impossible for one so experienced as Machiavelli, but it had one serious limitation. He could not be really sure, despite his correspondence with Vettori, what kind of ruler Lorenzo was or intended to be. Part of the secret behind the production of *Il Principe* lies in Machiavelli's creation of the possible rôles of the tract's recipient—the task of Italian liberation remaining, however, as the most worthy of them and the one most called for by the necessity of the times. Florence was at a turning point for either good or bad, and Machiavelli could not tell whether Lorenzo was going to be *uno buono uomo*, was going to fulfill a similar role to Cosimo's or Lorenzo I's, or even to drag the republic further toward ruin, as a tyrant. *Il Principe* was written under the shadow of possibilities, just as much as realities, and its ambiguities arise from a mixture of the Florentine's immediate reactions to the special context of 1512–3 and the application of his theories about political and constitutional change.

Machiavelli had moments of such deep despair about his own age, cf. esp. *Disc.* II,*proem.* (vol. 4, pp. 7–8), that hopes of a savior might seem far from his thoughts. Yet he harbored such hopes nevertheless, probably even as late as 1527. It is remarkable, moreover, how Florentine-centered they were, and how, before a dying Italy, he believed in a future greatness for his beloved city. A savior-prince might have an Italian basis of power, but it was above all a Florentine one. A key model for such a prince was Cesare Borgia, who swept with remarkable speed through the Romagna, acquiring territory as he went. Borgia was just a model, however, and not the "good man" of his dreams and theory. (See *Princ.* vii,3ff. From the point of view of republicanism, Cesare was no hero: cf. S. Anglo, *Machiavelli: A Dissection*, London, 1971, pp. 30ff., and see C. Clough, "Niccolò Machiavelli and the Francesco Troche Episode" in *Mediaevalia et Humanistica* XVII,1966, esp. p. 143. Concerning Machiavelli's hopes of a national leader emerging from Florence, Francesco Guicciardini estimated his position correctly: cf. *Considerationi* I,xii.) The "good man" was required to achieve much more than Cesare if Italian *libertà* was to be preserved and the foreigners removed. With the Spanish presence in Florence and Italy in and after 1512, all the crucial turning points in Machiavelli's chief recurrence models seem to converge. Everything—the *rovina* of Italy in general and of Florence in particular, the emergence of *uno buono uomo*, prince or tyrant, the recovery of Florentine republicanism—was contingent on the extent and permanence of Spanish rule. Much of Machiavelli's brilliance lies in the fact that he could offer constructive, practical advice about the situation while at the same time eliciting forms of political and constitutional recurrence which, despite differing possibilities, would be confirmed in the future.

# Excursus 6

# Notes on Sixteenth-Century *Metabolē* Theory and Age Theory

1) Ideas of recurrence in constitutional history were not confined to such models as the Machiavellian *cerchio*. If few were prepared to subscribe to a cycle of governments, many were still interested in the most prevalent types of constitutional change. Machiavelli had suggested certain parallels between Venice and Sparta, in, e.g., *Disc.* I,5 (vol. 3, p. 245); 6 (pp. 248, 251–2), and those Venetians concerned to extol their city-state's stability explored the connections in greater detail; Giannotti widened the parallelism by ranking not only Venice and Sparta together but also Florence and Athens. [On parallelism in the works of Giannotti, Gasparo Contarini, and Paruta especially, see Rawson, op. cit., pp. 144–8, 150–1. For some paralleling of Athens and Florence in Machiavelli, cf. *Disc.* I,53 (p. 371).] Later sixteenth-century authors, preoccupied with growing monarchical centralism, wrote of a recurrent tendency in nations to find stability by submitting to a lord. This is the line taken by the Florentine G. B. Guarini in *Trattato della Politica Libertà* (1599), Venice, 1818, who illustrated his point from the history of the Jews, Athenians, Spartans, Romans, Swiss, etc., as well as from that of Florence. This line is also strong in Bodin, of course (so, above, Chapter 5, sect. A, pt. 6).

For all his stress on variety, Bodin was capable of formulating rules of thumb about constitutional change. One illustration comes to mind. In the *Methodus* (op. cit., p. 217), he argued that "a kingdom has almost always been changed without force into a tyranny; aristocracy into oligarchy, democracy into ochlocracy [basically an Aristotelian line]: but the change from a tyranny into a popular form of government always has been violent, that is, the tyrant has been slain."

It is noteworthy that the ideas of monarchy's degeneration into tyranny, and of tyranny's impermanence, remained widely held. See, e.g., P. de Commynes (ca. 1450–1511) on Charles VIII in *Mémoires* (1498, though they were compiled over a long period; cf. Calmette's edn.; *Les Classiques de l'histoire de France en Moyen Age*, Paris, 1964, vol. 1, pp. xii ff.), VI,12 (vol. 2, p. 340); cf. also above,

Chapter 5, sect. B, pt. 2; Erasmus, *The Education of a Christian Prince* (ET), B.445 (ed. L. K. Born, *Records of Civilization XXVII*), New York, 1936, pp. 172–3); "Junius Brutus," *A Defence of Liberty against Tyrants* (ET), London, 1924 edn., pp. 87ff.; cf. J. Calvin in the 1536 edn. of the *Institutes* (see M.-E. Chenevière, *La Pensée politique de Calvin*, Geneva, 1937, p. 186); and on such *metabolē* in Bodin, see *Methodus* (pp. 215–6). Cf. also Fulke Greville, "On Monarchy," stanzas 80ff. (in *The Remains*, ed. G. Wilkes, London, 1965, pp. 55ff.), and J. Lydgate, *A Treatise Showing the Falles of Sundry Princes* (from Boccaccio), London, 1554, etc. Theologians continued to insist that divine punishment awaited tyrants (even if they differed as to whether the tyrant's subjects were to be God's retributive agents!). [See esp. Luther, "An Exposition of Psalm 101 (vs.6)" (cf. Philadelphia edn. of Luther's *Works*, 1956–, vol. 13, pp. 213ff.), "Whether Soldiers, too, can be saved" (1526) (in ibid., vol. 46, pp. 105ff.), where Luther writes of God's punishment of the Jews through the Assyrians and of the Romans through the Goths, as key examples; Calvin, whose early commentary on Seneca's *De clementia* is pertinent: cf. G. Beyerhaus, *Studien zur Staatanschauung Calvins*, Berlin, 1910, pp. 8ff.; John Knox: see his "History of the Reformation in Scotland" in *The Works of John Knox*, Edinburgh, 1846, vol. 1, p. 411; cf. also Erasmus, op. cit., 44B (p. 173).] And one of the most important developments in this connection in the sixteenth century was that would-be reformers and Protestants came to write of the Catholic hierarchy as tyranny, even as opposed by God: cf. Erasmus *Querela pacis* (1517) (ed. W. J. Hirton), New York, 1946, p. 30, etc.; Luther *Admonitio* (1522); Calvin *Institutes* IV,vii, 18f., etc., and note how Paolo Sarpi considered that the Council of Trent had sanctified the conversion of the Church from a polity to a tyranny (*Istorie del Concilio Tridentino*, London, 1619, vol. 3, esp. pp. 47–53, 232, and cf. above, Chapter 5, sect. B, pt. 4).

2) a) The most famous restatement of the world-empire doctrine in the sixteenth century was made by Thomas Müntzer (ca. 1490–1525) in his "Sermon to the Princes," 1524. Müntzer interpreted Daniel 2 in a rather conventional fashion, identifying the four kingdoms as Babylon, the Medes and Persians, the Greeks, and Rome. But he rather skillfully extracted reference to a fifth kingdom from the multi-metallic image, the feet of clay and iron coming to represent a final earthly kingdom which God was about to destroy: *Sermo* vii, in *Spiritual and Anabaptist Writers* (ed. G. H. Williams and A. M. Mergal) (*Library of Christian Classics XXV*), London, 1957; and for discussion, G. H. Williams, *The Radical Reformation*, Philadelphia, 1962, p. 54. In the sixteenth century the idea of world empires was not uncommonly used to legitimate existing régimes without concern to convey the impression of a divinely-governed succession; cf. (on the work of Trithemius of Sponheim and Gerard Geldenhauer) B. R. Reynolds, "Latin Historiography: A Survey, 1400–1600" in *Studies in the Renaissance* II, 1955, pp. 20, 30, 51.

b) Concerning Age theory proper in the sixteenth century, a good example of the Great Week schema (the first and the last Ages being taken as paradisal) may be found with Anthony Pocquet, who was attacked by Calvin in his *Contre les sects phantastiques* in *Opera* (ed. G. Baum et al.) (*Corpus Reformatorum* XXXV), Berlin, 1863–1900, vol. 7, p. 237. Cf. also (Thomas) *Cooper's Chronicle*, London, 1560, p. 378$^{r}$; John Stow, *The Annales, or Generall Chronicle of England* (completed by Edward Howes), London, 1615, p. 948. L. van Vives modified Augustine's chronology of the seven Ages into three double millennial periods (under Nature, Law, and Grace). This is an old modification already touched on (e.g., in Excursus 4), and it had its variants during the Renaissance and Reformation. Gianotto Manetti revived the Eusebian idea of the worthy Ages of the Patriarchs and the early Church, both separated by the middle period of Law, externality, and temporalism; *Contra Iudeos et Gentes* (1454); cf. C. Trinkaus, *"In Our Image and Likeness": Humanity and Divinity in Italian Humanist Thought*, London, 1970, vol. 2, pp. 730–4. Later, the so-called Spiritualist, Caspar Schwenckfeld (1490–1561), proffered a similar doctrine—that there were Christians before Jews with the pure pre-Mosaic faith recaptured by early Christianity; cf. G. H. Williams, *Radical Reformation*, p. 289. On the related views of Guillaume Postel, see sect. B, pt. 4 (of Chapter 5). We may also note that John Foxe hoped (but failed) to show that there had been four periods of persecution, each 300 years in length, from Christ to the Reformation (cf., on persecution succession, Chapter 4, sect. D, pt. 3); so argues H. Baker in *The Race of Time: Three Lectures on Renaissance Historiography*, Toronto, 1967, p. 57, who also has some useful points to make about ideas of the last Age and the dissipation of the last world empire.

Ages or millennia were certainly not forgotten by the more apparently secular historians. On Biondo's treatment of the "Middle Ages" as a millennium, note the discussion in W. K. Ferguson, "Humanist Views of the Renaissance" in *The American Historical Review* XLV, 1939, p. 15 (cf. also Excursus 4); and on Bodin's argument that civilization flourished for two thousand years in southern regions (Mesopotamia, Egypt) and for two thousand years in northern ones (Greco-Roman and Christian civilization), see Huppert, op. cit., p. 95.

On notions of a Great Year reemerging during the Renaissance and Reformation, note esp. the Jewish writer Leone Ebreo, *Dialogi del Amore* (ed. S. Carmelle), in *Scrittori d'Italia* CXIV, Bari, 1929, pp. 241, 245ff., and the Hermeticist Tommaso Campanella; cf. F. Yates, *Giordano Bruno*, pp. 381ff.

# Select Bibliography

## Texts: Editions and Collections

### *Greco-Roman*

Editions of Polybius used included:
T. Buettner-Wobst (ed.), *Polybius: Historiae* (*Bibliotheca Scriptorum Graecorum et Romanorum Teubneriana*), Stuttgart, 1962–7, 5 vols.
W. R. Paton (ed.), *Polybius: The Histories* (Loeb Classical Library), London, 1922–7, 6 vols.
J. Schweighaeuser (ed.), *Polybii Megalopolitani Historiarum*, Leipzig, 1795, 8 vols.
J. L. Strachan-Davidson (ed.), *Selections from Polybius*, Oxford, 1888
Cf. also P. Pédech (ed.), *Polybe, Histoire Livre XII*, Paris, 1961
E. S. Schuckburgh (trans.), *The Histories of Polybius*, London, 1889, 2 vols.

For Greek and Latin authors, extensive use was made of the Scriptorum Classicorum Bibliotheca Oxoniensis, the Loeb Classical Library, Collections des Universités de France (L'Association Guillaume Budé), Bibliotheca Scriptorum Graecorum et Romanorum Teubneriana (Academia Scientiarum Germanica Berolinensis), and texts reissued by the German publishers Georg Olms (Hildesheim).

Collections of fragmentary material included:
H. Diels and W. Kranz (eds.), *Die Fragmente der Vorsokratiker*, Berlin, 1953 edn., 4 vols.
O. Hense and C. Wachsmuth (eds.), Stobaeus' *Anthologium*, Berlin, 1958 (from 1884–1912 ed.), 5 vols.
F. Jacoby (ed.), *Die Fragmente der griechischen Historiker*, Berlin, 1926–58, 3 pts.
G. Kaibel (ed.), *Epigrammata Graeca ex Lapidibus Conlecta*, Berlin, 1878
J. von Arnim (ed.), *Stoicorum Veterum Fragmenta*, Stuttgart, 1902–24, 4 vols.
F. Wehrli (ed.), *Die Schule des Aristoteles: Texte und Kommentar*, Basel, 1967–9, 10 vols.

### *Biblical*

Editions of the Bible included:
G. D. Kilpatrick et al. (eds.), Η ΚΑΙΝΗ ΔΙΑΘΗΚΗ, London, 1958
G. Kittel (ed.), *Biblica Hebraica*, Stuttgart, revised edn., 1939
A. Rahlfs (ed.), *Septuaginta*, Stuttgart, n.d., revised edn., 2 vols.
Various editions of apocryphal texts were used, and as collections, cf.:
R. H. Charles (ed.), *The Apocrypha and Pseudepigrapha of the Old Testament*, Oxford, 1963 (reissue), 2 vols.
E. Hennecke, *New Testament Apocrypha* (with W. Schneemelcher and R. McL. Wilson) (trans. R. McL. Wilson), London, 1965, 2 vols.
Related editions and collections:
D. Barthélemy, J. T. Milik, et al., *Discoveries in the Judaean Desert* (esp. I, Oxford, 1956) (Jordan Department of Antiquities), and subsequent issues by the Palestine Archaeological Museum
S. Schechter (ed.), *Documents of the Jewish Sectaries*, Cambridge, 1910, 2 vols.
G. Vermes (ed.), *The Dead Sea Scrolls in English*, Harmondsworth, 1962
Cf. also the editions of the works of Josephus (ed. H. St. J. Thackeray et al., Loeb Class. Lib., 9 vols.), and of Philo Judaeus (F. H. Colson et al., Loeb Class. Lib., 12 vols.)

### *Patristic and Medieval*

Major collections of importance included:
J. P. Migne (ed.), *Patrologiae Cursus Completus, seu Bibliotheca Universalis, Integra, Uniformis, Commoda, Oeconomica, Omnium SS. Patrum, Doctorum Scriptorumque Ecclesiasticorum, etc., Series Graeca*, Paris, 1857–68), 161 vols.

——, *Series Latina*, Paris, 1844–91, 221 vols. and supplements
B. G. Niebuhr et al. (eds.), *Corpus Scriptorum Historiae Byzantinae*, Bonn, 1828–97, 50 vols.
G. H. Petz et al. (eds.), *Monumenta Germaniae Historica inde ab anno Christi quingentesimo usque ad annum millesimum et quingentesimum auspiciis Societatis aperiendis fontibus rerum: Scriptores*, Berlin, 1826–96, 9 vols.
——, *Epistolae*, Berlin, 1891–7, 8 vols.
——, *Poetae Latini*, Berlin, 1881–96, 5 vols.
C. Wurstisen (ed.), *Germaniae Historicorum Illustrium*, Frankfurt, 1670, 2 vols.
Cf. also the French Collections: Sources Chrétiennes, Collection Byzantine, Les Chefs d'Oeuvre Historiques et Littéraires au Moyen Age, as well as the Turnhout editions of *Corpus Christianorum: Series Latina* (1954–6, 176 vols.); and *Continuatio Mediaevalis* (1971ff., 22 vols., +); O. Stählen, *Die griechischen christlichen Schriftstellen der ersten drei Jahrhunderte*, Leipzig, 1897ff.; H. Wace, P. Schaff, et al. (eds.), *A Select Library of Nicene and Post-Nicene Fathers of the Christian Church*, Oxford, 1890 (reissued Grand Rapids), 14 vols.

### *Renaissance and Reformation*

Editions of Machiavelli included those of:
M. Bonfantini (ed.), *Opere* (*La Letteratura Italiana: Storia e Testi XXIX*), Milan, 1963
N. Conti (ed.), *Opere*, Florence, 1818–21, 10 vols.
In English translation:
A. Gilbert (ed.), *Machiavelli: The Chief Works and Others*, Durham, N.C., 1965, 3 vols.
L. J. Walker (ed.), *The Discourses of Niccolò Machiavelli*, London, 1950, 2 vols.

A great variety of Renaissance and Reformation works were examined. Original texts and editions of greater importance include:

B. W. Bates (sel. and ed.), Louis le Roy's *De la Vicissitude ou varieté des choses en l'Univers* (Princeton Texts in Literature and the History of Thought), Princeton, 1944
Jean Bodin, *Les Six Livres de la République* (*avec l'Apologie de R. Herpin*), Paris, 1583 (facsimile reproduction, Aalen, 1961)
V. de Caprariis, Francesco Guicciardini's *Opere* (*La Letteratura Italiana: Storia e Testi XXX*), Milan, 1961
D. Hay (ed.), *The Anglica Historia of Polydore Vergil, AD. 1485-1537* (Camden Society Third Series LXXIV), London, 1950
Martin Luther, *Werke: Kritische Gesamtausgabe* (ed. J. C. F. Knaake et al.), Weimar, 1883ff., 110 vols. (unfinished)
J. W. O'Malley (ed.), "Fulfilment of the Christian Golden Age under Pope Julius II: A Text of a Discourse of Giles of Viterbo, 1507 (*De Ecclesiae Incremento*)" in *Traditio* XXV, 1969, pp. 265–338
J. Poujol (ed.), Claude Seyssel's *La Monarchie de France et deux autres fragments* (Bibliothèque Elzeverienne N.S.: Études et Documents), Paris, 1961
Paolo Sarpi, *Istorie del Concilio Tridentino* (ed. G. Gambarin), Bari, 1935, 3 vols.
T. van Braght, *The Bloody Theater or Martyr's Mirror* (ed. E.B. Underhill, for Hanserd Knollys Society), London, 1850, 2 vols.

## Secondary Works

### *General*

Bauer, C., J. Boem, and M. Müller (eds.), *Speculum Historiale: Geschichte im Spiegel von Geschichtsschreibung und Geschichtsdeutung*, Munich, 1965
Bolgar, R. R., *The Classical Heritage and Its Beneficiaries*, Cambridge, 1965
Brandon, S. G. F., *History, Time and Deity*, Manchester, 1965
Bury, J. B., *The Idea of Progress: An Enquiry into Its Origin and Growth*, London, 1924
Cairns, G. E., *Philosophies of History: Meeting of East and West in Cycle-Pattern Theories of History*, New York, 1962
Collingwood, R. G., *The Idea of History*, Oxford, 1946

Eliade, M. *Cosmos and History: The Myth of the Eternal Return* (trans. W. R. Trask), New York, 1959
Franck, E., *Philosophical Understanding and Religious Truth*, London, 1945
Glacken, C. J., *Traces on the Rhodian Shore: Nature and Culture in Western Thought from Ancient Times to the End of the Eighteenth Century*, Berkeley and Los Angeles, 1976 edn.
Heer, F., *The Intellectual History of Europe* (trans. J. Steinberg), London, 1966
Löwith, K., *Meaning in History*, Chicago, 1949
*Man and Time: Papers from the Eranos Yearbooks* (*Eranos-Jahrbücher*) (trans. R. Manheim), London, 1958
Nisbet, R., *History and Social Change: Aspects of the Western Theory of Development*, New York, 1969
Rehm, W., *Der Untergang Roms im abendländischen Denken* (*Das Erbe der Alten XVIII*), Darmstadt, 1930
Spranger, E., "Die Kulturzyklentheorie und das Problem des Kulturverfalls" in *Deutsche Akademie der Wissenschaften, philosophisch-historisch Klasse* XXXV–XXXVI, 1926, pp. 35ff.
Toulmin, S., and J. Goodfield, *The Discovery of Time*, Harmondsworth, 1967
van Doren, C., *The Idea of Progress* (Concepts in Western Thought Series), New York, 1967

## *Greco-Roman*

Burnet, J., *Early Greek Philosophy*, London, 1930
Bury, J. B., *Ancient Greek Historians*, London, 1909
Cole, T. H., "The Sources and Composition of Polybius VI" in *Historia* XIII, 1964, pp. 440ff.
Edelstein, L., *The Idea of Progress in Classical Antiquity*, Baltimore, 1967
Eisen, K. F., *Polybiosinterpretationen: Beobachtungen zu Prinzipien griechischer und römischer Historiographie bei Polybios*, Heidelberg, 1966
Gatz, B., *Weltalter, goldene Zeit und sinnverwandte Vorstellungen* (*Spudasmata XVI*), Hildesheim, 1967
Gomme, A. W., *A Historical Commentary on Thucydides*, Oxford, 1945, 3 vols.
Graeber, E., *Die Lehre von der Mischverfassung bei Polybios* (*Schriften zur Rechtslehre und Politik LII*), Bonn, 1968
Guthrie, W. K. C., *In the Beginning: Some Greek Views of the Origins of Life and the Early State of Man*, London, 1957
——, *A History of Greek Philosophy*, Cambridge, 1962–9, 3 vols.
Häussler, R., *Tacitus und das historische Bewusstsein* (*Bibliothek der klassischen Altertumswissenschaften N.S. II*), Heidelberg, 1965
Immerwahr, H. R., *Form and Thought in Herodotus* (*Philological Monographs XXIII*), Ohio, 1966
Kajanto, I., *God and Fate in Livy* (*Annales Universitatis Turkuensis LXIV*), Turku, 1957
Kirk, G. S., and J. E. Raven, *The Presocratic Philosophers: A Critical History with a Selection of Texts*, Cambridge, 1969
Laistner, M. L. W., *The Greater Roman Historians* (*Sather Classical Lectures XXI*), Los Angeles and Berkeley, 1947
Lehmann, G. A., *Untersuchungen zur historischen Glaubwürdigkeit des Polybius* (*Fontes et Commentationes V*), Münster, 1967
Lovejoy, A. O., and G. Boas, *Primitivism and Related Ideas in Antiquity* (*A Documentary History of Primitivism and Related Ideas, Vol. 1*) Baltimore, 1935
Mioni, E., *Polibio* (*Problemi d'Oggi III*) Padua, 1949
Momigliano, A., "Time in Ancient Historiography" in *Quarto Contributo alla Storia degli Studi Classici e del Mondo Antico* (*Storia e Letteratura CXV*), Rome, 1969, pp. 13ff.
Mugler, C., *Deux Thèmes de la cosmologie grecque: devenir cyclique et pluralité des mondes* (*Études et Commentaires XVII*), Paris, 1953
Naudé, C. P. T., "*Fortuna* in Ammianus Marcellinus" in *Acta Classica* VII, 1964, pp. 70ff.
O'Brien, D., *Empedocles' Cosmic Cycle: A Reconstruction* (Cambridge Classical Studies), Cambridge, 1969
Pédech, F., *La Méthode historique de Polybe*, Paris, 1964
Petzold, K.-E., *Studien zur Methode des Polybios und zu ihrer historischen Auswertung* (*Vestigia IX*), Munich, 1969

Philip, J. A., *Pythagoras and Early Pythagoreanism* (*Phoenix: Journal of the Classical Association of Canada, Supplementary Vol. VII*), Toronto, 1966

Pöschl, V., *Römischer Staat und griechisches Staatsdenken bei Cicero: Untersuchungen zu Ciceros Schrift De Re Publica* (*Neue Deutsche Forschungen Abt. klassische Philologie V*), Darmstadt, 1962 (reissue)

Reinhardt, K., *Von Werken und Formen*, Godesberg, 1948

Romilly, J. de, "Le Classement des constitutions d'Hérodote à Aristote" in *Revue des Études Grecques* LXXII, 1959, pp. 81ff.

Rose, H. J., "World Ages and the Body Politic" in *Harvard Theological Review* LIV, 1961, pp. 131ff.

Ryffel, H., **ΜΕΤΑΒΟΛΗ ΠΟΛΙΤΕΙΩΝ**: *der Wandel der Staatsverfassungen* (*Noctes Romanae II*), Bern, 1949

Sambursky, S., *Physics of the Stoics*, London, 1959

Solmsen, F., *Aristotle's System of the Physical World: A Comparison with His Predecessors* (*Cornell Studies in Classical Philology XXXIII*), Ithaca, 1960

Swain, J. B., "The Theory of the Four Monarchies: Opposition History under the Roman Empire" in *Classical Philology* XXXV, 1940, pp. 1ff.

Taeger, F., *Die Archaeologie des Polybios*, Stuttgart, 1922

Täubler, E., *Tyche: historische Studien*, Leipzig, 1926

van Groningen, B. A., *In the Grip of the Past: Essay on an Aspect of Greek Thought* (*Philosophia Antiqua VI*), Leiden, 1953

Verbeke, G., "Les Stoiciens et le progrès de l'histoire" in *Revue Philosophique de Louvain* LXII, 1964, pp. 12ff.

von Fritz, K., *Aristotle's Contribution to the Practice and Theory of Historiography* (Howison Lecture, 1957), Berkeley and Los Angeles, 1958

——, *The Theory of the Mixed Constitution in Antiquity: A Critical Analysis of Polybius' Political Ideas*, New York, 1954

Walbank, F. W., *A Historical Commentary on Polybius*, Oxford, 1957–67, vols. 1–2

——, *Polybius* (*Sather Classical Lectures XLII*), Berkeley and Los Angeles, 1972

Weil, R., *L'"Archaeologie" de Platon* (*Études et Commentaires XXXII*), Paris, 1959

Zeller, E., *Die Philosophie der Griechen in ihrer geschichtlichen Entwicklung*, Hildesheim, 1963 (reissue), 3 pts.

## *Biblical*

Ackroyd, P., *Exile and Restoration: A Study of Hebrew Thought of the Sixth Century BC*, London, 1968

Albrektson, B., *History and the Gods: An Essay on the Idea of Historical Events as Divine Manifestations in the Ancient Near East and Israel* (*Coniectanea Biblica, OT Ser. I*), London, 1967

Barr, J., *Biblical Words for Time* (*Studies in Biblical Theology XXXIII*), London, 1962

——, *Old and New in Interpretation: A Study of the Two Testaments* (Currie Lectures, 1964), London, 1966

Barrett, C. K., *Luke the Historian in Recent Studies*, London, 1961

Bowman, T., *Das hebräische Denken in Vergleich mit dem griechischen*, Göttingen, 1954 ed.

Cadbury, H. J., *The Book of Acts in History*, London, 1955

——, The Making of Luke-Acts, London, 1958 ed.

Canick, H., *Mythische und historische Wahrheit: Interpretationen zu Texten der hethitischen, biblischen und griechischen Historiographie* (*Stuttgarter Bibelstudien XLVIII*), Stuttgart, 1970

Conzelmann, H., *The Theology of Luke* (trans. G. Buswell), London, 1960

Cullman, O., *Christ and Time: The Primitive Christian Conception of Time and History* (trans. F. V. Filson), London, 1962 ed.

Daube, D., *The Exodus Pattern in the Bible* (*All Souls Studies II*), London, 1963

Dentan, R. C. (ed.), *The Idea of History in the Ancient Near East*, New Haven, 1955

Dibelius, M., *Studies in the Acts of the Apostles* (trans. H. Greeven), London, 1956

Eichrodt, W., *Theology of the Old Testament* (trans. J. A. Baker), London, 1961–7 edn., 2 vols.

Evans, C. F., "The Central Section of St. Luke's Gospel" in *Studies in the Gospels: Essays in Memory of R. H. Lightfoot* (ed. D. E. Nineham), Oxford, 1957, pp. 37ff.

Flender, H., *St. Luke: Theologian of Redemptive History* (trans. R. H. and I. Fuller), London, 1967

Goodenough, E. R., *An Introduction to Philo Judaeus*, New York, 1962

Goulder, M. D., *Type and History in Acts*, London, 1964
Haenchen, E., *Die Apostelgeschichte* (*Kritisch-Exegetischer Kommentar über das Neue Testament*), Göttingen, 1965
Hengel, M., *Judaism and Hellenism: Studies in Their Encounter in Palestine during the Early Hellenistic Period* (trans. John Bowden), Philadelphia, 1974, 2 vols.
Jeremias, J., *Jesus als Weltvollender*, Gütersloh, 1930
Keck, L. E., and J. L. Martyn (eds.), *Studies in Luke-Acts* (Paul Schubert Festschrift), London, 1968
Knox, W. L., *St. Paul and the Church of the Gentiles*, Cambridge, 1939
——, *Some Hellenistic Elements in Primitive Christianity* (Schweich Lectures, 1942), London, 1944
Lampe, G. W. H., and K. J. Woollcombe, *Essays on Typology* (*Studies in Biblical Theology XXII*), London, 1957
Marshall, I. H., *Luke: Historian and Theologian*, Exeter, 1970
Morgenthaler, R., *Die lukanische Geschichtsschreibung als Zeugnis*, Zurich, 1949, 2 vols.
North, C., *The Old Testament Interpretation of History* (Fernley Hartley Trust Lectures), London, 1946
Noth, M., *Überlieferungsgeschichte Studien I: die sammelnden und bearbeitenden Geschichtswerke im Alten Testament*, Halle, 1943
Östborn, G., *Yahweh's Words and Deeds: A Preliminary Study into the Old Testament Representation of History* (*Uppsala Universitets Åarskrift VII*), Uppsala, 1951
Plümacher, E., *Lukas als hellenistischer Schriftsteller: Studien zur Apostelgeschichte* (*Studien zur Umwelt des Neuen Testaments IX*), Göttingen, 1972
Rohde, J., *Rediscovering the Teaching of the Evangelists* (trans. D. M. Barton), London, 1968
Rowley, H. H., *Darius the Mede and the Four World Empires in the Book of Daniel*, Oxford, 1935
Rudolph, W., *Chronikbücher* (*Handbuch zum Alten Testament*), Tübingen, 1955
Talbert, C. H., *Literary Patterns, Theological Themes and the Genre of Luke-Acts* (*Society of Biblical Literature Monograph Series XX*), Missoula, 1974
Trompf, G. W. "La Section médiane de l'Évangile de Luc: l'organisation des documents" in *Revue d'Histoire et de Philosophie Religieuses* LIII, 1972, pp. 141ff.
von Rad, G., *Old Testament Theology* (trans. D. Stalker), Edinburgh, 1962–5, 2 vols.
Welch, A. C., *The Work of the Chronicler: Its Purpose and Its Date* (Schweich Lectures, 1938), London, 1939
Wijngaards, J. N. M., *The Dramatization of Salvific History in the Deuteronomic Schools* (*Oudtestamentische Studien XVI*), Leiden, 1969
Wolfson, H. A., *Philo: Foundations of Religious Philosophy in Judaism, Christianity and Islam*, Cambridge, Mass., 1948, 2 vols.

## *Patristic and Medieval*

Bainton, R., *Early and Mediaeval Christianity*, London, 1965
Baron, H., *The Crisis of the Early Italian Renaissance*, Princeton, 1955, 2 vols.
Beck, H. G., *Theodoros Metochites: die Krise des byzantinischen Weltbildes im 14. Jahrhundert*, Munich, 1952
Bloomfield, M. V., "Joachim of Flora: A Critical Study of His Canon, Teachings, Sources, Biography and Influence" in *Traditio* XIII, 1957, pp. 249ff.
Boas, G., *Essays on Primitivism and Related Ideas in the Middle Ages* (*Contributions to the History of Primitivism*), Baltimore, 1948
Chaux-Ruy, J., *Saint Augustin: temps et histoire*, Paris, 1956
Cochrane, C. N., *Christianity and Classical Culture: A Study of Thought and Action from Augustus to Augustine*, Oxford, 1940
Cohn, N., *The Pursuit of the Millennium*, London, 1957
Doren, A., "Fortuna im Mittelalter und in der Renaissance" in *Vorträge der Bibliothek Warburg* II, pt. 1, 1922–3, pp. 71ff.
Downey, G., "The Perspective of the Early Church Historians" in *Greek, Roman and Byzantine Studies* VI, 1965, pp. 60ff
Emerton, E., *Humanism and Tyranny: Studies in the Italian Trecento*, Cambridge, Mass., 1925
Funkenstein, A., *Heilsplan und natürliche Entwicklung: Gegenwartsbestimmung im Geschichtsdenken des Mittelalters*, Munich, 1965

Goez, W., *Translatio Imperii; ein Beitrag zu Geschichte des Geschichtsdenken und der politischen* ——, *Theorien im Mittelalter und in der frühen Neuzeit*, Tübingen, 1958
Grumel, V., *La Chronologie (Traité d'Études Byzantines I)*, Paris, 1958
Guilland, R., *Essai sur Nicéphore Grégoras: l'homme et l'oeuvre*, Paris, 1926
Hammer, W., "The Concept of the New or Second Rome in the Middle Ages" in *Speculum* XIX, 1944, pp. 50ff.
Heer, F., "Die 'Renaissance'—Ideologie im frühen Mittelalter" in *Mitteilungen des Instituts für Österreichische Geschichtsforschung* LVII, 1949, pp. 23ff.
Köhler, O., "Der Neue Äon" in *Saeculum* XII, 1961, pp. 181ff.
Ladner, G. B., *The Idea of Reform: Its Impact on Christian Thought and Action in the Age of the Fathers*, Cambridge, Mass. 1959
Leff, G., *Heresy in the Later Middle Ages: The Relation of Heterodoxy to Dissent c. 1250-c. 1450*, Manchester, 1967, 2 vols.
Masai, F., *Pléthon et le platonisme de mistra*, Paris, 1956
Milburn, R. L. P., *Early Christian Interpretations of History* (Bampton Lectures, 1952), London, 1954
Mommsen, T. E., *Medieval and Renaissance Studies* (ed. E. F. Rice, Jr.), Ithaca, 1959
Newald, R., *Nachleben des Antiken Geistes im Abendland bis Beginn des Humanismus: ein Überschau*, Tübingen, 1960
Panofsky, E., *Renaissance and Renascences in Western Art* (*Figura* X), Copenhagen, 1960
Patch, M. R., "The Tradition of the Goddess Fortuna in Mediaeval Philosophy and Literature" in *Smith College Studies in Modern Languages* III, 1922, pp. 131ff.
Patterson, L. G., *God and History in Early Christian Thought (Studies in Patristic Thought)*, London, 1967
Reeves, M., *The Influence of Prophecy in the Late Middle Ages: A Study in Joachinism*, Oxford, 1969
Robbins, F. E., *The Hexaemeral Literature*, Chicago, 1912
Spangenberg, H., "Die Perioden der Weltgeschichte" in *Historische Zeitschrift* CXXVII, 1923, pp. 1ff.
Taylor, J., *The "Universal Chronicle" of Ranulf Higden*, Oxford, 1966
Trompf, G. W., "The Concept of the Carolingian Renaissance" in *Journal of the History of Ideas* XXXIV, 1973, pp. 3ff.
Wallace-Hadrill, D. S., *Eusebius of Caesarea*, London, 1960

## *Renaissance and Reformation*

Allen, J. W., *History of Political Thought in the Sixteenth Century*, London, 1957
Anglo, S., *Machiavelli: A Dissection*, London, 1971
Baker, H., *The Race of Time: Three Lectures on Renaissance Historiography*, Toronto, 1967
Bietenholz, P. G., *History and Biography in the Work of Erasmus of Rotterdam (Travaux d'Humanisme et Renaissance LXXXVII)*, Geneva, 1966
Bouwsma, W. J., *Concordia Mundi: The Career and Thought of Guillaume Postel (1510-1581)*, Cambridge, Mass., 1957
——, *Venice and the Defense of Republican Liberty: Renaissance Values in the Age of the Counter Reformation*, Berkeley and Los Angeles, 1968
Chabod, F., *Machiavelli and the Renaissance* (trans. D. Moore), London, 1958
Church, W. F., *Constitutional Thought in Sixteenth Century France* (*Harvard Historical Studies XLVII*), New York, 1941
Ferguson, W. K., *The Renaissance in Historical Thought: Five Centuries of Interpretation*, Cambridge, Mass., 1948
Gilmore, M. P., "'Fides et Eruditio': Erasmus and the Study of History" in *Teachers of History: Essays in Honour of Laurence Bradford Packard* (ed. M. S. Hughes), Ithaca, 1954, pp. 9ff.
——, "Freedom and Determinism in Renaissance Historians" in *Studies in the Renaissance* III, 1956, pp. 49ff.
Gundersheimer, W. L., *The Life and Works of Louis le Roy (Travaux d'Humanisme et Renaissance LXXXII)*, Geneva, 1966
Harbinson, E. H., *Christianity and History: Essays*, Princeton, 1964
Hay, D., *Polydore Vergil: Renaissance Historian and Man of Letters*, Oxford, 1952

Headley, J. M., *Luther's View of Church History* (*Yale Publications in Religion VI*), New Haven, 1963
Hexter, J. H., "Seyssel, Machiavelli and Polybius VI: The Mystery of the Missing Translation" in *Studies in the Renaissance* III, 1956, pp. 75ff.
Klempt, A., *Die Säkularisierung der universalhistorischen Auffassung: zum Wandel des Geschichtsdenken im 16. und 17. Jahrhundert* (*Göttingen Bausteine zum Geschichtswissenschaft XXXI*), Göttingen, 1960
Littell, F., *The Origins of Sectarian Protestantism*, New York, 1964
Mazzeo, J. A., *Renaissance and Revolution: The Re-making of European Thought*, London, 1965
Meyer, F., *Der Kirchenbegriff der Schwärmer*, Leipzig, 1939
O'Malley, J. W., *Giles of Viterbo on Church and Reform: A Study in Renaissance Thought* (*Studies in Mediaeval and Reformation Thought V*), Leiden, 1968
Pocock, J. A., *The Machiavellian Moment: Florentine Political Thought and the Atlantic Republican Tradition*, Princeton, 1975
Rawson, E., *The Spartan Tradition in European Thought*, Oxford, 1969
Reynolds, B. R., "Latin Historiography: A Survey, 1400–1600" in *Studies in the Renaissance* II, 1955, pp. 7ff.
Rousseau, G. S., "The *Discoursi* [sic] of Machiavelli: History and Theory" in *Journal of World History* IX, 1965, pp. 143ff.
Schäfer, E., *Luther als Kirchenhistoriker*, Gütersloh, 1897
Seeberg, E., *Grundzüge der Theologie Luthers* (*Theologische Wissenschaft*), Stuttgart, 1940
Simone, F., "La Coscienza della Rinascità negli Umanisti" in *La Rinascità* II, 1939, pp. 838ff.; III, 1949, pp. 163ff.
———, *La Coscienza della Rinascità negli Umanesti Francesci* (*Letture di Pensiero e d'Arte*), Rome, 1949
Stauffer, E., "The Anabaptist Theology of Martyrdom" in *Mennonite Quarterly Review* XIX, 1945, pp. 179ff.
Strauss, L., *Thoughts on Machiavelli*, Glencoe, 1958
Weisinger, H., "Ideas of History during the Renaissance" in *Journal of the History of Ideas* VI, 1945, pp. 415ff.
———, "The Renaissance Theory of the Reaction against the Middle Ages as a Cause of the Renaissance" in *Speculum* XX, 1945, pp. 461ff.
———, "The Self-Awareness of the Renaissance as a Criterion of the Renaissance" in *Papers of the Michigan Academy* XXIX, 1944, pp. 561ff.
Whitfield, J. H., *Discourses on Machiavelli*, Cambridge, 1969
Williams, G. H., *The Radical Reformation*, Philadelphia, 1962
Wray, F. J., "The Anabaptist Doctrine of the Restitution of the Church" in *Mennonite Quarterly Review* XXVIII, 1954, pp. 186ff.
Yates, F. A., *Giordano Bruno and the Hermetic Tradition*, London, 1964

# INDEX


Aachen, 226, 228, 246
Aalders, G. J. D., 46
Abelard, Peter, 213
Abenzoar, 282
Abijah, king, 160, 162, 163
Ablabius, 76, 203
Abraham, 169, 208, 209, 213, 215, 217, 218, 220, 221, 222, 224–5, 301–2, 331
Academicians. *See* Platonic school
Achaeus, satrap, 105
Achaia, Achaian League, 4, 25, 30, 38, 49, 53, 58, 64, 69, 70–1, 73, 81, 88, 91, 100, 108–9, 150, 292, 319
Achan, betrayer, 159
Achilles, 67, 77, 221
Achtemeir, P. J., 151
Ackroyd, P., 138, 157, 158
Acominate, Nicetas, 242
Acts, the Book of. *See* Luke-Acts
Adam, 128, 207, 208, 209, 211, 215, 217, 218, 219, 220, 221, 226, 229, 299, 301, 302, 331, 335, 336
Adams, Brooks, 237
Adkins, A. W. H., 21
Adler, A., 55, 207
Ado of Vienne, 213
Adversity, idea of: general, 64, 88, 207, 216, 240, 284; private, 64–5, 285; public, 65, 103, 110, 194–5. *See also* Fortune, misfortune
Aegatis Islands, 90
Aelianus, Claudius, 244
Aemilianus, emperor, 199
Aeneas, 53
Aeschines, 46, 99, 113
Aeschylus, 16, 25, 93, 94
Aetolia, 72, 73, 98, 100, 101, 109
Africa: general, 290; northern, 55, 103, 189, 203, 217, 223, 231, 237. *See also* Egypt; Libya; *African countries by name*
Agamemnon, 78
Agathius, 239, 242
Agathocles of Alexandria, 101, 105
Age(s): Age Theory, 175–8, 180, 184, 200–21, 232, 295–303, 314, 335–7, 343–5; cosmic Ages, in Hesiod, 17, 75, 201–4; cosmic Ages, in Plato, 10–11; cosmic Ages, in Stoicism, 82, 201; cosmic Ages, in Zoroastrianism, 114, 118, 202, 204; cosmic Ages, in other, 62, 67, 81, 229–30; historical Ages, 75–7, 81–2, 114, 118, 139–40, 142–3, 154–5, 169, 174–8, 184, 196, 200–222, 224, 228, 290, 295, 298, 307–8, 335–6, 344–5; Golden Age, 76, 203, 210, 211–2, 215, 218, 224, 245–6, 248, 295, 297–9, 301–3, 308, 312; Iron Age, 203, 210–1, 215; silver and bronze, 210, 215; metal in general, 201, 221, 299. See also *Saeculum*
Agesilaus, king, 114, 245
Aggrandizement, aggression: imperial, 70, 96, 101–3, 113, 187, 232, 240, 289, 320; personal, 26–7
Agricultural existence, 42, 61, 62, 71, 149
Agrigentum, 89
Ahaz, king, 162, 163
Ahaziah, king, 162, 163
Ahura Mazda and Ahriman, 118, 204
Alaric the Goth, 217, 227, 236
Albizzi, Rinaldo degli, 270, 286
Albrektson, B., 119–20
Alcaeus of Mytilene, 88
Alcibiades, 245
Alcimus, high priest, 164
Alcmaeon of Croton, 21, 24, 82
Alcmene, 230
Alcuin, 246
Alemani, the, 219
Alexander of Aphrodisias, 82–3, 200
Alexander the Great, 65, 67, 70, 80, 93, 100, 103, 104, 114, 149, 183, 186, 187, 194, 228, 245, 282
Alexandre, C., 230
Alexandria, 167; Alexandrian school, 184
Allegory, 128, 183–4, 219, 335
Allen, J. W., 276, 293, 306
Allmen, J. J. von, 133
Alternation (fluctuation, undulation): alternation view of historical recurrence, 2, 61–3, 67, 82–3, 93, 95, 106–7, 119–20, 159, 164, 177, 238, 241, 249, 285; cosmic alternation, 8–10, 44, 61, 85–6, 167; constitutional, 13, 25, 32, 34–6, 42–4, 83, 253–5, 261, 266–9; general socio-political or religious, 78, 87, 88–92, 156–9, 161, 167–8, 170, 176–7, 187, 195, 197–200, 207, 214–6, 220, 229, 233, 237, 240, 256, 264–5, 273–4, 289–90, 336; other, 172, 219
Amaziah, king, 162, 163
Ambrose, St., 128, 184, 335

America, 229, 302
Ammianus Marcellinus, 183, 188, 191, 192, 200, 207, 233, 243, 245
Ammon(ites), 157
Amon, king, 162, 163
Amos, book of, cited, 144, 168, 171
Amphytrion, 230
Anabaptism, Anabaptists, 282, 303–10
*Anacyclōsis*. *See* Cycles, ideas of, cycle of governments
Ananias, high priest, 172, 173, 174
Ananias and Sapphira, 173
Anaxagoras, 16
Anaximander, 8, 86, 93
Anaximenes of Lampsacus, 99
Andreas of Regensburg, 226
Andrew, St., apostle, 328
Andrewes, A., 26, 31
Angels, angelology, 124, 170, 176, 333
Angilbertus, 226
Anglo, S., 341
Anicius, Lucius, 71
Animal: animal-like conditions, 6, 15, 18, 20–3, 28, 32, 36, 38–40, 43–4, 49, 111, 224; animals compared with humans, 16, 17, 20–1, 68, 253; Man as political animal, 21
Anjou, House of, 290
Annas, high priest, 174
Annaken of Rotterdam, 305
Anselm of Havelberg, 214, 216
Anthropology, ancient Greek, 15–23, 37–43, 181, 253
Antigonus II Gonatus, 'the Great', 94, 108, 318, 319
Antigonus III, 104
Antioch: Syrian Antiochene schools, 184; Pisidian, 170
Antiochus of Ascalon, 42
Antiochus III, 'the Great', 65, 99, 103, 264
Antiochus IV Epiphanes, 164, 165, 171, 232, 306
Antiphon of Athens, 41
Anti-Semitism, 171
Antoninus Pius, emperor, 199
Antonius, Marcus (Mark Antony), 113, 197
Anthony, St., 220
Apelles the Macedonian, 100
Aphraates, 208
Apocalyptic literature, 116–8, 145, 149, 164, 168, 175–7, 204, 207, 222, 280–1, 298, 301, 314, 335
Apollodorus of Athens, 69, 150
Apollonius of Rhodes, 155
Appian, 54, 79, 186
Aquinas, Thomas, 216, 238, 253, 266, 274
Arabia, 147
Aragon, House of, 290
Aratus of Sicyon, 76, 100
Araxes River, 87, 96
Arcadia, 22, 32
Archaeology: Polybian, 41, 49, 51–3, 58, 102, 181; Dionysian, 181–2
Arches. *See* Cycloids
Archias, betrayer, 173
Archytas of Tarentum, 28, 46, 317
Arendt, H., 313
Argo, argonauts, 77
Argos, Argives, 14, 38, 57
Arians (followers of the heresiarch Arius), 219, 226, 235, 236
Aristagoras the Ionian, 96
Aristarchus of Samos, 12
Aristides (of Athens), 244
Aristides, Aelius, 154
Aristocracy, 5, 23–5, 28–30, 33–6, 39–41, 43–5, 50–52, 54, 56, 107–8, 180–2, 187, 252–3, 257, 261–2, 267–8, 275–8, 312, 340, 343; aristocratic elements, 46–7, 54–6, 260, 311–2, 317; tendencies, 238, 294
Aristotle: cosmology and catastrophe theory, 9–15, 17, 201, 244; constitutional theory, 18–9, 21, 23–33, 37–8, 57, 114, 252–3, 274–5, 277, 317, 319, 343; theory of social change and regularities, 62–3, 66–8, 70, 76, 82, 88, 94, 119–20; of cultural cycles, 17, 244, 281; of cause, 44; ethics, 86, 93–4; mentioned, 77, 282
Aristotle, pseudo-, 67–8, 119–20, 201
Aristotelian (or Peripatetic) school, 6–7, 9–10, 12, 14, 20, 26–7, 37, 41–2, 44, 65–8, 70, 81–2, 151, 200, 229, 277, 279, 343
Arius Didymus, 23, 25, 42, 180
Armenia, 198
Arndt, W. F., 171
Arnim, J. von, 9, 13, 46, 76, 176
Arnobius of Sicca, 224, 237–8
Arrian, 67, 94, 151, 183
Artabanus, 97, 114
Artabus, 227
Artemisium, battle of, 187
Artemidorus, 322
Arts and skills, 11–2, 16–7, 22, 40, 42, 244, 247, 282; and letters, 281
Asa, king, 160, 162, 163
Asclepius, Latin, 200
Asia: boundary between Asia and Europe, 103–4, 189, 197; continent, 290, Asia Minor, 103. *See also* Middle East
Aspasia, 113
Assyria, 79–80, 137, 165, 186–7, 209, 219, 222–4, 227, 280–1, 344
Astin, A. E., 5
Astral (or planetary) influences and movements, astrology, astronomy, 10–1, 61–2, 68,

77, 178, 188, 201–7, 211, 229, 240, 280, 292; planets named, 201, 206
Athenaeus, 53, 94, 185, 232–3
Athenagoras, 114
Athens, Athenians, 11, 14, 24–7, 31, 39, 45, 57–8, 70–1, 73, 80, 87, 91, 96, 102, 108, 113–4, 147, 149, 187, 195, 232, 240, 247, 268, 277, 295, 343; Duke of Athens, 268, 286
Atlantis, 11, 231, 302 (as Atlanticus)
Atomism, 9, 16, 20. *See also* Epicurus, Epicureanism
Attaliates, 242
Attic Scolion, 24; Attic tragedy, 244
Augusta, empress, 239
Augustine, St., 185, 187–8, 200, 205, 208–17, 220, 222–5, 227–9, 235, 237, 238, 253, 287, 313, 335, 345; Augustinian Order, 299
Augustus (Octavius), emperor, 23, 114, 145, 187, 189–90, 192, 197–9, 202–3, 211, 214, 243, 245, 282, 294; Augustan period, 180, 190, 198
Aulus, tribune, 232
Aurelian, emperor, 199, 234, 245
Aurelianensis, Toinardus, 301
Aurelius, Marcus, emperor, 9, 93, 166, 196, 199, 205, 233, 234, 244, 264, 265
Aurelius Victor, Sextus, 151, 185–6, 187, 190, 260, 264
Auspices, the, 51
Austria, 290
Averroes, 282
Avicenna, 282

Ba'al(s), 156
Babel, 223
Babylon, Babylonians, 165, 201, 222–4, 227–8, 344; city of Babylon, 113, 134, 144; Babylonian New Year Festival, 119; Babylonian exile of the Jews, 118, 134–7, 144, 157–8, 160, 162–5, 171, 208, 213, 220–1, 283, 295, 331
Bacchus, 230 (on two Bacchuses)
Bacher, W., 207
Bacon, Francis, 294, 296
Baghdad, 228
Bailey, C., 65, 93
Baillie, J., 117
Bainton, R., 205, 208, 304, 308
Baker, H., 288, 294, 345
Balance (or equilibrium), idea of, 46–7, 55, 57, 70, 86–7, 88–92, 95–6, 102, 107, 167, 181, 259, 261, 268, 272, 276; shifting balance, 63, 87, 91, 167, 207, 209, 288. *See also* Rectified mean
Balbinus, emperor, 199
Baldeschi, L. C., 248
Baldry, H. C., 76
Balsdon, J. P. V. D., 53, 98
Baluzius, Stephanus, 301
Banks, R., 134
Barbarians: Greek conceptions of, 14, 16, 27; Roman and Byzantine, 225, 227–8, 236–8, 246, 265, 273, 277, 295; Renaissance Italian, 248, 272, 281, 338, 341; idea of new Barbarism, 237
Barber, G. L., 80
Barbu, Z., 61
Bardesanes, 206, 211, 229
Barker, E., 116, 118, 175, 212, 275, 318
Barnabus, Epistle of, 128, 207, 212
Baron, H., 266
Barr, J., 117, 119–20, 128, 332
Barrett, C. K., 121, 148, 333
Barth, G., 322
Bartholomew of Pisa, 219
Basil, St., 207
Basil II, emperor, 239
Bates, B. W., 280, 281–2
Bathsheba, 159
Battifol, P., 208
Baudrus, Paulus, 301
Bauer, C., 119, 226
Baum, G., 298, 345
Baur, E., 298
Bavaria, 290
Beard, Thomas, 294
Beare, F. W., 322
Beck, H. G., 239, 240, 242
Becker, C., 16
Beckwith, J., 246
Bede, the Venerable, 209, 210, 213, 216, 238
Bede, pseudo-, 225
Belus, king, 77, 209, 210, 299
Benardete, S., 94
Bender, H. S., 303, 305, 306
Benedict, St., 218, 219, 220
Benz, E., 206
Berengaudus, 220
Bergk, W. T., 62
Bernard, St., 184, 226. *See also* Cistercian Order
Bernhard of Moles, 226
Bernheim, E., 186
Berossus, 201
Besilarius, 239
Bethel, 158
Bethsaida-Julius, 132, 330
Beyerhaus, G., 344
Beza, Theodore, 310
Biblical tradition: general, xi, 1–2, 107, 112, 116–121, 128–9, 145, 147, 156, 159, 177, 179, 183–5, 204, 210–13, 218, 221–2, 229, 232–3, 246, 248, 274, 278, 287, 298, 303, 309–10, 313–4, 323, 331–3, 335; Old Testament, 116–20, 134–9, 140–2, 144, 146–8, 156–64, 166, 168, 169–72, 174–5, 180, 184, 234, 246,

300, 305–6, 308, 330–1; New Testament, 121–34, 139–55, 170–80, 207, 246, 305, 307, 311; Extra-Biblical, 149, 164–70, 175–7, 179, 307
Bietenholz, P. G., 298
Billerbeck, P., 141
Biography, 113, 148, 151, 244–5
Biological principles. *See* Cycles, ideas of, biological
Biondo, Flavio, 229, 247, 248, 336, 345
Bithynia, 72, 98
Bloch, J., 239
Bloomfield, M. V., 218
Boas, G., 16, 67, 76, 77, 207, 214
Boccaccio, Giovanni, 243, 283, 344
Bodin, Jean, 276, 277–8, 280, 281, 283, 296, 343, 344, 345
Boehm, J., 119
Boeotia, 65, 72, 109, 231
Boer, W. den, 187, 189, 190
Boethius, 235
Bohun, E., 296
Boissonade, 242
Bolgar, R. R., 253
Boman, T., 117, 120
Bonadeo, A., 292
Bonaventura, St., 184, 213, 335
Bondanella, P. E., 295
Bonfantini, M., 251
Boniface III, Pope, 297
Borgia, Cesare, 315, 341–2
Born, L. K., 344
Bornkamm, G., 322
Botticelli, Sandro, 298
Boundaries, transgression of, 87, 96, 103, 148–9, 155, 197. *See also* Asia; Europe
Bouterweck, K. W., 307
Bouwsma, W. J., 290, 301, 302, 310, 311, 312
Bouyer, L., 298
Bowman, J., 331
Brabant, F. H., 216
Brack, H., 226
Braght, Thielman van, 305, 306
Braitmichel, Caspar, 308
Brandon, S. G. F., 61, 118
Braunert, H., 173
Bréhier, E., 167
Briggs, C. A., 160
Brink, C. O., 7
British, Britons, 186, 279. *See also* England
Brockley, R. C., 233, 243
Broek, R. van den, 202, 203
Brooke, C. F. T., 288
Brown, A. M., 295
Brown, F. E., 160
Brown, R. E., 131
Brown, S., 334
Brown, T. S., 26, 77
Bruce, F. F., 333
Bruni Aretino, Leonardo, 242, 243, 247, 248, 251, 273, 283
Bruno, Giordano, 251
Brutus, Lucius Iunius, 112, 189
Brutus, Marcus Iunius, tyrannicide, 112, 153, 266
Buckingham, Thomas, Duke of, 287
Buecheler, F., 76
Buettner-Wobst, T., 5, 54
Buffière, F., 82
Bultmann, R., 117, 121, 322
Bunsen, C. C. J., 160
Burnet, J., 8
Bury, J. B., xi, 61, 94
Bury, R. G., 19
Busnelli, M. O., 312
Butterfield, H., 295
Buttrick, G. A., 156
Bywater, J., 82, 85, 86, 93, 95
Byzantines: empire, 225, 227–8, 235, 237, 239, 240, 247; thought, 212, 228–31, 235–6, 238–42, 249, 275
Byzantium, 226, 240, 242, 243

Cabala, Cabalism, 251, 299, 301
Cadbury, H. J., 121, 123, 141, 148, 152
Caesarea, 130, 131, 324
Caesarea-Philippi, 132
Caesars. *See* Principate, Roman
Caiaphas, high priest, 174
Cain, 306
Caird, G. B., 140
Cairns, G. E., 77, 210
Cajetan, St., 298
Calabria, 216
Caligula, emperor, 199, 203
Callahan, J., 61
Callicrates of Leontium, 71
Calmette, J., 290, 343
Calpurnius Siculus, 76
Calvin, Jean, 297–8, 310, 344, 345
Camarina, 89, 90
Cambyses, king, 87, 96
Campanella, Tommaso, 345
Campen, Jacob van, 305
Campenhausen, H. von, 237
Camus, P. M., 200
Canaan(ites), 135, 157, 282–3
Cancik, H., 165
Cannae, battle of, 52, 55, 56, 58, 65, 73, 88, 102, 187, 315
Cantacuzenus, John VI, emperor, 240
Cantacuzenus, Matthew, co-emperor, 231, 242
Cappadocia, 101
Capponi, Neri di Gino, 270

Caprariis, V. de, 276
Caracalla, emperor, 199
Carcopino, J., 203
Carinus, emperor, 199
Carmelle, S., 345
Carmody, F. J., 213
Carneades, 42
Carolingian Renaissance: Carolingian rulers, 277. *See also* Renaissance, Carolingian Renaissance
Carthage, Carthaginians, 54–5, 65–6, 78, 80, 88–91, 100, 102–3, 109, 114, 185, 195, 199, 223–4, 227, 232; constitution of Carthage, 24, 45, 54, 57–8, 71, 73, 275, 317; fall of Carthage, 73–4, 79, 101, 105, 182, 189, 199, 231, 240, 245, 264; idea of a second Carthage, 247. *See also* Punic Wars
Carus, emperor, 197, 199
Cary, E., 181
Cassiodorus, 245
Cassius, Spurius, 265, 267
Cassius Longinus, tyrannicide, 152, 266
Castiglione, Baldassare, 283
Castruccio Castracani, 268
Catastrophes (or cataclysms), catastrophe theory: in Plato and Aristotle, 10–14, 17–9, 38, 40, 42, 75–6, 78, 201, 229; in Polybius, 13–6, 18, 40, 42–4, 81; in Ocellus Lucanus, 14–5, 76; in ancient Greek thought generally, 7, 10, 117, 119, 185, 200–1, 302; in Judeo-Christian tradition, 176, 203–4, 224, 229, 236, 238, 295; in Machiavelli, 253, 279. Catastrophes as floods, 7, 10–13, 15–6, 176, 201–3, 279 (*see also* Flood, the); fire, 10, 12, 15, 176, 202–4, 224; famine, 7, 15, 203, 236, 238, 279; other natural disasters, 150, 203, 236, 238, 279; other types of disaster, 220–1, 302
Cato Major, 52, 53, 71, 185, 245
Cato Minor, 152–3
Causation, historical, 32, 44–5, 83–4, 91–4, 96–8, 106–7, 112, 178, 231–2, 254, 274, 293–4; final causes, 44
Celsus, 201, 205, 207
Censorinus, 12, 62, 201, 202, 216
Century, idea of. See *Saeculum*
Cephas. *See* Peter, St.
Chabod, F., 255
Chaeronia, battle of, 187
Chalcedon, Council of, 307
Chalcidius, 200
Chaldea(ns), 219, 222
Chance. *See* Fortune
Change (*metabolē*, mutation, transience), Greco-Roman ideas of: general, 8, 17, 47, 60, 66, 69, 81–3, 85–6, 99, 116, 147–8, 168, 180, 188, 245; *metabolē* theory concerning, 3, 6, 25–37, 42, 106–10, 181; cosmic, 8–10, 14, 44, 59, 61–2, 66–8, 82, 85–6; into opposites, 25, 42, 48, 63, 82–3, 85–6, 181, 291; from more to less or *vice versa*, 42–4, 82, 86; for the worse, 50, 78, 104, 106–9; remarkable, 63, 148; desire for, 107, 109; forestalling, 41, 47, 66, 74, 191, 194–5, 255; variations of, 11, 38, 75, 97, 106, 110, 181, 183; internal-external relations and, 72–4, 91–2, 107, 185–6. Biblical ideas of: general, 116–7, 119, 122, 147–9, 166–8, 175, 180; continuity and, 138–9, 164, 174; *metabolē* theory concerning, 149, 167–8 (extra-biblical); cosmic, 166–8; into opposites, 167; forestalling, 169. Christian ideas of: general and cosmic, 183–4, 222–9, 235, 240–1; continuity and, 223–4, 226, 246; forestalling, 227, 248; variations of, 223, 241. Renaissance humanist ideas of: general and cosmic, 274, 278–9, 281, 284, 293, 303, 308, 310; *metabolē* theory concerning, 251–6, 261–78, 285, 290, 339–45; into opposites, 290–1; for the worse, 275; variations of, 276–8, 283, 293–4; internal-external relations and, 255, 262, 288–90. *See also* Constitution, changes between simple types of; Fortune, mutability of; Law; Reciprocity, reciprocal processes of change; Reenactment
Charlemagne, emperor, 212, 220, 226, 227, 246, 247, 281, 282, 336
Charles the Bald, emperor, 246
Charles V, emperor, 300, 339
Charles VIII, king, 247, 295, 339, 343
Châtelet, F., 205
Chauviré, R., 277
Chaux-Ruy, J., 214, 237
Chavasse, C., 134
Cheilon, revolutionary, 319
Chenevière, M.-E., 344
China, xi, 315
Chios, 62
Chrimes, K. M. T., 47
Christian: attitudes to change, history and time, 112, 117–34, 139–55, 168, 170–89, 200, 204–42, 245–9, 279–83, 287–8, 294–314, 321–37, 343–5. Church, early, 121–7, 129–34, 139, 144–8, 150, 154–5, 170–4, 176, 283, 297–8, 300, 304–8, 311–3, 322, 326, 332, 345; patristic and medieval, 183–4, 203, 214–5, 217, 224–7, 235–6, 298, 300; Renaissance and Reformation, 298–312; more generally, 218–9, 225–8, 296, 306, 308–11. Christian civilization, 219, 345; Church councils, 303, 310–1, 344; magistracies, 303, 307
Christianity, earliest, 118–34, 139–55, 170–80, 183, 222, 279, 283, 295, 297–8, 302–4, 306–8, 321–3, 326, 345; patristic, 179, 183–6, 189, 204–14, 222, 228, 233–5, 245–6, 279, 298;

medieval, 179, 183–5, 207, 209, 214–20, 222, 225–9, 230–1, 235–42, 246–9, 297, 298, 313; Renaissance, 220–1, 247–8, 278, 281, 286, 287–300; Reformation and Counter-Reformation, 278, 299–312
Christology, Christological ideas, 121, 123, 140–1, 154, 184, 207–9, 211–2, 216–9, 221, 224–5, 235, 299, 321, 325, 329, 334
Chronicler, the, 118, 135–9, 145, 148, 160–4, 166, 169, 175, 178, 223; books of, cited, 119, 136–9, 143, 145, 160–4, 166, 170, 331, 332, 333
Chroust, A.-H., 117
Chrysippus, 9, 13, 46, 76
Chrysostom, John, 184, 228, 234, 239
Church, W. F., 276, 280
Cicero, Tullius, 7, 13, 21, 42, 49, 51, 52, 53, 62, 67, 74, 76, 82–3, 94, 113, 152, 153, 180–1, 186, 189, 192, 200, 201, 202, 233, 234, 238, 243, 244, 253, 260, 262, 266
Ciompi, the, 268
Circumstances, ideas concerning, 47, 49, 57, 60, 88, 95, 125, 232, 257–8, 274, 284, 293–4, 315
Cistercian Order, 226
City-State. *See* Political society
Cius, 72, 109
Civilization, ideas of, 11, 14, 16, 78, 187, 244–6, 248, 279, 315, 345
Civil War. *See* Factions
Clasen, C.-P., 307
Classical tradition. *See* Greco-Roman tradition
Claudian, 186, 212, 245
Claudius, Appius, 265, 266–7
Claudius, emperor, 199
Claudius Gothicus, emperor, 199
Cleisthenes, 25
Clement of Alexandria, 9, 212
Clementine Epistles, pseudo-, 298, 307
Clements, R. E., 136
Cleomenes I, 96
Cleomenes III, 108, 272–3, 318–20
Cleomenic War, 320
Cleon, demagogue, 114
Clopas, disciple, 307
Clough, C., 341
Cochrane, C. N., 87, 96, 110, 111, 186, 205, 234
Cohn, N., 210, 212, 218, 305, 309
Cole, A. T., 16
Cole, T. H., 23, 25, 27, 30
Collingwood, R. G., 84, 120, 205, 274
Collins, J. J., 176, 204
Colonna, Giovanni, 228
Columbus, Christopher, 302
Columbus, Joannis, 301
Commodus, emperor, 199
Commun(al)ism, 155, 304, 307–8
Commynes, Philippe de, 290–1, 343
Comte, Auguste, 107
Conciliarism, 303
Constans I, emperor, 236
Constantine the Great, 212, 220, 224, 225, 234, 235, 236, 237, 302, 306, 307
Constantine II, 236
Constantine VIII, 239
Constantinople. *See* Byzantium
Constantius I, 199
Constitution(s): types of simple constitution, 5–6, 19, 21–4, 27, 41, 44, 70, 252, 259, 275–8, 311–2; changes between simple types, 5–6, 14–5, 18–44, 48, 50–3, 71, 83, 107–9, 114, 149, 180–2, 252–5, 258, 261–70, 273, 275–7, 311–2, 317–20, 339, 340–3; mixed constitutions, general, 41, 45–6, 51, 259, 268, 276, 283, 291, 296, 312, 317–8, 338, 340, 342; Spartan, 39–41, 46–7, 49–50, 57–8, 108, 317–20; Roman, 41, 45–52, 54–8, 69–71, 181–2, 253, 259–62, 266, 275, 317 (also referred to simply as the Roman constitution, 7, 24, 41, 45–58, 65, 71, 73, or as the Roman Republic, 192–4, 196, 245, 248, 251, 259–68, 273, 337); Carthaginian, 45, 54–5, 58, 71, 317; other, 45, 72, 268–74 (with references to Italian republics, 248, 251, and the Florentine Republic, 268–72, 338–43). *See also* Cycles ideas of, cycle of governments; Plato, on ideal republic
Consulate, Roman, 51–2, 55, 260–1, 267, 275, 289; consular elements, 47, 56
Contarini, Gasparo, 343
Contarini, Nicolò, 290
Conti, N., 251, 252–73, 278–9, 283–6, 289, 292, 295–6, 309, 338–40
Conzelmann, H., 130, 131, 132, 140, 142, 155, 171, 175, 217, 322, 324, 333
Cooper, Thomas, 288, 345
Corbin, H., 118
Corbinelli, Jacopo, 293
Corinth, 149
Coriolanus, Gnaeus, 245
Cornelius, centurion, 133, 323
Cornford, F. M., 63, 94
Corruption, social (socio-political and religious evils, license, depravity, lawlessness, sin, injustice, disorder, sedition, demoralization, overindulgence), 8, 11, 21, 23, 26–30, 32, 39, 50–1, 55–6, 70–1, 73–4, 80, 82, 87, 92, 96, 100–1, 104, 107, 152, 156, 158–60, 166, 168, 170, 181–2, 185, 187–8, 190–1, 195–8, 214–5, 232–42, 246, 253–4, 256, 258, 260–1, 263, 266, 267–9, 271, 274, 276, 281, 284, 287–8, 290, 292, 294, 296–7, 302, 304, 340–1; idleness, inertia, 74, 92, 190–1, 288–90; passions,

98, 185, 258, 263, 278, 291–2; boredom, 107; surfeit, 109. *See also* Decay; Factions; *Hybris*; *Stasis*
Cosmic dissolution and reconstitution, ideas of, 7–10, 12–4, 44, 66–7, 76, 81–2, 85, 117, 176, 200–2, 279
Cosmology: Greco-Roman, 7–15, 20, 61–2, 66–8, 75–7, 82, 85–7, 95, 176, 178, 188, 191, 200–7, 213, 229, 279; biblical and Middle Eastern, 116–8, 166–9, 171, 176, 207; patristic and medieval, 188, 206–9, 213, 229–30; Renaissance and Reformation, 279–81, 295, 301, 345
Côtelier, J. B., 208
Coulton, G. G., 184
Counter-Reformation Catholicism, 286, 298, 306, 310–2, 344
Cozzi, N., 290
Cranz, F. E., 214
Crawford, R. M., 285
Creation, ideas of, 2, 10–1, 117, 175, 205–6, 212–3, 218, 220–1, 230, 288, 314, 335
Crete, 45, 69, 81–2, 317
Critias, 16, 21
Critolaus the Achaian, 114
Critolaus, the Peripatetic, 70
Croce, B., 277, 315
Croesus, king, 87, 95, 96, 97, 114, 235
Cropsey, J., 339
Cross, F. M., 138–9
Crusades, the, 226, 247, 295
Ctesias, 80, 186
Cullmann, O., 118, 128, 323
Cumont, F., 201, 203, 204
Cuntz, O., 25, 73
Cuperus, Gisbertus, 301
Curtius, Quintius, 67, 183, 193, 196, 197
Cycles, ideas of: general, xi, 1–2, 61–2, 64, 68, 81, 84–8, 92–3, 106–7, 111–2, 114, 117–20, 122, 127, 156–7, 159, 166–7, 169, 177–8, 180, 183, 185, 195, 200, 204–8, 221, 228–31, 241, 248–51, 282, 309, 313; cosmic, 8–15, 44, 75, 81–2, 85, 118–9, 170, 178, 185, 188, 201–2, 205, 213, 229–30, 301, 345; macro-historical, 10, 12–5, 42–4, 48, 67, 75–8, 81, 118, 176, 212, 218, 220, 229, 300, 311–2 (*and see* Ages); biological, 22–5, 33, 35–6, 42–4, 48, 51, 54–7, 62, 66–75, 77–8, 83, 92, 111, 167–8, 177, 188, 190, 206–7, 214, 227, 237, 249, 255–7, 259, 262, 273, 279–83; life cycle analogy, 181, 183, 188–92, 197–8, 207, 213–4, 221, 227, 244, 276, 279, 301; cycle of governments (*anacyclōsis*), xi, 4–6, 12–52, 57–60, 63, 69, 72, 77–8, 81–3, 92, 107–9, 111, 116, 156, 180–4, 249, 251–65, 267–8, 271, 273–4, 277–8, 310–2, 320, 339–40, 343; of imperial rise and fall, 75–82, 92, 96, 167–8, 170, 176–8, 180, 183, 185–95, 206, 252, 256–8, 264–5, 273–4, 280–1, 311; of cultures or civilizations, 81–3, 83, 166, 196, 243–6, 252, 281–2, 287; of war, 228; of fortune, 62–7, 74, 83, 87, 88, 91, 98, 194–200, 229, 249, 251, 257, 285–7; hybristic cycles, 87, 92, 98, 166, 233, 285–8; lectionary or liturgical cycles, 127, 184; vegetation cycles, 68; cycles as circles, 81–2, 86, 288
Cycloids (curves, arches), 67–8, 76, 88, 95
Cyclops, 20, 38, 39, 40, 78
Cynaetha, 72, 73, 100, 109
Cynics, Cynicism, 194
Cyprian, St., 237
Cyprus, 173, 242
Cyril of Jerusalem, St., 184
Cyrus (I) the Great, 87, 96, 113, 114, 145, 223, 227, 228, 282, 300, 339

Dacia, 198
Damascus, 131, 144, 332
Dan (city), 158
Danes, Danish, the, 279
Daniel: author of book of, 116–8, 186, 207, 222, 280, 295–6, 332; hero of book, 221; citations of book, 164, 168, 171, 176, 214, 222, 332, 344
Daniélou, J., 208, 211
Dante Alighieri, 212, 229, 243, 247, 248
Danube River, 87, 96
Darius I, 31, 37, 87, 96
Dark Ages, idea of, 225–6, 243, 248, 297, 302, 337
Dati, Goro, 283
Daube, D., 123, 134, 152
David, king, 128, 135–8, 145–6, 148, 151, 159–63, 208, 213, 215, 220, 221, 246–7, 305, 308
Davies, W. D., 123, 146, 152
Davis, K. R., 309
Dawson, C., 117
'Day of Yahweh', 118
Death(s), types of, 93, 100–1, 152–4, 158, 164, 172–3, 233–4, 236–7, 286, 327; death as fate of all, 166–7; suicide, 100, 152–3, 172. *See also* Jesus of Nazareth, crucifixion and death of; Martyrs
Deborah, judge, 157
Decay, decline, degeneration: general and cosmic, 8, 10, 17, 24, 44, 69, 81, 83, 85, 177, 185–6, 189, 207, 297; constitutional, 5, 11, 19, 24, 27–30, 32–3, 35–6, 39, 43, 48, 50–1, 54–7, 70–4, 80–1, 104, 106–9, 180–2, 185–9, 255–6, 258, 260–3, 265–6, 272, 275, 317–20; general socio-political, religious or moral, 18, 30–2, 39, 41, 43, 50, 56, 65, 70–4, 78, 80–1, 92, 94, 101, 104, 147, 177, 185–99, 202, 208, 210, 222, 224, 226–7, 233, 246, 248, 255–8,

260, 263–5, 280–2, 293, 297, 299, 302, 307, 312, 315, 336
Decemvirs, 51, 52, 54, 181–2, 262, 265, 266, 275, 276, 278
Decius, emperor, 199, 234
Delphic Oracle, 86, 94
Demagogy, 30–2, 36, 55, 109, 114, 254, 263, 318
Demaratus, king, 96
Demetrius I, 113
Demetrius of Phalerum, 63, 65, 66, 72, 80, 99
Democracy, 5, 23–5, 27, 29–41, 43, 45, 49–52, 56–8, 71–3, 107–9, 114, 168, 181, 252–4, 257, 261, 263, 268–9, 275–8, 311, 318, 340, 343; democratic elements, 46–7, 54–5, 267, 311–2, 317; democratic or popular tendencies, 54–6, 71–2, 81, 182, 259, 262, 270
Democritus, 16, 24
Demosthenes, 24, 93, 113, 244, 282
Denton, R. C., 157
Destiny, ideas of, 63, 81, 94–5, 97, 152, 188–9, 192–3, 206, 284
Deuteronomic historian(s), 118, 134–5, 138, 145, 147–8, 151, 153, 156–60, 162, 169–70, 175, 178, 287, 329, 330–3; books of cited, 119, 129, 134–7, 142–3, 145–6, 148, 155–61, 164–6, 170, 331–2
Diaspora, Jewish, 148, 169–70, 204; other, 307
Dibelius, M., 121, 148, 178, 322, 323, 324
Dicaearchus, 9, 15, 17, 20, 37, 42, 44, 46, 80, 188, 203, 244, 318
Dictatorship, 27, 51, 55, 182, 244
Didius, emperor, 199
Diels, H., 8, 9, 16, 21, 24, 41, 62, 66, 82, 85, 86, 93, 169, 200
Dindorf, L., 208
Dinkler, E., 176
Dio Cassius, 103, 114, 185, 196, 233, 294, 321
Dio Chrysostom, 63, 66, 154, 194, 202
Diocletian, 198, 199, 203, 224, 234
Diodorus Siculus, 9, 16, 17, 20, 21, 63, 65, 86, 91, 94, 98, 105, 106, 111, 113, 185, 187, 193, 194–7, 202, 232–3, 242, 252, 288, 322
Diogenes Laertius, 8, 9, 44, 46, 67, 151, 152, 154, 155
Dionysian mysteries, 94
Dionysius of Halicarnassus, 21, 26, 54, 112, 181–2, 185, 186–7, 192, 193, 233, 244, 262, 265, 275
Diphilus, 63
Dix, G., 184
Dobschütz, E. von, 120
Dodd, C. H., 149, 175, 322, 324, 330
Dodds, E. R., 205
Dominic, St., 296
Domitian, emperor, 199, 203, 234
Donati, Corso, 268
Dorcas, disciple, 127, 327
Doren, A., 283
Doren, C. van, 248
Dorians, the, 38, 40, 244
Downey, G., 236
Downing, J., 174
Drepana, 90
Drews, R., 106, 232
Driver, S. R., 160, 216
Driver, T., 117
Drury, J., 129, 174, 330
Ducas of Phocaia, 213
Dudley, D. R., 194
Duhem, P., 61
Dühring, I., 11
Dupont, J., 121, 132
Dutch, the. *See* Netherlands

Eadmer, 238
Ebreo, Leone, 345
Ebro River, 103
Ecclesiastes (Qoheleth), 119, 120, 166–7, 178; citations of, 166–7, 220, 229
Ecclesiasticus: author of (Ben Sirach), 166; citations of, 144, 164, 166, 170
Eclipses, 152, 202, 240
Ecnomus, 89
Ectbatana, 228
Edelstein, L., 2, 16, 61, 185
Eden. *See* Primitive life, primitivism
Edom, 183
Education, 17, 20–2; schools and programmes of study, 183–4, 291, 296, 298
Edward IV, 287
Egypt, Egyptians, 11, 77, 81, 87, 96, 100, 134, 149, 165, 167, 168, 175, 186, 231, 247, 292, 306, 319, 345; Egyptian captivity, 134, 183, 219, 282, 308; 'the Egyptian', 174
Ehrenberg, V., 25, 319
Ehrhardt, A. A., 123, 148
Ehud, judge, 157
Eichrodt, W., 117, 333
Eisen, K. F., 33, 49, 52, 65, 79, 80
Eisenstein, E. L., 204
Eissfeldt, O., 166, 167, 176, 331
Ekkehard of Aura, 226
Elagabalus, emperor, 199
Elert, W., 303
Elferink, M. A., 200, 239
Eli, judge, 157
Eliade, M., 61
Elijah (Elias), 134, 135, 141, 142, 143, 144, 219, 220, 329, 331, 336
Elisha, 134, 142, 143, 218, 219, 329, 331
Elizabeth, mother of John the Baptist, 219
Elizabethan literature, 288, 294, 344–5
Elliott-Binns, L. E., 133

Ellis, R. L., 294
Elymas the magician, 173
Emerton, E., 220, 266
Emmaus, 123, 140, 153, 326
Empedocles, 8, 9, 10, 25, 41, 62, 85, 93, 205
Emperors. *See* Principate; Rome, Holy Roman Empire
Empires, Rise and Fall of, 75, 77–82, 101–2, 119, 167–8, 174–8, 180, 183, 185–93, 195, 204–7, 214, 222–9, 232–3, 251, 257, 273, 278–82, 300, 312, 344–5. *See also* Succession, of empires
Englebert of Admont, 226
England, 264, 279, 290, 294, 310. *See also* British
Enguerrand of Montrelet, 242
Ennius, 112, 186, 222
Enoch, books of. *See* Pseudepigraphical literature (biblical)
Entrèves, A. P. d', 253, 266
Epameinondas, 64, 114
Ephesus, Ephesians, 124. On St. Paul's letter to, *see* Paul of Tarsus
Ephicrates, 114
Ephorate, Spartan, 100, 317–9
Ephorus, 26, 80
Ephraim of Nisibis, 208
Epictetus, 65, 67, 93, 151
Epicurus, Epicureanism, 9, 65, 72, 93, 95, 99, 155, 193, 200, 253, 286, 288. *See also* Atomism
Epstein, I., 183
Equilibrium, ideas of. *See* Balance
Erasmus, Desiderius, 283, 290, 294, 298, 344
Erigena, John Scotus, 217
Erskell, H., 196
Eryx, 90
Eschatology, 116–8, 121, 140, 143–5, 150, 154, 169, 171–7, 206–9, 211–2, 215–8, 220, 222, 224–6, 229–30, 234–5, 237, 281, 288, 297, 300–2, 305–6, 308, 314, 320, 333–5, 345; and historical linearity, 2, 116–8, 170, 205, 221, 297. *See also* Jesus of Nazareth, parousia; Millennium
Eternity, ideas of: eternal cosmos, 7–10, 13–4, 20, 67, 119, 178, 191, 206, 216, 227, 229–30; eternal laws of nature, 280; eternity of God, 227–8, 238, 280, 314; of truth, 184, 274, 311; of Christianity, 248; of Rome, 181, 186, 188, 190–2; endless world history, 206
Ethical ideas, moral values, in connection with historical recurrence: Plato, 19–20, 40; Stoics, 13–4, 21–2, 152, 154, 185, 188–9; Polybius, 15–8, 21–2, 26, 33, 40, 44, 53, 71–2, 82, 93–4, 97–106, 115, 148; Greco-Roman, other, 62–3, 86, 93–6, 112, 154, 185–200, 232–3, 242, 284; Greco-Roman, harmony, 47, 54, 85, 92; Greco-Roman, moderation, 86, 88, 92, 96, 102–4, 195, 232. Biblical, 137–8, 142–4, 149, 150–1, 153–4, 156, 158–161, 164, 165–74, 178, 233, 303–4; moderation, 167. Patristic and medieval, 183, 233–43; moderation, 240. Renaissance and Reformation, 256–7, 259–60, 263, 268–9, 281–4, 289–90, 295, 301, 303–9, 345; moderation, 278, 285. *See also* Excess; Moral order
Etruria, Etruscans, Tuscans, 76, 202, 203, 279, 299, 300
Etzioni, A., 315
Eucherius (son of Stilicho), 236
Eudemus of Rhodes, 9, 66, 67, 200
Eugyppius, 213
Euripides, 26, 63, 72, 244, 282
Europe, European, 87, 226, 248, 280, 290, 297, 302, 303, 304; boundary between Asia and, 104, 149, 197. *See also* France; Italy; *European countries by name*
Eusebius of Caesaria, 121, 147, 201, 204, 205, 208, 209, 213, 219, 224–5, 235, 302, 307, 326, 335, 345
Eutropius, 233, 234, 236
Euxine Sea, 103
Evagrius, 236
Evans, A. P., 227
Evans, C. F., 127, 128, 129, 133
Events, types of, complexes of, 3, 64–5, 67–8, 84–5, 88, 90, 94–8, 105–7, 110, 113, 126–8, 136, 159–60, 165, 174, 177–8, 188, 206, 243, 251, 257–8, 286, 289, 292–3. *See also* Significance in historical events
Excess, ideas concerning, 83, 86–7, 92–101, 181, 190, 194–5, 197–8, 232, 263, 276, 281. *See also* Ethical ideas, moderation
Exemplars from history, 242–3, 294–5
Exile, idea of, 134–7, 143, 158, 160, 171. *See also* Babylon, Babylonian exile
Exodus, the, 134, 141, 170, 183, 220; the new, 210, 247; book of, cited, 119, 134, 135, 141, 142, 287, 330, 331, 332
Ezekiel, 143, 333; book of, cited, 134, 143, 331, 332, 333
Ezra, 136, 138, 160, 331; citations from I Esdras, 139; II Esdras, 176, 177, 207; 4 Ezra, 151, 208, 331. *See also* Chronicler

Fabius Pictor, 53, 91
Factions, factionalism, civil dissension, 31, 72, 80, 107, 109, 181, 255, 263, 268–9, 270–1, 275–6, 281, 285, 318. Civil (mainly Roman) Wars, 90, 189–90, 195–9, 202–3, 221, 293. *See also* Corruption; *Stasis*
Falco, G., 336
Family: in social development, 20, 23, 27, 73; leading, 81, 85
Farmer, W. R., 323
Farrer, A., 124

Fate, fatalism, 83, 93–5, 97, 105, 119, 152, 165–6, 173–4, 193, 195, 205–6, 233, 238–9, 241, 257, 287, 295
Favorinus, 194
Ferdinand I of Austria, emperor, 306
Ferguson, A. B., 250
Ferguson, J., 193
Ferguson, W. K., 243, 336, 345
Festivals, feasts, 61, 119, 134, 137; Passover, 124, 134; Passover as the Last Supper, 125, 141, 304, 327
Festugière, A. J., 193, 200
Feyel, M., 75
Fichtenau, H., 246
Ficino, Marsilio, 298
Finley, J. H., 114
Firmicus Maternus, 77, 201, 204
Flamininus, Titus, 244
Flaminius, Gaius, 55
Flender, H., 123, 129, 134, 322, 323
Fliess, P. J., 111
Flood, the: in Greco-Roman cosmology, 7, 10–12, 77, 202; in Judeo-Christian tradition, 128, 176, 204, 207–10, 213, 221, 223–4, 297, 301–2
Florence, 247, 251, 252, 256, 290, 291; constitutional history, 261, 268–74, 338–42, 343; military matters of, 268, 294, 338–42. Florentine thought mentioned, 266. *See also* Guicciardini, Francesco; Humanism; Machiavelli, Niccolò
Florianus, emperor, 199
Florus, 112, 183, 185, 186, 189–92, 196–8, 202, 203, 207, 233, 248
Fluctuation. *See* Alternation
Flusser, D., 176
Foresight, 47, 90, 102, 259, 284, 293. *See also* Prognostication
Fornana, A., 96
Fortune: wheel, turning, altering of, 62–3, 64, 69, 73–4, 77, 83, 87–8, 91, 96, 98, 101, 111, 119, 166, 177, 187, 190, 192–200, 223, 228–9, 238–40, 242, 249, 251, 257, 285–8, 318; as guardian of the moral order, 63–6, 74, 84, 87, 93–4, 96, 98–100, 103–5, 148, 165–8, 193–7, 200, 232–3, 235, 240, 259, 264, 283–6, 288, 291; as umpire between combatants, 88, 90–1; as capricious, fickle chance or luck, 63–6, 84, 95, 98–9, 103, 169, 193–4, 196, 200, 235, 240, 253, 259, 270, 283–8; good, as prosperity, 47, 64–5, 95, 103–4, 151, 158, 197–8, 240, 256, 259, 264, 285, 287; misfortune, as adversity, 64–5, 73, 80, 100, 157–8, 161, 164–6, 198–9, 240, 290, 318; fortune and internal-external relations, 72–4, 88–92, 195–6, 288–9; and Rome, 88–91, 99–105, 192–200, 259, 284; other references, 48, 84, 97, 150, 167, 174, 193, 198, 260, 274, 278, 283, 315. *See also* Adversity; Prosperity
Fosdick, H. E., 305
Foxe, John, 345
Fracassetti, J., 336
France, the French, 264, 272, 275–7, 290–1, 293, 294
Francia, the Franks, 226–7, 246
Francis of Assisi, St., 180, 220, 296, 309, 336
Franciscan Order, 184; Spirituals (Joachites), 219, 302, 307, 335. *See also* Joachim of Fiora
Franck, E., 117
Frankfort, H., 118
Fraser, J. T., 61, 117
Frederick I Barbarossa, 226
Frederick II, emperor, 220
Freedom (equality, liberty, liberation), 29–30, 39, 50–1, 71, 83, 98, 109, 113, 157, 248, 251, 260–2, 265–71, 274, 276, 281, 310, 339, 342; loss of freedom, 199; free will, 239
Freeman, D. N., 138
Friedländer, P., 10, 11
Friedmann, M., 216
Friedmann, 305, 308
Fritz, K. von, 4, 42, 52, 244, 262, 318
Froissart, Jean, 242
Fronto, Marcus, 99
Fruchtel, L., 206
Fueter, E., 248
Fuks, A., 29
Funkenstein, A., 117, 208, 214, 225, 227, 242, 247
Future, foretelling. *See* Prognostication; Prophecy, fulfillment

Gabrielli, Jacopo, 268
Gaertringen, F. H. von, 151
Gaguin, Robert, 294
Galatia: Galatian Gauls (Celts), 98; St. Paul's letter to, *see* Paul of Tarsus
Galba, emperor, 183, 199
Galen, 151
Galerius Maximian, emperor, 198, 199, 234
Galilee, 122, 125–6, 130–33, 141, 295, 325, 328
Gallienus, emperor, 199
Gamaliel I, 'the elder', 174
Gambarin, G., 311
Gasque, W. W., 121
Gaster, M., 229
Gaston, L., 171
Gatz, B., 203
Gaul, 100, 186, 199, 237; Gallic Wars, 53, 91, 199
Gaza, 147
Geden, A. S., 140
Gelden, H. A. E. van, 288
Geldenhauer, Gerard, 344
Gellius, Aulus, 9

Gelon, tyrant, 232
Gelzer, M., 5, 30, 58, 81
Generations, human, 20, 29–30, 33, 36, 41–2, 44, 61, 69, 75, 109, 156–7, 159, 172, 175–6, 201–3, 209, 218–9, 253–4, 282, 287, 331, 333
Genesis, book of, cited, 151, 330, 331
Genoa, 290
Genthius, king, 71, 108
Gentiles (in biblical and Jewish thought), 132, 133, 144, 147, 149, 151–3, 155, 166, 169, 171, 173–4, 177, 179, 204, 215, 226, 313; Gentile Mission of early Christianity, 130, 133, 147, 150, 154–5, 215
Gerasa, Gerasenes, 132
Germans, 226, 227, 282, 290. *See also* Bavaria, Westphalia; *German districts by name*
Gerson, Jean, 247, 297
Gese, H., 120, 157
Geta, emperor, 199
Gethsemane, 125, 154
Giannotti, Donato, 276–7, 340, 343
Gibbon, Edward, 187
Gideon, judge, 157
Gilbert, A. H., 338–9
Gilbert, F., 277, 340
Gilboa, battle of, 221
Giles of Viterbo, 212, 298–300
Gill, D., 126
Gilmore, M., 242, 290, 294, 298
Gilson, E., 247
Gingrich, F. W., 171
Ginsburger, M., 143
Giorgone, 295
Glaber, Rodulfus, 226
Glacken, C. J., 247
Glover, T. R., 71
Gluntz, H. H., 335
God, gods: Greco-Roman ideas of, 10–1, 17, 20–1, 38–40, 42, 62, 67, 75, 77, 86–7, 93–6, 105, 188, 193, 195–6, 200, 203, 206, 210, 232–4, 293, 301; biblical, 118, 123, 125–7, 129, 135–7, 139, 141–2, 144–5, 150, 153–61, 164–5, 167–8, 170–1, 173–4, 177, 204, 207, 329, 330, 332–3; ancient Near Eastern, 118, 156–7; patristic and medieval, 200, 204, 206–11, 214–9, 224, 227–8, 230, 232, 234–6, 238–9, 283; Renaissance and Reformation, 259, 274, 279–80, 286–7, 290–310, 344. Ideas of divine inspiration, 40, 50; monotheism, 117, 178, 210–1, 224, 235, 313–4; fortune as divine, 63–4, 90–1, 93, 99, 167–8, 193, 195–6, 200
Goez, W., 226
Gombrich, E. M., 295
Gomme, A. W., 111
Gonfalonier, office of, 340
Goodenough, E. R., 167, 168
Goodfield, J., 206
Goodyear, F. R. D., 74
Gordian I, II and III, emperors, 199
Gorgias, 21
Gorgons, the, 231
Goths, the, 219, 224, 237, 239, 245, 344
Gould, J., 19
Goulder, M. D., 122, 124, 125, 127, 128, 130, 136, 138, 146
Gracchi, the, 186, 190, 197, 263, 264, 278; Caius Gracchus, 182
Graeber, E., 21, 22, 44, 46, 47, 57, 58, 71, 81
Graffin, F. and R., 206
Grant, F. C., 328
Grant, M., 58
Gratian emperor, 203, 236
Grayson, C., 276, 279, 286, 287, 293
Great Commission, the, 304, 326
Great Hours model of history, 213
Great men in history, ideas about, 70, 151–4, 228, 230, 237, 242, 285. *See also* Imitation
Great Week model of history, 207–14, 217, 220–2, 282, 296, 301, 309, 335–6, 344–5
Great Winter and Summer, idea of, 11–2, 201
Great Year, idea of, 11–2, 62, 67, 76, 201–2, 295, 345
Grebel, Conrad, 303
Greco-Roman tradition: general, xi, 1–2, 5, 60, 65, 67, 77, 80–1, 92–4, 107, 111–2, 116–7, 119, 121, 147, 154–5, 173, 179–80, 185, 201, 206, 231–2, 244–6, 248–9, 251, 257, 274–6, 278–9, 281–3, 288, 291, 295, 301, 309–10, 313–4, 322, 323, 332, 345; Greek thought, 16–7, 20–2, 24–5, 30–1, 42, 46, 60–2, 109, 149, 160, 164–6, 168, 172–4, 176, 182, 186, 193, 204, 242, 291; Roman or Latin thought, 76, 186, 191, 193, 201, 204, 213, 224, 237, 243, 247, 284; Greek language, 151
Greece (Hellas), 4, 11, 19, 27–9, 31, 38–40, 42, 45–7, 49–53, 62, 72–4, 78–80, 87–8, 93, 95–6, 100–1, 110, 113–4, 147, 149, 187, 219, 222, 242, 244–5, 247, 318; Magna Graecia, 108; Hellenism, 239, 241–2, 249. *See also* Athens; Sparta; *Greek cities by name*
Greenleaf, W. H., 294
Gregoras, Nicephorus. *See* Nicephorus Gregoras
Gregory bar Hebraeus, 206
Gregory of Cyprus, 242
Gregory of Elvire, 208
Gregory of Nyssa, 207
Gregory of Tours, 209, 213
Gregory the Great, Pope, 214, 335
Grenfell, B. P., 234
Greville, Fulke, 280, 344
Griffith, F. L., 210, 212, 217
Groningen, B. A. van, 206
Groslot de l'Île, Jerôme, 312

Growth: as formation, 70; as expansion, 69–70, 73–4, 96, 222, 224, 275; biological, *see* Cycles, biological
Grumel, V., 212
Grundmann, 321
Grundy, G. B., 111
Gruyter, W. de, 169
Gualterus Mapes, 226
Guarini, G. B., 343
Guicciardini, Francesco, 276, 279, 280, 286–7, 293–4, 314, 341–2
Guilland, R., 230, 240, 241
Gundersheimer, W. L., 280, 281, 298
Güterbock, M. G., 157
Guthrie, W. C. K., 61, 75, 93
Gyndes River, 96, 113

Hadrian, emperor, 190, 198, 199, 203
Haenchen, E., 121, 155
Hagentahl, H., 253
Haggai, book of, cited, 118
Hagiography, 238
Hahn, F., 129
Halys River, 87, 96
Ham, son of Noah, 302
Hamilcar Barcas, 90
Hammer, W., 225, 226
Hammond, N. G. L., 81, 150
Hamp, V., 119
Hannah, mother of Samuel, 145, 330
Hannibal, 46, 54, 55, 64, 65, 66, 91, 100, 102–4, 114, 236, 294, 315. *See also* Punic Wars
Hanson, R. P. C., 184
Harbinson, E. H., 250, 297, 298
Harder, R., 14, 42, 71, 76
Harnack, A. von, 330
Harrington, W. J., 334
Harvey, Gabriel, 282
Hasdrubal, last ruler of Carthage, 114
Hasenberg, K. E., 304
Hasmonean House. *See* Maccabees
Hastings, Sir William, Lord, 287
Hatch, E., 166
Häussler, R., 183, 188, 191, 277
Havelock, E. A., 16, 61
Hay, D., 248, 287
Hayduck, M., 200
Headley, J. M., 297, 303
Heath, D. D., 294
Heath, T., 12
Hebrew(s) (Hebraic, Israelites, Israel, Jews): general, 117, 119, 121, 142–7, 169–70, 207, 219, 247, 330, 332, 343–4; Hebraic thought and language, 120, 159–60, 165–6, 177, 180; early Hebrews, 159, 161, 169, 170; Israelites, 134–8, 156–7, 168–72, 175, 211, 219, 246; Jews, 136–8, 148, 160–71, 175, 219, 330; Jews of New Testament times, 127, 131, 133, 139, 142–5, 149–50, 154–5, 165–75, 177, 195, 214–5, 219, 226, 330; Epistle to the Hebrews cited, 175, 177, 228, 229. *See also* Israel; Judaism; Patriarchs
Hecataeus, 16, 17, 20, 21, 77
Heer, F., 245, 247
Hegesippus, 307, 326
Heiric of Auxerre, 246
Held, M. J., 372
Hellanikos, 97
Hellenization, process of, 2, 117, 164, 166, 195, 204
Hellespont, 95, 96, 113, 149
Hempel, C. G., 107
Hengel, M., 176, 186
Hennecke, E., 209
Henry VI, king, 287
Henry VII, emperor, 212, 247
Henry of Cossey, 213
Hense, O., 26, 46, 317
Heraclidae, 26, 27
Heraclitus, 9, 12, 62, 82, 85–6, 87, 93, 95, 167, 168
Heraclitus, pseudo-, 82
Hercules, 113; two, 230–1, 241
Hereditary rule, 4, 26–7, 108, 182, 237, 244, 253, 264, 271–2, 277–8, 319
Hermaecum, 89
Hermas, Shepherd of, 307
Hermeias the Seleucid, 105
Hermeticism, 201, 251, 345
Hermocrates, 114
Herod Agrippa I, king, 123, 131, 173
Herod Agrippa II, king, 173
Herod Antipas, tetrarch, 126, 131, 173, 328
Herodians, 124, 126, 127, 148, 173
Herodotus, 25, 26, 27, 28, 30, 31, 37–8, 46, 51, 61, 62, 74, 77, 79–80, 82, 86, 87, 93–7, 103, 109, 112, 113–4, 147, 150, 151, 186, 252, 282
Herzog-Hauser, G., 63
Hesiod, 8, 17, 21, 37, 42, 61, 62, 63, 69, 75–6, 78, 83, 85, 93, 201–4, 210, 231
Hesychasticism, 240
Hexter, J. H., 252, 273, 276
Hezekiah, king, 136, 137, 160, 223
Higden, Ranulf, 213
Higgins, A. J. B., 121, 322, 323
Hildebertus of Lavardin, 247
Hippocrates, Hippocratic school, 111
Hippodamus, pseudo-, 15, 26, 27, 38, 46
Hippolytus, St., 208, 211, 212, 222
Hirton, W. L., 344
History: As historiography, Greco-Roman, xi, 1, 77, 87, 92–6, 120–1, 147–9, 155, 159, 174, 177, 180, 193, 200, 213, 220, 232–4, 243–5, 251, 282, 284, 321–2, 332–3; methods, pre-

suppositions and accuracy, 45, 70, 72, 74–5, 78, 90–1, 105–6, 134, 155, 166, 180–3, 185–200, 231–3, 241–2; universal history in Polybius, 4–5, 66, 74, 78–82; pragmatic history, especially in Polybius, 15, 45, 60, 66, 70, 81, 83–4, 97, 101, 242–3, 258, 292. Biblical, general, 117, 119–21, 134, 147–8, 174; ancient Near Eastern, 119; Old Testament, 118, 134–9, 145, 147–8, 156–64, 169, 175, 178, 234, 331, 333; Jewish extra-biblical, 149, 164–6; New Testament, 128–9, 134, 146–55, 169–78, 234, 321–4. Christian, general, 185, 206, 233, 241, 248–9; patristic, 179, 206, 209, 228, 234–7; medieval, 95, 179, 206, 213, 219, 223–9, 235–43, 246–7, 249, 283, 314; Renaissance, 247–8, 251–95, 309; Reformation, 282–3, 288, 296–314. As the past, Greco-Roman views of, 12–5, 26–7, 42, 65–6, 66–9, 75–80, 93, 97, 117–8, 147–8, 151, 154, 196, 201–5, 242, 333; biblical, 117–8, 138–9, 141–2, 146, 155, 158, 169–70, 183, 323, 333–4; patristic and medieval, 185, 205–10, 213–4, 216–7, 219, 222, 228, 234, 239, 241–2; Renaissance and Reformation, 185, 220, 274, 278, 287–8, 290–2, 297, 299–304, 312; general, 315

Hlothere, king, 287

Hofmeister, A., 226

Hohenstaufen(s). *See* Rome, Holy Roman empire

Holtz, T., 144

Holy Spirit, 129, 144, 146, 174, 214, 216–9, 330–1, 333–4

Holyoake, G. J., 180

Homer, 61, 62, 78, 86, 88, 94, 154

*Homoousios* party, 235

Honoré d'Autun, 213

Honorius, emperor, 236

Hooff, A. J. L. van, 232

Hooke, S. H., 118

Horace, 76, 282

Horatius Cocles, 53, 243

Houlden, J. L., 122

Housman, A. E., 202

Howes, Edward, 345

Huart, P., 97

Hugh of St. Victor, 213

Hugo of Fleury, 283

Hull, J. M., 151

Hultsch, E., 49

Humanism, Renaissance, 220–1, 241, 243, 247–51, 257–8, 266, 269, 273, 278, 287, 295–6, 298, 302, 309–10, 335–7. *See also* Guicciardini, Francesco; Machiavelli, Niccolò; *humanists by name*

Hunt, A. S., 234

Huppert, G., 282, 284, 345

Hurd, J. C., 330

Hus, Jan, 307, 308

Hussey, J., 239

Hutterites, the, 307, 308

*Hybris* (political insolence, arrogance), 28, 30, 39, 47, 50, 87, 89, 92, 94–5, 98, 102, 107, 109, 166–7, 194–5, 232–4, 240, 242, 261–3, 267, 285–7, 289. *See also* Cycles, hybristic cycles

Hydaspes, pseudo-, 224

Hyginus, 201

Hyman, A., 296

Iamblichus the anonymous, 10, 21, 155

Illyria, 69, 71, 100, 108

Imitation, ideas of, 1, 113, 115, 183–4, 243, 292, 308–9

Immerwahr, H. R., 79, 96

Inachos the Argive, 14

Incalculable, the. *See* Fortune

Inequality between rich and poor, 21, 31, 71, 109, 195, 276, 287

Innocent I, Pope, 307

Ion of Chios, 46

Ionia(ns), 96, 244

Irenaeus, St., 207, 208, 209, 212, 220

Isaac, patriarch, 128, 184, 219

Isaiah, 141, 218, 219; book of, cited, 119, 141, 144, 150, 164, 166, 168, 229, 326; targum of, 142

Ishanad Vempeny, 117

Isidore of Seville, 213

Islam, 226, 302

Isocrates, 16, 17, 20, 21, 24, 26, 28, 30, 31, 32, 46, 69, 93, 94, 113, 317

Israel: geographical references, 130 (Palestine), 132, 136; as Northern kingdom, 136, 158; idea of new, 145. *See also* Hebrews

Italy, Italians, 64, 89, 90, 100, 102, 103, 108, 197, 217, 236, 241, 242, 243, 247–8, 251, 255–7, 270–4, 277, 279–80, 294, 302, 314, 338–42. *See also* Florence; Rome; Venice; *Italian cities by name*

Jackson, F. J. Foakes, 121, 141, 184

Jacob, patriarch, 219

Jacoby, F., 26, 69; works of, cited, 32, 53, 86, 94, 99, 112, 185

Jaeger, W., 10, 22, 63, 244

Jael (wife of Heber the Kenite), 164

Jahn, O., 62

Jairus (and daughter of), 127, 327

Jal, P., 190

James, St., *adelphos* of Jesus, 124, 131, 325–6

James, St., apostle, 124, 131, 328

Janus, 299, 300

Japheth, son of Noah, 302

Jason of Pherae, 114

Jehoahaz, king, 162, 163

Jehoiachim, king, 162, 163
Jehoiachin, king, 145, 162, 163
Jehoida, king, 136, 162, 163
Jehoram, king, 162, 163
Jehoshaphat, king, 160, 162, 163
Jephthah, judge, 157
Jeremiah, 143; book of, cited, 143, 166, 172, 233, 331, 332
Jeremias, J., 118, 175, 183
Jeroboam I, king, 158, 165
Jerome, St., 208, 213, 222, 224
Jerusalem, 123, 125–6, 130–4, 136–7, 141, 147, 164, 172, 304, 325; fall(s) of, 143–4, 149, 158, 165, 171–2, 333; temple of, 118, 123, 127, 135–7, 150, 164, 170, 329, 330, 332; destruction(s) of the temple of, 112, 136, 144, 165, 171, 213; heavenly, 207, 308
Jesuits, 298, 301
Jesus of Nazareth: life and ministry, 121–7, 129–33, 139–47, 150, 170–5, 183–4, 213–5, 217, 219–21, 224, 296, 298, 300, 302, 305, 307–9, 321–3, 326, 329, 331, 334–5, 338, 345; crucifixion and death of, 122–8, 131, 141–2, 151–4, 173, 183, 202, 206, 306, 328–30, 335; transfiguration, 141; resurrection, 122, 124, 126–7, 131–2, 140, 142, 151–2, 306, 321, 325, 328–9; ascension, 131–2, 141–3, 151–2, 202, 334; parousia, 322, 333
Jews. *See* Hebrews; Judaism
Joachim of Fiora, 33, 213, 216–20, 297, 301, 302, 308, 312, 335
Joachites. *See* Franciscan Order, Spirituals
Joanna the Virgin, 301
Joash, king, 136, 162, 163
Job, book of, cited, 119, 233
John, St., apostle and evangelist, 125, 127, 321, 325, 328, 329; Gospel of, cited, 125, 127, 133, 141, 151, 153, 174, 233, 246, 325, 326, 334
John of Salisbury, 214, 238
John the Baptist, 124, 125, 142, 143, 144, 172, 173, 219, 220, 334, 336
Jonah, 184, 332; book of, cited, 332
Jonathan, pseudo-, 143
Jones, A. H. M., 30, 318
Jones, C. P., 264
Jones, C. W., 213
Jordan River, 134, 147
Joris, David, 308
Joseph, patriarch, 169, 170
Josephus, Flavius, 74, 112, 132, 139, 149, 151, 153, 164–6, 169, 172, 173, 174, 176, 186, 229, 322, 332; Slavonic, 326
Joshua, 134, 136, 156, 159
Josiah, king, 158, 160, 162–3, 164
Jotham, king, 136, 160, 162, 163
Jovian, emperor, 233, 234, 236
Judaism: general, 128, 134; post-exilic, 118, 136–8, 160–4, 166, 168–9, 175, 331, 334; later, 139, 142–3, 146, 164–73, 175, 177, 179, 195, 334; rabbinic, 183, 207, 222, 301, 331, 335; Renaissance and Reformation, 299, 345. *See also* Rabbinical scholarship and literature
Judas, betrayer, 152, 172–3
Judas the Galilean, 174
Judea, Judah, 127, 130–2, 134, 137, 148–9, 158, 160–1, 171, 223
Judeo-Christian tradition. *See* Biblical tradition; Christianity; Hebrews
Judges, the, 156–8, 161, 164
Judith, book of, 164
Jugurthine War, 228
Julian the apostate, emperor, 199, 233, 236, 247
Julian of Toledo, 213
Julio-Claudian emperors, 199
Julius Africanus, 207, 208
Julius Caesar, emperor, 112, 114, 152, 182, 189, 190, 197, 228, 245, 264, 265, 266–7, 269, 271, 273, 282
Julius II, Pope, 212, 299
Junius, Lucius Pullus, 90
'Junius Brutus' (pseudonym), 344
Justice: as divine or higher principle, 94–6, 98, 100–1, 160, 165, 167, 172, 232, 285, 287–8; other, 20, 47, 100, 253
Justin(us), Roman historian, 21, 187, 194, 210, 222, 223
Justin Martyr, 153, 207, 208
Justin Martyr, pseudo-, 155
Juvenal, 76, 186, 202

Kahn, C. H., 8
Kaibel, G., 62
Kajanto, I, 63, 105, 193, 196
Kamlah, W., 216
Kapelrud, A. S., 121
Käsemann, E., 121
Keck, L. E., 121, 131, 155, 322, 324
Kerenyi, K., 193
*Kerygma*, the (early Christian), 121–2, 321–3, 328
Kiessling, T., 239
Kilpatrick, G. D., 140
Kings, kingship, 5, 15, 17–29, 32–43, 45, 47, 49–53, 56, 58, 70–1, 73, 80, 94–5, 101, 104, 107–8, 113, 129, 135–8, 145–6, 152, 158, 160–4, 168, 173, 181, 183, 188–9, 192, 210, 213, 215, 219, 222–4, 237, 239, 246, 260–2, 264–7, 274–5, 277–8, 290, 317–8, 339, 344; kingdom of God, 126, 140, 150, 155, 170. *See also* Monarchy, as one man rule
Kirk, G. S., 8, 16, 62, 66, 67, 82, 85, 86, 93, 95
Kittel, G., 183
Klassen, P. J., 308
Klein, G., 333

Klempt, A., 296
Klostermann, E., 206, 216
Knaake, A., 283
Knaake, J. C. F., 297
Knapp, C., 227
Knauss, B., 11
Knowledge (science, technology) in connection with recurrence, 16–7, 69, 185, 281–2, 302. *See also* Arts and skills; Progress, ideas of
Knowles, D., 184
Knox, John, 344
Knox, W. L., 144, 154, 176, 201, 324
Koch, J., 212, 245
Koerte, A., 63
Köhler, O., 217
Kolenkow, A. C. B., 176
Kornemann, E. K., 46
Krahn, C., 307
Kranz, W., 8, 16, 21, 24, 41, 62, 66, 82, 85, 86, 93
Kristeller, P. O., 295
Kronos, 10, 11, 17, 21, 42, 76, 201, 210
Kümmel, W. G., 171

Labuske, H., 58
Lacedaemon. *See* Sparta
Laconia, 27
Lactantius, 183, 188, 189, 193, 202, 204, 207, 209–12, 224, 225, 229, 234–6, 301, 302, 313
Ladner, G. B., 191, 201, 245
Lainez, Diego, 298
Lake, K., 121, 141, 184
Lami, J., 229
Lampe, G. W. H., 128, 143, 144
Lasaulx, E. von, 312, 313
Lascaris, Janus, 276
Last Supper. *See* Festivals, Passover
Latini, Brunetto, 213
Laurence, St., 220
Laurentin, R., 131
Law, social and religious, 23, 39, 86–7, 96, 99, 107, 134–5, 137, 139, 142–3, 161, 165, 169–70, 187, 196, 209, 217–8, 225, 256, 259–60, 268–9, 278, 301, 305, 334, 345; as historical regularities, 107, 120, 178, 258, 280, 289, 293–4, 302, 312, 343; legislator, 47, 129, 143, 169, 271–2, 274, 285; lawyers, 134. *See also* Justice; Corruption, social
Leaney, A. R. C., 146
Lefèvre d'Étaples (Jacobus Faber), 298
Leff, G., 184, 336
Lehmann, G. A., 75
Lehmann, P., 216, 336
Lemerle, P., 149
Leo X, Pope, 272, 299, 300, 340
Lerner, M., 254
Le Roy, Louis, 280–2, 283, 288, 302
Lessons from (or utility of) the study of the past, ideas concerning, 3, 60–1, 66, 70, 74–5, 81, 97–8, 101, 105–6, 111, 158–60, 165, 178, 206, 232, 241–3, 249, 251, 285, 291–5, 314
Leuctra, battle of, 318
Leutsch, E. L., 62
Levant, the, 130, 147, 149
Leviticus, book of, cited, 330
Lewalter, E., 211
Libya, 89
License, rule of. *See* Mob rule
Liebeschuetz, W., 186, 243
Lightfoot, R. H., 325
Lilybaeum, 89–90
Lindars, B., 143, 334
Linear (as distinct from recurrence) views of history, xi, 2, 112, 117–20, 157, 167, 169–70, 178–9, 183, 185, 204–9, 217, 223, 227, 250–1, 281–2, 288, 308–9, 313; rectilinearity, 67–8, 76
Lipara, 89
Lisowsky, G., 137, 160
Littell, F., 304, 307
Livy, Titus, 49, 72, 103, 152, 185, 186, 189, 193, 196, 200, 202, 203, 233, 242–3, 252, 259–62, 264, 266, 273, 300, 319
Lobel, E., 88
Lohmeyer, E., 325
Lohse, E., 129, 323
Lombards, the, 219, 339. *See also* Milan
Loserth, J., 304
Lot, nephew of Abraham, 221
Louis I the Pious, 246
Louis XI, 276, 339
Love, ideas of, 8, 302
Lovejoy, A. O., 16, 67, 76, 77
Löwith, K., 112, 117, 205, 216
Lucan, 186, 202
Lucca, 270
Luccioni, J., 19
Lucian, 83, 151, 153, 242
Lucifer. *See* Satan
Luck. *See* Fortune
Lucretius, 20, 21, 25, 26, 109, 253
Luke-Acts, xi, 2, 116, 120–35, 139–55, 169–78, 204, 218, 279, 298, 303–4, 310, 314–5, 321–34; date and provenance, 121; Luke's reasons for writing, 173; his methods and presuppositions, 121–7, 129–35, 139–55, 170–8, 184, 321–34; his reliability, 121–2, 129–30, 132, 171, 321–2; reenactment in Luke-Acts, 122–34, 139–55, 180, 183–4, 305, 308; retribution in, 170–4, 234, 287; Age theory and imperial rise and fall in, 174–7, 217
Lumpkin, W. L., 304
Luther, Martin, 283, 295, 297–9, 303, 306, 308, 310, 344

Lutheranism, 297, 303
Lycurgus, the legislator, 40, 47, 49, 57, 102, 114, 245, 254–5, 259, 262, 317–20, 339
Lycurgus, king, 318, 319
Lydgate, J., 344
Lydia, 79, 96
Lysander, 245
Lysicus the Aetolian, 100

Maccabees, the (Hasmonean House), 164, 220; Simon Maccabeus, 146, 220; Judas Maccabeus, 146, 164; authors of I-II Maccabees, 164; of IV Maccabees, 165; books of, cited, 143, 146, 153, 164–5, 171, 174, 306
Macedon, Macedonia, 32, 65, 69–71, 73–4, 78–80, 99–101, 103–5, 108, 149, 165, 186, 187, 189, 195, 203, 223, 224, 227, 231, 264, 319, 323
Machiavelli, Niccolò: theory of constitutional change, 251–75, 289–90, 296, 310, 338–42; on Roman constitution, 259–68; Florentine constitution, 256, 268–74, 338; more general political and military change, 252, 256, 272, 280–2, 284, 289, 291, 294, 296, 312; on political ruin, 255–6, 264–5, 272, 338–9, 341–2; internal-external relations, 185, 255–6, 271, 288–90, 340–2; military matters, 268, 286, 289–90, 293, 338–9; on fortune, 283–7; on a good man (*buono uomo*), 254, 269, 271–2, 339–42; on Italy in general and Italian city-states, 255–7, 270–1, 286, 295, 338–42; on religious matters, 259, 283, 286, 293, 296; on human nature, 257–8, 291–3; his eclecticism, 258; his pragmatism, 258, 285, 289, 291–3; mentioned, 2, 92, 180, 249, 250, 251, 310, 314, 315, 319–20
Mackay, C., 332
McKelvey, R. J., 145
McKeon, R., 12
MacMurray, J., 117
MacRae, G., 151
Macrinus, emperor, 199
Macrobius, 203, 234
Maddox, R., 129, 149
Maelius, Spurius, 266–7
Malachi, book of, cited, 144
Malalas, Joannis, 208, 212
Mamertines, 91
Manasseh, king, 136, 137, 158, 162, 163
Manetti, Gianotto, 345
Manlius Capitolinus, 266–7
Mannerism, 282
Mantinea(ns), 100
Manuel I, king, 299
Marathon, battle of, 96
Marcellus, Marcus Claudius, 102
Marcellus of Ancyra, 216
Marcus, emperor. *See* Aurelius
Margaret of Anjou, queen (of England), 287
Marianus Scotus, 213, 226
Marius, Gaius, 197, 263, 266–7
Mark, St., evangelist, 125, 171, 322, 325, 329; Gospel of, cited, 123, 125, 126, 127, 129, 132, 133, 140, 141, 142, 144, 151, 152, 153, 154, 155, 171, 172, 175, 305, 322, 325, 326, 328, 330, 331, 332, 334; pseudo-Mark, 126, 334
Marshall, I. H., 134, 146, 322
Marsilius of Padua, 238, 253
Martial, 192, 203
Martin, C., 275
Martin, R. P., 121
Martyn, J. L., 121, 131, 155, 322, 324
Martyrs, martyrdom, martyrology, 123, 154, 165, 170, 173, 207, 234, 305–8. *See also* Persecutions
Marx, Karl: Marxism, 33, 107, 218, 314–5
Mary, mother of Jesus, 326, 330
Masai, F., 230
Mascezel, 236
Mattathias, 164
Matthew, St., apostle and evangelist, 124, 129, 144, 146, 171, 172, 173, 176, 218, 321, 325, 331; Gospel of, cited, 123, 125, 126, 127, 129, 132, 133, 140, 141, 142, 144, 151, 152, 153, 154, 171, 172, 174, 175, 183, 209, 219, 300, 304, 305, 325, 326, 330, 331, 332, 334
Mauersberger, A., 5, 64
Maximian, emperor, 234
Maximian Herculius, emperor, 199, 234
Maximilian I, emperor, 339
Maximus (correspondent), 230, 241
Mazzeo, J., 250, 251, 273, 295
Media, 79, 80, 186, 219, 222, 224, 227, 280, 344
Medici, de', House of, 268, 271, 284, 338; Cosimo, 270, 271, 294, 341; Lorenzo I, 270, 271, 295, 338, 341; Lorenzo II, 270, 271, 272, 338–9, 340, 341; Piero, 270. *See also* Leo X, Pope
Mediterranean Sea, 131, 232
Meinecke, A., 63
Melanchthon, Philipp, 296
Melissus of Samos, 82,
Melito of Sardis, 224
Menander, 63
Mendels, D., 108
Mercenaries, 90; Mercenary War, 91
Mergal, A. M., 304, 344
Merovingians, 277
Merton, T., 128
Mesopotamia(ns), 119, 157, 345. *See also* Middle East
Messana (Sicily), 89, 91
Messene (Peloponnesus), 38, 57, 108
Messiah, ideas of, 142, 145, 183, 209, 334; Messianic Age, 169, 175, 178

*Metabolē. See* Change, *metabolē* theory concerning
Metempsychosis, 61, 66–7, 206, 229, 230, 251; special translation, 219
Meteorology (storm, wind, weather, etc.), 12, 83, 241, 290
Metochites, Theodore, 228, 239–42, 249, 275
Metzger, H., 171
Meyer, E., 120, 121, 186
Meyer, F., 307
Michael IV, emperor, 239
Middle Ages: concept of, 218, 243, 246–7, 336–7, 345; general references to, 180, 208, 214, 222, 283, 301, 309; medieval ideas of recurrence, 2, 179, 183, 207, 212–20, 235–42, 257, 283, 289, 291, 308–9; aspects of medieval thought, 207, 218, 221, 225–6, 235, 238, 242, 246–9, 251–3, 266, 273–4, 300, 310, 314, 335 (*see also* Christian Church, patristic and medieval; Christianity, medieval). Medieval monasticism, orders, 184, 218–9, 226, 277, 299, 302, 307, 309–10, 335
Middle East, 74, 75, 76, 80, 81, 101, 147, 186, 204, 300; Middle and Near Eastern thought, 117, 119, 157, 160, 178–9, 204, 207. *See also* Asia; Hebrews; Mesopotamia; Persia
Midian(ites), 157, 219
*Midrash(im)*, 129, 138, 164
Mierow, C. C., 227
Migne, J. P., 183; citations of works published by, 188, 200, 207–11, 213–4, 216–7
Milan, 270, 272–3, 286. *See also* Lombards
Milburn, R. L. P., 214
Miles, G., 174, 203
Miletus, 124
Milik, J. T., 176
Millennium, millennia, ideas of, 207–11, 223, 225, 301, 336, 345
Minear, P. S., 131, 330
Minucius Felix, 224
Mioni, E., 42, 64
Miracles, 124, 126–7, 130, 143–4, 151, 220, 324, 327–8, 330–1
Miranda, A. A. de, 232
Mixed constitution(s). *See* Constitution, mixed
Moab(ites), 157
Mob rule (ochlocracy, rule of license), 5, 16, 23–5, 30, 32, 34–6, 39–41, 43–4, 48, 50–1, 56, 71–4, 107–9, 180, 254, 261, 263, 275, 277–8, 318, 343; as license in Machiavelli's works, 252–8, 263–5, 269–71, 273, 340
Moderation. *See* Ethical ideas, moderation; Excess
Modoin, 212, 226, 246
*Moira*, 86, 94, 188
Molpagoras of Cius, 109
Momigliano, A., 2, 61, 117, 183, 188, 233
Mommsen, T. E., 216–7, 223, 224, 237, 336
Monarchy: primitive, 4–6, 15–6, 19–24, 27–8, 31–3, 36, 38–41, 49, 51–2, 54, 56, 109, 210, 254, 261, 318–9; as one man rule, 4, 7, 20–1, 24, 27–33, 35, 37, 39, 44–5, 48–9, 118, 135–8, 145–6, 160–3, 166, 171–3, 187, 189, 191, 215, 224, 252–3, 257, 260, 263–4, 267–8, 271–3, 275–8, 312, 318–9; monarchical elements, 46–7, 54–6, 275, 311–2, 317, 340; world monarchy, 186–7, 222–3, 225, 280, 282, 299, 302, 309; mixed, 52, 275; new, 339, 343
Monnier, F. le, 276
Montaigne, Michel de, 294
Montano, Cola, 270
Montereau, Chevalier de, 282
Moore, J. M., 71, 262
Moral order, 87, 92–106, 109, 111, 160, 165–6, 178, 195–6, 232–42, 244, 288, 323; and fortune, 63–6, 73–4, 84, 94, 193, 195, 200, 232–3, 235, 239–40, 283–4, 286–7, 291; and providence, 84, 96, 99, 139, 165, 174, 188, 195–6, 210, 217, 232–3, 235, 238–41, 281, 286–8, 290–1, 302, 315; and divine foreknowledge or plan, 153, 205, 208–9, 228, 235; and other-worldly requital, 233–4, 237–9, 241. *See also* Ethical ideas; Retribution
Moravia, 308
Moreau, J., 219
Morgenthaler, R., 122
Morris, L., 128
Morse, W. E., 307
Moses, 128, 134–6, 138, 140–4, 146, 151, 158–9, 167, 169–70, 215, 220, 225, 292, 295, 301, 335, 336, 339, 345
Moule, C. D. F., 143, 151, 322
Moulton, W. F., 140
Mountford, J. F., 211
Mowinckel, S., 117, 118
Mugler, C., 11, 12
Muller, C. J., 239
Müller, F. Max, 118
Müller, M., 119
Munck, J., 170
Münster(ites), 282–3, 305, 307
Müntzer, Thomas, 344
Muratori, L., 283
Murchison, L., 330
Muslims. *See* Islam
Myers, J. M., 137, 156
Mylae, 89
Myres, J., 120, 157
Myth, mythological material, 10–1, 14, 20–1, 38–40, 42, 75–7, 117, 119, 154, 204, 206, 210, 301, 315

Naaman the Syrian, 330
Nabis of Sparta, 108, 318, 319
Nain, widow of, 329
Namatianus, Rutulius, 245
Naoma, wife of Noah, 301

Naples, Neapolitans, 339
Nation(s), ideas of: nationalism, patriotism, 38, 40, 69, 71, 74, 81, 93, 96, 100, 102–3, 149–50, 157, 160, 171, 174–5, 177, 183, 190, 204, 232, 290, 338–9, 341–3
Nature, natural processes, 14, 20, 22, 36, 41, 44–9, 51, 56–7, 66, 68–71, 73–4, 81, 83–4, 86, 92–4, 96, 100–1, 103–4, 107–8, 110–1, 113, 119, 159, 166–9, 177, 188, 191–2, 194, 207–8, 210, 220, 227–8, 234, 240, 249, 254, 257–60, 274, 278–80, 282, 293, 296, 302, 319, 335, 345. *See also* Cycles, ideas of
Nau, F., 206
Naudé, C. P. T., 193, 200
Navone, J., 124
Near East. *See* Middle East
Nebuchadnezzar, king, 171, 175
Necessity, 14, 17, 22, 36, 44, 47, 83, 153, 166, 168, 193, 195, 205, 254, 256–8, 279, 284–6, 289, 292, 302, 315, 329
Needham, J., 61
Neff, C. W., 305
Nehemiah, 136, 138–9, 160–1. *See also* Chronicler
*Nemesis*, 94, 98, 240, 285
Nemesius, 200, 205
Nepos, Cornelius, 244
Nero, emperor, 183, 199, 203, 220, 234, 265, 266
Nerva, emperor, 190, 198, 199, 264
Netherlands, Netherlanders, 305
Neubauer, A., 216
Neusner, J., 222
Newald, R., 243
Newman, W. L., 24
Nicaea, Council of, 307
Nicephorus Gregoras, 229–31, 238–42, 247, 248, 249, 275, 313, 315
Nicholson, E. W., 135
Nicodemus, Apocryphal Gospel of, 307
Niebuhr, Reinhold, 117, 313
Nietzsche, F., 61
Nigidius Figulus, 201
Nile River, 96
Nilsson, M. P., 234
Nineham, D., 124, 128
Ninus, Nimrud, king, 77, 186, 187, 209, 210, 223, 277, 282
Nisbet, R., 37
Nithard, 238
Noah, 209, 210, 215, 220, 221, 301–2, 335, 338
Nock, A. D., 183, 200, 203, 234
Nogara, B., 247
Nogent, G. de, 242
Norden, E., 154, 324
Norin, W., 205
Normans, the, 279, 301
North, C., 156, 175
North, Thomas, 294
Noth, M., 117, 118, 121, 157, 158, 175
Notker the Stammerer, 247
Novatian, emperor, 245
Numa Pompilius, king, 191, 192, 245, 265
Numantia, Numantine War, 189, 190, 197–8
Numbers, book of, cited, 135, 142
Numerian, emperor, 199
Numidia, 198

Obermann, H. A., 296
Obolensky, D., 181
O'Brien, D., 8
Ocellus Lucanus, pseudo-, 14–5, 42, 44, 71, 76, 200
Ochlocracy. *See* Mob rule
Octavius. *See* Augustus
Odovocar, Scirian king, 227
Oesterley, W. O. E., 166
Ogygus, 108
Oligarchy, 5, 23–4, 27, 29–30, 33–7, 39–41, 43–4, 50–2, 54, 56, 107–9, 180, 182, 252, 254–5, 258, 261–2, 265, 275–8, 318, 343
Oliverotto da Fermo, 286
Olivet, 326
Olivi, Peter, 335–6
Olschki, L., 295
Olympiodorus, 200, 205
O'Malley, J. W., 299, 300
O'Neill, J. C., 330
Onias, high priest, 220
Origen, 119, 176, 178, 185, 200, 201, 204, 205, 206, 207, 220, 224, 229–30, 239, 313
Origins (human), ideas concerning, 7, 13, 16, 21, 206, 253, 279, 288
Orléans, House of, 290
Oroetes the Persian, 96
Orophernes, king, 101
Orosius, 150, 209, 213, 219, 223–5, 227, 228, 236–8, 247, 287, 313
Orpheus, 61
Östborn, G., 135, 138, 157
Othniel, judge, 157
Otho, emperor, 199
Otto of Freising, 213, 220, 226–8, 238
Otto, W., 193
Ottonians. *See* Rome, holy Roman empire
Ovid, 15, 62, 76, 210, 282

Pachymer, George, 242
Packard, D. W., 186
Page, D. L., 88
Palamas, Gregory, 240
Palestine. *See* Israel
Pamphilius, 206
Panaetius of Rhodes, 7, 9, 20–1, 22, 46
Pannenberg, W., 149
Panofsky, E., 246

Panormus, 89
Papacy, Roman, 217, 245, 294, 297, 289, 310, 311–2, 338, 340
Papias, 208
Paradigms, paradigmatic qualities, 2–3, 60–1, 68–75, 105–6, 111, 119, 121, 173, 178, 192, 232, 242, 248, 251, 278, 283, 288, 291–2, 309, 315. *See also* Cycles, ideas of; Seasons; Theatre; Tidal analogy; Woven cloth analogy
Parallels, parallelism, uses of in conveying ideas of recurrence, 3, 97, 113–4, 122, 126–9, 135–9, 143, 148, 151–4, 170, 172, 177, 183, 192, 218–9, 223, 227–8, 234, 244–5, 251, 253, 269, 277, 291–2, 295, 299, 302, 306, 317, 327–30, 332, 343
Paris, city of, 247
Paris, Matthew, 213
Parratt, J., 333
Parthia, 198
Paruta, Paolo, 276, 343
Paschoud, F., 188
Pasquier, Estienne, 282, 284
Patch, M. R., 283
Paton, W. R., 5, 50, 71
Patriarchs, the Hebrew, 170, 215, 225, 335, 336, 345. *See also* Abraham; Isaac; *patriarchs by name*
Patristic thought. *See* Christianity
Patterns, educed from history, 2, 10, 14–5, 33, 57, 60, 83, 85, 88, 90, 95, 110–1, 122, 127, 134, 136, 138, 147–8, 150, 155–6, 160–1, 164, 169–70, 178, 198, 208–9, 216, 218, 224, 228, 231, 242, 258, 274, 288, 292, 294, 301–3, 306–7, 312, 323. *See also* Cycles, idea of
Patterson, L. G., 207, 237
Paul (Saul) of Tarsus, St., 121, 123–8, 130–1, 133, 144–5, 147, 149–50, 153–5, 170–4, 220, 301, 324–5, 327, 329, 334; epistles of, cited, 121, 128, 155, 175, 216, 229, 326, 329, 335
Paullus (Macedonicus), Aemilius, 264
Pausanias, 26, 151
Peace, ideas concerning, 92, 190, 198, 194, 202, 224, 256, 288; pacificism, 306
Pearson, L., 155, 183
Pédech, P., 5, 24, 25, 46, 97, 99, 105, 106, 232
Peiper, R., 235
Peisistratus, Peisistratidae, 25, 31, 268
Peloponnesus, 64, 80
Pentecost, 130, 220, 323
Pepagomene (correspondent), 230
Pericles, 114, 295
Periods, periodicity, periodization, 7–10, 12, 14, 17, 66–7, 76–8, 117, 119, 155, 158, 160, 164–5, 175–7, 180, 185, 188–90, 201, 203, 214, 218, 220, 229–30, 244, 251, 279, 290, 335–7, 345
Peripatetic school. *See* Aristotle; Aristotelian school
Persecutions, 219, 228–9, 233–6, 297, 305, 345. *See also* Martyrs
Perseus, hero, 231
Perseus, king, 65, 73, 104, 105, 108, 114, 231, 235, 242
Persia, 39, 40, 65, 79, 96, 101, 165, 186, 187, 195, 219, 222, 227, 247, 280, 344; fall of, 94, 101, 103; Persian Wars, 79, 87, 94, 96, 102, 113, 187. *See also* Darius I; Xerxes I
Pertinax, emperor, 199
Pesch, R., 123, 328
*Pesher(im)*, 129
Pessimism, 17, 61, 166, 186, 188, 190, 192, 196, 225–6, 235, 237, 302, 341
Peter (Simon, Cephas), St., the apostle, 122–5, 127, 131, 176, 300, 325–9; epistles of, cited, 124, 176, 207, 223; apocryphal Gospel of, 132, 328, 329: St. Peter's Church, Rome, 299, 300
Petrarch, Francesco, 218, 243, 248, 297, 336–7
Petzold, K. E., 58, 111
Peuckert, W.-E., 229
Pfeiffer, R. H., 164
Pfligersdorfer, G., 185
Pharsalia, battle of, 190, 197
Pheretima of Egypt, 96
Philemon (poet), 63
Philinus, 91, 99
Philip the evangelist, 130, 133, 333
Philip II of Macedon, 70, 80, 104, 114, 187, 232, 240
Philip V of Macedon, 32, 65, 70, 99, 100, 102, 104, 107–8, 114
Philip II of Spain, 306
Philip, Roman emperor, 199
Philip, J. A., 12, 61
Philipp van Haveng, 213, 214–6
Philippi, 127, 149
Philistia, Philistines, 157, 247
Philo Judaeus, 9, 70, 164, 167–70, 175, 176, 180, 195, 203, 204, 228, 239, 279, 307, 313
Philomenus the Phocian, 232
Philopoemen, 64, 66, 244
Philostratus, 17, 124, 150, 151, 154
Phocas, emperor, 297
Phoenicia, 130, 131
Phoenix, the, 202, 203
Phylarchus, 94, 105
Piccinino, Niccolò, 286
Pierozzi, A., 336
Pierro, E. de, 247
Pindar, 21, 62, 86
Pisa, 247, 290
Pitti, Luca, 270
Plataea, battle of, 187
Plato: cosmology, 9–10, 62, 69, 230, 295; catastrophe theory, 10–5, 19, 75–6, 78, 176, 200–2, 210, 279; on society and ethics, 17, 19–22,

26–32, 37–42, 47, 50–1, 54, 57, 84, 93–4, 152, 181–2, 252, 254, 263, 277, 317–9; on change, 67, 72, 88, 107, 113, 166, 206–7; on ideal republic, 11, 18, 19, 40–1; mentioned, 244, 282, 307

Platonic school, Neo-Platonism, 6, 9–10, 12, 14, 21, 42, 241, 248, 279, 295, 298, 311. *See also* Celsus; Plotinus; *Platonists by name*

Plekhanov, G. (N. Beltov), 314

Plethon, Gemisthius, 229–30, 241, 247

Pliny the Elder, 193

Pliny the Younger, 190

Plotinus, 205

Plümacher, E., 148, 324

Plumptre, E. H., 167

Plutarch, 9, 62, 63, 65, 66, 68–9, 79, 94, 113, 150, 151, 152, 153, 185, 186, 192–4, 200, 201, 202, 212, 230, 233, 234, 239, 244–5, 264, 282, 284, 317, 319; early English translation of, 294

Pocock, J. G. A., 271, 277, 281, 285, 314

Pocquet, Anthony, 345

Poggio Bracciolini, 283

Political society, polity, polis, state: beginnings of, 16, 18, 253–4; establishment of, 10, 18, 22, 27, 29, 38, 43, 48, 253; conditions necessary for, 17, 19, 21, 23–5, 82, 255; and magistrates, 29, 38–40, 269; in relation to rural life, 62, 71; church as, 311; breakdown of (*see* Corruption; Decay); general references, 69–70, 113, 281

Polos, 17

Polybius of Megalopolis: reasons for writing his history, 4–5, 65, 147–8, 322; attitudes toward cosmology, 10, 12–5, 44, 78, 82, 203, 232, 279; anthropology of, 15–24, 181, 253; theory of constitutional change, 5–6, 18–45, 48–59, 69, 70–4, 77–8, 83, 107–9, 116, 180–2, 184, 194, 249, 252–5, 257–63, 265, 273–4, 278, 317–20; on Roman history, 41, 45–58, 64–6, 71, 73, 79, 81–2, 88–92, 98–9, 148, 149, 150, 155, 169, 177, 182, 185, 187, 192, 194, 197, 243, 253, 260–2, 276, 317; on political and military changes, 69–74, 78–82, 88–92, 97–106, 111–2, 114, 166, 173, 195, 255, 274, 288–9, 291, 318–9; on ethics and history, 93–4, 97–106, 178, 194, 237, 288; on fortune, 63–6, 72–4, 97–105, 148, 193, 196, 318; on religion, 78, 232; on pragmatic history, 15, 45, 60, 66, 70, 81, 83–4, 97, 101; his eclectic tendencies, 13, 17, 20, 22–5, 28, 32–3, 36–7, 42–3, 45–6, 58–9, 74, 78, 84, 99, 103, 112, 177, 293, 302; other references, xi, 2–3, 67, 120–1, 129, 132, 151, 231–2, 275, 310, 314–5, 321

Polycrates of Samos, 62, 85, 95

Pompey the Great, 190, 197, 245, 263, 266, 282

Pontano, Giovanni, 286

Pontus, the, 13

Porcari, Stefano, 286

Porcia, wife of Brutus, 153

Porphyry, 9, 66, 155, 200

Portugal, 290, 299

Pöschl, V., 51, 52, 181

Poseidonius, 21, 76, 82, 94, 120, 148, 178, 185, 193, 201, 232

Postel, Guillaume, 297, 301–3, 308, 314, 345

Pötscher, W., 16

Poujol, J., 275

Pratesi, L., 283

Prato, 270

Prefiguration, instances of, 124, 128, 146, 184, 219

Pre-Socratic philosophers, 8–10, 12, 14, 16–7, 20–1, 85–6. *See also* Heraclitus; Pythagoras

Press, G. A., 117

Preuss, M., 297

Previtera, C., 286

Priam, 78, 79

Priestly source (Bible), 175

Primitive life, primitivism: prepolitical conditions, 6, 14–6, 19, 22, 24, 39–40, 81–2, 253 (*see also* Animal, animal-like conditions); pastoral idyllicism, 42, 149; important primeval events, 10–1, 14, 20–1, 38–40, 42, 75, 76, 302; Eden, 176, 301–2; return to primitive Christianity, 180, 300, 303, 305–8, 311–2. *See also* Monarchy, primitive; Reversion, return

Princedom, 253–4, 264, 268, 269–74, 284, 312, 338–42

Principate, Roman, 183, 188, 192–4, 202–3, 209, 245, 262–4, 275; as the Caesars, 180, 191, 246, 265, 267, 272, 276; as emperors, 81, 189, 268, 307, 336; Byzantine, 237, 239. *See also* Julius Caesar; Augustus; *individuals by name*

Pritchard, J., 75, edited work by, cited, 119

Probus, emperor, 199

Procacci, 293

Procas, king, 223

Proclus, 200

Procopius, 200, 206, 228, 238, 239, 242, 243

Prodicus, 16, 17, 20

Prognostication, 6, 13, 27, 48, 51, 57–8, 71–2, 74, 292–4

Progress, ideas of: general, xi, 16–7, 22, 223, 315; of knowledge and science, 16–7, 247, 281–2, 302; of technology, 17, 20, 185, 281–2; socio-political, 20, 226; moral, 185; spiritual, 208, 214, 216–7, 226–7, 301–2, 336

Prophecy: classical, 80, 173, 201 (*see also* Delphic Oracle); biblical, 135, 142, 150, 172–3, 299, 305, 306, 308, 330–2, 334–5; patristic, 224; prophecy fulfillment, 128–9, 139–42, 144, 161, 171, 321, 333; biblical

prophets, 129, 135, 139–40, 142–5, 154, 158, 164–6, 170, 219
Prosperity: general, 47, 64, 166, 207, 216, 240; social, 47, 50, 54, 69, 71, 92, 100, 160, 164, 169, 195, 197, 290; individual, 62, 64–5, 95, 167, 233. *See also* Fortune, good
Protagoras, 16, 17, 20
Protestantism. *See* Reformation; Reformers, Protestant
Providence. *See* Moral order
Prudentius, 192, 207, 245
Prusias II of Bithynia, 98
Psalms, 140, 329; book of, cited, 119, 207, 233
Psellus, Michael, 228, 238
Pseudepigraphical literature (biblical), cited, 143, 164, 168, 175–6, 202, 207, 209
Ptolemaeus, Claudius, 186
Ptolemy II Philadelphus, 169
Ptolemy IV Philopater, 99, 101, 105
Publicola, 245
Publius, official at Malta, 127, 328
Puech, H. C., 205
Punic Wars, 46–7, 49, 52–5, 74, 88–91, 100–4, 189, 199, 262
Pupienus, emperor, 199
Purpose, human (purposive causes, human decisions, determination, etc.), 22, 44, 47, 64, 72, 83–4, 91, 94, 96–7, 100, 103–4, 110, 168, 195, 257–8, 274, 278, 280–1, 283, 285–6, 293
Pyrrhus, king, 199
Pythagoras, Pythagoreanism, 9, 12, 14–5, 28, 66, 75–7, 84, 86, 93, 119–20, 155, 200–1, 203, 205–6, 220–1, 225, 230, 250–1, 282, 307

Qoheleth. *See* Ecclesiastes
*Querelle* between ancients and moderns, 281, 295
Quinctius, Lucius, 51
Quispel, G., 205
Qumranite literature, 129, 146, 164; cited, 129, 143, 170, 176

Raab, F., 264
Rabanus Maurus, 209, 213, 214, 216, 217
Rabbinical scholarship and literature, 183, 207, 222, 301, 331, 335; literature cited, 170, 175, 176, 183, 207, 209, 216, 331
Rad, G. von, 75, 118, 121, 134, 136, 137, 138, 157, 164
Radagaisus the Goth, 236
Rainhald of Dassel, 226
Raleigh, Walter, 288, 294
Rambeau, 243
Rationality, reason: in connection with recurrence, 15, 17–9, 21, 27, 40, 47, 70, 84, 86, 97, 99, 167, 239, 299; rationalism, 78
Raven, J. E., 8, 16, 62, 66, 67, 82, 85, 86, 93, 95
Rawson, E., 277, 343
Rebirth. *See* Renaissance
Recapitulation, ideas of, 146, 209
Reciprocity, reciprocal processes of change, 2, 85–107, 155–74, 231–41, 252, 256, 272–4, 283–91
Reckford, K. J., 76
Rectified mean, 2, 85–93, 167. *See also* Balance
Recurrence: historical as against cosmological, 6–15, 22, 204–7, 229–30, 313; exact, numerical or identical, 9, 15, 66–8, 75, 77, 84, 110, 119, 126, 165, 178, 200–1, 211, 220–1, 230–1, 242, 294–5, 303; eternal, 2, 9, 178, 185, 204, 209, 221, 229–30, 250–1, 291–2, 315; event-complexes repeated 'many times' (*pollakis*), 11, 13, 166–7, 230; general references to historical recurrence, xi, 1, 6, 27, 37, 42, 44–6, 58–61, 81, 84–5, 87, 90, 92, 94–5, 97–8, 104–7, 109–11, 113–4, 119–20, 122, 126, 128, 134, 138–9, 144, 146, 148, 156–61, 165, 168–9, 171, 174–7, 179–81, 183–5, 190, 192, 194, 198, 200, 203, 205, 206, 208–9, 212, 214, 216–21, 224–8, 232–4, 237, 241–2, 244, 246, 251–2, 254, 258–9, 266, 272–4, 276, 278–9, 282–3, 286–91, 293, 295–300, 303, 308–9, 311, 313–5, 342–3
Red Sea, 134
Redpath, H. A., 166
Reenactment, ideas of, xi, 1, 3, 69, 113; in Luke-Acts, 122–34, 140, 142–3, 146–7, 149, 151–2, 154–5, 164, 177–8, 183–4, 331; in Old Testament histories, 134–9, 148, 160, 164; in medieval thought, 184, 247, 336; in Reformation thought, 303–10
Reeves, M., 216, 219, 220, 335
Reformation, the, xi, 1, 180, 185, 212, 250, 278, 280, 291, 297–8, 303, 308, 310, 336–7, 345; radical, 2, 184, 303–10; views of reform, 243, 296, 298, 303
Reformers, Protestant, 294, 296–8, 302–4, 306–8, 310–1, 344
Regress, historical regression, ideas of, 11, 14, 17, 19, 22, 39, 51, 75, 248, 273, 297, 302; pejorism, 76. *See also* Decay
Regulus, Marcus, 55, 89, 98, 263
Rehm, W., 73, 79, 80, 84, 214, 224, 225, 226, 247, 265
Rehoboam, king, 162, 163
Reicke, B., 172
Reidemeister, K., 8
Reincarnation. *See* Metempsychosis
Reinhardt, K., 16, 87, 185
Renaissance: as an idea of recurrence, xi, 1, 3; as instances of renewal, rebirth, revival, 69, 81, 114, 243–9, 251; as revival of antiquity and learning, 278, 283, 291, 295, 298–9, 303, 309; as revival of Christian antiquity in par-

ticular, 295, 298, 303, 309; as religious revivals, 296–7, 299; Carolingian Renaissance, 226, 228, 246–7; Ottonian, 226; Byzantine, 230, 239, 241; early classic, 2, 179–80, 200, 231, 247–8, 273–4, 283, 309, 336–7; classic (general references), xi, 180, 231, 241, 250, 298, 309, 336, 345; high classic, 249, 250–1, 278, 290–1, 295, 303, 337
Rengstorf, K., 141, 146
Renovation, restoration, ideas of, 3, 69, 114, 118, 136–8, 144, 146, 148, 160–1, 164, 175–6, 189-90, 211, 224, 245–6, 266, 269, 281–3, 297–8, 301–2, 306–7, 309, 311, 318, 340
Restitution, ideas of, 301, 308
Retribution, requital in history, ideas of, xi, 1, 2, 85–8, 92–106, 137, 139, 144, 155–74, 176, 178, 180–1, 188, 194, 196, 203, 205, 214, 229, 231–42, 283, 285–7, 290, 300, 302, 306, 344
Reuchlin, Johann, 251
Revelation, book of, 207; cited, 123, 164, 223
Reversal, ideas of, 10, 63, 66, 83, 101, 174, 181
Reversion, return, ideas of: to original principles, 262, 271–3, 341; to good government, 191, 312; to kingship, 183, 191–2, 264, 275, 278; to childhood, 189, 302; to Canaan (as recurrence idea), 282–3; to early Christianity, *see* Primitive life
Reynolds, B. R., 276, 282, 344
Rhetoric, rhetoricians, orators, 106, 113, 244–5, 299, 330
Rhoda, disciple, 124
Rhodes, 69
Rhythm (dance, rhapsody), 61, 288, 336
Rice, E. F., 217, 298
Richard III, king, 287
Richard de Templo, 283
Richardson, P., 145
Ridemann, Pieter, 304
Rise, A., 76
Robbins, F. E., 208
Robert of Auxerre, 217
Roberto da Rimini, 285
Robertson, C. M., 230
Robinson, J. M., 322
Robinson, T. H., 166
Robinson, W. C., 131
Rohde, E., 61, 154
Rohde, J., 178, 322, 323
Romagna, the, 315, 341
Romanus III, emperor, 239
Rome: Roman empire, xi, 4, 55, 58, 64–6, 70–1, 73–4, 77–82, 88–92, 98–105, 109, 114, 122, 147–50, 165, 177, 183, 186, 188–203, 219–20, 223–5, 227–8, 231–2, 235–7, 240, 242, 244–7, 252, 260, 264–5, 268, 280–1, 284, 288–9, 300, 302, 343–4; Roman constitution, 24, 41, 45–8, 51–8, 69–71, 73–4, 81, 92, 108, 259–60, 275, 277, 289, 317, 319; constitutional history, 45, 47, 49, 51–6, 58, 71, 114, 151, 169, 181, 183, 187–99, 202, 259–60, 273, 275–7, 295; military system, 45, 53, 55, 88–92, 102–3, 190, 194, 287, 294; judicial system, 127, 147–8, 150; culture, 76–7, 151–3, 279, 287; decline and fall (in both thought and event), 79, 81–2, 104–5, 148, 182, 185–98, 200, 214, 217, 219, 222, 224–6, 233, 236–7, 248, 263–4, 276; Rome and Christianity, 126–7, 130, 133, 149–53, 170, 175, 191, 207, 209, 213, 219, 223, 225, 227, 233, 236, 246, 323–4, 336–7; eternal Rome, 181, 186, 188, 190–2, 225, 246; a second, 226, 246–7; Holy Roman empire, emperorship, 212, 219–20, 226–7, 232, 246, 268, 282, 302; medieval and Renaissance Rome, 228, 300, 339; Church as Roman, 300
Romilly, J. de, 46
Romulus, 49, 51–2, 54, 56, 150–2, 181, 188, 189, 190, 192, 198, 199, 202, 223, 245, 260–1, 264, 265, 272, 273, 276, 277, 339; and Remus, 150–1
Ronconi, A., 76
Rose, H. J., 85, 202, 230
Rosen, K., 233
Rosini, G., 277
Ross, W. D., 10, 11, 37
Rost, L., 120
Rotation. *See* Alternation; Cycles
Rothmann, Bernst, 282–3, 305
Rottendorf, B., 283
Rotterdam, 305
Rousseau, G. S., 274, 289
Roveri, A., 41, 55, 56, 98, 111
Rowe, J. G., 250
Rowley, H. H., 138, 222
Rubenstein, N., 289
Rucellai gardens, 276
Rudolph, W., 137
Runciman, S., 239
Rupert of Deutz, 213, 216, 217
Russell, D. A., 113, 148
Russell, D. S., 175
Russell, J. L., 117
Ryffel, H., 6, 14, 24, 25, 27, 28, 30, 42, 68, 107

Sabatier, S., 184
Sabbatini, R., 253
Sabellicus (Marcantonio Coccio), 336
Sacraments, Christian, 297, 304, 307, 311. *See also* Festivals
*Saeculum, saecula*, 76, 202–3, 210, 221
Salamis, battle of, 187
Sallust, 21, 74, 107, 186, 193
Sallustius, 183, 200, 203, 234
Salutati, Coluccio, 220–1, 266, 281, 288, 337
Salvianus, 237–8

Samaria, Samaritans, 130, 132, 133, 136, 158, 229, 302, 330
Samos, 79, 96
Samson, judge, 157
Samuel, judge, 151, 157, 335
San Casciano, 341
Sanctis, G. de, 25
Sandbach, F. H., 7
Sanhedrin, Jewish, 123, 126
Santini, E., 247
Saracens, 282
Sarah, wife of Abraham, 219
Sardinia, 89
Sardis, 96
Sarpi, Paolo, 298, 310–2, 344
Satan, Lucifer, 207, 299, 334
Sattler, Michael, 304
Saturn(us), 76, 77, 210, 299, 301. *See also* Astral influences
Saul, king, 153, 161, 162–3, 221
Savonarola, Girolamo, 266, 314, 340
Scala, R. von, 42, 46, 73
Sceva, the sons of, 173
Schäfer, E., 297
Schechter, S., 331
Schleitheim Confession, 304, 306
Schlier, H., 151
Schlosser, J. von, 245, 282
Schmidt, K. L., 131
Schneemelcher, W., 209
Schoene, A., 208, 209
Schubert, H. von, 216
Schultz, J. T., 211
Schweighaeuser, J., 5, 23
Schweizer, E., 324, 325
Schwenckfeld, Caspar, 345
Science. *See* Knowledge
Scipio Aemilianus, 4, 51, 55, 66, 74, 79, 231
Scipio Africanus, Publicus Cornelius, 55, 65, 100, 102–4, 114, 148, 155, 231, 245, 281, 295
Scopas the Aetolian, 101
Scotland, 290
Scott, E. J. L., 282
Scott, R. B. Y., 166
Scylas the Scythian, 94, 96
Sealey, R., 96
Seasons, analogous to historical change, 61, 62, 68, 81, 86, 117, 119
Sebaste, 133
Sebastius, 245
Secret, F., 300
Seeberg, E., 297
Seleucia, Seleucids, 99, 103, 105, 164. *See also* Antiochus
Seligman, P., 86
Sellasia, 319
Semiramis, queen, 223
Senate, Roman, 51, 55–6, 181, 259–61, 267, 275, 317; senatorial elements, 47, 54–6, 182, 191, 245
Seneca, Lucius, 13, 21, 22, 67, 68, 74, 76, 94, 99, 152, 153, 183, 185–6, 188–93, 198, 201, 202, 203, 210, 224, 233, 344
Seneca, pseudo-, 62, 76
Sennacherib, king, 137
Septuagint, uses of the, 141, 145, 147, 150, 169, 209, 330–3
Serra, A. T. Y., 210
Servetus, Michael, 307, 308
Servite Order, 310
Servitude, 83, 134, 165, 268–9, 273. *See also* Egypt, Egyptian captivity; Babylon, Babylonian exile
Servius, commentator, 211, 221
Servius, Tullius, king, 181
Sesostris, pharoah, 282
Setton, K. M., 241
Sevčenko, I, 240
Severus Alexander, emperor, 199, 234
Severus, Sulpicius, 219
Seyssel, Claude, 275–6, 279, 294
Seznec, J., 301
Sforza, Francesco, 270, 286
Sforza, Galeazzo Maria, 270
Sforza, Ludovico il Moro, 270
Shepherd, M. H., 124
Sherrard, P., 241
Shimron, B., 320
Sibylline Books: Roman, 76, 201, 210, 220, 224; Jewish, 168, 177; cited, 168
Sicarii, the, 174
Sicily, 72, 77, 80, 88, 89–90, 102, 113, 114, 189, 203, 232. *See also* Panormus, Syracuse
Sidonius Apollinaris, 76, 203, 229
Siegfried, W., 79
Siena, 290
Sigebertus of Gembloux, 213
Significance(s) in historical events, educed, 64, 75, 94–8, 106, 112, 124, 138–40, 146–7, 149, 152, 154, 164, 169, 175, 178, 180, 206, 214, 217, 219, 236, 286, 288, 292, 315
*Signoria*, Florentine, 340
Silas, disciple, 127
Silius Italicus, 203
Silvester (I), St., Pope, 299, 300
Silvestri, Domenico, 220
Similarities in historical events, 125, 128, 165, 211, 227, 230, 241, 258, 291–2, 294–5, 305; striking, 3, 95, 113–4, 218, 244, 292, 294–5
Simon, son of Clopas, 307
Simone, F., 243
Simonides, 94
Simons, Menno, 307
Simplicius, 9, 86, 200

Simpson, C. A., 156, 157
Sirach, ben. *See* Ecclesiasticus
Skemp, J. B., 9
Skinner, G. W., 315
Smalley, B., 184
Smith, J. R., 243, 283
Smith, K. F., 201
Socrates, historian, 235, 236, 237
Socrates, philosopher, 31, 152, 153, 155
Soderini, Niccolò, 270–2, 338, 340
Sodom and Gomorrah, 176, 204, 221; new Sodom, 306
Solmsen, F., 12
Solomon, king, 135–8, 146, 148, 158–63, 165, 166, 246
Solon, 11, 30, 31, 97, 114, 245, 254–5
Sophists, the, 16–7, 20–1, 27, 30, 106
Sosicrates of Rhodes, 69
Sotion of Alexandria, 155
Soury, G., 234
Sozomen, 236
Spain, Spanish, 91, 103, 189, 203, 271, 290, 299, 338–9, 341–2
Spampanato, V., 251
Spangenberg, H., 336
Sparks, H. D. F., 330
Sparta, Spartans, 38, 40–1, 57, 79, 80, 87, 89, 96, 100, 110–1, 114; Spartan constitution, 39, 45, 46–7, 49–50, 57–8, 70, 108, 187, 232, 245, 259, 273, 295, 343
Spatianus, 203
Spedding, J., 294
Speil, A., 296
Speiser, E. A., 157
Spengler, O., 61, 312
Spiazzi, R. M., 275
Spirals, ideas of, 191, 277
Spitz, L., 251
Stählin, G., 123, 329
Stählin, O., 206
Starr, C. G., 61, 117
*Stasis*, 107–10, 318; social distress, 63
State: State-Church relations, 226–7, 235, 306; general idea of the state in Machiavelli, 252. *See also* Nations; Political society
Stauffer, E., 305, 306, 326
Stenning, J. F., 142
Stephen, St., martyr, 122, 123, 127, 144, 170, 173, 183, 329
Sticker, B., 61
Stigen, A., 17
Stilicho the Vandal, 236
Stobaeus, 15, 26, 28, 38, 46, 180, 317
Stockdale, W. H., 250
Stoics, Stoicism, 6–9, 12–5, 21–2, 44, 66, 70, 76–7, 81–2, 93, 119–20, 151–3, 155, 176, 178, 185, 188–91, 200–1, 205–6, 210, 213, 220, 225, 244, 250, 279, 288
Stow, John, 345
Straaten, M. van, 7, 20, 21
Strabo, 201
Strack, H. L., 141
Strato, 67
Strauss, L., 253, 339
Strelan, J., 128
Strife, ideas of, 8, 10, 85–6, 96. *See also* War
Stroheker, K. F., 26
Strozzi, Andrea, 270
Stubbs, W., 283
Stübler, G., 193
Stüve, G., 200
Succession, ideas of: general, 2, 9, 14, 117, 176, 203, 223, 241; fixed sequence, series, stages, 37–9, 44–5, 47, 77, 84, 86, 93, 107–8, 127, 156, 181, 212, 257, 262, 268, 273–4, 276–8, 288, 292; succession of Ages, 116, 118, 174–5, 180, 200, 202–8, 214, 221, 228, 335; succession and translation of empires, 79, 116, 168, 176, 186, 207, 222–4, 226–7, 279–83, 300, 302, 344; succession and translation of knowledge or its bearers, 69, 155, 247; succession of generations, 68–9, 201; of civilizations, 248; of kings, 237; of the empire by the church, 300; translation within church history, 300; succession of revelations, 216; troubles, 228; disobedience, 170; persecutions, 219, 228–9, 345
Suetonius, 183, 203, 243
Suffolk, William, Lord, 287
Suidas, 55
Suleiman, emir, 300
Sulla, 114, 186, 197, 245, 263, 266, 278, 294
Superstition, ideas concerning, 16, 78, 155
Sura, Aemilius, 80, 186, 209
Swain, J. B., 186, 187, 222
Swiss, Switzerland, 345
Syme, R., 193
Syme, R. J. B., 198
Symmachus, 203
Syncellus, 212
Syracuse, Syracusan, 26, 91, 104, 195. *See also* Sicily
Syria, 130, 147, 330

Tacitus, emperor, 199
Tacitus, historian, 21, 26, 49, 81, 83, 95, 132, 183, 186, 190, 193, 247
Taeger, F., 45, 49, 51–3, 79, 265
Taio, 213
Talbert, C. H., 122, 127, 148, 151, 155
Tarentum, 72, 108, 109
Tarquinius, Collatinus, 189
Tarquinius Superbus, 49, 51, 54, 57, 112, 188, 199, 234, 258, 266–7
Tarquins, the, 260, 261, 278

Tarsus, 130, 131
Tasso, 295
Tatian, 205
Täubler, E., 5, 58, 81, 97
Taylor, A. E., 12
Taylor, H. O., 290
Taylor, J., 213, 243
Taylor, M., 22
Taylor, V., 323
Teacher of Righteousness (Qumranite), 146
Technology. *See* Arts and skills; Knowledge
Teleology, 14, 36, 38, 116–8, 208, 217, 221, 227, 301; entelechy, 44
Teleutias, 114
Terrien, S., 233
Tertullian, 204, 207, 208, 214, 219, 224, 237
Thales, 8, 282
Thallus, 209, 210
Theatine Order, 298
Theatocracy, 39–40
Theatre, image of history as, 239, 242, 315
Thebes, 45, 65, 70, 72, 80, 108, 245
Theiler, W., 71
Theodatus the Goth, 239
Theodoret, 239
Theodoric the Great, king, 246
Theodosius I the Great, emperor, 201, 212, 225, 236, 245–6
Theodulf of Orléans, 246
Theognis, 62, 63, 86, 93, 94, 207, 233
Theophilus of Antioch, 208
Theophrastus, 9, 16, 26, 46, 99
Theopompus, 32, 112
Theramenes, 114
Therapeutae, the, 307
Theron, 26
Theseus, 113, 151, 154, 245, 339
Thessalonika, 275
Theudas, rebel leader, 174
Thomas à Kempis, 184, 309
Thomas Aquinas. *See* Aquinas
Thomas, K., 238
Thracians, 244
Thrupp, S. L., 297
Thucydides, 26, 28, 30, 31–2, 68, 74, 77, 80, 83, 86, 87, 88, 93, 94, 96–7, 108, 110–4, 147, 206, 242–3, 258, 292, 322
Tiberius, emperor, 183, 190, 198, 199
Tibullus, 62, 188
Tidwell, N. L. A., 175
Tidal analogy of history, 228, 250
Tillich, P., 117
Timaeus of Tauromenium, 26, 86, 94, 105
Time, views of: Greco-Roman, 10–13, 117, 120, 204–7; Judeo-Christian, 117, 119, 177, 206–7, 212, 216, 223–4, 298, 301–3, 306, 308, 311, 335; neo-pagan, 230; Renaissance, 280, 293, 336
Timocracy, 23, 39, 41
Tinsley, 184
Titans, the, 39–40, 78
Titus, emperor, 172, 199, 264
Tonkin, J. M., 297
Torah. *See* Law
Toulmin, S., 206
Toynbee, A., xi, 312
Trajan, emperor, 189, 190, 192, 198, 199, 245
Trankle, H., 193
*Translatio* theory. *See* Succession
Transmigration of souls. *See* Metempsychosis
Trebizond, Basil, 240
Trebonianus, emperor, 199
Trent, Council of, 310–1, 344
Treu, M., 58
Tribuneship, 51–2, 182, 244, 261–3
Trier, 226
Trinkaus, C., 242, 345
Trinity, the, Trinitarianism, 216–8; anti-Trinitarianism, 307
Trithemius of Sponheim, 344
Trocmé, E., 121, 174
Trogus, Pompeius, 21, 187, 194, 209, 223
Trojans, Troy, 68, 77–9, 96, 221
Trompf, G. W., 119, 120, 121, 123, 126, 133, 134, 137, 148, 155, 160, 161, 172, 174, 246, 301, 324, 325, 326, 334
Tudor literature, 288
Turks, Turkish empire, 228, 240, 247
Turner, H. E. W., 184, 205
Tuscans. *See* Etruria
Tyndaris, 89
Typology, 122, 128–9, 133, 137, 139, 180, 183–4, 209, 221
Tyranny, tyrants: as constitution, 5, 18–9, 21–9, 31–6, 39–41, 43, 49, 51, 54, 56–8, 73–4, 107–8, 113, 165, 181–3, 187, 238, 245, 252–5, 258, 260–78, 283, 286, 306, 311–2, 318–9, 341–4; general, 11, 39, 87, 152, 168–9, 182, 238, 258, 263, 265–7, 269–74, 276–7, 283, 286, 306, 317, 341, 344
Tyre, 295

Ullmann, B. L., 220
Ullmann, W., 247
Ulysses, 154
Undulations. *See* Alternation
Unexpectedness in human affairs, 12, 58, 63, 66, 73, 84, 90–1, 108, 151, 167, 195, 233, 239, 259, 284
Ungar, W. W., 250
Uniformity of human nature, uniformitarianism, 3, 96–7, 100, 106, 110–2, 258, 278, 287, 291–5
Uniqueness of historical events, 46, 112, 117, 126, 146–7, 168, 174, 231, 293, 306, 313, 315;

notions of 'the great exception', 101–6, 169, 174, 227
Unnik, W. van, 121
Untersteiner, M., 16, 17, 20
Ure, P. N., 150
Urstisius, C., 226
Utica, 153
Utility of the study of the past. *See* Lessons
Uzziah, king, 136, 160, 162, 163, 219

Vacalopoulos, A., 241
Vahlen, I., 186, 222
Valens, emperor, 245
Valentinian I, emperor, 236
Valerianus, emperor, 199, 234
Valerius Maximus, 185, 186, 244
Valero the Arian, 236
Vandals, the, 219
Variation. *See* Change
Varro, Marcus, 188, 202, 216, 222
Vasari, Giorgio, 282, 283, 287
Vasiliev, A., 212
Vatican hill, the, 299, 300
Veazie, W., 86
Veh, O., 239
Velleius Paterculus, 107, 186, 244, 247
Venice, Venetians, 285, 290, 295, 301, 310, 339, 343; patriarchate of Venice, 310
Vergil, Polydore, 279–80, 287–8
Verbeke, G., 185
Vespasian, emperor, 199
Vettori, F., 341
Vicissitudes, or upward and downward movements, in history, 64–5, 88, 116, 166–9, 180, 195, 197–200, 206, 216, 223, 225, 228, 238–9, 256–7, 268, 280–1, 283–5, 313. *See also* Alternation; Change
Vico, Giambattista, xi, 237, 277, 312
Vidal-Naquet, P., 117
Vienna, 300, 306
Vigne, André de la, 247, 295
Villani, Giovanni, 229, 243, 248, 289
Vincent de Beauvais, 335
Virgil, 76–7, 202–3, 211–2, 220–1, 298, 300
Virtue, civic and socio-religious, 22, 72, 90, 97–9, 101–5, 115, 148, 151, 165, 182, 185, 188, 191–4, 196–7, 232–3, 236, 242–3, 245, 253, 256, 260, 264–5, 272, 280–1, 284–5, 290, 295, 341; pre-civic, 20, 42; general, 53, 257, 268, 294
Visconti, Filippo, 270
Visconti, Giangaleazzo, 266
Visconti, House of, 290
Vitellius, emperor, 199
Vittigis the Goth, 239
Vives, Juan L., 295, 345
Vlastos, G., 86
Voegelin, E., 209
Vööbus, A., 329
'Vopiscus', 114, 192, 196–200, 233

Waerden, B. L. van der, 67
Walbank, F. W., 5, 7, 18, 24, 25, 26, 30, 41, 46, 54, 75, 78, 80, 81, 90, 91, 99, 109, 148, 320
Walker, A., 184
Walker, L. J., 264
Wallace-Hadrill, D. S., 225
Wallace-Hadrill, J. M., 246
Walsh, P. G., 186, 193
Walter von der Vogelweide, 226
War, 70, 72–4, 80, 88–92, 160, 164, 169, 238, 281, 288–90, 307. *See also* Gaul, Gallic Wars; Persia, Persian Wars; Punic Wars; Strife, ideas of
Wardman, A., 244
Webb, G., 184
Wehrli, F., 9, 17, 20, 37, 42, 44, 46, 63, 65, 66, 67, 72, 80, 200, 244
Weil, R., 11
Weinstein, D., 296–7
Weis, P. R., 164
Weisinger, H., 243, 250, 280, 293
Welch, A. C., 137
Wendel, T. O., 229
Wendland, P., 83
West, E., 118, 176, 186
West, M. L., 61, 62
Westlake, H. D., 114
Westphalia, 305
Wheare, D., 296
Wheel, as analogy of human events, 61–2. *See also* Fortune, wheel of
White, P., 197
Whitfield, J. H., 252, 266, 338
Whybray, R. N., 121
Wieder, N., 146
Wijngaards, J. N. M., 135
Wilamowitz-Moellendorf, U. von, 42
Wilckens, U., 149, 324
Wilcox, D. J., 242, 266
Wilcox, M., 121, 140, 324, 330
Wilderness, discussed in connection with recurrence, 135, 159, 170, 308
Wilken, R. L., 184
Wilkes, G. A., 280, 344
Wilkins, E. H., 337
Will, human. *See* Purpose
William of St. Thierry, 184
William of Tyre, 242
Williams, G. H., 303, 304, 307, 308, 344, 345
Williamson, H. G. M., 136
Wimmer, F., 99
Wimpfeling, Jacob, 282–3

Winckler, E. A., 315
Winiarski, W., 339
Wisdom literature of the Bible, 164, 166–7
Wittenbach, D. A., 321
Wolfson, H. A., 167, 169
Women, referred to in connection with historical recurrence, 124, 127, 153, 157, 159, 164, 219, 223, 239, 287, 305, 325–6, 327, 329–30
Woodhead, A. G., 97
Woodward, W. H., 242
Woolcombe, K. J., 128, 184
World, ideas concerning the: in Polybius, 4, 64–6, 70, 73–4, 78, 80–2, 102–4, 148; in Stoicism, 185, 189–90, 200–1, 206, 232; in Luke-Acts, 134, 145, 150, 152, 154–5, 170, 175, 323, 333; in Philo, 168–9; in others, 118, 191, 194, 197, 209, 213–4, 216, 220, 222–3, 225–6, 230, 278, 280–1, 293, 295–9, 301–2, 344–5
Woven cloth analogy of history, 231, 241
Wray, F. J., 307, 308
Wright, G. E., 138
Wroebel, E., 200
Wyclif, John, 308

Xanthippus, 89
Xenophanes of Colophon, 8, 16, 21, 85
Xenophon, 27, 46, 93, 94, 114, 152, 155, 252
Xerxes I, 53, 54, 80, 87, 93, 95, 101, 113–4, 262

Yahweh (YHWH), 118, 119, 135–7, 156, 158–61, 168, 170, 175, 232, 332–3. *See also* God, biblical
Yates, F. A., 201, 251, 310, 345

Zama, battle of, 100, 102–3
Zarepheth, women of, 329
Zechariah, book of, cited, 330–1
Zecheriah, father of John the Baptist, 219
Zedekiah, ruler over Judah, 161–3
Zeller, E., 9, 93
Zeno the Stoic, 9, 76
Zephaniah, book of, cited, 164
Zeux, 11, 21, 210
Ziegler, K., 5
Zijpp, N. van der, 305
Zimmerli, W., 134
Zohar, the, 301
Zonari, chancellor, 220
Zoroaster, Zoroastrianism, 75, 116, 118, 202, 204, 230, 244; literature of Zoroastrians, cited, 118, 176, 186
Zosimus, 102, 187–8, 203, 233, 234, 236
Zwingli, Huldreich, 283, 308

Compositor: Freedmen's Organization
Printer: Malloy Lithographing, Inc.
Binder: Malloy Lithographing, Inc.
Text: Compugraphic Goudy
Display: Typositor Perpetua
Cloth: Holliston Roxite B 53565
Paper: 50 lb. Glatfelter Natural